THE ECONOMIC GROWTH OF SOUTHEAST ASIA

This is the first comprehensive analysis of Southeast Asian globalization and development since 1870. Interpreting over 150 years of Southeast Asian economic history, Gregg Huff traces the impact of a first period of globalization from the 1870s to 1929, the effects of Japanese occupation during World War II and its aftermath, and a second wave of globalization since the late 1960s. He uses vent-for-surplus, dual economy and plural society concepts and argues that the response of those in Southeast Asia to periods of transport revolutions, innovation and opportunity in the world economy translated into rapid export-led growth. Recent swift growth enabled Southeast Asia to start to 'catch up' with the world's leading countries for the first time in its history. Achievements include industrialization, genuine social progress and numerous large urban regions. Nevertheless, the book contends that Southeast Asian development in its 'miracle economies' remains incomplete.

GREGG HUFF is a Senior Research Fellow at Pembroke College, University of Oxford, and author of *The Economic Growth of Singapore* and *World War II and Southeast Asia*.

THE ECONOMIC GROWTH OF SOUTHEAST ASIA

Trade, Globalization and Development since 1870

GREGG HUFF

Pembroke College, University of Oxford

CAMBRIDGE
UNIVERSITY PRESS

CAMBRIDGE
UNIVERSITY PRESS

Shaftesbury Road, Cambridge CB2 8EA, United Kingdom

One Liberty Plaza, 20th Floor, New York, NY 10006, USA

477 Williamstown Road, Port Melbourne, VIC 3207, Australia

314–321, 3rd Floor, Plot 3, Splendor Forum, Jasola District Centre, New Delhi – 110025, India

Cambridge University Press is part of Cambridge University Press & Assessment, a department of the University of Cambridge.

We share the University's mission to contribute to society through the pursuit of education, learning and research at the highest international levels of excellence.

www.cambridge.org
Information on this title: www.cambridge.org/9781108487429
DOI: 10.1017/9781108766814

When citing this work, please include a reference to the DOI 10.1017/9781108766814

First published 2026

Cover image: Photo by AMAURY PAUL/AFP via Getty Images)

A catalogue record for this publication is available from the British Library

Library of Congress Cataloging-in-Publication Data
Names: Huff, W. G. author
Title: The economic growth of Southeast Asia : trade, globalization and development since 1870 / Gregg Huff.
Description: Cambridge, United Kingdom ; New York, NY : Cambridge University Press, 2026. | Includes bibliographical references.
Identifiers: LCCN 2026002431 (print) | LCCN 2026002432 (ebook) | ISBN 9781108487429 hardback | ISBN 9781108720267 paperback | ISBN 9781108766814 ebook
Subjects: LCSH: Economic development – Southeast Asia – History | Southeast Asia – Economic conditions | Southeast Asia – Economic policy
Classification: LCC HC441 .H838 2026 (print) | LCC HC441 (ebook) | DDC 338.959–dc23/eng/20260311
LC record available at https://lccn.loc.gov/2026002431
LC ebook record available at https://lccn.loc.gov/2026002432

ISBN 978-1-108-48742-9 Hardback
ISBN 978-1-108-72026-7 Paperback

For my teachers
Andrew Bain, Richard DuBoff and Mike Montesano

CONTENTS

FIGURES

TABLES

ACKNOWLEDGEMENTS

Southeast Asianists tend to write about the region's post-1870 history and development either stopping at World War II or starting in one of the decades after it. Few are economists and not many more are economic historians, and those that are generally specialize in one country or another. This book had its genesis during a discussion of these problems during lunch at Pembroke College, Oxford, with Kevin Fogg and Lucy Rhymer. She said that Cambridge University Press had been looking unsuccessfully for someone to write an economic history to cover all of modern Southeast Asia and to span both the decades before and after World War II. Both Kevin and I said that was not us but I thought to myself this would be something that, in time, I might try. The original remit was a book of 120,000 words. That this book is considerably longer owes much to the patience, advice and faith of Michael Watson who took over the project at Cambridge University Press and saw it to completion. My thanks go to him for his patience and belief. Thanks also to Rosa Martin, Natasha Whelan, Margaret Humbert and Lou Attwood, who saw the book through its production stages at Cambridge University Press with tact, skill and remarkably good humour.

Many people have contributed to the book. None more than my three teachers – Andrew Bain, Dick DuBoff and Mike Montesano – to whom the book is dedicated. Andrew Bain, a professor of finance at the University of Glasgow, read the entire manuscript, much of it more than once and most pages reflect his sharp mind, insistence on clarity and insightful comment. Dick DuBoff, my first economics teacher as a freshman at the University of Pennsylvania, has ever since remained a close friend and reader. He was educated in the Penn tradition of economic history and has brought that to bear in his many comments on this book. Mike Montesano has an astonishingly comprehensive knowledge of Southeast Asia across all disciplines and has been my patient teacher in questioning numerous parts of the book and correcting my mistakes. Thanks also go to an anonymous referee who made, in an understated way, suggestions which caused me to rethink and rewrite important parts of the book. A number of other people have read or helped with specific parts of the book. They include Blessing Muyiwa Ali, Anne Booth, Richard Leete, Pierre van der Eng and Michael Yeo.

My heartfelt thanks go to Kathleen McCully, who did a brilliant and painstaking copyediting job, making no less than 1,487 queries or changes to the original manuscript and correcting numerous errors. Mike Shand, University of Glasgow, drew all the maps. His mapmaking skill is a joy to behold. Tanya Izzard compiled an excellent and comprehensive index, which is much appreciated.

Figure F.1 Southeast Asia, 2025

Introduction

If the twenty-first century is to remain the century of Asia, Southeast Asia will continue as integral to that eastwards shift. The region, an area of some 1.7 million square miles, stretches from the Philippines in the east to Myanmar (Burma until 1989) in the west. In between are Thailand, Malaya (now the separate states of Malaysia and Singapore) and Indochina, consisting of Vietnam, Cambodia and Laos. At the region's southernmost extension is the Indonesian archipelago. Bounded by India and China, and with economies that are increasingly integrated with both those countries as well as with one another, Southeast Asia has shared in the rapid economic growth known as the Asian Miracle and founded on an upsurge in manufactured exports: many of the components and finished manufactures produced in Asia and shipped globally come from Southeast Asia. Swift growth is not, however, a new phenomenon in the region. Much of it was frontier in 1870, after which it grew rapidly until the 1930s, when the depression, Japanese World War II occupation and then civil war and revolution put growth into reverse. In the later 1960s, swift growth resumed, spreading throughout much of the region.

This book tells the story of economic transformation in Southeast Asia since 1870. Whereas historians generally treat the pre- and post-World War II periods in Southeast Asia separately, either ending in 1939 or beginning with the 1950s, or even later, this book's focus is on long-term historical forces and flows and an integrated global history. Here, for the first time, Southeast Asian economic history since the late nineteenth century is analysed as a whole, through a comparative and, where possible, quantitative analytical approach. In every economic history, including this one, the geography and politics of countries are, of course, fundamental to an understanding of the story.

The book begins in 1870 because Southeast Asia's integration into the global economy followed a path markedly different from its development in decades preceding that landmark year. Globalization – although, as often observed, long a feature of a region astride the world's main east–west trade route – moved to a scale qualitatively different from earlier periods. After 1870, trade and migration began to increase enormously. Transport and communications innovations bound Southeast Asia to the world economy more comprehensively than ever before, facilitating greater flows of goods, people and capital. These enhanced global flows have been instrumental in shaping modern Southeast Asia's economies and its political systems. By the 1870s, Southeast Asian history had, as Benda emphasizes, entered a 'new epoch'.[1] This beginning, and the World War II boundary on the far side, for Pluvier, 'clearly stand out as a distinct period in the history of South-East Asia'.[2] Sweeping late nineteenth-century changes, paralleled by further waves of innovations beginning from the 1950s, could not have occurred without revolutions in transport and communications.

While the book adopts a long-term perspective in focusing on post-1870 globalization, economic development as part of long-term global change had as its corollary openness to short-term fluctuations. And just as the first gave pattern to Southeast Asian economic history, so the second punctuated this with booms and slumps. The latter include the 1930s depression, the Asian financial crisis of 1997 to 2000 and the 2019 Covid pandemic. The book devotes relatively little space to these events because, although important, over the span of over 150 years, downturns generally proved comparatively brief interruptions to a long-term upwards trend. A fall of 10 or even 15 per cent in national income may not be disastrous for a whole economy if it has previously been growing, but fluctuations of these magnitudes may be quite serious for the poorest in a population. That may help to explain why many historians have devoted considerable attention to Southeast Asia's downturns, and their social and economic impact.

The book argues that between the late nineteenth and early twenty-first centuries, Southeast Asian economic history has three clear divisions. In all of these, global forces were exogenous to Southeast Asia, and in each the way that those in the region reacted to external change is basic to the narrative of Southeast Asian development. During the first of the divisions – a period of rapid globalization from 1870 to 1939 and the subject of Part I of the book – Southeast Asia was fully drawn into the world economy. By World War II, and arguably even by 1913, export-led growth had brought such great economic and social alterations that substantial parts of the region would likely have been almost unrecognizable to most people of the 1870s.

World War II and its early repercussions form Part II of the book and constitute a second main segment of Southeast Asian history. The war, Japanese wartime occupation and the aftermath of both encompass a mere decade from 1941 to 1950, but the impact of these years on the region's history was considerable. Occupation and the war's dislocation disrupted a pre-World War II regional historical unity and altered the course of both social and economic development. Events during the 1940s, as well as accelerating the realization of Southeast Asian political independence, led to a basic re-ordering of internal politics and economic policies in Burma, Indonesia and Vietnam, although less so in the rest of Southeast Asia. Part II shows how World War II and its

[1] Benda, 'Structure', p. 127.
[2] Pluvier, *South-East Asia*, p. 4.

immediate aftermath are crucial to an understanding of both the pre-1940 and post-1950 decades.

The decades from the 1950s onwards mark a third main division in Southeast Asian history. During this period, if not shortly before, all countries in the region gained independence. Once independent, Southeast Asian countries could chart their own courses. These diverged, with regimes attempting either some version of socialism, the so-called inward-looking countries, or capitalism, the outward-looking countries. Part III of the book analyses socialist Southeast Asia and Part IV its capitalist counterpart. The chapters in Part III concentrate on Burma, Indonesia and Indochina (Vietnam, Cambodia and Laos) which chose socialist or communist approaches to development, while Part IV compares and contrasts the market-oriented economies of, first, Malaysia and Thailand and, then in the next chapter (Chapter 14), the Philippines and Singapore. All the chapters in Parts III and IV examine the development paths and strategies followed by Southeast Asian countries from 1950 until the late 1980s.

By the 1990s, once inward-looking Southeast Asia, except Myanmar, had effectively abandoned its socialist experiments, Southeast Asia can, as from 1870 to 1939, be analysed as a whole. The book's Part V considers, in four chapters, the impact on Southeast Asian development and urbanization of a second swift globalization phase which began in Singapore in the late 1960s and spread to other Southeast Asian countries from the 1970s. Once again, globalization and the trade accompanying it fundamentally transformed Southeast Asia, and once again growth was export-led. Throughout the book, attention is drawn to the parallels and contrasts between these long late nineteenth- and late twentieth-century swings in global history and their effect on Southeast Asia.

The Introduction's next section deals with Southeast Asia as a region, its geography and populations. The second section looks at world communications since the late nineteenth century and how developments in these created conditions allowing Southeast Asia to be linked inexorably to the world economy. Changing political arrangements in Southeast Asia are the subject of the third section. The fourth section considers how those in the region, as well as outsiders coming to it, responded to new opportunities in the world economy. The fifth section presents main concepts which appear throughout the book. A sixth section sets out the book's plan.

Regional Identity and Population

Before World War II, the description Southeast Asia was 'mainly a geographic convenience, a logical product of "South" and "East" Asia'.[3] World War II and the Japanese occupation encouraged the concept of regional identity, because,

[3] Emmerson, '"Southeast Asia"', p. 7.

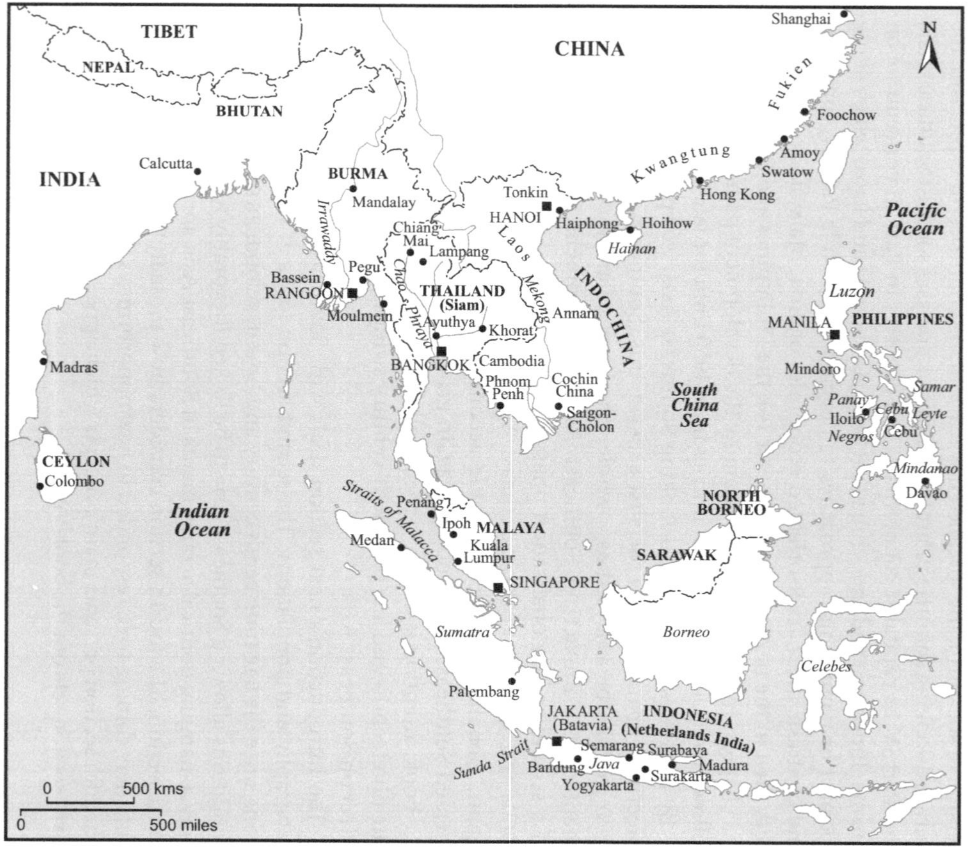

Figure I.1 Southeast Asia, 1940

after Japan took control of the region in early 1942, it was designated in 1943 an Allied operational theatre, under Admiral Lord Louis Mountbatten's South-East Asia Command.

Southeast Asia splits geographically between Burma, Thailand and Indochina, together forming the southernmost extension of continental Asia but separated from it by mountains, and the three insular areas of Malaya (peninsular Malaysia), Indonesia and the Philippines (Figures I.1 and F.1). The Malay Peninsula and Indonesia's combined land area (747,000 square miles) is similar to that of continental Southeast Asia. However, insular Southeast Asia sprawls over much more of the map than its land area and, including intervening seas, covers approximately the extent of the contiguous United States.[4] The archipelagos of Indonesia and the Philippines include thousands of small islands.[5]

Always more the receiver than giver of cultural and social forces, Southeast Asia can be divided into Indianized, Sinicized and Philippine elements.[6] This last refers to the Philippines, colonized by Spain in the sixteenth century as an act of devotion and inheritor of a Spanish Catholicism akin to that in Latin America.[7] Although four-fifths Catholic, the Philippines includes in Mindanao and nearby islands a sizeable Muslim population.[8] Similarly, Thailand has, in Buddhism, a large religious majority, but in the south, near the border with Malaysia, a significant Muslim population. Nearly all Burmans (about 70 per cent of the total population) inhabiting Myanmar are Buddhists, but the country has over 30 other ethnic groups, including the Chins, who are predominantly Christian, and the Karens. Most of the latter practise a blend of Buddhism and animism but have a significant Christian minority. There is also a considerable Muslim population in Rakhine (Arakan) state, including the Rohingya, and a variety of hill people such as the Kachin and Shans.

Indonesia is mainly Muslim and Malaysia almost exclusively so in its ethnic Malay inhabitants. However, because of large inflows after 1870 of Chinese and Indians to British colonial Malaya, only some three-fifths of Malaysia's population today are Malays, and other systems of beliefs and religions figure importantly. Javanese account for about two-fifths of Indonesians, but Indonesia has some 350 identified ethnic groups and, reflecting this, a significant presence of minority religions. In Vietnam, the nineteenth-century promotion of Catholicism by the French challenged the traditional three religions of Buddhism, Taoism and Confucianism, and over the course of the twentieth century contributed to major political and social divisions.

4 Dobby, *Monsoon Asia*, p. 199.
5 Chandler et al., *In search*, p. 3.
6 Benda, 'Structure', pp. 112–20.
7 Chandler et al., *In search*, p. 45.
8 Chandler et al., *In search*, p. 45.

Long-term rapid expansion in aggregate GDP is typically accompanied by substantial population growth, and that was so for Southeast Asia. In 1870, the population of Southeast Asia was some 62 million, of whom three-quarters lived in Indonesia (largely Java) and Indochina (mainly northern Vietnam). By 1913, population had increased to 109 million and in 1940 to 157 million. Before World War II, in Malaya, Burma and Thailand, mass international immigration from southeast China and south India was the main contributor to population expansion. Elsewhere in the region, population grew more slowly, and depended chiefly on natural increase. Southeast Asia accounted for just 4.9 per cent of world population in 1870, but this rose to 6.1 per cent in 1913 and 6.8 per cent by 1940, principally due to immigrant inflows.

After 1940, population continued to grow, despite catastrophic wartime loss of civilian life due to famine and forced labour during the Japanese wartime occupation. Continuous post-war population growth, now almost entirely owing to natural increase, and the settlement of the frontier, changed Southeast Asia from a land- to a labour-abundant region. Southeast Asia's population increased from about 157 million in 1940 to over 680 million by 2022, amounting to about 8.5 per cent of the global total.

Global Forces and Communications

The shaping of Southeast Asian history as an outcome of globalization from the later part of the nineteenth century onwards had three major constituents. One was the lessening of barriers to the free international flow of goods, labour and capital; a second, divergent levels of economic development across the global order; and a third, responses within Southeast Asia to the forces in the global economy unleashed by the reduction in barriers and different world developmental levels. These constituents, to which transport and communication revolutions were key, appear, if in varying guises and of differing importance, throughout this book, and help to provide themes around which it is organized. Throughout Southeast Asia's post-1870 history, growth and development in the region have been crucially affected by alterations in world communications, by demand for Southeast Asian products coming from the economies of industrialized countries, and by the choices of these countries for war or peace.

After 1850, and increasingly from the 1870s, innovations in world transport and communications, together with the extension of colonialism throughout nearly all of Southeast Asia, created the conditions for the region to be drawn ever more closely into the international economy. Sweeping changes, paralleled by further waves of innovations beginning from the 1950s, would not have occurred without revolutions in transport and communications.

Construction of the Suez Canal and completion of the Union Pacific railway across the United States, both in 1869, were central to breaking down global communication barriers. Suez cut the distance between London and Singapore by a third, to 8,326 nautical miles from the 11,740 nautical miles for the sea route around the Cape of Good Hope, opening 'at a stroke' the eastern trade to steamships.[9] Prior to Suez, steamships had to remain close to the shore to obtain coal, and long stretches of open sea on the Cape route made coal bunkering difficult and expensive and put water at a premium.

The impact of the Suez Canal was magnified by innovations in shipping technology, and together these changes revolutionized world shipping. Beginning in the 1860s, adoption of the compound engine economized on the use of coal, greatly reducing fuel costs for steamships and allowing more space for cargo. Improvements in 1870 in the surface condenser further saved on fuel and freed space for cargo. Until the surface condenser's minimization of evaporation, steamships had to carry large quantities of fresh water, because sea water corroded ships' boilers. In the 1880s, new, lighter steel vessels displaced less sea water, allowing them to carry more cargo than iron ships.[10]

During the 1880s, world and intra-Southeast Asian freight rates began to fall sharply and journey times to shorten. An index of tramp real freight rates for grain and sugar from Southeast Asia to London almost halved from 141.1 in 1871/75 to 74.1 in 1910/13.[11] By 1900, the voyage from Europe to India, which took three months for sailing ships using the Cape route, could be accomplished in two weeks by steamer through Suez.[12] Quicker voyages reduced commodity spoilage costs and the expense of financing trade.

The Suez Canal and switch to steam relocated the main world east–west shipping route, and channelled vessels though the Straits of Malacca rather than the Sunda Strait between Java and Sumatra. World shipping now passed within a few miles of Singapore, at the southernmost extension of the Asian land mass and through the centre of Southeast Asia (Figure I.1). Singapore became 'the gate to the east', and its trade and population grew rapidly. Three streams of east-bound shipping converged on Singapore – one using the Suez Canal, a second taking the Cape route and joining the Suez stream in the area of the Indian subcontinent, and a third beginning in the Indian area. Beyond Singapore, shipping fanned out, partly to termini in Thailand, Indochina, British Borneo and Indonesia, and partly as a main stream to Far Eastern ports. When returning and then sailing 'homewards' in the direction of the United Kingdom, these streams of shipping again converged at Singapore.[13]

Rice was first shipped through Suez in 1872, marking the 'starting-point of present-day [1920] conditions' in Burma.[14] However, rice was still carried

[9] Fletcher, 'Suez Canal', p. 558. And for the mileage figures, see Rabino, 'Statistical story', p. 526.
[10] Knowles, *Economic development*, pp. 17–18.
[11] Mohammed and Williamson, 'Freight rates', table A3A.
[12] Knowles, *Economic development*, p. 316.
[13] Imperial Shipping Committee, *British shipping in the Orient*, pp. 5–9.
[14] Furnivall, 'Industrial agriculture', p. 91.

mainly by sailing vessels taking the Cape route until the 1880s, when technical developments in shipping and falling freights gave steamships a decisive advantage.[15] The cities – Rangoon, Bangkok and Saigon-Cholon – that functioned as continental Southeast Asia's main steamer ports expanded through becoming centres for the sale and export of rice.

The Atlantic and Pacific Oceans meet, via the Indian Ocean, at Singapore, and the opening of the Panama Canal in 1914 linked Southeast Asia ever more firmly to the global economy. Panama was especially important for the Philippines in allowing direct shipping connections to the United States east coast, near the centres of American industrialization. Shipping through Panama reduced journey times and shipping freight rates to refineries in the eastern United States, which was the chief market for Philippine sugar.[16] In the inter-war period, some four-fifths of sugar from the Islands went via Panama.[17] By then, too, Malayan and Indonesian rubber exported from Singapore was carried mainly by eight shipping lines on a 'round the world' route which started from the Atlantic coast of the United States and, before calling at Singapore, sailed westwards by the Panama and Suez Canals.[18] At the same time as Suez and steamships increasingly drew Southeast Asia into the global economy, the spread of the telegraph put European merchants and, during the late nineteenth century, increasing numbers of Asian dealers and up-country producers, in telegraphic touch with world markets.[19]

Rapid technological change in world transport and communications, which began in the 1950s and accelerated from the 1970s, again reduced communication barriers between Southeast Asia and the rest of the world, strengthening the region's geographical advantages. A further revolution in world transport began with the introduction of the long-distance jet aircraft in 1958 and, more important, the introduction of the wide-body jet in 1967. Between 1955 and 2004, air transport costs in 2000 US$ fell from US$3.87 per ton-kilometre to under US$0.30, making air freight commonplace.[20]

World air traffic, like shipping, runs predominantly east–west. For Southeast Asia, global air routes essentially reproduced world shipping patterns; Singapore and Bangkok became world air hubs. Air freight minimized Southeast Asia's effective distance from markets in the United States and Europe and enabled the rapid, low-cost shipment of items like electronics and electrical goods with high value to weight ratios, where timeliness and

15 Cheng, *Rice industry*, pp. 13–15; Ingram, *Economic change*, p. 42; Manarungsan, *Economic development*, pp. 52–53.

16 Larkin, *Sugar*, p. 59.

17 Cutshall, 'Trends of Philippine sugar production', p. 156.

18 Imperial Shipping Committee, *British shipping in the Orient*, pp. 9, 87.

19 Ellis, 'Brief account of the Malay tin industry', p. 11; Cheng, *Rice industry*, p. 226; Owen, *Prosperity*, p. 189.

20 Hummels, 'Transportation costs', pp. 137–38.

reliability are essential. Electronics components air freighted from Singapore, Malaysia or Thailand on one day could, by the next, be almost anywhere in the world, with a consequent saving in time and inventory costs.

New shipping technologies also decreased trade barriers, just as they did after 1870. In 1950, the average merchant ship was between 5,000 and 10,000 tons, while by the twenty-first century it was 150,000 tons or more. Shipping methods changed with the introduction of bulk carriers, roll-on-roll-off vessels designed to carry wheeled vehicles like cars, supertankers and container ships. These last continuously increased in size to be able to convey as many as 24,000 containers by the 2020s. Large tankers were valuable to Southeast Asia as an oil exporter, and container vessels important to Southeast Asian exporters such as Vietnam and Cambodia of low-value goods like wooden furniture and footwear. For apparel and other fashion items, a mix of ocean and air shipping enabled a rapid response to demand shocks, and a real hedge to market volatility.[21] Singapore, along with Hong Kong, became one of the most technologically complex communications hubs in Southeast Asia, allowing the instantaneous transmission of detailed plans. Just as technological innovations in communications reduced distance costs for Southeast Asia, so too did the spread of English as an international language. As former British colonies, Singapore and Malaysia had a tradition in English, which helped to explain their attractiveness for multinationals and consequent rapid growth.

World tariffs and quantitative trade restrictions fell dramatically after the establishment of the General Agreement on Tariffs and Trade in 1947 (renamed the World Trade Organization in 1995), and through eight subsequent rounds of trade negotiations. The Kennedy Round, completed in 1967, brought a 50 per cent across-the-board reduction in tariffs. By the mid-1990s, world tariffs were less than 10 per cent of their 1947 level.

Southeast Asia Political Arrangements

Political configurations in Southeast Asia have always reflected, and often been a product of, differential developmental levels across the world. During the late nineteenth century, the emergence in Europe and the United States of the 'modern state' – characterized by the centralization of state power, an incorporation of civilian and military bureaucracies, the creation of national markets, and a unity forged through culture and mass politics – had sweeping consequences for Southeast Asia.[22] For the most powerful modern states, which included Britain, France, the Netherlands and the United States, the late nineteenth-century communications and transport revolution and

[21] Hummels, 'Transportation costs', pp. 137–38.
[22] Analysis of the modern state draws on Iriye, 'Japan's drive', pp. 721–28.

technological advances in armaments gave national defence a global imperative. Imperialism – the political and/or economic domination of economically weak and less developed parts of the world by stronger nations to create spheres of influence – became important to state power, prestige and prosperity. In pursuit of these goals, Britain was the most successful modern state; 'the Empire, and not merely Great Britain, became a world power … not a mere congeries of races under the British flag but a *world unit*'.[23]

Imperialism, although before the 1870s long evident in Southeast Asia, was easily extended to the entire region due to the disparity between the power of local political entities and modern states. Political organization in pre-colonial Southeast Asia was weak and often marked by fragmentation and ethnic, linguistic and religious divisions. In Southeast Asia, the 'state' was:

> a rather grandiose title for what was essentially a knotting together of the leading ends of strands of vertically-shaped personal relationships. The institutions of state and governance were informal, impermanent, personal, malleable and negotiable, and always prey to contestation from courtly aristocrats or local potentates. Accordingly, administrative control was characteristically weak, diffuse, irregular and decentralized; effective power outside the core of the state was usually the preserve of territorial chiefs or quasi-autonomous tributaries.[24]

The usual preference of pre-modern Southeast Asian rulers for maintenance of the power of the court and the existing social order was at the expense of economic growth. In fifteenth- and sixteenth-century Southeast Asia, weak or absent property rights, Reid argues, blocked the development of a propertied middle class and was a main reason why Southeast Asians remained poor relative to early modern Europe.[25] Colonialism led to a consolidation of law and order over wide areas of the region, and virtually ended dynastic and inter-principality rivalry and martial interaction.[26] Throughout Southeast Asia, 'traditional ruling classes were shorn of the instrumentalities of sovereignty, especially of the power to wage war, one of their principal *raisons d'etre*'.[27]

By the turn of the century, Southeast Asia, Thailand apart, had been divided among four colonial powers – Britain (Burma and Malaya); the Netherlands (Indonesia); France (Indochina); and the United States (the Philippines). Although avoiding formal colonialism, Thailand was part of Britain's informal empire and semi-colonial.[28] Colonial rule implemented modern, centralized

[23] Knowles, *Economic development*, p. 15 (emphasis original).
[24] Elson, 'International commerce', pp. 127–28.
[25] Reid, *Southeast Asia*, vol. 2: *Expansion and crisis*, pp. 129–31, 267–70.
[26] Benda, 'Structure', p. 127.
[27] Benda, 'Structure', p. 129.
[28] Aldrich, *Key to the south*, pp. 1, 4–7, 15, 25–30; Callis, *Foreign capital*, p. 59.

administrative and legal systems modelled on Europe and staffed at the top by Europeans, established property rights and forced open local markets to world trade. Through imposing political rule, the late nineteenth-century extension of colonialism over Southeast Asia created the stable political and social framework that economic growth demands but without the flexibility associated with modern economic growth.[29] In parts of Southeast Asia like Indonesia and some of Malaya and Indochina, colonial powers retained indigenous social and political structures, resulting in so-called indirect rule as opposed to direct rule's wholesale destruction of pre-colonial political systems.

Although many Southeast Asians resisted colonial incursion, in every country classes or entire ethnic groups actively aligned themselves with the European power.[30] After the imposition of colonialism, there were episodes of peasant rebellion. These were, however, distinct from nationalism and were often part of a tradition borne out of rising peasant irritations and a longing to return to some idealized past.[31] Instability was not, however, the norm: in colonial Southeast Asia 'Western-style law and a kind of order was imposed'.[32]

Europe came close to complete free trade for only about a decade in the 1860s and 1870s.[33] By contrast, Southeast Asian colonial regimes, while not strictly laissez-faire, were free trade for exports, though not imports. Typically, Southeast Asian governments maintained their free trade policies until the early 1930s.

Southeast Asian countries on the whole had to wait until the post-1945 period for independence. The Tydings–McDuffie Act of 1934 created the Commonwealth of the Philippines, with a 10-year timetable for full independence. Elections the next year chose a Commonwealth president and marked the inauguration of the Commonwealth. Independence was in turn granted in July 1946. But in other Southeast Asian countries, except Thailand, Japan's late 1941 and early 1942 military sweep through Southeast Asia and occupation of the region until August 1945 greatly accelerated the process of decolonization. Burma gained independence in 1948 and Indonesia in 1949. Ho Chi Minh declared Vietnamese independence in September 1945 and, after a lengthy war with the French, this was accepted in the 1954 Geneva Accords which also dissolved Indochina, and led to independence for Cambodia and Laos. After another long war, this time with the United States, Vietnam was unified under a communist government in 1975. Malaya secured independence in 1957 as, in 1965, did Singapore as a city state, following a two-year union as part of Malaysia.

[29] Cf. Kuznets, 'Modern economic growth', p. 254.

[30] Trocki, 'Political structures', pp. 75–79; Tarling, *Nations and states*, pp. 58–63.

[31] Benda, 'Peasant movements', pp. 423–33.

[32] Trocki, 'Political structures', p. 104.

[33] Cameron and Neal, *Concise economic history*, p. 293.

In the process of decolonization and independence, the six pre-World War II Southeast Asian countries became 11 (Figure F.1). Burma (Myanmar), Thailand and the Philippines retained their geographical boundaries, as did the French Indochinese administrative divisions of Vietnam, Cambodia and Laos, but as separate states. By 1965, Malaya had split into Malaysia, Singapore and Brunei (independent in 1984). East Timor, after separating from Indonesia, gained sovereignty in 2002. The book does not deal with Brunei, a tiny, extremely wealthy, petroleum economy, or Timor, small, tragically poor and undeveloped. Both are special cases and need separate consideration.

Globalization and Southeast Asian Growth

Parallels between Southeast Asia's two phases of rapid globalization and growth, in the late nineteenth and late twentieth centuries, afford the book a coherent comparison across both time and geographical space. In both globalization phases, trade was in response to growing markets in developed countries and served as an 'engine of growth'. Just as the export of natural resource-intensive products conferred a commonality of regional commodity composition throughout the first phase, so manufactures assumed the same role during the second. The two globalization phases were similar in that for both growth was chiefly extensive, depending on ever greater inputs, not intensive through technical progress.

These two globalization phases differ in the extent of industrialization and economic structure of Southeast Asian countries. Remarkably little manufacturing developed before World War II, and Southeast Asia's economies remained overwhelmingly agricultural. Beginning in the 1970s, however, manufacturing for export fuelled growth at historically unprecedented rates, and by the early 2000s throughout the region GDP became more industrial than agricultural.

Pre-World War II Economic Responses to Globalization

Beginning in the late nineteenth century, the lowering of barriers to transport and trade, growing external markets and political stability were necessary, but not sufficient, conditions for Southeast Asia's rapid economic transformation. Change and growth also required responsiveness from those in Southeast Asia to the forces of globalization. Traditionally, two main strands in Southeast Asian society were the old elites (Benda's 'Great Tradition') and the peasantry (the 'Little Tradition').[34] While colonialism neutralized, or even eliminated, the former, it enhanced the scope of the peasantry to respond to economic opportunity. During post-1870 globalization, the speed and extent of peasant response,

[34] Benda, 'Structure', p. 114.

in migrating to frontier areas and planting export crops, was fundamental to Southeast Asia's economic and social transformation. Throughout Southeast Asia, as in Burma, 'unspectacular peasant pertinacity and courage … not less than the demands of the world market and European capital, in three generations turned the vast desolation of the Delta swamps and jungles into the greatest export granary of the East'.[35] Massive inflows of peasant migrants from India and China added fundamentally to the strength of this economic response.

Three further components were also key to Southeast Asian commercial response. Two were a large, vibrant network of Asian traders, and, complementary to it, European merchants located in the ports and larger cities and towns. Asians, mostly Chinese, collected hinterland produce; Europeans linked Southeast Asia to world markets for the sale of exports and a return flow of manufactures. The last of these three further components was European plantation and mining enterprise. While rice remained a crop of peasant farmers, plantations were important for rubber in Malaya, Indonesia and Vietnam. Often, plantations were organized through merchant houses which then functioned, along with their other business, as agents to sell rubber and procure supplies for the plantations. Because of the enhanced role as agents, these merchant houses became known as agency houses. Tin mining turned into a predominantly European enterprise because of its access to finance and technology. That also explains why Indonesian oil production was in European hands. Where Europeans were responsible for output, they already had links to the hinterland, and so also marketed exports.

Post-1945 Economic Responses to Globalization

Pre-World War II Southeast Asian development was a response of markets; post-war development was much more one of governments. After 1945, governments throughout the region intervened, to a greater or lesser extent, to promote development through import-substitution strategies. These followed the then prevailing development orthodoxy, and were easily justifiable because of the region's limited pre-war industrialization and the need to provide employment for rapidly growing populations in the early post-war years.

Because approaches to intervention varied greatly in the extent of government involvement and ideological approaches to the economy, for over four decades after World War II, Southeast Asian economic history cannot be analysed as a whole. The region no longer had its pre-World War II unity of a group of highly globalized, export-dependent, commodity specialized economies. Malaya, Thailand and the Philippines had relatively benign encounters with colonialism, and Japanese wartime efforts to encourage nationalism were largely unsuccessful. These countries all opted for continuity with pre-war

[35] Spate, 'Burmese village', p. 543.

globalization, economic openness and a pro-Western orientation as part of the 'Atlantic system'.[36] By contrast, before World War II, strong anti-colonial feeling existed in Burma, Indonesia and Vietnam. Between 1942 and 1945, nationalisms grew, and the means to realize them, through revolution or social upheaval, appeared as a consequence of wartime disruptions and, in Burma and Indonesia, Japanese-trained local armies. Beginning in the later 1940s, Burma, Indonesia and Vietnam turned decisively away from the global economy and inwards economically to try to develop as socialist or communist economies.

From the late 1960s onwards, historical unity began again to be restored in Southeast Asia, as an outcome of new opportunities in the global economy and government responses to these. Opportunity arose as a new wave of globalization, facilitated by the series of innovations in transport and communications, drew the world more and more tightly together. At the same time, Western multinational corporations began to search worldwide for cheap labour which, soaked up by post-1945 growth, no longer existed in developed countries. In response, Southeast Asian countries, through government policy shifts, could utilize their new factor endowment of abundant labour, the result of continuous post-World War II population growth and the settling of the frontier. Beginning with Singapore in the late 1960s, followed by Malaysia, Thailand and the Philippines during the 1970s, almost all Southeast Asian governments turned away from attempting to industrialize on the basis of import substitution and looked more towards manufacturing for export. By making components, often for electronics and electrical goods, as part of global supply chains organized by multinationals, and through work on garments and footwear, Southeast Asian countries provided jobs for the unemployed and shifted workers out of low-productivity agriculture and services and into manufacturing.

All countries industrialized, all countries grew more rapidly than ever before, and in all the structure of GDP changed from predominantly agricultural to industrial. Heavy economic dependence on manufactured exports to the global economy, reliance on a narrow range of these goods, utilization in their production of the region's abundant factor endowment of labour and industrialization combined to create a new phase in Southeast Asian development. Together, excepting Myanmar and, for long periods, Indonesia, this phase gives the region's economic history, once more, a unity that allows it largely to be considered as a whole.

Concepts and Themes

This section discusses several themes that recur continuously throughout the book. These are all concepts of, or responses to, or the results of, globalization – the principal idea around which the book is organized. One, the frontier, is a concept. Three are responses: staple commodities, vent-for-surplus and migration

[36] Benda, 'Japanese interregnum', pp. 69–74; Bastin and Benda, *History*, p. 156.

including international immigration. The other two are results: 'the so-called "Plural Society" [and] the myth and reality of the "Dual Economy"'. Both were labelled *problematik* by Benda, who added, 'these are urgently awaiting a new generation of historians of Southeast Asia'.[37] Although that was several decades ago, relatively little has been written on either in a Southeast Asian context.

Frontier Southeast Asia

Globalization associated with innovations in transport and industrialization in Europe and the United States made it profitable to open and exploit the Southeast Asian frontier by creating a major new demand for the food and raw materials that it could produce. Because globalization led to the opening of frontier areas in this way, from the later nineteenth century it emphasized a unity of Southeast Asian economic and historical geography. In the 1870s, large parts of all Southeast Asian countries had in common low population densities and large frontier areas abundant in natural resources (Figure I.2).

As in much of the Americas and Africa, late nineteenth- and early twentieth-century globalization turned late nineteenth-century Southeast Asian history into the Age of the Frontier. In the 1860s, Malaya was still sparsely populated, largely unexplored and in large part jungle.[38] At that time, too, Sumatra and Borneo, part of Indonesia's Outer Islands (all islands other than Java and, before World War II, Madura), were lightly populated. Sumatra and Borneo became, along with Malaya, the world's leading world producers of rubber. In the closing decades of the nineteenth century, large areas of the Philippines, subsequently to specialize in sugar, remained frontier.

In continental Southeast Asia, frontier areas consisted of the deltaic plains deriving from two of the world's great rivers, the Irrawaddy in Burma and the Mekong in Indochina, and from Thailand's Chao Phraya Delta region. Between the 1870s and World War II, Southeast Asia's three delta areas became the 'rice bowl of Asia'. Beginning in the late nineteenth century, the phenomenal flow of peasants into frontier delta lands, Benda emphasizes, 'constitutes one of the most important ... periods in the social and economic history of modern Burma, Vietnam and Thailand'.[39]

The Southeast Asian frontier comprised relatively small parts of most countries and did not include Java or northern Vietnam, before World War II Southeast Asia's only densely populated areas. Economic historians of Indonesia

37 Benda, 'Structure', p. 132.

38 In this book, 'jungle' means an area which is lightly, if at all, settled and covered with some mixture of dense vegetation, trees and undergrowth making it difficult to navigate. Jungle areas, as in the deltas of Burma, Thailand and southern Vietnam, may also include swampy land. Jungle requires clearing prior to its widespread cultivation. For a similar use of 'jungle', see Elson, *End*, pp. 112, 129, 131, 154.

39 Benda, 'Structure', p. 132.

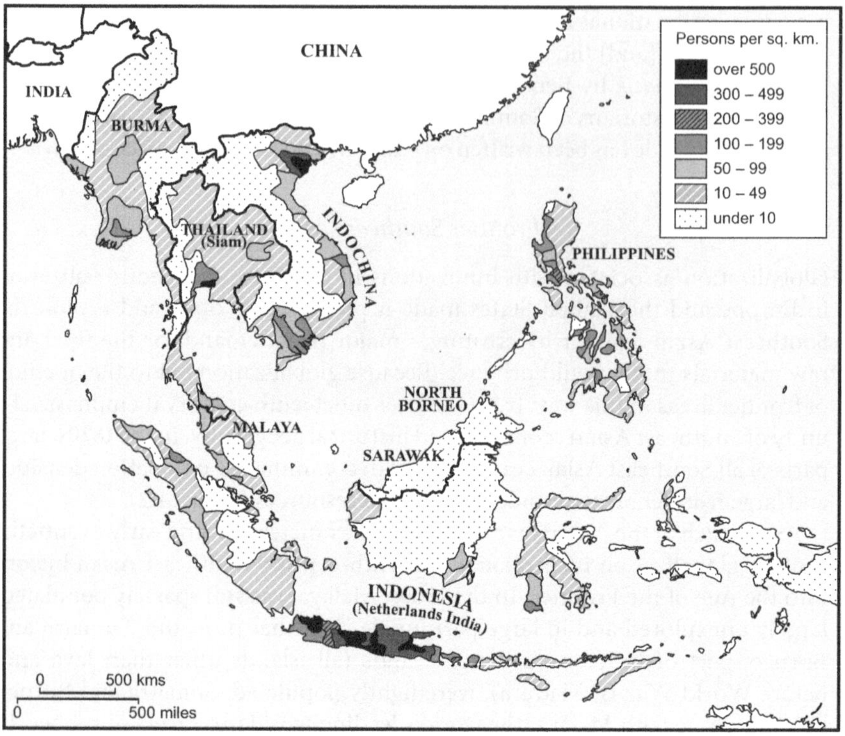

Figure I.2 Southeast Asia population distribution, 1940
Source: Broek, 'Diversity and unity', p. 180.

customarily treat its Javanese centre and the Outer Islands separately. Exceptional volcanic richness in mid-Java helped to make the island, even in the late nineteenth century, among the world's most thickly populated agricultural regions. By the 1930s, population density averaged 318 persons per square kilometre, but in parts of central Java densities were between 500 and over 750 per square kilometre, comparable to the most peopled regions of India and China (Figure I.2).

Northern Vietnam, made up of Tonkin and North Annam, had densities in five provinces in the Red River Delta of between 500 and over 800 people per square kilometre. In the north, unlike land-abundant Cochinchina – the southernmost of the three French administrative divisions of Tonkin, Annam and Cochinchina and including the Mekong Delta region – labour abundance resulted in an intricacy of rice cultivation that, observed a French civil servant, made difficult an incorporation of yet more labour. It was already like gardening.[40]

[40] AOM, Indochine nouveau fonds (hereafter INF) 2749, 'Principes généraux de la future économie Indochinoise', p. 10.

Staples and Vent-for-surplus

The staples and vent-for-surplus theories of growth are closely related. Staples are a single commodity, or a few commodities, that dominate a country's exports. As a leading sector, staples set the pace of growth and, because of the institutions and linkages that grow up around them, leave their particular imprint on an economy and society.[41] Often, staples are primary commodities whose production depends on abundant natural resources. In pre-World War II Southeast Asia, these were frontier land and mineral deposits. Just four main exports, one or two in each country, were basic to economic growth: rice, rubber, tin and sugar. These four, together with coconut products and petroleum, gave Southeast Asia a pattern of high export commodity concentration. Rice was overwhelmingly the chief export of Burma, Thailand and Indochina. Rubber and tin dominated the Malayan economy, and, along with sugar, were principal Indonesian exports. The Philippines developed into primarily a sugar economy, but additionally was the world's chief source of abaca and became a major producer of coconuts.

Although less appreciated in the literature, staples can also be manufactures if they are central to exports and become a leading sector. In much, but not all, of post-1970 Southeast Asia, electronics and electrical products and/or garments and footwear became the new Southeast Asian staples. The production of the new staples utilized, not an abundance of natural resources, but abundant labour, which, with the settling of frontier land and population increase, had become Southeast Asia's main factor endowment. Specialization was, as before World War II, pronounced, changing the region from agricultural to industrial economies.

The common characteristic of the 'vent-for-surplus' and staples theories is that, in both, growth involves the mobilization of resources that for the domestic economy lack alternative uses of significant economic value. In Southeast Asia before World War II, the resources were land, mineral deposits and labour, but by the 1970s became underemployed and unemployed labour. International trade provides a 'vent' or outlet allowing productive use of otherwise surplus resources.

During the pre-World War II phase of Southeast Asian vent-for-surplus growth, the exploitation of the region's natural resources drew on W. A. Lewis's unlimited labour.[42] Placed in an international context, Lewis's model is closely related to the concept of vent-for-surplus.[43] The exploitation of previously underutilized natural resources yields windfall gains, or rents, defined

41 Watkins, 'Staple', pp. 143–45; Caves, '"Vent-for-surplus" models' and 'Export-led growth'; Hirschman, 'Linkages', pp. 217–19; Baldwin, 'Patterns' and 'Export technology'.
42 Lewis, 'Economic development'.
43 Caves, '"Vent-for-surplus" models', p. 96.

as returns above the competitive average, as part of the venting process. These rents can be distributed between capital and labour depending on the extent to which a natural resource boom exerts upwards pressure on wages. In Southeast Asia, however, the prevalence of Lewis's unlimited labour effectively ruled out rents accruing to labour, and the issue becomes the realization among capitalists of rents and their reinvestment or not in the domestic economy.

Before World War II, workers came to Southeast Asia's staple-producing regions through internal migration and, even more, through international immigration from China and India. Surplus labour was again important during the manufacturing vent-for-surplus phase. In that phase, Southeast Asia in effect exported labour surpluses by virtue of their embodiment in labour-intensive goods produced for export.

Post-1970 Southeast Asia divided into migrant-receiving and migrant-sending countries. The most successful exporters of manufactures – Singapore, Malaysia and Thailand – needed more workers and mobilized labour surpluses through inter-Southeast Asian and Asian migration. For underemployed or unemployed workers in the less successful exporters and the more labour-abundant countries, there were three choices: remain at home, migrate to other Southeast Asian countries or migrate outside the region. Large numbers of workers chose either the second or third alternatives.

Southeast Asia's economic reliance on global markets for the venting of surpluses – both natural resources and labour – reappears throughout this book as a principal result of globalization. That, and the importance of a few staples to both social and economic development in Southeast Asia, give a commonality and continuity to the region's economic history, and a basis for the pre- and post-World War II comparisons which this book attempts. Through the combination of a mobilization of surpluses and international trade, Southeast Asia increased production and consumption, and the latter became much more varied.

Staple theory often focuses on GDP, not GDP per capita, and extensive rather than intensive growth.[44] In this book, however, GDP per capita is the main concern. It provides a gauge of welfare, overcomes the problem of different rates of population growth and offers a measure of Southeast Asian success in 'catching up' with income in the world leaders.

Vent-for-surplus, Staples and Growth

Few would imagine that Southeast Asia could have advanced so rapidly in the absence of export-led growth. Much of the book is about the two periods – from 1870 to 1929 and after 1967 – when, for most countries in the region, globalization and staple exports combined to fuel swift growth. The argument for these

[44] Caves, 'Export-led growth', pp. 405, 422–23; Dales et al., 'Primary products', p. 876.

parts of the book is that the venting of surplus resources, in some combination of land and labour, gave Southeast Asia a comparative advantage in the production of a few staples. The response of those in the region and export of these staples during the two globalization phases explains the pattern of growth, its acceleration and amplitude. Growth depended heavily on the specialization and division of labour engendered by the dynamic effects of exporting staples. They began expanding incomes in the home economy by hitherto unmatched volumes and redirecting labour into sectors of the economy servicing foreign demand.[45]

The vent-for-surplus and staples approaches are theories of regional growth.[46] Accordingly, the book concentrates on the dynamic, vent-for-surplus regions and sectors within Southeast Asian countries and, for the most part, leaves aside more traditional areas. While anthropologists have shown these areas as enterprising and vibrant, they do little to account for growth upsurges that have marked Southeast Asia's history.

Migration, Immigration and Plural Societies

Southeast Asia offered probably the world's best pre-World War II examples of plural societies, in which ethnic groups remain separated occupationally, residentially and socially: 'Each group holds by its own religion, its own culture and language, its own ideas and ways. As individuals they meet, but only in the market-place, in buying and selling … Even in the economic sphere there is a division of labour along racial lines.'[47]

A basis for plural societies already existed in pre-colonial Southeast Asia, because local rulers encouraged Chinese immigration, or resorted to kidnapping and slavery of ethnically different Asians to offset low population densities and so labour scarcity.[48] After 1870, colonial rule, economic expansion and large immigrant inflows to Southeast Asia combined to amplify plural societies. Colonialism had this effect in two important respects. One was that often, as in Burma and Indonesia, ethnic groups sharply distinguished by language and culture were subsumed within new borders established by colonial rule. The

[45] North, *Economic growth*, pp. 1–14, 68–69; Caves, '"Vent-for-surplus" models', pp. 109–11 and 'Export-led growth', pp. 405–06, 419–24.

[46] Buckley, 'Role of staple industries', p. 443; see also Bruchey, 'North on American economic growth', pp. 150–51; Engerman, 'North's *Economic growth*', pp. 251–52; Easterlin, 'Review of North', pp. 124–26.

[47] Furnivall, *Colonial policy and practice*, pp. 304, 353. The term race, although strictly incorrect, is long sanctioned by Southeast Asian usage to refer to Chinese and Indians as well as 'indigenous' regional groups. However, this book uses the term ethnic group to denote Chinese, Indians, Malays and so on rather than race.

[48] Trocki, 'Political structures', p. 106.

second was that colonial policy in Malaya and Burma actively promoted mass immigration, while it was virtually unrestricted in Thailand until the 1930s. Chinese immigration, though sizeable, was smaller in Indonesia, Indochina and the Philippines, because of restriction by the authorities. In addition to large numbers of Chinese and Indian immigrants, colonial rule and economic growth drew some Europeans, as administrators or for business.

Before World War II, ethnic tensions in Southeast Asia, though with exceptions, remained in check. After the war, however, they frequently boiled over. How to manage an inheritance of ethnic diversity became a problem confronting the region's newly independent nations. Malaysia, through a post-war bargain of Chinese economic dominance and Malay political control, found an early, though temporary, reconciliation, but some other countries did not. Burma forced Indians to leave as did Vietnam for many Chinese, but the Myanmar government fought ongoing wars with the country's ethnic minorities.

While during the first globalization phase immigration was fundamental to the peopling of Southeast Asia, after World War II, rapidly expanding populations and increasing land scarcity fuelled cityward migration. Southeast Asia changed from a little-urbanized region to one of several large cities and three megalopolises. The region also became, not a recipient of large population inflows, but a provider of them, because migrants either left home to work in other, wealthier Southeast Asian countries or for jobs outside Southeast Asia.

Dualism

The concept of dualism – the split of an economy, society or geography into distinct parts – is elusive, because it applies to a number of interrelated social science disciplines, and often blurs them. Societal splits in two are seldom, if ever, neat. One half overlaps with and links to the other, something true of all aspects of Southeast Asian dualism.

For economists, the dual economy divides into modern and traditional economic sectors. That is inappropriate for Southeast Asia, since most exports, including rice, were produced by peasants and small farmers using traditional methods. Although these producers were drawn into considerable specialization and a money economy, they could not otherwise be described as being part of a modern sector.[49] In this book, the modern sector refers to plantation organization, industry dependent on a degree of technology, some of which was advanced like tin smelting, and parts of the larger urban areas. The modern sector of cities included the commercial apparatus of European banks and business houses, along with a relatively small number of Asian businesses and

[49] The book adopts the broad terminology 'peasant', although in reality many such individuals became small farmers.

banks. Because Southeast Asian development relied heavily on peasant exporters, the region, like pre-World War II Nigeria and Ghana, does not fit the development literature's concept of 'enclave economies'. Those are economies like South Africa's, in which 'foreign capital, entrepreneurship, and modern technology have developed the economy and in which there is a relatively large flow of workers from the traditional to the modern economy'.[50]

The Southeast Asian traditional sector, as defined here, has the ambivalence that it encompasses, as well as peasants producing for export, others not chiefly engaged in, or dependent on, export production. That included a large share of the population, because export production typically concentrated in relatively small parts of each country. Many of those in the traditional sector were subsistence or near subsistence producers, for example the populations in a large part of the agricultural sectors in Indonesia, the Philippines or northern Vietnam.

Before World War II, Tonkin and the north of Annam in Vietnam could be described as 'a sluggish, rather self-contained economy resembling China … rather than Southeast Asia [while] Laos and Cambodia were isolated and backward'.[51] Nevertheless, throughout Southeast Asia the traditional sector, although producing little for export, had vibrant local markets, and sold some output to the modern sector as well as buying from it manufactured imports like simple implements. In Burma's Shan States, for example, 'hill-rice, reared on flights of small terraces in the gentler valleys, is the chief subsistence crop, while where the railway is accessible potatoes, flowers, oranges and soft fruits are grown for Rangoon and hill-station markets'.[52]

Dualism in Southeast Asia also had geographic and social dimensions. These overlapped and reinforced each other. The location of pre-World War II export-oriented production was typically explained by some combination of suitable natural resources and existing transport links; both had quite uneven geographical distributions within countries. Immigrants tended to locate either where export production centred or in cities, while the population of traditional areas was generally disproportionately indigenous. Export-led growth that favoured geographically as well as economically lopsided economies was, as Nurkse argued, 'surely better than no growth at all'.[53] But the unevenness of growth showed up one of the limitations of vent-for-surplus trade as an 'engine of growth'.

Plural societies strengthen a social dualism of occupational specialization and residential location. Different ethnic groups tended to specialize in certain occupations, because others from their group, already engaged in an occupation, could help in securing employment in the same occupation. The tendency

50 Helleiner, *Peasant agriculture*, pp. 135–36.
51 Reynolds, *Economic growth*, p. 135.
52 Spate, *Burma setting*, p. 19.
53 Nurkse, *Patterns*, p. 18.

of ethnic groups to specialize occupationally encouraged a geographical concentration of that group, since its members needed to be near their work and preferred to live with others who spoke the same language, ate the same food and practised the same religion.

Distinct labour markets developed as an aspect of plural societies. The markets persisted, often beyond the pre-World War II years, because for much of the region's history an oversupply of workers allowed employers to continue to choose employees from a pool of a like group or religion. The occupational concentration of ethnic groups depended partly on the supply price of their labour. Immigrants originating from different areas had different supply prices. More arrivals in Southeast Asia from the same ethnic group drove down wages, and the plural society's selectivity worked to solidify inter-group economic inequality.

In pre-World War II Southeast Asia, economic, geographical and social dualism were all apparent in a split between a few large urban centres and rural areas. Before World War II, Southeast Asia's population remained overwhelmingly rural. Each pre-war country had one or two large port cities – the first usually twice or more the size of the country's second city – that grew as administrative centres and around the provision of handling, processing and finance services for primary commodity exports. In 1913, and much more by 1939, Southeast Asia had modern banking systems, good port facilities, networks of railways and roads, schools and hospitals. However, this infrastructure concentrated in the main port cities. Because of the dominance in Southeast Asia's economies of at most a few exports, the large port cities that handled these exports, including Rangoon, Bangkok, Singapore and Saigon-Cholon, can be thought of as staple ports.

Cultural and social dualism as a contrast between elements of the modern and the traditional is exemplified in the differences between Rangoon and Mandalay. Rangoon was 'the cosmopolitan sea-port, busy and flourishing, yet a little shoddy and second-hand, grafted on to the country rather than growing from it'. Mandalay, although Burma's second city, was an 'overgrown village dreaming of a religious and monarchical past, and for the rest untidily stagnating'.[54]

Mass Chinese and Indian immigration to Southeast Asia added to an association between geographical dualism and cultural and social dualism. Singapore and Bangkok became Chinese cities and Rangoon an Indian one. Saigon-Cholon, Manila, and Indonesia's main cities all had a large Chinese commercial presence. Everywhere in Southeast Asia, immigrant groups – Indians in Burma, Chinese elsewhere – not indigenous ones, dominated commerce, along with European trading houses and banks.

[54] Spate, *Burma setting*, pp. 32–33.

Southeast Asia's pre-war urban dualism had a global dimension. Late nineteenth-century globalization divided the world into a small group of industrialized countries in Europe and the United States and a much larger number of primary producing countries. Southeast Asia became a component of the latter. The main Southeast Asian cities were, as major ports, situated on the fringes of their respective countries and in function and ethnic composition distinct from the countryside. Accordingly, these urban centres could be regarded as peripheral to their countries which, in turn, were peripheral to the world economy, the periphery of a periphery.

Still in 2025, Southeast Asia had a large rural component, despite several major cities. Some of the largest, Jakarta, Manila and Bangkok, qualify as megalopolises. Just as before World War II, large Southeast Asian cities differed sharply in modernity and function from most of rural Southeast Asia. The region's major cities, and others still sizeable but further down an urban hierarchy, displayed a dualism of their own. Substantial modern, Westernized areas co-existed with numerous poor inhabitants, often dwelling in slum or squatter areas and working in an informal economy rather than its organized, modern sector.

Plan of the Book

Seven chapters comprise Part I of the book on the pre-World War II period. Chapter 1 sets out a vent-for-surplus model and quantifies economic growth. The subjects of Chapter 2 are the Southeast Asian frontier, flows of migrants and immigrants to it and trade expansion. Business structure and finance are considered in Chapter 3, while industrialization is assessed in Chapter 4. The fifth chapter deals with infrastructure, including education, and foreign investment. Chapter 6 examines urbanization, and Chapter 7 offers a pre-World War II development assessment.

Part II of the book, in Chapters 8 and 9, looks at the World War II Japanese occupation and its political and economic impact on Southeast Asia. Together with some of the legacies of colonialism, wartime occupation had a major role in dividing Southeast Asia between the inward-looking nations of Indonesia, Burma and Vietnam, which rejected globalization, and their outward-looking counterparts of Thailand, Malaysia, Singapore and the Philippines, which continued actively to engage in the world economy. Because of this split and the need to assess countries individually, the book's Part III, in Chapters 10 through 12, focuses first on inward-looking, socialist Vietnam, Cambodia and Laos and then on Myanmar and Indonesia. The book turns, in Part IV, to the experiences of the outward-looking countries.

Part V again deals with all of Southeast Asia because, starting from the 1970s, countries in the region began to look to global markets for export-oriented industrialization as the engine for swift economic growth. Chapters 15 and 16 investigate the genesis and results of post-1970 industrialization and growth. Driven by multinationals and exports, this phase of globalization transformed Southeast Asia into a region for which manufacturing became the chief source of growth. Gains in GDP per capita were accompanied by marked improvements in life expectancy, the expansion of education and poverty reduction. A result of rural–urban migration and industrialization has been rapid urbanization and the creation of Southeast Asian cities of 10 million or more. Chapter 17 analyses this urbanization. The concluding chapter offers an appraisal of Southeast Asian development after 1950 and considers themes and commonalities which, since 1870, allow the region's economic history to be treated as a whole.

PART I

Southeast Asia, 1870–1940

1

Vent-for-surplus and Growth Trends

In the vent-for-surplus model, international trade affords a vent, or outlet, for potentially productive, but surplus, land and mineral resources as well as possibly also for surplus labour. Utilization of these endowments in response to external demand allows exports to increase rapidly. Specialization in one or two primary commodity staples accompanies this expansion, and is based on comparative advantage in commodities that exploit the region's resource surpluses. There is not a binding capital constraint, because technologies remain simple and ever greater output draws on the surpluses, not on technological advance.

In accounting for pre-World War II Southeast Asian growth, a vent-for-surplus model is the explanation preferred by several economists, if sometimes with qualification as to whether surplus labour as well as surplus land existed. Lewis indicates vent-for-surplus as apposite for Burma and Thailand; Findlay and Lundahl specify Burma and mention Malaya. So too does Maddison, who further extends the analysis to Indochina and Indonesia. Booth, and even more Touwen, elaborate on the latter's vent-for-surplus nature, while Power and Sicat, as well as Hooley, draw attention to this pattern of growth in the Philippines. Articles by Drake and Hayami give credence to all these instances. A recent, interesting application of vent-for-surplus is provided by López Jerez.[1]

This chapter's first section sets out a formal vent-for-surplus model applicable to pre-World War II Southeast Asia. A second section considers the roles of exports, investment and government in Southeast Asia's pre-war economies, and argues that exports were the driving force in growth. The chapter's third section presents GDP and population data for the 1870s to World War II. Growth was rapid in vent-for-surplus areas, although markedly slower in countries as a whole, because of still large traditional sectors.

[1] Myint, 'Gains' and '"Classical" theory'; Lewis, 'Development economics', p. 123; Findlay and Lundahl, 'Natural resources and economic development' and 'Staples theory', p. 71; Maddison, 'Colonial burden', p. 364 and *Historical statistics: 1-2008 AD*, p. 98; Booth, *Agricultural development*, p. 205; Touwen, *Extremes*, p. 30 and throughout; Power and Sicat, *Philippines*, p. 15; Hooley, 'Century', p. 269; Drake, 'Natural resources', pp. 951–62 and 'Vent for surplus'; Hayami, 'Ecology', pp. 177–81; López Jerez, 'Factor endowments'.

Vent-for-surplus Model

The importance to Southeast Asian growth of international trade which enabled the region to 'vent' or export factors of production surplus to domestic use appears throughout this book. The formal vent-for-surplus model in this section provides a framework to aid an understanding of the mechanisms of pre-World War II Southeast Asian growth and expansion. While the model does not generalize to the rapid growth in Southeast Asia underway by the 1970s, the concept of vent-for-surplus does. Vent-for-surplus has not previously been extended to recent economic growth in Southeast Asia or elsewhere, but, as pointed out, it is a notion that 'cries out for full generalization to the exportation of labor in the form of industrial goods'.[2] Later chapters in the book extend the vent-for-surplus concept to show Southeast Asia's incorporation of labour surpluses in post-1970s growth.

The development process in the vent-for-surplus model combines Adam Smith's venting, through bringing into production some previously unused resource, and Ricardian reallocation of factors of production according to comparative advantage. Unlike earlier vent-for-surplus models, however, the model in this section carefully delineates the vent-for-surplus model's Smith and Ricardo phases and incorporates consumer preferences. By stressing these and delineating a more complex set of production possibility frontiers than previously, the model gains in reality by more fully explaining trade and 'de-industrialization' in pre-World War II vent-for-surplus countries. These economies did not simply specialize in one or two staple exports and exchange these for manufactured goods. Rather, they produced even greater quantities of the vented staple than earlier models suggest. Some of this output was used to import preferred, non-manufactured, goods, and more of these or other goods than possible with home production. Consideration of consumer preferences, and freeing them from an assumption of constancy, allows the model to explain both a lack of industrialization and regional trade in vent-for-surplus economies. Intra-regional trade in these economies depended principally on trade in food rather than an exchange in manufactures.

In the model, the economy consists of two sectors (Figure 1.1). One comprises locally produced manufactured goods, measured along the vertical axis and described as handicrafts. The other sector, along the horizontal axis, produces food, consumed at home, and also an export staple, which may be the food but may also be another primary commodity. Initially, the country exists in autarky; the domestic economy exchanges handicrafts for food. The line MX reflects total person hours available and the labour required for each unit of handicrafts and food. It is shown as a straight line. The supply of land is not a constraint: over a large range of production, and for a considerable

[2] Ranis, 'Comment', p. 146.

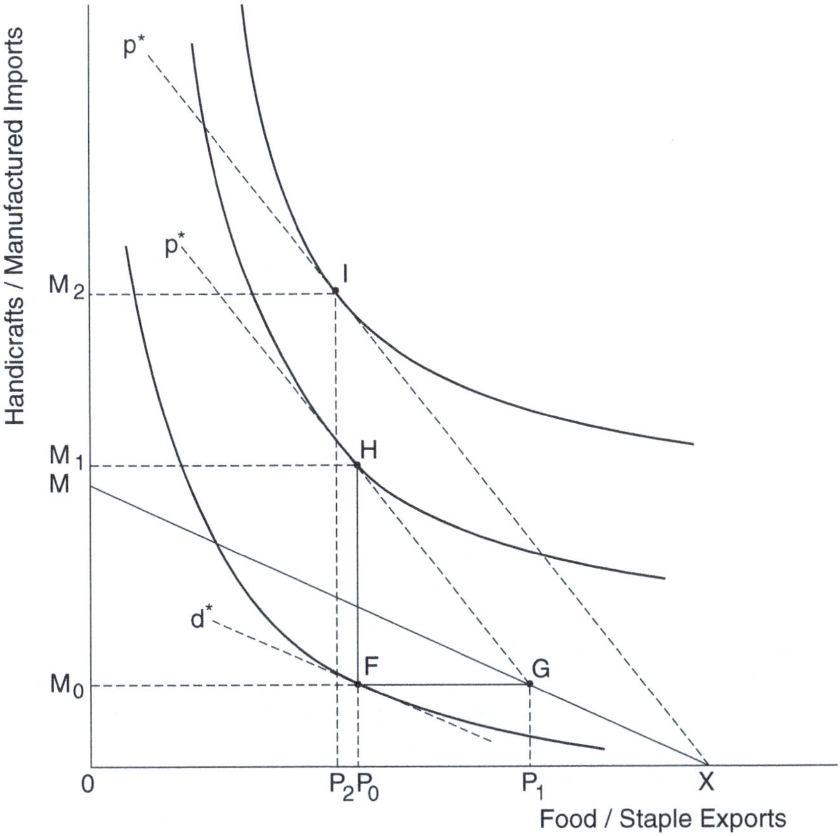

Figure 1.1 Vent-for-surplus with consumer preferences

time, the ready availability of good quality land avoids diminishing returns. Furthermore, even when frontier land is no longer of the best quality, it remains abundant and surplus to purely domestic economy requirements. There is no capital constraint, because it is assumed that any required tools are simple and available to the labour force in the desired quantities. Technology is not considered; expansion occurs through the exploitation of surplus natural resources with virtually unchanged techniques.[3]

The economy begins with both surplus land and surplus labour. As neither have domestic uses regarded as worth the effort of mobilization, the economy is not producing on the production possibility frontier MX but somewhere

[3] Myint, '"Classical" theory'; and see the formal models of Helleiner, *Peasant agriculture*, pp. 10–12 and Findlay, *Trade and specialization*, pp. 70–76. The model presented here is owing to Andrew Bain.

inside, at point F. The line d*, parallel to MX, shows the terms of trade at the underemployment equilibrium F. At F, with the economy in autarky, production is identical to consumption for both food and handicrafts. Since the opportunity cost of leisure is the same for both outputs, and producers could, if they wished, switch between the two, this is a point of consumer equilibrium and the indifference curve at F must be tangential to terms of trade line d*.

When international trade opens, variously described as 'unlocking' or 'opening up' the tropics, this creates a vent or outlet for surpluses of land and labour and so a chance to mobilize them.[4] The opportunity that foreign markets afford to exploit underutilized resources sets in train a process stretching, as Myint stressed, over 'many decades'.[5] During these, trade expands the productive capacity of the economy by widening the market and supporting specialization, through promoting the development of transport and other social overhead capital, creating linkages associated with exported commodities and strengthening an institutional framework conducive to stability and commerce. Once trade is opened, a new, improved terms of trade (the segment GH) becomes available and consumption in the economy can move to point H. At H, the economy produces OP_1 of food and staples, divided between OP_0 of food for domestic consumption and P_0P_1 of staples for export, and consumes OM_1 of handicrafts/manufactures, consisting of OM_0 of domestic handicraft production supplemented by M_0M_1 of imported manufactures. The trade triangle FGH, showing the exchange of FG of staples for FH of manufactures, represents the Smith effect. This initial Smithian venting phase is pure gain through the mobilization of unemployed resources of both land and labour. Through trade, the economy can consume at point H, above F. However, leisure must be sacrificed to produce staples, FG, destined for international markets. An increased opportunity cost of leisure induces this sacrifice. Opportunity cost rises because consumers can obtain, in exchange for staple exports, as well as more goods broadly comparable to the handicrafts produced by the economy, new items, the 'novelties hitherto unknown in the subsistence economy' emphasized by Myint.[6] Imports such as cotton piece goods replace handicrafts as a cheaper way of satisfying existing wants. Moreover, a greater range of goods, including, in time, capital items, like sewing machines, bicycles and small trucks as well as construction materials for houses, stimulates new wants and is a dynamic force in the expansion of exports.[7]

The Smith effect, described above, is a statement of the use of unutilized resources to produce commodities which, once vented, allow an economy to import goods regarded as being of greater value, FH of imports in Figure 1.1.

[4] Knowles, *Economic development*, pp. 138–52; Myint, '"Classical" theory', p. 324.
[5] Myint, 'Neoclassical resurgence', p. 121.
[6] Myint, 'Neoclassical resurgence', p. 121.
[7] Touwen, *Extremes*, p. 319.

The effect does not, however, take into account any adjustments that people might want to make once vented output creates the possibility of obtaining the additional imports. In Figure 1.1 the trade-off in production is now shown by the line p*, passing through point H. Consumption of food remains at OP_0, consumption of handicrafts and manufactures is OM_1. This is not a consumer equilibrium position for two reasons. First, other than by coincidence, the consumer indifference curve passing through H will not have the slope of p*: in Figure 1.1 the consumer equilibrium lies above and to the left of H, implying that the consumer would prefer to give up some food consumption to obtain even more manufactures. Second, as Ricardo showed, H is not a producer equilibrium. Domestic production of handicrafts has become an obsolete technology which will be superseded by producing staples (food such as rice, rubber or some other staple in which the economy specializes) and obtaining manufactured goods by trading these staples for imports.

In continued adjustment during this second, Ricardian, phase, domestic consumers and producers re-adjust preferences and reallocate production in line with comparative advantage. The production possibility frontier has moved upwards and to the right to become the straight line p* through X. In Figure 1.1, the indifference curve touches the p*X frontier at I and P_2X of staples are exchanged for OM_2 of manufactures.[8] Domestic production of handicrafts will gradually fall towards zero and the economy tend towards full specialization in food and staples production, the food for home consumption (OP_2) and the staple (P_2X) exported. All the economy's manufactures (OM_2) will be imported.

With unchanged labour supply and no reduction in the cost of producing food domestically, real food consumption would be likely to fall, though in economies like Southeast Asia's any reduction might be small. Moreover, if imported food became available as a cheaper or superior substitute, food consumption could be maintained or increased while the labour applied to production of food for domestic consumption diminished. The Southeast Asian reality was an extensive trade in food, because tastes were particular and country production costs different; Asia's three great rice-exporting economies of Thailand, Burma and Indochina produced a wide variety of types and grades of the grain. In turn, these rice producers imported food from other Southeast Asian countries or beyond. Regional trade in food enabled economies to cut back on domestic food production to produce more of the vented staples, and at the same time, indirectly, adjust food consumption by importing superior and/or cheaper substitutes for domestically produced food. An outcome (as happened in non-food-specialized Southeast Asia) of this possibility of importing

8 With unchanged preferences (stable indifference curves) and since the labour force is now fully employed, people have less leisure. Accordingly, its marginal utility of leisure will rise and P2 will lie to the left of P0.

both food and manufactures may be a reduction in food production as well as the likely relegation of handicraft production to a small, specialized sector.

A theme of late nineteenth- and early twentieth-century swift 'de-industrialization' runs through the Southeast Asian literature. Preferences help in two respects to illuminate this issue and explain why during the late nineteenth century Southeast Asian economies quickly became so specialized and so little industrialized. In the first of these respects, supply- and demand-side considerations work together. Since H is not a point of equilibrium, consumers may, even in the initial Smithian phase, prefer to give up food to supply staples in exchange for manufactures, while consumers demand more of these cheaper and possibly better quality goods. Second, a preference for fewer handicrafts, reflecting their rudimentary nature and relatively high cost, would shift G down the XM line, implying even less local handicraft production, and therefore de-industrialization, a Ricardian effect in a Smithian phase.

A third phase of vent-for-surplus development is again a venting one, and thus Smithian. Continued migrant inflows and natural population increase lead to ever more settlement of the frontier. As more surplus land is brought under cultivation and/or mineral resources further exploited, the production possibility curve shifts to the right. The gains from trade promote growth through widening and deepening markets, paying for the import of capital goods and enabling countries to borrow abroad. Many of the gains were, however, linked to expanding the production and processing of staples and few to local industrialization.

Macroeconomy and Gains from Trade

Southeast Asian growth, as the vent-for-surplus model postulates, was export-led. Exports were chiefly responsible for fluctuations and long-term trends in growth. When exports collapsed in the 1930s, so did growth. This section examines, first, the macroeconomic aggregates of net exports, investment and government spending in pre-World War II Southeast Asia, and then indicates how exports contributed to widening and diversifying economies in the region.

In the vent-for-surplus model – and in Southeast Asia between the 1870s and World War II – exports set more rapid growth in motion, and remained the dominant factor in it.[9] Most Southeast Asian countries ran large surpluses on their trade balances and also, probably, their current accounts. The remitted profits of foreign business and pension obligations to colonial civil servants held down local consumption. Throughout Southeast Asia, colonial currency board systems that required 100 per cent foreign exchange backing for local currencies kept consumption spending highly dependent on income. It, in turn, depended principally on exports (Chapter 5).

[9] Cf. Ingram, *Economic change*, pp. 203–8, 227; Power and Sicat, *Philippines*, pp. 13–16.

Private investment spending was checked by four main circumstances. One was the predominance of peasant production in Southeast Asia, most notably in the three main rice-producing countries. In the rice industry and for other crops grown by peasants, the main investment inputs were not financial capital but own and family labour, which kept formal private investment expenditure low. Second, weakly developed financial systems restricted borrowing to invest. A lack of financial intermediaries to mobilize capital helped to explain why, for example in pre-World War II Thailand, '[I]nvestment in industrial projects is extremely limited'.[10]

The third circumstance limiting investment expenditure in Southeast Asia was that the region had relatively little modern industry, apart from processing the primary commodities exported in response to external demand (Chapter 4). In the three rice-exporting countries, with the partial exception of Vietnam, modern industry consisted of rice mills and not much else. Nor was investment in export processing industries necessarily large. Rubber processing required relatively little investment; rubber mills were generally part of rubber estates or small, Chinese-owned establishments. Only a few main export industries required substantial investment: estate crops, especially rubber, oil production and processing in Sumatra and Borneo, sugar centrals (factories) in the Philippines and the Malayan tin industry after about 1910.

Fourth, relatively modest requirements for infrastructure curbed investment expenditure. Southeast Asia relied heavily on water transport and settlement was predominantly rural with few large cities. These aspects of the region restricted the need for expensive transport infrastructure like railways and for urban amenities such as electricity, gas, lighting, streets and sewers. In contrast, the late nineteenth- and early twentieth-century newly settled areas of North and South America needed large investment in transport and urban infrastructure, and together these accounted for much of their capital formation (Chapter 5).

Southeast Asia's dual economies also served as a check on infrastructure spending as well as being perpetuated partly by the selective nature of expenditure on infrastructure. That was to some extent due to government policies not to build infrastructure in advance of demand. More important, infrastructure did not spread evenly through entire countries, but concentrated in comparatively small parts of Southeast Asia, where it catered for the needs of exports or served a few major cities.

Government spending, including on infrastructure, was restrained by the financial orthodoxy of the Southeast Asian colonial state. As a rule, colonial governments had a policy of balancing the budget, and restricting borrowing and public investment to stay within this guideline (Chapter 5). That

[10] Yang, *Multiple exchange rate system*, p. 14.

conservative approach limited the contribution state spending could make to incomes and demand in the economy, effectively constraining an impact of government expenditure on GDP to a balanced budget multiplier.

Trade Gains

The vent-for-surplus model illuminates how surplus land and/or labour can drive growth in the early stages of development. A part of this growth comes through the full utilization of available factor inputs and then the static gains of trade through a reallocation of resources. However, much of growth normally depends on two empirical considerations: the linkages generated by increased production of, and specialization in, one or more staple commodities and trade's indirect or dynamic gains. Different commodities have varying linkages; in Southeast Asia rice had only weak linkages, but tin and rubber stronger ones.

The dynamic gains from increased staple exports, which move the production possibilities outwards, are well known: the benefits of specialization with the attendant gains due to a greater division of labour and economies of scale; foreign exchange earnings allowing the import of capital goods; contact with and the transmission of new ideas, skills and technologies; and the stimulating effects of competition.[11] And yet, like linkages, these gains do not follow automatically from more staple exports but are contingent on the character of the staple and its multiplier effects as well as on human agency and its responsiveness to the market. Southeast Asian and expatriate European firms were quite alert to new opportunities but elsewhere in the world that may not always be so.

Trade's dynamic nature and its indirect benefits were fundamental to Southeast Asian growth. These indirect benefits appear throughout the book's subsequent chapters. They show how, as exports expanded, the size of economies grew, and along with this growth, opportunities arose for a greater division of labour and specialization. Trade added to growth through widening and deepening markets for locally produced goods and services. Market expansion promoted domestic manufacturing in import-substitution industries, created specialized services, especially in the marketing of staple exports, encouraged urbanization and helped to finance infrastructural development. Transport networks, including railways, extensive Southeast Asian intra-regional shipping and, by the inter-war years, motorized transport, all augmented growth in their own right. Through generating forward and backward linkages, transport gave rise to specialization gains, setting up further, new sources of growth and augmenting trade's dynamic effect. The spread of transport allowed large areas to be drawn into vent-for-surplus production, and so economies of scale to realize their productive capacity more fully.

[11] Haberler, *International trade*, pp. 10–15.

GDP and Population Growth

Southeast Asia's lopsidedness, in which countries were split between modern and traditional sectors but data collected on the basis of colonial (or for Thailand national) boundaries, causes countrywide statistics to mask, for vent-for-surplus areas, the speed of GDP per capita and population growth. Since the modern, or export, halves of the region's economies were usually small, rates of GDP per capita growth in them were well above those for countries as a whole. However, in vent-for-surplus Southeast Asian countries that attracted large immigrant inflows, GDP per capita growth lagged well behind GDP increases.

This section's first sub-section looks at estimates from the Maddison Project of Southeast Asian GDP per capita between 1870 and the late 1930s. A second sub-section shows data from another set of GDP per capita data that derive from Bassino and van der Eng. They reach figures quite different from Maddison's. The third sub-section analyses population data taken from Maddison. The data indicate the rapidity of population increase in some countries, and, by implication, much swifter GDP than GDP per capita growth. Because of this disparity, and to give a better idea of the rapidity with which national product expanded in parts of pre-war Southeast Asia, a fourth sub-section provides further population information. These data are drawn mainly from country censuses, and help to pinpoint population change in some of Southeast Asia's specifically vent-for-surplus regions.

Extreme caution should be used in interpreting any historical national income data for Southeast Asia. Comparison of the data discrepancies in the present and next sub-section shows this. GDP per capita estimates cannot be more than approximate, in view of the low levels of development in Southeast Asia in the late nineteenth century, and, subsequently, a lack of data for some economies and different methodologies of constructing estimates. Another reason to approach GDP data with care is that, Indonesia apart, only benchmark figures are available for Southeast Asia. Furthermore, data compiled by the Maddison Project use a single year of prices to arrive at benchmark figures, and the data derive from many different scholars, not always using estimation methods consistent with one another.

Maddison GDP per Capita

Between 1870 and 1900, according to the Maddison data, GDP per capita income gains were modest and Malaya had negative growth. That is explained by massive immigrant inflows. However, some of Southeast Asia grew as fast as, or even faster than, major European countries. Singapore's per capita income increased at 1.5 per cent annually and Indonesia's at 1.2 per cent, the latter especially boosted after an 1870 abandonment of the Culture System of forced deliveries of commodities to the state and the liberalization of foreign trade (Table 1.1).

Table 1.1 *Southeast Asia and metropolitan country GDP per capita, 1870–1938*

(a) GDP per capita (2011 US$)

	1870	1900	1913	1929	1938
Burma	803	1,114	1,092	1,438	1,180
Thailand	969	–	1,341	1,264	1,317
Malaya	1,055	818	1,289	3,220	2,515
Singapore	1,423	2,206	1,812	3,323	3,363
Indonesia	810	1,151	1,361	1,702	1,655
Philippines	995	1,073	1,575	2,252	2,295
Vietnam	805	–	1,159	–	–
Japan	1,580	2,123	2,431	3,665	4,257
United States	4,803	8,038	10,108	11,954	10,526
United Kingdom	5,829	7,594	8,212	8,772	9,988
Netherlands	4,422	5,306	6,454	9,068	8,368
France	2,990	4,584	5,555	7,508	7,119
Germany	2,931	4,758	5,815	6,457	7,960

(b) Growth of per capita GDP (2011 US$) per annum (%)

	1870–1900	1870–1913	1900–1913	1900–1929	1929–1938
Burma	1.1	0.7	−0.2	0.9	−2.2
Thailand	–	0.8	–	–	0.5
Malaya	−0.8	0.5	3.6	4.8	−2.7
Singapore	1.5	0.6	−1.5	1.4	0.1
Indonesia	1.2	1.2	1.3	1.4	−0.3
Philippines	0.3	1.1	3.0	2.6	0.2
Vietnam	–	0.9	–	–	–
Japan	1.0	1.0	1.0	1.9	1.7
United States	1.7	1.7	1.8	1.4	−1.4
United Kingdom	0.9	0.8	0.6	0.5	1.5
Netherlands	0.6	0.9	1.5	1.9	−0.9
France	1.4	1.5	1.5	1.7	−0.6
Germany	1.6	1.6	1.6	1.1	2.4

Notes: Growth rates for Burma and the Philippines are calculated for the years for which data are available, as noted below. *Burma*: The figure for 1900 is for 1901 and the 1929 figure is for 1931. *Philippines*: The figure for 1900 is for 1902. *Malaya* includes Penang but excludes Singapore.
Source: Maddison Project Database, 2020.

During the early settling of the rice frontier between 1870 and 1901, Burma recorded growth of 1.1 per cent per annum, but after the turn of the century, failed to find sources of growth other than rice. After 1900, Burma's per capita income growth lagged distinctly behind other Southeast Asian countries except Thailand, the other Southeast Asian laggard and also a rice economy. By 1913, the rice boom in Thailand was ending and, as in Burma, no new staple emerged to take the economy forward. In Thailand, GDP per capita stagnated after 1913. Income per person had actually declined somewhat by 1929, but recovered in 1938 again to reach its 1913 level. Inter-war expansion of Thailand's tin and rubber industries was too small to make a major contribution to growth.

Southeast Asian countries as a whole had their fastest long-term growth over the three decades 1900 to 1929. During this period, Malaya grew at 4.8 per cent annually, Indonesia at 1.4 per cent, Singapore at 1.4 per cent and the Philippines at 2.6 per cent. These growth rates were above, or on a par with, European income increases. Much of Southeast Asian growth is explained by the rubber export boom in Malaya and the Indonesian Outer Islands and the expansion of Philippine sugar production in response to preferential access, at above world prices, to the United States market. The opportunity to sell sugar to the United States on a preferential basis (unlimited exports from 1913 to 1933 and quotas either side of those dates) encouraged a partial modernization of sugar production in the Philippines.[12] Maddison does not have data for Vietnam but most probably, like the other rice export-dependent economies, it grew slowly after 1913.

The 1930s collapse in the world economy effectively halted growth in Southeast Asia, and for Burma and Malaya put it sharply into reverse. Southeast Asian economies, all heavily dependent on world markets for primary commodities, had no answer when demand for these plummeted. For Southeast Asia, the 1930s was the beginning of at least two, and for a number of countries even more, dismal decades. Economic advance was replaced, first, by at best stagnation and, then, during the Japanese occupation, by precipitate decline. Relative to the United States, Southeast Asian countries began the 1950s at income levels far behind those of 1929 and further still adrift of 1870 (Table 1.1).

Bassino and van der Eng GDP per Capita

For twentieth-century Southeast Asia, Bassino and van der Eng have made purchasing power parity estimates of GDP per capita that differ considerably from the Maddison data (Table 1.2). Malaya offers the most striking divergence between the Maddison and Bassino–van der Eng figures. By 1929, Malaya had a per capita income almost equivalent to Japan's according to the Maddison data, but the work of Bassino and van der Eng shows that in 1922 Malayan income was twice Japan's, and in 1938 over 80 per cent higher. This Malaya–Japan income

[12] Power and Sicat, *Philippines*, pp. 14–16; Golay, *Philippines*, pp. 133–35.

Table 1.2 *Southeast Asia and Japan GDP per capita, 1913–38*

(a) Current PPP Japanese yen	1913	1922	1938
Japan	98	271	377
Burma	86	152	231
Thailand	–	–	152
Malaya	262	563	691
Indonesia	103	145	146
Vietnam	78	167	159
Philippines	166	294	262
(b) Japan = 100	**1913**	**1922**	**1938**
Japan	100	100	100
Burma	87	56	61
Thailand	–	–	40
Malaya	267	207	183
Indonesia	104	53	39
Vietnam	80	62	42
Philippines	168	108	69

Source: Bassino and van der Eng, 'Asia's "little divergence"', p. 197.

difference suggests how fast vent-for-surplus growth could be and is explained by Malaya's small population and by the substantial proportion of its people engaged in producing rubber and tin for export. By contrast, Japan had a large, low-productivity agricultural sector and, although with considerable exports, concentrated on building an industrial economy. While that effort may have kept growth below what it might have been, it did build an economy that, by 1941, had become able to wage total war in the Pacific. Bassino and van der Eng find, however, lower Malayan growth from 1913 to 1938 than does Maddison. In both sets of estimates, inclusion of Singapore, then integral to the Malayan economy, to yield pan-Malayan data would increase a pan-Malayan GDP per capita figure.

The Bassino and van der Eng estimates, which have data for Vietnam but not Thailand, appear broadly to confirm for the inter-war years a slow-growth story for the three rice exporters.[13] Only the Maddison Project has data for 1929 and 1938, which hinders comparison with Bassino and van der Eng. However, their data, if 1913 and 1938 are compared, suggest a 1930s contraction in Southeast Asian per capita incomes not too dissimilar from that shown in the Maddison estimates.

13 Bassino and van der Eng, 'Asia's "little divergence"', p. 201.

Population Growth

Population grew rapidly in the countries of mass immigration, and considerably more slowly in Indonesia and the Philippines; in both, restrictions limited inflows from abroad. Between 1870 and 1913, the 2.5 per cent annual increase in Burma's population implies a doubling about every 28 years. That corresponds to the decades when, on the Burma frontier, good rice land was still available. In Thailand, population never grew so fast as in Burma, probably because the main employment opportunities for immigrant Chinese were in Bangkok. Increase in Thailand was most rapid after 1900, when the main growth in rice cultivation occurred. The same was true of the relationship from 1870 and 1900 between rice and population expansion in Burma.

Until the inter-war years, Malaya and Singapore recorded negative population growth through natural increase but that was more than offset, for most of the decades after 1870, by the arrival of large numbers of Chinese and Indian immigrants. In all the periods from 1870 onwards shown by Table 1.3, Malaya's population expanded swiftly. It grew at over 3 per cent annually between 1870 and 1913, and thereafter at more than 2 per cent. In response to the 1930s slump and collapse in rubber prices, immigrant inflows to Malaya and Singapore were replaced by mass exodus. Nevertheless, in both Malaya and Singapore from 1929 to 1940, population increased by over 2 per cent annually, substantially due to natural increase as sex ratios normalized.

For most of the years after 1870, Indonesian growth rates remained at about 1 per cent. Until the turn of the century, rates in the Philippines were also around 1 per cent, but increased markedly thereafter as the economy, boosted by preferential access to the American market for sugar, expanded at a quicker pace. In much of Southeast Asia in 1870, population was tiny in absolute terms. Despite seven decades of sustained growth throughout the region and rapid increase in several countries, in 1940 populations remained small in all countries except Indonesia and Indochina, where settlement concentrated in Java and northern Vietnam respectively.

GDP and Population

The addition for a given period of GDP per capita increase and population growth yields approximately the rate at which GDP grew. The difference between growth rates of GDP per capita and GDP was considerable in the Southeast Asian areas of mass international immigration. This sub-section matches, for Burma and Malaya, country per capita income data from Maddison (Table 1.1) with rates of population increase from the same source (Table 1.3) to indicate how rapidly GDP grew in the Southeast Asian countries with large immigrant inflows. Between 1870 and 1900, Burma's population expanded at an annual rate of some 3.0 per cent and Malaya's at 3.5 per cent.

Table 1.3 *Southeast Asian population, 1870–1940*

(a) 000 persons

	1870	1900	1913	1929	1940
Burma	4,245	10,174	12,326	14,364	16,594
Thailand	5,775	7,320	8,689	12,058	15,513
Malaya	800	2,232	3,084	4,316	5,434
Singapore	84	215	323	575	751
Indonesia	32,743	45,100	51,637	61,019	74,376
Philippines	5,063	7,324	9,384	12,890	16,585
Indochina	13,623	–	23,796	–	28,071

(b) Growth of population per annum (%)

	1870–1900	1870–1913	1900–1913	1900–1929	1929–1940
Burma	3.0	2.5	1.5	1.2	1.3
Thailand	0.8	1.0	1.3	1.7	2.3
Malaya	3.5	3.2	2.5	2.3	2.1
Singapore	3.2	3.2	3.2	3.5	2.5
Indonesia	1.1	1.1	1.0	1.0	1.8
Philippines	1.2	1.4	1.9	2.0	2.3
Indochina	–	1.3	–	–	–

Notes: 1. Indochina includes Vietnam, Cambodia and Laos. The figure for 1940 for Indochina is estimated. 2. Malaya includes Penang but excludes Singapore.
Source: Maddison Project Database, 2020.

The addition of these rates and GDP per capita increase implies, for 1870 to 1900, for Burma, GDP growth of 4.1 per cent, and for Malaya, of 2.7 per cent. In fact, the pace of GDP increase must have been even faster than 4.1 per cent in Burma's main vent-for-surplus region of Lower Burma, since, between 1870 and 1900, population increase in Lower Burma (2.5 per cent annually between 1871 and 1901) largely accounts for Burma's overall rise in population. Cochinchina, Vietnam's rice frontier, added people at a pace comparable to Lower Burma's, with 2.8 per cent annual population growth during the last decades of the nineteenth century (Table 1.4).

The time of spectacular Southeast Asian GDP per capita expansion was from 1900 to 1929, and for these years some of the country differences between increases in GDP and GDP per capita were large. The addition of Malaya's annual per capita income growth of 4.8 per cent and its 2.3 per cent population growth indicates that GDP increased annually at 7.1 per cent, equivalent to a doubling every 10 years. High exports, a booming economy and mass Chinese

Table 1.4 *Southeast Asia growth of population, 1871–1938*

(a) Population, 000 persons

	1871	1881	1891	1901	1911	1921	1931	1938
Burma: Lower Burma	2,747	3,737	4,603	5,580	6,393	7,047	7,964	9,066
Burma: Total	–	–	7,722	10,491	12,115	13,212	14,667	16,824
Thailand	5,775	6,200	6,670	7,320	8,266	9,207	11,506	14,464
Malaya	–	–	1,710	2,085	2,651	3,327	4,348	5,004
Indonesia: Outer Islands	–	–	–	7,851	–	14,366	19,009	–
Indonesia: Java and Madura	–	–	–	30,353	–	34,984	41,718	–
Indochina: Cochinchina	–	1,679	–	2,937	3,004	3,797	4,484	4,620
Indochina: Total	–	12,000	–	–	16,395	18,800	21,450	23,030
Philippines	–	6,122	–	7,635	8,835	10,314	13,405	16,000

(b) Annual growth (%)

	1871–1901	1881–1901	1901–1911	1901–1931	1931–1938
Burma: Lower Burma	2.5	3.6	1.4	1.2	1.3
Burma: Total	–	–	1.4	1.1	1.4
Thailand	0.8	0.8	1.1	1.5	3.3
Malaya	–	–	2.4	2.5	1.8
Indonesia: Outer Islands	–	–	–	3.6	–
Indonesia: Java and Madura	–	–	–	1.1	–
Indochina: Cochinchina	–	2.8	0.2	1.4	0.6
Indochina: Total	–	–	–	–	0.7
Philippines	–	0.9	0.8	2.0	2.0

Table 1.4 (*cont.*)

Notes and Sources:

Growth: rates refer to the nearest available dates from panel a, as described below.

Population:

Burma: Figures for Lower Burma refer to the 1872 census area. The figure for 1938 refers to 1941. Hlaing, *Study*, p. 13.

Indochina: Figures for 1880 and 1911 are from Brocheux and Hémery, who point out that they are orders of magnitude. The figure for 1911 refers to 1913 and that for 1938 refers to 1936. Brocheux and Hémery, *Indochina*, p. 254; Indochina, *Annuaire statistique 1943–1946*, p. 271. Population figures for Cochinchina refer for 1881 to 1880, for 1901 to 1900 and for 1938 to 1936. Figures for 1880 and 1900 are from Sansom, *Economics of insurgency*, pp. 259, 261; 1910: Coquerel, *Paddys et riz*, p. 225; 1921 and 1931: Indochina, *Annuaire statistique 1923–29*, p. 61; *1931–32*, p. 53, *1943–46*, p. 271.

Thailand: For 1881–1901 figures are from Skinner and refer to 1880, 1890 and 1900. Skinner, *Chinese society*, p. 79. Subsequent figures are from Thailand, *Statistical yearbook, 1937–38 and 1939–40*, p. 46 and refer to the census returns for 1919, 1929 and 1937.

Malaya: The 1881 population is estimated by assuming that population grew at the same rate as in 1891–1901. For 1891 and 1901 figures are estimated for the Unfederated Malay States (UMS) only. Estimation is on the basis of the 1911 census figure of a UMS population of 899,968 persons and backwards extrapolation assuming that during both decades the population grew at 0.65 per cent per annum. A basis for this assumed rate of UMS population growth is Dodge, 'Population estimates', pp. 457–74. Data for 1891–1911 are from Federated Malay States, *1911 census*, pp. 18, 95; Malaya, *1921 census*, p. 18. For 1921 onwards data are from Malaya, *1947 census*, p. 39. The 1938 population figure is an estimate and assumes proportional population growth between 1931 and the 1947 census figure of 5,848,910 persons.

Indonesia: The figure for 1881 refers to 1880. Indonesia, *Statistical pocketbook of Indonesia 1941*, p. 5. Figures for 1901, 1921 and 1931 refer to 1905, 1920 and 1930. Boomgaard and Gooszen, *Population trends*, pp. 117–21, 133–37, 224–30.

Philippines: For 1881 the figure refers to 1877. It is the census figure for that year for 'civilized people' (5.567 million) plus the 1903 census figure for 'wild people' transformed into an estimate for 1877 under the assumption of population growth of 0.60 per cent per annum. Philippines, *Census of the Philippine Islands 1903*, vol. 2, pp. 19, 123. The 1901 figure is for 1903 and from the census for that year. *Census of the Philippine Islands 1903*, vol. 2, p. 123. The 1921 figure refers to 1918 and is the census figure. Philippines, *Census of the Philippine Islands 1918*, vol. 2, p. 19. The figure for 1931 is an estimate from Philippines, Bureau of the Census and Statistics, *Yearbook of Philippine statistics 1940*, p. 24. For 1931 the figure refers to 1930. The figure for 1938 is for the census taken on 1 January 1939 and is from Philippines, Commission of the Census, *Special bulletin no. 1, 1939 census*, p. 3.

and Indian immigration complemented one another. That was not always the case. Although, after 1913, Thai rice exports, and so GDP, expanded markedly, per capita income gains, and also urban wages, were depressed by continued large immigrant inflows from China.

Conclusion

As will become apparent in the course of Part I of this book, the production of vent-for-surplus staples shaped virtually every aspect of Southeast Asia's social and economic development. Rapid export expansion drew large numbers of migrants and immigrants to export areas. These newcomers, many of whom were Europeans, Chinese or Indians, and ethnically distinct from indigenous inhabitants, created probably the outstanding world examples of the plural society. Immigrants dominated the external trade of the region and its business structures. Infrastructure developed to serve export regions and concentrated in them, largely to the exclusion of traditional parts of what became dual economy structures.

Industrialization was slight, and much of it involved processing the vented commodities. Comparative advantage in staple exports led to extreme specialization in a few primary commodities. The profitability of producing these commodities, combined with the sharp economic fluctuations to which they gave rise, discouraged the production of manufactures. Southeast Asia attracted relatively little foreign investment because vent-for-surplus output relied chiefly on using the surpluses of abundant land and labour. Vent-for-surplus commodities were principally exported through one main port city in each country. These cities grew on the basis of shipping, handling and commercial functions associated with staple exports, and gained population disproportionately to other cities, skewing Southeast Asia's urban structures towards its port 'gateways' to the global economy.

2

Growth Patterns, Specialization and Migration, 1870–1940

Pre-World War II Southeast Asian growth is a story of expansion onto frontier land, export specialization and the often transient, sometimes marginal, people fundamental to it. Late nineteenth-century Southeast Asia, with extensive frontier areas, was land-abundant. Only Java and northern Vietnam were densely populated. Frontier land, together with large numbers of migrant and immigrant workers, combined to provide the vent-for-surplus model's abundant land and surplus labour components. This chapter analyses pre-war Southeast Asian growth in the context of the first chapter's vent-for-surplus model, in which international trade affords a vent for surplus land and labour.

In Southeast Asia, workers came to the region's frontier areas through a combination of internal population shifts and massive international immigration, mostly from China and India. Significant inflows of French to Cochinchina and Dutch to Java notwithstanding, Southeast Asia was not a region of white settlement; Europeans emigrated mostly for business or government, and few of them intended to remain permanently, as was also true of the majority of Chinese and Indian immigrants. Most immigrants were attracted by high wages relative to China and India in Southeast Asia's export sectors and by commercial opportunities in the region's swiftly growing cities.

Although export economies based on vent-for-surplus staples brought spurts of rapid growth and a higher standard of living than anywhere in Asia except Japan, Southeast Asia developed as a collection of narrowly specialized, primary commodity-dependent mono-economies. Growth was extensive, not intensive, and accompanied by only limited technical progress or industrialization.

This chapter looks first at the land and labour surpluses integral to Southeast Asian vent-for-surplus production. The first section describes Southeast Asia's frontier lands and the second and third sections their migrant and immigrant settlement. The vent-for-surplus model predicts a swift expansion of exports and specialization in one or two primary commodities. That these predictions are correct is demonstrated in the fourth and fifth sections.

Migrant and immigrant settlement patterns complemented and reinforced geographical and economic divisions in Southeast Asia, giving rise to pronounced demographic intra-country differences and reinforcing Southeast Asian dualism. The sixth section focuses on Malaya, where the demographic impact of immigration was especially marked, because of exceptionally large immigrant inflows of Chinese and Indians and their difference from the indigenous Malay population.

The seventh and eighth sections assess aspects of Chapter 1's vent-for-surplus model. The seventh section argues that Southeast Asia's vent-for-surplus economies faced no serious capital constraint until about 1910, but after then, the production of some commodities, although continuing to draw on abundant natural resources, also depended on substantial inputs of foreign capital and technology. Although technical change in the rice and rubber industries was slight or even nearly non-existent, it was essential in tin mining and petroleum production. In Java, a non-vent-for-surplus area, there were technical improvements in sugar production, but these did not extend to the Philippine sugar industry. The eighth section analyses Southeast Asia's large regional trade, much of it in rice, which was partly a response to vent-for-surplus specialization in non-rice-specialized economies and, in turn, fundamental to their specialization.

Southeast Asian Frontier

Throughout Southeast Asia, the venting of land and settlement of the frontier, depicted in the model in Figure 1.1, was dramatic. In the 1860s, large parts of Southeast Asia were uninhabited or sparsely populated. Typically, the region's potentially richest natural resource areas were also the least settled, because they were jungle or semi-swampland, and unattractive for settlement prior to a demand for the commodities that could be produced there. Globalization was integral to drawing settlers to these areas and to defining them as resource abundant. Through creating a demand for products suited to Southeast Asia's climate and soil types, globalization made the land for producing these products economically valuable.

Opening the Frontier

A 'moving frontier' was basic to Southeast Asian growth. Across Southeast Asia, 'the huge expansion in cultivation for export' was 'achieved almost entirely by bringing into production vast tracts of previously uncultivated land'.[1] The timing of frontier development was broadly defined by demand in the world economy, favourable prices for Southeast Asian staples and empty land still available for settlement. In 1881, population densities in much of Southeast Asia were low, ranging from as few as 25 persons per square mile in Malaya to 67 in the rice-exporting area of Cochinchina. Java and Madura, with an 1881 density of 388 persons per square mile, was one exception to the general Southeast Asian pattern and the other was the Red River Delta settlement in northern Vietnam, for which data are not available (Tables 2.1 and 2.2).

[1] Brown, *Economic change*, p. 213.

Table 2.1 *Southeast Asia area cultivated with export crops, 1870–1938*

(a) Area cultivated, 000 hectares

	1870	1880	1890	1900	1913	1927	1938
Burma (rice)	702	1,255	2,329	3,460	4,181	4,735	5,011
Thailand (rice)	907	995	1,192	1,293	2,162	2,928	3,370
Thailand (rubber)	–	–	–	–	2	53	185
Indochina (rice)	376	522	854	1,174	1,766	2,000	2,200
Indochina (rubber)	–	–	–	–	15	79	127
Malaya (rubber)	–	–	–	2	435	1,052	1,331
Indonesia (rubber)	–	–	–	1	215	987	1,708
Indonesia (copra)	–	410	511	652	964	1,286	1,629
Philippines (three main export crops)	–	–	–	438	768	1,324	1,573

(b) Annual growth (%)

	1870–1938	1870–1900	1900–1938	1900–1913	1913–1938	1913–1927
Burma (rice)	3.4	5.5	1.0	1.5	0.7	0.9
Thailand (rice)	2.3	1.2	2.6	4.0	1.8	2.2
Thailand (rubber)	–	–	–	–	19.9	26.4
Indochina (rice)	3.1	3.9	1.7	2.8	1.0	1.0
Indochina (rubber)	–	–	–	–	8.9	12.6
Malaya (rubber)	–	–	–	51.3	4.6	6.5
Indonesia (rubber)	–	–	–	51.2	8.6	11.5
Indonesia (copra)	–	–	–	3.1	2.1	2.1
Philippines (three main export crops)	–	–	–	5.2	2.9	3.5

Notes and Sources: Acres are converted to hectares as one hectare = 2.471 acres and rai to hectares as 6.25 rai = one hectare. Growth rates for Indochina and the Philippines are calculated for the years for which there are data, not necessarily for the years shown in the table headings. Data exceptions to the years shown in the tables are noted below.

Burma: Grant, *Rice crop*, p. 44; Cheng, *Rice industry*, pp. 242–43.

Indochina: The figure for 1913 for rice refers to 1915. Murray, *Development*, p. 180; Indochina, *Annuaire statistique, 1937–1938*, pp. 95–96.

Thailand: Thailand, *Statistical yearbook of Thailand, 1916*, p. 214; *1921*, p. 254; *1923*, p. 265; *1937–38* and *1938–39*, p. 423, *1939–40 to 1944*, p. 466; Wilson, *Handbook*, p. 118.

Table 2.1 *(cont.)*

Malaya: Figart, *Plantation rubber industry*, p. 277; Malaya, *Rubber statistics handbook 1940*, p. 15.
Indonesia: van der Eng, 'Growth and productivity change in Indonesian agriculture', table A.1.2.1. For 1940, Bauer, *Rubber industry*, pp. 379–80 gives figures for the total mature and immature area in Indonesia as: 1934: 1,297 and 1940: 1,929. These compare with van der Eng's estimates of: 1934: 1,511 and 1940: 1,928. Creutzberg, *Changing economy in Indonesia*, vol. 1, p. 93 gives 1,293 thousand hectares as the 1938 rubber hectarage.
Philippines: The three export crops are abaca, sugar and coconuts. The figure for 1900 refers to 1902 and for 1927 to 1929. Philippines, Bureau of Commerce, *Statistical bulletin, 1920*, pp. 23–24; *1929*, pp. 45–46; Golay, *Philippines*, p. 35.

Table 2.2 *Southeast Asia population density, 1881–1938 (persons per square mile)*

	1881	1901	1921	1931	1938
Burma: Lower Burma	46.2	69.0	87.1	98.5	112.1
Burma: Total	28.8	44.9	56.6	62.7	72.1
Indochina: Cochinchina	67.2	117.6	152.0	179.5	184.9
Indochina: Total	42.0	–	65.8	75.0	80.6
Thailand	31.0	36.6	46.0	57.5	72.3
Malaya	24.7	36.8	58.8	76.8	88.4
Indonesia: Outer Islands	–	11.5	21.0	27.8	–
Indonesia: Java and Madura	388.1	594.8	685.5	817.5	–
Philippines	53.3	66.5	89.9	116.7	139.3
Japan	270.8	300.5	383.9	443.4	481.1

Sources:
Area:
Burma: Andrus, *Burmese economic life*, pp. 24–25. Lower Burma consisted of the four southern administrative divisions of Arakan, Irrawaddy, Pegu and Tenasserim.
Indochina: Indochina, *Annuaire statistique 1931–32*, pp. 53–54.
Thailand: Ingram, *Economic change*, p. 7.
Malaya: Malaya, *1921 census*, p. vi.
Indonesia: Indonesia, *Statistical pocketbook of Indonesia 1941*, p. 2.
Philippines: Philippines, Bureau of the Census and Statistics, *Yearbook of Philippine statistics 1946*, p. 10.
Population: As for Table 1.4.

Until Lower Burma, with its vast Irrawaddy-Sittang delta plains, came under British rule in 1852, the export of rice was prohibited. Land in the 1860s remained a 'free gift of nature', so abundant and 'of so little value as scarcely to be worth appropriating'.[2] In 1869, cultivators grew rice mainly for their own families.[3] The opening of Suez transformed this, and between 1870 and 1938, land cultivated with rice increased sevenfold to 5 million hectares. Rapid expansion was confined to the late nineteenth century, and depended mainly on demand in Europe, as its industrialization gained scale, and the nearby provinces of India as they increasingly relied on imported food. Between 1870 and 1900 in Burma, land hectarage cultivated with rice grew at an annual rate of 5.5 per cent, but over the next four decades at around 1.0 per cent. By 1921 in the Irrawaddy Delta, where the rice export economy centred on just 13 districts, the supply of 'good land culturable without large capital expenditure has come almost to an end' (Figure 2.1).[4]

The cultivation in Indochina of rice for export concentrated in Cochinchina, the southernmost of Vietnam's administrative divisions and including the Mekong Delta (Figure 2.2). In 1860, Cochinchina was a '"new land", a true frontier'.[5] As this frontier opened, the late nineteenth-century increase in rice hectarage was rapid, averaging 3.9 per cent annually from 1870 to 1900. There was also a marked increase between 1900 and 1913, which reflected increased demand in Southeast Asia, due to the early growth of the rubber industry and to exports to China. At the heart of the Mekong Delta was Nam Bo (literally 'the southern part of Vietnam' and comprising the six provinces conquered by France in the 1870s). Its resemblance to 'all the world's great deltas in that the boundaries between water and land are often indistinct' had previously discouraged settlement, but rice cultivation brought large numbers of migrants.[6] 'Like many pioneer areas, western Nam Bo, and the whole of the South generally [was] settled by marginal elements'. Many of the newcomers were economic migrants, lured by the promise of riches. They included people from southern Vietnam, political refugees and social misfits from South China, northern and central Vietnam and Cambodia. There were also 'all sorts of undesirable elements, voluntary exiles as well as penal criminals'.[7] The Southeast Asian frontier, like its nineteenth-century American counterpart, served as a social safety valve.[8]

2 Furnivall, 'Land as a free gift', p. 561; and see Cheng, *Rice industry*, pp. 5–8.
3 Furnivall, 'Safety first', p. 28.
4 *Census of India, 1921. vol. X, Burma* part 1. *Report*, p. 94; Burma, *Report of the Burma Provincial Banking Enquiry Committee, 1929–30*, vol. 1, pp. 17–18, 30.
5 Brocheux and Hémery, *Indochina*, p. 121.
6 Brocheux, *Mekong Delta*, p. 2 and see p. 223 for the history of Nam Bo.
7 Tai, *Millenarianism*, p. 9.
8 The idea of migration affording a 'safety valve' is often first associated with F. J. Turner writing in the 1890s, although it was by then already well known among American historians. Dorfman, *Economic mind*, p. 347.

Figure 2.1 Burma 13 principal rice districts and other main geographical divisions
Sources: India, *Census of India, 1931. vol. XI. Burma. Part I, Report*, p. between pp. x and 1; India, *Census of India, 1921. vol. X. Burma. Part I. Report*, p. 2; Cheng, *Rice industry*, p. xxvi.

In Thailand, around 1850, three-quarters of land in the Chao Phraya Delta region, a complex of streams crisscrossing the country's central plain and its rice frontier, remained unused (Figure 2.3).[9] At that time, land was so abundant

[9] Baker and Phongpaichit, *History of Thailand*, p. 82; Robertson, 'Rice export', p. 250.

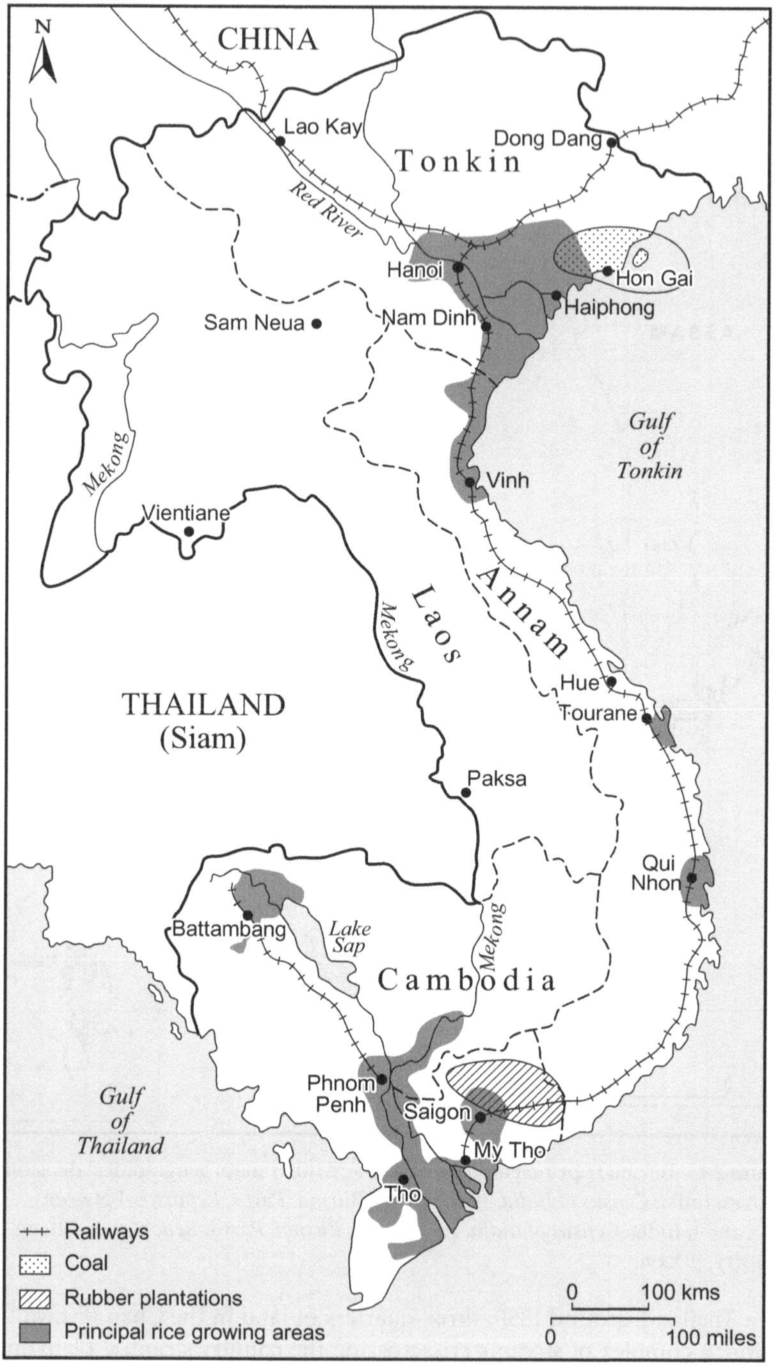

Figure 2.2 Indochina rice-growing areas
Source: Brocheux and Hémery, *Indochina*, p. 183.

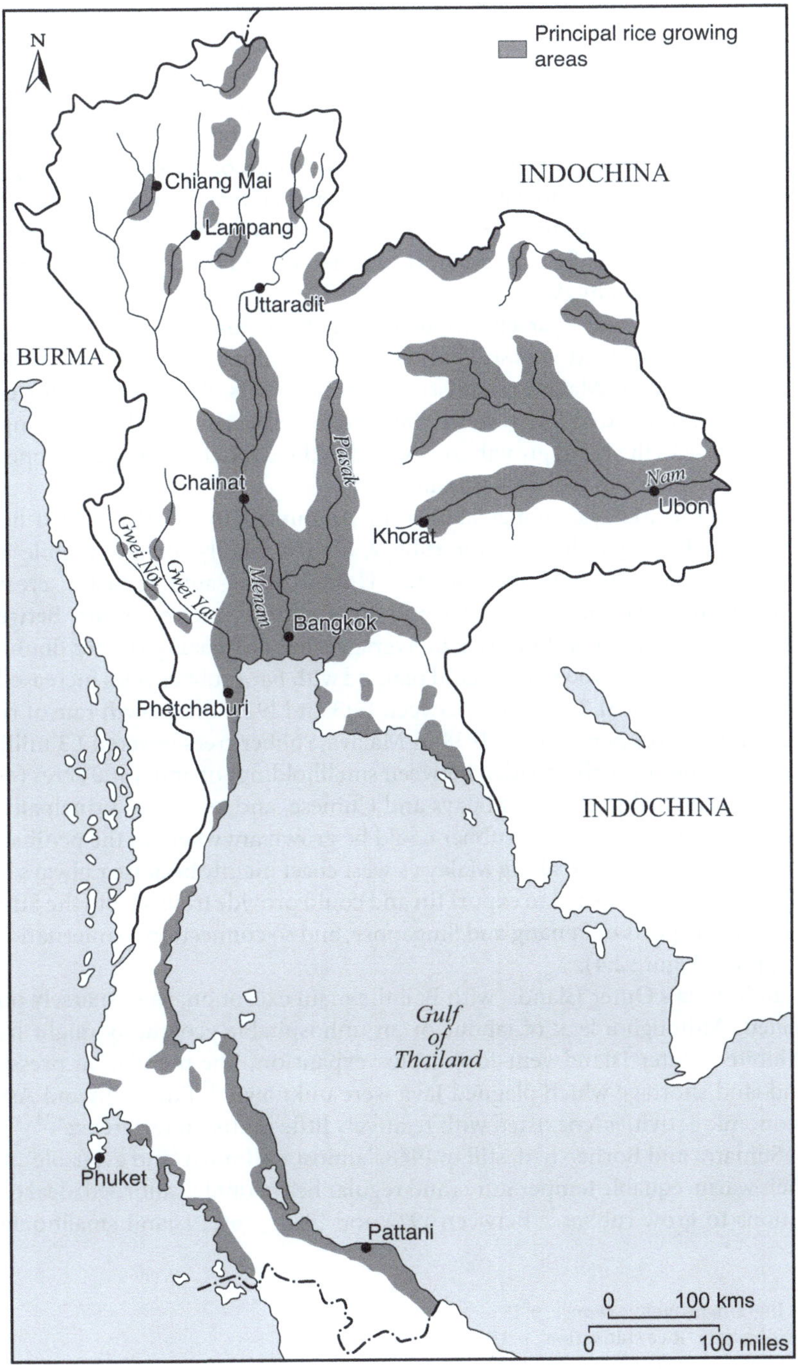

Figure 2.3 Thailand rice-growing areas
Source: Fisher, *South-East Asia*, p. 498.

that it had little, if any, value.[10] The rice frontier opened after the 1855 Bowring Treaty with Britain forced a liberalization of foreign trade. The Thai frontier was reminiscent of the United States wild west, and during its 1890s and 1900s boom years 'in every direction the land was cleared of the heavy jungle grass which afforded shelter to wild elephants'.[11] Land cultivated with rice increased from 907,000 hectares in 1870 to 1,293,000 hectares in 1900 and then, growing at 2.6 per cent annually over the next four decades, practically tripled to reach 3,370,000 hectares by 1938.

Malaya remained sparsely populated in the 1870s. The area was largely unmapped, and 'land was so abundant and readily available that it had no value'.[12] However, Malaya possessed rich tin deposits. By the turn of the century, tin mines dotted the western Malay states, especially Perak and Selangor, in response to the rapid growth in demand in the United States and Europe for the metal, mainly to fabricate tin cans.

In 1900 in Malaya, rubber cultivation amounted to less than 2,000 hectares, but thereafter demand for rubber, almost wholly for automobile and truck tyres, and principally from the United States auto industry, created a Southeast Asian boom industry and large natural resource rents. Between 1900 and 1910, the London price of average standard quality rubber doubled. In response, from 1900 to 1913, land planted with *para* rubber trees increased at an annual rate of 51.3 per cent; between 1913 and 1927, the growth rate of rubber land was 6.5 per cent. By 1938 in Malaya, rubber trees covered 1.3 million hectares, about equally divided between smallholdings of under 100 acres (40.5 hectares) owned mainly by Malays and Chinese, and by estates principally in European ownership. *Para* rubber could be grown anywhere in the peninsula, but cultivation centred along Malaya's west coast mainly because railways had already been established to export tin and could provide transport to the Straits Settlements ports of Penang and Singapore, and so connection to international shipping (Figure 2.4).

Indonesia's Outer Islands, with Bali the main exception, were sparsely populated. Although a lack of labour or an unhospitable geography might have inhibited Outer Island vent-for-surplus expansion, 'the population pressure and land shortage which plagued Java were unknown'.[13] European and Asian economic activities 'coexisted with relatively little mutual interference'.[14]

Sumatra and Borneo had, still in 1948, 'almost unlimited land available', and their warm, equable temperatures and regular heavy rainfall afforded ideal conditions to grow rubber.[15] Between 1927 and 1938, Outer Island smallholders,

10 Ingram, *Economic change*, p. 15.
11 Johnston, 'Rice cultivation', p. 111.
12 Gullick, 'Entrepreneur', p. 59.
13 Touwen, *Extremes*, p. 319 and see pp. 30, 46, 228 325, 337.
14 Touwen, *Extremes*, p. 308.
15 Bauer, *Rubber industry*, p. 69.

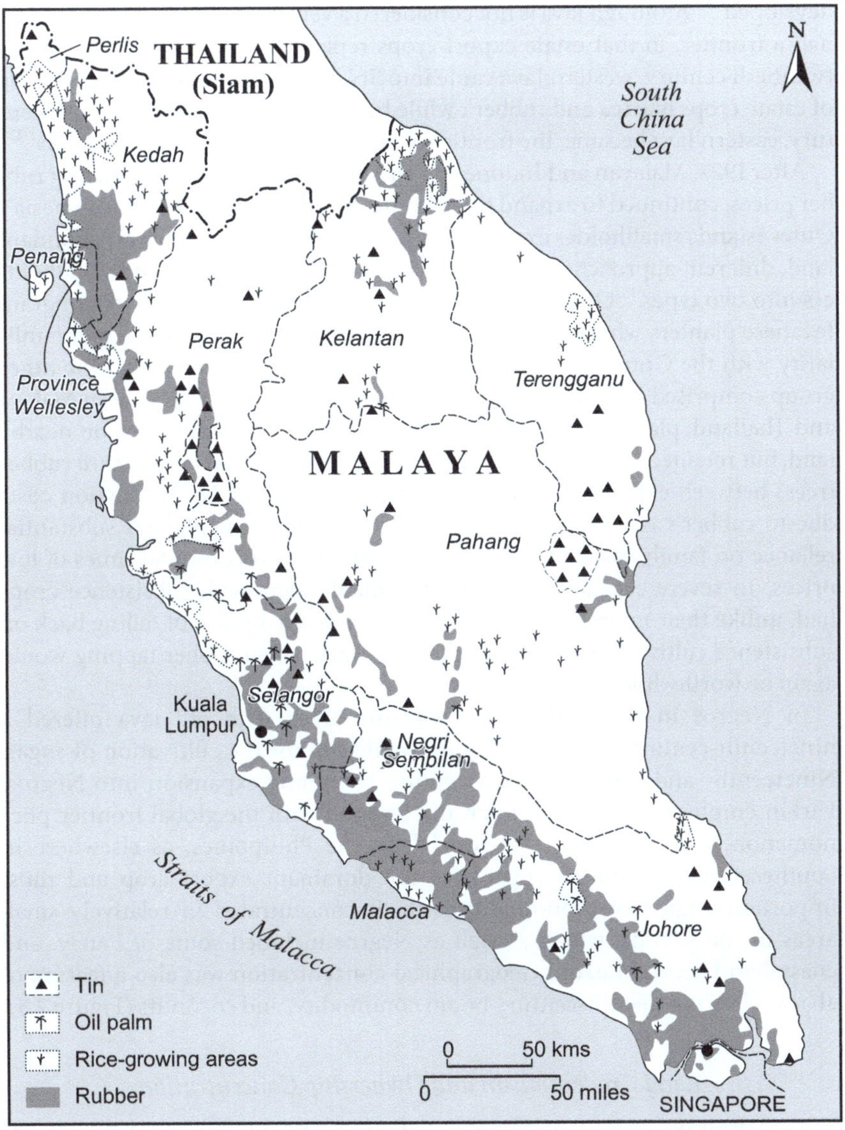

Figure 2.4 Malaya distribution of primary commodity production
Source: International Bank for Reconstruction and Development, *Economic development of Malaya*, p. 125.

responding to high mid-1920s rubber prices, were largely responsible for a near doubling of land planted in rubber and, because of this, for Indonesian rubber hectarage larger than Malaya's. In the 1950s, the 'great interest of Sumatra lies in the fact that there is still a pioneer land with huge areas which can be settled and developed'.[16] Although Java is not considered a vent-for-surplus area, the island had a frontier, in that estate export crops replaced earlier cultivation. In the twentieth century, western Java came into 'its own as a frontier for the planting of estate crops like tea and rubber', while beginning in the late nineteenth century, eastern Java became 'the frontier of an expanding plantation economy'.[17]

After 1927, Malayan and Indonesian smallholders, despite plummeting rubber prices, continued to expand their rubber holdings. Although in Indonesia's Outer Islands smallholder expansion, as in Malaya, relied heavily on abundant land, different approaches to land utilization divided Outer Island smallholders into two types.[18] One, less numerous, group of smallholders were migrant Javanese planters who, because they lacked agricultural experience and familiarity with the Outer Islands, tended to specialize solely in rubber. The other group comprised previously established farm households, which, as in Malaya and Thailand, planted rubber near their houses or, predominantly, on nearby land, but retained earlier subsistence crops or inter-planted *hevea* (*para* rubber trees) between existing subsistence crops. Low smallholder production costs due to rubber's relatively non-onerous labour requirements and substantial reliance on family work made rubber an attractive crop, even at times of low prices. In severe economic downturns, smallholders with subsistence crops had, unlike their migrant Javanese counterparts, the option of falling back on subsistence cultivation and waiting for recovery, when rubber tapping would again be worthwhile.[19]

In Negros in the Philippines, volcanic areas with old lava offered a nineteenth-century frontier of highly fertile soil for the cultivation of sugar. Nineteenth- and early twentieth-century economic expansion into Negros, Larkin emphasized, 'shared much in common with the global frontier phenomenon taking place at this time'.[20] In the Philippines, as elsewhere in Southeast Asia, although sugar was the dominant export crop and most important engine of economic growth, it concentrated in relatively small areas of the Islands, which as well as Negros included some of Panay, and coastal and central Luzon. Geographical concentration was also a feature of abaca, a late nineteenth-century boom commodity, and coconuts (Figure 2.5).

Land Credentialism and Ownership Concentration

For much of the nineteenth century in large parts of Southeast Asia, excepting densely populated Java and northern Vietnam, land was plentiful and

[16] Stamp, *Asia*, p. 447.

[17] Dick et al., *Emergence*, pp. 119–20 for the first quote and Naval Intelligence Division, *Netherlands East Indies*, vol. 2, p. 347 for the second.

[18] van der Eng, *Agricultural growth*, pp. 234, 236; see also Pelzer, *Pioneer settlement*, pp. 24–25.

[19] Bauer, *Rubber industry*, pp. 5–7, 66–67.

[20] Larkin, *Sugar*, p. 60.

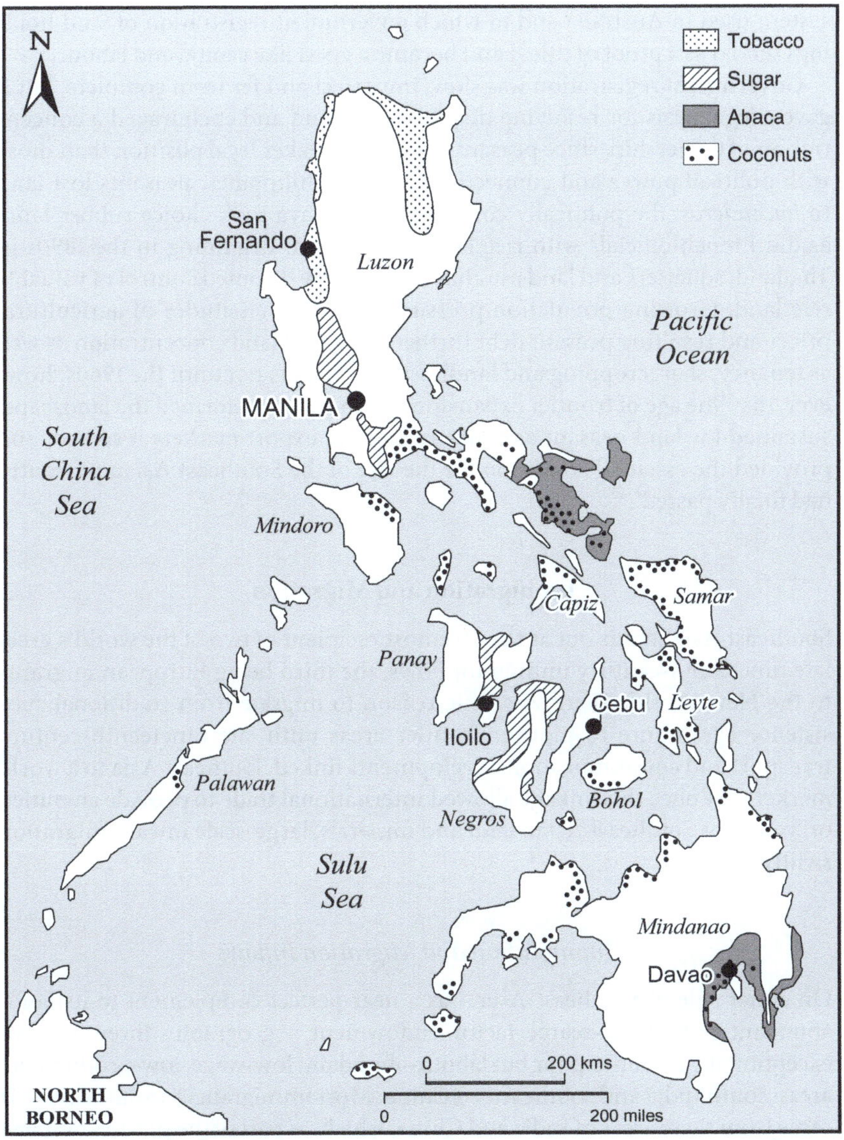

Figure 2.5 Philippines geographical distribution of principal export crops
Source: Robequain, *Malaya, Indonesia*, p. 280.

essentially valueless. Property rights were unknown; 'land, like air, water and forest, was there for the taking'.[21] By the 1890s as frontiers were opened, governments began to register land, in most countries adopting the Torrens

[21] Elson, *End*, p. 125.

system used in Australia and in which government registration of land holdings served as a proof of title. Land became a good like capital and labour.

Government registration was slow, imperfect and far from complete, but it gave a legal basis for resolving disputes over land and encouraged a concentration of ownership, since peasants were in a weaker legal position than those with political power and connections. In the Philippines, peasants lost land to *hacenderos*; the politically connected in Malaya took choice rubber land, as did French officials with rice land in Vietnam. Beginning in the 1890s in Thailand, squatters and land purchasers endlessly disputed control of valuable rice land. Growing population pressure and the vicissitudes of agricultural prices and resulting peasant debt further increased land concentration as well as tenancy, sharecropping and landlessness.[22] It was not until the 1960s, however, that 'the age of frontier expansion which had transformed the landscape, sustained lowland peasant agriculture and the export markets it served, and provided the essential condition for the rise of the Southeast Asian peasantry had finally passed'.[23]

Immigration and Migration

Southeast Asia stands out as the foremost recipient of two of the world's great late nineteenth-century immigrant flows, the third being European migrants to the New World. There was little reason to migrate from traditional subsistence agriculture to pioneer frontier areas until late nineteenth-century transport and communication developments linked Southeast Asia to a world market. But once this linkage allowed international trade to provide an outlet, or 'vent', for Southeast Asian land and minerals, large-scale inward migration swiftly followed.

Immigration and Migration Inflows

On either side of Southeast Asia – as a near perfect complement to its land-abundant but labour-scarce factor endowment – geography threw up two exceptionally resource-poor but labour-abundant, low-wage, low-productivity areas: south India and southeastern China. Most immigrants to Southeast Asia came from these areas of India and China, which, as part of the process of Asian globalization, served as 'hinterlands' of surplus labour, sending workers to a 'centre' of land-surplus Southeast Asia.

The bulk of Chinese and Indian immigration to Southeast Asia was to Burma, Thailand and, especially, Malaya. Burma received chiefly Indian immigrants,

22 Elson, *End*, pp. 128–41; Hiscock and Allan, 'Law modernization', pp. 518–19.
23 Elson, *End*, pp. 92–93.

and Thailand mainly Chinese. Malaya, about equidistant between China and India, attracted vast numbers of both Chinese and Indians. Until the 1930s, immigration to Malaya was unrestricted, apart from temporary controls during part of World War I, and in Burma there were no restrictions on the immigration of Indians until 1938.[24] Thailand did not limit Chinese immigration until 1932, when residence and permit fees were imposed and officials used literacy requirements arbitrarily to block immigrants.[25]

Malaya's export industries of tin and rubber relied mainly on immigrant labour; 'indigenous' Malays stayed largely in traditional agriculture and fishing, but also grew smallholder rubber. Malay immigrants from Indonesia, mainly Javanese and attracted by employment opportunities and the possibility of acquiring land, greatly augmented Malaya's ethnic Malay population.[26] In 1891, the Malay population of the Federated Malay States was 232,000. The author of the 1931 census calculated that of the total number of Malays enumerated, 350,000 were 'native' Malays and 244,000 were immigrants or their descendants.[27] In Malaya as a whole, only the Malay population in the north-east states of Kelantan and Terengganu, components of Malaya's traditional economic sector, could be regarded as not heavily immigrant in origins and truly 'indigenous'.[28]

Apart from Malaya, migration (the internal movement of population as distinct from immigration across international borders) by indigenous groups furnished most of those who cultivated vent-for-surplus crops. Burma was a partial exception. Urban labour was principally Indian, but so too were many of those who cultivated rice. Part of this labour force came to Burma seasonally to work in gangs and perform specialized tasks. In Thailand, Chinese supplied most urban labour, especially in Bangkok, making that city a Chinese one, just as Rangoon was mainly an Indian one. The great majority of those who grew rice in Thailand were Thai.

In Burma, Thailand and southern Vietnam, migrants from the traditional sectors of these economies quickly responded to the opportunity to settle new land and cultivate rice. Burma's late nineteenth-century rice boom depended on the migration of peasants, described as a 'Rice Rush' of Burmese farmers from southern and central Burma to the Irrawaddy Delta in the far south, where, in just 13 districts, Burma's rice export economy centred (Figure 2.1). Indochina and Thailand followed the Burma example, with peasant rushes to

24 Malaya, *Census of British Malaya, 1921*, pp. 21–22; Purcell, *Chinese*, p. 203.

25 Skinner, *Chinese society*, p. 177; Landon, *Chinese in Thailand*, pp. 206–7 and 'Problem of the Chinese', p. 153.

26 Federated Malay States, *Census of population, 1901*, p. 32 and *Federated Malay States census, 1911*, pp. 18–23, 95, 127.

27 Vlieland, 'Population', p. 64; Malaya, *British Malaya, a report on the 1931 census*, p. 60.

28 Malaya, *Malaya: a report on the 1947 census*, p. 60.

their own deltaic plains.[29] Rice cultivation in Vietnam depended on an incessant flow of migrants from Nam Bo's central and eastern provinces.[30]

Indonesian and Philippine export expansion also relied on large internal migration to frontier areas. Some Javanese migrated to the Outer Islands, but many more left Java to become labourers on plantations in East Sumatra and Borneo or went to Malaya. The movement of Javanese to the Outer Islands, either through government policies of resettlement or, more important, as estate workers, was Southeast Asia's largest early twentieth-century internal migration.[31] Between 1845 and 1914, population in the sugar-producing frontier of Western Negros grew at an annual rate of 3.4 per cent as migrants streamed there. They arrived from depressed areas such as Bohol, Cebu and Antique and the textile towns. Most migrants sought a better life, but others came to avoid the law, military draft or taxes and labour obligations.[32]

Labour Surpluses and Supply Price

Between 1880 and 1939, Burma, Malaya and Thailand received over 15 million Chinese and Indian immigrants, more than these countries' total 1881 population (Tables 2.3 and 1.4). The arrivals were part of Lewis's highly elastic labour supply: the 'unlimited supply of Indians and Chinese willing to travel anywhere to work on plantations for a shilling a day'.[33] That was recognized at the time: Singapore, a resident wrote in 1931, was near 'two unlimited sources of supply for cheap labour, namely India and China'.[34] For the five decades beginning in the 1880s, Malaya averaged immigrant inflows per decade of 826 persons per 1,000 resident population, almost five times the immigration rate to Argentina, which had higher rates than any other New World country. Immigrant inflows to Burma and Thailand were on a par with, or above, New World rates (Table 2.3). For Asia, stretching from the emigrant-sending part of India, across Burma, Thailand and Malaya and to southeastern China, there existed an equilibrium relationship between wages in sending and receiving areas and so an integrated labour market.[35]

Clearly some migrants from traditional areas left productive jobs, and not all labour responsible for the new export industries was surplus, but much of it was. Labour from the traditional sectors of the Burmese and Thai economies was surplus, in having zero or low marginal products per person before moving into producing for export. To expand rice hectarage, cultivators in Burma,

29 Dobby, *Monsoon Asia*, pp. 182–83.
30 Brocheux, *Mekong Delta*, pp. 2–58, 223.
31 Booth, *Colonial legacies*, p. 61.
32 Larkin, *Sugar*, p. 60.
33 Lewis, *Evolution*, p. 15.
34 Rotary Club of Singapore, *Singapore*, p. 2.
35 Huff and Caggiano, 'Globalization'.

Table 2.3 *Southeast Asia and New World immigration, 1881–1939*

(a) Immigration to the United States, Burma, Malaya and Thailand, 1881–1939 (millions of persons, total flow per decade)

	1881–1910		1911–1929		1930–1939	
	Gross	Net	Gross	Net	Gross	Net
United States	5.91	4.10	3.20	2.15	0.70	0.21
Burma	1.45	0.26	3.27	0.50	2.64	0.17
Malaya	1.87		2.75	0.78	1.62	-0.07
Thailand	0.34	0.12	0.81	0.27	0.50	0.12
Total Southeast Asia	3.66		6.83	1.55	4.76	0.22
Southeast Asia as % of United States	61.9		213.0	72.1	680.0	104.8

(b) Southeast Asia and New World immigration rates by decade, 1881–1890 to 1931–1939 (per 1,000 mean population)

	1881–1890	1891–1900	1901–1910	1911–1920	1921–1930	1931–1939
Burma	85.3	138.4	219.7	240.9	277.2	167.8
Thailand	22.4	39.6	75.9	74.3	102.1	30.8
Malaya	921.9	994.5	993.5	838.9	859.7	346.0
United States	91.6	52.5	103.8	57.2	35.3	3.6
Canada	193.4	67.1	268.4	216.3	130.4	13.6
Argentina	267.4	163.8	292.9	150.1	133.2	39.7
Brazil	40.2	69.8	33.2	31.9	27.4	7.3

Sources:
Burma: Baxter, *Report*, p. 121; Cheng, *Rice industry*, pp. 262–63.
Malaya: Indians: Saw, *Singapore population*, p. 52; *Chinese*: Straits Settlements, 'Protector of Chinese', *SSAR*, 1881–1911; Malaya, *1921 census*, p. 21 and *1931 census*, p. 113: 'Chinese affairs', *SSAR*, 1930–38; Straits Settlements, 'Progress of the Straits Settlements', *SSAR*, 1934–38.
Thailand: Skinner, *Chinese society*, pp. 61, 173; Manarungsan, *Economic development*, pp. 207–8.
United States: United States Department of Commerce, *Historical statistics*, part 1, pp. 8, 105–6; Kuznets and Rubin, *Immigration*, pp. 94–96. Net immigration figure for 1880–1910 as estimated by Kuznets and Rubin.
Canada: Urquhart and Buckley, *Historical statistics*, pp. 14, 23.
Argentina: Díaz-Alejandro, *Essays*, pp. 421, 424.
Brazil: Brazil, 'O Brasil em numeros', pp. 5, 12.

as well as working longer hours, 'made use of formerly under or unemployed familial labor'.[36] In the 1920s in Burma, at the start of the rice cultivation season, migrant flows from poorer regions generally created 'a surplus of men who have found no engagement as farm labourers'. These men, with almost no bargaining power, had no choice but to take land as tenants on unfavourable terms.[37] In Thailand, workers, perhaps of necessity as cheap European imports flooded in, left the handicraft sector or other traditional production. Nevertheless, a shift of labour from other employment to rice cultivation 'could not have been very great'. Rather than through giving up earlier work, the supply of labour 'received important additions as the existing rice growers gave up leisure' in favour of spending time on cultivating more land.[38]

In Burma, Thailand and Malaya, between the opening of large-scale international trade and World War II, long-term unskilled wages (real income) in the export sector remained more or less constant at about the shilling a day (US$0.26) suggested by Lewis.[39] Around this amount, wages varied considerably according to occupation and time. In general, labourers in Lower Burma rice cultivation were better off than tenants. Competition among labourers was keen, and the 'iron law of wages' was said to apply until at least the 1930s. Nevertheless, for the ordinary labourer, the usual rate of wages was well above subsistence, and the labourer could save. During Burma's early development, labourers were normally engaged on a ten-month contract, and a labourer able to save or borrow enough to live on for a year could clear a patch of jungle and raise his own crop.

Dating from the late nineteenth century, increased Indian immigration and labour specialization in the different stages of rice cultivation led to a fall in wages, possibly by about 20 per cent.[40] It became more difficult to save from wages, buy a yoke of cattle or even become a landowner. A large increase in crime in Burma may have been mainly due to the growing poverty of labourers.

Rangoon and Bangkok were heavily immigrant, and in both wages were below rural levels. In Rangoon, 'No employer has any interest in raising the wages of the coolies huddled in the coolie barracks of Rangoon on pay that is far below subsistence.'[41] Ingram concluded that in the 1930s in Thailand, the real wage in terms of rice, despite a sharp rise with the onset of the depression,

[36] Adas, *Burma Delta*, p. 59, see also p. 26.

[37] Furnivall, 'Industrial agriculture', p. 94.

[38] Ingram, *Economic change*, p. 54 and see p. 55 on regional migration.

[39] Lewis, 'Economic development', pp. 140–52. Lewis, *Evolution*, pp. 14–16, emphasizes that his analysis of an infinitely elastic labour supply refers to the long run.

[40] Furnivall, *Introduction to the political economy*, pp. 75–77; Hlaing, 'Trends of economic growth', pp. 120–21.

[41] Furnivall, *Colonial policy and practice*, pp. 352–53 and on wages, see Feeny, *Political economy*, pp. 18, 21, 29, 132–33; Huff and Caggiano, 'Globalization'; Ingram, 'Thailand's rice trade', p. 115; Manarungsan, *Economic development*, pp. 164–68.

remained within the range set in the seventeenth century.[42] Despite export expansion, for a large number of Southeast Asians none of this suggests any large twentieth-century rise in living standards, and for a number of ordinary Southeast Asians possibly the reverse.

Whether through international immigration, migration from an economy's traditional sectors or some combination of the two, migrant labour came at a supply price dictated by the opportunity cost of labour (its marginal product in subsistence agriculture) plus some mark-up to cover migration costs and risk. Figure 2.6 presents a stylised version of the markets for unskilled labour in Malaya, Burma and Thailand. The distaste of indigenous groups for wage labour is indicated by the figure's steep domestic labour supply curve, while the responsiveness of immigrant Chinese and Indian workers to wages and job opportunities in Southeast Asia made labour supply highly elastic along W^*, where the supply price of labour, W_s, equals the wage received, W_r, and both remain unchanged as employment increases from N_1 to N_2 along the immigrant labour supply curve. Employment of indigenous labour is limited to no more than $0N_1$ and N_1N_2 unskilled jobs are filled by immigrants. Even if Southeast Asian employers, themselves often Indian and Chinese, were willing to hire indigenous (non-Indian or Chinese) workers, there was no reason to pay above the equilibrium unskilled immigrant wage, W^*. In Malaya, it was pointed out, 'any very great increase in wages must wait upon a similar rise in the reservoirs of over-abundant and, therefore, cheap labour in India and China'.[43]

Just as virtually unlimited immigration from India and China to Burma, Thailand and Malaya ensured the long-term elastic supply of labour at an essentially constant real wage, elsewhere in Southeast Asia internal migration from the traditional sectors of dual economies had a similar effect.[44] Labour in Cochinchina was scarce and the rice and rubber industries turned to the densely populated north for workers. Even so, during the rice harvest, labour was always insufficient and supplied by migrant gangs of workers. Payment was almost always in kind, but harvesters occasionally demanded cash. When they did, the daily wage was US$0.80 without food, or about 3 shillings a day, but in a good year it might rise to US$1.10 to US$1.50 without food.[45]

[42] Ingram, 'Thailand's rice trade', p. 112.

[43] Furnivall, *Political economy*, pp. 75–77; Hlaing, 'Trends of economic growth', pp. 120–21; Feeny, *Political economy*, pp. 18, 21, 29, 132–33; Huff and Caggiano, 'Globalization'; Ingram, 'Thailand's rice trade', p. 115; Runes, *General standards of living*, pp. 10–11, 31. On Thailand and Burma, see also Manarungsan, *Economic development*, pp. 164–68.

[44] Robequain, *Economic development*, pp. 53–59; Brocheux, *Mekong Delta*, p. 23; Murray, *Development*, pp. 224–31; Feeny, *Political economy*, pp. 42–43; Boomgaard and Gooszen, *Population trends*, p. 54; Lindblad, 'Late colonial state', p. 140; Larkin, *Sugar*, pp. 60–61; Adas, *Burma Delta*, pp. 41–57.

[45] Brocheux, *Mekong Delta*, pp. 57–59.

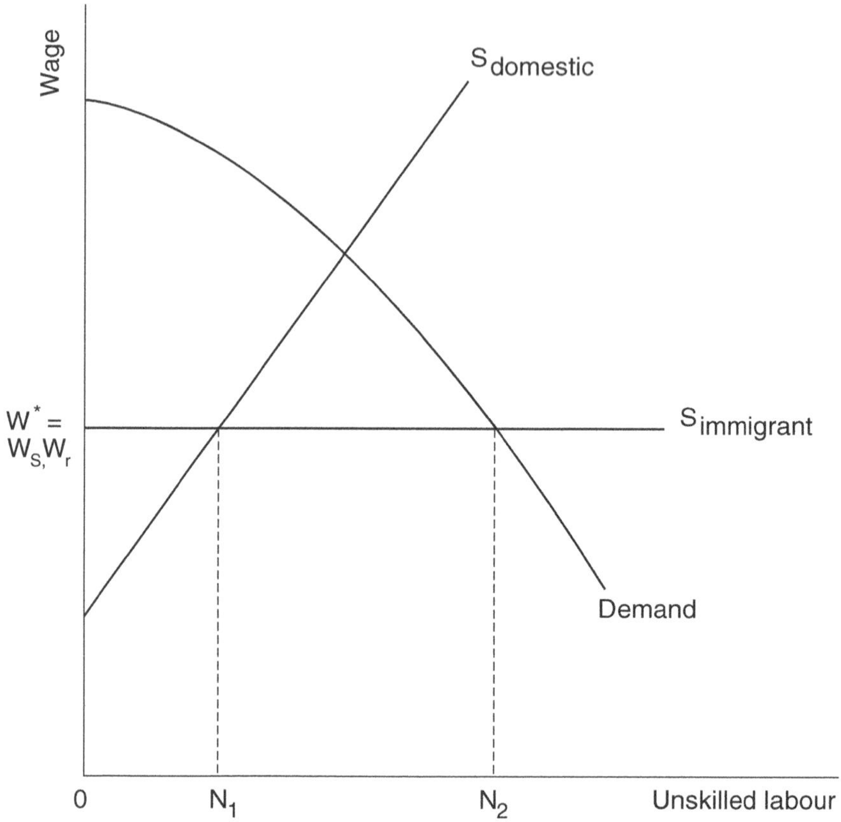

Figure 2.6 Immigration and the market for unskilled labour in Burma, Malaya and Thailand
Source: Huff and Caggiano, 'Globalization, immigration', p. 56.

By the late 1920s in Vietnam, rubber plantation workers numbered some 75,000, divided between 46,000 contract workers on three-year contracts and 29,000 non-contract workers.[46] Contract workers were recruited in northern Annam and Tonkin and 'were for all intents prisoners on the plantations [and] forced to endure the brutal and ferocious exploitation of the companies for 0.30 to 0.40 piastres a day (about US$0.20) until the adoption of the first "contractual labor" regulation in 1927'.[47] Wages were negotiated between the colonial government and the Union des Planteurs de Caoutchouc, which included the largest rubber companies. Wages of US$0.40 for men and US$0.30 for women plus daily rice rations and lodging may have been subsequent to

46 Murray, *Development*, p. 284.
47 Brocheux and Hémery, *Indochina*, p. 127.

regulation. Non-contract workers received lower wages than their contracted counterparts. However, due to labour shortages during the boom years of 1924 to 1929, non-contract workers were able collectively to demand US$0.60 a day, but without rice rations or lodging.[48]

Although Indonesia restricted immigration, large labour surpluses were available in Java. Outer Island plantations in East Sumatra, which grew rubber, tea or oil palm, and rubber plantations in Borneo relied heavily on Javanese migrants as workers. Almost all of the about 300,000 coolies working on East Sumatran rubber plantations were indentured Javanese.[49] Their nominal wages of roughly US$0.10 a day plus housing and other benefits remained more or less unchanged from the beginning to the end of the inter-war period, but real wages rose by about half in the 1930s, due to a fall in the price of rice.

It was anticipated that transmigration from Java would both solve its problem of overpopulation and augment Outer Island labour supply. However, transmigration never materialized to anything like the anticipated extent, and Outer Island smallholder rubber cultivation depended mainly on resident populations putting in additional labour hours and effort. For those, including smallholders, in the Outer Islands hiring workers, the supply price of labour was US$0.10 to US$0.20 a day, but no more than a fifth of that in the slump.[50]

In the Philippines, unskilled wages were higher than elsewhere in Southeast Asia because immigration was restricted, because the same abundance of labour as in northern Vietnam and Java was lacking and because labour legislation had some force. When sugar prices were low, some planters talked of bringing in 'Oriental labor', but that did not happen.[51] Even without imported labour, wages were still dictated by the opportunity cost of output in the Philippines' traditional agriculture, and miserably low. *Sacadas* (sugar migrants) 'from neighboring islands risked travel to Negros on crowded vessels to accept poor wages because they could earn more than by staying at home'.[52] For planters in Negros, the movement of unskilled ('hand' or manual) labour was particularly important, since the island's sugar industry lacked Luzon's well-established system of tenants. In Luzon, permanent hand labour could be obtained from tenants who lived on the land with their families and perhaps had a team of carabao. The usual wage for these tenants was US$1.25 a week plus seven kilos of rice.[53]

Daily wages in the Philippines, as everywhere in Southeast Asia, are difficult to establish accurately, since employment might be for part of the year, and remuneration include more than cash. In purely sugar-producing regions,

[48] Murray, *Development*, p. 284.
[49] Booth, *Colonial legacies*, p. 61.
[50] Bauer, *Rubber industry*, p. 71.
[51] Larkin, *Sugar*, p. 178.
[52] Larkin, *Sugar*, p. 179 and see p. 78n.
[53] Larkin, *Sugar*, pp. 177–78.

farm workers found employment for eight months, and for the other four were practically idle.[54] Wages in 1919 on Philippine sugar estates, according to the *Manila Times*, were US$0.25 a day, but that did not include use of the land or the availability of rice and cash loans.[55] In 1929, daily farm wages for men averaged US$0.39 with a maximum of US$0.55. The average wage for women was US$0.26 and the maximum US$0.35, while for children these figures were US$0.22 and US$0.31.[56]

Origins and Methods of Immigration

Although for Malaya, Thailand and Burma the trend in immigration was upwards, it was subject to extreme fluctuations. The unmistakeable impression for each of the countries is of a highly mobile immigrant population, alert to economic signals and taking decisions on this basis. Swings in immigration were greatest during the inter-war years, and at their most extreme in Malaya. In that country, between 1926 and 1932, the net loss through migration was 650,000 persons, equal to 20 per cent of the 1921 population.

Typically, Chinese and Indian immigrants to Southeast Asia intended to stay from three to at most five years. Due to the transient nature of much immigration, between 1881 and World War II in Southeast Asia, immigrant retention (net as proportion of gross immigration) compares poorly with the United States where most immigrants intended to stay (Table 2.3). But in Southeast Asia, new arrivals more than replaced departures and, together with greater natural increase, continuously augmented labour supply.

Most Indian and Chinese emigrants to Southeast Asia came from relatively small areas, the Madras Presidency in India and southeastern China. Neither was far from Southeast Asia. Negapatam, the great port of Tamil emigration from the Madras Presidency, was only a little over 900 nautical miles from Rangoon, and about half as far again from Penang, the destination for most Indians coming to Malaya. Just west of Southeast Asia lay the provinces in southeastern China of Kwangtung (Guangdong) and Fukien (Fujian), no further from Singapore than 1,500 nautical miles and about a week's sailing. Even by the 1880s, these parts of India and China, with histories of hardship and periodic famine, were surplus labour areas.[57] Emigrants from India and China were almost all unskilled, largely men, and mainly from agricultural regions.

[54] Runes cited in Larkin, *Sugar*, p. 220 and see Runes, *General standards of living*, pp. 10–11, 31.

[55] Larkin, *Sugar*, p. 78.

[56] Larkin, *Sugar*, pp. 177–78.

[57] See, for example, India, *Census of India. 1901. vol. XV. Madras*. Part I. *Report*, pp. 27–32; India, *Census of India. 1921. vol. X. Burma*. Part I. *Report*, p. 31 and *Census of India. 1931. vol. XI. Burma*. Part I. *Report*, p. 61; Kumar, *Land and caste*, pp. 104–05, 144, 161–67; India, *Census 1931, Madras Report*, part I, p. 93; Buck, *Land utilization*, pp. 76–77, 125–28.

Immigration to Thailand, Malaya and Burma was largely voluntary. Indentured immigration never existed in Thailand, and in Malaya ceased to be significant long before its final abolition for Indians in 1910 and Chinese in 1914.[58] In Burma, experiments with importing indentured coolies 'speedily became obsolete in view of the spontaneous growth of a free market which in an automatic, smooth, and self-regulating fashion connected the infinitely elastic supply of labour in India with Burmese requirements'.[59]

Chinese and Indian immigration was conducted through a variety of methods. A principal one was personal recruitment, which depended either on individuals returning from the region to persuade others from their home area to emigrate, or on professional recruiters. Personal recruitment, for Chinese known as credit ticket immigration, usually bound the immigrant to specific employment until the debt for passage expenses could be repaid. For many Indians, emigration was through a *maistry* system and so with a personal recruiter, known as a *kangany* (an experienced Indian worker acting as a labour recruiter and supervisor). He took the labourers from India to the place of work in Malaya. This arrangement and associated provision of finance lifted poverty as a barrier to emigration, as organized recruitment did for many Chinese.

In Burma, employment might be arranged through the *maistry* system but not always.[60] One aspect of organized immigration was gangs of seasonal Indian immigrants which could be booked in advance, allowing farmers in Burma to be sure of work at fixed dates and avoid having to find their own labourers.[61] However, Indian labourers travelling to Burma do not seem to have had any serious problem in finding work even if they had not emigrated in the company of a *kangany*. For Indians wishing to stay in Burma after the main rice harvest, however, employment became less certain, and many drifted towards Rangoon to look for work.[62]

Credit ticket and *maistry* systems of immigration were clearly open to abuse. Although not formal indenture, they could be manipulated to create a hold over labourers once in Southeast Asia. Debt incurred for passage, food and lodging before immigrants started to work might be unreasonably inflated, and when sold on to employers, further increased through the monopoly sale of goods, supply of opium, or rigged gambling games. Abuse remained common and considerable. But its severity, and so accompanying labour tying devices, appear to have lessened markedly by the 1880s in Thailand and Burma, and in

58 Skinner, *Chinese society*, p. 53; Cheng, *Rice industry*, pp. 117–24; Saw, *Singapore population*, pp. 46, 48; Sandhu, *Indians*, pp. 89–108; Blythe, *Methods and conditions*, pp. 91, 97–98.

59 Bernardelli, 'New Zealand and Asiatic migration', p. 41.

60 Adas, *Burma Delta*, pp. 92, 120.

61 Furnivall, 'Industrial agriculture', p. 95.

62 Baxter, *Report*, pp. 51–56.

Malaya after 1890. Once in Southeast Asia, immigrants who did not themselves pay their passage seem generally to have succeeded in working free of debt and to have been at liberty to move to other jobs. Even by the late nineteenth century, and increasingly thereafter, the picture is one of a substantially free Southeast Asian labour market and mobile workforce.[63] That was further encouraged by the increasing number of emigrants able to pay for the journey to Southeast Asia themselves. During the late 1880s in Malaya, there was an 'increase in the number of immigrants who could pay their own passages, either because they were helped by friends and relatives who already had made some money from the tin mines or elsewhere, or because they were Chinese labourers returning to the Straits to make more money'.[64] The 1931 Madras census pointed to 'a strong current which is simply emigration in its natural sense, a movement abroad of people who depart when they like and return when they like; no agency assists their passage or controls their stay in the new country'.[65]

In 1907, Indian immigration to Malaya began to be organized under government auspices to ensure a supply of cheap labour. All employers of Indian workers (effectively, European rubber planters) were obliged to contribute to an Indian Immigration Fund. It met all an immigrant's expenses, whether travelling individually from India to Malaya or, as the great bulk did, with a *kangany*. *Kanganies* received a fee from employers who, in turn, claimed back recruiting allowances from the Fund. Immigrants arrived in Malaya without debt and free to change jobs subject to a month's notice. The decision to finance Indian immigration recognized the impossibility of enforcing any type of contract in Malaya's open labour market and aimed to make labour readily abundant and so avoid any upwards wage pressure.[66]

Export Expansion

Merchandise exports of the six Southeast Asian countries, presented in Table 2.4 as three-year annual averages deflated to constant 1913 US$, and centred around the cyclical peaks of 1872, 1883, 1889, 1912, 1926 and 1937, showed swift, long-term expansion. Over the five-and-a-half decades 1871/73

[63] Bernardelli, 'New Zealand and Asiatic migration', p. 41; Blythe, *Methods and conditions*, pp. 1–3; Andrew, *Indian labour*, p. 37; Bennison, *Report of an enquiry*, pp. 75–80; Skinner, *Chinese society*, pp. 53–58; Feeny, *Political economy*, p. 163 and 'Extensive versus intensive', p. 697; Cheng, *Rice industry*, pp. 123–24; Baxter, *Report*, p. 75; Vlieland, 'Population', p. 66; Bauer, *Rubber industry*, pp. 217–18; Wong, *Malayan tin industry*, pp. 67–76; Look Lai, 'Asian contract', pp. 233–35, 256–58.

[64] Wong, *Malayan tin industry*, pp. 66–67.

[65] India, *Census 1931, Madras Report*, part I, p. 80; and see Madras, *Report of the census of the Madras Presidency, 1871*, p. 75; Bennison, *Report of an enquiry*, pp. 75, 76, 80.

[66] Bauer, *Rubber industry*, pp. 220–22; Parmer, *Colonial labor policy*, pp. 38–39; Saw, *Singapore population*, pp. 46, 48.

Table 2.4 *Southeast Asia merchandise exports, 1871/73–1936/38*

(a) Annual averages in 1913 US$, millions

	1871/73	1898/1900	1911/13	1925/27	1936/38
Burma	17.6	59.9	119.6	194.4	273.7
Indochina	14.4	31.7	50.7	87.6	129.8
Thailand	4.8	20.3	34.8	81.5	100.8
Malaya	37.1	133.6	196.1	489.1	545.3
Indonesia: total	62.7	118.9	241.1	490.0	556.8
Indonesia: Outer Islands	*9.5*	*35.1*	*102.9*	*256.2*	*368.5*
Philippines	16.1	25.1	48.4	106.4	182.3
Southeast Asia	152.7	389.5	690.6	1,449.0	1,788.7

(b) Annual growth rates (%)

	1871/73–1925/27	1871/73–1898/1900	1871/73–1911/13	1898/1900–1925/27	1925/27–1936/38
Burma	4.6	4.6	4.9	4.5	3.2
Indochina	4.3	5.1	4.4	3.8	3.6
Thailand	5.4	5.5	5.1	5.3	2.0
Malaya	4.9	4.9	4.3	4.9	1.0
Indonesia: total	4.1	2.7	3.7	5.4	1.2
Indonesia: Outer Islands	*6.7*	*5.6*	*6.6*	*7.6*	*3.4*
Philippines	3.6	1.6	2.8	5.5	5.0
Southeast Asia	4.3	3.5	3.8	5.0	1.9

Notes: 1. For Indochina, 1871/73 refers to 1883. 2. For Malaya, 1871–1913 refers to the Straits Settlements only. 3. For Indonesia, 1871/73 refers to 1874–76. 4. For the Philippines, 1871/73 refers to 1872–73 only and 1898/1900 refers to 1899–1901.

Sources:

Burma: Shein, *Burma's transport*, pp. 263–64; Burma, Office of the Chief Collector of Customs, *Annual statement*, 1912–13, 1914–15, 1920–21; Andrus, *Burmese economic life*, p. 183; Furnivall, *Study*, statistical appendices, VIb, 29–31, VII, 40–41, VIII, 49–52.

Indochina: Frézouls, 'Tableau', p. 274; Indochina, *Situation*, vol. 1, pp. 407, 448–49; Arnaud, 'Taux', p. 267; Leurence, 'Étude', p. 143; Indochina, *Annuaire statistique, 1942–44*, p. 290; Stover, 'Tropical', p. 48.

Thailand: Ingram, *Economic change*, pp. 333–34.

Malaya: Malaya, *Return of foreign of imports and exports*, 1921–28; Malaya, *Foreign imports and exports*, 1930–37; Malaya, *Foreign trade of Malaya 1939*.

Table 2.4 *(cont.)*

Indonesia: Korthals Altes, *General trade statistics*, pp. 50–56, 69–75.
Philippines: Philippines, *1903 census*, vol. 4, pp. 564–65; Philippines, Bureau of Commerce, *Statistical bulletin 1918*, p. 32; *1920*, p. 125; Philippines, Division of Statistics, *Bulletin 1938*, p. 324; Philippines, *Yearbook 1940*, p. 415.
Deflators: Data are converted into US dollars using exchange rates in van der Eng, 'Silver standard', pp. 27–28 and deflated with the index for tropical exports in Lewis, *Aspects*, pp. 49–50.

to 1925/27, Southeast Asian real exports grew at an annual rate of 4.3 per cent, equivalent to a doubling in volume every 16 years. Although separate GDP figures are not available for Indonesia's Outer Islands, their dynamism is evident from a rapidly growing share of Indonesian exports. In 1874/76, Outer Island exports accounted for 15.2 per cent of the Indonesian total. But thereafter, and during a time when Indonesian real exports grew ninefold, the Outer Island share rose to 42.7 per cent of Indonesia's total in 1911/13 and reached two-thirds by 1936/38. Data for Malaya in Table 2.4 tell a remarkable story of export-led growth. Between 1871/73 and 1925/27, Malayan exports grew at 4.9 per cent per annum, equivalent to a doubling in volume about every 14 years.

Volume is, in several respects, a more telling measure of trade expansion than total value, since all commodities were subject to marked price fluctuations, and for rubber these were extreme (Table 2.5). After 1870, a few vented commodities – rice, tin, rubber, coconut products and sugar – increased swiftly in importance to provide, even by 1911/13, the lion's share of Southeast Asia's exports. Production for export of these commodities started from virtually nothing to register, typically in the space of two or three decades, extraordinary increases in volume. In all countries except Indonesia, production concentrated in just one or two main export commodities.

While price affected volume, its influence varied between commodities and countries. In response to the 1930s slump, rice production fell in Burma and Thailand, but not in Indochina. Rubber output remained stable for Malayan smallholders and, in Indonesia, increased. Smallholder supply was normally more elastic than estate because smallholders could turn to alternative sources of earnings. Even in the worst of the 1930s slump, however, smallholders maintained output because of their low, peasant production costs relative to the price of rice and because of rubber's assured saleability.[67]

The value of Southeast Asia's exports dropped from US$2,923 million in 1928 to US$1,034 million in 1935 and recovered only slightly in 1938 to US$1,132 million. However, Southeast Asia, due partly to the increases in the volume and low supply elasticities for most of its exports, maintained almost the same share of world trade at the end of the 1930s as it had a decade earlier.

[67] Bauer, *Rubber industry*, pp. 28–30, 59–62 and 'Some aspects', pp. 196–97.

Table 2.5 *Southeast Asia export volume of main commodities, 1871/73–1935/37 (000 metric tons)*

	1871/73	1900/02	1911/13	1925/27	1931/33	1935/37
Burma						
Rice	0.4	2,330.3	2,530.9	3,137.2	3,456.8	2,134.1
Thailand						
Rice	95.8	643.1	809.3	1,468.0	1,555.8	1,387.6
Rubber			0.1	4.4	6.0	34.4
Malaya						
Rubber		0.1	24.3	264.70	479.9	457.9
Tin	4.6	49.8	52.3	52.9	38.9	66.5
Indonesia						
Sugar Java and Madura	199.1	533.5	868.9	1,355.4	913.9	723.6
Rubber Outer Islands	0.0	0.2	3.2	205.2	221.2	278.1
Copra Outer Islands	0.0	54.2	159.1	328.5	415.7	492.3
Tin Outer Islands	5.3	19.7	28.6	38.7	23.4	39.4
Petroleum Outer Islands	0.1	173.3	813.6	2,313.3	3,929.0	5,488.9
Indochina						
Rice	271.5	696.2	1,287.0	1,594.0	1,153.7	1,698.0
Rubber			0.2	8.8	15.1	38.6
Philippines						
Sugar		73.4	187.8	503.8	949.4	762.4
Coconut products			87.2	295.4		

Notes:
Burma: 1. For Burma the figure for 1871/73 is for 1870–71 only. For 1870 and 1915/16–1928/29 figures are for rice and paddy in terms of rice and so differ slightly from data for other years. 2. The figures for rice and paddy in terms of rice for 1880 are 850,000 tons compared to 884,000 tons for rice and paddy not expressed in terms of rice, and for 1913/14, 2,653,348 tons if in terms of rice, and 2,744,000 tons if paddy is not expressed as the rice equivalent. 3. Figures for 1929/30–1935/36 are for exports of rice and paddy to foreign ports and Indian ports (excluding Burma) and differ slightly from earlier years. 4. The figure for exports for 1928/29 from this series is 2,767 tons as compared to 2,797 tons for the same year from the 1915/16–1928/29 series taken from Grant, *Rice crop*, p. 52.
Malaya: The figure for 1871/73 is for 1874 only and for rubber the figure for 1900/02 is for 1905. Rubber includes rubber latex. Tin refers to tin blocks, ingots, bars or slabs.
Malaya volume of tin exports: 1. Figures refer to tin-in-concentrates. 2. For 1874–97 the figures are for tin production which moved similarly to exports but in most

Table 2.5 (*cont.*)

years slightly exceeded them. Production figures (in tons) for 1898–1900 were: 1898: 41,167; 1899: 38,960; 1900: 43,111.
Indonesia: Figures for 1871/73 are for 1874. Petroleum includes petroleum products.
Indochina: For 1871/73 and 1900/02, rice exports are for Cochinchina only. These constituted the great bulk of exports. For 1911/13, rice and rubber exports are for 1913 only. In 1860, rice exports from Cochinchina were 58,045 metric tons.
Philippines: Coconut products include copra and coconut oil.
Sources:
Burma: Grant, *Rice crop*, p. 52 (for 1870 and 1915/16–1928/29); Shein, *Burma's transport*, p. 265 (for 1880/81–1914/15); Burma, *Report on the administration of Burma*, 1929/30–1935/36 (for 1929/30–1935/36); Andrus, *Burmese economic life*, p. 164 (for 1937/38 onwards).
Thailand: Wilson, *Handbook*, pp. 212–17.
Malaya:
Straits Settlements total merchandise exports/imports (Straits dollars): Straits Settlements, *Blue book*, 1898, 1899; Straits Settlements, *Return of imports and exports*, 1908–10; Straits Settlements, *Blue book*, 1912, 1913; Straits Settlements, *Return of imports and exports*, 1914–27.
Malaya imports and exports: Malaya, *Return of foreign imports and exports*, annual series, 1921–28; Malaya, *Foreign imports and exports*, annual series. Malaya volume of rubber exports 1905–09: Drabble, *Rubber in Malaya*, p. 220; 1910–19: McFadyean, *History of rubber regulation*, pp. 226–27; 1920–41: Drabble, *Malayan rubber*, p. 309.
Malaya volume of tin exports: 1874–97: Wong, *Malayan tin industry*, p. 246; 1898–1940: Yip, *Development of the tin mining industry*, pp. 397–98.
Indonesia: Korthals Altes, *General trade statistics*, pp. 50–75.
Indochina: Coquerel, *Paddys et riz*, p. 264; Indochina, *Annuaire statistique, 1943–46*, pp. 283, 297, 300.
Philippines:
Merchandise Exports/Imports pesos: Philippines, Bureau of Commerce, *Statistical bulletin no. 1*, pp. 15, 17, 24, 27; Philippines, Bureau of Commerce, *Statistical bulletin of the Philippine Islands 1922*, pp. 52–53; *Statistical bulletin* 1929, pp. 161–62; Philippines, Department of Agriculture and Commerce, *Statistical Review*, vol. 4, no. 4 (1937), p. 452.
Sugar for 1930–41: Port of Manila, *Year book 1940*, p. 64. Volume sugar figures for 1939 and 1940 are from Larkin, *Sugar*, p. 202.

In 1928, Southeast Asia accounted for 5.3 per cent of total world exports, and in 1938, 5.2 per cent. Malaya and Indonesia were the principal Southeast Asian exporters, with 1.9 per cent and 1.5 per cent respectively of world exports in

1928, although these figures, and those for Southeast Asia as a whole, involve an element of double counting, since exports sent to Singapore or Penang and then exported from these ports were counted as exports from them as well as from Malaya or Indonesia.[68]

Commodity Specialization

The vent-for-surplus model predicts that during the second Smithian phase, as production extends onto surplus land, primary commodity specialization becomes extreme, and this accords well with Southeast Asian reality. Southeast Asian countries specialized in one or two commodities to a degree that could have been possible only through importing food from other Asian countries and not just manufactures from the West, Japan and India. Some crop and mineral diversification occurred, mainly in inter-war Thailand and Burma, but insofar as Southeast Asian countries diversified this was mainly a post-1950 story and a limited one. Even in the later 1960s, as Myint observed, although the outward-looking countries had diversified somewhat, 'all the Southeast Asian countries are still highly dependent on a few exports'.[69]

Between 1911/13 and 1935/37, Indonesia apart, shares of two or at most three commodities in exports changed relatively little, or increased (Table 2.6). Rice, rubber and tin accounted for over 80 per cent of Thailand's exports. Until the 1930s, the great preponderance of exports were rice. In 1935/38, however, its share of total exports fell to just over half, because rice prices were low and because the Kingdom's rubber and tin industries, though still relatively small, had gained in importance. By the 1930s, agriculture employed over 80 per cent of the labour force and 95 per cent of cultivated land in the Kingdom was planted with rice.[70]

From 1911/13 onwards in Burma, rice accounted for 71 per cent of the total acreage under crops and, together with petroleum, made up over three-quarters of exports. Petroleum did not emerge as a major export until the 1930s, and, even then, was an enclave industry. Much of the drop in rice as a proportion of exports was explained by a halving of rice export prices between the mid-1920s and later 1930s.[71] Burma's dependence on rice, along with rice milling, which was virtually the sole industrial venture, explains why GDP growth rates were at best anaemic after 1911/13, when the frontier began to close and rice production grew slowly, or negatively. In Cochinchina, responsible for almost the whole of Indochinese rice exports, rice occupied 90 per cent of land under cultivation in the early 1920s, and still about three-quarters of the cultivated

68 League of Nations, *Network of world trade*, pp. 142–43.
69 Myint, 'Inward and outward looking countries', p. 281.
70 Ingram, *Economic change*, pp. 50, 236–37.
71 Robertson, 'Rice export', pp. 244–45.

Table 2.6 *Southeast Asia export commodity concentration, 1911/13–1935/37 (% of total merchandise exports)*

	1911/13	1925/27	1931/33	1935/37
Burma (rice, petroleum)	82.6	72.3	78.7	75.3
Thailand (rice, rubber, tin)	81.9	82.1	82.5	83.3
Malaya (rubber, tin)	–	70.9	49.2	71.2
Indonesia (sugar, rubber, copra, tin, petroleum)	62.3	–	64.2	77.7
Indochina (rice, rubber)	62.0	72.3	57.3	59.9
Philippines (sugar and coconut products)	44.6	56.3	57.1	63.2

Notes:
Burma: Figures are for 1913/14, 1926/27, 1931/32 and 1935/36.
Philippines: Coconut products include copra and coconut oil.
Indochina: The figure for 1911/13 is for 1913 only. Figures are estimated as follows: Indochina (1927–48), *Annuaire statistique, 1941–1942*, pp. 296, 303 shows rice and rubber as percentages of total merchandise exports. These percentages times the values of total merchandise exports give approximate values in each year for rice and rubber exports and these values are combined to arrive at average values of rice and rubber for each period.
Sources: As for Table 2.4.

area at the end of the 1930s, despite the expansion of rubber growing. Rice and rubber normally accounted for around 60 per cent and at times over 70 per cent of Indochinese exports.[72]

Tin and rubber dominated Malaya's economy. In 1925/27, the two commodities made up 71 per cent of Malayan merchandise exports, but 49 per cent in 1931/33, due to the collapse in rubber prices (Table 2.6). Inter-war Malaya began to diversify into oil palm, chiefly in Johor, but in 1939 the industry remained in its infancy.

Of Philippine exports, sugar and coconut products (both copra and oil) climbed from under half in 1911/13 to more than three-fifths in 1935/37. Sugar, the Islands' chief export, was boosted by American policy which left large amounts of land in the hands of a few owners and allowed preferential access to the United States market. By 1927 to 1932, the Islands ranked as the world's largest sugar exporter after Cuba.[73]

Indonesia alone had, at least by Southeast Asian standards, a diversified commodity-based economy and exported a variety of tropical produce. In 1935/37, however, five commodities – sugar, rubber, copra, tin and

[72] Copeland, *Rice*, p. 258; Robertson, 'Rice export', pp. 244–45; Elson, *End*, p. 83.
[73] Stamp, *Asia*, p. 442.

petroleum – made up some 78 per cent of Indonesian exports (Table 2.6). Nor was this entirely a vent-for-surplus story, since sugar was largely grown on estates in Java. However, the other four Indonesian exports all came largely, or almost entirely, from the land-surplus Outer Islands of Borneo and Sumatra.

As well as forming a highly specialized component of the global economy, Southeast Asia had global dominance in a number of its exports. By the inter-war period, Burma, Thailand and Indochina accounted for over two-thirds of world rice exports and fed large parts of the rest of Asia.[74] In 1940, Southeast Asia supplied 85 per cent of world rubber exports.[75] Most of world output of natural rubber at that time, and for a few years afterwards as immature rubber acreage came into bearing, depended on Malaya and Indonesia. Each country had, in 1940, just under two-fifths of world rubber acreage; Southeast Asia accounted for 91.3 per cent of world hectares planted in rubber. Including the smaller Southeast Asian producers of Thailand and Burma, 65.1 per cent of all tin production was in Southeast Asia, most of which came from Malaya and Indonesia. In 1937, when world tin output amounted to 211,033 metric tons, Malaya produced 78,787 tons and Indonesia 40,417 tons, more than half of the world's total.[76]

Although Southeast Asia grew and exported large quantities of sugar, Southeast Asian exports of the commodity lacked the global prominence that the region had for rubber and tin. However, the Philippines was the world's largest producer of coconut products.[77] The Islands also had a virtual world monopoly in the production of abaca due to unique soil conditions in the Bicol region of southern Luzon and Davao in Mindanao. The fibres of abaca were the only natural fibres that would not swell in salt water, and because of this quality abaca was essential for naval and shipping use.[78]

Malayan Settlement and Economic Patterns

In Southeast Asia, because migrants moved primarily in response to the prospect of work and higher earnings, they settled predominantly in areas specialized in producing for export, or in cities and towns. Since export areas were only parts of each country, and because they generally overlapped with more urbanized areas, migration, and especially immigration, created ethnically differentiated regions within countries. Malaya was the extreme example of the

74 Burma, *Interim report of the Committee to Enquire into the Rice and Paddy Trade*, p. 4.

75 Bauer, *Rubber industry*, p. 391; Knorr, *World rubber*, p. 249.

76 International Tin Research and Development Council, *Statistical year book 1938*, pp. 12–13; Commodity Research Bureau, *Commodity year book 1939*, pp. 574, 578.

77 Nyberg, 'Growth in the Philippine coconut industry', p. 42.

78 Hainsworth and Moyer, *Agricultural geography*, p. 29; Hartendorp, *Japanese occupation*, p. 357.

correlation between economic, geographical and social dualism. This section examines Malayan settlement and economic patterns and how they evolved.

The population of Malaya, excluding Singapore, in 1940 divided into 45.5 per cent Malay, 38.1 per cent Chinese, 14.8 per cent Indian and a tiny proportion of others (Table 2.7). Malays were overwhelmingly rural dwellers, and comprised the bulk of settlement in the 'traditional' parts of Malaya. These included Malaya's east coast states, none of which was more than partially drawn into the tin and rubber export economy, and Kedah and Perlis in the far north-west. Although many Malays were rubber smallholders, the majority followed other, more traditional pursuits which, as well as rice cultivation, included fishing. Chinese settled disproportionately in a 'tin and rubber belt', which began in southern Kedah and continued southwards along the entire peninsular west coast to Singapore. In this tin and rubber belt, a high proportion of Chinese resided in large cities or sizeable urban settlements. While Malays comprised almost three-quarters of the population in Malaya's 'traditional' areas, Chinese accounted for almost half of those living along the west coast, where Malaya's export economy predominated. In that part of Malaya, many Chinese were rubber smallholders or tin miners. Because Indians, chiefly Tamils from the Madras Presidency, provided the bulk of the labour force for European-owned rubber estates, they were concentrated along Malaya's west coast, and especially in Selangor and Perak. The 1931 Malayan census found that three-fifths of Malaya's Tamil population were employed on rubber estates.[79]

Corresponding to Chinese settlement in both Malaya's export-oriented and more urbanized region, Chinese also tended to live in the country's wealthier areas, and had higher average pre-war incomes and more assets than Indians and Malays. Reflective of this wealth distribution, Malayan Chinese society included, particularly by the inter-war years, a significant middle class.

Indian estate labourers, numbering some 370,000 in the later 1930s, had almost always come to Malaya as contract workers, and often alone. When a demand for rubber disappeared, so too did their jobs. In the 1930s slump, Indians lacked their own resources to pay the passage home and most relied on an entitlement given by the Malayan government to return at no cost to India. Between 1930 and 1933, there was a net outflow of 243,100 Indians from Malaya, equivalent to well over a third of that group's 1929 Malayan population.[80] Malays were generally financially better off than Indians, and among Malays, the best-off group were *kampong* (village) Malays, since they owned land or had access to it.[81]

79 Malaya, *British Malaya: a report on the 1931 census*, p. 85.
80 Huff, 'Entitlements', pp. 306–07.
81 ANM, 1957/0290683 Sel. CA 232/46 BMA, Nutrition Unit report, Jan./Feb. 1946, pp. 5–6.

Table 2.7 *Malaya population by industry and ethnic groups, 1940 (000 persons)*

		Malays	Chinese	Indians	Others	Total
Traditional and rice states	Kedah	340.2	108.4	61.8	14.9	525.3
	Perlis	46.9	8.6	1.2	2.1	58.8
	Kelantan	338.9	30.9	11.5	9.0	390.3
	Terengganu	185.7	18.7	2.1	1.4	207.9
	Pahang	128.5	73.9	17.0	2.1	221.8
Total traditional		1,040.3	240.6	93.8	29.4	1,404.1
% of ethnic group in traditional		74.1	17.1	6.7	2.1	100.0
West coast tin and rubber	Perak	335.4	450.2	196.1	11.1	992.7
	Selangor	152.7	339.7	193.5	15.6	701.6
	Negri Sembilan	106.0	125.8	59.3	4.9	296.0
	Malacca	110.0	90.2	28.3	3.7	232.2
	Johore	309.5	346.6	76.2	5.2	737.6
	Penang and P. Wellesley	117.5	225.9	60.7	7.8	411.8
Total tin and rubber		1,131.0	1,578.4	614.1	48.4	3,371.8
% of ethnic group in tin and rubber		33.5	46.8	18.2	1.4	100.0
Total Malaya		2,171.3	1,819.0	707.9	77.8	4,776.0
% of ethnic group in Malaya population		45.5	38.1	14.8	1.6	100.0

Note: Columns and rows may not add to totals due to rounding.
Source: Malayan Union, *Report of the medical department 1946*, p. 11.

Production Functions and Capital Constraints

Production functions of vent-for-surplus economies like Southeast Asia's are modelled with no separate capital constraint, because production often required only simple tools and seeds and was self-financing. It is further assumed that economies of scale are not a significant issue. Throughout the late nineteenth and early twentieth centuries, these assumptions of the model remained largely true of Southeast Asia. Even in the 1920s and 1930s, rice and smallholder rubber were produced with traditional methods and employed much the same technologies as used decades previously.[82] During the twentieth century, however, Southeast Asian economies had increasingly to look to international financial

[82] Ingram, *Economic change*, pp. 48–49, 209; Manarungsan, *Economic development*, p. 81; Hlaing, *Study*, pp. 18, 120–21; Cheng, *Rice industry*, pp. 28–36; Adas, *Burma Delta*, p. 128; Drabble, *Malayan rubber*, pp. 5–6; Wong, *Malayan tin*, pp. 156, 170.

markets to avoid a serious capital constraint and continue to vent surplus land and attract surplus labour. The production of sugar, plantation rubber, tin and petroleum all involved sizeable amounts of foreign capital.

Nineteenth-century Production Functions

Until after about 1910 in Southeast Asia, the dominant, almost the sole, production model for export staples utilized abundant land and more or less unlimited cheap, unskilled labour. Technical change was minimal; expansion was almost entirely through increased land and labour inputs. For the most part, small parcels of land were available to those willing to settle them. In Southeast Asia, colonial land policy, rather than economic or technical advantages, could have made large-scale production the mode, as happened in parts of Cochinchina. However, governments generally favoured small production units, encapsulated in a colonial rhetoric of the nobility of peasant cultivators or, in the Philippines, the ideal of the yeoman farmer.[83]

In Burma, Thailand and Indochina, methods of growing rice changed little as more land was cultivated although, as discussed below, there were improvements in rice milling. By 1930 in Burma, 10 million acres of swamp had been cleared and planted with rice through 'the sustained effort of millions of peasants working only with bullocks or buffaloes and the simple, locally made ploughs and implements they had evolved in their own way over the centuries'.[84] Chinese miners in Malaya relied on large labour inputs, used basic tools and did not require much capital. In 1903 in Malaya, the exploitation of rich alluvial tin deposits yielded 51,000 tons of the metal, over half of world output. Production at this time depended on some 224,000 miners, virtually all Chinese and equipped with little more than shovels and simple pumps. Because rubber smallholders often planted trees on nearby land and tended them at the same time as maintaining earlier, subsistence production, so long as land was available, the main cost was the effort of planting rubber and maintaining the trees. In Indonesia, a large proportion of smallholder rubber was planted as a by-product of rice cultivation, which made the cost of adding rubber 'negligible in terms of cash or effort'.[85] Until after the end of the Spanish period (effectively 1902) in the Philippines, sugar production 'was a matter of small landholdings, small mills, primitive methods, and fairly widespread participation in the fruits of production and export'.[86]

Surplus land and natural resources, traditional cultivation and mining techniques and labour-intensive production functions allowed late

83 Larkin, *Sugar*, p. 68; Furnivall, 'Industrial agriculture', p. 92 and *Colonial policy*, p. 493.
84 Dobby, *Southeast Asia*, p. 173.
85 Bauer, *Rubber industry*, p. 67.
86 Spencer, *Land and people*, p. 203.

nineteenth-century Southeast Asian production to be essentially self-financing. Rice cultivation, as in Thailand, required only 'a very small cash outlay'.[87] In Indochina, rice growing was 'left to the natives who worked practically without capital'.[88] Initial investment by rice cultivators and, during the twentieth century, by rubber smallholders, consisted mostly of their own and family labour time. Finance to buy seeds and simple tools to clear land came from personal savings or borrowing from family, relatives, traders, paddy dealers or local shopkeepers.[89] Both workers and financers could be paid when tin was found or rubber sold. Once production was underway, the main need was for circulating capital or produced inputs (as opposed to fixed or durable inputs), which are used up in one period of production and include 'wage fund' advances paid to workers at the outset of the production cycle. The cycle was typically short – under a year for land developed for rice production or with established rubber and coconut, and even less for tin mining. Finance was self-sustaining. Principal recouped and profits from one cycle provided finance for the next and, moreover, new capital to extend the export production frontier, so long as the rent created by clearing new land at least equalled the interest cost of the wage fund.[90] Investment was likely to be productive since, as Bauer emphasizes, it was made by people with a direct interest in the returns and who, furthermore, supervised their own work effort.[91]

Twentieth-century Production Functions

In the twentieth century, Southeast Asian production functions became more varied, and often more complex. Beginning in the 1890s, petroleum production in Indonesia began to require large amounts of capital after a merger of two companies to create Royal Dutch Shell. Together with Standard Oil of New York and Standard Oil of New Jersey, operating through various subsidiaries in Southeast Asia, the three oil giants dominated petroleum exploration, refining and distribution.[92] As well as petroleum production, tin mining, plantation rubber and sugar processing had to look to international financial markets to avoid a capital constraint.

In Malaya, substantial capital expenditure for most tin mining awaited the exhaustion of easily won tin alluvial deposits and a need for deeper mines.

87 Ingram, *Economic change*, p. 66.
88 Robequain, *Economic development*, p. 160.
89 Ingram, *Economic change*, p. 65.
90 Drake, 'Natural resources' and *Currency, credit*; Findlay and Lundahl, 'Natural resources and economic development'. On the nature of circulating capital, see Eltis, *Classical theory*, pp. 75–76.
91 Bauer, *Subsistence to exchange*, pp. 12–13.
92 Huff, *Economic growth*, pp. 237–40.

Deeper mining involved dredging, with its associated high capital requirements for dredges and other mining inputs, and so a growing importance of European mines. In Malaya, Chinese miners, though with more capital than their late nineteenth-century counterparts, continued to account for a substantial share of tin output, but beginning about 1910 European mines largely supplanted Chinese, and increasingly fell under the control of international mining companies with their ready access to finance and technology.[93]

Indonesian tin mining centred on two small islands, Bangka and Billiton, near Singapore. Mines were in the hands of large Dutch companies, employed comparatively few workers and existed as an enclave with few linkages to other parts of the economy. In 1920, the introduction of bucket dredgers on Billiton allowed 150 men working three eight-hour shifts to move as much earth and tin ore as had formerly required 4,000 or 5,000 workers. In Thailand, tin production concentrated on both sides of the peninsula in the south and on the island of Phuket. As in Malaya, by World War II, mining depended largely on bucket dredging and European companies.

Malay and Chinese smallholders in pre-World War II Malaya grew around two-fifths of rubber with only small capital inputs, but plantation agriculture produced the rest and required substantial amounts of capital to grow the same crop as smallholders. Malayan and Indonesian smallholders with less than 15 acres brought rubber into bearing for no more than a twelfth of the capital outlay required to open a European estate.[94] Rubber cultivation on the Sumatran east coast was dominated by large, European-owned estates, but in Sarawak was carried out almost entirely by smallholders, and in Borneo divided about equally between smallholders and estates. While rubber in Thailand was a smallholder crop, in southern Vietnam it became chiefly a plantation one, mainly organized through large financial and industrial groups.

Rubber plantations needed finance, not because of any appreciable difference in agricultural tools, but to feed and supervise a labour force while clearing land, planting trees, waiting about seven years for them to bear, and then maintaining an estate and marketing its output. In contrast, smallholders could use mainly family labour and this largely accounted for their lower outlay in bringing rubber into bearing and marketing it. Capital for Malayan plantation rubber came principally through the floatation of rubber companies on the London stock market, but also from Shanghai and Ceylon.[95] An initial rush to acquire a stake in Malayan rubber, beginning in 1909 and lasting into 1910, set off the then greatest new share boom in the London market's history.

93 Fermor, *Report*, pp. 25–26.

94 Figart, *Plantation rubber industry*; Bauer, *Rubber industry*, pp. 67–68.

95 See, for example, Thomas, 'Intra-empire capital transfer'.

Singapore Chinese entrepreneurs managed to sidestep much of the capital needed to bring estate rubber into bearing by organizing sharecroppers to plant rubber trees and also grow a catch crop of pineapples. Sharecroppers tended the growing rubber trees in exchange for a share of the profits from selling pineapples and a fixed fee. The fee, about enough to guarantee subsistence, protected the sharecropper against downside risk to pineapple crops, while a stake in the sale of the pineapples gave an incentive for their cultivation. When the rubber trees matured, the sharecroppers cleared the land of pineapples, again for a fixed fee, and the entrepreneur had a yielding rubber estate. In this way, rubber estates could be established for about £14 an acre rather than the £70 required for European-owned estates. As a by-product of the entrepreneur-sharecropper arrangement, Malaya became the world's largest exporter of tinned pineapples, then a favourite food in Britain. A number of the Chinese entrepreneurs became the core of inter-war Singapore's legendary wealthy Chinese businessmen. They used some of their rubber profits and rents to invest in manufacturing and founded, or became closely involved with, local Singapore Chinese banking.[96]

Sugar requires processing near where it is grown, and that, together with economies of scale, dictated the large, centralized, expensive installations of sugar centrals to process cane. The Philippines, however, moved slowly to establish centrals, and remained the last major producer of cane sugar without them. Finally, after 1911, sugarmen in the Philippines progressively implemented modern milling techniques to satisfy the requirements of the lucrative North American market for better quality sugar.[97]

Agricultural Technical Change

In pre-World War II vent-for-surplus Southeast Asian agriculture, sweeping technical change was never economic or practicable. Predominantly small farm units, together with a continued ready availability of land and cheap labour, minimized economic pressures to mechanize agriculture.[98] At the same time, the continued ability to access land, even if perhaps of poorer quality and at relatively higher prices, worked against the adoption of any revolutionary biological package of technologies using fertilizers and scientifically improved crops like that disseminated in inter-war Taiwan and Korea under Japanese colonialism.[99]

96 Huff, 'Sharecroppers, risk, management'.

97 Larkin, *Sugar*, pp. 54–57, 97–99, 148–53.

98 There were a few pre-World War II experiments in mechanization but, with one or two exceptions, these failed. One exception was rice cultivation in Thailand undertaken by Chinese from Penang. Federated Malay States, *Report on the Rice Cultivation Committee*, vol. 2, p. 178. For an analysis of the obstacles to mechanization, see Copeland, *Rice*, p. 253. An interesting example of failure can be found in Main, 'La culture', pp. 323–24.

99 Ho, 'Agricultural transformation', pp. 327–33; Hayami, 'Conditions', pp. 143–45.

Six decades of economic expansion led to continuously increasing Southeast Asian population densities. By the 1930s, the number of persons per square mile was between double and treble 1881 levels (Table 2.2). While in some countries population pressure was evident in vent-for-surplus areas like Burma's delta, in most, opportunities still existed for vent-for-surplus growth through bringing new land under cultivation with established techniques. So long as this obtained, as generally remained true until at least the 1950s, relative factor prices made other avenues of agricultural development difficult to justify.[100]

Substantial technical advance occurred in the processing of the chief vent-for-surplus exports. Innovations were characteristically a response to international marketing requirements. The introduction of standard grades of rubber in Malaya (where, in Singapore, most Outer Province rubber was also processed) and better milling methods greatly reduced marketing transaction costs, and helped to prevent sheet rubber from rotting en route to overseas markets.[101] In Thailand, mechanization began to replace hand mills in 1858, and from the late 1880s white rice was produced to meet taste preferences in Southeast Asian markets.[102] Likewise, in Burma, improved rice-milling technology was increasingly adopted, first to replace cargo (rice in husks) with white milled rice and, beginning about 1915, also to produce parboiled rice popular with Indian consumers.[103]

Intra-regional Trade

The vent-for-surplus model developed in Chapter 1 explicitly allows for intra-regional trade. Intra-regional exchange was fundamental to Southeast Asian growth through allowing greater economic specialization and widening the market in both non-food and food-specialized countries. Food imports were essential for the countries that specialized in non-food commodities, while for food-producing countries, regional trade catered for food preferences, filled dietary gaps and offered a more varied choice of foods. Most items of food consumed in Southeast Asia came from within the region or from elsewhere in Asia, apart from relatively small trades in Western foods demanded by Europeans and, to a much lesser extent, by an urban Asian middle class. Rice, sugar and dried fish were the main food items traded within Southeast Asia, but

[100] In the 1950s there was still a good deal of land available in Malaya and the Indonesian Outer Islands. On the ready availability of land in Thailand and the Philippines, see respectively Manarungsan, *Economic development*, p. 16 and Hooley, 'Century', p. 269. Land remained available in Malaya even in the 1960s (Bruton, *Sri Lanka and Malaysia*, p. 277) and in the Philippines until the mid-1960s (Dohner and Intal, 'Marcos legacy', pp. 376, 574.)

[101] Huff, *Economic growth*, pp. 195–207.

[102] Manarungsan, *Economic development*, pp. 68–69.

[103] Cheng, *Rice industry*, pp. 95–97.

the list extended to a variety of other foods, including dried fruits and vegetables, eggs, seaweeds, beans of various kinds, ginger, sago and salt.

Rice dominated Southeast Asian regional trade as the main export of three of the region's six countries and the staple food throughout Southeast Asia. While the three specialized rice producers relied on the income from exporting the grain to purchase manufactures and foods, the three non-food producers used their export incomes to buy rice, other food items and manufactured goods. The trades in sugar and dried fish were often linked with regional rice shipments, and these were conducted, especially until 1913, chiefly through Singapore Chinese traders.

The pattern of Southeast Asian rice exports emphasizes both Southeast Asia's economic integration and the extent of the region's globalization. While Burma, Thailand and Indochina were the main source of the food required by workers in the Malayan and Indonesian export industries and those in towns and cities, none of the three rice producers relied chiefly on a Southeast Asian market. By the inter-war years, the three rice-specialized economies accounted for about four-fifths of world exportable rice surpluses.[104] The largest share of Southeast Asian rice exports went to China and India, but Southeast Asia also provided rice to markets in Sri Lanka and Japan, along with less important Asian destinations, as well as meeting a substantial demand in Europe. Burma sent most of its rice to India, notably Bengal, although large quantities also went to Europe; Indochina supplied China, as did Thailand.

Late Nineteenth- and Early Twentieth-century Rice Trade

Between the 1870s and World War I, Southeast Asia took no more than about a fifth of rice exports from Burma or Indochina, although about a third to as much as two-fifths of shipments from Thailand. Within Southeast Asia, the pattern of trade in rice was largely dictated by market proximity (Table 2.8). Burma, in the west of Southeast Asia, exported principally to Malaya, only a short distance away, while Cochinchina increasingly looked to a market in the Philippines as the nearest rice-consuming country, although it had significant markets in Indonesia, and also Singapore. The main regional outlets for Thailand, centrally located in Southeast Asia, were directly to the south, in Malaya and Indonesia.

As an entrepôt, Singapore occupied a key role in the inter-regional Southeast Asian market for rice, by bridging regional demand for rice and its supply. All three rice exporters shipped rice to Singapore which then, although drawing on some of these supplies for its own consumption, distributed rice to Malaya and Indonesia, although not the Philippines. The Philippines remained

[104] van der Eng, 'Productivity and comparative advantage', p. 348.

Table 2.8 *Burma, Thailand and Cochinchina rice exports, 1872–1911 (000 short tons)*

(a) 1872/81	Burma	Thailand	Cochinchina
Malaya	75	65	33
Indonesia	0	0	43
Philippines	0	0	10
Others	832	133	229
Total	907	198	315
Southeast Asia % of total exports	8.3	32.8	24.1
(b) 1882/91	**Burma**	**Thailand**	**Cochinchina**
Malaya	179	106	39
Indonesia	3	–	18
Philippines	0	–	53
Others	913	223	386
Total	1,095	329	496
Southeast Asia % of total exports	16.6	32.2	11.5
(c) 1892/1901	**Burma**	**Thailand**	**Cochinchina**
Malaya	241	210	58
Indonesia	3	–	57
Philippines	0	–	56
Others	1,401	362	475
Total	1,645	572	646
Southeast Asia % of total exports	14.8	36.7	17.8
(d) 1902/11	**Burma**	**Thailand**	**Cochinchina**
Malaya	307	347	36
Indonesia	84	–	96
Philippines	7	–	159
Others	2,013	607	502
Total	2,411	954	793
Southeast Asia % of total exports	16.2	36.4	16.6

Source: Owen, 'Rice industry', pp. 98–101.

peripheral to a Southeast Asian regional market because of distance from the other Southeast Asian countries, because of close ties to the United States and because it produced much of its own rice. Even so, Philippine imports from Indochina and Singapore's key distributive role ensured an integrated Southeast Asian rice market and facilitated that market's integration to the world rice market.[105]

Rice accounted for the bulk of Singapore's imports from Thailand, Burma and Indochina. Because of the taste of Thai rice and the quality of the product in cooking as separate grains, rice from Thailand was favoured by consumers in Singapore, Malaya and the Outer Islands. In these areas, Thailand's rice was known as 'Singapore rice'.[106] Thailand was Singapore's main source of rice, and Singapore a major outlet for Thailand's rice. In 1880/84, Singapore took half of Thailand's rice exports, and in 1900/04 more than a third.[107] Along with Penang, Singapore's importance to Burma's rice exports was sufficient to lead Rangoon traders to market a grade known as Straits Quality.[108]

Inter-war Regional Integration and Rice

By the inter-war years, although Singapore's importance as an entrepôt in Southeast Asian economic integration had declined, earlier patterns of intra-regional exchange persisted. In comparison to pre-1913 decades, integration may even have increased, because the region itself became ever more specialized. Where Southeast Asia was most integrated, along a Thailand–Malaya–Indonesia axis, a high proportion of this integration was through Singapore and, to a lesser extent, Penang. Integration continued to centre around the exchange of rice. The importance of the two Straits Settlements ports as entrepôts for the rice trade substantially accounts for Malaya's high share of intra-regional imports as a proportion of its total imports (Table 2.9). The much lower share of Malayan intra-regional imports in total imports, approximately a fifth, has two main explanations. One is that during the inter-war years, more of the rice trade was direct between Southeast Asia's producing and consuming countries; the other, that manufactures imported by the two Straits ports for regional distribution came from the West and Japan, and these added to intra-regional exports but not to imports.

As during the years of emerging late nineteenth-century specialization, trade flows along the Thailand–Malaya–Indonesia axis included, as well as rice, a variety of basic consumer goods and manufactures, especially textiles. These were the items mainly required by rubber growers and urban residents in Malaya, Thailand and Indonesia, principally the Outer Islands. As Malaya and the Outer Islands became increasingly specialized in rubber, Thailand looked more to them as a market for rice, and its export within Southeast Asia largely

105 Latham and Neal, 'International market', pp. 264–65.
106 *SSTC* II, p. 859, and see II, p. 390.
107 Ingram, 'Thailand's rice trade', p. 107.
108 Burma, *Interim report of the Committee to Enquire into the Rice and Paddy Trade*, pp. 7, 65.

explains the high proportion of Thai exports with an intra-regional destination. Intra-regional trade accounted for three-fifths to three-quarters of Thailand's total exports and a third to two-fifths of imports (Table 2.10). Much of this trade was via Singapore. In 1925/27, mainly reflecting rice exports, Singapore handled two-fifths of Thailand's exports. By 1937/39, rice made up a much smaller proportion of Thailand's exports to Singapore, although it still took almost one-third of all Thailand's exports, because of the growth of shipments of tin ore and rubber.[109]

Roughly a quarter to a third of Indonesia's exports were intra-regional although no more than about a fifth of imports were, partly because Java bought a high proportion of consumer goods directly from Europe. Indonesia's intra-regional export trade had two main components. The Outer Islands sent rubber to Singapore for processing and onwards sale, and Java exported sugar to most of Southeast Asia except the Philippines. A substantial share of Javanese sugar went to Singapore where, as well as being exported, it was used in pineapple canning and the manufacture of biscuits and sweets. Sugar came from Java already refined. But so-called sugar refineries in Singapore, numbering 18 before World War I and 15 in 1926, made the Javanese product into sugar candy, and re-boiled the liquid left from this process into what was called Singapore brown sugar.[110]

Table 2.9 does not offer a good picture of Burma's intra-regional trade, because data are for the whole of India. It is clear, however, that Burma had a substantial intra-regional rice trade, and exported rice chiefly to Penang, its nearest Straits port, and to Sumatra, where large numbers of plantation workers relied on imported food. Although Burma and Indochina sent rice to Singapore, it was not of great importance to either country. Singapore remained, however, a clearing house that balanced supply and demand for rice throughout Southeast Asia and furnished various foods and manufactures in exchange. Indochina was much more integrated with China than with Southeast Asia. The Philippines stood largely apart from Southeast Asian trade, and looked to the United States as its main market and source of consumer goods.

A pan-Asian feature of the structure of Singapore's trade was the importance of China (including Hong Kong) and India. Trade with both areas was essentially an extension of the Southeast Asian regional economy. Imports from China were principally food and simple manufactures to meet the demand created by Chinese workers in Malayan and Indonesian export industries. Similarly, India provided a range of goods required by Indian

[109] Kingdom of Thailand, *Annual statements of the foreign trade and navigation*, 2468 (1925–26) and 2469 (1926–27), pp. 77–80, 87, 96, 158; *Foreign trade and navigation of the Kingdom of Siam* (1938–39), pp. 105–11, 118–20, 195; Landon, *Chinese in Thailand*, p. 137.

[110] *SSTC*, II, pp. 650, 811, 860, 891, V, p. 129; *SSLCP 1931*, 'Report on the Pineapple Conference', p. C225.

Table 2.9 *Intra-Southeast Asian imports and exports, 1928–38 (US$ million)*

(a) Intra-Southeast Asian imports, 1928–1938

	Burma		Malaya		Indochina		Indonesia		Philippines		Thailand		Other Southeast Asia	
	1928	1938	1928	1938	1928	1938	1928	1938	1928	1938	1928	1938	1928	1938
Burma			72	25	8	3	33	11	1	1	11	4	1	0
Malaya	35	17			6	2	91	23	2	1	28	14	26	13
Indochina	12	0	22	8			15	1	4	1	0	0	0	0
Indonesia	114	10	279	85	12	2			5	3	13	3	1	2
Philippines	1	0	1	1	0	2	1	0			0	0	0	0
Thailand	2	0	99	49	1	1	11	2	0	0			0	0
Other Southeast Asia	1	1	36	15	0	0	2	1	0	0	0	0	1	2
Total Southeast Asia	165	28	509	183	27	10	153	38	12	6	52	21	29	17
Intra-imports as % total Southeast Asia imports			61.0	58.3	16.0	18.2	22.4	14.2	6.0	5.4	38.5	38.2	90.6	94.4

(*continued*)

Table 2.9 *(cont.)*

(b) Intra-Southeast Asian exports, 1928–1938

	Burma		Malaya		Indochina		Indonesia		Philippines		Thailand		Other Southeast Asia	
	1928	1938	1928	1938	1928	1938	1928	1938	1928	1938	1928	1938	1928	1938
Burma			35	15	12	0	119	5	1	0	3	3	1	1
Malaya	63	23			18	8	227	81	1	1	100	49	38	14
Indochina	11	4	9	1			2	1	0	0	1	0	0	0
Indonesia	30	8	87	21	14	1			0	0	7	1	1	1
Philippines	3	1	2	1	4	1	4	4			0	1	0	0
Thailand	10	2	28	9	2	0	5	2	0	0			0	0
Other Southeast Asia	1	0	17	8	0	0	1	1	0	0	0	0	0	2
Total Southeast Asia	118	38	178	55	50	10	358	94	2	1	111	54	40	18
Intra-exports as % total Southeast Asia exports			21.8	16.9	25.6	12.3	33.4	24.4	0.8	0.9	60.0	71.1	87.0	78.3

Notes: 1. Values are in US 'new gold dollars', which is the current US dollar and equivalent to 0.5906 of the dollar when the US went off the gold standard in 1934. 2. Burma includes India and Ceylon, which overstates its trade with Southeast Asia. The main factor in this overstatement is the shipment of gunny bags to Thailand, Indochina and Indonesia for the transport of rice and sugar. 3. Other Southeast Asia includes British Borneo, British North Borneo, Brunei, Sarawak and Portuguese Timor.
Source: League of Nations, *Network of world trade*, pp. 106–08, 143–47.

workers, while gunnies from Bombay mills were sent via Singapore to Indochinese and Thai-Chinese rice exporters and to Javanese sugar exporters. However, specie accounted for about half of imports from India, and opium another quarter. The opium was used by Chinese labourers throughout the region, as well as in Singapore, where 60 per cent of coal coolies were said to be smokers.[111] Opium, rice and sugar accounted for a considerable proportion of exports to China, which otherwise consisted largely of tropical produce, also the main exports to India.

Conclusion

Beginning in the late nineteenth century in Southeast Asia, two inputs – surplus natural resources and surplus labour – complemented each other to yield the swift growth and staple specialization outlined in the vent-for-surplus model in Chapter 1. Globalization provided a catalyst for this growth when, in opening world markets and creating a demand for Southeast Asian exports, it offered a way to vent both land and labour. By about 1910, capital and technology entered Southeast Asia's vent-for-surplus story and enabled Southeast Asia more fully to exploit its own resources. An essential growth ingredient in the venting process was the responsiveness of Southeast Asians to economic opportunity. They were, along with Chinese, Indian, Indonesian and European immigrants, the authors of two of the most remarkable economic events in late nineteenth-century world history: the opening of the Southeast Asian frontier and the mass migration and immigration of millions of people to new lands.

111 United Kingdom, *Commission to Enquire into the Use of Opium*, I, p. 12.

3

Business Structure and Finance

Global supply chains are not new, and before World War II were fundamental to commerce in Southeast Asia. A web of European merchants, agency houses, commission agents and banks located in Southeast Asia linked the region to markets in the United States and Europe. Even more complicated networks of Asian dealers, sub-dealers, brokers and commission agents assembled commodities from the hinterland either for delivery to the European merchants and agency houses or for distribution within Asia. Equally intertwined commercial networks imported food and manufactured goods and distributed them within Southeast Asia. Almost all the Asian intermediaries and principals were Chinese or, in Burma, Indians and Chinese. Southeast Asia's mercantile structures as well as those financing trade and providing other services divided along ethnic lines characteristic of plural societies. The first section of this chapter analyses Southeast Asia's differing mercantile arrangements and considers them from the viewpoint of commodities and production structures.

Financial development is the subject of the chapter's second section. By the early twentieth century, Southeast Asian governments had established stable monetary systems regulated, except in Indochina, by colonial currency boards which required 100 per cent, and in practice generally more, foreign exchange backing for local currencies. European banks dominated formal finance, although after 1900 local Chinese-owned banks emerged and became especially strong in Singapore. Unlike their European counterparts, the Chinese banks were willing to lend for industrial projects. Lending was, however, constrained by the monetary rigidity of the currency board system, the inherent instability of mono-economies and quickness of depositors to withdraw funds. The peasant nature of much of Southeast Asian production was reflected in a heavy reliance on informal finance and in interlinked deals, often facilitated through multiple intermediaries. The co-existence of formal and informal finance created a clear financial dualism although often, as in trade, the two sectors were complementary and interdependent.

Business Structure

Mercantile structures depended on methods of production and export markets. European merchants, typically with head offices in Europe or the United States, controlled exports to, and imports from, these countries. When European merchants acted as agents for European hinterland producers and so also functioned as agency houses, they organized production or had other close ties with the producers. Through agency contracts as well as more informal relationship ties, European merchants controlled the marketing chain for the output of European estates and mines. When Asians produced export crops, Europeans, although still often the exporters to the West, relied on Asians, as principals or intermediaries, to extend finance to producers, collect hinterland produce and sometimes also process it. This section discusses, for major Southeast Asian exports, the region's differing mercantile structures, and compares and contrasts their variations.

Exporters, whether European merchants or Asians, were at the apex of an often pyramidal mercantile structure. For European merchants, oligopoly tended to be the rule. In acquiring a hold on trade, European firms had frequently gained competitive power through first-mover advantages of early or mid-nineteenth-century establishment in Southeast Asia and then enhanced an early lead by becoming large. They further added to their size and market dominance through the acquisition of agencies for manufacturers in metropolitan countries and/or taking on the role of shipping agents by virtue of the cargoes they could offer as large exporters. Shipping agents profited through shipping commissions as well as by exporting, and possibly also by means of rebates from shipping companies given in exchange for support of conferences (cartels) organized by the shipowners. Everywhere, most of the leading European merchants had the same national affiliation as the colonial power.

Because of these ties to nation, individual merchant houses, although perhaps with offices in a number of countries, were generally among the principal firms in no more than two countries. The main European firms in Malaya were British, and included Guthrie and Company, Boustead and Company, Paterson, Simons and Company and the Borneo Company. This last also had a major role in Thailand, where it was one of the four British trading firms among the six most important European ones; one of the other two being the Danish East Asiatic Company.[1]

Thailand's timber industry was virtually entirely in foreign, chiefly British, hands, and, along with the Borneo Company, major firms that extracted and shipped teak were the Bombay-Burmah Trading Corporation and the Anglo-Siam Corporation.[2] The importance of European companies in importing goods in the teak industry did not extend to rice, where Chinese handled most exports.

In Indochina, the foremost merchant exporters were French or Chinese: 40 Chinese trading houses and, especially, 11 French concerns controlled more than 80 per cent of exports. The main French merchant houses, among which

[1] Mitchell, *Industrialization*, p. 171.

[2] Callis, *Foreign capital*, pp. 63–64.

those based in Bordeaux were notable, included Denis Brothers and Renard. Because of the role of Chinese in exporting rice and the reliance of trade on European finance, 'It was said in Cochinchina that "Cholon belongs to the Banque de l'Indochine through the intermediary of the Chinese".'[3]

The 'big four' Dutch firms of Handelsvereeniging Amsterdam, Maatschappij tot Voortzetting der Zaken van der Linde & Teves en Stokvis (Lindeteves-Stokvis), Handelmaatschappij Borneo-Sumatra (Borsumij) and Internationale Crediet & Handelsvereeniging Rotterdam (Internatio) were leaders in Indonesia. In the Philippines, the dominating merchant houses were American and British, such as Ker, and Warner, Barnes and Company. Several of the main British firms had nineteenth-century origins, as also did American houses, although two of the latter, leaders for much of the century, went bankrupt towards its end.[4]

Merchants in Burma were principally British, reflective of the country's status as a province of India, and generally operated elsewhere in that country, although usually not in other parts of Southeast Asia. Steel Brothers was probably the most important of the European merchants. As well as a major miller and exporter, it had interests throughout the Burmese economy and, along with the Bombay-Burmah Trading Corporation, Steel Brothers was a leading teak firm. Steel Brothers and three other principal European houses that milled and exported rice formed the Bullinger Pool in 1921 to function as a cartel and manipulate rice prices. The Pool's members purchased about a quarter to a third of rice, and to an unknown degree augmented this market share through financing various up-country millers. Although often referred to as 'notorious', the cartel's success in price manipulation and exercising control over railway freights to the detriment of up-country mills remains unclear.[5]

Rice and Peasant Crops

The collection of peasant crops necessitated dealing with numerous small growers, and in Southeast Asia this created an often-complex structure of intermediaries. Usually, these intermediaries were Chinese. Smallholder rubber, rice and tropical produce were collected and reached exporters, both European and Chinese, through networks that might include brokers, dealers, commission agents and up-country storekeepers. Brokers, although described as such at the time and subsequently, were generally more accurately termed dealers, because as well as bringing together buyer and seller they assumed ownership of the commodities. The storekeepers might function as some combination of dealers, sellers of imported goods and often financiers.

[3] Brocheux and Hemery, *Indochina*, p. 122.
[4] Larkin, *Sugar*, pp. 48–50, 71.
[5] Cheng, *Rice industry*, pp. 67, 91, 94; Andrus, *Burmese economic life*, p. 144.

In Singapore, the Asian commercial network was layered and hierarchical, one layer linked to and dependent on others both above and below it. Most commonly, the structure of trade was vertically complementary and horizontally competitive, although those in one layer always looked to usurp the functions of those above or below them in the commercial network. Asian dealers, typically financed by European merchants, collected the produce and, perhaps through sub-dealers or local storekeepers, also extended finance to producers. Of Singapore's Asian mercantile structure, even the five-volume Straits Settlements Trade Commission had to admit that: 'The reticulation of dealers and sub-dealers, commission agents and brokers … is too elaborate and various for concise description.'[6] 'The principal agent', it was observed, 'of this vital, valuable and complex organization is the Chinese dealer.'[7] The same complexity of mercantile interrelationships obtained in Indonesia, where an intricate structure distributed manufactured imports to Asian producers.

The marketing of rice in Burma, like Furnivall's 'industrial agriculture' description of its rice cultivation and harvesting, gave rise to especially complex specialization, at least partly because the size of the harvest and the export of so much of it encouraged a division of labour.[8] Most commonly for big rice mills (200 to 500 tons per day capacity), jungle (up-country) brokers obtained paddy from growers and sold this to local dealers or various speculators. Mill brokers, numbering 10 to 12 for big mills and genuine brokers, bought the paddy for their employers, the mill, but probably also traded some on their own account. Every stage of marketing depended on credit, which smaller dealers and brokers generally looked to Chettiars, a caste of Indians, to provide. Chettiars supplied about two-thirds of the working capital from their own reserves and drew on European banks for some of the rest.[9]

All paddy sent to Burma's four rice export ports, of which Rangoon was by far the largest, came by water transport unless this possibility did not exist. Paddy was carried mainly by thousands of small, sail or oar propelled, country boats (paddy gigs or *tonkin*), not Irrawaddy Flotilla Company vessels. In districts where water transport was infeasible, mills set up along the railway lines and from January to March heaps of 1,000 to 2,000 tons of paddy destined for Rangoon were a common sight along the lines.[10]

6 *SSTC*, I, p. 41.

7 *SSLCP 1932*, 'Report of the Customs Duties Committee', p. C158.

8 The description of rice marketing is based on Burma, *Report of the Burma Provincial Banking Enquiry Committee, 1929–30*, vol. 1, pp. 102–7; Grant, *Rice crop*, pp. 27–31; Cheng, *Rice industry*, pp. 48–64, 95.

9 Burma, *Report of the Burma Provincial Banking Enquiry Committee, 1929–30*, vol. 1, pp. 105, 213–17; Cheng, *Rice industry*, pp. 69, 95.

10 Grant, *Rice crop*, p. 27.

Much of the output of small mills (10 to 75 tons per day capacity), located up-country and in Burmese, Indian or Chinese ownership, was for local consumption. Mill owners were often also moneylenders, landowners and shopkeepers. These men might bargain for paddy themselves or rely on jungle brokers as the first link in a marketing chain.

The market was integrated: cultivators 'know the ruling local price and they know very quickly whenever the Rangoon price rises or falls; and there is generally enough competition amongst buyers to give them [cultivators] a fair deal even in somewhat remote places'.[11] In Rangoon, rice and finance for exports to Asia gave rise to a vibrant market.

> Moghul Street, Rangoon's Wall Street, and the centre of the Indian Rice Merchants' Association, presented a striking scene during business hours. Thousands of prosperous merchants and their clerks, principally Hindus, dressed in Gandhi caps and homespun, thronged the streets, conducting a great deal of their brokerage business in the open air.[12]

All Chettiar moneylenders were located along a short stretch of Mogul Street. Its money market was linked to the main cities in India as well as Colombo, Penang, Singapore and Saigon-Cholon, the chief destinations for Burma's rice exports.[13] Although Rangoon was a world market for rice, and by 1900 had a futures rice market, this was never so developed as Singapore's futures market for rubber, and traded in only one grade of rice.[14]

In Thailand, rice cultivators sold or – often having taken advances in the form of goods – bartered rice with local paddy dealers or sub-dealers. These were almost all Chinese. The paddy dealer and his family typically lived on a boat and used it or a cart to go to the villages of central Thailand to buy rice. The grain, as paddy, was taken by rail or, more usually, by boat to Bangkok, where mills concentrated.[15] Millers rarely sent their own buyers into the country, although the thousands of small up-country mills often did to buy directly from growers. As with the other two main rice-exporting countries, Europeans handled exports to non-Asian markets and Chinese millers the bulk of those to Asian destinations. Significantly for the ethnic make-up of business structure and so also for the Kingdom's 1930s and later development policies, Thai participated in the rice trade only as growers.[16]

[11] Burma, *Report of the Burma Provincial Banking Enquiry Committee, 1929–30*, vol. 1, p. 103.
[12] Christian, *Burma*, p. 72.
[13] Burma, *Report of the Burma Provincial Banking Enquiry Committee, 1929–30*, vol. 1, pp. 186, 194–95.
[14] Cheng, *Rice industry*, p. 74.
[15] Zimmerman, *Siam rural economic survey*, pp. 175–77; Andrews, *Siam, 2nd rural economic survey*, pp. 313–14.
[16] Ingram, *Economic change*, pp. 71–73.

Rice marketing in Cochinchina, except for export to Europe, concentrated in Chinese hands. Chinese bought most rice straight from the field.[17] For the whole of marketing 'Cholon's powerful Chinese middle class ... controlled the complex system of paddy collection and storage, the small river craft for transportation, Cholon's factories ... and pricing and sales'.[18]

Estate Rubber, Tin and Petroleum

Estate crops of rubber and sugar had a simpler marketing structure than peasant ones. European merchants could deal directly with estates and had no need for Asian intermediaries. Similarly, European tin miners and petroleum producers did not require Asian intermediaries. From tin mines in Malaya, ore could be delivered to smelters in the Straits ports; the international oil companies that dominated Indonesian production oversaw the processing and storage of their output ready for distribution to consumers.

Estate rubber was marketed through different departments of the same firm when, as for most Malayan estate rubber by the 1930s, European merchants were agency houses that managed the estate, handled the sale of its produce and secured estate supplies. Commissions were payable for each of the merchant's services. Since the most powerful houses were also shipping agents with a further commission for this service, a reason for Malaya's oligopolistic European mercantile structure is apparent.

Because of the development of standard grades of rubber, by the inter-war period Singapore physically handled little estate rubber. The city remained, however, the centre of Malaya's rubber trade, and by 1918 was firmly established as a world market for rubber. In the morning, overnight orders from London and New York were cabled to up-country Malaya from Singapore. Throughout the day, Singapore firms, including some 20 European dealers and seven brokers, were in constant touch with all of Malaya by telegraph and telephone. Although the Singapore auction handled minute quantities of rubber, it performed an important information function. Up-country people, explained a rubber dealer, watched the auction very closely. They 'know exactly what is paid in the auction and if anybody goes into that auction and puts up the price it affects almost the whole of Malaya at once'.[19]

In Southeast Asia, the Philippine sugar industry was unusual in the labour structure of estates and high proportion of indigenous estate owners. Sugar production depended on a broad base of transient labourers and tenant farmers, above whom were a smaller number of peasant proprietors and then, many fewer still, large landowners. After annexation of the Philippines, in an attempt

17 Brocheux and Hémery, *Indochina*, p. 309; Robequain, *Economic development*, p. 309.
18 Brocheux and Hémery, *Indochina*, p. 122.
19 *SSTC*, II, p. 354.

to prevent efficient sugar production in the Islands, United States sugar beet and cane interests supported a law limiting the amount of land that could be alienated. Because of this – although many latifundia from the Spanish era remained in family ownership and grew sugar – numerous Filipino peasant proprietors, with an average of two to five hectares, cultivated sugar, as did tenant farmers.[20] Tenants worked estate land, much of which was owned by an elite consisting of a small number of Filipino families and a further large share by American corporations. Luzon had about equal contingents of peasant proprietors and tenant farmers. In the Visayas, haciendas employing transient labourers (*sacadas*) predominated, but there were also many peasant proprietors.[21]

The marketing of peasant sugar output differed from peasant crops like rice and smallholder rubber in lacking the same network of intermediaries. Sugar cane requires processing near where it is grown, and that, together with economies of scale, dictated the delivery of cane, whether grown by peasants or on estates, to sugar centrals for milling. European merchants bought the milled product and its export, overwhelmingly to the United States, was chiefly through them.[22]

Estate ownership in the Philippines was unusual in Southeast Asia in its high indigenous participation, since prominent Filipino families retained ownership of sizeable tracts of land under American colonialism, despite a law to limit land holdings. Sugar centrals require large and certain supplies of cane, and the land owned by these families enabled them to meet the necessary supply requirements; either they could themselves finance the construction of centrals or borrow funds to build them. While this meant that, compared to Asians elsewhere in Southeast Asia, Filipinos obtained a greater share of profits from the export staple, these did not come primarily from exporting sugar. Export was still handled principally by European merchants. Family ownership of land and centrals did, however, create a 'supra class of millers'.[23] The large Filipino landowners and millers constituted a wealthy and powerful elite. Preferential access for sugar to the United States market at above world prices created a stream of rents for this elite, which could have promoted Philippine diversification and development by investing the profits and rents from sugar in manufacturing industry. It is unclear how much of the gains for trade were invested domestically, but, insofar as they were, investment was typically in sugar.

Financial Development

Self-sustaining, technologically based growth has always been accompanied by a process of financial transition which, as defined by Raymond Goldsmith,

[20] Friend, 'Philippine sugar industry', p. 181 and *Between two empires*, p. 8.
[21] Friend, 'Philippine sugar industry', p. 181; Larkin, *Sugar*, pp. 6, 90, 171–72.
[22] Larkin, *Sugar*, pp. 48–50, 53, 71.
[23] Larkin, *Sugar*, p. 170.

entails an increase in the financial superstructure to a status in the economy comparable to that in the leading countries of North America and Western Europe.[24] Development along this transitional path may, of course, differ, for example in the contributions of bank- or market-based financial systems. But all countries, Goldsmith observed, trace a similar transitional path in the increase in their superstructure of financial instruments and institutions relative to an infrastructure of output and wealth. Although, beginning in the later nineteenth century, Southeast Asian countries acquired several of the basic elements of a modern financial structure, including stable monetary systems and commercial banking structures, by 1940 the region had moved only a short way along the path to financial development.

This section argues that three main reasons largely account for the pattern of Southeast Asian financial development and explain why the region remained in the relatively early stages of financial transition. One is that abundant natural resources discouraged internal financial development. Highly export-dependent Southeast Asian economies, able to achieve substantial growth through venting primary commodities, confirmed European financial and mercantile institutions in a strong orientation towards the foreign trade sector, which principally required short-term self-liquidating finance. A second, related reason for limited financial transition is that financing methods depend crucially on the distribution and nature of capital formation. Throughout Southeast Asia, predominantly small rural production units, needing only small amounts of finance with consequent screening, monitoring and enforcement problems, restricted any role for formal or institutional finance.

The last of the three reasons accounting for limited Southeast Asian financial development is the laissez-faire stance of governments. They did, if for the most part only after 1900, fulfil a major function of the financial superstructure, in providing good systems of money. But adoption of the colonial or classic currency board system worked against the development of local Asian banking. These banks apart, virtually all modern financial institutions in Southeast Asia were owned and operated by metropolitan interests, often with headquarters in the ruling colonial power.

Gold-exchange Standard and Currency Boards

Until about 1875, the Mexican dollar, then ubiquitous in Asia, and silver-based coins afforded a unified money over the trading areas of Southeast and East Asia.[25] During the late nineteenth century, however, Southeast Asia's monetary systems became increasingly uncertain and piecemeal due to a progressive

[24] Goldsmith, *Financial development of India, Japan*, pp. 1–2 and *The financial development of Japan, 1868–1977*, p. 69n.

[25] King, *Money*, p. 10; Drake, 'Southeast Asian monies', pp. 90–96.

breakdown in the silver standard, and so also in the use of the Mexican dollar for domestic as well as international payments. The uncertainty forced Southeast Asian governments into some regulation of the monetary system. Twentieth-century monetary policies instituted the gold-exchange standard and currency boards, making Southeast Asia part of the prevailing international monetary system. Although operative in Indonesia by the later 1870s, the gold-exchange standard and currency boards did not begin in Burma until 1898, and only after the turn of the century in the Philippines, Malaya and Thailand. As Keynes observed in 1913, during 'the last ten years the gold-exchange standard has become the prevailing monetary system of Asia'.[26] Although until 1930 Indochina stayed on a silver – rather than moving to a gold – standard, in deference to large rice exports to China, also a silver country, legal requirements for a high foreign currency backing for its piastre made the Indochinese monetary system similar to the rest of Southeast Asia's.[27]

The gold-exchange standard linked the exchange rate of Southeast Asian countries to gold by fixing it to the metropolitan currency, and so could be described variously as the sterling-, dollar- or guilder-exchange standard.[28] Maintenance of the value of the Southeast Asian currency was assured by high foreign reserve backing (mostly or wholly in the metropolitan currency), which in British colonies (and Thailand) was 100 per cent, and often 110 per cent.[29] Similar backing obtained in Burma, where three Presidency banks in India (from 1921 to 1934 the Imperial Bank of India) acted like a currency board.[30] In Indonesia, the government gave a private bank, the Java Bank, the exclusive right to issue currency, subject to a high reserve backing. The Bank safeguarded exchange rate fixity with the Dutch guilder through discount policy but, like currency boards, could not control Indonesia's domestic monetary policy.[31]

Under the colonial board system, full adjustment of the quantity of local high-powered money to foreign reserves was automatic, since by law the local currency had to be fully backed by foreign reserves. Reserves, not government, effectively determined the quantity of local high-powered money, M0; a positive trade balance created the possibility of expanding the local monetary base,

[26] Keynes, *Collected writings: Indian currency*, p. 25.

[27] Nevin, *Capital*, p. 6; King, *Money*, p. 30; Keynes, *Collected writings: Indian currency*, p. 25; Schwartz, 'Currency boards', p. 167.

[28] Bloomfield, *Monetary policy*, p. 14.

[29] For a discussion of variations in currency board requirements, including reserve ratios and composition, in Indochina, Indonesia and the Philippines, see Schwartz, 'Currency boards', pp. 164–67; Robequain, *Economic development*, pp. 142–49; Prince, 'Monetary policy', pp. 59–68.

[30] Keynes, *Collected writings: Indian currency*, pp. 24–25; Bloomfield, *Monetary policy*, p. 14; Tun Wai, *Burma's currency*, pp. 88–90.

[31] van Laanen, 'Between the Java Bank', p. 252; Prince, 'Monetary policy'.

a negative trade balance automatically extinguished equivalent base money. The currency board's passivity in merely responding at the fixed exchange rate to changes in the demand for notes and coins made it similar to the 'classical' gold standard.[32] In fact, the colonial currency board system, as operated in Southeast Asia, effected a particularly rigid form of the gold standard: monetary reserves kept in the currency of the metropolitan country rather than gold gave less leeway than the classical gold standard for adjustment to disequilibria in the balance of payments.[33]

Currency boards had the advantage of credibility, through practically eliminating exchange rate risk and guaranteeing stability of Southeast Asian currencies relative to that of the colonial power. Stability was important for foreign investors and European banks in repatriating capital and/or profits, and probably also maximized capital inflows. For colonial authorities, constantly anxious that colonies should pay for themselves, a currency board represented an essentially costless and administratively easy way to provide local currency.

A further attraction of the currency board system for Southeast Asia's governments, which tended to favour laissez-faire, was that it minimized the state's regulatory role. Legal stipulation that the currency board could not create credit precluded it from acting as a lender of last resort; nor did the currency board regulate the banking system.

Heavily backed by foreign reserves and identical to metropolitan currency apart from the printing on the notes, the new Southeast Asian currencies gained an almost instant credibility, as for example in Malaya and the Philippines, and this encouraged the rapid spread of unified systems of money. Almost as soon as the government in Malaya began to issue paper money, the Treasurer reported that 'The public confidence, including that of all classes of natives, in the Government paper is so great, that it will certainly, hereafter, represent the bulk of our local Currency.'[34] In the Philippines, within 20 months of its introduction in late 1903, the new gold-based currency successfully replaced the variety of monies circulating in the Islands.[35]

Under a currency board system like those in Southeast Asia, foreign reserves and so base money supply could change in three possible ways.[36] One of these – government deficits or surpluses – was unimportant, since colonial authorities typically favoured closely balanced budgets, even in the 1930s depression. A second – net foreign capital movements – had a role

[32] Hanke and Schuler, *Currency boards*, p. 41.

[33] Bloomfield, *Monetary policy*, p. 14; Friedman and Schwartz, *Monetary history*, p. 359.

[34] 'Currency note issue', *Straits Settlements annual report 1903*, p. 19.

[35] Philippines, *Annual report of the Chief of the Division of Currency, 1903–04*, pp. 11–19; Philippines, *Third annual report of the Secretary of Finance and Justice*, pp. 22–24.

[36] Walters, 'Currency boards', p. 111.

in secular money supply growth at times of heavy investment in plantation agriculture or mining, and probably helped to overcome a currency board's 'start-up' problem of securing sufficient hard currency reserves to establish a realistic monetary base. But at times of low commodity prices, foreign investment acted, if anything, pro-cyclically. All European banks were branches, and in downturns could have drawn on their metropolitan head offices to import capital and counter the severe liquidity squeeze required under a currency board. Banks do not, however, appear to have done so; a senior Bank of England official observed in the 1950s that it was 'unlikely that overseas banks in Malaya could run a head office overdraft to dodge a squeeze'.[37] Nor, as discussed below, did most European banks venture much beyond the traditional 'exchange bank' functions of financing foreign trade and associated foreign currency dealings. As a result, demand deposits (chequing accounts) were relatively unimportant and money supply in Southeast Asian countries remained predominantly base money, M0.[38] The third possibility – changes in the current account in the balance of payments – was, especially by the interwar years, the principal factor influencing the base money supply.[39] It, in turn, largely reflected price fluctuations in Southeast Asia's main export commodities, and so cycles of boom and bust.

European Banks

In later nineteenth-century Southeast Asia, formal finance consisted chiefly of branches of European banks, characteristically with head offices in metropolitan countries. These banks, of which the most important were British, almost entirely restricted themselves to financing the region's trade with Western countries and, due to this orientation and associated currency dealings, became known as 'exchange banks'. Three main British banks – the Hongkong and Shanghai Banking Corporation (an exception to European banking patterns in having its head office in Hong Kong), the Chartered Bank of India, Australia and China and the Mercantile Bank of India – operated throughout Southeast Asia. Even in non-British colonies these banks financed much of trade, which gave them a degree of monopoly power, and exchange banking in the region an oligopolistic structure. As late as 1917 in the Philippines,

37 Bank of England Archive OV65/10, Notes on 'The Report on a central bank(s) for Malaya', 17 April 1956. The official was G. M. Watson and his report was being summarized by E. B. Bennett of the Overseas and Foreign Office.

38 Bank of England Archive OV65/10, Notes on the Hongkong and Shanghai Banking Corporation by G. M. Watson, 8 February 1956.

39 Hazelwood, 'Economics', pp. 299–301; Short, 'Indigenous banking', pp. 65–69; International Bank for Reconstruction and Development, *Economic development*, pp. 473–74.

'American banking capital has never taken any deep root ... the great English-oriented institutions – the Hongkong & Shanghai, and the Chartered Bank of India, Australia and China – have long exerted a dominating influence in the local banking field'.[40] This situation persisted into the inter-war period, when, although more non-British banking competition had emerged, Hongkong and Shanghai Bank records show that in Southeast Asian countries the bank normally financed between about a fifth to a third or more of imports and exports.[41] Other major exchange banks – the Banque de l'Indochine, the Java Bank, the Netherlands Trading Society and the National City Bank of New York – although usually operating in more than one Southeast Asian country, tended to be less international than their British counterparts in spreading throughout the region.[42]

In the decades before World War II, European, and especially British, banking ventured little beyond its nineteenth-century exchange bank origins. Four considerations discouraged change: an oligopolistic banking structure; more or less assured business growth in step with export expansion; restricted lending opportunities due to a lack of industrialization and difficulty in judging risk associated with loans to Asians, which discouraged lending to them.

A member of the Radcliffe Committee, the economist A. K. Cairncross, was 'a little puzzled that such a high proportion of your funds appeared to be employed in London when you simultaneously had opportunities for very advantageous use of the money in the East?' In response, the London manager of the Hong Kong and Shanghai Bank explained that 'A good deal of the business done by indigenous banks would not be handled by us at any rate of interest [because of] the nature of the business and the impossibility of controlling many orientals.'[43] Although faced with weak Southeast Asian capital markets, local Asians, probably mainly for fear of a dilution of control over business ventures, seldom clubbed together to finance manufacturing. Instead, Asians had to turn to their own banks, as discussed in the next sub-section, or to informal arrangements.

Mobilization of finance by European banks was limited. As an internal Bank of England report observed of Malaya in 1956, 'British banks do not tap the general public to any great extent'.[44] Apart from risk, a mobilization function

40 Willis, 'Philippine', p. 410.

41 HSBC Group Archive, LII, 121 and 122. Inspector's reports for 1924 on Rangoon, Bangkok, Singapore, Batavia and Saigon.

42 A notable exception was Lloyds Bank, which, as a big financier of English firms through its London office and a substantial lender to Chettiars, had a prominence in Burma not matched elsewhere. Tun Wai, *Burma's currency*, p. 26.

43 United Kingdom, *Report of the Committee on the Working of the Monetary System*, minutes of evidence, p. 327, paragraphs 4637–38.

44 Bank of England, OV65/10, Notes on the Hongkong and Shanghai Banking Corporation by G. M. Watson, 8 February 1956.

was also curtailed, at least in British colonies, by European business practice.[45] In evidence to the Radcliffe Commission, representatives of the Eastern sector of the British Overseas Banks Association described the behaviour of 'the sort of British company who owns estates and tea gardens and so on. The moment they earn surplus funds the tendency is to bring the funds back to this country [Britain]. They do not invest them locally.'[46]

A preference for financing foreign trade, notable especially among the British banks, and the tendency of European plantation and mining interests to remit funds and not invest locally, left Southeast Asia a surplus area for bank funds: local deposits exceeded bank loans.[47] The consequent repatriation of funds from Southeast Asia is generally regarded as sizeable; until the 1950s, European banks 'presided over a substantial transfer of funds from the colonies to the London capital market'.[48] Throughout Southeast Asia, as in Malaya, and also, for example, in Indonesia, the tendency was to transmit a high proportion of operating surpluses abroad.[49]

Official recognition in the Philippines of the dominance of British banks which, together with one American bank, 'employed only a very limited amount of their capital in the development of the natural resources of the Philippines, but chose to confine themselves chiefly to financing the export and import trade through exchange transactions', led to the establishment of the Philippine National Bank in 1916.[50] The Bank, a commercial, government-controlled institution, aimed to lend long-term to local agriculture and industry. To do so, the Bank temporarily departed from the currency board requirement of 100 per cent backing for the Philippine peso, and instead used an increasing proportion of reserves to make loans to sugar plantations in the Philippines. Problems soon arose when post-World War I macroeconomic instability and loan defaults

45 On the banks' concentration on foreign trade, see, for example, Straits Settlements, *Reports of the commissions, 1921*, appx. 1, pp. 169–70, 174–77; *SSTC*, III, pp. 415–17, 423, IV, p. 414; Burma, *Report of the Burma Provincial Banking Enquiry Committee, 1929–30*, vol. 1, pp. 36, 42; Murray, *Development*, pp. 115, 132–33.

46 United Kingdom, *Report of the Committee on the Working of the Monetary System*, minutes of evidence, p. 331, paragraph 4751.

47 Nevin, *Capital*, pp. 47–51.

48 Drake, 'Vent for surplus', p. 101. In 1956 European banks in Singapore and the Federation of Malaya held over 40 per cent of their assets as 'overseas assets', very largely in London and denominated in sterling. Watson and Caine, *Report*, pp. 18–19. In evidence to the Radcliffe Committee, the general manager of the Chartered Bank and the London manager of the Hong Kong and Shanghai Bank stated that at least 90 per cent of their London resources came from overseas, the majority of these from Malaya. United Kingdom, *Report of the Committee on the Working of the Monetary System*, minutes of evidence, pp. 326–27, 329.

49 van Laanen, 'Between Java Bank', p. 250; Golay, 'Southeast Asia', p. 373; Lindblad, 'Foreign investment', pp. 195–96 and *Foreign investment*, pp. 82–83.

50 Luthringer, *Gold-exchange*, p. 87, and see pp. 86, 88, 117–21; Willis, 'Philippine', pp. 410–12; Kemmerer, 'Agricultural', pp. 263–64.

led to the depreciation of the peso from 1919 through 1921. By 1922, however, its value vis-à-vis the US dollar had been restored. The next year the government borrowed to fully back the currency and, under American pressure, the Philippines returned to a gold-exchange-based currency board system.[51]

Up to 1939, the international or European banking system remained the largest source of institutional finance in Southeast Asia; local stock exchanges were either insignificant or dated only from the 1950s. Pre-World War II stock exchanges included the Manila Stock Exchange, which had a small volume of transactions before World War II, almost all in mining shares, and the Rangoon Stock Exchange.[52] Owing to the 'small volume of transactions' the latter was 'of little importance'.[53] In other cities, for example Singapore, certain firms handled shares in local companies, but this did not amount to an organized market.[54]

Agency houses were a principal conduit for foreign investment, and linked Southeast Asia to the London capital market, not just for Malayan and Indonesian rubber plantations, but also for the Burmese teak industry. They floated shares on the London market on the strength of their reputation and then, partly as a guarantee to investors, generally assumed a management role in, and became agents for, the new enterprise, hence the description 'managing agency house'. Southeast Asia's agency houses could also have furnished industrial finance. The obvious model was India. There, agency houses, effectively substitutes for non-existent investment banks, were 'of crucial importance' in developing the modern, industrial sector of the economy, including cotton and jute mills.[55] But in Southeast Asia, European business apparently judged as unprofitable investment outlets outside the traditional ones of trade, shipping, banking and property. Singapore's largest agency house, Guthries, 'time and again toyed with the idea of undertaking local manufacturing activities, especially rubber goods, but did not act'. Ultimately, Guthries gave primacy to a need for liquidity and, insofar as it invested in Malaya rather than London, chose to acquire local land and godowns (warehouses) as the best collateral available should it become necessary to borrow in Malaya.[56]

51 Schwartz, 'Currency boards', pp. 164–66; Claudio, *Profligate colonial*; Larkin, *Sugar*, pp. 57, 98, 156–57.

52 United Nations, *Mobilization*, p. 192.

53 Burma, *Report of the Burma Provincial Banking Enquiry Committee, 1929–30*, vol. 1, p. 287.

54 HSBC Group Archive, LII, 121. Inspector's Report, Singapore; *SSTC*, I, p. 227.

55 Goldsmith, *Financial development of India*, p. 18 and see pp. 53–56.

56 Drabble and Drake, 'British', pp. 310, 311. The decision-making process of Guthries may be traced in the firm's letter books for 1916–20 in Guthrie Corporation Archives. See in particular: G/COR/3 F. J. D. Jenkins to Guthrie, London, 29 November 1918; G/COR/4 letter S/857 Guthrie, Singapore to Guthrie, London, 15 November 1919; G/COR/4 letter T/334 Guthrie, Singapore to Guthrie, London, 24 March 1920; G/COR/5 Guthrie, Singapore to Guthrie, London, letter U/035 on glass manufacture, September 1920.

In Southeast Asia, financial institutions that did develop to facilitate long-term investment in primary production, such as the agency houses and agricultural banks in Indonesia, remained heavily oriented towards European enterprise. Thus, Asian entrepreneurs, principally Chinese, had, with few exceptions, to look elsewhere than European banks to finance plantation agriculture or industry. In Malaya, Chinese who developed estates relied on 'very limited amounts' of finance from European banks against security like house mortgages; credit came chiefly from storekeepers and Chettiar moneylenders.[57]

Chinese Banks

After 1900, the emergence of local Asian banks in major urban areas, including Singapore, Penang, Rangoon, Bangkok, Saigon and Manila, provided a domestic alternative to Southeast Asia's otherwise heavy reliance on European institutions. European banks lent, typically through compradors when dealing with Chinese, to a comparatively small number of important Asians.[58] Chinese banks were generally formed along dialect lines (e.g. Hokkien or Teochew) and by leading merchants. The success of these men helped to inspire the public confidence necessary to persuade a wider public to entrust deposits to Chinese banks. Both depositors and lenders tended to be concentrated among members of the same dialect group. Even so, Asian banks tapped a new, much wider market than their European counterparts. In Singapore, for example, Asian banks encouraged the 'banking habit' and mobilized additional finance, since even in the inter-war period 'the European banks had an air about them which intimidated many local people … [and] would not accept small accounts'.[59] Likewise, the importance of two Chinese banks, the China Banking Corporation and the Mercantile Bank of China, established in Manila in the 1920s, was that 'not many Chinese could avail themselves of the services of [European] commercial banks in the Philippines'.[60]

One of Thailand's first indigenous banks, originally in 1904 the Book Club and from 1907 the Siam Commercial Bank, was started by a brother of the King of Thailand to foster economic development. During the first decade of the twentieth century, three Chinese banks opened in Bangkok: Yü Sheng, Yüan Fa Li and, with the strong backing of rice millers, the Chino-Siamese Bank. The successful operation in Singapore of solely Chinese banks on Western lines encouraged their establishment in Thailand and probably elsewhere.

[57] Rowe, *Studies*, pp. 17–18.

[58] See, for example, HSBC Group Archive, LII, 121, Inspectors Report Singapore 1924, pp. 7, 9, 12, 17, 19–20, 26, 31, 33 and in LII, 120 Inspectors Report Batavia 1924, pp. 20–21; Inspectors Report Bangkok 1924, p. 6; Inspectors Report Saigon 1924, pp. 12–14.

[59] Yap, *Scholar*, p. 36, and see pp. 28 and 37–38.

[60] Wong, *Chinese*, p. 131.

Another Chinese bank in Thailand, the Wang Lee Chan Bank, was incorporated in 1933.[61] Indochina had three Chinese banks and a small Vietnamese bank, the Société Annamite de Crédit.[62] Burma had no indigenous (Burmese) banks.[63]

Asian banks showed a greater willingness than European banks to lend more widely to Asian communities and to local Asian entrepreneurs and industrialists, often among them the directors of the banks. Lending was, however, restricted by the comparative smallness of Asian banks and the institutional environment. The currency board system and an absence of good Asian bank connections to the international capital market practically guaranteed that these banks would remain small. Any export slump led to a liquidity crisis which left the Asian banking sector highly vulnerable to insolvency: because the region had no central banks (the antithesis of a currency board system) to serve as lender of last resort, because Asian banks lacked access to an external wholesale credit market and because depositors were quick to withdraw funds. By contrast, the head offices of European banks in Europe or New York could, if necessary, act as a central bank. For Asian banks, uncertainty over the timing and extent of monetary contractions, with a consequent cash drain but no recourse to a central bank, seriously curtailed the scope for lending. Asian banks normally kept at least 50 per cent of current account deposits liquid by depositing them with European banks, which partially but imperfectly substituted for a central bank.[64]

In the 1930s depression, the observation was amply borne out that 'balance of payments problems take the same form as bank liquidity crises'. Because 100 per cent backing in the metropolitan currency was mandatory for legal tender, balance-of-payments difficulties caused an automatic fall in the money supply to pay for an excess of imports compared to exports. Banks' reserves, also denominated in the currency of the metropolitan country, contracted as firms drew on them to pay for imports and cover losses, threatening the banks with a liquidity crisis and endangering their viability. In 1932, Singapore's three main Chinese (Hokkien) banks were forced into a merger, forming the Oversea-Chinese Banking Corporation, while in Manila the local Chinese-owned Mercantile Bank of China failed entirely in 1931.[65]

61 Skinner, *Chinese society*, pp. 108–9; Emery, *Financial institutions*, pp. 567–68; Siam Commercial Bank, *1904–1932 laying the foundations of Thai banking*; Lowy, *Century of growth*.

62 On Chinese banks in Indochina, see Brocheux and Hémery, *Indochina*, p. 141.

63 Burma, *Report of the Burma Provincial Banking Enquiry Committee, 1929–30*, vol. 1, p. 36, 186.

64 *SSTC*, III, p. 416; Grove and Exter, 'Philippine Central Bank Act', p. 939; Bank of England Archives, OV65/10 Memorandum on the Oversea Chinese Banking Corporation.

65 King, *Money*, p. 94, and see Hazelwood, 'Colonial', p. 299; Wong, *Chinese*, pp. 142–48.

Financial Development Measures

By 1913, monetization in Southeast Asia had already progressed much of the way towards meeting the requirements of external trade. While, Thailand apart, the ratio of base money, M0/Trade, was still appreciably less than in Japan (the prototype of a rapidly developing financial system), over the next 25 years the ratio rose and in some countries reached, by 1938, approximately the level in Japan (Table 3.1). Increases in the ratio in Southeast Asia almost certainly reflected not so much the monetization required for external trade as a continuing process of internal monetization due to a rising need for money to buy food and consumer goods, created by greater export specialization. Between 1913 and 1938, M0 measured in 1913 US$ rose rapidly throughout Southeast Asia, and on average M0 per capita approximately doubled (Table 3.2). After 1913, per capita growth in M0 was slowest in Burma because there, by World War I, export specialization, and with it accompanying internal monetization, was largely complete. High M0 per capita in Malaya reflected its residents' exceptionally high degree of economic specialization.

Comparison of the M0/Trade ratios for 1913 and 1938 shows Malaya as an outlier (Table 3.1). Low ratios there were chiefly because of the Straits Settlements' (especially Singapore's) large entrepôt trade with Indonesia, principally in rubber, and this trade's large barter element. Similarly, between 1933 and 1938, M0/Trade rose less in Indonesia than elsewhere because of barter via Straits ports for rice and simple manufactures.

In Table 3.1, ratios of M0/GDP – an alternative to M0/Trade in measuring money's use as a medium of exchange and therefore monetization – fail to show the clear patterns evident for M0/Trade. To some extent, this may reflect margins of error in benchmark GDP estimates used. A notable feature of the M0/GDP panel in Table 3.1 is the unusually high ratio for Burma, in 1938 substantially in excess of both the United States and Japan. This arose from the practice in Burma, well developed by the inter-war years, of buying all principal crops with notes:

> Dealers going out to buy paddy from cultivators at harvesttime commonly take one-half of their money in notes of ten rupees, the balance in notes of a hundred ... from December 1923 to March 1924 nearly 5½ crores of additional money [some 7 per cent of Burma's annual GDP at the time] were issued by the Currency Department in Burma in response to the annual demand for additional currency to finance the paddy trade.[66]

The striking difference between money supply in Southeast Asia compared to Japan and the United States – the last taken as the prototype of a developed financial system – was in their contrasting financial depth (Table 3.2). Since M1

[66] Burma, *Report of the Burma Provincial Banking Enquiry Committee, 1929–30*, vol. 1, p. 47.

Table 3.1 *Southeast Asia, Japan and the United States ratios of monetary aggregates to trade and GDP, 1913–38*

(a) Ratios of monetary aggregates to trade

	1913		1929		1938		
	M0/ Trade	M1/ Trade	M0/ Trade	M1/ Trade	M0/ Trade	M1/ Trade	M2/ Trade
Burma	0.21	–	0.31	–	0.26	0.35	0.41
Indochina	0.21	–	0.42	–	0.36	–	–
Thailand	0.54	–	0.43	–	0.58	0.75	0.80
Malaya	0.05	–	0.06	–	0.08	0.16	0.20
Indonesia	0.24	0.30	0.22	0.30	0.26	0.41	–
Philippines	0.25	0.30	0.20	0.30	0.41	0.56	0.73
Japan	0.42	1.08	0.40	1.31	0.43	1.37	–
United States	0.44	2.73	0.40	2.76	1.10	6.00	8.97

(b) Ratios of monetary aggregates to GDP

	1913		1929		1938		
	M0/ GDP	M1/ GDP	M0/ GDP	M1/ GDP	M0/ GDP	M1/ GDP	M2/ GDP
Burma	–	–	–	–	0.179	0.241	0.286
Indochina	–	–	–	–	–	–	–
Thailand	0.076	–	0.110	–	0.052	0.067	0.072
Malaya	0.057	–	0.046	–	0.089	0.180	0.226
Indonesia	0.077	0.094	0.089	0.120	0.076	0.119	–
Philippines	–	–	–	–	0.044	0.060	0.078
Japan	0.127	0.220	0.130	0.433	0.123	0.395	1.070
United States	0.048	0.292	0.037	0.256	0.065	0.355	0.530

Source: Huff, 'Monetization', p. 323.

differs from M0 essentially in the inclusion of cheque account money created by the banking system as a result of deposits, the small differences in Southeast Asia between M1 and M0 indicate the restricted role of banks as local deposit takers. In 1938, Southeast Asian ratios of demand deposits (D) to M0 were on the order of 0.3 to at most 1.0 compared to about 2.2 in Japan and 4.5 in the United States. Southeast Asian data for M2, which adds to M1 by including time or savings deposits, are not available until the 1930s. But even then, the region's banking system, taken as a whole, still had at most a limited role in mobilizing

Table 3.2 *Southeast Asia, Japan and the United States measures of money supply, 1913–38 (1913 US$)*

(a) Monetary aggregates ($m)

	1913		1929		1938		
	M0	M1	M0	M1	M0	M1	M2
Burma	–	–	–	–	105	141	167
Indochina	24	–	79	–	77	–	–
Thailand	41	–	67	–	91	117	125
Malaya	25	–	53	–	95	192	241
Indonesia	111	136	210	282	258	402	–
Philippines	25	33	57	84	160	217	282
Japan	314	804	567	1,882	516	1,656	–
United States	1,887	11,570	2,298	15,716	3,765	20,608	30,813

(b) Ratio of commercial bank demand deposits to M0 (D/M0) and M0 per capita ($)

	1913		1929		1938	
	D/M0	M0 per capita	D/M0	M0 per capita	D/M0	M0 per capita
Burma	–	–	–	–	0.34	6.23
Indochina	–	1.45	–	3.73	–	3.22
Thailand	–	4.72	–	5.84	0.29	6.05
Malaya	–	9.19	–	12.16	1.02	18.89
Indonesia	0.22	2.24	0.34	3.52	0.56	3.79
Philippines	0.30	2.75	0.49	4.42	0.36	10.10
Japan	1.56	6.08	2.32	8.96	2.21	7.17
United States	5.13	19.33	5.84	18.80	4.47	28.86

Source: Huff, 'Monetization', p. 324.

and allocating more (and probably also longer-term) capital to entrepreneurs, and finance remained shallow. In the United States, M2/GDP was some eight times M0/GDP but in Southeast Asia the difference was at most about double.

Informal Finance

Neither a rural banking network nor cooperative societies developed to any very meaningful extent in Southeast Asia. European and local Asian banks remained concentrated in the main port cities. That left informal finance to provide, from the late nineteenth century onwards, a large share of rural financial accommodation. Interlinked deals, encompassing 'barter', the extension of credit, an element of insurance and an ongoing trading relationship, were central to much of informal finance.

During the late nineteenth century, outside the enclaves of European bank and merchant house business – that is, through most of Southeast Asian commerce – interlinked deals predominated and reflected shortages of money and lack of a unified monetary standard. In pioneer economies, like late nineteenth-century Southeast Asia's, where peasants produced almost all exports, interlinked deals were an effective, and probably the only feasible, way to finance export expansion. At every level of the region's Asian marketing chains, with their perhaps three or more intermediaries, interlinked deals contained a large element of barter, and were interlinked in that the provision of manufactured goods, credit and marketing of primary commodities all formed part of a single transaction. Asian – often Chinese – dealers and storekeepers advanced rice and simple manufactures against future deliveries of commodities in this system of barter, furnishing the necessary credit as well as inducement goods to greater export production, and largely obviating a need for money in rural areas. Dealers and storekeepers generally lived near, and typically had close personal knowledge of, those with whom they traded. When advancing goods, these intermediaries frequently sought to minimize transaction costs by obtaining a 'lien' on the green crop to serve as a collateral substitute. The knowledge of dealers, liens and profits on both sides of a trade kept transaction costs low and minimized their importance.[67]

After 1900, the main change in rural finance was that, as good systems of money reduced the need for barter, agricultural production came to be financed chiefly through interlinked credit-marketing arrangements. Barter remained predominant only at the level of trade between storekeepers and growers.[68] The exception was Burma, where the Chettiars, who specialized in moneylending, dealt directly with cultivators. Chettiars extended about two-thirds of all finance for agriculture and used notes to buy paddy.[69]

Low transaction costs aside, two additional features of the credit-marketing interlinkage allowed it to substitute for formal financial and insurance markets, so long as new land remained sufficiently abundant and could be exploited by

[67] Huff, 'Barter, money', pp. 170–74; Tun Wai, *Burma's currency*, pp. 84–88; Brocheux, *Mekong Delta*, pp. 48–49, 66–72, 88.

[68] Inter-linked deals are described in Andrews, *Siam, 2nd rural economic survey*, pp. 305–09, 314–15, 332–33; Owen, *Prosperity*, pp. 89–93; van Laanen, 'Between the Java Bank', pp. 257–58; Huff, *Economic growth*, pp. 92–98, 202; Murray, *Development*, pp. 453–55.

[69] Burma, *Report of the Burma Provincial Banking Enquiry Committee, 1929–30*, vol. 1, pp. 47–53, 67.

a broad base of small cultivators. One feature was that, as in the late nineteenth century, interlinked deals continued effectively to meet the wage fund need. It was still the main requirement for a large share of export crop expansion, and was met by credit given to cultivators through networks of Asian dealers and storekeepers. Profits created throughout the credit-marketing chain made increasing amounts of finance available, and for both dealers and storekeepers who gave credit, its continued further extension avoided the danger that outstanding debts would be paid and so end business relationships. These were cemented by a 'tie in' of ongoing credit. Burma was again an exception to this pattern. Chettiars there dealt on a formal, legal basis with their clients, and lacked this 'tying' incentive or the additional one of storekeepers: that more credit simultaneously increased total profits due to the greater supply of provisions and manufactured goods. However, Chettiars tended to roll over loans so long as interest repayments were not too irregular and borrowers offered good security, especially developed land.[70]

The other feature that facilitated the substitution of credit-marketing interlinkages for formal finance was a partial replacement of formal market mechanisms to deal with risk. Credit functioned as an insurance substitute and means of consumption smoothing, since a considerable scope for deferred payment or 'time elasticity' associated with interlinked deals meant that intermediaries would generally allow more or longer-term finance at times of unfavourable prices, poor harvests or a grower's individual difficulties. In Thailand, for example, a farmer with an established relationship with a paddy buyer 'often borrows rice for food from [him] when prices are high and pays it back [in rice] without interest after harvest when prices are lower'.[71] More important, as in the Philippines for abaca, 'It seems to have been understood that if any disaster befell the cultivator or the crop, or if the market fell, the loan would simply not be repaid until times were better ... Moreover, the giver of the original advance was often obliged to provide a supplementary advance at such times if he ever hoped to have any of the debt repaid.'[72] The effect was to ease borrowing constraints, even at times of substantial income declines. Nor was it to the advantage of debtors ultimately to default since, in Southeast Asia's closely knit business communities, future borrowing opportunities would at the least be seriously prejudiced. Probably for this reason, Singapore traders, who financed much of production in the Indonesian Outer Islands as well as Malaya, did not find default a problem, although forced to extend credit for lengthy periods in a depression.

[70] Burma, *Report of the Burma Provincial Banking Enquiry Committee, 1929–30*, vol. 1, pp. 64–65, 68, 73, 78, 83–84, 88–89, 200.

[71] Andrews, *Siam, 2nd rural economic survey*, p. 333, and see Zimmerman, *Siam rural economic survey*, p. 200.

[72] Owen, *Prosperity*, p. 92.

While interlinked credit was probably the single most important way in which cultivators gained protection against idiosyncratic and aggregate shocks, consumption smoothing was also achieved through a variety of other methods. These included, as ways to save, crop storage and the accumulation of consumer durables, land or gold and possibly work animals. Such arrangements promoted the economic specialization essential to growth, but saving in tangible assets worked against a departure from pre-modern finance.

Within the range of available pre-World War II saving options, saving in the form of crops tended to be expensive and difficult, due to poor storage facilities.[73] Work animals must be fed, are subject to disease and may also represent a large undiversified investment. In Burma, for example, a single bullock cost about US$30, which was a considerable expense for a cultivator with 15 acres – roughly the area normally worked by a yoke of animals.[74] Among the more affluent, the purchase of additional land or the rebuilding of houses – recognized assets against which to borrow in the future – were frequent outlets for windfall gains from high commodity prices. But further down the income ladder, transitory income, as in Malaya at times of high rubber prices, was increasingly likely to find its way into consumer durables or jewellery which could be pawned in a downturn.[75]

As a way to smooth consumption, the advantage of saving in jewellery, especially with some gold content, was a maintenance of value on international markets, and so the option of having good collateral for future loans, whether from individual lenders, Chettiars or pawnshops. With growing export specialization, recourse to pawnshops, usually run by Chinese, was increasingly important in allowing Southeast Asians without large assets to even out consumption. In Indonesia, where the pawnshops were state controlled, the value of goods pawned rose to US$1.8 million after poor harvests in 1926 but fell to US$109,000 by 1928. Between 1931 and 1935, the auction of unredeemed pledges led to the export of gold jewellery equivalent to over 7 per cent of merchandise imports.[76]

73 For example, see Brocheux, *Mekong Delta*, p. 68; Burma, *Report of the Burma Provincial Banking Enquiry Committee, 1929–30*, vol. 1, pp. 112–13.

74 Burma, *Report of the Burma Provincial Banking Enquiry Committee, 1929–30*, vol. 1, pp. 25, 56, 80, 137.

75 On these preferences, see Fruin, 'Popular', pp. 161, 169; Burma, *Report of the Burma Provincial Banking Enquiry Committee, 1929–30*, vol. 1, pp. 69, 82, 132, 233, 266–69; Landon, *Siam*, p. 66; Brocheux, *Mekong Delta*, p. 72. Swift, 'Accumulation', p. 328 and Gamba, 'Poverty', pp. 37–38 describe the practice among Malayan smallholders of buying consumer goods convertible into cash at a pawnshop.

76 Fruin, 'Popular', p. 169; Burma, *Report of the Burma Provincial Banking Enquiry Committee, 1929–30*, vol. 1, p. 263. The Bank of England noted the same practice of hoarding gold in the form of jewellery but estimated exports at about half of Fruin's figure. Bank of England Archives, OV85/12, 'Dutch East Indies. Currency and foreign exchange', 18 October 1938.

The effectiveness of market-based informal arrangements in meeting the needs of small cultivators further dissuaded institutions, already wary because of asymmetric information and high transaction costs, from venturing into rural areas. Dawson's Bank in Burma, with its head office in Pyapon and eventually 11 branches, was the principal instance of European banking in rural Southeast Asia. The bank was unique in Southeast Asia as a European-owned agricultural bank, and one which, rather than financing trade, lent long-term to Burmese rice growers against the security of land.[77] Although the bank countered information and enforcement problems by having branches near cultivators and employees with a personal knowledge of borrowers, it was nevertheless forced into major re-structuring in 1931–32.[78]

Cooperatives, begun by all governments, although with varying enthusiasm, did not meet with much success, partly because the frontier character and large population movements in vent-for-surplus areas discouraged effective community organization. In Thailand's rice export areas, for example, many families made several moves in a lifetime; peasants 'who felt overwhelmed by debt dues and tax arrears disappeared in the middle of the night and sought out new land'.[79] An exception was Java, where more settled communities and economies of scale associated with high population density created characteristics consistent with an ethos of cooperation and with institutional finance for borrowers needing only small sums of money. The Dutch built on these advantages, with considerable efforts to establish credit facilities through networks of regulated pawnshops and village banks.[80] But in 1939 in Southeast Asia as a whole, including Indonesia's Outer Islands, Asian cultivators continued to rely almost entirely on informal finance from such sources as village storekeepers, moneylenders and rotating saving and credit associations.

Conclusion

In Southeast Asian production, especially peasant production, trade and finance were so intertwined that they have been considered in the same chapter. There is not strong evidence that a lack of finance hindered primary commodity production. When finance was needed, the market supplied it, often through informal financial sector adaptations. It may have been, however, that if institutional credit had been more available to peasants or if they could have cooperated more effectively to form credit cooperatives, some of

77 Burma, *Report of the Burma Provincial Banking Enquiry Committee, 1929–30*, vol. 1, pp. 44–45; Tun Wai, *Burma's currency*, pp. 71–75.

78 Tun Wai, *Burma's currency*, pp. 74–75.

79 Phongpaichit and Baker, *Thailand: economy and politics*, pp. 21, 32.

80 van der Eng, *Agricultural growth*, pp. 131–33.

the unfavourable outcomes, especially in Burma, of capitalist agricultural expansion, with widespread land loss and chronic indebtedness, could have been avoided.

A test for financial transition is the extent to which elements of dualism are continuously eliminated as countries develop a unified modern financial system that expands at the expense of informal finance. That was only partially accomplished in pre-war Southeast Asia, leaving the region well short of financial transition. Although there was progressive monetization throughout the region and indigenous banks emerged, economies in every country continued to rely heavily on informal finance. Several factors combined to restrict financial development and perpetuate financial dualism. These included a continued ability to tap natural resources, the laissez-faire stance of governments in financial matters as exemplified by the currency board system and the uncertainty that it, and Southeast Asia's boom-and-bust economies, created for local Asian banks.

Southeast Asia's informal financial sector proved flexible and inventive. These attributes were important in promoting rapid Southeast Asian economic growth through furnishing credit, improvising arrangements to counter idiosyncratic shocks and providing insurance. Access to insurance substitutes and ways to smooth consumption help to explain the workings of the vent-for-surplus model and also to answer the question of why some peasants, even if risk-averse, proved willing to respond to new economic opportunities and to 'devote the whole of their available resources to export production'.[81]

[81] Myint, '"Classical" theory', pp. 328–30, and see *Economics*, p. 39.

4

Industrialization

In the mid-nineteenth century, virtually no modern manufacturing industry existed in Southeast Asia, and although by 1940 the region had some modern factories, the base of Southeast Asian manufacturing remained narrow. After almost three-quarters of a century of growth, Southeast Asia had in no way become an industrial region. Even the development of many basic industries progressed to only a limited extent, and a high proportion of manufactures required by Southeast Asia came as imports. Throughout Southeast Asia, the bulk of modern manufacturing in all sectors was in European, not Asian, hands. Although more industry oriented towards local markets would have developed, as it did after independence, behind protective tariffs or other restrictions, these were, with just a few exceptions, not possible under the region's colonial regimes or Thailand's semi-colonial regime. This chapter's first section assesses Southeast Asian industrialization and de-industrialization, while the second considers attempts in the 1930s to establish more industry.

Industrialization

A broad pattern of industrialization was characteristic throughout Southeast Asia. As the vent-for-surplus model predicts, beginning in the late nineteenth century, handicrafts and artisan industries declined precipitately. In every country, the chief industries involved processing the main vented commodities. A range of import-substitution light industry emerged, producing articles like building materials and consumer goods. Industry mainly concentrated in the urban centres and was organized by both Asian and European entrepreneurs. Industrialization, however, extended only to a limited degree to intermediate and capital goods. If these industries existed, they often depended on linkages associated with the processing of vented exports. Although governments had made little or no effort to promote industrialization, and Europeans shunned industry, that changed in the 1930s because of the sharp downturn in demand for the region's vented staples, and as multinationals began to arrive and set up assembly and production operations.

This section discusses these industrialization patterns. It begins by recounting the contraction of handicrafts. The narrative then deals, in successive sections and sub-sections, with processing industries, import substitution, including the failure to develop a substantial modern textile industry anywhere in Southeast Asia, de-industrialization and, lastly, the region's 1930s departures from earlier industrial policies.

Handicrafts

A large contraction in artisan and handicraft industries occurred as traditional activities were abandoned in favour of export specialization. During the latter part of the nineteenth century in Thailand, home weaving began to contract as 'the people turned to imported cloth'.[1] By 1940, handweaving had almost disappeared from Thailand's central and southern regions, and dyeing had been almost wiped out.[2] Indonesia's indigenous textile industry was said to have 'declined almost to the vanishing point' until a 1930s government programme breathed new life into it.[3] Likewise, in the late 1880s in the Philippines, Glasgow textiles were 50 per cent cheaper than the local handwoven ones; these latter became luxuries 'only the rich could afford'.[4]

Despite decades of decrease, handicraft and artisan production persisted and employed large numbers of people. Production in almost all industries was, however, generally far from sufficient to cater for consumption in the entire country, notably in regard to textiles, apart from a few narrow, specialized ranges of clothing. Before World War II, Burma had just over 100,000 industrial workers and no tobacco 'factories'. There were, however, 23,000 people making cheroots at home or in tiny workshops. Some 42,000 workers and 144,000 'working dependents' engaged about equally in cotton spinning and in handloom weaving. Typically, these were part-time occupations of younger women of agricultural families.[5] The Ilocos provinces in the Philippines produced some 5 million yards of cotton goods, such as piece goods, blankets and towels, but that output and a few textile factories met only a fraction of Filipino needs.[6] Most textiles came from abroad and, as a share of total imports, ranked second only to steel products and machinery, accounting by value for 20 per cent, and in some years for as much as 30 per cent, of all Philippine imports.[7]

1 Ingram, *Economic change*, p. 115.

2 Mitchell, *Industrialization*, p. 169, citing Thompson, *Thailand: the new Siam*, p. 443.

3 Mitchell, *Industrialization*, p. 206.

4 Constantino, *History*, p. 137.

5 Spate, 'Beginnings', pp. 77–78; see also Furnivall, 'Industrial agriculture', p. 92 on the decline of weaving.

6 NARA, RG226, entry 19, box 0412, J. Bartlett Richards, 'Textile manufacture in the Philippines', 24 January 1945; UP, Roxas Papers, Teodoro, 'Philippine manufacturing industries', 12 July 1945, p. 9.

7 Doeppers, *Manila*, pp. 17–35; UP, Roxas Papers, Teodoro, 'Philippine manufacturing industries', 12 July 1945, p. 9; United Nations, *Economic reconstruction: Philippine Republic*, p. 9.

Table 4.1 *Southeast Asia distribution of employment, 1930s (%)*

	Agriculture	Industry	Other	Total
Burma (1931)	69.6	11.0	19.4	100.0
Thailand (1929)	84.2	2.2	13.6	100.0
Malaya (1931)	60.8	12.3	26.9	100.0
Indonesia (1930)	70.0	10.4	19.6	100.0
Philippines (1939)	69.0	12.2	18.8	100.0

Source: Booth, *Colonial legacies*, p. 30.

In 1939, textiles made up half of Indochina's imports of manufactures, while in 1940/41 in Burma, cotton manufactures, principally piece goods, and textiles, comprised 30.1 per cent of general imports.[8]

Data on the percentage of the labour force in industry are patchy and inconsistent across countries, but available data, set out in Table 4.1, are misleading in regard to modern or large-scale manufacturing, and so the actual extent of Southeast Asian industrialization. The broad category of 'industry' in the table probably includes transport and communications, considered in Chapter 5 of this book, as well as mining and handicraft and artisan production. Manufacturing, defined as factory employment, whether modern or not, employed relatively small percentages of the labour force categorized in Table 4.1 as industrial, and most manufacturing industries in Southeast Asia could not be classed as 'modern'. Of a working population of 20.87 million, a 1936 estimate of 'industrial' employment by the Indonesian Department of Economic Affairs counted, excluding agriculture and extractive industries, 120,000 workers in mechanized factories with some claim to modernity. Another estimate indicates 2.8 million in some form of industry, of which 2.5 million were in small-scale industry. Full-time employment in handicrafts was 1.54 million.[9]

The 1939 Philippines census enumerated 11.3 per cent of the labour force in manufacturing, but of these individuals just 250,000 of 601,335 were employed in manufacturing of any size and much of industrial employment was part-time or seasonal.[10] In the same year, modern industry manufacturing for the domestic market engaged just 3,645 workers.[11] The bulk of Manila 'manufacturing' was low-productivity, low-wage handicraft production. Cigar making, embroidery

[8] Borg, 'French considering industrialization', p. 45; Andrus, *Burmese economic life*, pp. 174–75.

[9] Rothe, 'Industrial development', pp. 6–7; Sitsen, *Industrial development*, pp. 14, 22–23, 41; Mitchell, *Industrialization*, p. 214; Shepherd, *Industry*, pp. 81–82.

[10] Mitchell, *Industrialization*, p. 221.

[11] Brown, 'Some comments on industrialization', p. 210.

and *tsinela* (slipper or wooden clog) manufacture employed tens of thousands of metropolitan Manila workers organized in establishments ranging from large factories to individual workers in a putting out system.[12] In Thailand, the 1937 census showed 1.6 per cent of the labour force in manufacturing industries including rice and lumber milling, although an unofficial estimate suggested the proportion was possibly larger. Most of the manufacturing was on a very small scale.[13] Burma, where rice milling was the main industry, had no more manufacturing than Thailand and probably less.

Processing Industries

The main industrial linkage that vent-for-surplus exports created was their processing. These processing industries were, in all Southeast Asian countries, the principal constituent of a modern manufacturing sector. The development, or absence, of other large modern industries depended substantially on linkages created by the principal processing industries.

Primary commodities are advantageously processed near the point of production if this reduces bulk and so minimizes transport costs or is necessary to prevent spoilage. Milling paddy to eliminate husks results in substantial bulk and weight loss, and almost all rice exported from Southeast Asia had been milled there. The same reduction in bulk applied to sugar cane, while rubber grew mould on a long sea voyage, unless smoked and rolled into sheets before export. Because of a greater weight of coal than ore, tin smelting, alone in Southeast Asia's main processing industries, owed its location in the region to tariff protection, discussed below.

The Southeast Asian pattern was for the large port city to serve as the principal location for rice milling and to have the largest mills. Port cities had the locational advantages of cost savings of a place where large volumes of commodities were collected for export, changed modes of transport and were bulked for overseas shipment. Millers could further build on these advantages of the port as a collection and shipment point for rice to realize scale economies in milling and grading. Even so, in all countries, numerous smaller mills dotted the producing areas. Almost all these up-country mills were Asian-owned. In Burma, this included Burmese, Indians and Chinese but in Thailand and Indochina largely only Chinese. Mills in Bangkok and Saigon-Cholon were mainly in the hands of local Chinese who controlled the collection of rice and financing of rice cultivators. European mills in Bangkok found difficulty in competing with the Chinese. However, Europeans owned practically all the big

[12] UP, Roxas Papers, Teodoro, 'Philippine manufacturing industries', 12 July 1945, p. 9; United Nations, *Economic reconstruction: Philippine Republic*, p. 9.

[13] Ingram, *Economic change*, pp. 144–47.

Rangoon mills, most of which belonged to the four large firms that had formed the Bullinger Pool, a cartel to manipulate rice prices.[14]

Burma's 600 to 700 rice mills accounted for over half of all its factories and the industry's 42,000 workers for nearly half of total industrial employment.[15] Sawmilling, employing another about 12,500, was Burma's other main industry.[16] Together, the milling of rice and logs provided more than half to about three-fifths of factory employment in Burma. The first steam rice mill opened in 1861, and until about 1900 milling was principally carried on in the ports, especially Rangoon, and by Europeans. During the early 1920s, the availability of inexpensive German machinery and a supply of cheap capital led to the establishment of numerous small up-country mills, operated by Burmese or Indians. These mills cut into the dominance of the great mills at the ports, partly through the availability of plentiful supplies of low-cost labour and savings on transport costs to ports from milling in growing areas, and partly because of the competitive effect on milling charges of a 1920s over-expansion in the industry.[17] Even so, Rangoon remained the centre of milling, and in the 1930s, 31 of the 72 rice mills that employed over 100 workers were still located there.

The largest Indochinese industrial concentration of milling was in Cholon, adjacent to and to the west of Saigon, where some 30 rice mills, 27 of them utilizing more than 100 horsepower, were situated. Cholon's mills were several storeys of corrugated iron with high chimneys, visible for miles. The mills operated with imported American or German machinery, as did six saw mills. Northern Vietnam had few rice mills; there the more important industry was provided by two major French coal-mining companies with their own power plants and railways to the nearest port.[18]

Although Bangkok's first steam rice mill was built in 1858, it was not an immediate success, and in 1867 the city had just four important mills. By the late 1870s, mills had started to locate in the rice-producing districts, but these were much smaller than the Bangkok mills, which in 1939 accounted for 72 of Thailand's about 600 mills. Most Bangkok mills were steam-driven.[19]

Sugar centrals were not successfully established in the Philippines until 1912, making it the last major world sugar producer to have them. Because by 1920 the Philippines had its great network of family-owned sugar plantations, Filipinos could supply the large amount of cane needed by centrals throughout

[14] Spate, 'Beginnings', p. 82; Cheng, *Rice industry*, pp. 67–68, 77–103; Mitchell, *Industrialization*, p. 173; Ingram, *Economic change*, pp. 69–71.

[15] Mitchell, *Industrialization*, p. 194.

[16] Mitchell, *Industrialization*, p. 195.

[17] Spate, 'Beginnings', pp. 77–82, Cheng, *Rice industry*, pp. 93–95.

[18] Shepherd, *Industry*, pp. 14–15.

[19] Ingram, *Economic change*, pp. 69–71; Mitchell, *Industrialization*, p. 173.

the milling season, and so control a large share of the processing industry. Capital to set up Filipino-owned mills came from the United States and from the Philippine National Bank after its founding in 1916.[20] At the end of the interwar period, the Philippines had 46 sugar centrals and four refineries. Almost half of sugar mills were Filipino-owned.[21] There were 18 coconut oil factories, with American companies responsible for about 80 per cent of production, and 40 coconut crushing factories.[22]

Tin smelting and rubber milling accounted for much of Malayan processing industry. Two large European enterprises dominated tin smelting: the Straits Trading Company with smelters on Pulau Brani, an island near Singapore, and at Butterworth in Province Wellesley, Penang, and the Eastern Smelting Company in Penang. Tin smelting owed its location in the two Straits ports to the Malayan government decision to keep the smelting of tin in Malaya and to do so by imposing in 1903 a duty on the export of tin ore. In non-ferrous metallurgy, ore has almost invariably moved to fuel, as ore is the more weight-losing material in smelting. The two European companies were able to circumvent this economic consideration and conduct highly efficient operations that smelted a large share of world tin, because Singapore and Penang, as major ports and coaling stations on the main world east–west shipping route, could import coal from the cheapest world sources. A few small Chinese companies also smelted tin, but increasingly fell under the control of the European smelters.[23]

Rubber mills operated throughout Malaya, but the largest concentration was in Singapore. In part, that was because much of Indonesian Outer Island rubber was milled in Singapore, and also because the city could collect and bulk sufficient quantities of scrap rubber from up-country mills for its milling to be economic. In 1929, Singapore had 25 mills, more than a dozen of which employed between 100 and 500 persons. Employment in rubber milling of upwards of 5,000 persons was a major addition to the city's industrial sector.

In 1929, Java had 179 sugar factories, many with excellent modern equipment, but the sugar industry's 1930s collapse and government restrictions on export left just 43 factories in 1935 and still only 64 in 1937. The number of boilers in Java sugar factories dropped from a high point of 1,291 in 1920 to 672 in 1937. By comparison, in private industry other than sugar factories and excluding ships, locomotives and government enterprise, there were 1,284 boilers in 1910 and 1,975 in 1937. For the same dates, but including sugar factories, there were 804 and 1,806 boilers respectively in the Outer Islands.[24]

20 Larkin, *Sugar*, pp. 54–60, 97–100, 155–57.
21 Shepherd, *Industry*, p. 94; Mitchell, *Industrialization*, pp. 227–28.
22 Mitchell, *Industrialization*, pp. 96, 227–28.
23 Huff, *Economic growth*, pp. 60–63.
24 Naval Intelligence Division, *Netherlands East Indies*, vol. 2, pp. 190–91, 274, 280.

Import Substitution

Except for processing industries and their linkages to other industry, potential for greater Southeast Asian industrialization lay mainly in replacing imports. As late as 1940, however, that had occurred only to a limited extent. No Southeast Asian country was near completion of the first or 'easy' stage of import substitution. Supplies of most basic consumer goods, including textiles, came chiefly from abroad. Although Singapore probably had Southeast Asia's largest concentration of industry, it was not an industrial centre, nor close to being a large regional industrial agglomeration. Malaya, Singapore included, was 'dependent upon importation for all machines, plant, iron and steel, raw materials, etc.'.[25] Singapore, like the rest of Southeast Asia, lacked a substantial base of capital, chemical and other intermediate goods industries.[26] In Southeast Asia, scope did not exist for an industrial 'big push', suggested for lagging regions in some of the development literature.[27]

The main import-substitution industries that, without subsidies, tariffs or quotas, emerged in Southeast Asia were those with some natural protection. One strand of this industry, primary commodity processing, has already been discussed. The other type likely to have some natural protection occupies much of this sub-section: the manufacture of goods with simple technologies, no large-scale economies and often sufficiently high weight-to-value ratios to make transport costs prohibitive.

All Southeast Asian countries had, in varying degrees, the usual range of industries in any economy in the very early stages of industrialization. Some of these industries, together accounting for a substantial share of employment, were very closely tied to consumer markets, and were major activities even before export expansion – woodworking and furniture making, building and clothing manufacture. The majority of Southeast Asian import-substituting industries, although not strictly tied to the consumer market, were advantageously carried on in close proximity to it, typically due to their low value and high weight. These industries included the manufacture of bricks and tiles, cement products, earthenware, iron pans, pipes, metal bedsteads, inks, oxygen, acetylene and other gases, patent medicine, aerated water, beer, biscuits, cigarettes, toothpaste, motor car polish, sugar candy and other foodstuffs. Many of the consumer goods in this list were principally for European or Europeanized markets in the larger urban areas. An exception was cigarettes. In all countries, these were largely made by small Asian firms and catered for local tastes and

[25] ANM, 1957/0572698, 'Technical estimates of requirements for rehabilitation of government and public utility undertakings for Malaya', 12 June 1944, p. 1; OSS, R&A 2137, *Industrial facilities in Malaya*, p. 3.

[26] ANM, 1957/0571877, ALFSEA conference, item 9c, 'Sponsored industries', *c.* 15 December 1945, p. 1.

[27] Rosenstein-Rodan, 'Some problems'.

pockets. In Singapore, a modern cigarette factory opened by British American Tobacco, and in 1930 with 1,200 employees, found that continued production required tariff protection. The cigarette industry was denied this, and the factory soon closed.[28]

Other import substitution depended substantially on linkages spawned by processing industries. In Burma, the Burmah Oil Company at Yenangyaung included, among its 6,000 workers, a number engaged in engineering. Mining in the Namtu silver-lead area in the northern Shan States also employed engineers. Otherwise, engineering work concentrated in or around Rangoon and Mandalay where the Burma Railway and Irrawaddy Flotilla Company had shops.[29]

Rice milling, although linking backward to growing, had limited forward linkage effects, apart from some need to repair machinery. Partly because of few linkages, rice mills stood out as main instances of industrial development in Southeast Asia's rice-producing countries. Additionally, the lack of industry in these countries is explained by the weak impetus of rice cultivation to urbanization, owing to the small and dispersed markets afforded by a multitude of peasant growers. In Burma, apart from rice milling, saw milling and the other substantial extractive industry of oil refining, industrial development was 'negligible'.[30] Thailand had 'virtually no manufacturing industries'.[31] Siam Cement, able to develop with the natural protection of high transport costs, was almost the only modern manufacturer apart from the rice mills.[32] Nor was there much industrialization in Cochinchina other than rice mills.

The Philippines, too, developed little industrially outside the milling of sugar. Its share of manufacturing value added increased from 13 per cent in 1902 to a third in 1938. The Philippines exported significant amounts of iron, chromite, copper, silver and zinc, but as ores rather than as processed metals.[33] Although an overwhelmingly agrarian economy, just one firm in the Philippines made farm implements, and it employed fewer than 100 people.[34] Modern industry other than primary commodity processing included the manufacture of shoes and shirts, and the San Miguel brewery. Additionally, a few textile factories operated, some with obsolete machinery.[35] Philippine industrialization was sufficiently slight to occasion the observation that industrial production 'has not yet outgrown the handicraft stage'.[36]

28 *SSTC*, I, p. 146.
29 Spate, 'Beginnings', p. 88.
30 Spate, 'Beginnings', p. 88; Hlaing, 'Trends', p. 106.
31 Mitchell, *Industrialization*, p. 166.
32 Mitchell, *Industrialization*, p. 173.
33 Hooley, 'American economic policy', pp. 469–70.
34 Rōyama and Takéuchi, *Philippine polity*, p. 282.
35 UP, Roxas Papers, Teodoro, 'Philippine manufacturing industries', 12 July 1945, p. 9; United Nations, *Economic reconstruction: Philippine Republic*, p. 9.
36 Kurihara, *Labor*, p. 9.

Malaya, although otherwise with little industry, showed how commodity processing could have linkage effects leading to the development of other major industries. Engineering was the most important import-substituting industry in Singapore arising from linkages created by tin and rubber. United Engineers was the principal of a considerable number of Malayan engineering firms, and also Southeast Asia's largest engineering enterprise, with branches in Burma and Thailand as well as throughout Malaya. In 1929, in Singapore alone, United Engineers employed almost 2,000 workers. The firm manufactured gravel pumps for mining and was a large maker of stout-riveted steel pipes to convey gravel- and silt-laden water. By 1932, United Engineers had built 12 important tin dredges in Singapore, as well as redesigning and reconstructing a number of dredges built abroad.[37]

The rubber industry contributed to the growth of Singapore's engineering sector mainly through the need for processing equipment in the form of rubber factories. The demand was considerable, since factories were to be found on practically all of Malaya's several thousand estates and there were numerous Chinese mills treating smallholder rubber. By the inter-war years, United Engineers had become a large manufacturer of sheeting machines, rubber mangles, scrap washers and smoke houses; supplied and erected plant for lighting, power and water schemes; and built turnkey rubber factories. In the 1930s, 'many of the principal estates throughout the rubber growing area [of Malaya] are equipped with U. E. machinery, housed in U. E. structures'.[38]

Weak Southeast Asian Industrialization

Why didn't Southeast Asia have more industry? Comparative advantage is not static: staple exports, as well as often directly creating opportunities for industry, make an indirect contribution to industrialization, by widening the market as more producers are drawn into export production, and by deepening the market through increasing local and hinterland incomes. Export-induced market demand, and capital accumulation resulting from retained export earnings, work to shift comparative advantage away from primary production towards industrial production and to stimulate import substitution. This section argues that high wages and the distribution of profits were principal reasons why Southeast Asia did not industrialize more.

The most striking gap in the list of import-substituting industries in Southeast Asia is the absence of a strong textile industry and heavy reliance on imports from the West and Japan. A partial exception was Indochina, but even there the manufacture of cotton goods accounted for only about half of annual consumption.[39] The Philippines imported over 80 per cent of its textile

[37] *Singapore manufacturers' exhibition*, pp. 111–15.
[38] *Singapore manufacturers' exhibition*, p. 111.
[39] OSS, R&A 2594, *Selected industrial installations in Indo-China*, p. 42.

requirements and Malaya probably an even higher percentage.[40] From the late nineteenth century onwards, textiles were Thailand's major import.[41]

Textiles help in understanding reasons for slight Southeast Asian industrialization, because the production of cotton goods was a frontier industry for all countries to advance in the early stages of industrialization.[42] Furthermore, everywhere in Southeast Asia cotton goods accounted for a large share of imports, suggesting an opportunity to replace imports and ruling out market size along with scale economies as explanations for a lack of import substitution. Technology and technical ability were not major impediments. The technology of setting up weaving mills was well known and easily within the capabilities of Asian enterprise.

Only Thailand and Burma grew sizeable amounts of cotton for local weaving, although by no means most of this raw material; other countries would have had to rely almost entirely on imported cotton. Southeast Asia's lack of local supplies of cotton was not, however, an important barrier to textile production, since for cotton weaving transport costs are about the same for importing the raw material and the finished product. Nor, with large groups of enterprising Asian immigrants in each country, is a dearth of entrepreneurship a convincing explanation. The same is true of power supplies, since enterprises often arranged their own machines to generate power.[43] In the rice-producing countries, the Philippines and Java, small engines could use paddy husks or sugar cane after extraction of the juice for fuel.

Until the 1930s, governments did not attempt to direct Southeast Asian development along the path of industrialization, and even then certainly not one similar to Japan's. Southeast Asian industrialization would have had to occur under a free trade regime. However, historically, tariff autonomy allowing infant industry protection has not been decisive. Tropical countries with no import tariffs, and unhampered by colonial restrictions, could still move towards industrialization so long as wage levels were competitive.[44] By 1913, unaided by tariffs, a number of tropical countries, including Ceylon, had become self-sufficient in cottons.[45]

Indochina was a Southeast Asian exception to low or no tariffs against imports. The 1892 Méline Tariff put Indochinese manufactures at a strong disadvantage, because Indochina, as an assimilated colony, had the same tariffs as applied to foreign goods entering France, increasing the price of imported components needed for local production. Although a 1928 Act gave Indochina a method of adapting the tariff structure to its own needs, this legislation resulted

40 OSS, assemblage 43, R&A 2280, *Handbook of Japanese industry*, pp. 107–8.
41 Ingram, *Economic change*, pp. 119–20.
42 Lewis, *Growth and fluctuations*, p. 220.
43 Shepherd, *Industry*, pp. 80–81.
44 Lewis, *Growth and fluctuations*, pp. 200–1.
45 Lewis, *Growth and fluctuations*, pp. 200–1; Craig, 'Ceylon', p. 245.

in harsher protectionism than before, as well as harming Asian consumers, by increasing tariff rates against imports from Japan and China.[46]

Government policy in Indochina also discouraged industrialization. The 'persistence of opposition to the establishment of secondary industries as a major feature of French economic policy' meant that modern manufacturing would have had largely to depend on French capital. It, however, chose 'to apply itself in the main to the primary production of raw materials'.[47]

Wage costs were a key explanation for weak Southeast Asian industrialization. Southeast Asian wages were high by the Asian standard set by India and China. High wages were a fundamental driver of immigration to Southeast Asia. As the Straits Settlements Trade Commission pointed out, immigrants came to Singapore from India, Hong Kong and China because of the prospect of higher wages.[48]

Only Java and Tonkin, areas of dense population, had sufficiently low wages effectively to compete on this basis. Textile production around Haiphong in Vietnam had the advantage of a nearby abundance of workers and so low labour costs. Given these, producers became competitive through the combination of large mechanized French mills manufacturing cotton thread, selling it to large numbers of weavers working in homes and small workshops, and, additionally, the benefit of a tariff on imported Indian fabrics. In 1940, the Société Cotonnière had four large mills employing 14,000 and supplying 50,000 weavers in the Red River Delta. The company's factory in Saigon, opened in 1924, had 10,000 spindles and 400 looms.[49]

In Southeast Asia, wage pressure was further created by varying degrees of Dutch disease. This arose from Southeast Asia's heavy reliance on a handful of staple exports and their volatile prices, and was worsened by the region's lack of financial development. Booms in staple export industries forced up prices of non-tradeables. Higher non-tradeable prices, which included wages, the cost of many services and land, raised manufacturing costs and ensured that for substantial periods local manufactures would be uncompetitive. In a bust, markets shrank, and, due to this contraction and falls in consumer purchasing power, local manufacturing became unattractive. Moreover, when commodity prices turned downwards, Asian entrepreneurs who had borrowed were likely to be caught up in a liquidity crisis. European banks, although with recourse to external sources of finance, were not interested in lending to industry, while local Asian banks that were willing to lend to industry were always subject to severe liquidity constraints and the sharp contraction in

46 Robequain, *Economic development*, pp. 128–33, 323; Murray, *Development*, pp. 105–6, 196–99.

47 Shepherd, *Industry*, pp. 13, 17; see also Mitchell, *Industrialization*, pp. 151–60.

48 *SSTC*, I, p. 149, and see I, pp. 150, 119, III, p. 271, V, p. 72.

49 Brocheux and Hémery, *Indochina*, p. 125.

money supply which, under the currency board system in Southeast Asia, resulted from any export contraction.[50]

In Southeast Asia, if more profits had been in Asian hands there would likely have been more industrialization. Singapore provides an example of this. Chinese in the city had a substantial stake in the production of rubber through the development of estates by using the system of a catch crop of pineapples and sharecropper labour, and they also dominated rubber processing. The Chinese stake in these industries led to the development of some domestic (i.e. Singapore-based) manufacturing by promoting the emergence of entrepreneurs, putting profits and rents in their hands and therefore creating a large new source of finance for industrial expansion. As a European representative of the Singapore Manufacturers' Association pointed out, 'It is to the Chinese merchants of the City that Singapore is largely indebted for its industrial development.'[51] Men like Tan Kah Kee, Lim Nee Soon, Tan Ean Kiam, Tan Lark Sye and Lee Kong Chian used their profits from rubber to become the city's, and some of Southeast Asia's, leading industrialists and assume a pioneering role in the development of local Chinese banks.

De-industrialization

Two processes, both described above, occurred as part of 'de-industrialization'.[52] First, specialization in primary commodities, as the vent-for-surplus model predicts, came at the expense of basic industrialization self-sufficiency. Many of the consumer items (handicrafts in the model) which had traditionally been sourced locally no longer were. Local textile (and other traditional consumer goods) industries ceased to serve the bulk of the market and, instead, arrived chiefly as imports. As a result, in 1939 no country even approached the realization of first-stage import substitution or came close to self-sufficiency in textiles. Although local textile (and other traditional) industries survived, they did so by catering for only small, specialized segments of the market such as for elaborate weaves or patterns and clothing for special occasions.[53]

Second, the composition of industrial goods changed. There was the early acquisition of a modern manufacturing sector, of which the processing of staple exports was a major component. Because of this emergence of modern manufacturing, the share of industry, defined as all activity other than

50 Huff, 'Boom-or-bust commodities', pp. 1087–105.

51 Cresson, *Industrial Singapore: handbook*, p. 59.

52 See also Huff, '"Vent-for-surplus"', p. 8. The term 'de-industrialization' was popularized by Williamson, *Trade and poverty*, pp. 70–71 and *Globalization*, pp. 65–86.

53 van der Eng, 'Why didn't colonial Indonesia', pp. 1039–40, 1042–43; Frederick and van Nederveen Meerkerk, 'Local advantage'.

agriculture and services, did not necessarily fall. A more or less constant share of industry, broadly aggregated to include its traditional and modern sectors, appears to have existed in Indonesia and the Philippines.[54]

1930s Industrial Departures

Only in the 1930s, and even then not in Burma or Singapore, was there much governmental interest in establishing industry, although still not comprehensive industrialization. In Indonesia, for example, it was observed in 1938 that '[T]he government has always considered that a rapid and extensive industrialization … is neither desirable nor possible.'[55] During the 1930s, however, government policies in Southeast Asia towards industry altered to a greater or lesser extent for three main reasons. One was to try to counter sharp increases in unemployment created by the depression, mainly, although not exclusively, through a revival of handicraft and artisan industries. The governments in Indonesia and Indochina were especially active in this regard.[56]

Second, the 1930s downturn, by making apparent Southeast Asia's lack of industry and extreme dependence on primary commodity exports, led to policies to expand modern manufacturing as a supplement to agricultural economies, not to replace them. Indonesia went furthest in this regard in 1933, enacting protectionism to foster industrialization, but also to keep out Japanese imports.[57] The Philippines, after becoming a Commonwealth in 1935 with its own government, revived its first National Development Company (1919–27) as a vehicle for government participation in industry.[58] In Thailand, the 1932 revolution invigorated earlier ideas of extensive state involvement in, and sponsorship of, Thai manufacturing. These ideas gained momentum in 1938, after Prime Minister Phibun assumed the premiership and incorporated Thai manufacturing into his nationalist, anti-Chinese, modernizing agenda. The anti-Chinese element had, however, to be modified due to the need for Chinese entrepreneurial participation to develop industry to work towards modernizing the economy, a government–Chinese partnership that marked the beginnings of Thailand's bureaucratic capitalism. However, implementation of industrialization and the flowering of bureaucratic capitalism largely awaited the World War II Japanese occupation and, even more, the 1950s.

Acceptance of the move to more industrialization was not, however, universal. In the early 1930s, the Governor of the Straits Settlements, Sir Cecil Clementi, pushed for Singapore to become 'a great centre for manufacture'.[59]

[54] van der Eng, 'Real domestic product'; Hooley, 'American economic policy'.
[55] Rothe, 'Industrial development', p. 5.
[56] Sitsen, *Industrial development*, p. 38; Mitchell, *Industrialization*, pp. 200–5.
[57] Shepherd, *Industry*, pp. 50–57, 61.
[58] Shepherd, *Industry*, pp. 113–14.
[59] *SSLCP 1932*, 'Address by His Excellency the Governor', pp. B100–B102; *Straits Times*, 11 January 1932.

It was high time, he argued, to have 'a greater measure of self-sufficiency than we possess at present'. To this end, he advocated import substitution, extending to textile mills, a tin plate factory and even a local steel industry. The initiative met stiff opposition in free trade Singapore, and never got off the ground. More important, the Colonial Office reacted to Clementi's proposed tariff protection with annoyance and some alarm; London was unwilling to encourage colonies to develop any industries that might compete with those in the United Kingdom.[60]

Near the end of the decade, a third government departure towards more industry was to push for some degree of country self-sufficiency in preparation for war. French colonial government promotion of Indochinese industrialization began in 1938, reversing the long-standing metropolitan opposition to colonial manufacturing. The government in France now saw colonial industry as important for national defence and self-sufficiency, and began to direct the economy towards these goals.[61] In the 1930s, the Dutch colonial government was already promoting considerably more industrialization, and in 1933, erected protective walls behind which industry could develop. Beginning in 1940, the Dutch made further plans to establish substantial manufacturing in Java to avert the shortages that would result from an inability to import manufactured goods due to the outbreak of war in Europe. Industrialization was to be balanced. Light industry would cater for Indonesian consumers in combination with heavy and metallurgical industries to provide manufactured materials and capital goods.[62] Japanese occupation, however, cut short industrialization plans in most of Southeast Asia except Indochina, where the French colonial government remained in place until March 1944, and in Thailand through joint Thai–Japanese ventures.[63]

By the 1930s, a number of foreign firms, typically multinationals, had begun to set up assembly industries in Southeast Asia, and usually sited these in the main cities, owing to their large urban markets and good distribution facilities. Singapore attracted a sizeable industry in bicycle assembly. In 1926 in Singapore, Ford established an automobile assembly plant with a capacity of 100 cars a month, although the refusal by the Singapore Municipal Commissioners to give General Motors a licence for a factory site because it bordered on a residential area led that company to locate in Jakarta's port of Tanjung Priok.[64] After the 1933 imposition of tariff and quota restrictions,

60 NA, CO 273/582/92080, file on Singapore manufacturers' exhibition, *passim*. Clementi's speech was reported in the *Straits Times*, 2 September 1931.

61 'I. G. M. I.', 'L'effort d'industrialisation', pp. 161, 163; 'L. A.', 'L'Indochine depuis la guerre', pp. 6, 16.

62 Department of Economic Affairs, Batavia, 'Economic condition of Indonesia', p. 123; van der Eng, 'Government promotion', pp. 176–200; Sato, 'Relocation', p. 253.

63 Kubo, 'Higashi Ajia', p. 65.

64 *SSTC*, I, pp. 146, 50, II, p. 192, IV, p. 108.

Java had an influx of multinationals, including General Motors, Unilever, Goodyear and Bata.[65]

Conclusion

In 1850, Lewis observes, there were no signs of modern industrialization in Thailand, Indochina or the Indonesian archipelago, apart from Java.[66] At that time, too, almost all of the Malay Peninsula was jungle, while much of Lower Burma and Cochinchina was jungle or semi-swamp. Between the 1870s and World War II, relatively little import-substitution industry developed, although Southeast Asia did not de-industrialize. A more accurate assessment than de-industrialization is that globalization and staple exports transformed 'industry' in Southeast Asia: it destroyed much artisan, handicraft and cottage industry, but led to the emergence of a new industrial sector appropriately described as manufacturing.

For any country, manufacturing for export is a difficult step, and in inter-war Southeast Asia there was no particular reason to expect the emergence of export-oriented industry. One possible basis for such industrialization is low wage costs, but most of Southeast Asia did not have these. Nor did Southeast Asia possess any marked advantage from its ready access to raw materials, which is typically the other possible basis for success in manufacturing for world markets. Large rubber production offered some possibility of export-oriented industrialization based on raw material access, and to some extent this was realized. Both Singapore and the Philippines exported some locally made rubber goods, including shoes and technical rubber goods such as plugs, valves, hoses and belting for use in engineering industries. The advantage of rubber's availability as a raw material was not, however, great. Manufacturers in other countries could use rubber at not much greater cost than in Southeast Asia, since in manufacture it was not a high weight-losing raw material, and this minimized the importance of transport costs.

The 1930s depression and then acute World War II shortages left a strong desire among many Southeast Asians for more industrialization. Options to realize this without protective tariffs were economically much the same as before the war. Politically, however, an industrialization strategy no longer had its pre-war limitations of foreign rule and free trade policies. As a result, beginning in the 1950s, industrialization began to be pursued behind protective walls to shelter import-substitution industries, examined in Parts III and IV.

[65] Sitsen, *Industrial development*, p. 27; van Eeghen, 'Beginnings of industrialization', p. 131; Mitchell, *Industrialization*, p. 209.

[66] Lewis, *Evolution*, p. 9.

5

Infrastructure and Foreign Investment

For the region's vent-for-surplus commodities, infrastructure concentrated around transport in the modern sectors of Southeast Asia's dual economies. Railway systems, almost non-existent in 1870, were established throughout Southeast Asia over the next six decades. Like roads, railways inevitably focused on the main ports as the outlets for exports, but only Java had a well-developed rail system. A large share of the other infrastructure, including the buildings of the principal European banks and businesses, concentrated in the principal urban centres, giving them a modern look which was already evident by the early years of the twentieth century.

Human infrastructure was also patchy and poorly developed. In 1870, widespread education was not offered outside Burma and Thailand. Both had long traditions of education, and nearly every village had a monastery school which almost all boys attended. Although the opening of Suez gave an impetus to education as well as to commerce, schooling in all of Southeast Asia began to be provided on a substantial scale only after 1900, when it was first seen as an instrument of progress.[1] Yet subsequent educational expansion often fell short in building the human infrastructure fundamental to development, because of a lack of absorptive capacity for the kinds of schooling available and little demand for technical education in the absence of industrialization.

While Southeast Asia might be supposed to have received substantial foreign investment, this was not the case. One reason was the lack of extensive industrialization in the region, another that rich natural resources and cheap labour available through mass migration obviated the need for large amounts of foreign capital. Much of late nineteenth-century foreign investment in less developed areas was in railways and urban infrastructure. Southeast Asia did not attract a great deal of investment on either score, because water transport often substituted for rail, and urbanization was limited. Additionally, European enterprises controlled a considerable share of business retained earnings. These enterprises had little interest in Southeast Asian industry, and a large share of the profits of many European businesses were remitted as dividends to shareholders living abroad.

[1] Furnivall, *Educational progress*, pp. 36–48.

This chapter focuses on stocks and flows of investments of four kinds and the associated capital accumulation. The chapter first examines the building up of physical capital in the form of infrastructure. Next, the chapter assesses, in the second and third sections, the nature and extent of Southeast Asia's development of human capital through educational provision and flows of foreign investment in the region. A fourth section shows that Southeast Asia, rather than investing in its own development, was a net capital exporter.

Infrastructure

Geography provided, ready-made, the basis for much of Southeast Asia's post-1870 physical infrastructure. Governments built on this geographical inheritance and reinforced it. Determining geographical features were the region's good access to water routes, both the sea and internal river systems, and the strongly north–south configuration of Malaya, as well as mainland Southeast Asia's countries of Burma, Thailand and Indochina. The cheapness of water transport compared to rail or road explained mainland Southeast Asia's heavy reliance for the conveyance of goods on the three river systems of the Irrawaddy, the Chao Phraya and the Mekong, as well as the extensive use by the Malay Peninsula and the island countries of Indonesia and the Philippines of coastal vessels for intra-country transport.

Southeast Asian transport routes were, with the exception of Indonesia, north–south. In the mainland Southeast Asian countries of Burma, Thailand and Vietnam, this was the orientation of their great river systems, whose delta areas and points near the southern termination of these maximized the scope for inland water transport and gave the best access to east–west ocean shipping routes. Similar access considerations applied to Singapore as the terminus of coastal shipping routes at the southernmost extension of the Malay Peninsula. The expansion of coastal shipping routes and development of trunk railway lines paralleled major rivers and coastlines. This transport network strengthened the existing north–south orientation, although in mainland Southeast Asia trunk railway lines additionally branched to form tree-like configurations (Figure 5.1). A north–south Southeast Asian transport pattern was further reinforced by mountain ranges and jungles, which formed near-impenetrable east–west barriers across Indochina and into Thailand, between Thailand and Burma, from one coast of the Malay Peninsula to the other, and across Sumatra. In 1941, almost no east–west roads or railways crossed the borders of mainland Southeast Asian countries, while for their island counterparts, inter-regional transport was necessarily by sea.

In adhering to Southeast Asia's north–south geography, infrastructure construction ensured that internal communications focused on a single port city in the south. Rather than providing an alternative to a historic reliance on

Figure 5.1 Southeast Asia railways, 1939
Source: *Burma*: OSS, R&A 1286.1, *Additional strategic objective*; R&A 1992A, *Burma (situation report no. 1)*, pp. 7–16; and R&A 1992, *Burma (New Delhi area report no. 1)*, pp. 1–11. *Malaya*: Federated Malay States Railways, *Fifty years of railways*, p. 2. *North Borneo*: Naval Intelligence Division, *Netherlands East Indies*, vol. 2, p. 483. *Thailand*: Kakizaki, *Laying the tracks*, p. 36; Ingram, *Economic change*, pp. 85–86. *Indonesia*: Reitsma, *Gedenkboek der Staatsspoor- en Tramwegen*, pp. 72–73, 75–76; Naval Intelligence Division, *Netherlands East Indies*, vol. 2, maps between pp. 428–29. *Indochina*: Indochina, *Annuaire statistique*, 1937–38, fold-out map; JISPB, *Joint Army-Navy intelligence study of Indochina*, chapter 7, section 'Transport and telecommunications'; Naval Intelligence Division, *Indo-China*, p. 423. *Philippines*: Spencer, *Land and people*, p. 76; Worcester, *Philippines*, pp. 622–23, end map.

water transport and its north–south bias, railways strengthened the nodality of Rangoon, Bangkok, Saigon and Singapore. Already, these ports had the advantage of being near the world east–west shipping route that bisected Southeast Asia after the inauguration of the Suez Canal. North–south railway configurations and the economics of ocean shipping contributed significantly to Singapore's growth and help explain the extreme urban primacy of Bangkok and Rangoon.

Southeast Asia's colonial governments and Thailand's semi-colonial one built infrastructure mainly to serve export areas, and in so doing could often economize on construction. One source of available economies was that the region's natural geographical configuration and advantages limited a need for built infrastructure, and a second that most infrastructure was directed towards export sectors of economies, and so relatively small parts of each country. Only in Java did the Dutch build an extensive railway network with the aim of closely interlinking island communications.

As a rule, infrastructure projects needed to satisfy at least one of two criteria. One was to meet existing (or sufficient potential) demand; the other to serve military or political objectives of control over regions distant from the centre of government. Unless one of these objectives was met, infrastructure was, typically, not built in lagging, traditional regions.

In Indochina, the French undertook large-scale late nineteenth-century investment in dredging and the construction of canals in Cochinchina to create the basis for a rice export economy, which would enable the colony to pay for itself and benefit France. That Laos should finance itself was the immediate goal of its French administrators for a decade after 1894.[2] In Thailand, the pre-World War I government decided, partly for financial reasons, against investing in irrigation, even though this would have extended rice cultivation. Slight urbanization in Southeast Asia also restricted infrastructural investment, since much of this infrastructure was in cities, including all the largest ones, in the form of power stations for electricity and gas provision, street lighting, water supply, roads, sewers, and trams and trolleybuses (Chapter 6).

Measured as track kilometres as a proportion of population, only Indonesia, where railway construction was largely confined to Java, and Burma had built most of their pre-World War II railways by the turn of the century (Table 5.1). Elsewhere in Southeast Asia, the principal burst of railway expansion was between 1901 and 1913. After that, Thailand alone greatly extended its railway system, mainly for political/strategic reasons. In Malaya, kilometres of railway per person fell substantially, because continued high net immigrant population inflows outpaced considerable railway building.

[2] Stuart-Fox, 'French in Laos', p. 122.

Table 5.1 *Southeast Asia, West Africa and Latin America kilometres of railways per 100,000 population, 1901–38*

	1901	1913	1929	1938
Burma	14.4	20.6	21.2	19.7
Indochina	1.6	11.8	11.2	14.7
Thailand	2.5	11.6	24.6	21.4
Malaya	20.9	46.6	38.4	34.4
Indonesia	10.1	12.8	12.1	10.3
Philippines	2.6	12.4	9.6	8.5
Ghana	3.4	16.7	25.5	21.4
Nigeria	1.5	9.6	14.4	13.4
Chile	145.4	232.9	196.6	178.5
Bolivia	54.5	64.0	89.1	86.3
Peru	58.3	76.8	61.4	45.5
Costa Rica	121.1	162.5	136.0	112.7
Guatemala	70.3	84.7	67.9	56.1
Honduras	22.0	41.6	157.2	119.6
Nicaragua	51.8	56.3	48.2	46.8
Cuba	116.7	157.6	138.3	117.2

Source: Huff, 'Globalization, natural resources', p. 142.

In 1870, the telegraph between Europe and India was extended to Singapore, and in the 1880s this telegraphic communication spread to the Malay states.[3] By 1908, Malaya had 1,654 miles of operating telegraph line.[4] Thailand was connected by telegraph to Burma and Saigon-Cholon in 1883, and from there to the rest of the world.[5] In 1897, the Philippines had 65 telegraph offices, of which 49 were in Luzon, and 1,750 miles of telegraph line, while after 1902 the Islands' telegraph network greatly expanded.[6]

During the twentieth century, additions to up-country telegraph communications and the spread of the telephone added to the immediacy of communications. 'Sumatra and Borneo Indonesians', explained a contemporary observer, 'are shrewd and keen business men and many of them will gladly discuss with you the trends of the London and New York produce markets: in fact, quite a number of them in small townships, 100 miles inland, get their daily

[3] Turnbull, *History of Singapore*, p. 90.
[4] Kesner, *Economic control*, pp. 135–39.
[5] Manarungsan, *Economic development*, p. 57.
[6] Worcester, *Philippines*, p. 613.

price quotations of world markets by telegram from their brokers or bankers in the harbour towns.'[7] In Malaya, up-country Chinese rubber dealers relied on the telephone and telegraph. They received official price quotations three times a day through a Reuters service and kept constantly abreast of the Singapore rubber auctions.[8]

Mainland Southeast Asia: The Three Rice Economies

Predominantly self-reliant peasant cultivation and the option of depending substantially on water transport limited infrastructural development in the rice-specialized regions of Burma, Thailand and Indochina. The striking exception was the extensive late nineteenth-century programme of hydraulic engineering which made possible the Cochinchina rice economy.

Thailand

Consistent with its slow pre-1940 economic growth and slight urbanization outside Bangkok, Thailand had, apart from its rail network, less modern infrastructure than any other Southeast Asian country. The Kingdom had fewer roads than even the Philippines, although an area nearly twice as large. No trunk road connected Bangkok to the rest of the country; motor vehicles could comfortably travel at most 20 miles beyond central Bangkok. In 1941, the city itself had 2,000 motor vehicles and the rest of Thailand no more than that. Bullock caravans were the chief means of road transport outside Bangkok.[9]

Exports travelled mainly by water routes which converged on Bangkok as Thailand's only large port. Goods, including about four-fifths of rice, were carried chiefly by punt-like boats along a network of rivers, canals and small channels. Teak from the north was floated down the main rivers.

Compared to other Southeast Asian countries, Thailand opted for fairly extensive railway construction, and by 1940 had 1,925 kilometres of 1 metre gauge track. However, it was partly because of railway expenditure that the government rejected a proposal for infrastructure spending for a large irrigation scheme recommended in 1902 by the Dutch engineer, Homan van der Heide. Irrigation would have enabled the commercial cultivation of more rice land and raised yields on existing land. However, even apart from a preference for railway extension, the benefit of adding yet further to Thailand's mono-rice economy may have seemed unclear to the government. Nor, given the Kingdom's extremely conservative approach to finance and reluctance

[7] Hart, 'Recent development', p. 93.
[8] *SSTC*, II, p. 354.
[9] Dobby, *Southeast Asia*, p. 285; Ouyyanont, 'Bangkok', p. 101; Stamp, 'Siam', p. 218; International Bank for Reconstruction and Development, *Public development programme*, p. 120.

to borrow, is it entirely apparent that funds for an irrigation project were available. Although railways brought economic benefits and extended agricultural specialization, the Thai government opted for rail lines chiefly to extend and secure Bangkok's reach into more distant areas of the Kingdom and knit together the polity.[10] Thailand's railway mainly catered for passengers, but before World War II these numbered fewer than 1 million each year, about one-fifteenth of the population.

In its financial and developmental conservatism, Thailand was as much a British colony as any of the formal British colonies. 'London bankers would have only been too glad to give new loans to Thailand' in light of its strong financial record if the Kingdom had wanted.[11] However, it did not, and Ingram concludes that the Thai government failed to furnish the essential public works of railways, power, electricity and irrigation; and that educational provision was 'seriously inadequate'. In all these regards, the government's 'conservative monetary and fiscal policies became significant'.[12]

Burma

The pre-war transport network concentrated in Burma's centre, the delta and dry zone, and to a greater or lesser extent neglected peripheral regions.[13] The Irrawaddy River, navigable for 874 miles all year round, and a further 105 miles for seven months of the year, provided Burma's chief transport artery for goods. A European enterprise, the Irrawaddy Flotilla Company, formed in 1865 and managed by P. Henderson of Glasgow, dominated Burma's river transport for passengers and transported some rice, although most rice was carried by small craft (Chapter 3). The company operated a fleet of about 600 ships, including its signature paddle steamers, some as large as 326 feet long and with a 76-foot beam.

Railway construction in Burma began in 1877, soon after the opening of the Suez Canal. Initially, the railway ran between key ports and towns in Lower Burma, but after the third Anglo-Burmese War in 1885, the line was extended northwards to Myitkyina in Upper Burma, mainly for military reasons.[14] In the northern hills, away from both the Irrawaddy and the one rail line to Myitkyina, transport was mostly by mule.[15]

The completed rail network, 2,058 miles in 1934, came at little, if any, immediate capital cost to Burma's provincial government, since it was undertaken mainly by British and American companies and then, as the

[10] Kakizaki, *Laying the tracks*, pp. 6–9: Brummethuis, *King of waters*, pp. 161–95.
[11] Callis, *Foreign capital*, p. 60.
[12] Ingram, *Economic change*, p. 212.
[13] Fisher, *Southeast Asia*, p. 444.
[14] Silverstein, 'Politics and railroads in Burma', p. 80.
[15] Spate, *Burma setting*, pp. 9–10.

Burma Railway Company, was bought in 1928 by the Government of India. Rather than running parallel to the Irrawaddy, the trunk railway from Rangoon to Mandalay followed the Sittang Valley, and by 1903 extended to Lashio. A different route than along the Irrawaddy allowed the railway to avoid the same intense competition with shipping characteristic of much of internal transport in inter-war Southeast Asia. However, Burma's main road, running from Rangoon to Lashio via Mandalay, duplicated the route of the railway and crisscrossed it.

During the 1920s, motorized transport became a severe competitor to the railway, leading to the Burma Railway Company's dissolution and its purchase by the government. Still, in 1940, as well as a large passenger traffic of 19.8 million people, or a little more than Burma's total population, the railways transported sizeable amounts of rice from areas where water routes were infeasible. The rice, known as rail paddy, was of lower quality than boat paddy grown in the rich alluvial soil of the delta. On the eve of World War II, Burma had 4,440 miles of main roads, out of a total of 17,000 miles of vehicular roads, and 20,000 motor vehicles.[16]

Indochina

The main lines of communication in Indochina stayed close to its long coastline; the transport network penetrated the interior to only a limited extent.[17] When in the later 1930s the Transindochinois railway finally connected Hanoi and Saigon-Cholon and linked Indochina north–south, the rice trade continued to be conducted largely by coastal shipping, although rough seas hampered ships for almost half the year (Figure 5.1). Two main infrastructure projects – financed by a combination of private French enterprise, three large loans raised by the government and taxation of the general population – stand out in pre-1940 Indochinese economic history. One was the construction of an intricate system of canals in Cochinchina; the other the Transindochinois.

In Cochinchina, early French colonists found 'a new country still half wild' and a terrain of low, marshy land, seldom more than 2 metres above sea level at high tides, on which good roads were difficult to build and maintain.[18] Development required the construction of canals. In the French manner, their ordered construction partitioned the Cochinchina landscape into geometrical sections. Canal construction began in 1866, and until the mid-1890s relied largely on manual labour. Beginning in 1893, a five- to 10-year public works programme started, and contracts for canal construction were let to private companies, which used powerful mechanized dredging equipment. By 1940, Cochinchina

16 Burma Intelligence Bureau, *Burma*, vol. 2, pp. 224–26; Andrus, *Burmese economic life*, pp. 226–40; Fisher, *Southeast Asia*, pp. 443–45; Dobby, *Southeast Asia*, pp. 194–95.

17 Brocheux and Hémery, *Indochina*, p. 120.

18 Robequain, *Economic development*, p. 110 and see p. 221.

had 1,300 kilometres of main canals dug to an upper width of 22 metres and a depth of over 2 metres at low tide. Secondary canals branched off the main ones and made possible the permanent cultivation of almost the entire delta as part of a network that provided, as well as transport, drainage and irrigation. Water transport, converging at Cholon, was the most economic way to move rice and corn. Numerous small vessels, barges, junks, of which 2,600 were over 16 tons burden, 200 motor launches and a fleet of steam launches, with 191 of more than 30 tons, carried Chochinchina's trade and passenger traffic.[19]

While in Cochinchina canals provided an infrastructural basis for Indochina's export economy, in nineteenth-century Tonkin the French also built major infrastructure. Two main rivers, the Red River and Thai Binh, flow through the Red River Delta. If these rivers were contained only in their natural levees, most of the delta would be flooded. During the nineteenth century, French engineers added to existing Vietnamese-built infrastructure to create an extensive system of large dykes. These allowed Tonkin's rice production to expand, and its delta area to become one of the world's most densely populated regions.

Railway construction in Indochina was more strategic and political than economic, although the first line, from Haiphong to Kunming, built between 1904 and 1910 over near impossible terrain, mainly reflected early French hopes to develop a China trade (Figure 5.1). The Transindochinois, 1,860 kilometres long and running close to the coast, was completed in successive stages from 1905 to 1936. Used more by passengers than freight, railway construction helped to unify Vietnam, but did relatively little in that regard for Indochina as a whole. Cambodia had a rail line from Phnom Penh towards Bangkok, but before the war this railway did not quite connect to the Thai capital. In late 1941, the Japanese closed the gap between the Thai railways at Aranyaprathet and the Phnom Penh–Mongkolborey line. Laos had no railways.[20]

Insular Southeast Asia: Rubber, Tin and Sugar

Philippines

Philippine geography dictated a heavy reliance on coastal shipping. A collection of 7,083 islands, the Philippines, from a practical viewpoint, divided among several large islands and had a mountainous terrain often extending to near the sea and covered by dense forest. These geographical features were reflected in Southeast Asia's fewest railway track kilometres per person and just 14,250 miles of road, of which only 7,500 miles were first-class roads (Table 5.1). Two-thirds of first-class roads were in Luzon, mostly around Manila.[21] For the

19 Robequain, *Economic development*, pp. 110–11, 220–21.

20 Robequain, *Economic development*, p. 385.

21 NARA, RG226, entry 16, box 1004, 'Report on railroads of the Philippine Islands', October 1943, pp. 1–3.

economies of other islands in the Philippines, coastal shipping was essential. In 1938, 3,337 vessels engaged in inter-island trade, of which 67, with an aggregate net tonnage of over 50,000 tons, were steamers. These connected the islands, and carried much of the seaborne freight as well as a large passenger traffic. Shipping, which included sailing *bancas* (boats of traditional Philippine design, about 50 to 70 feet in length), were able to carry just a fraction of the freight needed to supply Philippine industries.[22]

Two main rail lines, together running much of the length of Luzon, centred on Manila's Tutuban Central Terminal (Figure 5.2). A northern segment of railway, established by an 1886 Spanish royal decree and developed by the Manila and Dagupan Railway Company (later the Manila Railroad Company) and British capital, showed the tree-like configuration common to Southeast Asian railways, and ran through most of Luzon's main sugar-producing area, and eventually reached the port of San Fernando in northwest Luzon during the 1930s slump. The southern rail segment, built by the Philippine Railway Company and again by British capital, covered the remainder of Luzon's main sugar area. The Philippine Railway Company also built the lines in Panay and Cebu.[23] The Panay line, extending between Iloilo and Capiz, served that island's sugarland and showed, as in Luzon, how sugar substantially determined the siting of railway infrastructure. The pattern was not, however, repeated in Negros, since its sugar region and main road ran along the coast, and the crop could move without a rail network. Before World War II, sugar exporters shipped mainly across the Guimaras Strait to Panay for onwards shipment.[24] By 1919, all Philippine railways had been purchased by the government.[25]

Indonesia

Javanese geography and infrastructure contrast markedly with the strongly north–south patterns in most of the rest of Southeast Asia (Figures 5.3 and 5.4). Political decisions were central to Java's extensive infrastructure development. The Dutch colonial government determinedly built a comprehensive inland transport network, partly with the intention of balancing food availability across the island, and financially supported inter-island shipping services to link Indonesia's many islands. The first Javanese railway opened in 1867, and by 1894 a continuous rail line connected Jakarta and Surabaya. By the 1930s, Java's rail system crisscrossed the island, and had a density comparable

[22] NARA, RG226, entry 16, box 208, 'Economic conditions in the Philippines', 15 October 1942, p. 8; see also Hartendorp, *Japanese occupation*, p. 198.

[23] Worcester, *Philippines*, pp. 622–23.

[24] Larkin, *Sugar*, pp. 9–17.

[25] Corpuz, *Economic history of the Philippines*, pp. 245–46.

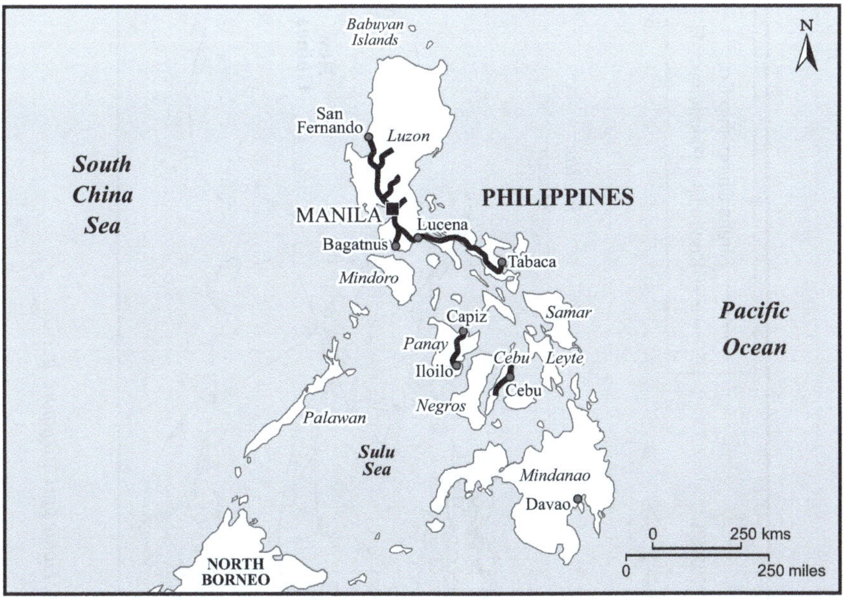

Figure 5.2 Philippines railways, 1939
Sources: Spencer, *Land and people*, p. 76; Worcester, *Philippines*, pp. 622–23, end map.

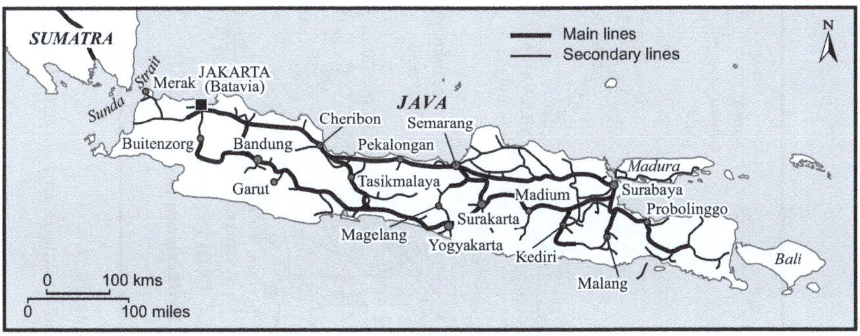

Figure 5.3 Java railways, 1939
Sources: Reitsma, *Gedenkboek der Staatsspoor- en Tramwegen*, p. 73; Naval Intelligence Division, *Netherlands East Indies*, vol. 2, pp. 415–17.

to European countries (Figure 5.3). Railways connected not just Java's large cities but numerous smaller towns 'by what may be fairly called a metropolitan network of railways'.[26]

[26] Fisher, 'Economic myth', p. 184 and see Naval Intelligence Division, *Netherlands East Indies*, vol. 2, p. 414, figure 7.

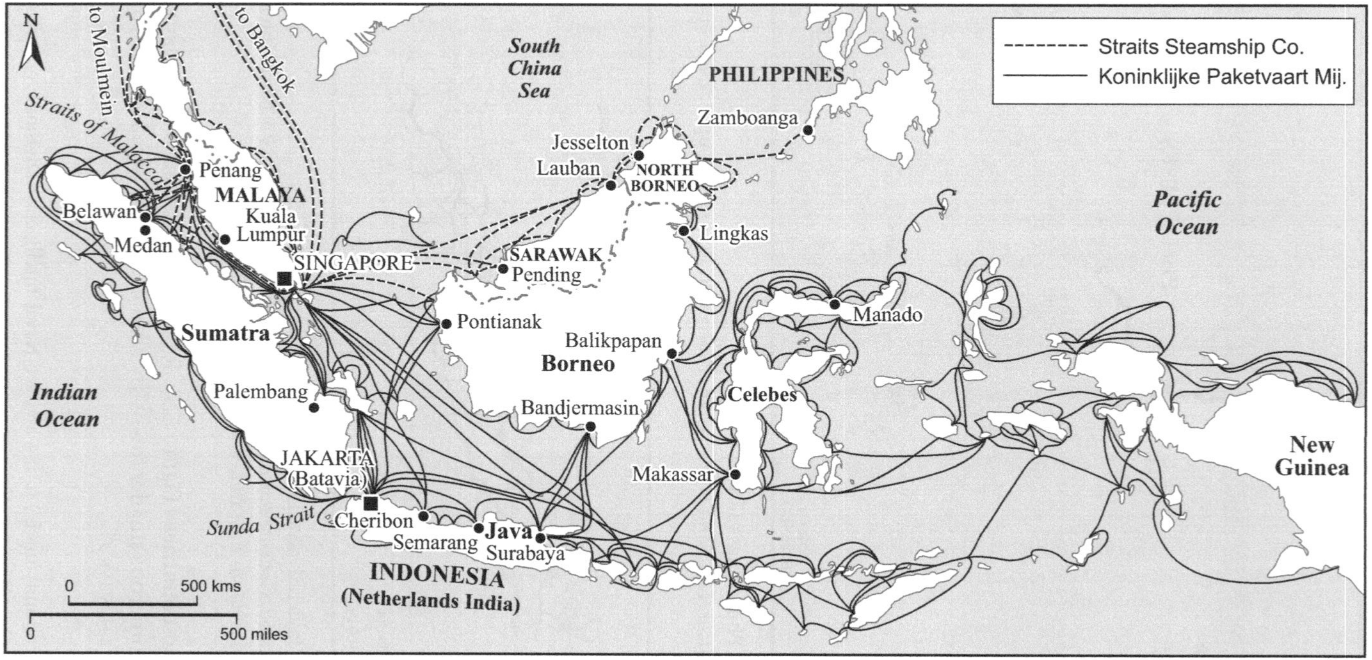

Figure 5.4 Indonesia local shipping, 1939

Sources: de Boer and Westerman, *Een halave eeuw paketvaart*, p. 119; Tregonning, *Home port Singapore*, p. 162.

The Indonesian islands were linked to one another and to surrounding parts of Southeast Asia by a dense network of steamer services and small vessels. Many of the smaller Outer Islands relied on outside supplies of food, and without the Dutch government subsidies supporting the shipping network, would have been dangerously isolated. Steamers were mainly owned by two companies. One was the Dutch-controlled Koninklijke Paketvaart Maatschappij (KPM) (Figure 5.4).[27] The KPM was central to intra- and inter-island communications. It had 134 ships, and called at every major Indonesian port and most of the minor ones. The other was the Singapore-based Straits Steamship Company, which operated 55 of 81 local steamers based in Singapore, and provided services covering 78 ports in the region, including many in Indonesia. There were, in addition, several small Chinese steamer companies.

Malaya

Transport development in Malaya illustrates how so much of infrastructure in Southeast Asia developed in response to vent-for-surplus growth and then enhanced it through facilitating the opening of new land. In Malaya, a network of local shipping and then railway construction worked in tandem. Between 1885 and 1895, railways, built along Malaya's west coast to serve tin mines, took the form of short, east–west lines that connected each of the main tin mining districts with its coastal port: Port Weld (1885), Klang (1888), Port Dickson (1891) and Telok Anson (1895). Local shipping linked these ports to Singapore and Penang.

Even before the turn of the century, the railway system, following the major valleys, began to turn north–south, and so towards Singapore. By 1903, the north–south pattern was well established. After the turn of the century, as the railway extended north–south, the rubber industry gravitated towards it. One reason for rubber growers to locate along Malaya's west coast was that the foothills where tin was mined afforded good natural drainage for rubber trees. Moreover, the railway provided transport to ports for rubber, firmly siting the axis of rubber production along Malaya's west coast.[28]

During the inter-war years, the main Malaya railway was linked north–south to create a continuous Singapore–Bangkok line, and extended though the peninsular interior to an east coast terminus near the Thailand border. Construction of an east coast line, branching off the main line at Gemas and running to Tumpat in Kelantan near the Thai border, began in 1903 and was completed in 1931. At its full extension, the east coast route gave the Malaya railway a total of 1,067 miles (1,717 km) of running line, mainly single track, and 254 miles (409 km) of second line and siding. Not just the 1930s slump

[27] *SSTC*, I, p. 96, IV, p. 250.
[28] Dobby, *Southeast Asia*, pp. 131–33.

but the emergence of strong competition with motorized transport halted further railway construction in Malaya, as elsewhere in Southeast Asia.[29] The capital cost of the entire railway was £230 million, of which about £80 million was financed by surplus revenues of the Federated Malay States Railway and government.

The experience of Malaya, like other Southeast Asian infrastructure development discussed in this section, supports economic development theories of unbalanced growth and leading-sector linkage effects, as opposed to a 'big push' stressing simultaneous creation of a large number of infrastructure projects and industries in a balanced development effort.[30] In Malaya, development began with the rapid growth of one staple – tin – which led to another – rubber – and the expansion of the output of both staples created transport, processing and trade linkages. During this process, the whole west coast Malayan economy shifted onto a higher development plane, while Malaya's east coast lagged behind, giving rise to the familiar Southeast Asian 'lopsided pattern of development' of dual economies.[31]

Educational Provision

Education divides into an investment good capable of raising productive capacity and a consumption good which increases human enjoyment, awareness and possibly also tolerance. In Southeast Asia, the demand for education was almost entirely to invest in the possibility of obtaining a better job. That preference, together with limited employment opportunities for technical education, restricted the contribution that education, despite its considerable post-1900 expansion, made to pre-World War II Southeast Asian development. Nevertheless, an institutional framework for modern systems of education was established where none had previously existed.

Table 5.2 shows three main features of educational provision in Southeast Asia. One is a great increase after 1900 in primary education throughout the region. Much of this instruction was in the language of the colonial power, but there was also considerable 'vernacular' (teaching in an Asian language) schooling, especially in Malaya (Malay and Chinese) and Indonesia (Javanese). All schools in the Philippines taught in English. However, for the majority of

[29] Fisher, 'Railway geography', pp. 124–28; *Reports on the Federated Malay States for 1901*, p. 3; *Reports on the Federated Malay States for 1903*, p. 22; Federated Malay States Railways, *Fifty years of railways*, pp. 3, 7, 42; NA, CO273/677/10, 'Straits. F.M.S railways report by L. M. Smart'; Sanders, 'Malayan railway', p. 25.

[30] For a discussion of these theories, see Rosenstein-Rodan, 'Some problems', pp. 202–11; Hirschman, *Strategy of economic development*, pp. 29–75 and 'Generalized linkage approach'.

[31] Nurkse, *Patterns*, p. 18; see also Nurkse, 'International investment to-day', p. 753.

Table 5.2 *Southeast Asia, Japan and the United States comparative primary school enrolment rates, 1890–1939 (per 10,000 population)*

	1890	1900	1910	1920	1930	1939
Burma	–	–	–	–	206	316
Indochina	–	–	–	–	190	260
Thailand	–	–	9	179	552	939
Malaya	–	–	–	–	–	548
Indonesia	57	62	96	161	267	338
Philippines	–	188	970	1,038	936	1,267
Japan	772	984	1,240	1,508	1,550	1,695
United States	1,985	1,969	1,828	–	–	–

Note: Malaya refers to the Straits Settlements and Federated Malay States only.
Sources: Easterlin, 'Why isn't the whole world', pp. 18–19; Indochina, *Annuaire statistique 1943–46*, p. 274; Furnivall, *Educational progress*, p. 111.

Filipinos with some years of schooling, familiarity with English did not translate into fluency in it.[32] In Thailand, instruction was in Thai which, unlike Asian-language teaching elsewhere, was not a barrier to obtaining the highest level of jobs.

Second, except in the Philippines where the Americans arrived committed to an education agenda, still in the 1930s at most about half of Southeast Asians had a primary education. Comparison with the United States and with Japan, as the leader in Asia, shows how badly Southeast Asia lagged in the spread of primary education. In 1930, education, the Philippines apart, was well short of the Japanese level of 1890, and was a fraction of 1890s United States schooling (Table 5.2).

Third, government expenditure on education varied markedly. In primary schooling, the Philippines and Thailand were well in advance of the rest of Southeast Asia. Spending per capita on education as a share of total expenditure was highest in the Philippines and lowest in Burma, where it was only about a fifth of the Philippines level. Even in the Philippines, however, at some 4 shillings per person per year, expenditure was large only in comparison to much of the rest of Southeast Asia (Table 5.3). Partly as a result, for most of the region, as in Thailand for example, educational provision has been judged to have been 'seriously inadequate'.[33]

32 Rafael, 'War of translation', p. 285.
33 Ingram, *Economic change*, p. 212.

Table 5.3 *Southeast Asia education expenditure, late 1930s*

	Burma	Thailand	Malaya	Indonesia	Indochina	Philippines
	1938/39	1939/40	1937	1938	1936/37	1938
Population (m)	16.0	14.9	5.3	68.4	23.5	16.3
Exports (£m)	36.4	19.7	106.5	81.6	20.5	34.6
Total government expenditure (£m)	11.5	11.3	18.0	74.2	12.1	16.4
% spent on education	6.0	11.0	5.0	6.0	12.0	20.0
Education expenditure per capita (£)	0.04	0.08	0.17	0.07	0.06	0.20

Source: Furnivall, *Educational progress*, p. 112.

Everywhere in Southeast Asia, numbers in school fell away sharply at the secondary level. The great bulk of those in primary education were in levels 1–4; few continued to levels 5–7. Only small numbers were enrolled in vocational education, and even fewer in universities (Table 5.4 a). The large gap between literacy levels of Indonesians and Chinese in 1930, shown by Table 5.4 b, suggests two observations. One is the importance of Chinese initiatives to organize their own schools or travel abroad for education; the other is that literacy differentials help explain the dominance of Chinese in commerce and the professions in Indonesia. Relatively high literacy levels in Burma (and, although not shown, Thailand) reflected their traditions of monastic education (Table 5.4 c).

Educational provision made less of a contribution to development than it might have, because almost the only demand on the part of Southeast Asians for schooling was to obtain a good job, and practically the only employment for the kind of literary language demanded was low-level clerical government and commercial work. There were few takers for technical or, when it began to be offered, agricultural training. In 1900, there was a shortage of clerks, and clerical work attracted high wages. European employers complained at having to pay so much for poor or indifferent work, 'clerks "neither in *esse* nor in *posse*"' (neither in qualification nor performance).[34] By the inter-war years, as educational provision expanded, clerical occupations became heavily oversupplied. Unemployed clerks and others in clerical work on low wages, mired in debt

[34] Furnivall, *Educational progress*, p. 67.

Table 5.4 *Southeast Asia school enrolment and literacy, 1930s (000 and %)*

	Burma	Thailand	Malaya	Indonesia	Indochina	Philippines
(a) School enrolment	1936/37	1939	1938	1938	1936/37	1938
Population (000)	13,100	14,900	3,460	68,410	23,000	16,250
Schooling: total	513.8	1,564.7	16.0	2,290.3	473.5	1,738.9
Schooling: primary: elementary and levels 1–7	498.8	1,564.7	–	2,269.7	471.6	1,659.1
Schooling: secondary	15.0	–	16.0	20.6	1.9	79.7
Higher academic	0.5	0.9	–	–	0.6	7.7
Vocational: total	2.5	–	3.9	34.2	3.0	15.9
Vocational: technical	2.1	–	3.1	33.1	2.6	13.3
Vocational: higher	0.4	–	0.8	1.1	0.4	2.6
% of population in schools	5.5	10.7	7.8	3.4	2.5	11.5
(b) Literacy: Indonesia 1930	Java: Indonesians	Java: Chinese	Java: all groups	Outer Islands: Indonesians	Outer Islands: Chinese	Outer Islands: all groups
% of population literate: men	9.7	47.5	10.7	13.4	33.2	14.5
% of population literate: women	1.4	16.0	1.9	4.0	7.7	4.2
% of population literate total	5.5	33.5	6.2	8.7	24.7	9.5

(*continued*)

Table 5.4 (*cont.*)

(c) Literacy: Burma 1940 and Malaya 1931	Burma	Malaya
% of population literate: men	56.0	35.5
% of population literate: women	16.8	7.6
% of population literate total	36.8	24.1

Notes: 1. For Thailand, secondary schools are included under primary. 2. For Indonesia, higher academic is included under higher vocational and the data for all schools exclude non-recognized schools.
Source: Furnivall, *Educational progress*, pp. 56, 66, 76, 111.

and living hand to mouth on advances from moneylenders, became common throughout Southeast Asia.[35]

In Southeast Asia, a greater supply of people with formal qualifications than jobs led to a situation familiar in today's developing countries of an emphasis on obtaining a diploma. When one diploma level lost its value and likely yielded only unemployment, the demand for education escalated to ever rising levels, right up to university degrees. While not all of those with high-level diplomas found jobs, if 'the worst comes to the worst, they can become lawyers'. The number of lawyers further increased, because anyone bringing a case had to do so before a European court and required a lawyer's help. Although Southeast Asia needed doctors and engineers, it had far too many lawyers: 'The Philippines are overrun with lawyers; in Indochina the annual output of lawyers is "a menace to social equilibrium"; under British rule the plague of lawyers is a general complaint.'[36]

Attempts were made to provide technical education, but it attracted little interest, apart from courses in mechanics to learn to repair motor cars and bicycles. Demand was low because Southeast Asia's lack of industrialization meant there were few jobs for the technically trained outside the Western community, where employers required Europeans. An agricultural college opened in Burma in 1924, but recruitment ceased in 1932 due to an inability to attract cultivators. The agricultural school established in 1931 in Malaya gave preference to Malays, but had to offer stipends to attract them and, in any event, seems to have had very little success in helping farmers to work the land more profitably. Great efforts were made in the Philippines to promote vocational and especially agricultural training, but no more than a small proportion of students on these courses found jobs. Only the Dutch in Indonesia had moderate success in teaching techniques of agricultural improvement.[37]

A strong positive contribution of educational expansion, for all its limitations, was to lay the basis for a modern system of education. It offered an institutional framework for education and the spread of literacy on which post-1945 Southeast Asia could build. Universities were established throughout the region, mostly after 1900. In Malaya, Raffles College (1928) in Singapore conferred degrees to university level. Typically, universities such as the University of the Philippines and the University of Malaya, which were founded under colonialism, are the oldest, and now usually regarded as the best, in their respective countries.

[35] See, for example, *Census of India, 1931. vol. XI. Burma. Report.* Part I, pp. 137–38; *SSLCP 1923*, 'Report of the Committee to consider the problem of destitution among various sections of the community', pp. C237–C238; *SSLCP 1929*, 'Supply Bill', p. B144.

[36] The quotations are from Furnivall, *Educational progress*, p. 116.

[37] Furnivall, *Educational progress*, pp. 59, 6, 69, 78–79, 92–94, 109, 116–17.

Foreign Investment

The geographical distribution of foreign investment associated with late nineteenth- and early twentieth-century globalization was strikingly uneven. Between 1865 and 1914, three-fifths of British, and two-thirds of trans-European, foreign investment went to regions of recent European settlement or the New World, with only a tenth of global population; just over a quarter of capital went to Asia and Africa, where two-thirds of people lived.[38] A distinguished literature, traceable from Alfred Marshall to Clemens and Williamson, stresses natural resources and large inwards migration as key explanatory factors in disproportionate foreign investment in the New World. Marshall ranked natural resources first among the determinants attracting foreign capital.[39] Similarly, Nurkse emphasized the synergy between natural resources and capital flows.[40] Clemens and Williamson explain the uneven world distribution of late nineteenth-century investment flows as capital 'chasing natural resources, educated populations, migrants, and young, urban populations'.[41]

Why then between the 1870s and World War II did rapidly expanding, resource-rich Southeast Asia receive little foreign investment, despite having the abundant natural resources and heavy inward migration identified as fundamental to explaining capital inflows to the New World? The main aim of this section is to provide at least a partial answer to that question. After initially setting out data on foreign investment, this section goes on to argue that four main reasons account for the relatively small amounts of foreign investment in Southeast Asia. One involves substitutes: that both natural resources and cheap labour effectively substituted for foreign borrowing. Second, Southeast Asia's particular geography allowed much of transport to be water-borne, obviating the need that arose in countries with large land masses for railways and foreign capital to finance them. A third reason is that Southeast Asia was relatively little urbanized, reducing demand for costly urban infrastructure (Chapter 6). Fourth, the institution of colonialism and its associated preferences for light taxation and, if possible, small surpluses, or at least balanced budgets, severely circumscribed fiscal capacity and therefore government borrowing for investment in social overhead projects.

Foreign Investment Data

Two main features are apparent in the 1930 stock of foreign investment in Southeast Asia (Table 5.5). One is an uneven distribution across countries. More

38 Edelstein, *Overseas investment*, p. 40; Stone, *Global export*, pp. 23, 414.
39 Marshall, *Principles*, p. 668.
40 Nurkse, *Patterns*, pp. 17–18.
41 Clemens and Williamson, 'Wealth bias', pp. 304, 333.

Table 5.5 *Southeast Asia foreign investment, 1930*

	Current US$, m	Direct, %	Portfolio, %
Burma	220	95.5	4.5
Indochina	280	91.1	8.9
Thailand	132	56.8	43.2
Malaya	560	79.8	20.2
Indonesia	1,997	80.1	19.9
Philippines	385	77.9	22.1
Total	3,574	80.8	19.2

Source: Callis, *Foreign capital*, p. 108.

than half of investment went to Indonesia, partly due to its size; partly due to an extensive transport infrastructure of railways and shipping; and partly due to European capital in sugar, tea and rubber plantations, as well as petroleum production and tin mining. Malaya and the Philippines were the other two main recipients of foreign investment. Although in Malaya smallholders accounted for 44 per cent of rubber output, there was considerable European investment in rubber estates and tin mining and smelting. In the Philippines, American sugar interests and coconut oil factories were the main components of foreign capital.

Southeast Asia's rice economies attracted markedly less foreign capital than their non-rice counterparts. Rice cultivation did not offer much scope to overseas capitalists, because it depended heavily on peasants, who needed only small amounts of finance. Extending credit in these quantities would entail disproportionately high transaction costs. Furthermore, rice milling was mostly in local hands. Only Burma had a large European-owned rice-milling industry, while in Indochina and Thailand rice mills were mainly controlled by local Chinese (Chapter 3). There was more investment in Indochina than Thailand, partly because of French-owned rice plantations in Cochinchina and French industries in Tonkin, including textiles and coal mining. One explanation for more foreign capital in Burma than Thailand was the former's European rice mills; another, that Indian Chettiars advanced considerable sums to rice cultivators for production but also for unproductive purposes, taking land as security and charging high interest rates to offset transaction costs.

Table 5.5's other main feature is that most investment was direct, defined by Callis as entrepreneurial or business investment, and explained as mostly capital in export and import sectors, including production, merchant houses and banks. Thailand apart, direct investment accounted for about four-fifths or more of total investment in Southeast Asia. Only about a fifth of investment was portfolio or rentier investment such as government or corporation bonds, which in Southeast Asia were a usual way of financing infrastructure projects.

The high proportion of portfolio investment in Thailand compared to elsewhere in Southeast Asia resulted from a relatively large programme of railway construction financed by bonds and limited foreign investment in business or industry, due mainly to a lack of opportunities for foreign capital in the rice industry (Table 5.5).[42]

Two features stand out when comparing per capita exports and foreign investment in Southeast Asia with temperate, or New World, regions. One is rapid export growth in both groups of countries. The other is a sharp divergence in capital inflows: they were large to the New World and slight to Southeast Asia, where as late as 1913 export expansion occurred with minimal foreign investment. Taking the ratio of per capita exports to per capita foreign investment as a measure, in 1913 and 1930 the average export–investment ratio for Southeast Asia was far higher than for the New World. By 1938, the difference in ratios had narrowed somewhat, but the export–investment ratio in Southeast Asia was still four times higher than in the New World (Table 5.6).

Substitutes

This and the next three sub-sections offer an explanation of why rapid export expansion in Southeast Asia was accompanied by relatively little foreign investment. A principal attraction of Southeast Asia for international investors was the exploitation of natural resources. Plantation agriculture requires substantial amounts of finance, and therefore often foreign capital, to finance labour, supervision and administrative costs to establish and then maintain an estate and market its output. Mining enterprise also typically relies on foreign technology, and with this overseas investment. In Southeast Asia, however, peasant agriculture accounted for a large share of production: all of rice cultivation, almost half of rubber output and a large share of coconuts. Only sugar, tea, about half of rubber production and, in the inter-war years, a small oil palm industry were plantation crops. Malayan tin mining did not require much capital until after 1910.

Southeast Asian peasant production could be largely self-financing because it drew on the resource abundance of a highly elastic supply of fertile frontier land and large amounts of cheap migrant and immigrant labour (Chapters 1 and 2). These inputs served as substitutes for foreign capital. Technology was not an issue, since peasants and plantations used nearly identical technologies; both relied on traditional agricultural tools. Although estates might have developed new and better technologies, abundant labour discouraged capital-intensive techniques and moves to innovate.

[42] Callis, 'Capital investment' and *Foreign capital.*

Table 5.6 *New World and Southeast Asia exports and foreign investment per capita, 1871–1938 (1990 US$)*

(a) Exports per capita (annual averages)	1871/73	1900/02	1911/13	1925/27	1936/38
Canada	230	641	605	1,116	831
Argentina	260	621	851	666	431
Australia	891	1,098	1,249	1,005	1,084
South Africa	–	377	699	449	554
Indochina	–	37	46	51	41
Outer Islands (Indonesia)	35	79	146	176	118
Malaya	471	1,071	1,064	1,319	868
Philippines	27	61	79	101	87
Thailand	12	50	61	88	54
Burma	44	107	144	157	120

(b) Foreign investment per capita	1900	1913	1930	1938
Canada	226	385	377	359
Argentina	290	266	140	104
Australia	308	275	300	229
South Africa	157	202	–	145
Indochina	–	9	8	11
Indonesia (Java and Outer Islands)	7	12	16	18
Malaya	–	58	61	50
Philippines	–	10	14	13
Thailand	–	6	5	5

(c) Per capita exports/foreign investment	1900	1913	1930	1938
Canada	2.8	1.6	3.0	2.3
Argentina	2.1	3.2	4.8	4.1
Australia	3.6	4.5	3.4	4.7
South Africa	2.4	3.5	6.4	3.8
Weighted average	–	3.0	4.0	3.5
Indochina	11.3	5.1	6.4	3.7
Indonesia (Java and Outer Islands)	–	12.2	11.0	6.6
Malaya	–	18.3	21.6	17.4
Philippines	–	7.9	7.2	6.7
Thailand	–	10.2	17.6	10.8
Weighted average	–	16.2	18.2	13.3

Table 5.6 (*cont.*)

Notes Panel (b): Canada: 1938 figure refers to 1939; *Argentina*: 1930 figure refers to 1929; *Australia*: 1913 figure refers to 1914, and 1930 figure refers to 1929; *South Africa*: 1938 figure refers to 1935; *Indochina*: 1913 figure refers to 1914; *Outer Islands (Indonesia)*: foreign investment data refers to all of Indonesia. Investment in the Outer Islands was a small proportion of these totals; 1913 figure refers to 1914, and 1938 figure refers to 1937; *Malaya*: 1913 figure refers to 1914, 1930 figure refers to 1929, and 1938 figure refers to 1937; *Philippines*: 1913 figure refers to 1914, and 1938 figure refers to 1935; *Thailand*: 1913 figure refers to 1914, and 1930 figure refers to 1929.

Sources Panel (a) for trade statistics:

Burma: Shein, *Burma's transport*, pp. 263–64; Burma, Office of the Chief Collector of Customs, *Annual statement*, 1912–13–1920–21; Andrus, *Burmese economic life*, p. 183.

Indochina: Frézouls, 'Tableau', p. 274; Indochina, *Situation*, pp. 407, 448–49; Arnaud, 'Taux', p. 267; Leurence, 'Étude', p. 143; Indochina, *Annuaire statistique*, 1942–44, p. 290; Stover, 'Tropical', p. 48.

Thailand: Ingram, *Economic change*, pp. 333–34.

Malaya: Chiang, *History of Straits Settlements foreign trade*, pp. 174–75; Malaya, *Return of foreign imports and exports*, 1921–28; Malaya, *Foreign imports and exports*, 1930–37; Malaya, *Foreign trade of Malaya 1939.*

Indonesia: Korthals Altes, *General trade statistics*, pp. 50–56, 69–75.

Philippines: Philippines, *Census of the Philippine Islands, 1903*, vol. 4, pp. 564–65; Philippines, Bureau of Commerce, *Statistical bulletin of the Philippine Islands, 1918*, p. 32, *1920*, p. 125; Philippines, Division of Statistics, *Bulletin of Philippine statistics 1938 (Fourth Quarter)*, p. 324; Philippines, *Yearbook of Philippine statistics, 1940*, p. 415.

Argentina: Ferns, *Britain and Argentina*, pp. 492–93 for trade 1870–1910; Díaz-Alejandro, *Essays*, pp. 2, 461, 475–76, 484.

Australia: Butlin, *Australian domestic product*, pp. 410–11, 436–37, 441, 443, 470. Exports include gold until 1938 and *exclude* gold thereafter. In the three years 1936–38 gold exports averaged £12.9m. Beginning in 1914/15 data are for fiscal years.

Canada: Urquhart and Buckley, *Historical statistics*, pp. 173, 183. Data are for calendar years after 1919, fiscal years ending 31 March of the year given from 1908–19 and for fiscal years ending 30 June of the year given for 1868–1906. The total for 1907 is for the nine months ending 31 March 1907. Exports include gold.

South Africa: Mitchell, *International historical statistics: Africa, Asia and Oceania*, p. 521 (1902–07) *and* includes Cape of Good Hope, Natal, Orange Free State and Transvaal; Katzen, *Gold and the South African economy*, pp. 46, 60–61, 71 (from 1908). Exports include gold.

Sources Panel (a) for population: Table 2.2 and:

Argentina: Díaz-Alejandro, *Essays*, p. 421; *Australia*: Mitchell, *International historical statistics: Africa, Asia and Oceania*, pp. 64–65; *Canada*: Urquhart and Buckley, *Historical statistics*, pp. 14–16; *South Africa*: Mitchell, *International historical statistics: Africa, Asia and Oceania*, pp. 5, 49.

Sources Panel (b): Twomey, *Century of foreign investment.*

The international trade literature on the Leontief Paradox shows that natural resources and capital may be either complements or substitutes.[43] If, as for a number of export industries in Southeast Asia, the elasticity of substitution between labour and natural resources on the one hand and foreign capital on the other is quite high, and the implicit wage low, labour-intensive production is likely to offer the economically least cost and most technically efficient solution. So it proved in Southeast Asia before World War II. When capital- and managerial-intensive European undertakings competed with small Asian enterprises, the latter were almost always the more economically viable. Such efficiency rendered foreign investment to finance capital-intensive raw material production (though not necessarily complementary infrastructure) largely redundant. There was no reason for capital to flow to export industries in Southeast Asia if it could not profitably be employed there.

As soon as world demand for tin increased sharply (due mainly to the innovation of tinned food), European companies raised capital in Britain and repeatedly tried to establish Malayan mining ventures. They were, however, unable to compete with Chinese miners until after 1910, when a depletion of rich alluvial deposits gave scope for costly dredging equipment. Before then, Europeans failed to appreciate that 'technological efficiency was not synonymous with economy, and that the condition [alluvial nature] of tin deposits favoured small scale mining by simple labour-intensive technique'.[44]

The great deltaic rice-growing regions of Southeast Asia had the natural resource of soil so fertile that it 'has long been marvelled at'.[45] Combined with cheap labour, this gave the region's farmers a clear edge over United States rice production. In Burma's late nineteenth-century rice industry, efficiency, measured as total factor productivity, equalled that in the American South.[46] Large-scale United States rice production, labour-saving devices and efficient milling were insufficient to overcome high American wages and create the competitive strength to challenge Southeast Asian producers in world export markets.[47]

Geography and Urbanization

The second possible reason for large international investment in Southeast Asia was lending for social overhead projects such as plant and equipment for railways, tramways, docks, telecommunications, and gas, electric and water works. Between 1865 and 1914, this social overhead investment, of which railways made up three-fifths, accounted for 61.8 per cent of new issues raised on British stock

[43] Naya, 'Natural resources, factor mix', pp. 567, 570.
[44] Wong, *Malayan tin industry*, p. 153.
[45] Coclanis, 'Distant thunder', p. 1065.
[46] Coclanis and Komlos, 'Time in the paddies'.
[47] Cole, 'American rice-growing industry'.

exchanges. The composition of lending by other major nineteenth-century capital exporters was similar to that in Britain.[48] This sub-section argues that two important reasons for the relatively low levels of foreign investment in Southeast Asia compared to the New World were that to a considerable extent in Southeast Asia water transport substituted for rail and that the region was overwhelmingly rural.

Between 1865 and 1914, railway expansion absorbed 42 per cent of British capital exports.[49] Geographical considerations significantly influenced the distribution of this investment. Where water routes were difficult or infeasible and labour costs high, railways soon became essential as the only serious alternative to human or wagon transport. That was true in countries of late nineteenth-century settlement like Argentina and Brazil as well as Australia, the Canadian prairies and the western United States.

Conversely, in Southeast Asia a more favourable geography than usual in New World countries made it possible to avoid large commitments of railway investment, and yet still achieve rapid export expansion. Fundamental features of Southeast Asia's development were its maritime character, together with the region's many navigable rivers and high rainfall. The spread of cultivation in some areas required, first, lumpy investment in infrastructure, as in the construction of a network of canals in Cochinchina to drain the land, and in Thailand, where canals helped to distribute floodwater. Subsequently, however, the new waterways afforded a cheap means of internal transport. Coastal, riverine or island shipping fulfilled a similar role elsewhere in Southeast Asia. The Irrawaddy in Burma and the Mekong in Indochina provided main transport routes for the export of rice and timber. In the Philippines, the network of islands and seas afforded sheltered domestic waterways. Malaya's peninsular shape allowed the use of railways in conjunction with coastal shipping.

In Southeast Asia, once vent-for-surplus expansion was underway, railways helped to promote it, as for example with rice in Thailand, Burma and Indochina and rubber in Malaya. Even so, export expansion could get started without railways, and when they were built, staple exports continued largely to use water transport for its cheapness. By the inter-war period, motorized transport provided a more flexible, lower-cost alternative to rail.

Cities and accompanying industrialization require large amounts of infrastructure. In Southeast Asia, all of the main cities and some of the smaller ones had a modern infrastructure of power and water supplies, transport and communication facilities, roads and drainage systems. Southeast Asia was, however, little industrialized, as well as being one of the world's least urbanized regions, and the need for foreign capital to finance urban infrastructure was correspondingly less. Malaya was the only country where more than 10 per cent

[48] Edelstein, *Overseas investment*, pp. 37–38.
[49] Stone, *Global export*, p. 10.

of people lived in cities, and in some countries the share of rural dwellers was well over 90 per cent (Chapter 6).

Governments

The argument in this sub-section is that governments would have had to sponsor much of foreign investment and have been willing to pay for it. They were not, however. One reason was limited tax revenues and another the conservatism of the fiscal and monetary policies of colonial governments. The sub-section first discusses taxation and then colonial finance.

Social overhead projects tend to be lumpy, and before World War II their size and a small pool of local savings generally necessitated long-distance finance and foreign savers. Capital markets in London, other European centres and after 1914 the United States, where finance was available, usually demanded the involvement of government in the borrowing countries: 'the organizing and taxing power of governments, backed by [a] monopoly of violence, was necessary to impress the required mass of overseas investors'.[50] From 1865 to 1914, government and mixed government-private enterprise took 65 per cent of British social overhead capital issues invested overseas. And from 1918 to 1931, lending to public authorities accounted for 69 per cent of British overseas investment.[51]

In countries at Southeast Asia's embryonic level of financial development, financial markets relied heavily on foreign investment. Governments organized much of this.[52] Railway construction and social overhead projects largely devolved to governments or some measure of state participation. Insofar as foreign investors, typically through joint stock companies, came forward, they almost invariably dealt through Southeast Asian governments, and required, as for example with railway construction in Burma, a large amount of government finance as well as interest guarantees on investment.[53]

For Southeast Asian countries to have received per capita foreign investment not much less than their high per capita exports would suggest, colonial governments would have had to borrow for social overhead projects, including railways. Fully 75 per cent of pre-1914 British foreign investment was in public utilities, government securities and railways, and this same proportion of lending took the form of debentures and preference shares.[54] But the composition of foreign capital in Southeast Asia, shown by Table 5.5, is remarkable for the paucity of portfolio and government borrowing. The Southeast Asian pattern, with the partial exception of Thailand, is the polar opposite of the New World.

50 Edelstein, *Overseas investment*, p. 38.
51 Atkin, *British overseas investment*, pp. 130–31.
52 Davis and Gallman, *Evolving financial markets*, pp. 721–22.
53 Shein, *Burma's transport*, pp. 44–53.
54 Stone, *Global export*, pp. 23–24, 31.

In most of Southeast Asia, government borrowing to finance infrastructure was restricted by low tax ratios (tax as a percentage of GDP) and by the determination of colonial governments to avoid deficits. Table 5.7 shows Southeast Asian tax ratios in support of this argument. In 1913, ratios of around 5 per cent to 7 per cent, although low, were not entirely out of line with the 10 per cent or so in Western countries. The big difference came in the inter-war years, when developed country tax ratios rose to 20 per cent or more, but the Southeast Asian tax take lagged behind. Burma, where taxes reached 16 per cent of GDP, showed that Southeast Asian governments could tax. However, as much as half of Burmese revenue was transferred to the Imperial government in Delhi, with minimal return benefit.[55] Comparatively high tax ratios in Thailand are also misleading in that a substantial share of government revenues went into a near obsessive accumulation of foreign reserves. Tax ratios in Indonesia, roughly the same as Thailand's by the inter-war years, are a better guide to government spending. The colonial exception was Malaya. Tax ratios there were already 12.1 per cent by 1913 and, if with the help of a 1930s fall in GDP, stood at over 15 per cent in 1937. Revenue came disproportionately from the Federated Malay States, where the export sector of peninsular Malaya's economy centred, but in 1931 with just 1.7 million of Malaya's 4.3 million inhabitants. The combination of extremely low population and abundant resources also made the Federated Malay States, as Schwulst observed, a 'special case' of quite high per capita government spending.[56]

Lewis's observation that before World War I tropical governments could do all they wanted with taxes at around 5 per cent of GDP does not hold for all countries in Table 5.7.[57] But it applies to the majority before the war. Even afterwards, the horizons of Southeast Asia's colonial and semi-colonial governments remained low. Although a source of revenue might have been tariffs to tax imports, Southeast Asian governments, at least until the 1930s, tended to keep tariffs to a minimum. For the Philippines, Hooley emphasizes the absence of tariffs, and that 'Government revenues during the entire American period approximated 7 per cent of GDP, which was little more than already achieved under the [pre-1898] Spanish regime.'[58]

The restrictive fiscal approach of colonial governments, and with this limited capital imports from metropolitan countries, is explained by four main considerations. First, a fundamental tenet of colonial policy was that government revenue from taxes and other sources had to cover recurrent expenditures.[59] These expenditures, including administration, police, defence and pensions, and in

[55] Hlaing, 'Trends of economic growth'.
[56] Schwulst, 'Report', pp. 43, 53, 58.
[57] Lewis, *Growth and fluctuations*, p. 218.
[58] Hooley, 'American economic policy', p. 472.
[59] Edelstein, 'Imperialism: cost and benefit', p. 210.

Table 5.7 *Southeast Asia tax ratios, 1913–37 (government revenue as a % of GDP)*

	1913	1929	1937
Indochina	1.6	1.6	1.4
Indonesia	6.1	11.1	9.8
Malaya	12.1	10.9	15.5
Philippines	7.0	17.0	7.0
Thailand	9.6	9.1	12.2
Burma	15.7	11.6	14.2

Notes: 1. Indochina refers to Vietnam only and figures include central government revenues and revenues of local budgets. The figures omit an estimate of corvée labour, which was not insignificant. 2. For 1913 Malaya includes the Straits Settlements (SS), Federated Malay States (FMS) only and for later dates also the Unfederated Malay States (UMS). For this last, revenue was mainly from Johore and not large in 1913 since that state was still little developed before World War I. In 1929, UMS revenue was 24.6 per cent of SS and FMS revenue and a similar proportion is assumed to estimate Malayan revenue for 1937.

Sources:

Revenue and expenditure:

Burma: Shein et al., '"Provincial contract system" of British Indian Empire', pp. 25–26; Shein, *Burma's transport*, pp. 273–74; Hlaing, 'Public finance', p. 5 (for 1937–38 only).

Thailand: Birnberg and Resnick, *Colonial development*, p. 316; Wilson, *Handbook*, pp. 242–49.

Malaya: Straits Settlements, 'Report on the Straits Settlements', *Straits Settlements annual reports*, issues 1903, p. 589, 1904, p. 189; 1909, p. 439; 1911, pp. 459–60; 1937, I, pp. 1017, 1019; 1938, II, pp. 248–49; Straits Settlements, *Statistical summary 1934*, p. 20; Federated Malay States, *Table of taxes, duties, fees, etc.*, p. 223; Fermor, *Report*, p. 88; Emerson, *Malaysia*, pp. 187, 196, 300; FMS, *Report by the auditor on revenue and expenditure 1939*, p. 1.

Indochina: Bassino, 'Public finance in Vietnam', pp. 287–88.

Indonesia: Creutzberg, *Public finance*, pp. 59, 64–67. Figures are estimated actual revenue and expenditure in Indonesia as opposed to revenue and expenditure relating to Indonesia but expended in the Netherlands.

Philippines: All figures are taken from the general estimate by Hooley, 'American economic policy', p. 472. For revenue figures, see Birnberg and Resnick, *Colonial development*, p. 307.

Gross Domestic Product:

Burma: Hlaing, 'Trends of economic growth', p. 143. Figures are for Net National Product. For 1913 the figure is for 1911/12 and for 1929 it is for 1926/27.

Table 5.7 (*cont.*)

Thailand: van der Eng, private communication, recalculation and extension of GDP figures in Manarungsan, *Economic development*, 1989, p. 251.
Malaya: Nazrin, 'Historical statistics of Malaya', p. 41. These estimates are in current prices but are for peninsular Malaya and exclude Singapore. GDP to include Singapore is estimated by assuming that Singapore's GDP was 39.6 per cent of peninsular Malaya's (the proportion in 1956). GDP for Singapore in 1956 is from Oshima, 'Growth and unemployment', p. 49, and for peninsular Malaya from Lim, *Economic development*, p. 317.
Indochina: Jean-Pascal Bassino, private communication, 1 October 2004.
Indonesia: van der Eng, 'Indonesia's growth performance', pp. 171–72 and using the reflator provided by van der Eng.
Philippines: For GDP figures in 1985 prices, see Hooley, 'American economic policy', pp. 480–81.

which wages and salaries loomed large, took the bulk of available revenues.[60] Low tax ratios, often in deference to European merchant lobbies, and high standing expenditure commitments left little room for additional spending and circumscribed debt service capacity.[61]

The second and third of the four reasons were closely linked, and seem to have had much greater importance than any rate of return analysis in evaluating possible capital projects. One was that such capital spending as occurred had to be consistent with the usual aim of colonial governments to balance budgets over a short period and, if possible, run an overall surplus. The other reason was that government revenue moved with the value of international trade – also its largest single source – and wide fluctuations in commodity prices, not just over a few months but years, encouraged caution.

Over the period 1900 to 1939, all six Southeast Asian countries registered cumulative budget surpluses. With few exceptions, the orthodox and prudent tenets of colonial fiscal policy prevailed. In the inter-war depressions of 1920–22 and 1930–32, only Malaya and Indonesia found themselves with large fiscal deficits. During 1930–32, three of the six countries had healthy surpluses of revenue over expenditure and none ran a deficit bigger than 14 per cent of revenue for the three years.

Not all Southeast Asian countries strictly conformed to this colonial ideal, and some, mainly non-British possessions did not unfailingly wish to do so. Indochina had periods of significant government borrowing in the decade after 1900, and again in the 1930s with the ascendancy of the doctrine of *mise en valeur*, which advocated state-controlled colonial development and spending

[60] Schwulst, 'Report', p. 53.
[61] Hlaing, 'Public finance', pp. 4–5; Booth, *Indonesian economy*, p. 147.

on public works and development if likely to benefit France. In Southeast Asia, Indonesia was exceptional in government's willingness to contract debt. Between 1898 and 1939, Indonesia ran budget deficits in 19 of these 41 years.[62] After the depressions at the beginning of the 1920s and 1930s, government debt stood at over a fifth and two-fifths respectively of GDP.[63] From 1898 to 1920, Indonesian government spending significantly exceeded revenue, almost entirely owing to outlays in the inflationary years 1918–20. But surpluses that accumulated between 1921 and 1939 far outweighed the pre-1921 deficit. Even in Indonesia, government spending never strayed too far or for too long from a balanced budget.[64] Throughout Southeast Asia, commodity-based export economies and the aim of governments to limit borrowing gave little scope for deviation from a policy of being sure of balancing budgets.

The fourth and final reason for the restrictive fiscal approach of colonial governments was that after the turn of the century each of the Southeast Asian economies except Indochina operated a strict, or colonial, currency board system. Under it, the balance of payments almost entirely determined local money supply, and this increased the risk for Southeast Asian governments of contracting fixed interest external debt if they were anxious to avoid the counter-measure of borrowing abroad. Unless capital inflows materialized to offset a fall in export revenue from low commodity prices, the already considerable effect that these price declines had in forcing deflation on Southeast Asia's economies would have been further magnified.

Southeast Asian Capital Export

Investment need not be foreign, and the potential availability of domestic finance in Southeast Asia should also be considered. Maddison estimates that in India, between 1921 and 1938, about one-third of net savings were transferred abroad as remitted profits, government pensions and so forth.[65] Nor, he adds, is it 'clear that India's experience was worse than that of other colonies'. This section shows that Southeast Asian countries exported a significant part of their savings, and suggests reasons for this. Capital export from Southeast Asia shown in this section is similar to the point made by Sultan Nazrin Shah that Malaya failed to benefit from a significant share of the growth its economy generated.[66]

A stages theory of the balance of payments posits that developing regions, in need of capital, first move forward through being international borrowers and,

62 Creutzberg, *Public finance*, pp. 59, 64–67.
63 Booth, *Indonesian economy*, p. 146.
64 Dick et al., *Emergence*, p. 123.
65 Maddison, 'Historical origins of Indian poverty', p. 52.
66 Shah, *Charting the economy*.

like the United States beginning in 1914, become creditors when economically developed.[67] Contrary to this theory, Southeast Asian countries seem from the start generally to have run large current account surpluses, and so always to have been net lenders. Trade data are the best available guide to the balance of payments, and appear to confirm a picture of net capital outflows to the rest of the world (Table 5.8). Over the decades 1870 to 1939, with the exception of Indochina from 1900 to 1909, Southeast Asian countries ran substantial and growing export surpluses.

For the impression suggested by Table 5.8 of Southeast Asia as a net capital exporter to be wrong, imports of services and precious metals, along with invisibles, would have had to be sufficiently large to offset on the current account unrequited transfers on the trade account. But four considerations make it difficult to believe that unrequited trade account transfers as large as the ones shown in the table would have been offset. First, the convention of valuing imports c.i.f. and exports f.o.b. already encompassed a significant part of the services to be recorded as a debit on Southeast Asian countries' current account balance. Second, while it might be argued that dividends, interest and profits from earlier investment created a charge on the balance of payments sufficient to render the current account zero, this seems unlikely. In the late nineteenth century, no net transfer of funds to Southeast Asian countries occurred.

Third, in Southeast Asia, especially Burma, Malaya and Thailand, immigrant remittances added to invisibles. Even in Burma, however, with both Chettiar and Chinese business, as well as large immigrant labour transfers, total outflows never surpassed 30 per cent of Burma's trade surpluses, and would not make up for transfers on the trade account. Figures for Chinese remittances from Southeast Asia are at best imprecise but, with the possible exception of Malaya, appear to have been a smaller proportion of trade surpluses than in Burma.[68]

Fourth, a colonial currency board system flourished in five of the six Southeast Asian countries, and the system had, in practice, to be supported by continuing surpluses on the current account of the balance of payments (Chapter 3). Just as for much of the 1800s, and until World War II, Britain was a large net lender, so too, it would seem, were Southeast Asian countries.[69] They surely, however, contributed to reducing Britain's net lending, since London must have been the destination of a substantial proportion of Southeast Asian capital outflows.

In Southeast Asia, institutional and structural considerations of the dominance of expatriate enterprise, local capital market failure and, in several countries, a heavy reliance on immigrant workers all contributed to the export of

[67] Samuelson and Nordhaus, *Economics*, pp. 673–75.
[68] Huff, 'Monetization'.
[69] Edelstein, 'Foreign investment', pp. 175–76.

Table 5.8 *Southeast Asia average ratio of exports (f.o.b.) to imports (c.i.f.), 1870–1939*

	1870–1879	1880–1889	1890–1899	1900–1909	1910–1919	1920–1929	1930–1939
Burma	134.1	113.2	142.7	158.3	155.5	170.6	227.1
Indochina	–	–	121.5	84.4	130.3	120.4	132.2
Thailand	161.6	188.5	187.7	157.7	141.7	126.9	142.1
Malaya	–	–	–	–	–	111.0[a]	109.9
Indonesia	159.2[b]	139.5	128.2	152.5	179.1	167.5	153.2
Philippines	113.5[c]	118.5	119.9[d]	101.8	110.2	114.8	120.0

Notes: [a] Includes 1921–29 only. [b] Includes 1874–79 only. [c] Excludes 1871. [d] Excludes 1896–98.
Source: As for Table 5.6.

capital. Europeans controlled the leading merchant, banking, shipping and insurance companies, and a high proportion of their equity was owned by overseas shareholders. To them, profit repatriation was automatic. Clearly, shareholders would not always have wished to reinvest in Southeast Asia. But shareholders who did want to invest would have found it practically impossible to do so, except through foreign intermediaries, because of these economies' weak and fragmented capital markets. Much of the immigrant labour drawn to Southeast Asia remained for just a few years, and a principal objective of these workers was to remit home.

Conclusion

Geography and institutional arrangements are at the core of economic development and history.[70] Analysis of infrastructure and foreign investment in Southeast Asia shows why this should be so. Earlier parts of the book demonstrated that rapid Southeast Asian export expansion depended on the geography of a moving frontier, while this chapter showed how geography was fundamental in determining patterns of Southeast Asian infrastructure development. By taking advantage of Southeast Asia's particular geographical features of insular configurations and great rivers, governments in Southeast Asia could avoid much of the heavy spending on infrastructure that would have been necessary under a less favourable geographical configuration. A geography of islands and water facilitated the early stages of Southeast Asian

[70] See, for example, Sokoloff and Engerman, 'Institutions, factor endowments'; McArthur and Sachs, 'Institutions'.

vent-for-surplus growth by offering accessible and low-cost transport, and during later phases of this development continued to limit the need for extensive investment in infrastructure by allowing transport to be mostly by water and not rail.

In Southeast Asia, the prevailing institution of colonialism, aided by a favourable geography, worked against government borrowing and in favour of colonial policies of low taxation, tariffs and financial conservatism. Limited urbanization and little industrialization further explain why, between 1870 and 1939, Southeast Asia received a tiny share of global foreign investment. Contrary to New World experience where natural resources attracted large capital inflows, slight foreign investment in Southeast Asia reflected the region's abundance of natural resources.

6

Urbanization

By 1870, Southeast Asia had experienced two centuries of de-urbanization.[1] There were only two cities, Mandalay and Manila, with possibly as many as 100,000 inhabitants. By the 1930s, although Southeast Asia's primary commodity specialization and lack of industrialization ruled out extensive urbanization, the region had 15 cities of 100,000 or more.

This chapter has two main aims. One is to analyse, in the first section, the emergence in post-1870 Southeast Asia of a few large cities. Other than Java, late nineteenth- and twentieth-century Southeast Asian urbanization was an outgrowth of vent-for-surplus development and the specialization it engendered. In five countries, one city stood out from the others. The five were Burma (Rangoon), Malaya (Singapore), Thailand (Bangkok), Indochina (Saigon) and the Philippines (Manila). Together with these five cities, two in Indonesia, Jakarta and Surabaya, comprised Southeast Asia's seven main cities. In the 1930s, the seven ranged in size from a quarter to over half a million (Figure 6.1). Each of Southeast Asia's seven largest cities served as 'gateways' through which exports passed on the way to overseas markets and through which imports arrived. In functioning as a bridge between hinterlands and foreign markets, these cities provided port, handling, shipping, commercial and financial services for exports and the return flow of imports.

The chapter's other main aim is to examine the growth in Southeast Asia of urban systems, defined as the hierarchical organization of centres based on their size and economic function. Gateway cities and their frontier hinterlands interact dynamically. Gateways are 'spearheads' that advance frontier settlement through the services that they provide.[2] After the gateway is established, lesser cities emerge in a logically and chronologically distinct second growth phase. Urban systems develop as the countryside fills in with smaller cities that provide traditional central place functions such as marketing and distribution to nearby producers. The 'filling in' of the frontier provides a basis for the maturation of gateways and smaller, regional centres into a stable, articulated urban system.[3]

1 Reid, *Southeast Asia*, pp. 1–2, 63–77, 302–3.
2 Burghardt, 'Hypothesis', p. 272.
3 Weiman, 'From old South to new', pp. 39, 46.

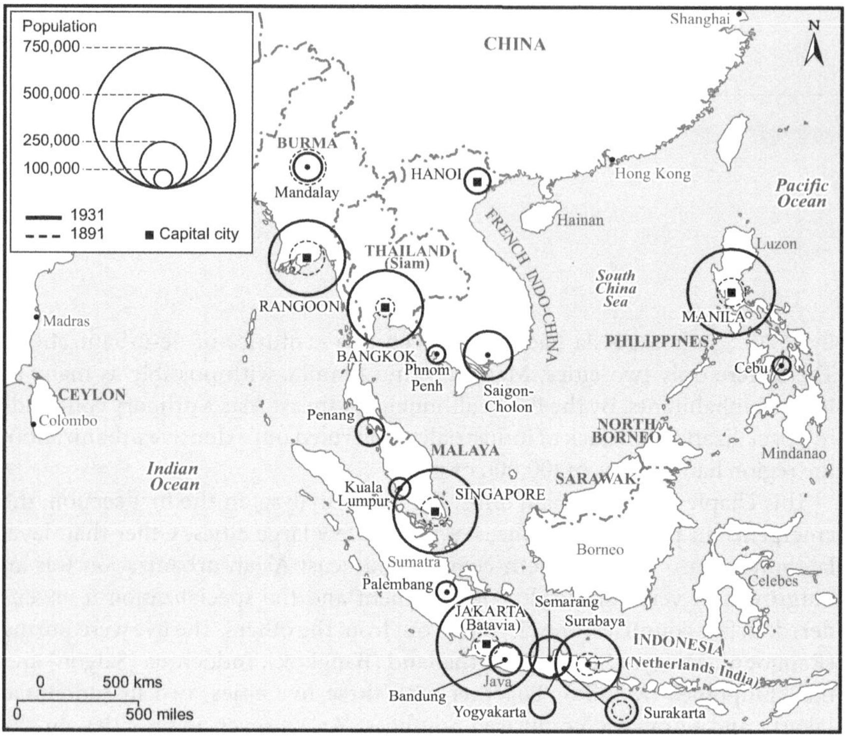

Figure 6.1 Southeast Asia cities of 100,000 and more, 1891 and 1931
Source: See Table 6.1.

This development of urban systems is examined in the chapter's second section. Rank-size distributions and transition matrices demonstrate that the evolution of urban systems differed considerably between countries in degrees of development and that the pace of change was markedly slower in rice-producing countries. By contrast, rubber had substantial urban spread effects. The section also assesses how other factors – geography, path dependence and government policy towards infrastructure development – shaped urban patterns in different Southeast Asian countries.

Gateway Cities

Southeast Asia's seven main cities stood in sharp contrast to a region that remained overwhelmingly rural. As late as the 1930s, in five countries only between about 4 and 8 per cent of Southeast Asians lived in cities of 10,000 or more; Malaya was the exception, with 23.4 per cent of its population in cities as large as, or larger than, 10,000. Very few Southeast Asians inhabited cities of over 100,000 (Tables 6.1 and 6.2). Each of Southeast Asia's main cities had some industry and all except Saigon and Surabaya were national capitals. What defined the principal cities, however, was their role, as Southeast Asia's 'gateways', in connecting the region to the global economy. The cities were all major ports, and had commerce as their main purpose.

The gateway city model, used in this section to analyse the development of Southeast Asia's main cities, applies to an open economic system like Southeast Asia's, geared to the externalization of trade and so its vent-for-surplus economies. Gateway cities grow through a combination of locational fundamentals and increasing returns that encourage a concentration of commercial services. Early gateway city development hinges on spatial, or 'first nature', advantage of transport nodality, through which the cities gain prominence as transport hubs. The cities evolve through self-reinforcing, 'second nature', advantages of population and built environment to establish themselves as centres for commerce and finance.[4] Increasing returns arising from the provision of these commercial services yield incentives for urban agglomeration.

Southeast Asian experience does not sustain the idea in the literature that, through agglomeration effects, initial city size is determinate.[5] In Southeast Asia, cities did not always retain dominance by virtue of being initially the biggest city. Although Manila remained a major city after 1870, Mandalay and Hanoi did not. The post-1870 export-led growth that drew Southeast Asia into the world economy decisively directed the region's main urban centres to peripheries of its export-producing frontiers.

Locational Advantages

Physical geography finds little place in the new economic geography, but physical considerations were fundamental to the post-1870 rise of Southeast Asia's seven main cities. In Southeast Asia, urban comparative advantage deriving from physical features dictated ports near the coasts of their respective countries and optimally located to link frontier areas to the global economy. Southeast Asian gateways were both economically accessible to ocean-going vessels and afforded the best available access to the largest possible frontier exporting regions. A situation that allowed Southeast Asia's gateways to receive, assemble and process primary commodity exports from a large hinterland also allowed efficient distribution of a return flow of manufactured goods and food to the exporting regions.

[4] Cronon, *Nature's metropolis*, p. 264; Weiman, 'From old South to new', p. 39; Krugman, 'First nature, second nature', p. 129.

[5] Krugman, 'Increasing returns', p. 487; Fujita and Mori, 'Role of ports', pp. 371–72.

Table 6.1 *Southeast Asia main urban centres and country populations, 1891–1947 (000 population)*

(a) Cities

	1891	1911	1931	1947
Burma: Rangoon	180.3	293.3	400.4	737.1
Burma: Mandalay	188.8	138.3	147.9	185.9
Burma: Moulmein	55.8	57.6	65.5	102.8
Burma: Bassein	30.2	37.1	45.7	77.9
Malaya: Singapore	153.5	259.6	445.7	679.7
Malaya: Penang	51.6	101.2	149.4	189.1
Malaya: Kuala Lumpur	19.1	46.7	111.4	176.0
Malaya: Ipoh	3.2	24.0	53.2	80.9
Thailand: Bangkok	100.0	130.0	400.0	781.7
Thailand: Chiang Mai	–	–	–	38.2
Thailand: Lampang	–	–	–	23.0
Thailand: Nakhon Ratchasima	–	–	–	22.3
Indonesia: Jakarta	126.7	–	533.0	1,050.0
Indonesia: Surabaya	118.0	–	341.7	400.0
Indonesia: Semarang	71.2	–	217.8	–
Indonesia: Bandung	18.1	–	166.8	–
Indonesia: Surakarta	100.3	–	165.5	–
Indonesia: Yogyakarta	57.5	–	136.6	–
Indochina: Saigon-Cholon	81.0	182.0	256.0	492.2
Indochina: Hanoi	–	114.0	135.0	238.0
Indochina: Phnom Penh	–	62.0	96.0	111.0
Philippines: Manila	154.0	234.4	462.9	983.9
Philippines: Cebu	–	–	95.0	167.5
Philippines: Basilan	–	–	–	110.3
Philippines: Iloilo	–	–	–	110.1

(b) Countries

	1891	1911	1931	1947
Burma	7,772	12,115	14,667	19,051
Malaya	1,710	2,651	4,348	5,900
Thailand	6,670	8,266	11,506	17,443
Indonesia	33,800	–	60,727	–
Indochina	13,400	16,395	21,450	31,397
Philippines	7,635	8,835	13,405	19,234

Table 6.1 (*cont.*)

Notes: Cities are the four largest in 1931 and 1947 but not always in earlier years. In Burma, Sittwe (Akyab) was slightly larger than Bassein from 1891 to 1911. In Malaya, Malacca was larger than Ipoh in 1891 and 1901. A number of Indonesian cities were bigger than Bandung in 1890. For 1891 for Indonesia and Indochina populations are interpolated and approximate.

Sources:

Burma:

Urban Population: Burma, Census Department, *Towns classified by population*, p. 2; India, *Census of India, 1931. vol. XI. Burma*, Part II, pp. 280–81; Saito and Lee, *Statistics on the Burmese economy*, p. 16. Figures for 1938 refer to 1941 and are from Murphey, 'New capitals', p. 22. *Population*: Hlaing, *Study*, p. 13; Saito and Lee, *Statistics on the Burmese economy*, p. 7 for 1938–83. For 1938 population data refer to 1941.

Malaya:

Urban Population: Straits Settlements, *Report on the census, 1891*, pp. 47, 87, 104; Straits Settlements, *Report on the census of the Straits Settlements, 1901*, pp. 30, 71; Federated Malay States, *Census of population, 1901*, pp. 28; Federated Malay States, *Review of the census operations, 1911*, p. 25; Malaya, *Report on the 1947 census*, p. 44; Huff, *Economic growth*, p. 158; Marriott, 'Population of the Straits Settlements', pp. 34–41; Malaya, *Population census, 1957*, pp. 8, 53; Arumainathan, *Report on the census of population 1970*, vol. 1: 231. The figures for 1938 refer to 1936 and for Penang and Kuala Lumpur are estimated assuming proportionate population growth between 1931 and 1947. *Population*: The 1881 population is estimated by assuming that population grew at the same rate as in 1891–1901. For 1891 and 1901 figures are estimated for the Unfederated Malay States (UMS) only. Estimation is on the basis of a 1911 census figure of a UMS population of 899,968 persons and backwards extrapolation assuming that during both decades the population grew at 0.65 per cent per annum. A basis for this assumed rate of UMS population growth is Dodge, 'Population estimates', pp. 457–74. Data for 1891–1911 are from Federated Malay States, *Review of the census operations, 1911*, pp. 18, 95; Malaya, *Census of British Malaya, 1921*, p. 18. For 1921–47 data are from Malaya, *Report on the 1947 census*, p. 39; Malaya, *Population census, 1957, Final report*, p. 3; Arumainathan, *Report on the census of population 1970*, vol. 1, p. 31. The 1938 population figure refers to 1936 and is an estimate which assumes proportional population growth between 1931 and the 1947 census figure of 5,848,910 persons.

Thailand:

Urban Population: Because data for Thailand are for municipal areas, I rely for figures for Bangkok's urban population on the calculations of Sternstein, 'Growth'. The figures for Bangkok include Bangkok and Thonburi. Thailand, *Statistical yearbook of Thailand, 1963*, p. 52 gives statistics for municipal areas;

Table 6.1 (*cont.*)

see also Wilson, *Handbook*, p. 38 for municipal data for 1947–70. Apart from Bangkok, the earliest available data for 'centres' are for 1943. These centres, for the larger of their number, correspond to a measure of municipal population (Sternstein, 'Critique', pp. 24–25). Before 1947 figures for Bangkok are estimated by applying a log scale to the vertical axis in the figure that shows Sternstein's ('Growth') estimates of the population of built-up Bangkok and reading the population from the regression line that he fits. Population estimates are for 1880, 1890, 1900, 1910, 1920, 1930 and 1940. In 1970, when Bangkok had a population of 2,495,312, Chiang Mai, the second city, had only 83,729 inhabitants. Wilson, *Handbook*, p. 27. *Population*: For 1881–1901 figures are from Skinner, *Chinese society*, p. 79 and refer to 1880, 1890 and 1900. Subsequent figures are from Thailand, *Statistical yearbook of Thailand*, issues for 1937–38 and 1939–40, and refer to the census returns for 1911, 1919, 1929 and 1937.
Indonesia:
Urban Population: Indonesia, *Koloniaal verslag 1892*, pp. 6–7; Indonesia, *Centraal kantoor voor de Statistiek*, pp. 23–25; Indonesia, *Volkstelling 1930*, vol. 1, pp. 122–23, vol. 2, pp. 146–49, vol. 3, pp. 124–25, vol. 4, pp. 142–43, vol. 5, pp. 141–42, vol. 8, pp. 78–81; Indonesia, *Statistical pocketbook of Indonesia 1941*, p. 13; Boomgaard and Gooszen, *Population trends*, pp. 220–21, 245. Data for 1891, 1921 and 1931 are for 1890, 1920 and 1930. Data for 1939 and 1948 for Jakarta and Surabaya are from Dick, *Surabaya*, p. 123. *Population*: Indonesia: Data for 1891, 1901, 1921 and 1931 are for 1890, 1905, 1920 and 1930. For 1890, Outer Province population is estimated by assuming that between 1890 and 1905 it grew at 1.25 per cent annually. The estimate is based on Gooszen, *Demographic history*, p. 8. She suggests Indonesian population growth rates in the range of 1 per cent to 1.25 per cent. Available statistics suggest that from 1890 to 1905 the population of Java and Madura grew at 1.56 per cent. Boomgaard and Gooszen, *Population trends*, pp. 117–21, 133–37, 224–30.
Indochina:
Urban Population: Indochina, *Annuaire statistique 1923–29*, pp. 30–31, 61, *1931–32*, p. 53, *1943–46*, p. 27. A population estimate for 1921 indicated the following: Cholon 200,000 of which 130,000 were Chinese, Saigon 100,000, Hanoi 100,000 and Phnom Penh 100,000 (Indochina, *Annuaire statistique 1923–29*, p. 28). For Saigon-Cholon data for 1891, 1902, 1911, 1921, 1931 and 1938 are for 1890, 1902, 1910, 1921, 1930 and 1936 and for Hanoi data are for 1900, 1910, 1920, 1930 and 1936; and for Phnom Penh data for 1901, 1911, 1938 and 1946 are for 1900, 1910, 1936 and 1948. For 1946 for Saigon-Cholon and Phnom Penh data are for 1948. *Population*: Figures for 1880 and 1911 are from Brocheux and Hémery, *Indochina*, p. 254 and are orders of magnitude. The figure for 1911 refers to 1913 and that for 1938 refers to 1936. The 1901 figure is for 1906 and from Smolski, 'Les statistiques de la population', p. 56. For population figures for Cochinchina for 1880 to 1936, see Sansom, *Economics*, pp. 259, 261; 1910: Coquerel, *Paddys et riz*, p. 225; Indochina,

Table 6.1 (*cont.*)

Annuaire statistique 1923–29, p. 61, *1931–32*, p. 53, *1943–46*, p. 271. The 1946 Indochina population is for 1950.
Philippines:
Urban Population: The figure for 1891 includes rural areas of Manila township and is from Mitchell, *International historical statistics: Africa, Asia and Oceania*, p. 41. For 1901, 1921 and 1938 figures for Manila, and for Cebu and Iloilo for 1901 only, are for 1903, 1918 and 1939 and from Philippines, *Census of the Philippine Islands, 1903*, vol. 2, pp. 129–30; Philippines, *Census of the Philippine Islands, 1918*, vol. 2, p. 20; Philippines, *Census of the Philippines: 1939*, vol. 2, p. 59; Philippines, Bureau of the Census and Statistics, *Yearbook of Philippine statistics, 1946*, p. 10. The 1931 population of Manila is estimated by calculating the mean growth for Manila for 1918–39 and assuming that population grew at the same rate (0.0372) between 1918 and 1931. Data for 1911–31 for Cebu are from Murphey, 'New capitals', p. 227 and refer to 1910, 1918 and 1929. The 1931 population of Cebu is estimated by applying a 1929–41 growth rate (0.0410) to the 1929 population. The 1939 census shows Zamboanga as a city of 131,455 but in fact it was chartered to include an area of 1,139 square miles and the actual urban area contained only about 18,000 people. Wernstedt and Spencer, *Philippine island world*, p. 171. For 1948 population by cities is from Philippines, *Handbook of Philippine statistics 1903–1959*, p. 8. *Population*: For 1881 the figure refers to 1877. It is the census figure that year for 'civilized people' (5,567 million) plus the 1903 census figure for 'wild people' transformed into an estimate for 1877 under the assumption of population growth of 0.60 per cent per annum. Philippines, *Census of the Philippine Islands, 1903*, vol. 2, pp. 19, 123. The 1901 figure is for 1903 and from the census for that year (Philippines, *Census of the Philippine Islands, 1903*, vol. 2, p. 123). The 1921 figure refers to 1918 and is the census figure (Philippines, *Census of the Philippine Islands, 1918*, vol. 2, p. 19). Figures for 1911 and 1931 are estimates and from Philippines, Bureau of Commerce, *Statistical bulletin 1920*, p. 13 and Philippines, *Yearbook of Philippine statistics, 1940*, p. 24. For 1931 the figure refers to 1930. The figure for 1938 is for the census of 1 January 1939 and is from Philippines, Commission of the Census, *Special bulletin no. 1, Census of the Philippines, 1939*, p. 3. For 1948 population is from Philippines, *Handbook of Philippine statistics 1903–1959*, p. 5.

Gateway cities can be likened to positioning at the point of a fan.[6] For Rangoon, Bangkok and Saigon, river systems were the transport arteries around which gateway fans formed. Rangoon lay 21 miles from the sea, on one of the distributing mouths of the Irrawaddy River. Like other delta cities (Shanghai,

[6] Burghardt, 'Hypothesis', pp. 273–74.

Table 6.2 *Southeast Asia urbanization ratios, 1891–1947*

(a) % of population in cities of 10,000 and over

	1891	1901	1911	1921	1931	1947
Burma	7.8	6.7	6.2	6.5	7.5	11.5
Malaya	13.1	17.9	19.3	22.8	23.4	26.9
Thailand	–	–	–	–	–	6.3
Indonesia: total	–	–	–	5.2	7.0	–
Indonesia: Java	4.5	–	–	6.2	8.3	–
Indonesia: Outer Islands	–	–	–	2.6	4.2	–
Indochina	–	–	–	–	3.9	–
Philippines	–	–	–	–	–	–

(b) % of population in cities of 100,000 and over

	1891	1901	1911	1921	1931	1947
Burma	4.8	4.0	3.6	3.7	3.7	5.4
Malaya	8.9	9.3	13.6	14.2	16.2	17.7
Thailand	1.5	1.8	2.2	3.0	3.5	4.5
Indonesia: total	0.9	–	–	1.8	2.7	–
Indonesia: Java	1.1	–	–	2.6	3.7	–
Indonesia: Outer Islands	0.0	–	–	0.0	0.6	–
Indochina	0.0	1.7	1.8	1.4	1.8	2.7
Philippines	–	2.9	2.7	2.8	3.5	7.7

Notes: For 1881 the proportion of population in cities of 100,000 and over was 6.8 per cent in Malaya and 0.8 per cent for Thailand. For Burma 1947 refers to 1953.
Sources: See Table 6.1.

Rotterdam), Rangoon's location avoided some of the silting and strong currents of the main stream. Moreover, the city was the only point controlling both approaches to the heart of Burma, by the Irrawaddy and Sittang Rivers.[7] Rangoon gave 'access to almost the whole of the productive part of the country'.[8] Up-country from Rangoon, the Irrawaddy was navigable all year round for 874 miles inland. Saigon was similarly located on another of Asia's great rivers, the Mekong.[9] The port's natural advantage of location was then enhanced by

[7] Spate, *Burma setting*, p. 30.
[8] Murphey, 'New capitals', p. 232.
[9] Dobby, *Southeast Asia*, pp. 303–04.

large French infrastructural investment. Bangkok, the only significant port in Thailand, was situated where rice exports could be most economically assembled via the Chao Phraya River and its tributaries.[10]

Singapore, positioned at the tip of the Malay Peninsula and at the southernmost extension of continental Asia, controlled the shortest international water route between the Indian Ocean and South China Sea.[11] The port's central situation within Southeast Asia, and so its geographical advantage, was also evident. Partly because of location, Singapore pulled towards itself most of Malaya's trade, and also much of that of Sumatra and Borneo.

Manila, historically a trading centre, was like Singapore in possessing a magnificent natural harbour. The Philippines gateway was 'well situated to collect and ship' the products on which colonial Philippines trade was based.[12] For Indonesia, Jakarta, in conjunction with its port of Tanjung Priok five miles to the north-east, occupied 'by far the best location' for maritime communications, being at the head of a large bay and commanding the Sunda Strait.[13] Surabaya was as much a gateway as Jakarta. In the late nineteenth and early twentieth centuries, it became 'the gateway to the fertile valley of the Brantas River' as that region specialized in growing sugar for export. On that basis, Surabaya emerged as one of Asia's great port cities.[14]

Trade, Marketing, Information, and Banking Services

The late nineteenth-century industrial revolution dramatically increased international trade and commercial and financial services related to it. These services, by their nature subject to increasing returns, created incentives for urban agglomeration. This sub-section measures the density of banking in Southeast Asia's gateways, while the next sub-section quantifies the tendency in Southeast Asian countries for the gap between the largest and second city to widen.

All of Southeast Asia's gateway cities were the principal, and generally the only large, port in their respective countries. Although gateways initially provide physical services such as the handling and processing of primary commodities, if the city is to consolidate its importance and become a metropolis, it does so by intensifying economic centrality through the supply of higher order services. These include information, mercantile and financial services. Bigger trade volumes, arising from export-led growth and increased market size, led to

10 Murphey, 'New capitals', p. 234.
11 Lady Raffles, *Memoir*, p. 378; Raffles, 'Founding of Singapore', p. 74.
12 Robequain, *Malaya, Indonesia*, p. 293; Murphey, 'New capitals', p. 244.
13 Naval Intelligence Division, *Netherlands East Indies*, vol. 2, p. 343; Murphey, 'New capitals', p. 238.
14 Dick et al., *Emergence*, pp. xvii, 419, 434–35; Naval Intelligence Division, *Netherlands East Indies*, vol. 2, pp. 358–59.

a greater division of labour in service provision. With this specialization came increasing returns and the urban agglomerative effects. It was through providing these higher order services that Southeast Asia's gateway cities gained in importance and justify their description as metropolises.

At the same time as promoting urban growth by providing higher order services, the gateway helped to transform frontier into hinterland. By linking hinterlands to world markets, the gateway transmitted stimuli for increased primary commodity export production and hinterland economic growth. If staple exports are to be regarded as an engine of growth, Southeast Asian gateways functioned as the drive shaft of this process.

Merchant services, together with the complexity of such services that gateway cities promoted, have already been explored in Chapter 3. Financial services, including the European 'exchange banks', which had as their main function the financing of long-distance trade, concentrated in these cities. Everywhere except Malaya, gateway city banking density, measured as European- and Asian-owned banks per million population, was several times that in the country as a whole. In their respective countries, Bangkok, Rangoon and Saigon had half to two-thirds, Singapore 29.4 per cent and Manila 18.1 per cent of all banks. Banking in Indonesia concentrated in Jakarta and Surabaya and divided almost equally between them (Table 6.3).

Primate Cities

Between the 1870s and World War II, population size gaps between gateway cities and their respective second largest city typically widened. The suggestion, associated with Krugman, that an orientation towards external markets decreases urban concentration and produces two cities of equal size, is not borne out by Southeast Asian experience.[15] As the Southeast Asian metropolis emerged between the turn of the century and the 1930s, the ratio of the first to the second largest city widened throughout Southeast Asia except in the Philippines. The increasing size of almost all of Southeast Asia's largest cities relative to second biggest cities gave pre-World War II urban growth an undeniable 'lopsidedness'. That same imbalance is apparent when measuring the largest city as a percentage of the four biggest cities (Table 6.4).

Nevertheless, not all the largest Southeast Asian cities in each country were primate, or over twice the size of the second biggest city. While in each of Southeast's Asia's six main countries, four of the six most populous urban concentrations were primate cities, Jakarta and Saigon were not. Jakarta, at the west of Java, and Surabaya, on the island's eastern fringe, ranked about equally as Indonesia's major ports. Hanoi was the French colonial capital and, partly because of this administrative role, was more than half the size of Saigon.

[15] Krugman, 'Increasing returns', pp. 17–19.

Table 6.3 *Southeast Asia banks and banking density, 1940*

	No. of banks	Banks per million total population	Banks per million persons in largest city	% banks in largest city	No. of cities outside the largest with banks
Thailand	12	1.04	20.0	66.6	3
Burma	34	2.31	42.5	50.0	15
Indochina	23	1.07	19.5	47.8	11
Malaya	68	15.64	49.4	29.4	20
Indonesia	102	1.68	18.8	9.8	38
Philippines	72	5.40	28.1	18.1	50

Note: In Indonesia Surabaya had more banks (11) than Jakarta. All the banks in Surabaya were branches. Dick, *Surabaya*, p. 417.
Source: Bankers' almanac, 1941.

Urban Plural Societies

Gateway cities disproportionately attracted immigrants. Singapore and Bangkok were Chinese cities, Rangoon an Indian one. Chinese comprised three-quarters of Singapore's population, Indians half of those in Rangoon, and Chinese probably a like proportion in Bangkok. Mass immigration gave full expression to Southeast Asia's plural societies. Residential localization and occupational specialization reinforced each other. Chinese and Indian arrivals clustered in well-demarcated areas of the cities, concentrated in their centres and in specific lines of work. In Rangoon, Burmese were 'crowded out of the centre of the town and lived in areas where the sprawling city merged into garden land and rice fields';[16] Malays were pushed to the fringes of Singapore. Throughout Southeast Asia, Asians in business were generally Chinese or Indian and often immigrants, but immigrants also largely supplied menial labour, work that indigenous groups shunned.

Throughout urban and rural Southeast Asia, part of the explanation for the persistence of the plural society's several non-competing economic groups and their different remuneration levels was a sense of group cohesion: employees and employers alike supported maintenance in the workplace of sharp ethnic and language cleavages. As one group or another arrived, it gravitated to areas where people spoke the same language or dialect as the newly arrived immigrants did, ate the same food and had the same system of beliefs or religion. There were also people with whom a new arrival could stay while finding a job, and

[16] Christian, *Burma*, pp. 71–72.

Table 6.4 *Southeast Asia indexes of centralization and primacy, 1891–1957*

(a) Ratio of the first to second largest city

	1891	1901	1911	1921	1931	1938	1947	1957
Burma	1.0	1.3	2.1	2.3	2.7	3.1	4.0	–
Malaya	3.0	2.1	2.6	2.8	3.0	–	3.6	2.9
Thailand	–	–	–	–	–	–	20.5	25.9
Indonesia	1.1	–	–	1.6	1.6	–	–	2.9
Indochina	–	1.6	1.6	2.2	1.9	1.7	2.1	–
Philippines	–	7.1	–	4.4	4.9	4.0	5.9	5.9

(b) Population of the largest city as a % of the largest four cities

	1891	1901	1911	1921	1931	1947
Burma	39.6	46.1	55.7	57.5	60.7	66.8
Malaya	63.8	57.6	60.2	59.3	58.7	60.4
Thailand	–	–	–	–	–	90.3
Indonesia	30.5	–	–	38.7	–	42.3
Indochina	–	–	–	–	44.3	–
Philippines	–	–	–	–	–	71.7

Notes: For Burma 1947 refers to 1953; for Indonesia data in panel b are for 1890, 1920 and 1930 and in panel a 1957 refers to 1961; for the Philippines 1947 refers to 1948 and 1957 to 1958; and for Indochina 1931 in panel b refers to 1936.
Source: See Table 6.1.

who might help in obtaining one, probably in the same line of work as many in the group already undertook. Most immigrants and migrants lacked job experience and skills appropriate to Southeast Asia, and tended to be pushed into certain jobs according to their ethnic affiliation.[17] A group might originally specialize in an occupation because its time of arrival coincided with that occupation's expansion. Subsequently, new arrivals expected, and were expected, to seek jobs associated with their particular group. The presence of their fellows in these jobs made it natural to do so, and continuous labour force turnover through immigration and migration perpetuated the process and provided its rationale.

The other main reason for the continued ethnic segmentation of the plural society and the differences in remuneration for different groups derived from

[17] Cf. Vaughan, *Manners and customs*, pp. 15–16; Hodder, 'Racial groupings', pp. 27, 33, 34.

divergences in the supply prices of labour in areas of emigration. Once in Southeast Asia, ethnic groups sought to exclude other, lower-waged groups to avoid wages being bid down. Ethnic group exclusion, reinforced by language and cultural differences, was sufficiently strong that groups from the poorest areas found themselves largely confined to the provision of marginal labour in Southeast Asia. The arrival of more of those in a poorly paid group only further swelled its numbers, eroding Southeast Asian remuneration levels until these equalled the group's labour supply price at home.[18]

In Rangoon, over 90 per cent of semi-skilled and unskilled workers were Indian, including nearly all dock labourers, rickshaw pullers and sweepers and scavengers. Indian labour in Rangoon faced chronic underemployment and was willing to work for wages so low that few Burmese would accept them, ensuring indigenous group exclusion.[19] Indian immigrants to Burma reflected the divisions and divergent living standards of their home population. Each different group disproportionately followed certain occupations. Bengalis worked as clerks and in a subordinate capacity in government; a large share of Chittagonians were engaged in sampan and small craft traffic; and Uriyas (from the district of Ganjam in the Madras Presidency and from Bihar and Orissa) furnished the bulk of labour for railways and public works. The Gujaratis and Suratis formed Rangoon's mercantile community. At the bottom of the wage hierarchy, the Telugus, who came principally from the Coromandel coast and Ceded Districts in Deccan (now the Rayalaseema region of Andhra Pradesh), worked in mills and factories, as porters, carriers and rickshaw pullers. Those from the area's Nellore district belonged to the scavenging class and furnished most of Rangoon's sweepers.[20]

Singapore Chinese split into the Chinese and the English-educated, forming 'two solid and distinctive classes'.[21] Among the majority Chinese-educated, a complex ethnic division of labour obtained among *pang* or dialect groups. Hokkien is the dialect pronunciation for Fukien (Fujian), but the overseas Chinese known as Hokkiens came only from the area around the port of Amoy in that province. It was significant for understanding the Singapore division of work along ethnic lines that inter-intelligible dialects were spoken by Hokkiens and Teochews, the latter originating from that part of Kwangtung (Guangdong) province near the port of Swatow and adjacent to the Fukien border. The other Chinese groups, speaking dialects understood by no group in Singapore but themselves, were the Cantonese from Kwangtung province; the Hainanese from the island of Hainan off Kwangtung; and the Hakka from the provinces of Kwangtung and Fukien. The other dialect groups were mainly

[18] Lewis, *Racial conflict*, pp. 38–40, 53–54, 120.
[19] Baxter, *Report*, pp. 37, 53–54.
[20] Andrew, *Indian labour*, pp. 35–37.
[21] Yong, 'Preliminary study', p. 283.

the Hokchia and Hokchew, who were from northern Fukien including the area around the port of Foochow, and spoke dialects different from those of the larger groups.[22]

The Hokkien, who 'are of an urban habit and have a genius for trade and shopkeeping',[23] dominated Chinese commerce, including the rubber trade and banking.[24] Singapore Teochew achieved their greatest commercial presence in the trades in tropical produce, piece goods, rice and other foodstuffs.[25] Cantonese, reflecting what was considered to be a mechanical proclivity, supplied the bulk of artisans in Singapore;[26] while, at least until the late 1930s, most Cantonese women who joined the labour force became either domestic servants or prostitutes. In 1921, 'practically all the Chinese prostitutes are Cantonese'.[27]

Most rickshaw pullers in Singapore came from poor areas of China, and were the Hokchew and, especially, Hokchia, so that in 1931 Singapore Municipality contained well over half of all Hokchia in Malaya.[28] Furthermore, 'The Hokchia and Hokchew dialects control most of the night stalls in Singapore ... Their customers are mostly rickshaw pullers'.[29] Although Hainanese managed to establish themselves to some extent in shopkeeping and particularly the coffee shop trade, the majority 'engaged in domestic service, nine out of ten servants in European establishments belonging to this tribe'.[30] Hakka had more varied employment than other groups, probably because they came from scattered areas in China and often spoke a second dialect. However, Hakka ran most pawnshops and Chinese drugstores.[31]

Until well after World War II, a segmented labour market persisted in Singapore, with consequent large income differentials between the Malays, Indians and Chinese. Among the Chinese, income differentials were substantial. A 1953–54 survey found that 'The Hokkien are the best off, followed by the Hakka and the Teochew. The Cantonese are fourth, while the Hainanese come a very bad last.'[32] Labour market segmentation, like economic dualism, was a

22 Freedman, *Chinese family*, pp. 12–15.

23 Malaya, *Malaya, a report on the 1947 census*, p. 76, and see Malaya, *Census of British Malaya, 1921*, p. 79; Malaya, *British Malaya: a report on the 1931 census*, p. 80.

24 Goh, *Urban incomes*, p. 19; Tan, 'Chinese emigration', pp. 44–45.

25 Goh, *Urban incomes*, p. 19; Lee, *Chinese society*, pp. 100–6.

26 Bingham, *Report*, p. 3; Hodder, 'Racial groupings', p. 34.

27 Malaya, *Census of British Malaya, 1921*, p. 80.

28 Malaya, *British Malaya: a report on the 1931 census*, p. 82; Malaya, *Census of British Malaya, 1921*, p. 84.

29 *SSLCP 1932*, 'Hawker question', p. C27.

30 Malaya, *British Malaya: a report on the 1931 census*, p. 81, and see Malaya, *Census of British Malaya, 1921*, p. 83; Malaya, *Malaya, a report on the 1947 census*, p. 76.

31 Goh, *Urban incomes*, p. 19; Hodder, 'Racial groupings', p. 36; Malaya, *Malaya, a report on the 1947 census*, p. 75.

32 Goh, *Urban incomes*, p. 18, and see p. 19.

legacy that Singapore carried forward into the 1950s. Both were, however, to disappear under the pressure of rapid 1970s and 1980s economic growth.

Urban Systems

This section constructs rank-size distributions and transition matrices to analyse urban development beyond Southeast Asia's gateway cities.[33] The production characteristics of vent-for-surplus staples helped to shape patterns of urbanization, because they heavily influenced the way in which the frontier 'filled in' with cities as new areas were settled. In Burma, Thailand and Cochinchina, rice did little to fill in the frontier or further urban growth outside gateway cities. By contrast, in Malaya, finance and marketing arrangements associated with rubber promoted an expanding and increasingly interconnected urban system.

Java, like Malaya, gained a relatively articulated and integrated urban system. In Java, however, an insular geography, international transport cost minimization and an elaborate railway infrastructure were chief determinants of the urban system. As an island, Java afforded greater scope for small, coastal ports, and so urbanization, than mainland Southeast Asia. Furthermore, Dutch colonial policy, which led to the construction of a dense railway network, promoted Javanese urban integration.

Data Sources and Limitations

Data derive largely from censuses assembled from multiple sources. Two main data gaps exist. One is that for some countries not even skeletal censuses were taken until after the turn of the century. Nor were pre-1900 censuses always complete. Indonesia's 1890 census, largely just a population count, was only for Java. In omitting the Outer Islands, the census excluded a large area of Indonesia, although no cities as big as 100,000 and at most a few of over 10,000. In Thailand, initial attempts in 1904 and 1909 to take censuses were 'piecemeal'.[34] The 1936 Indochina census – reliant on capitation tax returns for persons aged 18 to 60 and the evaluations of local headmen – is approximate and probably understates Saigon-Cholon's population.[35] For Malaya, Burma and Indonesia, the last pre-war census was at the beginning of the 1930s. Almost nothing of the 1941 Burma census survives.[36]

[33] Urban is defined as an unbroken concentration of 10,000 inhabitants or more. While in Southeast Asia populations of 100,000 and over were clearly large cities, there is no universally accepted lower limit of urban size and 10,000 must be somewhat arbitrary. It satisfies, however, the criteria that an urban settlement is big enough to obtain sufficient data and avoids mistaking villages for towns.

[34] Skinner, *Chinese society*, p. 73.

[35] Smolski, 'Statistiques de la population', p. 60.

[36] Sundrum, 'Urbanisation', p. 113.

The second data gap is for the Philippines until the 1930s and for Thailand until the later 1940s. Data are, the very largest Philippine cities apart, for administrative districts ('municipalities') rather than urban areas of an unbroken concentration of buildings and habitation.[37]

Rank-size Distributions

Rank-size distributions provide an empirical measure of the development and maturity of Southeast Asian urban systems (Figures 6.2 to 6.5). To derive these distributions, the log of city size is regressed on cities ranked by size. Computationally, this may be expressed as $\log P = \log k - q(\log R)$ where P is population, R is rank and k and q are constants. Distributions which, when plotted, closely approximate a straight line with a slope of $-q$ can be regarded as lognormal. Lognormality would indicate a mature urban system in which the extensive interaction of cities with one another has given rise to an articulated urban structure.[38]

A special case of lognormality, and common benchmark to assess urban integration, has a slope of –1.00 and so perfect log linearity. Such a distribution, identified in the 1920s as often true of urban ordering and popularized by G. K. Zipf, conforms to the rank-size rule: the second largest in a series is half the size of the biggest or first-ranked, the third largest a third the size of the biggest, and so on.[39]

At one rank-size extreme – in Southeast Asia (and the world) most nearly true of pre-World War II Bangkok – a single city would contain all urban population. The slope of a regression of city size on rank would be infinite. The other extreme, a collection of equally sized cities and a regression line with zero slope, would reflect a grouping of small, autonomous urban areas without significant linkages to one another. In practice, no country of any size approaches, over its entire range of cities, this flat distribution. Often, however, within distributions there is a bunching of (usually relatively small) cities with a quite gently sloped, even plateau-like, distribution. At the upper end of city-size distributions for developing regions, a comparatively flat slope, generally thought of as around –0.50, often occurs. Flatness at the top, and concavity for the distribution as a whole, points to an immature and weakly integrated urban system.[40]

A reason for weak integration is that in natural-resource-dependent countries just starting to develop, the growth of major ports and transport nodes

37 Spencer, 'Cities of the Philippines', pp. 288–94; Sternstein, 'Growth', pp. 44–47; Wilson, *Thailand*, p. 27.

38 Berry and Horton, *Geographical perspectives*; Richardson, 'Theory'; Smith, 'Modern and premodern' and 'Types of city-size distribution'.

39 Zipf, *Human behavior*.

40 Smith, 'Types of city-size distribution', pp. 27, 41.

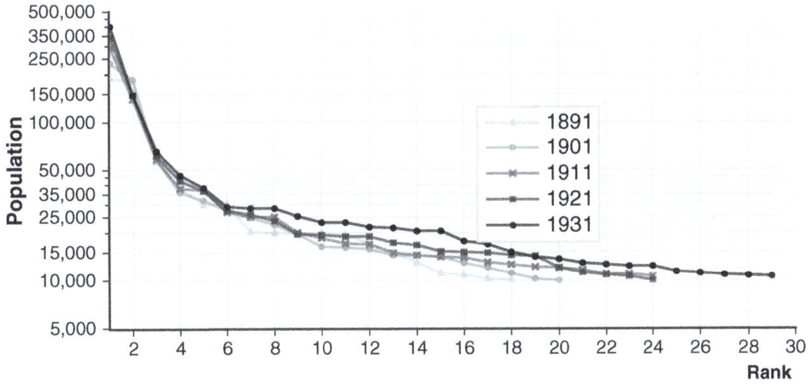

Figure 6.2 Burma rank-size distributions, 1891–1931
Source: See Table 6.1.

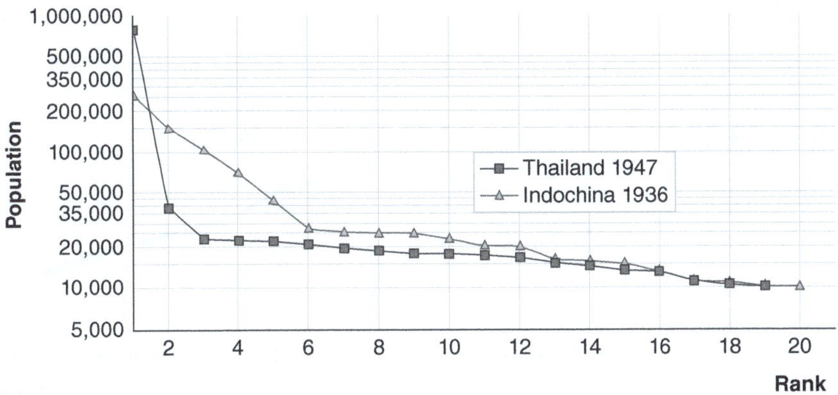

Figure 6.3 Indochina 1936 and Thailand 1947 rank-size distributions
Source: See Table 6.1.

provides the initial basis for urbanization.[41] The early growth of Southeast Asia's gateways fits that pattern. Vent-for-surplus growth depended on the natural resource of frontier land and, as the gateway model specifies, the frontier 'filled in' with cities only in the course of development.

Rank-size distributions of urban systems are subject to various irregularities.[42] They require, as de Vries and also Smith emphasize, careful,

41 Parr, 'Note on the size distribution', p. 208.
42 Parr, 'Class of deviations', pp. 285–92.

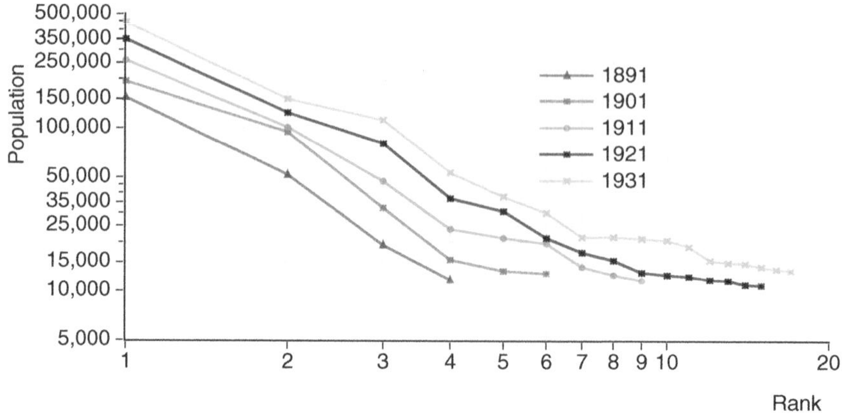

Figure 6.4 Malaya rank-size distributions, 1891–1931
Source: See Table 6.1.

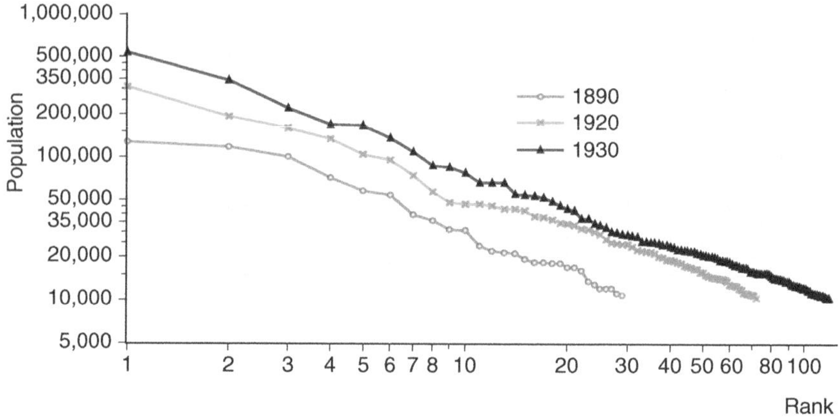

Figure 6.5 Indonesia rank-size distributions, 1890–1930
Source: See Table 6.1.

historically informed interpretation.[43] For numerous European and Asian pre-modern and developing countries, conformity (or not) to lognormality and a Zipfian slope of minus unity have been used as an investigative standard and the norm towards which city systems should trend. Although not previously applied to Southeast Asia, this standard, carefully treated, is helpful in assessing pre-war Southeast Asian urbanization. By the 1930s, some Southeast Asian city systems conformed – if sometimes for historically divergent reasons and perhaps over a limited number of cities – tolerably well to the rank-size rule.

[43] de Vries, *European urbanization*; Smith, 'Types of city-size distribution'.

But others did not, and their urban systems remained weakly integrated and unarticulated.

Figures 6.2 to 6.5 show rank-size distributions for the five Southeast Asian countries with available data for cities of 10,000 and over. When cities become larger, rank-size curves shift upwards. An increase in cities over 10,000 shifts a distribution rightwards. Changes in the slope of a curve, either as a whole or along its contours, indicate relative growth in different-sized cities.

Between 1891 and 1931 in Burma, the faster-than-average growth of Rangoon and decline of Mandalay transformed a flat-topped distribution into, by 1931, an approximately lognormal one with a slope of –0.94 (Figure 6.2). More striking, however, and indicative of a limited need for urban functions outside Rangoon, was that over four decades, rank-size curves shifted only slightly. The main shift occurred between 1921 and 1931, when cities of around 20,000 to 25,000 grew relatively rapidly to form a roughly plateau distribution. The move up-country of some rice milling after 1910, facilitated by the availability of new German-made machinery and easy finance, probably contributed to this plateau by promoting growth in several smaller cities (Chapter 4). However, these traded little among themselves, limiting urban development; Burma was 'essentially a country of villages'.[44] Rangoon remained the focus of marketing and finance for Burma's rice exports.[45]

The specification of an appropriate region is important in rank-size analysis. Exclusion from Burma's distribution of the one-time Burmese capital of Mandalay in north-central Burma on the (substantially true) grounds of limited integration with the 'modern' parts of the southern rice-exporting economy would create an urban distribution which at its top sharply descended from Rangoon (400,400 population in 1931) to the next largest city, Moulmein (65,500).[46] The slope, if less extreme, would look like the 1947 distribution for Thailand where (Figure 6.3) the distribution drops from Bangkok (400,000) to Chiang Mai (about 30,000).

In Thailand, the 1947 distribution's very gentle slope, beginning with the third city, reflects several small, relatively autonomous cities with limited central place functions. The gateway model's second 'filling in' phase remained largely absent. Looking at early 1950s Thailand, it is doubtful, Bangkok apart, whether any Thai population centre deserved the title of city: 'the nation possesses no middle-sized cities, no small cities, but only towns, the largest of which has a population of less than 50,000'.[47]

Indochina as a whole shows a flat-top, pre-modern distribution (Figure 6.3). But for Indochina's main rice-growing area of Cochinchina (4.8 million people

44 Spate, *Burma setting*, p. 28 and see page numbered 20 between pp. 25 and 26.

45 Grant, *Rice crop*, pp. 29–30; Spate, 'Beginnings', pp. 79–83.

46 On the contrast between Rangoon and Mandalay, see Spate, *Burma setting*, pp. 32–33.

47 Skinner, *Leadership and power*, p. 18.

in 1936), a distribution similar to Thailand's obtained. City size falls from Saigon-Cholon (256,000) to the market towns of Can Tho and My Tho with 27,000 and 25,000 inhabitants respectively and then to the 13,000 population of Vinh Long.[48] The feature common to Thailand, Burma and Vietnam – and a key element in explaining patterns of urbanization – was that rice dominated the export sectors, and so the entire economies, of all three countries. This point is taken up in the next sub-section.

The 1931 distribution for Malaya's seven largest cities is steeply sloped, with a coefficient of −1.24 (Figure 6.4). The steepness reflects both the geographical realities of strategic location on the Straits of Malacca and path dependence. In 1870, when much of Malaya remained a jungle of tangled vegetation and trees, the two largest Malayan settlements of Singapore and Penang were thriving cities. As Malaya developed, both Straits ports gained disproportionately in size through building on established positions as trading centres. Furthermore, both expanded their extra-Malayan roles, especially for nearby Sumatra and Borneo, on the basis of earlier trade and finance functions.

A characteristic of Malaya's rank-size distributions, particularly striking when compared to Burma's, is that over successive decades they move strongly upwards and to the right. Rapid urban growth accompanied Malaya's transition from a frontier economy. However, a better developed urban system would be considered to have a city distribution with a slope nearer to −1.00 than Malaya's −1.24. Excluding Singapore and Penang, the regression coefficient drops to −1.08, but it approaches lognormality for only a few Malayan cities. The expectation of lognormality over more than a limited number of cities is unrealistic. A distribution in strict accordance with the rank-size rule for 10 Malayan cities, with Singapore as the first-ranked, would imply urbanization amounting to almost a third of national population. That large an urban sector would have been inconsistent with an economy like Malaya's, in which agriculture, although the chief source of wealth and exports, did not grow primarily through technical change.

Analysis of Indonesia is, as in other respects, complicated by the contrasting natures of Java and the Outer Islands (Figure 6.5). By 1930, Indonesia displayed an integrated urban system largely because of Java: it had Southeast Asia's most integrated urban system and over two-thirds of the total Indonesian population. Additionally, substantial Outer Island urbanization occurred. Contributing to this urban expansion was the rapid increase in Outer Island exports (Chapter 2). Between 1890 and 1930 in Indonesia, swift growth in Jakarta and Surabaya, and even swifter growth in a number of smaller Indonesian cities, including several in the Outer Islands, converted a concave, pre-modern distribution into one, by 1930, not too far adrift of Zipf

48 Naval Intelligence Division, *Indo-China*, pp. 369–408, 470–77.

'normality' with slopes of –0.82 over all of Indonesia's 119 cities of at least 10,000, and –0.87 for the first 50.

Transition Matrices

This and the next two sub-sections use transition matrices to help explain the factors that shaped urban systems in Southeast Asia. This sub-section considers the three rice-exporting areas of Burma, Thailand and Cochinchina, and contrasts their urbanization with Malaya's, where rubber created substantial urban spread effects. The next sub-section focuses on Indonesia's geography- and infrastructure-dominated development, while the third sub-section looks at the Philippines.

Transition matrices provide an analytical means to trace city growth in Southeast Asia and assess the dynamism, or torpidity, of the region's urban systems. Did small cities of 10,000 to 20,000 in 1891 generally move, by 1931, into the proportionately larger grouping of 20,000 to 40,000, or even advance two categories to have 40,000 to 80,000 inhabitants? Or, in 1931, were cities in a particular Southeast Asian country much the same size as four decades earlier, making gateway cities increasingly appear 'over-large'?

For the three Southeast Asian countries with urban population data, city distribution by size category in 1891 is shown in the far right column of the transition matrices (Tables 6.5 to 6.7). The bottom row of the matrices gives the 1931 distribution of cities by categories of population size. In Burma, for example, the first row of the matrix (Table 6.5) shows 12 settlements of below 10,000 in 1891. The second and third columns indicate that in 1931, 11 of these 12 settlements had progressed to become cities of between 10,000 and 20,000 and that one moved up two size categories to over 20,000 inhabitants.

Burma is striking for its lack of urban growth and the increasing dominance of Rangoon. Between 1891 and 1931, most of Burma's 29 cities did advance but, with a single exception, by only one size category. Growth of the advancing cities was at roughly the same rate as for Burma's overall population, which doubled during this period. Many of the settlements of under 10,000 in 1891 that by 1931 had joined the urban category were only marginally within it. Two cities in the 10,000 to 20,000 grouping in 1891 had declined to fewer than 10,000 inhabitants in 1931. There was one city of over 20,000 in 1891; by 1931, it no longer met the urban qualification of a population of 10,000. Urban increase in Burma came largely from Rangoon, 'really the only modern city' in Burma.[49] It moved from the category of under 320,000 to a population size (400,400) well above that level. Between 1891 and 1931, Rangoon's population increased by 122.1 per cent, but urban population elsewhere in Burma by just 38.4 per cent.

[49] Spate, *Burma setting*, p. 30.

Table 6.5 *Burma urban transition matrix, 1891–1931 (distribution of cities of at least 10,000 sometime between 1891 and 1931)*

000 persons	<10	10–20	20–40	40–80	80–160	160–320	320–640	City distribution 1891
<10	–	11	1	–	–	–	–	12
10–20	2	3	5	–	–	–	–	10
20–40	1	–	2	1	–	–	–	4
40–80	–	–	–	1	–	–	–	1
80–160	–	–	–	–	–	–	–	0
160–320	–	–	–	–	–	1	1	2
320–640	–	–	–	–	–	–	–	0
City distribution 1931	3	14	8	2	–	1	1	29

Notes: The city that advanced two size categories was Maymyo, although with a population of 21,300 in 1931 it only just crossed the threshold. No city rose by three size categories. Yandoon fell by two size categories. Between 1891 and 1931 the only city of between 20,000 and 80,000 to rise a category was Bassein. Mandalay remained in the 160–320 range.
Source: See Table 6.1.

Urbanization in Malaya, unlike in Burma, rose substantially (Table 6.6). Smaller cities grew at a similar pace to the large ones of Singapore and Penang. Population in the medium-sized cities of Kuala Lumpur and Ipoh rose even faster than in the two Straits metropolises. A transition matrix that showed no urban change between its beginning and ending dates would form a diagonal from the upper left to the lower right corner. By contrast, entries for Malaya concentrate in the upper half of the matrix. The pattern is one of a frontier country that began with few cities but urbanized rapidly. All of Malaya's 17 cities moved up by at least one size category; no city declined to a lower grouping. Four cities jumped by two categories, and Kuala Lumpur and Ipoh by three. Kuala Lumpur gained through being the administrative seat of the Federated Malay States government; through being on the Malayan railway main line and a hub for three rail branches; but chiefly through functioning as a service centre for the rubber industry.[50]

[50] Federated Malay States, *Fifty years of railways*; Fisher, 'Railway geography', pp. 130–31; Bennett, 'Kuala Lumpur', pp. 327–29.

Table 6.6 *Malaya urban transition matrix, 1891–1931 (distribution of cities of at least 10,000 sometime between 1891 and 1931)*

000 persons	<10	10–20	20–40	40–80	80–160	160–320	320–640	City distribution 1891
<10	–	8	4	1	–	–	–	13
10–20	–	–	–	–	1	–	–	1
20–40	–	–	–	1	–	–	–	1
40–80	–	–	–	–	1	–	–	1
80–160	–	–	–	–	–	–	1	1
160–320	–	–	–	–	–	–	–	0
320–640	–	–	–	–	–	–	–	0
City distribution 1931	0	8	4	2	2	0	1	17

Notes: Cities rising by two size categories were Taiping, Johore, Seremban, Klang and Singapore. The cities rising by three size categories were Ipoh and Kuala Lumpur.
Source: See Table 6.1.

Ipoh, on Malaya's west coast railway line and near the state of Perak's rich tin deposits, rose to prominence as a mining centre. Until 1914, tin mining was predominantly a Chinese industry. Miners relied on mines advancers to finance the prospecting for, and mining of, tin. The Ipoh-based operations of many of these advancers enhanced the town's commercial role.

The contrasting processing, marketing and financial linkages of the staples of rice and rubber help explain why relatively little urban development occurred in Burma, Thailand and Indochina, while in Malaya vigorous city growth filled in the countryside. In Burma, nearly half of larger rice mills with over 100 workers were in Rangoon. Spread effects from rice milling in Cochinchina were similarly limited, since most large mills concentrated in Saigon (Chapter 4).

Rice, as paddy, could be transported some distance for milling without significant deterioration, but rubber, as raw sheet, could not. Although initially Singapore was a milling centre, by the inter-war period most Malayan rubber coming to the port was off-grades and scrap. Rubber was mainly milled up-country, either on European estates or in towns and cities. Moreover, finance and lower order marketing functions devolved to peninsular cities.[51] Rubber buying, explained the Chairman of the Singapore

[51] *SSTC*, III, p. 246, II, pp. 331–32.

Table 6.7 *Indonesia urban transition matrix, 1890–1930 (distribution of cities of at least 10,000 sometime between 1890 and 1930)*

000 persons	<10	10–20	20–40	40–80	80–160	160–320	320–640	City distribution 1890
<10	1	16	7	3	–	–	–	27
10–20	–	12	10	3	1	1	–	27
20–40	–	–	4	6	1	–	–	11
40–80	–	–	–	–	2	1	–	3
80–160	–	–	–	–	–	1	2	3
160–320	–	–	–	–	–	–	–	0
320–640	–	–	–	–	–	–	–	0
City distribution 1930	1	28	21	12	4	3	2	71

Notes: Cities rising by two size categories: In Java: Jakarta, Buitenzorg, Soekaboemi (Sukabumi), Garoet, Tarkinmalaja, Pemalang, Semarang (Samarang), Madioen (Madium), Kediri, Surabaya and Probolinggo. In the Outer Islands: Makassar, Manado and Teluk Betung. *Cities rising by three size categories*: In Java: Cirebon (Cheribon) and Malang. In the Outer Islands: Medan and Pontianak. *Cities rising by four size categories:* Bandung (Bandoeng) in Java.
Source: See Table 6.1.

Chamber of Commerce Rubber Association, 'is all done in the towns'. Kuala Lumpur had Malaya's greatest concentration of buyers. They, in turn, had representatives in bigger towns like Klang and Seremban with populations of around 20,000 by the 1930s.[52] The shift of finance to peninsular centres helps to explain why Malaya had easily Southeast Asia's highest banking density (Table 6.3).

Rice did not promote urban growth outside gateway cities, because it lacked the extensive marketing and formal, or institutional, financial functions associated with rubber and tin. The practice in Burma was to buy all principal crops with cash.[53] Likewise, in Thailand, rice marketing outside Bangkok necessitated little urban structure, and did not give rise to banks or other institutional finance that would have promoted urbanization. Paddy dealers or sub-dealers bought, or bartered for, rice from growers in the countryside and took it to the rice mills (Chapter 3).

52 *SSTC*, II, p. 750.
53 Burma, *Report of the Burma Provincial Banking Enquiry Committee, 1929–30*, vol. 1, p. 47.

It was consistent with rice's few linkages to formal finance that Thailand and Indochina had by some margin Southeast Asia's lowest banking densities (Table 6.3). A relatively high density in Burma is explained by the 11 branches of Dawson's Bank (Chapter 3).

Indonesia: Geography, Policy and Infrastructure

Comparison of the Indonesian censuses for 1890 and 1930 yields data for 71 cities (Table 6.7). Because nearly all of the 48 cities recorded in the 1930, but not the 1890, census were under 20,000, the transition matrix must considerably understate the post-1890 birth of new cities. Nevertheless, strong urban growth is a feature of the matrix. Indonesian urbanization – contrary to the law of proportionate effect, or Gibrat's Law, that all cities are equally likely to grow at the same rate – is striking in its selectivity. Of the 71 cities, 19 grew by two or more size categories. Adjusting for population, the Outer Islands contributed more of these fast-growing cities than Java and so added significantly to greater Indonesian rank-size regularity.

Three factors largely account for Java's city growth and urban integration. One is an insular geography which allowed, on the northern coast of Java, the gateways of both Jakarta and Surabaya, since each city could economically link to international shipping flows and because an open economy counteracted centripetal forces that might otherwise have encouraged concentration in a single city.[54] Indonesia's insular geography and dense network of local shipping conduced, in Java and the Outer Islands, to the growth of smaller port cities with their associated handling and marketing functions. Such cities included the large port of Semarang in central Java and a number of smaller ports such as Palembang, Pontianak and Makassar in the Outer Islands.

Internal transport systems, along with international shipping, also shaped patterns of Javanese urbanization. Political decisions were central to internal infrastructure development. Following the opening of the first Javanese railway in 1873, the Dutch colonial government determinedly constructed a comprehensive inland transport network, partly with the intention of balancing food availability across the island. By the 1930s, Java's rail system had a density comparable to European countries, and connected 'numerous smaller towns'.[55] Through efficiently linking ports to surrounding hinterlands, the rail network promoted the rapid expansion of Jakarta, Surabaya and Semarang. The traditional urban centre of Yogyakarta benefited from good rail connections and railway workshops.[56] Railway expansion was instrumental in the growth

[54] Cf. Krugman, 'Urban concentration', pp. 17–19.

[55] Naval Intelligence Division, *Indo-China*, p. 414; Fisher, 'Economic myth', p. 184.

[56] Naval Intelligence Division, *Indo-China*, p. 430.

of large inland urban centres, notably Bandung (headquarters of the western half of the state railway network), Malang and Surakarta in Java and Medan in Sumatra. Table 6.7 identifies 14 Javanese cities that grew by two or more size categories. Of the 14, 12 (including all cities rising by more than two categories) had been linked to the railway by 1899, and usually well before.

Javanese geography and infrastructure contrast markedly with the strongly north–south patterns in most of the rest of Southeast Asia (Chapter 5). The southwards extension from mainland Asia of Burma, Thailand and Indochina predisposed these countries to a predominantly north–south geographical configuration. Because Thailand was largely surrounded by the Asian land mass, its geography offered scant opportunity for smaller ports to develop, or for alternatives to Bangkok's extreme dominance.

In Malaya, Burma, Thailand and Indochina, the gateway ports were not just nature's gift: internal transport developments reinforced their geographically derived comparative advantage. Already, these ports were nearest to the world east–west shipping route that bisected Southeast Asia after the inauguration of the Suez Canal. Rather than providing an alternative to a historic reliance on water transport that focused on a single large city, railways strengthened the nodality of Rangoon, Bangkok, Saigon and Singapore. Since railway lines generally paralleled major rivers or the coastlines, and these ran north–south, infrastructure construction ensured that internal communications focused on a single port city in the south. North–south railway configurations and the economics of ocean shipping contributed significantly to Singapore's growth and help explain the extreme urban primacy of Bangkok and Rangoon.

Philippines Urbanization

The emergence of provincial centres in the Philippines had similarities to both Indonesia and Malaya. In the Philippines, as in Indonesia, an insular geography encouraged port development beyond the Manila gateway. The explanation for the expansion of medium-sized cities like Iloilo and Cebu relative to Manila was their acquisition of port and staple-export-related commercial functions.

Philippine urbanization resembled Malayan in that economic roles in processing, wholesaling and finance promoted secondary urbanization outside the main city. Sugar, like latex from rubber trees, underwent first-stage processing near the point of production. After 1918 in the Philippines, this swelled employment and incomes in the urban centres of sugar-producing districts. An example was Bacolod in Negros Occidental. It became, as a commercial centre for sugar, 'an attractive, bustling community with markets, department stores and amusements'. As part of the same urbanization process, other communities, especially those with large (sugar processing) centrals, 'harbored an active urban life', and even smaller towns obtained electric lights and a telephone service.[57] There were four banks in Iloilo and one in Bacolod; and the Philippines had Southeast Asia's highest banking density after Malaya (Table 6.3).

Conclusion

Pre-World War II Southeast Asia urbanized largely as a product of vent-for-surplus expansion. Its requirement for optimum access both to exporting hinterlands and world markets determined a locational pattern of gateways and, unlike pre-1870 urbanization, of the cities that would come to dominate Southeast Asia's urban structure. Favourable geography was a necessary component in setting this pattern. Gateways grew and became Southeast Asia's great cities through their role as centres performing a range of higher order services and agglomeration effects. The location of the gateways on the margins of each country added to the geographic dualism of Southeast Asia, just as the distinct ethnic compositions of these cities and their functions as ports and mercantile and financial centres did in regard to the region's social and economic dualisms.

Beyond Southeast Asia's gateway cities, urban growth was selective and, for the most part, followed a clear set of determinants. Geographically imposed economic realities were the primary considerations in the development of city systems: the production locations of vented staples and infrastructure to facilitate their production and export; commercial functions associated with export growth; and where governments decided to build infrastructure and establish administrative centres. These factors were instrumental in where and which cities increased in size, whether or not small cities grew sufficiently fast to promote the spread of urbanization and so the speed at which countries gained denser, more articulated urban structures.

[57] Larkin, *Sugar*, pp. 182–83, 73, 14–15; Wernstedt, 'Cebu', pp. 337–43; Ullman, 'Trade centers', pp. 212–13.

7

Development Assessment, 1870–1940

To say that from the 1870s to World War II trade was an engine of growth for Southeast Asia is something of an understatement. Trade acts as a transmission mechanism which induces growth and helps in the acquisition of physical and human capital and the advancement of technology and learning. In this handmaiden role, trade as an 'engine' promoted growth in pre-World War II Southeast Asia. By 1939, the foundations for development – rudimentary in much of Southeast Asia in 1870 – existed.

Between countries, however, trade as an engine, and the extent to which it supported growth, varied considerably, leaving differing development inheritances. The main aim of this chapter is to provide some assessment of what, in terms of development, individual Southeast Asian countries had accomplished by World War II. The World War II Japanese occupation forms a complicating overlay on Southeast Asian economic and political history but even before that the pre-war origins of the region's development need to be traced. Pre-war experience allows an understanding of the positions from which countries began after the war, and why they made the post-war choices that they did.

While vent-for-surplus growth tends to be swift in terms of exports, it is not, of itself, self-sustaining in the Kuznets sense of achieving modern economic growth.[1] Implicit in the chapter's analysis is how far countries travelled towards self-sustaining growth and why distances traversed differed. Why, despite decades of rapid export-led growth, did Southeast Asia end the 1930s still short of modern economic growth and trailing further behind the United States and Japan than in the late nineteenth century?

In its first section, the chapter discusses the 1870 starting points of countries. Since a venting of surpluses was, in all countries, the principal force motivating growth, the section considers how far vent-for-surplus conditions were met, as well as some of the factors in different Southeast Asian countries that promoted or hindered export growth. The second section explores how the gains from trade were used: it attempts to assess to what extent these gains laid the foundations for future development and how they were shared among the peoples of Southeast Asia.

[1] Kuznets, 'Modern economic growth'.

Starting Points and Export Growth

Where Southeast Asia Started

It is unrealistic to compare post-1870 Southeast Asian and Japanese development and ask why by 1940 Japan was much more developed. Southeast Asian countries began from markedly lower levels of development than Japan, and lacked its growth pre-conditions of an already considerable infrastructure and long history of a unified, educated population. In 1870, nearly all of Malaya was jungle; still, as somewhat romantically described, 'a savage and empty land'.[2] At that time, too, the areas of Burma, Cochinchina and Indonesia's Outer Islands which were to drive rapid development remained largely frontier. As late as 1870 in Burma, 'apart from barracks, jails and law-courts, built mostly with Indian immigrant or convict labour, the public works consisted of little more than five incomplete roads'.[3] Thailand, in 1890, had 'a tiny scattered population (perhaps 6–7 million), virtually no large towns outside Bangkok, no railways, and almost no roads'.[4] Late nineteenth-century Spanish colonialism largely neglected the Philippines. Before development there could get properly underway early in the twentieth century, the Philippines had to emerge from colonial neglect and the loss of some 200,000 Filipino lives, mostly of civilians, caused by over three years of the destructive Philippine-American War and by disease and famine.

Conditions for Growth

Pre-conditions for Southeast Asian growth were the imposition of internal peace and a freeing of trade and production from restrictions. Both these pre-conditions were in place by the time that rising incomes in the West, the opening of Suez in 1869 and falling shipping freights stimulated demand for Southeast Asian commodities. Colonial enforced peace was extended over Lower Burma after the second Anglo-Burmese War in 1852–53, and in Cochinchina by 1867, after a series of French conquests and a declaration that the whole of this part of Indochina was to be a colony of France. The British minimized barriers to migration to Lower Burma by allowing anyone to settle on unoccupied land without a complicated application process. Beginning in 1855, Thailand, under pressure from the United Kingdom, lifted a prohibition on exporting rice and abolished corvée labour and debt bondsmanship. These liberalization measures eliminated key obstacles to personal freedom and enabled the Thai to participate in the rice economy.[5] The Treaty of Pangkor, signed with the

[2] Allen and Donnithorne, *Western enterprise*, p. 259.
[3] Furnivall, *Educational progress*, p. 26.
[4] Falkus, 'Review', p. 142.
[5] Johnston, 'Rice cultivation', pp. 108–9.

Sultan of Perak – the ruler of a major tin-producing area – paved the way for an enforcement of the order of British rule in Malaya and formation of the Federated Malay States in 1895. Internal peace, as American colonialism, was re-established in the Philippines after the 1902 end of the Philippine-American War. Long before Suez, the Dutch were entrenched in Java, though not the Outer Islands.

Once internal peace was established, Southeast Asia, as much as any of the world's tropical regions and more than most, met the other conditions for rapid growth through exporting agricultural commodities: empty, well-watered land, transport and entrepreneurship. In late nineteenth-century economic history, tropical countries with the fastest export-led agricultural growth were those where these conditions obtained, and where governments enabled agriculturalists to respond to them.[6] If countries exported substantial quantities of minerals, this markedly boosted growth. Malaya was the outstanding example. Tin mining got growth underway, created an infrastructural basis for rubber and provided a key staple throughout the pre-World War II decades and after. Indonesia, with oil, was the only other country to have a major mineral export. Oil lifted Indonesian growth significantly, and supplemented Outer Island rubber as a growth source.

Southeast Asia, as part of monsoon Asia, had plentiful rainfall, and in 1870 vast expanses of empty land existed in large parts of every country. Not all land in any country was empty but large tracts in every country were sparsely populated or even empty, and it was these areas that afforded the best opportunities for rapid and dynamic change. Growth could get started without the need for elaborate transport because river and coastal shipping afforded links to ports for overseas export. Even as growth progressed, this same availability of water carriage reduced the need for infrastructural investment, and facilitated export expansion through providing cheap transport. Although export growth in Burma and Cochinchina was not held back by transport, it may have been hindered in Thailand. If railway construction had been more for economic rather than political reasons, and had reached further into potential rice-growing areas in the interior, the Thai economy would probably have grown faster, and possibly avoided, uniquely in Southeast Asia, a failure to register per capita income gains after 1913.

Entrepreneurship, in the form of a willingness of peasants to respond to the availability of land and pioneer it, was evident in the inward rushes of settlers in all the rice-exporting countries. In Burma and Cochinchina this came mainly through migration, while Thailand relied more on a mobilization of surplus labour time. Malaya and Thailand, along with Burma, attracted massive population inflows. Asian traders to whom cultivators could sell their produce were, as throughout Southeast Asia, mainly Chinese, who penetrated to

[6] The criteria and observation on tropical growth are set out in Lewis, 'Export stimulus'.

every part of up-country interiors and multiplied along with settlers. European merchants and agency houses linked Southeast Asian production to European and American markets, for both goods and capital, completing a triumvirate of (largely complementary) entrepreneurial response.

Exports and Growth

Malayan growth was the swiftest in pre-World War II Southeast Asia, because Malaya was initially sparsely populated and had two staple exports, at first tin and then rubber, the twentieth-century boom commodity. Malaya is an example of Lewis's observation that the post-1880 response of tropical countries to the growth of world demand 'was swiftest where new land was available for cultivation ... and the government removed obstacles to access'.[7] The British promoted rapid Malayan expansion through allowing unlimited international immigration, mainly of Chinese and Indians, although Malays had protected status beginning in 1914 with the establishment of Malay reservations. The law prohibited the sale by Malays of reservation land except to other Malays. While the British decision to 'protect' the Malays probably encouraged their marginalization and contributed to long-standing problems of inter-ethnic group inequality, the colonial policy of shielding an indigenous group is unlikely to have held back growth significantly.

At the other end of the spectrum, the stagnation of per capita income in Thailand after 1913 puzzles scholars. One reason for a lack of growth was the absence of a serviceable network of roads, which hindered population mobility and economic integration. Another reason for unchanged incomes was that unlimited Chinese immigration until the 1930s put downwards pressure on wages and also checked income gains by adding substantially to population. By keeping unskilled wages low, immigration discouraged Thai from leaving rural areas and a traditional way of life. Skills on which the economy could draw to increase productivity beyond the techniques of customary agriculture remained largely confined to whatever technologies Chinese and European immigrants brought with them. Unrestricted immigration does not, however, wholly explain low per capita incomes, since this was also true of Malaya. There, too, low immigrant wages gave little incentive for the indigenous Malays to leave agriculture, but Malaya had the good fortune of the boom commodity of rubber to support relatively high average incomes.

A telling, but far from the only, difference in explaining growth in Malaya and Thailand is that Malaya had the luck of rubber as a staple and Thailand did not. Rice, unlike rubber, did not have strong linkage effects, either forward from milling or in promoting urbanization, also a factor working against faster growth in Burma and Indochina. In Thailand, as elsewhere in Southeast

7 Lewis, 'Export stimulus', p. 28.

Asia, conservative monetary and fiscal policies held back development. British financial advisors in Thailand were the technicians implementing an extreme Bank of England-directed conservatism of a colonial currency board, and the Thai elite agreed with them.

Thailand's elite refused to spend on road, rail, electricity and power infrastructure to an extent unusual even in colonial Southeast Asia. More expenditure on infrastructure would have countered weak economic integration, encouraged industrialization and augmented growth through widening markets and promoting specialization gains. Given these changes, Thailand could have moved further along a path of growth and structural change. Adoption of van der Heide's scheme for canals to extend irrigation to service over half of Thailand's central plain would have had similar effects, through drawing additional Thai into the export economy and increasing rice exports. As it was, large areas of Thailand remained part of a traditional economy, keeping per capita exports relatively low by Southeast Asian standards.

When by the 1930s Burma's rice frontier closed, the economy had nowhere else to look for development. Industrialization, other than rice milling and saw milling, was almost non-existent. Foreigners, both Europeans and Indians, dominated the economy outside of rice cultivation. While Thailand's rice economy had similarly weak linkages, the Thai, unlike the Burmese, had their own government, which better placed them to develop the economy. Beginning in 1932 and accelerating thereafter, Thailand's government took steps to industrialize and diversify agriculturally, initiatives pursued during World War II and implemented after it.

The sale of large tracts of land in Cochinchina by the French to offset the cost of canal construction, especially in the western part of the Mekong Delta, resulted in a concentration of landholding among a relatively few (usually absentee) owners and rice cultivation dependent on tenants and itinerant labour. Innovative and more productive systems of hydraulic management could have been implemented if landowners had been resident on the land and knowledgeable in farming.[8] Output might also have been higher if cultivators had worked their own land, with corresponding incentives to invest more effort and capital in it.

Under American colonialism, preferential access for Philippine sugar to the United States – on a free trade basis from 1913 to 1933 and otherwise quotas – led to a rapid increase in sugar exports and provided the main vent-for-surplus staple. But sugar locked the economy into a low-value commodity which could be easily and more efficiently produced elsewhere. Coconuts, readily grown on sandy soils too poor for sugar, further drew the Islands into the international economy, and, by the inter-war years, the export of copra contributed importantly

[8] Brocheux, *Mekong Delta*, pp. 43–57; Robequain, *Economic development*, pp. 83–86.

to growth. Unlike in Malaya, Philippine growth was held back by a Chinese Exclusion Act, which was framed to avoid 'coolie wages', and which sharply limited immigration and so labour supply. More land would have been opened and growth would have been higher if the Filipino elite, the *cacique* class of landed wealth under the Spanish, had been more willing to invest sugar profits in opening up the interior, and if ordinary Filipinos had been more disposed to leave the social security of areas where land was plentiful.

In Indonesia, workers, mainly indentured, could be mobilized from labour-surplus Java for Sumatra plantations; export growth in Borneo depended chiefly on smallholder inter-planting of rubber between existing crops. Transmigration to the Outer Islands to open land there was never large. It has been suggested that Indonesia might have grown faster if, before the early twentieth century, the Dutch had been able to replace Sumatra's various principalities with Dutch rule and establish internal peace and build infrastructure.[9]

Developmental Foundations and Problems

Vent-for-surplus expansion comes at little opportunity cost in land or labour and, along with the allocative gains from trade, yields natural resource rents which must provide someone with a net increase in real income. Basic to development in vent-for-surplus economies is that enough of these income gains become available for investment and that this investment contributes to capital accumulation and lays foundations for future sustainable growth. This section asks, over seven pre-World War II decades, how, and how far, trade gains were used in Southeast Asia to create a basis for post-war development, and how the benefits of trade were distributed among the peoples of Southeast Asia. An assessment is organized in six topics. To what extent was: agricultural productivity raised; infrastructure built to create cities and urban systems; human capital created through education and training; a domestic entrepreneurial class fostered; financial capacity constructed; and trade gains shared? How did the levels reached by different countries compare?

Agriculture

Finite land limits vent-for-surplus growth. For growth to continue and progress towards being self-sustaining, Southeast Asian countries needed to raise productivity in both their export staples and traditional agricultural sectors. Southeast Asia's integration into the world economy after 1870 promoted dual economies in which well-developed export sectors co-existed with traditional economies. Unless traditional areas developed, this added to Nurkse's absence of the 'other conditions of progress' that he cites as a main barrier to

[9] van Leeuwen, 'Indonesia', pp. 278–79.

development in the tropics.[10] Dualism exercised a continual drag on the economy, denying it the full advantages of the agricultural contributions to development of an investable surplus, a source of labour and a market for domestic manufactures.[11] In Southeast Asia, the development of traditional agriculture remained an agenda largely to be tackled after World War II and political independence. Java, due to concerted Dutch efforts and the establishment of a network of agricultural extension services, affords the main Southeast Asian instance of technical improvements in agriculture, but the island was not a vent-for-surplus area and so unlike most of Southeast Asia.

Mining for Malayan tin evolved, of necessity, to use new, more productive, capital-intensive technologies. While Java successfully raised productivity in sugar cultivation, the Philippine sugar industry, with preferential access to the United States market at guaranteed prices, remained the least efficient of the major world sugar producers. Apparently, most Philippine growers 'did not even care to invest in better farming techniques to improve their profits'. Declining demand in American and European markets finally forced the Philippine producers to switch from producing muscovado (unrefined cane sugar). But until 1921 the export of muscovado exceeded centrifugal sugar, produced by refining cane to separate out molasses and obtain pure sugar crystals.[12]

Other than in Java, Southeast Asian agricultural expansion was always through extending land frontiers and planting more of the same crop using essentially unchanged traditional techniques. That continued where possible. In countries where it was not, or had become difficult, notably Burma, where the frontier had closed by the 1930s, growth rates slowed.[13] As in Burma before the 1930s, the principal reason for a failure to raise productive capacity in agriculture significantly was a lack of impetus to change and pioneer new technologies, especially more capital-intensive ones, so long as surplus land existed and labour at not too much above subsistence wages was available as a substitute for capital.

In the 1930s, the lagging movement in Southeast Asia towards technical improvements, which might otherwise have transpired, was likely reinforced by low commodity prices. Already by the late 1920s, prices of several of the region's main export commodities – rubber, tin and sugar – were declining due to world oversupply. Then, the sharp 1930s downturns in industrial country demand caused a collapse in prices.[14] Only minor crop diversification

10 Nurkse, *Equilibrium and growth*, pp. 243, 289.

11 Johnston and Mellor, 'Role of agriculture'; Timmer, 'Agricultural transformation', pp. 383–88.

12 Larkin, *Sugar*, p. 55 for the quote and see pp. 54–60.

13 Burma, *Report of the Burma Provincial Banking Enquiry Committee, 1929–30*, vol. 1, pp. 17–18.

14 Lewis, *Economic survey*, p. 196; Brown, *Economic change*, p. 216.

occurred, such as rubber cultivation in Thailand and Indochina. An increased production of coconuts in the Philippines was, however, an exception.

A further possible explanation for stagnant agricultural technologies was that a scientific revolution in agriculture did not occur until after World War II. Even so, the Dutch in Java excepted, governments took relatively little interest in agricultural research and its dissemination until the inter-war years. In 1909, the Philippines government opened a research station and agricultural school at Los Baños, but failed to back this up with an agricultural extension programme to disseminate research results.[15] An example of increased British inter-war interest is the foundation of the Rubber Research Institute in Malaya in 1925.

On the plus side, there was great improvement in marketing technologies for agricultural exports. The development of standard grades of rubber allowed Singapore to assume its inter-war status as a world rubber market, where the commodity was shipped directly to consumers without ever coming to the city for grading and inspection.[16] Burma had five main recognized grades of rice, leading to a reduction in marketing costs and facilitating Rangoon's role as a world market.[17]

Infrastructure

Compared to agriculture, much more was done in furthering development though building infrastructure, a great deal of it from scratch. The bulk of the capital accumulation that exports made possible went into the construction of infrastructure, most of which served the needs of trade and focused on urban areas.

Hinterlands were opened and extended through investment by governments in transport and roads, but a substantial part of the opening of new land depended on individuals. Often, these were peasants who cleared and upgraded the land they farmed through draining and bunding to grow rice and cut down trees to establish rubber smallholdings. French investment in Cochinchina's extensive network of canals to open up the region for rice cultivation was probably the outstanding example of colonial capital expenditure on agricultural improvement.

In 1870, Southeast Asia had almost no railways or roads, let alone any decent roads. Over the next decades, Southeast Asian countries constructed hundreds of kilometres of roads, long stretches of them metalled. At the start of the Pacific War, Malaya's good road system facilitated the movement of Japanese troops down the length of the peninsula to take Singapore in some

[15] Hooley, 'American economic policy', p. 471.

[16] Huff, 'Development of the rubber market', pp. 291–92.

[17] Cheng, *Rice industry*, pp. 103–07.

two months. Indochina had 'one of the finest road networks in East Asia'.[18] Thailand, where still in 1940 no road linked Bangkok to the rest of the country, was the Southeast Asian outlier in not having a serviceable road network. In Burma, while good access to water transport limited the need to spend on infrastructure, it was also partly responsible for the 'unsystematic development of Burma's communications'.[19]

By the 1930s, when the slump and road competition halted railway construction, all countries had fairly extensive rail networks, although Java alone had a dense one. In the later nineteenth century, the absence of railway transport had restricted the extent of exploitable areas, for example in Malayan tin mining, which in its early stages had to use bullock cart transport along muddy tracks to take ore to coastal ports.[20] Railways opened interior areas to export production for rice in Burma and Thailand, rubber in Malaya and sugar in the Philippines.

Since staple exports moved predominantly by water, possibly as important for development as the contribution of railways in increasing the size of the hinterland was that they facilitated the movement of people. Rail revenue from passengers was not infrequently greater than from goods. Urban systems developed along with the railways. Towns grew up where in up-country Burma rice was collected for onwards rail transport and where in Malaya railway feeder lines brought tin ore for shipment by coastal vessels.[21] Kuala Lumpur gained in nodality and size through its location on the Malayan railway main line and as a centre for rail branches.[22] Java's elaborate railway infrastructure was a chief determinant of its urban system.[23]

A limitation of railway construction for future Southeast Asian development was, as for all other infrastructure, its siting chiefly in export areas. Rail systems that by-passed traditional areas confirmed their status as Southeast Asia's 'non-modern' areas, and contributed to the post-war legacy of economic and geographical dualism. Large cities, especially the principal ports in each country, got the lion's share of infrastructural amenities such as hospitals, water supplies, street lighting and trams. Urban infrastructural advantage and focus was further strengthened during the late nineteenth century, when telegraph communication connected Southeast Asia's larger cities with the rest of the world. By the inter-war years, the telegraph extended even to remote up-country areas, but communications still went through the region's main cities.

18 Brocheux and Hémery, *Indochina*, p. 130.
19 Spate, *Burma setting*, p. 22.
20 Wong, *Malayan tin industry*, pp. 83–84, 93–94.
21 Spate, *Burma setting*, p. 29.
22 Federated Malay States, *Fifty years of railways*; Bennett, 'Kuala Lumpur', pp. 327–29.
23 Huff, 'Export-led growth, gateway cities', p. 1447.

These cities also benefited from the construction of larger, more modern port facilities, along with railways a major forward linkage created by exports. Port development increased the nodality of the principal urban centres and this, along with the accompanying growth of business and financial services, led to a further concentration of infrastructure. Singapore, already a natural harbour, complemented this advantage with world-class port facilities, continuously upgraded from the 1870s onwards. By contrast, late nineteenth-century Manila was notorious for its substandard port.[24] The port was, however, substantially upgraded under American colonialism. Bangkok was held back throughout the pre-World War II decades by a sand bar at its harbour entrance, which prevented access by larger ocean-going ships and partly accounts for so much of its trade being conducted through Singapore. Saigon, the port for the Chinese merchant town of Cholon, expanded from the late 1850s onwards to become the most active port on the northwestern shore of the South China Sea. Traffic at Saigon of 2.1 million tons in 1937 made it the sixth largest French port.[25]

Educational Provision

A major failing of colonialism was insufficient opportunities for education and technical training, together with a lack of incentives for local populations to seek education other than to become clerks. Relatively few Southeast Asians were technically trained, and those with technical training were too few in number to form the backbone of technologically driven economies. More education could have increased human capital, taught skills, added to the literate population and helped to build an administrative and managerial middle class for post-independence Southeast Asia.

Efforts to extend educational provision increased greatly after 1900. Expansion was least in Indochina and most in the Philippines, where the Americans were said to have come with rifles and school primers.[26] The Philippines moved farther than any other country towards universal primary education, but the record on secondary, tertiary and technical education was much poorer. Some Southeast Asian countries were held back in progress towards giving all their populations at least a primary education by high immigration of working-age males, the great majority of whom arrived without schooling. Malaya was most affected in this regard, but the age and educational composition of immigrants to Burma and Thailand were similar.

In substantial part, the limitations of education's pre-war infrastructural contribution reflected environments of strongly economically oriented,

[24] Storer, 'Philippines', p. 293.
[25] Brocheux and Hémery, *Indochina*, pp. 130–31.
[26] Keesing, *Philippines*, p. 85.

lopsidedly developed tropical societies, not just an absence of colonial government commitment. More government efforts towards education could have been realized, and more resolute attempts made to shift the educational focus from a literary one with its associated problems of oversupply. But so long as abundant land and labour existed, success in attracting cultivators to participate in agricultural education was problematic, as it was for technical courses in the absence of much industrialization. Despite the lack of interest that Southeast Asians showed in technical and agricultural education, governments might beneficially have developed short courses, for example six-month programmes to teach modern farming techniques.

Even in the Philippines, as Hooley puzzles, educational advances 'seem to have had little impact on productivity. The improvement in total factor productivity during the colonial period was marginal at best.'[27] While better education improved the quality of the labour force, Hooley suggests that the negligible effect on total factor productivity might have been due to unequal income distribution or institutional weakness such as the absence of an agricultural extension programme to improve agricultural techniques. In Southeast Asia during the late twentieth and early twenty-first centuries, educational provision and shares of the populations with formal qualifications expanded enormously. And yet, despite this undoubted improvement, low factor productivity persists, a seeming paradox considered in Part V of the book.

Pre-war educational provision set Southeast Asian countries on a road to widespread education and literacy, and furnished an institutional basis, including universities, to achieve these goals.[28] Singapore and Malaya are examples. On one level, the spread of education soon created an oversupply of clerks; at the top, however, it gave rise to a professional and political elite, whose members were often the products of English or Scottish universities.[29] These were men who, in Singapore and Malaya, as elsewhere in Southeast Asia, became leaders in their countries during and after a struggle for independence.

Entrepreneurship

Apart from the movement of peasants to become small farmers and produce export crops, Southeast Asian growth almost entirely failed to foster entrepreneurship among indigenous groups. For all Southeast Asian countries, once independent, the legacy of a pre-war dominance of commerce by non-indigenous entrepreneurs became an issue of resentment and, in Burma,

[27] Hooley, 'American economic policy', p. 471.

[28] For example, de Pleijt and Frankema, 'Deeper roots', pp. 10, 14 stress these developmental origins.

[29] Examples are well known and given in Yong, 'Preliminary study', pp. 262–66; and see Straits Chinese British Association, *Golden jubilee souvenir*.

Indonesia and Vietnam, led to violence against minority entrepreneurial groups. The demands of indigenous groups for greater economic roles ended the plural society in its pre-World War II form of tolerance of a generally accepted ethnic commercial order. A legacy of the politics of resentment, further exacerbated by the inability of indigenous groups to assume entrepreneurial functions quickly, slowed post-war growth and was frequently an important explanation for the expansion of state enterprise as a substitute for private entrepreneurs.

Before the war, expatriate Europeans, principally the large merchant houses, handled the import of almost all manufactured goods and the export of nearly all commodities except rice and foodstuffs for the local Asian market. Most rice exports had Asian destinations, and Chinese in Thailand and Indochina and Indians and to a lesser extent Chinese in Burma largely conducted this trade. Furnivall describes how European firms monopolized Burma's import and export trade, and because of this control had, by 1886, gained a large share in the distribution of imported foreign goods, driving out even prominent Burman merchants who had previously dealt in products for which foreign goods now substituted.[30]

The Chinese had little role in import and export trade with the West, but they dominated local networks of collection, credit and distribution. Chinese dominance in these business structures was because of linkages within them such as the dependence of collection of produce on an earlier extension of credit; because of long Chinese experience in commercial activities and so accumulated knowledge; and because of close, perhaps kinship, network connections with other Chinese. While Chinese control represented a vibrant entrepreneurial tradition in Southeast Asian commerce, it left almost no room for Asians who were not ethnic Chinese.

In the production of Southeast Asian staples and trade in them, Thailand exemplified the extreme indigenous exclusion from the modern sector typical in Southeast Asia: in 1940, the Thai 'remained almost as deeply entrenched in traditional agricultural pursuits as they were before 1850'. They participated in the rice trade only as growers.[31] That had major significance for the ethnic make-up of business structure and so the maintenance of the traditional, well-defined plural society. From the 1930s, it also fundamentally shaped the Kingdom's development policies, which sought Thai participation in the economy through a Thai government and Chinese business partnership, described as bureaucratic capitalism (Chapter 13). After Southeast Asian independence, the main entry to the modern economy for the region's aspirant indigenous entrepreneurs was through intermarriage, partnerships like that in Thailand, or state corporations which took over formerly European and Chinese business functions.

[30] Furnivall, 'Safety first', pp. 31–32.
[31] Ingram, *Economic change*, p. 215 and see pp. 71–73.

Finance

Formal finance, more than trade, was a European preserve. Because the region's European banks – the dominant financial institutions in all countries – were chiefly interested in financing foreign commerce and its requirement for short-term self-liquidating loans, capacities for the mobilization of an investable surplus and its reinvestment locally were limited. As well as the tendency for European firms to send profits back to their head offices, a large share of investable surpluses automatically flowed out of Southeast Asia as dividends to overseas shareholders and pensions to former colonial civil servants. These remittances help to explain why Southeast Asian countries regularly ran large trade surpluses. Even adjusting for deficits in the services component of the current account, these surpluses point to substantial remitted profits rather than reinvestment in the region.

Estimates of Chinese remittances are speculative and one suspects often subject to overstatement. Nevertheless, almost all of the many Chinese and Indian immigrants coming to Southeast Asia did so with the intention of remitting home. Remittances by Asians added yet further to the drain from Southeast Asia of investable surpluses.

Local Asian banks were the principal institutional means to mobilize finance and allocate funds to local entrepreneurs. In these functions, the banks were constrained by the risk posed by the inherent instability of mono-economies, and the additional contractionary effect in a downturn that Southeast Asia's currency boards exercised. Almost all the region's local Asian banks were Chinese. Singapore had the greatest concentration, and these banks and their branches constituted a substantial pre-war developmental foundation for Singapore and Southeast Asia more generally. The Siam Commercial Bank in Bangkok represented a similarly important inheritance on which to build. The foundation was, however, less firm in the Philippines where two local Chinese banks served a small Chinese constituency and only one of the banks survived the 1930s slump.[32]

Southeast Asian agriculturalists relied heavily on informal finance obtained from Asian traders, shopkeepers or moneylenders. The network, described in Chapter 3, was complex. Because of the importance of agricultural credit and internal trade and distribution networks in Southeast Asia's economies, and because a substantial proportion of this credit may have originally come from European agency houses, they may have played as important a role as the European banks in financing Southeast Asian production.

Banks for small Asian farmers were almost unknown except in Burma. However, Dawson's Bank, a model for financial provision to Burmese cultivators on fair terms, did not survive the 1930s depression. Few credit cooperatives

[32] Huff, 'Currency boards and Chinese banks'.

existed outside of Java. While informal finance was agile and adaptative, institutional finance, with reasonable lending rates and close monitoring, could have helped farmers to modernize and avoid crippling debt and loss of land. That sequence of problems was most serious in Burma, due to inter-war foreclosures by Chettiar moneylenders. The percentage of land in the 13 principal rice-growing districts occupied by non-agriculturists increased from 31.8 per cent in 1930 to 51.1 per cent in 1938; Chettiar occupation accounted for practically the whole of the increase.[33] Yet further land loss by Burmese rice cultivators fed an already strong dislike in Burma of foreigners and led to widespread civil unrest and rioting during the early 1930s.[34] After World War II, agricultural credit schemes organized by governments spread throughout Southeast Asia, but were usually unsuccessful because of insufficient monitoring, high default rates and lack of long-term lending commitment.

Trade Gains, Specialization and Distribution

The mobility of foreign factors – foreign enterprise, capital and, often, labour – was integral to Southeast Asia's vent-for-surplus development. Inflows of these factors created the means to absorb domestic surpluses – land and labour – and over the course of decades were instrumental in widening markets and transforming Southeast Asia into a collection of highly specialized economies. Specialization and a division of labour within countries were fundamental components of this process and of Southeast Asia's gains from trade, as well as trade's several indirect benefits such as the introduction of new technologies and improvements in infrastructure, public services, education and financial institutions. Earlier parts of this chapter considered how far and in what ways trade gains and natural resource rents were used to lay a basis for future development. This sub-section focuses on the distribution of natural resource rents and how trade gains were shared – the 'internal terms of cooperation between domestic and foreign factors in export production'.[35]

Southeast Asian developmental lopsidedness was not just economic, in extreme specialization in a few exports, and geographic, in a spatial concentration of export sectors. The region was also socially lopsided, in a division of labour between foreigners and Asians and among Asians as well. Because of inter-group economic specializations and social divisions – the plural society – aggregates of income and exports do not accurately indicate how trade gains were distributed relatively among Southeast Asia's three broad groups of Europeans, indigenous peoples and immigrant Asians, or the implications of

33 Baxter, *Report*, pp. 27–28.
34 For an excellent review of unrest and the issues behind it, see Montesano, 'Revisiting the rice deltas'.
35 Myint, 'Neoclassical resurgence', p. 122.

the pre-World War II Southeast Asian model of development for welfare and the acquisition of skills.

Much of Southeast Asian specialization was to meet the needs of export markets for trade, transport and port facilities. These activities were mainly overseen by Europeans and immigrant Chinese and Indians. Europeans generally left Southeast Asia once their employment ended and their departure led to an outflow of remittances to pay pensions.

Asians realized some of natural resource rents but most went to Europeans. Plantations and, by the early twentieth century, mines were largely established by Europeans. A high proportion of rents and profits that this development generated left Southeast Asia as remitted profits and dividends to overseas shareholders. Nineteenth-century Chinese owners of tin mines in Malaya benefited from rents, as did smallholders with bearing rubber acreage in the boom conditions of the mid-1920s. Exceptions to the European dominance in plantation agriculture and mining were the extensive sugar interests of a Filipino elite and the establishment of rubber estates by Singapore Chinese using catch crops of pineapples. While in the Philippines, insofar as its elite reinvested the gains from sugar, these went into sugar, Singapore Chinese used the gains from rubber to invest in manufacturing and banking.

Although relatively few Asian immigrants were economically or educationally successful, some were. Typically, they remained in Southeast Asia to form a growing, largely Chinese, business and professional middle class. Europeans and this Asian middle class dominated almost all the specialized activities created as part of Southeast Asia's export economies and received the great bulk of the benefits that they yielded. Chinese and Indians almost entirely filled the middle tier of Southeast Asia's pyramidal structure of commerce and separated indigenous Southeast Asians from contact with the upper layer of European business and the outside world.

Most indigenous Southeast Asians and the great mass of Chinese and Indian immigrants stayed at the bottom of production structures and in the roles that they had always occupied, as peasant cultivators or unskilled labourers. These occupations afforded limited, if any, opportunity to acquire new or transferable skills. There was little technology transfer or skill acquisition at the bottom of the production structure, because Southeast Asian export economies were built on unlimited supplies of cheap, undifferentiated labour and because, apart from the region's low level of industrialization, much of production involved extension along existing lines with existing techniques.

Abundant labour kept wages near what could be earned from remaining in the traditional agricultural sector. Numbers of unskilled workers and landless labourers increased as population grew, exerting downwards wage pressure. For the countries with mass Chinese and Indian immigration, wages were pushed towards levels in China and India, and may even have declined as the venting process continued and attracted more immigrant labour. While most, but not all, of the bottom layer of the social structure probably gained in terms of income and also opportunity compared to ruling levels in the 1860s, continued low wages precluded large gains.

The predominant experience of indigenous Southeast Asians, who formed the majority in every country, was similar. Malays in Malaya remained chiefly cultivators and fishermen, figuratively as well as literally 'sons of the soil'. Burmese, Thai and Vietnamese mainly participated in their respective economies as cultivators. So too did most Javanese and Outer Island Indonesians. Filipinos had a different experience from indigenous groups elsewhere in Southeast Asia because of an elite indigenous group of sugar planters and millers but here, too, even if in export industries, most of the population remained cultivators.

The implications for post-World War II Southeast Asian politics of the pre-war social distribution of gains from trade were considerable. Unequal sharing fed an 'economics of discontent' based on the perception of exploitation and domination by foreigners.[36] The World War II Japanese occupation added considerably to nationalist feeling and widened its popular base. After 1945, nationalism became a major factor in reshaping the political landscape in Southeast Asia and led to a radical transformation of economic policy in some countries.

Conclusion

Between 1870 and 1940, large parts of Southeast Asia evolved into specialized economies based on exporting to each other and to the rest of the world. Progress in moving towards self-sustaining development was evident, but substantial in only a few respects. Furthermore, over the seven decades, major structural problems emerged. Trade and development left Southeast Asian countries with undiversified agricultural economies, with entrenched economic, social and geographical dualisms and with a potentially fractious legacy of plural societies. Within this last were economically marginalized indigenous populations whose main role was in agriculture. Ethnic tensions, latent in the plural society but held in check by colonialism, gained force in independent Southeast Asia. Economic conflicts and associated political divisions were sometimes expressed as violent struggles. After independence, Southeast Asia's post-World War II history was fundamentally shaped by the economic and social ways governments tried to deal with inherited structures of agricultural specialization, dualism and pluralism.

Until 1940, in export sectors near monoculture persisted, mainly because comparative advantage gave no reason to move away from it. There was limited structural change from agriculture towards services and industry, especially modern manufacturing. Land extension, labour reallocation, specialization

[36] Myint, 'Interpretation', p. 149 and see pp. 151, 162.

and population inflows, the latter mainly from China and India through immigration, remained principally responsible for increased product per head. Generally rising per capita incomes suggest improved living standards, but improvement remained limited, partly because of downwards pressure on real wages for the bulk of the labour force due to large inwards migration from the desperately poor areas of India and South China, and partly because of still large traditional sectors. While incomes remained low even in vent-for-surplus areas, in most regions of countries, living standards were well above subsistence levels, although not for many people in densely populated northern Vietnam and Java. Probably the greatest improvement in living standards was reflected in the rise throughout Southeast Asia of a middle class of professionals, civil servants and the better-off merchants and traders, many of the latter Chinese or Indian.

All these outcomes were integral accompaniments to the growth that occurred, and the pattern of development implicit in the three models that were used in the book's first six chapters to help in understanding Southeast Asian development: Myint's vent-for-surplus concept, staple theory and W. A. Lewis's unlimited labour. The first two tell a story of extensive, resource-intensive growth like Southeast Asia's. The third helps to account for large immigration and migration; generally no more than relatively modest Southeast Asian per capita income improvements and wage increases; and the persistence of large traditional sectors.

This chapter has looked forwards, beyond immediate gains from exporting, to try to judge long-term advances in increasing productive capacities and enabling Southeast Asian countries to move away from vent-for-surplus dependent growth. The chapter made the point that Southeast Asia began in 1870 with very different initial conditions than in Japan. Rapid Japanese growth and structural transformation depended fundamentally on strong preconditions and a determined, development-oriented government. Southeast Asia lacked Japan's promising pre-conditions. A developmental state, even if it was realistic, was not possible under Southeast Asia's colonial governments and Thailand's semi-colonial one. Burma's government did the least to advance development. It oversaw a country of 'unbridled laissez faire capitalism' that after independence yielded to autarkic socialism.[37] The Philippines did the most. Even there, however, small fiscal revenues severely constrained capital formation. Although it was 'truly remarkable how much the American administration was able to achieve' with limited resources, 'a more extensive program of capital formation ... would have paid handsome economic returns, and would have vastly improved the prospects for Philippine development during the independence period that followed World War II'.[38]

[37] Taylor, 'Disaster', p. 48.

[38] Hooley, 'American economic policy', pp. 472–73.

A similar verdict applied throughout Southeast Asia, since governments are crucial to economic development. 'Fundamentally', Harry Johnson observed some 50 years ago, 'the process of initiating self-sustaining growth is a process of effecting internal social and economic changes. The external trading environment may be influential in determining the relative difficulty of the process, but it is not crucial.'[39] It is difficult to see what agency except government can initiate such changes.

An answer to the counterfactual that Southeast Asian countries, if left to themselves, would have developed more successfully than they did under colonialism is unknowable. There may be different answers for different countries or areas that in 1870 were yet to be formed into countries. As history transpired, colonial rule, if to varying degrees, laid foundations for development on which countries, once independent, could build. It is by no means obvious that the diverse territories comprising late nineteenth-century Southeast Asia would have done more to create developmental foundations. In 1870, Southeast Asia had almost no modern industry, lacked technology and had established almost no educational base for its implementation. If one supposes that Southeast Asia had been closed to the flow of goods but not knowledge, the lack of a tradition of technical education would have made the knowledge of limited value.

It has been suggested that if, after the mid-nineteenth century, Southeast Asian countries had had their own governments, they might have been developed more and gone further towards laying foundations for subsequent development. The only possible strategy for growth as that which Southeast Asia experienced, however, was the one followed under colonial rule of using abundant resources to produce primary commodities for export to the world market. That is the usual way development starts. It seems probable that an independent Southeast Asia, in response to the unprecedented late nineteenth-century wave of globalization and the demand of industrial countries for raw materials, would still have developed as export economies.

Growth in an independent, export-oriented Southeast Asia might not have been as swift as under colonialism, since it established internal peace and built infrastructure, both fundamental pre-conditions for growth. Independent governments might well have blocked the same unlimited Chinese and Indian immigration as in Malaya and Burma. Although this would have created upwards wage pressure to encourage technical change, the abundance of land would have worked against such an outcome. Higher wages would have slowed growth, since integral to rapid expansion was abundant land and cheap labour to bring it under cultivation. Balanced against perhaps slower economic growth in a Southeast Asia free to make its own choices, indigenous Southeast Asians would likely have had a greater role in whatever economies emerged.

39 Johnson, *Economic policies*, p. 65.

An absence of colonialism might have placed export trade in indigenous hands and this, along with the freedom to make political choices, would have removed major resentments against colonial rule.

Given the region's pre-colonial history, it can hardly be assumed that, free of colonialism, Southeast Asia would have emerged in 1939 as a collection of developed economies. Benda, almost caricaturing a Panglossian view of Southeast Asian history, makes clear his considerable doubts over the likelihood that 'had Indonesia been left free to develop normally, it would not only have more or less "naturally" developed into a wealthy and just nation state, but also into a bourgeoise democracy'.[40] An assessment similar to Benda's for Indonesia applies to the rest of Southeast Asia.

After independence, all Southeast Asian governments set out to implement change. But in some countries it took decades to regain per capita income levels of the 1930s and to move positively and decisively in the direction of self-sustaining development, in substantial part because of the effects of World War II and the Japanese occupation, discussed in Part II of the book. The Southeast Asian search for growth and development, as Parts III, IV and V of the book will show, was not a straight nor easy path but all too often a matter of blind alleyways and disastrous mistakes.

[40] Benda, 'Democracy', p. 452.

PART II

World War II and Aftermath

8

The World War II Japanese Occupation of Southeast Asia

Late in November 1941, Japan decided on war in the Pacific. The principal Japanese objective in invading Southeast Asia was to secure natural resources, especially Indonesia's oil, and create, as the Greater East Asia Co-Prosperity Sphere, an empire large enough to secure independence from the international economy. By May 1942, the Japanese military controlled virtually all of Southeast Asia. Japanese occupation swept aside colonial rule by Britain, the Netherlands and the United States. Although Thailand was occupied by the Japanese, its pre-war government remained in place as the Kingdom's nominal ruler. In Indochina, a pro-Vichy French colonial regime accepted Japanese occupation and was left to administer Indochina until a 9 March 1945 Japanese coup.

Japanese occupation for some three-and-a-half years – from the 7 December 1941 attack on Pearl Harbour and the start of the Pacific War to Japan's surrender on 15 August 1945 – marks the darkest period in Southeast Asian history. This chapter recounts the suffering, privations and mass deaths of Southeast Asians during the occupation; it shows how Japan's economic weakness, policies towards Southeast Asia, indifference with which those in the region were treated and continuously worsening Japanese military position after the spring of 1942 magnified the ordeal of Southeast Asians. The chapter's initial two sections examine Japanese policy in Southeast Asia and methods of social control. How Japan financed occupation is explained in the third section. A fourth section analyses the impact of war and occupation on Southeast Asia's economies and people and the fifth shortages and black markets. In a sixth section, Japanese construction of railways and defence installations in Southeast Asia and the use of Southeast Asians and Allied POWs as labour to build them are considered. The final section quantifies the death toll of Southeast Asian civilians.

Japan's Economic Position and Policy in Southeast Asia

Japan's early, stunningly swift conquest of Southeast Asia was misleading, and largely reflected skeleton, unprepared colonial armies. With a tiny economy and a limited capacity for war production, Japan was no match for the

United States in a long conflict. In 1940, United States GDP was nearly five times that of Japan. Japanese productivity per man hour in all manufacturing industries was a quarter of American.[1] The United States accounted for two-fifths of world capital goods output compared to a mere 3.5 per cent for Japan. Low productivity and such a small capital goods industry severely constrained Japan's scope to produce armaments. So too did Japan's 1940 GDP per capita of (2011 US$) US$4,882 compared to America's US$12,005 per capita, since the lower GDP per capita, the less the leeway to reduce civilian consumption and re-direct productive capacity towards war.

Three further economic constraints told heavily against Japan, all of which impacted on Southeast Asia. One was that in late 1941 Japan was bogged down in an unwinnable war in China, which had dragged on since 1937 and cost 185,000 Japanese lives and billions of yen. Second, the United States was Japan's principal source of vital raw materials, chiefly oil, iron and cotton, and also the main Japanese export market. In 1936/37, the United States provided just under a third of Japanese imports and took a fifth of Japanese exports. By comparison, Asia as a whole supplied only a slightly bigger proportion than the United States of Japan's imports.

Third, Japan's geography compounded its economic weakness. As a small island cluster largely devoid of raw materials and unable to feed itself, Japan was fundamentally dependent on shipping for survival. In the event of war, Japanese naval vessels would have to secure Asian sea lanes and protect Japan's coastline. 'No country', observed the US Strategic Bombing Survey, 'could have been further from self-sufficiency with respect to raw materials than was Japan'; this made it 'desperately vulnerable to blockade operations'.[2]

Japan had determined even before the start of the Pacific War to disregard the deprivations of occupation for Southeast Asians and to send no goods or food to the region. This policy was partly explained by Japan's weak, already stretched economy, partly by the resource demands of war in China and partly by an inherent racism. Japan's official November 1941 outline of administration in Southeast Asia made Japanese policy towards Southeast Asians clear: 'During the war, the great burdens which will fall on natives on account of the acquisition of natural resources and the process of making the army self-supporting must be borne with the utmost patience. Any requests regarding welfare, which are contrary to this object, will be refused.'[3] Southeast Asian countries, or even areas of countries, were expected to make themselves self-sufficient and prevented from legally trading with each other.

[1] Productivity figures are from Goldsmith, 'Power of victory', p. 79.

[2] USSBS, *Effects of strategic bombing*, pp. 12, 14, and see p. 41; *Summary report*, pp. 18–20; and *Oil in Japan's war*, p. 31.

[3] NA, WO203/6310, 'SEATIC Special intelligence bulletin', 1946, p. 2.

Social Control

At the outset of occupation, many of those in Southeast Asia, notably in Burma, Indonesia and Thailand, were either well disposed towards the Japanese or at least neutral. Soon, however, the Japanese promise of a cultural mission and an Asia for Asians lacked credibility, as Southeast Asia's economies were forced towards an environment of acute shortages, social decay and draconian social repression. Japanese rhetoric never carried much weight in the Philippines. Filipinos doubted the idea of Asian brotherhood and considered their Christian morality superior to the Japanese, undercutting Japan's call for Asian solidarity.

Japan had three main goals in Southeast Asia: resource extraction, maintenance of social stability and army self-sufficiency.[4] In administering Southeast Asia and controlling its peoples so as to meet these goals, Japan faced stark geographic, demographic and economic realities. The region was large, divided into several countries, overwhelmingly rural, and ethnically varied. Against this, Japan had available only relatively few administrators and limited manpower for military occupation, especially with so many administrators and soldiers required for the war in China, and few resources to expend on Southeast Asia.

In administering Southeast Asia, Japan had to find ways to economize on scarce resources and make up for a lack of knowledge of the region and its variety of pre-war administrative systems, customs and languages. For the most part, Japanese administration maintained colonial Southeast Asian boundaries. Where possible, as to a large extent it was, use was made of existing administrative structures. Japanese practice was to work through elite groups, and sometimes create them, which reduced the need for contact with the mass of the population and made less important the acquisition of local knowledge and language skills. Economically, the Japanese operated through monopolistic bodies. Monopoly was seen as efficient and rational, and it limited the number of organizations with which administrators had to deal.

A goal of social organization was, as in Japan, to make control self-enforcing through a neighbourhood system, the system of *tonari-gumi*, which was built on a base of units of about 10 to 20 houses collectively responsible for the behaviour of each of their members and for allegiance to Greater Japan. There were, of course, serious limitations to self-enforcement in societies which had their own cultural norms and which were diverse, and social control was maintained through three further methods. One, viable in Thailand and Indochina, was to let an existing, pre-occupation administration try to deflect dissent and bear a share of the responsibility for worsening conditions.

[4] NA, WO203/6310, 'SEATIC Special intelligence bulletin', 1946, p. 2; JM 103, *Outline of administration*, pp. 1, 42.

To some extent, a similar strategy was tried, but much less successfully, in Burma and the Philippines, with the creation during the latter part of 1943 of nominally independent governments. A second strategy was the use of food. The Japanese controlled a large share of what food was available in Southeast Asia. Food distribution as rations created a measure of dependency, especially when, in most of Southeast Asia, food was so scarce. Moreover, the Japanese could induce people, perhaps otherwise reluctant to work for them, to do so though giving larger, priority rations.

The third Japanese answer to the maintenance of social control and suppression of anything deemed 'anti-Japanese' was extreme repression. Units of the military police had relatively few men but made use of the former employees of colonial security services and large numbers of local informers, both ways of economizing on scarce Japanese resources. The Japanese had, it was reported to Dutch intelligence, 'native spies everywhere'.[5] Among Indochina's most effective Sûreté agents were *métis* (people of mixed Euro-Vietnamese heritage), abandoned by their French fathers but offered education and employment by the colonial government.[6] The military police in Malaya particularly used women working in restaurants, bars, brothels and offices as informers.[7] In Burma, as well as a system of informers, marketplaces had white wooden boxes in which people could leave names.[8]

The security services of the *kempeitai* and *tokkeitai* were the ultimate enforcers of social control and routinely employed extreme methods of interrogation and torture so brutal that few dared oppose or openly question Japanese rule. Numerous independent contemporary accounts of *kempeitai* torture, graphic and harrowing, suggest that it would have been better to die immediately than be tortured, even if one might have survived.[9] It was standard practice to inflict brutal torture on anyone suspected of transgression before interrogating them. Execution frequently followed torture, and Burma's prison population fell because of this.[10] To be suspected of any crime – for example, dealing in British or American currency, listening to the BBC or smuggling – was almost certain to lead to torture.[11] The pulling out of a victim's fingernails was frequent

5 NIMH, 010A/10, Netherlands Forces Intelligence Service, 'Interrogation of three Boeginese survivors of a ship-wrecked crew of 10', 24 July 1944, p. 1; Sukarno makes a similar point: Sukarno, *Autobiography*, p. 181.

6 Marr, *Vietnam 1945*, p. 72.

7 NARA, RG226, entry 19, box 147, R&A XL10747, *Interrogation on Malaya*, 1 June 1945, p. 5.

8 Khin Myo Chit, *Three years*, p. 18; OSS, R&A 1713, *Structure of the government of Burma*, pp. 49–50.

9 Hartendorp, *Japanese occupation*, pp. 606, 642.

10 Burma Intelligence Bureau, *Burma*, vol. 2, pp. 41–51.

11 Chin, *Malaya upside down*, p. 124; Malayan Union, *Annual report on education ... 1946*, p. 3; NARA, RG226, entry 16, box 144, 'Conditions in the Philippine Islands', 23 August 1942, p. 9.

and vicious beatings usual. Water torture, followed by jumping on the stomach until water came out of the victim's orifices, was said to be the most dreaded of the Japanese methods.[12] The response of the military police and army to protest by Southeast Asians was truckloads of troops and arrests.[13] In Singapore, someone in Bukit Timah raised a Chinese flag; two days later the Japanese came and 'took over and then they slaughtered all the Chinese in Bukit Timah'.[14] When informed (incorrectly) that a Singapore man and his brother were communists, the *kempeitai*, after arresting the suspects, burned alive several women and children in their house.[15]

In Singapore, despite the city's overwhelmingly Chinese make-up, acceptance of Japanese rule was total.[16] Burma's civilian population was described as 'thoroughly cowed'.[17] In both Singapore and Burma, the civilian reaction is unsurprising: under *kempeitai* control, even Shanghai, notorious for an extensive underworld, relapsed into comparative law and order.[18] While it was wise to avoid the military police at all costs, as one moved about Singapore any Japanese were to be given a wide berth. Military sentries might brutally slap a person and then require hours of standing in the sun for not bowing or not having bowed to satisfaction.[19] As a Singaporean recalled, '[I]t was just the law of the sword, they used to chop off heads and all that kind of thing ... a kind of strict military discipline control over the city.'[20] As stories of *kempeitai* torture and beheadings spread, people in Indochina wondered if even the oppressive French might have been better.[21]

Japan's approach to social control and shortages of food and goods erased any lingering incentive for Southeast Asians to believe in Japan's Co-Prosperity or in Japanese superiority. For Southeast Asians there was no escaping the heavy-handed methods and ethnic disdain practised by the occupying Japanese. Convinced that they were a superior race, the Japanese, Thein Pe Myint observed, 'treated Burmese arrogantly and thought nothing of slapping them about the face'.[22] The Japanese slogans used throughout Southeast Asia, 'Same race, same culture' and 'One colour, one race', had a hollow ring.[23]

12 He, *Syonan interlude*, p. 184.
13 Lucas, *One soul*, p. 49.
14 NAS, Oral History, Baey Lian Peck, pp. 20–21.
15 Low and Cheng, *This Singapore*, pp. 48–49.
16 OSS, R&A 2423, *Singapore under Japanese domination*, 8 September 1944, p. 1.
17 OSS, R&A 1713, *Structure of the government of Burma*, p. 50.
18 OSS, R&A 3186S, *Kempei*, p. 3.
19 NAS, Oral History, Wong Kee Hung, p. 36; see also Baey Liam Peck, p. 34.
20 NAS, Oral History, George Edwin Bogaars, pp. 26, 39.
21 Marr, *Vietnam 1945*, pp. 91–92.
22 Taylor, *Marxism and resistance*, p. 107.
23 Low, *When Singapore*, p. 121; Benda, 'Beginnings', p. 67 and see p. 70.

Japanese Extraction and Finance

Japan transferred resources to itself from Southeast Asia in three main ways: direct confiscation or plunder, labour extraction and 'market-purchases'. In this last, Japan seemingly paid for what it obtained, but in reality did not, since goods and services were 'bought' with money that the Japanese printed, or ordered to be printed, and for which Japan provided Southeast Asia with no goods in exchange. This section considers all three methods of extraction but concentrates on 'market-purchased' resource transfers, since these were the principal means of extraction. The printing of money to finance extraction had inflationary consequences which fundamentally affected post-war Southeast Asia.

Japan's plunder of commodities was not especially great – it included, for example, four months' supply of crude oil and about 39,000 tons of rubber from Indonesia and between 60,000 and 150,000 tons of rubber from Malaya. Plunder was, however, considerable in regard to all types of transport.[24] Rolling stock and rails were taken from around Southeast Asia for Japanese railway construction projects in the region. Throughout Southeast Asia, the Japanese military took most motorized transport and ships. Houses and buildings were occupied without compensation. Except possibly in Thailand, '[I]f someone suddenly set up a small wooden board, with something written in Japanese on it, at the gate of your house, you realized immediately [that it was needed by the army] and you quit promptly, bag and baggage.' Even in Bangkok, despite Thailand's alliance with Japan, the 'Thais looked on helplessly, as Japanese officers and civilians occupied every available building in the city'.[25] The Singapore Chinese Girls School became a 'comfort station' or brothel for Japanese use, as did the otherwise non-descript Tan Lock Hotel in Penang.[26]

Labour extraction was also substantial. Including temporary and 'voluntary' workers, perhaps as many as 15 million Southeast Asians worked at some point for the Japanese. Work was generally organized by the Japanese, but might also be by chance. An Indian journalist recalled that: 'If you happened to be taking a stroll and saw some Japanese soldiers unloading cases of ammunition from a fleet of lorries, you just rolled up your sleeves and helped the war effort. If you tried to walk away, you would not get far; you would be lying on the road

24 Milward, *War, economy*, p. 165.

25 Sivaram, *Road to Delhi*, p. 62. On the Japanese takeover of any business or residential property that they wanted, regardless of whether it belonged to enemy nationals, Thais or Chinese, see NARA, RG59, entry 205, box 5834, file 892.00 233, J. Holbrook Chapman, 'General report on conditions in Thailand Dec. 1941 to June 1942', 18 August 1942, p. 24; Reynolds, 'Anomaly', p. 253.

26 Malayan Union, *Report on the British military administration*, p. 102; Nakahara, '"Comfort women"', pp. 583, 587.

with a bleeding bayonet wound in your back.'[27] More important, large numbers of Southeast Asians, as discussed below, were co-opted as forced labour. That amounted often to death and, at the least, to a tax on Southeast Asians, since wages were typically below market rates, as were forced deliveries of food. Either by force or by deceit, some 20,000 Asian women became, as comfort women, sex slaves, joining about 80,000 of these women, almost all Asians, in Southeast Asia's comfort stations.

Even before the outbreak of war, Japanese financial policy was clear: Southeast Asians would themselves provide much of the finance for war in the region. Two possible ways to implement this were by selling bonds to banks and Southeast Asians and by taxation. Neither, however, offered much scope in Southeast Asia. Its financial markets were not well developed and, furthermore, soon after occupation Japan closed almost all the European banks, the main possible purchaser of bonds. The Japanese allowed local Asian banks to re-open during 1942 and 1943, but they were tiny compared to the European banks. Stock markets in Southeast Asia were skeletal or non-existent and so, like the banks, were not of much help. Nor could much finance be raised through taxation, since tax bases in the region depended heavily on exports, which contracted dramatically after occupation cut Southeast Asia off from global markets. That left printing money: Japan paid for both its military and civilian expenditures in Southeast Asia and also for its imports from the region chiefly by expanding the money supply.

The Japanese transferred resources to themselves in Malaya, Indonesia, the Philippines and Burma simply by printing the required amount of military currency (scrip). It was legal tender only in the occupied territory for which it was issued, cost the Japanese only the expense of printing and could be used to buy goods and services and to meet local military and administrative (occupation) costs. As before the war, currencies were denominated in rupees, dollars, guilders and pesos for Burma, Malaya, Indonesia and the Philippines respectively. With 'appropriate' pictures – banana plants for Malaya and Indonesia, pagodas for Burma – scrip looked markedly different from pre-war notes. Print quality was, the Japanese acknowledged, 'appalling' and it deteriorated as the war continued.[28] Before then, however, Japan's occupation currencies attracted derisive names: 'banana money' in Malaya and Indonesia, 'Mickey Mouse money' in the Philippines.

Acquiring currency to spend in Thailand and Indochina was slightly more complicated for the Japanese. However, the effect was like issuing scrip, since Japan gave no money or credits convertible into tangible goods in exchange

[27] Sivaram, *Road to Delhi*, pp. 63–64.

[28] NIDS, Nansei Gunsei–17 Japan, Southern Military Administration Chōsabu, *Report no. 23: Zairai tsūka kaishu mondai ni tsute* [Withdrawal of local money] by Higuchi Gorō (Singapore, December 1943), p. 7.

for local Thai or Indochinese currency. Japan used baht in Thailand and piastres in Indochina to buy goods it exported and to defray the costs of occupying the two countries. When Japanese officials, after some negotiation with the Thai or Indochinese governments, specified currency requirements, the Yokohama Specie Bank credited at the Bank of Japan in Tokyo the accounts of the Bank of Thailand or Banque de l'Indochine with the yen equivalent of baht or piastres to be given to Japan. These Southeast Asian 'central banks' then credited the Yokohama Specie Bank in Bangkok or Saigon with local currency for military use.[29]

Yen credited to Thailand were 'special' but, in reality, merely paper credits without practical use. They could be neither spent in Japan nor used to purchase imports from Japan. While in Malaya, Burma, Indonesia and the Philippines Japanese military administrations directly controlled finance and the issue of currency, the pre-war governments in Thailand and Indochina were left to determine how to pay for resource transfers specified by Japan. Because of the lack of scope to sell bonds or tax, that largely meant monetary expansion.

For Thailand, Indochina and Indonesia, wartime national income estimates and measures of the different ways that Japan financed occupation can be used to evaluate transfers for market 'purchases' as a share of GDP. Exploitation was substantial: at wartime exchange rates imposed after Japan arbitrarily devalued Southeast Asian currencies, Thailand's payments between 1942 and 1945 averaged 6 per cent of GDP, Indochina's rose from 9 per cent in 1942 to over 25 per cent by 1945, and Indonesia's reached 11 per cent in 1943. Using 1937 exchange rates, these figures for market purchases are significantly higher: 10 per cent for Thailand, nearly 35 per cent for Indochina in 1945 and over 20 per cent for Indonesia in 1943.[30] Japan's transfers from Indonesia declined after 1943 because Japan was cut off from Indonesian oil supplies during 1944 by systematic American submarine and air attacks, which decimated the Japanese tanker fleet.[31] Moreover, plunder and labour resource transfers to Japan cannot be reliably quantified, making 'market-purchased' resource transfers a lower bound of total transfers.

The monetary and inflationary consequences of Japanese financial policies for Southeast Asia would likely always have been severe, but were further worsened by three considerations. One was that Japan supplied Southeast Asia with almost no goods, leaving the region with only whatever stocks existed in

[29] BE, OV25/9, Extract from *Bangkok Times*, 'Japan-Thailand economic co-operation. New agreement now signed. The system of settlement', 4 May 1942; Kingdom of Thailand, *Report of the financial adviser 1941–1950*, p. 55; AOM, 1AFFECO/289, Franco-Japanese accords: 'Modalities d'application de l'exchange de lettres, 1942' and 'Note: Négociation d'un nouvel accord financier entre l'Indochine et le Japon', Vichy, 23 December 1942.

[30] Huff, *World War II*, p. 90.

[31] Nenryō Konwa Kai, *Kaigun nenryō shi*, Part one, p. 664; USSBS, *Effects of strategic bombing*, pp. 41–44.

late 1941 and relatively small amounts of goods made locally. Acute shortages soon developed, driving up prices and forcing the Japanese printing of even more money to obtain goods and services. Second, by mid-1943 the war turned badly against Japan. That further exacerbated shortages because of increased Japanese demand for local materials and labour to construct defence installations. Third, as the war continued and inflation rose, many Southeast Asians became increasingly unwilling to hold Japanese scrip. Inflation eroded its real value and as this fell Southeast Asians spent scrip ever more quickly with the effect of causing prices to rise faster and the real values to decline further.

From 1943 onwards, in Thailand and Indochina money creation financed half to three-quarters of total government spending.[32] The proportion of government finance obtained from printing money was almost certainly as large, and probably larger, in the four military-administered Southeast Asian countries, since there Japan had merely to issue scrip as required. Increasing recourse to finance through printing money led to high inflation everywhere and, in the countries with scrip, rocketing inflation or hyperinflation. In Malaya, the Philippines and Indonesia, the greater the quantities of currency that the Japanese printed, the more price rises outdistanced monetary expansion as Southeast Asians divested themselves of the currency ever more quickly. Malaya appears the extreme example: by the end of the war money supply had multiplied 25.1 times while prices were 11,000 times higher. However, the Philippines and Indonesia might well show similar money supply and price histories if data were available for the final weeks of the war, when the Japanese issued particularly large quantities of currency (Table 8.1).

Economic Impact

In 1940, Southeast Asian economies ranked among the world's most open and most specialized. Throughout the region, growth had been strongly export-led, and exports were almost wholly some combination of agricultural and mineral products. Together, primary production and trade accounted for three-fifths to two-thirds of GDP in most Southeast Asian countries and as much as three-quarters of GDP in Malaya, due to its exceptional openness. Because during the Japanese occupation nothing fundamentally changed these pre-war macroeconomic relationships and because there was little new investment or much government spending, the collapse in exports led directly to large falls in national income. Such Japanese investment as occurred was mainly aimed at patching up infrastructure, the provision of textile machinery redundant in Japan, and a concerted but futile attempt to build wooden boats, as well as greater efforts to turn pre-war Southeast Asian manufacturing capacity to war production.

[32] Cf. BT, Bank of Thailand, *Economic report, 1945*, p. 24: '[T]he Government resorted to printing paper money to meet their revenue deficits.'

Table 8.1 *Southeast Asia characteristics of money and inflation during the Japanese occupation, 1942–45*

	Burma	Malaya	Thailand	Indonesia	Indochina Saigon	Philippines
1. Ratio of prices at the end of occupation to prices at its beginning	1,856.5	11,226.5	6.9	32.0	3.6	889.3
2. Ratio of quantity of currency at the end of occupation to the beginning	16.4	25.1	7.1	11.0	5.7	28.0
3. Ratio of (1) to (2)	111.4	447.3	1.0	2.9	0.6	31.8
4. Average rate of rise in prices (% per month)	16.9	16.3	4.0	7.9	2.7	18.4
5. Average rate of rise in quantity of currency (% per month)	6.3	7.4	4.1	5.6	4.1	9.0
6. Ratio of (4) to (5)	2.7	2.2	1.0	1.4	0.7	2.0
7. Average rate of rise in prices during last year of occupation (% per month)	27.1	30.5	5.4	7.6	2.8	32.3
8. Ratio of (7) to (4)	1.6	1.9	1.4	1.0	1.0	1.8
9. Average rate of rise in prices during last two months of occupation (% per month)	72.1	86.8	–	14.0	–	37.2
10. Ratio of (9) to (4)	4.3	5.3	–	1.8	–	2.0
11. Real balances at end of occupation as a % of real balances at its beginning	0.9	0.2	102.7	34.3	171.8	3.2

Note: Apparent anomalies in lines 1 and 4 between the rise in prices and the average monthly rise in prices are because data are for different time periods for countries.
Source: Huff, *World War II*, p. 99.

Table 8.2 *Southeast Asia and Japan GDP per capita, 1870–1950 (1938 = 100)*

	Burma	Malaya	Thailand	Indonesia	Vietnam	Philippines	Japan
1870	68.1	47.0	73.6	48.9	60.7	43.3	30.1
1913	92.6	65.7	101.8	82.3	87.4	68.6	56.6
1938	100.0	100.0	100.0	100.0	100.0	100.0	100.0
1941	–	–	102.4	109.6	91.8	–	117.3
1942	–	–	90.0	87.6	83.9	–	115.1
1943	–	–	98.3	69.9	79.3	–	115.2
1944	–	–	91.9	54.8	62.0	–	108.6
1945	–	–	82.6	48.5	48.9	–	55.0
1946	–	–	86.7	49.9	57.0	44.9	59.0
1947	–	–	93.8	57.0	59.9	60.8	62.9
1948	–	–	101.5	65.7	61.6	68.9	70.4
1949	–	–	100.0	71.8	67.6	71.1	73.5
1950	53.5	114.7	101.2	74.2	79.1	74.3	78.4

Source: Huff, *World War II*, p. 118.

If anything, conventional government expenditure fell because, Thailand and Indochina apart, the Japanese relied on adapting existing administrative structures and cut pre-war programmes including education, health services and hospitals, welfare provision and malaria eradication. Military spending only partially replaced pre-war government expenditure.

The wartime collapse in national income in Southeast Asia was dramatic: one of the great macroeconomic crises in modern history.[33] By early 1944, as the crisis intensified, incomes had plummeted to late nineteenth-century levels (Table 8.2). 'Economic life receded from modernity' and countries retreated 'toward an isolation and autarchy that harked back to precolonial times'.[34] Only Thailand escaped relatively unscathed, benefiting from its alliance with Japan, government support for the economy and ability to sell smuggled rice to Malaya and Indonesia. In 1945, per capita income in Thailand remained at 82.6 per cent of its 1938 level. Elsewhere in the region, available data show plunges in real per capita Southeast Asian GDP of around 50 per cent during the Japanese occupation.[35] In all of Southeast Asia except Thailand, widespread malnutrition, severe economic dislocation, forced labour, and in Vietnam and Indonesia mass famines checked, or often temporarily reversed, population growth.

[33] Cf. Barro and Ursúa, 'Macroeconomic crises'.
[34] Bastin and Benda, *History*, p. 127.
[35] Anamwathana, *Thailand's economy*, pp. 53–64.

A relatively normal pre-war year in Indonesia was 1938. Between then and 1945, GDP per capita dropped by 50 per cent and became roughly equivalent to what it had been in 1870 (Table 8.2). A collapse in real prices of Indonesia's principal export crops undermined a main incentive to produce; and great disorganization reigned as the Japanese authorities struggled to find the best way to manage and re-shape estate production. In trying to accomplish this, Japan faced enormous transport difficulties due to the loss in Southeast Asia of ships, railway disrepair and the disruption or unavailability of what regular shipping services still existed.

In Indochina during the early years of the war, an expansion of local industries, explained by import-substituting industrialization promoted by the French administration, helped to support the Indochinese economy, and in 1943 GDP per capita remained at over four-fifths of the 1940 level. A 38 per cent drop in GDP per capita between 1943 and 1945 reflected severe transport disruption, US air attacks, famine in Tonkin and North Annam, and extreme instability resulting from the March 1945 Japanese coup, followed by the Indochinese Communist Party/Viet Minh revolution in August. By early 1945, industrial activity had ceased except in sectors important to the Japanese war effort. Faced with economic breakdown, 'the main problem was to ensure the survival of the population'.[36]

The Philippines and Burma suffered greatly. While data-based estimates for GDP are unavailable, damage to the capital stock makes it likely that in both countries the fall in GDP per capita may have exceeded half. Sicat extrapolates backwards for the Philippines to calculate a drop in 1940 GDP of 50 per cent by 1943 and 70 per cent in 1945. He considers, moreover, that even a fall of 70 per cent may be an understatement due to the decimation of capital stock.[37] That included the near total destruction of Manila and devastation in many other cities and larger towns, which in the latter 'left little but the names and the sites'.[38] Between 1938 and 1946, a fall of three-fifths in the combined index of Philippines physical production supports Sicat's estimate of a 70 per cent wartime contraction of Filipino national income and indicates that a drop of half, suggested above, may be a conservative figure (Table 8.3).[39]

In Burma, the 1946/47 volume of output was 60 per cent of that in 1938/39.[40] This may understate national income decline between the end of the 1930s and 1945 due to wartime falls in transport, services, utilities and trade. Omitting strictly military traffic, the Japanese occupation soon reduced Burma's foreign trade to probably less than 5 per cent of its normal pre-war level.[41] In 1950, GDP

36 Le, *Impact*, p. 270 and see pp. 270–72.
37 Sicat, 'Philippine economy' (2015), pp. 197, 201, 202.
38 Hartendorp, *History of industry*, p. 153.
39 Spencer, *Land and people*, p. 223; Steinberg, 'Ambiguous legacy', p. 180.
40 Burma, *National income*, p. 2.
41 Burma Intelligence Bureau, *Burma*, vol. 2, p. 173.

Table 8.3 *Philippines index of physical production, 1937–50 (1937 = 100)*

	Combined index	Agricultural	Manufacturing	Mining
1937	100.0	100.0	100.0	100.0
1938	98.2	85.3	109.1	129.4
1939	93.4	82.8	98.8	152.3
1940	109.9	98.0	117.1	165.0
1946	38.7	58.2	21.0	2.0
1947	75.6	79.5	77.5	16.8
1948	85.3	86.4	89.4	36.0
1949	91.3	92.2	94.7	49.1
1950	98.2	97.6	103.1	58.6

Source: Huff, *World War II*, p. 162.

per capita in Burma was just slightly above half that in 1938 and apparently well below what it had been in 1870 (Table 8.2). British intelligence reported a 'drastic decline in living standards'; Burma had to adjust to a 'lower, handicraft stage of existence'.[42] The country, concluded one scholar, returned to a standard of living last seen in the 1880s and 1890s.[43] 'Both in internal transport and external trade', according to another observer, 'Burma was thrown back a century, without warning or prior preparation'.[44]

Malaya underwent a severe contraction in GDP, probably by a half to three-fifths (Table 8.2). The pre-war Malayan economy had the world's highest per capita exports and depended heavily on selling rubber and tin to the West. Output of both commodities dropped precipitately, and they piled up largely unwanted except for some Japanese demand.

Declining output in Southeast Asia was caused by the loss of access to global markets and supplies from them, by the Japanese imposition of Southeast Asian country autarky, and by Japan's attempt to re-fashion Southeast Asia's economies to fit into a Greater East Asia Co-Prosperity Sphere. The reasons for autarky were to limit transport use and, for an army living off the land, to avoid the domino effect of a military loss in one region causing the loss of another due to food and material shortages. Deterioration in Japan's military situation led to country autarky becoming regional, or even sub-regional, autarky. By mid-1943, a lack of regional shipping and land transport further contributed to pushing Southeast Asian countries towards autarky. Pre-war Southeast Asian countries and regions were so economically integrated and so interdependent,

[42] Burma Intelligence Bureau, *Burma*, vol. 2, pp. 173–74, 193–94, 198.

[43] Christian, *Burma and the Japanese invader*, p. 355 and *Burma*, p. 124.

[44] Andrus, *Burmese economic life*, p. 335.

especially in regard to food, that the near disappearance of intra-regional commerce and collapse of inter-country trade associated with autarky and shortages of transport exacerbated the already steep economic decline caused by Southeast Asia's severance from the global economy.

Rice exports held up well in Indochina and, until 1944, in Thailand due to shipments to Japan but dropped to almost nothing in Burma because the Japanese lacked ships to uplift Burmese rice (Table 8.4). Exports from the three non-food-specialized countries of Malaya, Indonesia and the Philippines dropped sharply (Tables 8.3 and 8.5). Malaya and Indonesia produced rubber and tin for a global market, and Japan's economy was too small to use more than an insignificant fraction of either commodity. The acute disparity between Southeast Asian rubber production and Japanese needs led the bulk of the export sectors of the Malayan and Outer Island Indonesian economies to shut down. Nor did Japan want Indonesian or Philippine sugar as it was already amply supplied by efficient Taiwanese production. Before the war, rice from Southeast Asia's three rice-specialized countries had been essential in feeding Malaya and, to a lesser extent, Indonesia and the Philippines. This dependence of non-rice-specialized Southeast Asia on the region's main rice producers became crucial during the war: none of the three pre-war rice importers was able to shift to feeding themselves and their populations were left malnourished or worse.

As foreign trade collapsed, so too did transport, public services and manufacturing. Nowhere in pre-war Southeast Asia had industrialization been sufficiently advanced for the region to be self-sufficient in practically any of the basic necessities such as cloth, thread, shoes and sandals, soap, matches, paper, batteries, light bulbs and essential medicines. Pre-war Southeast Asia typically relied on imports for half to three-quarters or more of its annual consumption of textiles. Japan's failure to step in as an alternative source of supply left large gaps in the availability of almost all basic consumer goods, manufactured materials and capital equipment.

Southeast Asia became a 'stock economy', dependent for consumption on pre-war stocks of goods meant to supply populations for a relatively short period. Clothing became almost universally hard to obtain, especially outside urban areas where few pre-war stocks existed. In Burma, thieves did a thriving business in stolen articles of clothing.[45] Graves in Manila were robbed to obtain clothes from the corpses, as well as for gold teeth.[46] By late 1943, gunny bags normally used to transport rice and sugar began to be worn as clothing. In Indonesia, some people even clothed themselves in sheets of crude rubber or, as a last resort, banana leaves.[47] A proportion of the population in Burma wore

45 OSS, R&A 2015, *Japanese administration of Burma*, p. 43.

46 UP, Manuel A. Roxas Papers for the ms. Osmeña, 'Dear dad', p. 310; Agoncillo, *Fateful years*, pp. 583–84.

47 Stoler, *Capitalism*, p. 99.

Table 8.4 *Burma, Indochina and Thailand rice acreage, production and exports, 1937/39–1950*

(a) Area, production and exports

	Burma Area 000 acres	Burma Production 000 metric tons	Burma Exports 000 metric tons	Indochina Area 000 acres	Indochina Production 000 metric tons	Indochina Exports 000 metric tons	Thailand Area 000 acres	Thailand Production 000 metric tons	Thailand Exports 000 metric tons
1937/39	12,433	7,193	3,350	12,685	6,957	1,419	8,617	4,547	1,382
1940	12,518	6,894	3,123	11,816	6,846	1,586	9,518	4,923	1,326
1941	12,325	7,738		12,207	6,944	944	9,923	5,120	1,599
1942	10,697	5,752		12,133	7,222	974	10,948	3,854	991
1943	7,635	3,053	336	12,792	7,071	1,024	10,370	5,536	739
1944	6,501	2,545		12,419	5,971	499	10,155	4,928	477
1945	6,496	2,677		12,419	4,871	45	9,406	3,572	305
1946	7,910	3,844		12,419	5,966		9,955	4,442	684
1947	8,597	5,440		12,419	6,340		12,062	5,506	513
1948	9,798	5,164		12,419	6,016		13,029	6,835	1,019
1949	9,017	4,581		12,419	6,579		13,170	6,684	1,319
1950	9,150	5,403	1,378	12,419	7,151		13,850	6,782	1,843

(*continued*)

Table 8.4 (*cont.*)

(b) 1937/39 = 100

	Burma Area	Burma Production	Burma Exports	Indochina Area	Indochina Production	Indochina Exports	Thailand Area	Thailand Production	Thailand Exports
1937/39	100.0	100.0	100.0	100.0	100.0	100.0	100.0	100.0	100.0
1940	100.7	95.8	93.2	93.1	98.4	111.8	110.4	108.3	95.9
1941	99.1	107.6	–	96.2	99.8	66.5	115.2	112.6	115.7
1942	86.0	80.0	–	95.6	103.8	68.7	127.0	84.8	71.7
1943	61.4	42.4	10.0	100.8	101.6	72.2	120.3	121.8	53.5
1944	52.3	35.4	–	97.9	85.8	35.2	117.8	108.4	34.5
1945	52.2	37.2	–	97.9	70.0	3.2	109.1	78.6	22.1
1946	63.6	53.4	–	97.9	85.8	–	115.5	97.7	49.5
1947	69.1	75.6	–	97.9	91.1	–	140.0	121.1	37.1
1948	78.8	71.8	–	97.9	86.5	–	151.2	150.3	73.7
1949	72.5	63.7	–	97.9	94.6	–	152.8	147.0	95.4
1950	73.6	75.1	41.1	97.9	102.8	–	160.7	149.2	133.4

Source: Huff, *World War II*, p. 135.

Table 8.5 *Indonesia estate and cash crop production, 1936/38–1950 (1936/38 = 100)*

	Estate crops	Cash crops
1936/38	100.0	100.0
1939	115.1	101.0
1940	120.8	103.8
1941	126.1	110.5
1942	68.1	67.3
1943	40.1	49.6
1944	27.7	35.2
1945	10.1	21.3
1946	3.7	51.5
1947	3.2	71.3
1948	22.1	88.2
1949	43.6	85.0
1950	46.3	142.8

Source: Huff, *World War II*, p. 154.

gunny bags for clothing.[48] When plague broke out in Rangoon, the Japanese gave gunnies as a reward for delivering tails of rats as a proof of their death.

By 1944, if not before, pre-war supplies of goods were effectively exhausted and Southeast Asia was left economically stranded. Because of the lack of basic goods and often food, living standards for ordinary Southeast Asians probably declined even further than the roughly halving of GDP per capita. Utilities and transport contracted because items such as spare parts, tyres, fuel and lubricants previously obtained from abroad were almost entirely unavailable after late 1941. The local manufacture of many basic consumer goods became impossible because inputs were locally unobtainable except possibly on black markets. Apart from that, Southeast Asians had no choice but to try to fashion substitutes for a whole range of items including basic manufactured goods, medicines and textiles, but with little success because of the lack of a pre-war industrial base, low human capital, few skilled workers and reliance on imported components. The Japanese made little effort to develop Southeast Asian manufacturing until mid-1943, and then largely for the military.

Falls in the contributions of trade and commodity production to GDP were intensified by acute transport shortages, which, by 1943, developed throughout Southeast Asia, and by the collapse of public utility provision. As the

[48] Burma Intelligence Bureau, *Burma*, vol. 2, pp. 175–76, 193–94, 198.

war continued, insofar as transport and public utilities still functioned, their operation became patchy due to failures to repair or replace compounded by inadequate fuel stocks and a lack of spare parts. The Japanese monopolized available modern transport and it became virtually unavailable other than for military use. Coastal and inland shipping services on which most of Southeast Asia depended to move food and goods sharply declined or even disappeared. Growing shortages of spare parts, lubricants and fuel together with Allied bombing made transport progressively more inadequate. Before the war, 3,500 to 4,000 heavy goods vehicles had operated in Indochina but by April 1944 transport utilization had fallen by between a third and a half due to a lack of tyres, spark plugs and spare parts.[49] As early as August 1942, transport in Manila was essentially limited to *carromatas* (horse-drawn carriages), bicycles and electric street cars.[50] Fuel shortages soon forced Manila electricity and gas companies to burn coconut oil and shells and restricted power supplies.[51] In Rangoon, electric trams ran intermittently, and apparently trolley buses did not operate for the duration of the occupation.[52] Oil and kerosene to run buses was hard to obtain. Passengers frequently had to push buses to get them started.[53] Public transport in Singapore so deteriorated that by the latter half of 1944 only a third of trams and buses were in service. Singaporeans increasingly turned to rickshaws, bullock carts and horse carriages for transport.[54]

Japan's policy of enforced autarky worked in tandem with transport shortages to split national economies into localized enclaves. Japanese price controls added to the economic squeeze by reducing incentives for farmers to produce for local markets. Market segmentation probably widened income inequalities in most, perhaps even all, of the region. For Southeast Asia, enforced enrolment in the Greater East Asia Co-Prosperity Sphere disrupted trade, both external and internal, deterred specialization within agriculture and mining, and wiped out dynamic gains that had flowed from all trade.

The want of transport in Southeast Asia was paralleled by inadequate Japanese shipping to carry goods home or to Asian war theatres. Japanese planners and military strategists utterly failed to realize the precariousness of Japan's merchant shipping capability. At the start of the war Japan had no

[49] VNA, Fonds de la direction des finances 15154, 'Le problème économique et la question des transports', 18 April 1944, p. 26.

[50] NARA, RG226, entry 16, box 144, 'Conditions in the Philippine Islands', 23 August 1942, p. 50.

[51] NARA, RG226, entry 16, box 208, 'Economic conditions in the Philippines', 15 October 1942, p. 25.

[52] OSS, R&A 2753, *Japanese use of Burmese industry*, p. 36.

[53] Burma Intelligence Bureau, *Burma*, vol. 2, pp. 122–28.

[54] NA, CO273/673/2, 'Conditions in Singapore in the late summer of 1944', 5 February 1944, p. 4; National Archives of Singapore, *Syonan years*, pp. 220–21.

more, and probably less, merchant tonnage than it needed.[55] Increasingly as the war continued, Japan's lack of merchant shipping prevented the transport of even the Southeast Asian output that Japan could use. Out of the total of 10.1 million tons of shipping available to Japan during the war, the Allies sank or damaged beyond use 8.9 million tons, leaving just 1.2 million operable tons when Japan surrendered in August 1945.[56] By March 1945, Allied submarines, ships and aircraft had interdicted the transport of the oil from Indonesia that Japan needed to carry on the war, except as a hopeless, last-ditch effort.

Food supplies in Southeast Asia, especially outside rice-growing areas, were drastically reduced by ever more narrowly circumscribed autarky, mounting transport deficiencies, increased Allied bombing, and greater control over food distribution, which included delivery quotas for farmers and confiscation. The Irrawaddy Delta, Cochinchina in the south of Vietnam and Central Thailand produced great surpluses of rice that were essential in feeding much of the rest of Southeast Asia but which during the war became largely or entirely unavailable to many food-deficit areas. In the food-deficit (net food-importing) countries of Malaya, Indonesia and the Philippines, the Japanese had to ration rice virtually from the start of occupation and then progressively rationed other foods. Occupying administrations were forced into ever greater reductions in ration sizes. These fell to well below minimum calorie requirements in the largest cities, typically to even less in smaller cities, and to nothing in rural areas.

Numerous Japanese campaigns encouraged Southeast Asians to grow their own food. These and Japanese dissemination of information on the preparation of substitutes for foods no longer available, especially rice, at best only partially countered scarcities. Most Southeast Asians in non-rice-specialized areas, and some in those areas who survived occupation, ended it malnourished to a greater or lesser degree. Although Burma had large supplies of unsaleable rice, people in Lower Burma's rice areas suffered serious food deficiencies because the rice-producing delta could produce almost nothing else. Lower Burma had depended on other areas of Burma for other essential foods, but these became largely unavailable due to a lack of transport and autarky.

In 1944 and 1945, mass famines occurred in Tonkin and North Annam in Vietnam and Java in Indonesia, which were densely populated and with already delicately balanced pre-war food availability. Famine accounted for 1 million premature deaths in Vietnam and 2.4 million in Java.[57] To be certain of adequate food, Java and northern Vietnam needed to be able to call on outside sources of supplies but the war impeded this safety valve. In Vietnam,

[55] USSBS, *War against Japanese transportation*, p. 48, and *Effects of strategic bombing*, p. 41; Cohen, *Japan's economy*, pp. 251–55, 266.

[56] USSBS, *Summary report*, p. 11.

[57] Huff, 'Great World War II Vietnam' and 'Causes and consequences'.

those who died were predominantly the landless, and in Java estate and factory workers thrown out of work by the collapse in the economy.

In Java, the decisions of the occupying Japanese military led to mass famine. Indonesia's wartime Japanese rulers failed, unlike the colonial government, to appreciate the central role of prices in securing rice production and the need to transport large quantities of rice from surplus to deficit areas. When things began to go wrong, Japanese administrators relentlessly moved away from market solutions and enforced ever more restrictions; 'The more the Japanese tried to control rice marketing, the more it slipped out of control.'[58] By the latter part of 1943 it was probably too late to avoid major famine.

Japanese, French and Americans with options to avert Vietnam's famine may have viewed it as an unfortunate by-effect of war. The Viet Minh saw the positive aspects of the famine and had its own goals. The trauma of the famine and its enormous impact on the Vietnamese psyche, along with an Allied invasion, were recognized by the Viet Minh as fundamental pre-conditions for a communist revolution.

Shortages and Black Markets

Acute shortages of goods, inadequate or non-existent rations, high inflation and attempts at price controls made black markets, along with prostitution and corruption, a way of life in Southeast Asia. The Japanese themselves often resorted to black markets to secure otherwise unobtainable items like building materials, machinery, medicines and sometimes food. In Malaya, people came to think of it as normal: 'when the stage arrived at which the public was compelled to pay black market prices for such things as bus-tickets, railway-tickets, cinema-tickets, cloth-coupons, and even newspapers, the situation was beyond redemption'.[59]

Black markets spawned a new class of Southeast Asians. In Burma, occupation produced several Rangoon Indian millionaires and multimillionaires. One was said to have 'started business with a couple of lorries and a dozen rowdies, looted some of the big stores and godowns in Rangoon after their owners had fled, stored away the stuff secretly and become prominent in the black market after the Japanese occupation'.[60] Along with their accomplices, an easily distinguishable group of 'speculators and middlemen' emerged, Burma's 'New Order Brokers'. Typically, these men bought up scarce commodities, sold them to the Japanese army at a huge profit and benefited from favours from the military.[61]

58 Sato, *War, nationalism*, p. 203.
59 Chin, *Malaya upside down*, p. 37.
60 Sivaram, *Road to Delhi*, p. 150.
61 NARA, RG226, E154, box 81, f 1398, Japanese control of government finance in Burma, p. 10; IOR, Clague Papers, Mss Eur E252/44, 'Situation in Burma', p. 12.

Recognizable by the Shan bag or leather briefcase that they invariably carried, the New Order Brokers became 'the Nouveau Riche of New Order Burma'.[62] In Singapore, black market kings were known as mushroom millionaires.

Faltering Japanese rationing systems and restricted scope for urban cultivation left black markets with a major role in urban food provision. Throughout Malaya, black market food was 'crucial' in maintaining the health and welfare of the population.[63] Without black markets, malnutrition in many of the large cities of rice-deficit Southeast Asia would have been far worse, and in some mass starvation might even have occurred. Jakarta was the destination for heavy black market trafficking of rice organized through the city's underworld and by networks of smugglers. Attracted by prices some 10 times above village levels, rice smugglers relied on bribes, network organization and a degree of luck to circumvent legal prohibitions and the threat of severe penalties, even death, if apprehended with black market cargoes.[64] A common sight along the route into Manila's Tutuban railway station, where a black market in food centred, was smugglers throwing first sacks of rice and then themselves from moving trains. They were met by clusters of people begging to buy rice.[65] The inability of the Laurel government to control rice supplies from November 1943 left Manila heavily and increasingly dependent on the black market.[66]

As an offshoot of Singapore's wartime commerce and black market, Karimun-Bali, previously an obscure fishing island, functioned as the unofficial trade centre of Malaya, Sumatra and Java. Known as 'little Syonan' and just 28 nautical miles from its Singapore namesake, Karimun became home to over 100 firms, the port for a flotilla of small vessels and a hub of smuggling and black marketeering. Although well known to the Japanese military command, it turned a blind eye to Karimun, partly in the interest of food supplies for Singapore.[67]

Middle-class Southeast Asians sold pre-war assets on black markets in order to buy consumer goods and food. In Manila and Singapore, specialized city-centre markets acquired institutional status as centres for the sale of gold, jewellery and other valuables. One set of Singapore dealers, trading in jewellery and property and operating mainly in the High Street or Chulia Street off Raffles Place, bought from a middle class 'parting with family heirlooms in order to stay alive'.[68] A similar, flourishing jewellery mart grew up in Manila's Azcárraga Street between Rizal Avenue and San Bernardo.

62 Pe, *Narrative*, p. 67; see also Taylor, *Marxism and resistance*, p. 234.
63 Kratoska, *Japanese occupation*, p. 175 and see p. 254.
64 Cribb, *Gangsters*, p. 42; Kurasawa, 'Mobilization', pp. 133–34, 148, 164–65; Sato, *War, nationalism*, pp. 132–35, 143.
65 Agoncillo, *Fateful years*, pp. 545–47.
66 Hartendorp, *History of industry*, p. 83.
67 Twang, *Chinese business élite*, pp. 94–96; Kratoska, *Japanese occupation*, p. 254.
68 Lee, *Singapore story*, p. 66.

Labour and Transport

By mid-1943, as the military required more workers, labour shortages replaced early labour gluts. The Japanese recruited, or arranged the recruitment of, workers, on a voluntary or semi-voluntary basis, often with an inducement of food. Additionally, workers were also frequently obtained as forced labour, principally in Malaya, Burma and, especially, Indonesia. Deception might be used to recruit this labour, but Southeast Asian authorities regularly had a large role in procuring workers. Indonesians in positions of leadership, including Sukarno, the Republic's first president, actively helped to recruit, often as conscripts, large numbers of *romusha*, a term that in Japanese meant unskilled manual labourers, but who, in the context of the war, often amounted to forced labour.[69] Out of Java's population of about 50 million, the Japanese calculated a potential workforce of some 12.5 million. At one time or another a high proportion of these individuals worked for the Japanese, most on a temporary basis but 2.6 million as permanent *romusha*.[70] Data exist for 294,100 Indonesian *romusha* who were transported from their home areas. Of these, 120,000 were sent to Sumatra, 80,400 to North and South Borneo, 32,400 to the Soenda (Sunda) Islands and 31,000 to Malaya. Records show that of the 294,100 *romusha*, 77,000 returned home.[71] Probably at least half of all *romusha* taken from their homes died.

As the military outlook worsened, the Japanese needed more Southeast Asian labour to serve as auxiliaries to the military and to build railways, airfields and defence installations. Southeast Asia's north–south transport pattern ill-suited the requirement of the Japanese military; it needed instead rail links that connected Southeast Asia east–west by land. Although the Thai and Burma railway systems were only about 250 miles apart, they were not linked by road and were separated by a near-impenetrable barrier of mountains and jungle. Construction of the Thailand–Burma railway from Bangkok to Moulmein in Burma via Ban Pong and Three Pagodas Pass would afford Japan the quickest and most direct way to transport military supplies and soldiers to and from Burma (Figure 8.1). By avoiding shipment from Thailand or Indochina around the Malay Peninsula and then up to Rangoon, the 320-mile railway link across Thailand and through the jungle of Burma saved a 2,000-mile sea voyage each way. Two more of a total of five Japanese railway projects were motivated by the same east–west transport imperative: the Kra Isthmus railway, agreed with Thailand on 6 June 1943, to avoid having to sail down the east coast of Malaya past Singapore and then up the Straits of Malacca, and the central Sumatra

69 Sukarno, *Autobiography*, p. 192; Hill, *Journalism and politics*, pp. 25, 44.

70 Sato, *War, nationalism*, pp. 156–58.

71 IC, 400 2431, 'Numbers of *romusha* sent from Java from mid-1943 to mid-1945, registered by destination'; De Jong, *Collapse*, pp. 249–51; Friend, *Blue-eyed enemy*, p. 163; Raben, 'Indonesian *rōmusha*', pp. 208–10.

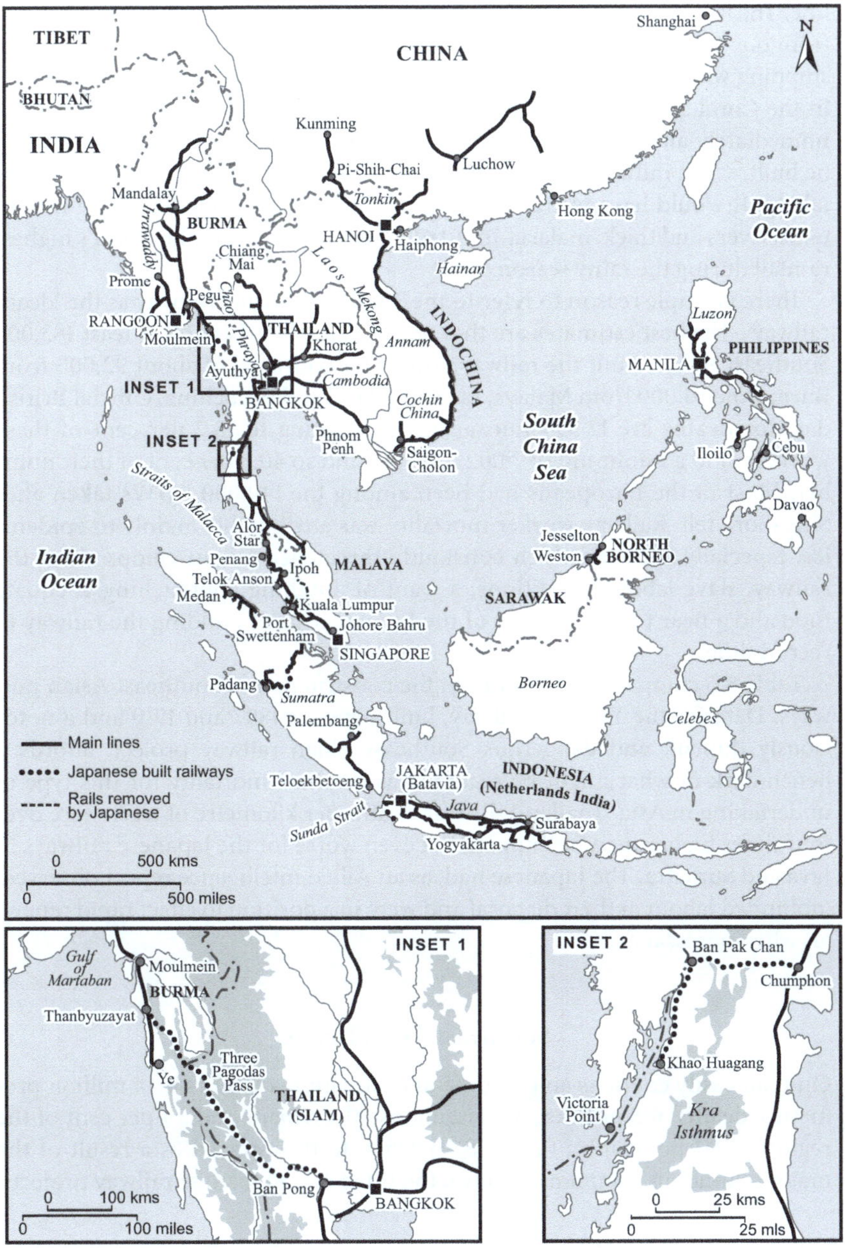

Figure 8.1 Thailand–Burma and Kra Isthmus railways
Sources: Rawson, 'Two new railways', pp. 85–88; Fisher, 'Thailand–Burma railway', pp. 85–97.

line. The lack of railways or roads across central Sumatra meant that transport from one side of the island to the other required sailing around it.[72] Japanese shipping was already under serious pressure due to naval setback in May 1942 in the Coral Sea and defeat during the first week in June at Midway. Almost immediately after that defeat, Tokyo ordered the Thailand–Burma railway to be built.[73] The railway was a monumental, seemingly near impossible, undertaking. It would have to traverse an extremely inhospitable terrain of mountains, rivers and thick, malaria-infested jungle with some of the world's highest rainfall during the rainy season.[74]

There is ample reason to refer to the Thailand–Burma railway as the 'death railway'. The best estimates are that 68,000 Allied POWs and at least 183,000 Southeast Asians built the railway. The latter consisted of about 92,000 from Burma and 91,000 from Malaya, Java, Thailand and Indochina. Official British data for deaths are 12,399 Europeans, amounting to 18.2 per cent of these workers, and a minimum of 74,025 Asians, and so 40.6 per cent of their number. Most of the Europeans had been among the 140,000 POWs taken after Singapore fell. Railway worker mortality was attributable mainly to epidemics, especially cholera, which constantly threatened labour camps along the railway, slave labour conditions, a want of anything approaching adequate food and a near total disregard of the human costs of building the railway in record time.

Table 8.6 compares death rates in the construction of Southeast Asian railways. Data for the Yunnan railway, built between 1897 and 1910 and a notoriously difficult and dangerous Southeast Asian railway project, affords a benchmark of what might be regarded as 'normal' mortality for this type of undertaking in Asia. Thailand–Burma deaths per kilometre of track were over four times higher than in Yunnan, but even worse for the Japanese railways in Java and Sumatra. The Japanese had, as an Allied intelligence report observed, 'unlimited labour at their disposal and were in a position to effect rapid renewals when necessary'.[75]

Southeast Asian Deaths

One can easily count as an outcome of occupation a total of 4.44 million premature deaths of Southeast Asians, almost all civilians and 3.1 per cent of the region's 1941 population (Table 8.7). Mass death occurred as a result of the major famines in Vietnam and Java, the three main Japanese railway projects,

72 De Jong, *Collapse*, p. 243.

73 NA, WO203/6325, SEATIC bulletin no. 246, 1946, 'Burma–Siam railway', pp. 3, 7.

74 *Japan Times and Advertiser*, 17 June 1942 cited in Reynolds, 'History, memory, compensation', p. 327; NA, WO203/6325, 'Burma–Siam railway', pp. 8–9.

75 NA, WO203/6325, 'Burma–Siam railway', p. 10.

Table 8.6 *Japanese World War II railways and Yunnan railway comparative construction deaths*

	Construction dates	Length km	No. of workers	No. of deaths	Deaths per km of railway
Yunnan railway (Lao Kay (Hekou) –Kunming)	1898–1910	464	60,000 at any one time	24,000	52
Thailand–Burma railway (Ban Pong –Thanbyuzayat): total	June 1942– Oct. 1943	402.3	250,503	86,424	215
Thailand–Burma railway (Ban Pong –Thanbyuzayat): Europeans	–	–	68,007	12,399	31
Thailand–Burma railway (Ban Pong –Thanbyuzayat): Asians	–	–	182,496	74,025	184
Bayah railway (Bayah–Saketi)	June 1943– March 1944	89.3	200,000	c. 35,000	392
Central Sumatra railway (Moeara –Pakan Baroe)	c. May 1944–15 Aug. 1945	221	Many *romusha*; 1,937 POWs	82,000	371

Source: Huff, *World War II*, p. 349.

the treatment of Indonesian *romusha* and an exodus of Indians from Burma to escape the Japanese. Additionally, many deaths occurred in Singapore in 1942 where, after occupying the city, the Japanese murdered some 22,000 Chinese, and in the Philippines during 1944 and 1945 before the Islands were liberated. Alternative, less conservative, estimates would produce totals of 5 or even 6 million premature dead. The United Nations Working Committee on Asia and the Far East, for example, estimated for Java 3 million deaths from execution by the Japanese, from hunger and disease and from a lack of medical attention, and a further 1 million deaths in the Outer Islands.[76]

[76] Dower, *War*, p. 296.

Table 8.7 *Premature deaths of Southeast Asians due to Japanese occupation, 1941–45 (000 persons)*

Cause of death	Number of deaths
Vietnam famine	1.000
Java famine	2.400
Java *romusha*	0.200
Singapore *sook ching* ('purification by elimination')	0.023
Japanese railways	0.191
Burma Indian exodus	0.030
Philippines	0.500
Others	0.100
Total	4.444

Source: Huff, *World War II*, p. 382.

As well as events involving death on a scale of 20,000 or more, there were numerous smaller instances ranging from the slaughter of a few thousand people to just one or two individuals who incurred Japanese displeasure. In all, such incidents may have added 100,000 to the wartime total of premature Southeast Asian deaths, on average about 17,000 per country but probably more than this in Burma, the Philippines and Indonesia. Whole villages in Burma were wiped out for harbouring offenders.[77] Everyone in a leper colony in Malaya was burned to death.[78] An October 1943 Chinese rebellion in British Borneo led to the systematic extinction by the Japanese of an entire tribe, the Suluk, who had assisted the rebels. Men were hunted down, some 4,000 in all, until there were no males left to transmit the cultural heritage. The torture and execution of all Suluk men and boys was judged to be the same or only a little worse than that of the Chinese, of whom some 700 were tortured and executed. Suluk women and children were either killed or deported elsewhere to work as slave labour. In the opinion of the British war crimes investigator, the treatment of the Suluk was standard for any people deemed to be 'anti-Japanese'.[79] The vast majority of 1,500 Indonesian, Chinese and Indian civilians arrested between October 1943 and June 1944 in Pontianak on suspicion of participating in an underground resistance movement were tortured and murdered, although some women

77 OSS, R&A 2015, *Japanese administration of Burma*, p. 39.

78 NARA, RG226, entry 16, box 1279, no. 112749, OSS, R&A Branch, Regular Intelligence Reports, 'General conditions in Malaya (Penang island), 11 January 1945', p. 5.

79 Totani, *Tokyo War Crimes Trial*, pp. 168–69; Ooi, *Japanese occupation*, pp. 99, 121.

were not killed but raped by members of the Japanese Naval Police and forced to become comfort women.[80]

Conclusion

Japan saw Southeast Asia as a treasure trove of natural resources, so easily available it would be like 'picking rice cakes off a shelf'.[81] However, the Japanese obtained little in the way of resources from Southeast Asia, and at a monetary cost that far outweighed gains. One main reason for this was the specialized nature of pre-war Southeast Asia's economies in which production concentrated in a few primary commodities for the world market. The Japanese economy, even if it had had shipping to carry commodities from Southeast Asia, was too small to use more than a tiny proportion of the region's output. Nor was Southeast Asia's industrial capacity sufficient to make more than a token contribution to Japan's need for manufactured goods and armaments.

Although Japan gained little materially from Southeast Asia, occupation turned the region upside down economically, politically and socially. The effects of occupation were fundamental in shaping Southeast Asian history after the Japanese surrender. In some countries, occupation changed politics in ways that led to basic departures from pre-war involvement with, and economic approaches to, the global economy. The next chapter draws out some of these legacies of the war to provide a bridge that links pre- and post-war Southeast Asian history.

[80] Tanaka, *Japan's comfort women*, p. 79; Ooi, *Japanese occupation*, pp. 102–17.
[81] Drea, *Japan's imperial army*, p. 209.

9

Aftermath of War: Economic and Political Legacies

War, occupation and its aftermath brought changes that accelerated the attainment of independence in Southeast Asia and led to new political regimes, enabling countries to determine their own economic future. Contrasting experiences of colonialism, together with different histories of occupation, shaped the political complexion of post-war Southeast Asian countries and so attitudes towards trade and development. A result was that, by the 1950s, while all the regimes throughout Southeast Asia sought to broaden their economies from the pre-war reliance on commodity exports as the growth engine and tried to industrialize, in some countries the departures became sufficiently radical to be one of kind, not merely degree. These disparities in approach defined Southeast Asian economic history for two decades or more, destroying its pre-World War II unity and making the war seem to many observers in the 1960s not just a political turning point but also an economic one.

The first section of this chapter quantifies the post-war recovery of GDP per capita in Southeast Asian countries and argues that, as severe as wartime destruction and displacement were, political ferment following the war explains why it took so long for most of the region to regain 1938 income levels. A second section analyses the mix of colonial inheritances, wartime experiences and independence struggles as determinants of the political complexion of independent Southeast Asian governments. Given the desire of all Southeast Asian countries to industrialize, the third section considers the options open to them and suggests that post-war exchange rate policy constrained the region to import substitution.

Wartime Destruction and GDP per Capita

Nowhere in Southeast Asia escaped wartime destruction. Much of wartime destruction in Malaya, assessed as 'widespread and serious', resulted from the attempts by retreating Allied troops to deny infrastructure and machinery to the Japanese and from Allied bombing.[1] In British Borneo, 70 per cent of the

[1] Federation of Malaya and Singapore, *Report of the War Damage Commission*, p. 4.

town of Jesselton (Kota Kinabalu) as well as almost all of its other main port of Sandakan were destroyed. So, too, was much of the railway, including locomotives, rolling stock and bridges.[2] Destruction in Thailand was mostly due to US bombing, as it also was in Indochina. Thailand's railway was a principal bombing target. Allied bombs had entirely destroyed or made unfit for further service 28 railway bridges (including the three largest), 22 principal stations, half the rolling stock, almost all repair shops, numerous buildings and enormous quantities of equipment.[3] Additional to this was damage to Thai industry and infrastructure other than building and transport equipment, assessed as 7.8 million 1945 US$. In comparison, damage in Indochina (chiefly Vietnam) was put in total at 2 billion 1945 US$. It included damage to industrial plants, the demolition of a third of all bridges, the inoperability of a large share of port installations and cuts in the railway so numerous that only short stretches of it could be used. About half of junks over 16 tons, private cars and motorcycles as well as 90 per cent of heavy vehicles were lost.[4]

The Philippines, Burma and Indonesia sustained the greatest wartime damage to physical infrastructure and cities. War damage in the Philippines extended to most of its physical capital being destroyed, damaged or depleted and was estimated at 1.6 billion 1945 US$. If not demolished, almost no factories and mines remained operable. At least four-fifths of Greater Manila was razed to the ground. Transportation facilities including railways, Manila's 100 street cars, bridges, the inter-island fleet of 160 ships, and wharves had been destroyed, and the power and communications infrastructure severely damaged.[5] Few factories in Manila, the main Philippines manufacturing centre, were left standing, and this was also true in other industrial cities like Cebu and Iloilo. Not much remained of many larger Philippine towns except their names.[6] A Committee on Industry and Manufacturing organized by the Philippines Chamber of Commerce summarized: 'what it took almost a half-century to build will have to be rebuilt again'.[7]

Allied bombing of Burma, together with Japanese disinterest and an inability to effect repairs, left Rangoon's entire dock area in ruin.[8] Rangoon itself had fallen into 'a state of indescribable filth [and] the City was in the hands of looters

2 United Nations, *Economic reconstruction: British Borneo*, p. 3.

3 Kingdom of Thailand, *Report of the financial adviser 1941–1950*, p. 47.

4 United Nations, *Economic reconstruction: Siam*, p. 3; United Nations, *Economic reconstruction: Indochinese Federation*, pp. 5, 20, 22, 24; Le, *Impact*, p. 272.

5 United Nations, *Economic reconstruction: Philippine Republic*, pp. 3, 21–24, 32; United States, Department of State, *Economic survey mission to the Philippines*, p. 6.

6 BE, OV149/1, 'Banking business in Philippines reported in chaotic condition', *New York Herald Tribune*, 24 April 1945; Hartendorp, *Japanese occupation*, pp. 153–54, 197; Friend, *Between two empires*, p. 231.

7 UP, Roxas Papers, box 39, Teodoro, 'Philippine manufacturing industry', 12 July 1945, p. 1.

8 United Nations, *Reconstruction: Burma*, p. 32; Tinker, *Union of Burma*, p. 286.

and bad hats'.[9] The Governor of Burma, Sir Hubert Rance, assessed Rangoon as 25 per cent destroyed.[10] Even after the organization of basic cleaning and restoration of greater order, Rangoon looked, in Collis's description, 'like a shanty town'.[11] Elsewhere, large parts of Burma were also damaged. Mainly due to British and American air raids, most towns 'were not just badly blitzed, they were completely laid waste, wiped off the map'.[12]

In Indonesia, colonial officials assessed direct damage as US$2.2 billion in 1938 values, and this rose to US$3.5 billion when account was taken of losses to food crops, commercial crops and mining output.[13] Damage to Indonesia's capital stock during the occupation and subsequent war of independence has been quantified by van der Eng using 1947 estimates of the destruction of physical capital in Indonesia. These put total damage at 4.1 billion florins. On the basis of pre-war replacement cost, this is equivalent to a loss of 34 per cent of the Indonesian capital stock. Included in the estimate are the defensive destruction of machinery and equipment by the Dutch colonial government in 1942 and the dismantling and shipment overseas of factories and railway stock by the Japanese military government, as well as damage sustained during the war of independence, particularly during 1946 and 1947.[14]

Destruction in Southeast Asia on the scale of World War II prevented an immediate recovery of GDP (Table 9.1). One approach to measuring lost GDP due to the war is to ask how much, using the PPP measure of 1990 Geary-Khamis $, GDP per capita fell below its 1938 level, a pre-war benchmark, in the years 1942 to 1947. Shortfall can then be defined as the difference between what the cumulative GDP per capita for 1942 to 1947 would have been if, in each of these years, incomes had been the same as in 1938 and the total for actual GDP per capita cumulated from 1942 to 1947. Taken as a percentage of GDP per capita in 1938 this difference is an indicative measure of lost years of income. It is only indicative, because losses after 1945 cannot be wholly attributed to occupation; because of changes in population; and although post-1945 national incomes were heavily influenced by war and occupation, internal political choices, ethnic conflict and revolution also played a part. These considerations became increasingly important in the late 1940s, and make it difficult after 1947 to attribute GDP losses wholly to Japanese occupation. Also, under conditions of no war, GDP per capita might have been expected to increase during the 1940s rather than remaining at its 1938 level, though it is difficult to gauge by how much.

9 MNA, 1/5 98 BMA Report, October 1945, Annexure A, 'Note on the achievements of the BMA in no. 1 area up to the 16 Oct.', p. 33; see also BE, OV79/17, A. K. Potter to C. E. Key, War Office, 29 September 1945.

10 'Burmese seek mastery of own country', *Daily Telegraph*, 1 November 1946.

11 Collis, *Last and first*, p. 263; see also Nu, *Saturday's son*, p. 215.

12 A correspondent [Dorman-Smith], 'Burma', p. 261.

13 United Nations, *Economic reconstruction: Netherlands Indies*, p. 3.

14 van der Eng, 'Capital formation and capital stock', p. 18.

Table 9.1 *Southeast Asia and Japan GDP per capita, 1870–1980 (1990 Geary-Khamis $)*

	Burma	Malaya	Thailand	Singapore	Indonesia	Vietnam	Philippines	Japan
1870	504	663	608	682	608	505	624	737
1913	685	939	841	1,367	869	727	988	1,387
1938	**740**	**1,452**	**826**	**2,070**	**1,057**	**831**	**1,440**	**2,449**
1939	–	1,708	826	2,379	1,038	886	1,508	2,816
1940	–	–	841	–	1,104	803	1,507	2,874
1941	–	–	846	–	1,158	763	–	2,873
1942	–	–	743	–	925	698	–	2,818
1943	–	–	812	–	738	659	–	2,822
1944	–	–	759	–	579	515	–	2,659
1945	–	–	682	–	512	407	–	1,346
1946	–	–	716	–	527	473	646	1,444
1947	–	–	775	–	602	498	875	1,541
1948	–	–	**838**	–	694	512	993	1,725
1949	–	–	826	–	758	562	1,025	1,800
1950	396	**1,665**	836	**2,219**	784	658	1,070	1,921
1956	490	1,505	930	2,333	955	764	1,410	**2,948**
1957	510	1,455	910	2,318	977	775	**1,442**	3,136
1959	555	1,467	992	2,186	987	792	1,501	3,554
1960	564	1,530	1,078	2,310	1,015	799	1,476	3,986
1962	606	1,637	1,149	2,520	1,025	**885**	1,537	4,777
1970	642	2,079	1,694	4,439	**1,231**	735	1,764	9,714
1978	**756**	3,271	2,422	7,752	1,740	806	2,262	12,585
1980	828	3,657	2,554	9,058	1,898	757	2,376	13,428

Note: The numbers in bold indicate years when Southeast Asian countries regained at least 1938 per capita GDP levels.
Source: Huff, *World War II*, pp. 374–75.

Table 9.2 *Thailand, Indonesia and Indochina, indicators of lost GDP per capita, 1942–47 (1990 Geary-Khamis $)*

	1938 GDP per capita	Average GDP per capita 1942–47	Average GDP 1942–47 as a proportion of 1938 level	Years of lost GDP per capita (cumulative shortfall as a proportion of 1938 level)
Thailand	826	748	90.5	0.57
Indonesia	1,057	647	61.2	2.33
Indochina	831	542	65.2	2.09

Source: See Table 9.1.

In Thailand, GDP per capita during the war never plummeted as elsewhere in Southeast Asia, and for 1942 to 1947 lost GDP per capita was just 57 per cent of a year of the 1938 level (Table 9.2). The loss in Indonesia was 2.33 years of 1938 GDP per capita and in Indochina 2.09 years. In Malaya, the Philippines and Burma, losses for 1942 to 1947 were probably at least as large as, or in excess of, those in Indonesia and Indochina but cannot be estimated due to lack of data.

After 1947, lost GDP cannot be attributed solely to the direct effects of war. Malaya, Singapore and Thailand were, however, the only countries in which by 1950 GDP per capita, in 1990 Geary-Khamis $, again matched that of 1938. These countries profited from sellers' markets arising from post-war shortages, Thailand for rice and Malaya mainly for rubber. Elsewhere in the region, GDP per capita more or less similar to the 1938 benchmark was not regained until well after 1950. The Philippines first recovered to a 1938 level in 1957 and Vietnam reached this mark in 1962 before sliding backwards with the escalation of the Second Indochina War. Indonesia nearly matched 1938 GDP per capita in 1960 but full recovery to the 1938 level occurred only in 1970, after the end of the Sukarno era. Burma finally regained 1938 income 40 years later, in 1978 (Table 9.1). Such slow recovery is largely explained by political change in Southeast Asia that grew out of pre-war and wartime histories.

Colonialism, Occupation and Political Change

The single unambiguous Japanese success in Southeast Asia was the destruction of Western colonialism. Japan lost a mere 3,500 men in the conquest of Malaya; for Burma the toll was another 2,000. The rest of Southeast Asia fell with few casualties. '[T]o destroy the British Empire in the Far East', Louis

Allen remarked, this was 'Not, surely, an inordinate price'.[15] Burma became independent in 1948, although Malaya not until 1957, followed by full independence for Singapore, as part of Malaysia in 1963 and as a city state in 1965. Although Thailand was only part of Britain's informal empire, for Thai supporters of Britain 'our collapse in the Far East came as a cruel disillusionment to those ... who had learnt to regard us as their special friends'.[16] United States legislation in 1934 had made the Philippines autonomous in domestic affairs and set out a 12-year timetable for full Philippines independence, which was granted on 4 July 1946.

Abject defeat at the hands of the Japanese marked the beginning of the end for Dutch colonialism in Indonesia and French rule in Indochina, although these two colonial powers hung on determinedly in the face of armed conflict with independence groups. Eventually in 1949, partly owing to the pressure of the United States threats to stop military and economic aid through the Marshall Plan, the Netherlands agreed to Indonesian independence.[17] In Vietnam, Ho Chi Minh announced independence on 2 September 1945, but this was soon followed by the First Indochina War, fought against the French. The conflict lasted until 1954, when, under a settlement negotiated in Geneva in July 1954, Vietnam was partitioned into an independent north and south divided at the 17th parallel. For Cambodia and Laos, Indochina's other pre-war constituents, Japanese occupation and the March 1945 coup marked the beginning of the end of French colonialism. The Geneva Accords opened the way for independence in the two countries.[18]

Political independence in Southeast Asia probably came sooner than it would have in the absence of war and the region was, arguably, more violent and politically unstable than it would otherwise have been. Every country except Thailand had civil war or revolution. As Lee Kuan Yew remarked of an area relatively less troubled than much of Southeast Asia, 'there was no return to the old peaceful, stable, free-and-easy Singapore'.[19] Even so, not all of Southeast Asia broke decisively with its pre-war past.

In the aftermath of World War II and subsequent conflict, Southeast Asia soon divided into two political and economic groups. One, consisting of Thailand, Malaya and the Philippines, remained part of what Benda calls the Atlantic system, and continued their pre-war orientation towards world markets.[20] In this group, the economy and industrialization remained substantially dependent

[15] Allen, 'Burma', p. 301.
[16] Crosby, *Siam*, p. 149.
[17] van der Eng, 'Marshall aid', pp. 335, 342–45; see also Friend, *Blue-eyed enemy*, pp. 222–23, 237, 267, 269.
[18] Stuart-Fox, *History of Laos*, pp. 55–59.
[19] Lee, *Singapore story*, p. 85.
[20] Benda, 'Japanese interregnum', pp. 69–74; Bastin and Benda, *History*, p. 156.

on private enterprise. The other group, comprising Burma, Indonesia and Vietnam, turned away from the global economy and towards some form of socialism, mixed with a strong dose of nationalism, and rejection of the West.[21]

The various guises of socialism in Southeast Asia shared, as in many developing countries in the 1950s and 1960s, preferences for state direction, central planning, a rejection of the price mechanism, heavy industrialization through import substitution, anti-Westernism and anti-globalization. Apparently, Paul Baran predicted that only the isolationist economic policies of Burma and Indonesia gave them any chance of sustained growth.[22] Import substitution and heavy industry were strongly influenced by the apparent success of the Soviet model as well as a desire for economic development and to break free of colonialism. A rhetoric, though often not the realities, of equity or even a strong central government, accompanied socialism in Southeast Asia.[23]

The Southeast Asian split corresponds to Myint's categorization of the region's outward- and inward-looking countries.[24] Varying colonial and wartime experiences, the strength of nationalism and associated ideologies, and different paths to independence help to explain this Southeast Asian economic division. The next two sub-sections consider the outward- and inward-looking countries respectively and contrast and compare their histories under colonial rule and during the Japanese occupation.

Thailand, Malaya and the Philippines

Outward-looking Thailand, Malaya and the Philippines shared two important historical features. One was relatively benign experiences of colonialism; the other that colonialism, together with wartime experience and Japanese occupation policies, did relatively little to promote nationalism. Thailand was only part of Britain's informal empire, and beginning with the 1932 revolution, a pattern of conservative, military rule was established. During the war, the Kingdom, allied with Japan, suffered less than other Southeast Asian countries and because of the alliance, and an existing Thai military, the Japanese did not attempt to establish a separate military force. In post-war Thailand, America replaced Britain as a patron, strengthening the country's conservative military rule.

The Philippines, and less so Malaya, were the only two Southeast Asian countries where in 1945 Southeast Asians viewed the return of colonial

[21] Elsbree, *Japan's role*, pp. 168–69.

[22] Woo et al., *Macroeconomic policies*, p. 27.

[23] Cf. Little, *Economic development*, pp. 30–31, 54–59; Booth, *Economic change*, p. 46.

[24] Myint, 'Inward and outward looking countries', pp. 1–13. Myint's 1967 list did not include either North or South Vietnam.

rulers in anything like a positive light. Filipinos welcomed back Americans as 'liberators'.[25] In Malaya, the Japanese encountered a relatively weak nationalism and the war did not augment this to the same extent as in some Southeast Asian countries.[26] During the war, Malaya had its own China- and India-oriented nationalism, but Malay nationalism remained relatively weak. Pre-war Philippine nationalism had been firmly under the control of a conservative elite: 'leaders of the middle and upper classes seized hold of nationalism early in the century, won the confidence of the masses, and never surrendered the issue or their following'.[27] The Japanese did not win Filipino allegiance, advance pan-Asian nationalism or create Filipino militancy.[28] Until the 1950s, nationalism in the Philippines was directed 'more against Oriental [Chinese and Japanese] minorities than against Occidental rulers'.[29] A pre- and post-war continuity of elites and conservatism in politics in Malaya and the Philippines ruled out wholesale political change even with the attainment of independence.[30]

Burma, Indonesia and Vietnam

Although nationalist movements existed in pre-war Burma, Indonesia and Vietnam, they did not seem likely to provide an effective force for early independence.[31] Nationalism derived almost entirely from the urban intelligentsia, and, unlike religious movements in the region, lacked roots in rural Southeast Asia and therefore a significant power base.[32] And yet within less than a decade after the end of World War II all three countries had more or less gained independence.

The experience of war and occupation in Burma, Indonesia and Vietnam built on and magnified particularly unhappy histories of colonial rule and made nationalism a strong force. Vietnam and Indonesia were Southeast Asia's two most repressed colonies, and in both a dislike of colonialism was widespread.[33] In Burma, nationalist feeling was strongest among the Burman majority, where anti-British and anti-Indian sentiments fused into a nationalism inspired, in many respects, by a hope to return to an idyllic pre-colonial past.[34]

[25] Friend, *Between two empires*, p. 272.
[26] Yoichi, 'Some aspects', pp. 264–66, 256.
[27] Friend, *Between two empires*, p. 34.
[28] Steinberg, 'Ambiguous legacy', pp. 179–83.
[29] Friend, *Between two empires*, p. 34.
[30] Bastin and Benda, *History*, p. 167.
[31] Silverstein, 'Importance of the Japanese occupation', p. 7 and see Trocki, 'Political structures', p. 104; Emerson et al., *Government*, pp. 15–35, 127.
[32] Benda, 'Structure', pp. 131, 135.
[33] Osborne, *Region*, p. 81.
[34] Guyot, 'Burma Independence Army', pp. 53–61; Silverstein, *Burma*, pp. 15–17; Taylor, 'Disaster', p. 56.

In the three countries, against a background of dislike of colonialism and pre-war nationalist movements, war and occupation fundamentally shaped post-war politics in two important ways. One was an impetus to Southeast Asian nationalism; the second the creation of Southeast Asian groups that could fill power vacuums which arose with Japan's sudden, unanticipated surrender, after which Allied forces took at least a month and a half to reach Southeast Asia in any numbers. In Burma and Indonesia, the groups in place and able to effect opportunistic political change were an elite core of Japanese-trained armies. Military training had an immediate and long-term impact in Burma and Indonesia, because it concentrated on majority ethnic groups previously by-passed by colonial governments; because it emphasized overtly military training, especially in Burma, and so created a revolutionary potential; and because it established a strong institution which could, and did, fill vacuums left by the Japanese surrender and discredited colonial regimes. Vietnam, where Japan did not train armies, had a different history but events during the war created the basis for revolution organized by the Viet Minh led by Ho Chi Minh.

The Burma Independence Army originated in the conjunction of the initiative of a Japanese officer, Colonel Suzuki Keiji, and the nationalism and ambitions for political independence of a small, elite group of Burmans. These men became Burma's much mythologized Thirty Comrades. In the Lenin-esque manner of a committed core, they constituted the commanding nucleus of the Burma Independence Army formed in December 1941.

War and occupation in Burma widened and increased a fervent ethno-nationalism among Burmans, who comprised some 75 per cent of the population and formed the basis of the army, renamed the Burma National Army. During the war, the Japanese allied with the Burmans, while minority groups, the Karens and various hill peoples, were recruited by the Allies. At least a dozen clandestine and para-military organizations operated in Burma, many of which were controlled from London or Washington. At one level, Selth points out, World War II in Burma was fought between the British and Japanese Empires, but at another, intra-country level, it became an ethnic Burma conflict, Burmans on one side, the minorities on the other. Within six months of independence, 'the Union of Burma was wracked by a number of insurgencies'. One was essentially intra-Burman due to communists being denied a place in the new government, but four others were inspired by ethnic antagonisms: the Karens, Kachins, Mons and the Muslims in Arakan all asserted separatist claims against the Burman-dominated government in Rangoon.[35] Because the war provided the reasons, and furnished the means, to mobilize separate ethnic identities in post-war Burma, 'ethnic politics [were] raised from

[35] Selth, 'Race', pp. 484 and 483 for the quotations; *passim* for the analysis set out in this paragraph.

the condition of inchoate aspiration to the pivot of political action'.[36] When the British returned to Burma they found the Burman-dominated Patriotic Burmese Forces (successor to the Burma National Army) 'the sole effective political organization in the country' and strong enough to impose its will on all other political groups.[37]

Two million Javanese in Indonesia received some military training from the Japanese, but the only group in receipt of genuine military training belonged to Peta, the Fatherland Defence Corps. Beginning in late 1943, it grew into a volunteer army of some 35,000, including about 1,500 in Bali. Peta officers were sent to elite training colleges in Indonesia set up by the Japanese. Training was founded on the Japanese spiritual virtues of sacrifice, self-reliance and endurance of hardship. Javanese trained by the Japanese or who taught in the School for Free Indonesia (*Asrama Merdeka Indonesia*), established in 1944, included most of the men who became generals and the principal politicians in independent Indonesia. Among their number were Sukarno, Mohammad Hatta and Suharto. In the 1970s, Peta officers remained the most significant element of Indonesia's political-military elite, and comprised three-quarters of the top ranks of the army.[38] As in Burma, Japanese military training in Indonesia gave rise to a new, and ultimately powerful, elite.[39]

In Indonesia, the Japanese interregnum had unloosed a 'whirlwind of a many-faceted-revolution'.[40] When, in March 1946, Dutch troops reached Java in any number, Indonesian Republican forces held sway in most of Java except in six large cities and part of a seventh.[41] Peta was a main basis for Indonesian Republican forces, which, armed largely with Japanese weapons, fought against both the British (until their departure beginning in March 1946) and the Dutch military attempting to regain control of Indonesia.[42] In the longer term, 'the drawn out struggle with the Dutch imbued political life generally with a radicalism and potential violence that proved difficult to contain'.[43] Added to the ferment was a strong religious current led by an Islamic elite, which the Japanese had done much to empower and which stood squarely behind the independence struggle.[44] When, in December 1949, Indonesia gained independence from the Netherlands, the revolution that followed was not revolution in the same sense as in the French, Russian and Chinese revolutions but 'certainly

36 Taylor, 'Perceptions', p. 9 and see p. 8; Smith, 'Burma and World War II'.
37 BNA, 1/5 86 British Military Administration Report, August 1945 (dated 29 September 1945), p. 8.
38 Lebra, *Japanese-trained armies*, pp. 176–77.
39 Benda, 'Indonesian Islam', p. 354.
40 Benda, 'Decolonization', p. 1061.
41 Cribb, 'Political dimensions', pp. 113–36.
42 Kahin, *Nationalism*, pp. 108–9; Anderson, *Some aspects*, pp. 97–98, 118–19, 126.
43 Bastin and Benda, *History*, p. 183.
44 Benda, *Crescent*, pp. 135, 175, 187.

involved a deeper shattering of social foundations' than in other post-war independence struggles, except Vietnam's.[45]

At the time of the Japanese coup in March 1945, the Indochina Communist Party, led by Ho Chi Minh, also the organizing force behind the Viet Minh, was not in a strong position.[46] However, the Viet Minh and Ho correctly identified three opportunities for revolution: the Japanese coup, the climax of the Pacific War, and the 1944–45 famine. After the 1944–45 famine struck, 'the Viet Minh came out of hiding and mobilized the population to seize rice that both the French and Japanese had stored in case of food shortages'.[47] Goscha summarizes: 'famine, more than anything else, ushered in change'.[48] The Viet Minh took control of Hanoi on the night of 19 August 1945 with at most 900 men and filled the power vacuum that existed until around mid-September, when Allied troops first arrived in significant numbers. Tens of thousands of peasants, activated by famine and revolution, immediately supported the revolution by marching on Hanoi, Haiphong and Hue. Ho Chi Minh publicly proclaimed independence on 2 September 1945. He was, like Sihanouk in Cambodia, Sukarno in Indonesia and Ne Win in Burma, a World War II creation.

In inward-looking Burma, Indonesia and Vietnam, war and occupation gave rise to a new social group: a military controlled by the population's principal ethnic component. The military in inward-looking Southeast Asia was 'born and tested in revolution and anticolonial war' and by virtue of this could lay claim to moral authority and legitimacy.[49] Power could be solidified largely due to an absence of other organized, disciplined and trained groups to contest military dominance.[50] At the same time as creating an ethnic-majority military elite, the Japanese interregnum widened and deepened nationalism. It grew from the preserve of the urban intelligentsia to incorporate rural Vietnamese and become a potent, countrywide force.[51] The Japanese-trained armies in Burma and Indonesia and the Viet Minh in Indochina could, and did, wrap themselves in post-war strident nationalism. Taking strength from nationalism, armed forces in all three countries assumed major political roles from independence onwards.[52]

45 Feith, *Decline*, p. 1.
46 Marr, *Vietnamese tradition*, p. 415.
47 Brocheux, *Ho Chi Minh*, p. 90.
48 Goscha, *Penguin history*, p. 211.
49 Bastin and Benda, *History*, p. 194.
50 Bastin and Benda, *History*; Huff, 'Finance and long-term development issues', pp. 58–61; Fenichel and Huff, 'Colonialism'; Brown, *Burma's economy*, pp. 3–4, 210.
51 See, for example, Benda, *Crescent*, p. 200; Yoon, 'Military expediency', pp. 264–67; Taylor, 'Disaster', p. 51.
52 For a study of the army's evolution into a political force in Indonesia, see Crouch, *Army and politics*, pp. 24–42.

Post-war military elites in the three countries became self-perpetuating military oligarchies able to enforce their views on the conduct of the economy and society. Military-political elites in Vietnam, Indonesia and Burma were analogous to the 'Brezhnev generation' in the Soviet Union, where wartime leaders, all ethnic Russians, retained their hold on the levers of power and dominated Soviet political life through the 1960s, 1970s and 1980s.[53] Among Burma's Thirty Comrades were Aung San, instrumental in bringing about Burma's independence in 1948, and Ne Win, elevated to command of Burma's armed forces in 1949 and the general who headed Burma's government after the army took control in 1958 and again in 1962. During the 1950s, the Indonesian army, strengthened by its role in the 1945–49 revolution, gained great power and could not be effectively challenged by any other social group. Army leaders had always refused to accept civilian control over military affairs and considered that the army embodied the revolution's spirit and fighting strength.[54] A State of Emergency in April 1957 allowed Indonesia's already socially dominant military to expand its activities into economic and political spheres.[55] In Vietnam, as late as 1985, the generation of Indochinese Communist Party members who 'had survived repression and jail in the 1930s, and who disseminated the Viet Minh message before August 1945' still commanded Vietnam's armed forces and governed the country.[56]

While in outward-looking Southeast Asia the Western superstructure created during the colonial era continued to function, for decades after World War II the military-dominated governments in Burma and Vietnam and to some extent in Indonesia pushed politics towards forms of socialism or communism and away from the global economy.[57] The Burman nationalist orientation was not to bend to global capitalism, including the rule of law, force of the market, international trade and the modern state, but to resist and reject it.[58] The military in Myanmar, with many of the direct successors of the World War II military, remained central to politics and outside the control of politicians.[59]

During the 1950s and 1960s, a chief objective of Burman nationalism and the military responsible for its political and economic expression was 'to erase capitalism'.[60] In Indonesia, radicalism fused with an Islamic revival originally encouraged by Japanese policies.[61] Independent Indonesia emerged as

[53] Harrison, 'Soviet Union', pp. 295–96.
[54] McVey, 'Post-revolutionary transformation, part I', pp. 131–32.
[55] McVey, 'Post-revolutionary transformation, part II', p. 147.
[56] Marr, *Vietnam 1945*, p. 552; and see Marr, *Vietnamese tradition*, pp. 411–12.
[57] Bastin and Benda, *History*, p. 180; Indonesia nationalized Dutch enterprises in 1957 and 1958.
[58] Taylor, 'Disaster', p. 56.
[59] Guyot, 'Burma Independence Army', pp. 51, 61.
[60] Silverstein, *Burma*, p. 32,
[61] Benda, 'Indonesian Islam', pp. 81–82.

resolutely opposed to the West, characterized as 'an independent nation sealed against neocolonialism'.[62] This was also true of Vietnam, which aligned with the Soviet Union, and after 1949 with China. While in outward-looking Southeast Asia the pre-war Western superstructure remained in place, the new governments in Burma, as also in Indonesia and Vietnam, liquidated most European economic interests.[63]

Change from an inward orientation in Indonesia and Vietnam came slowly, and in Myanmar haltingly and uncertainly. Under Sukarno, Indonesia had no real development strategy between 1948 and 1965, but beginning in 1966, after economic collapse into hyperinflation and Sukarno's overthrow, turned more outwards and towards the global economy under the New Order. Vietnam maintained a war economy between the end of World War II and 1975, and continued until a decisive Party shift in 1986 to implement a system like that in the Soviet Union and to plan the Vietnamese economy centrally. It was only after serious famine and malnutrition in the winter of 1987–88 that, in stages, Vietnam began to free the market, manufacture for the global market and again become a major world rice exporter.[64]

Economic Legacies

In Southeast Asia, economic legacies are not easily disentangled from political ones. Apart from the interruption to Southeast Asian growth, three substantially economic legacies require consideration. One was pressure to industrialize; a second the Japanese model of comprehensive government economic controls; and the third, internationally uncompetitive real exchange rates. Together they helped to determine post-war economic policy and to create a strong bias towards industrialization through import substitution. Although varying between countries, throughout Southeast Asia the difference between the state's pre- and post-independence roles was striking.

The wartime lack of basic consumer goods and demonstration of an extreme reliance on importing manufactured goods comprehensively exposed Southeast Asia's narrow economic specialization. War scarcities reinforced pre-war arguments for greater industrialization, already rooted in sharp 1930s falls in commodity prices and the examples of Japanese and Soviet economic development. Furthermore, a lesson not lost on Southeast Asian leaders was that Japan's industrialization enabled it to challenge the colonial powers and, as Asians, assert authority over other Asians.

Although strengthening a desire among Southeast Asians for industrialization, the Japanese occupation did not bequeath a significant industrial

62 Friend, *Blue-eyed enemy*, p. 257.
63 Bastin and Benda, *History*, p. 158.
64 Perkins, *East Asian development*, pp. 121–47.

inheritance on which to build, with the partial exceptions of Thailand and Vietnam. Post-war Thailand was able to make use of some of the machinery brought by Japanese companies, as well as a structure of state–private sector partnerships that these enterprises helped to promote, but gained little that advanced technological change or innovation. In Vietnam, more relevant than industrial plant left by the Japanese was that the small local Asian industries that emerged during the war became important for the Viet Minh government during the First Indochina War. The post-World War II government in the North favoured state-owned enterprises and heavy industry, but its survival strategy was based on local self-sufficiency in agriculture and handicrafts.[65]

Elsewhere in Southeast Asia, most notably the Philippines, the Japanese legacy was chiefly the destruction of pre-war industrial equipment. In Burma, contrary to a hoped-for post-war stimulus, wartime Japanese industries do not appear to have had much lasting impact. After the war, many of the spinning factories erected by the Japanese were looted for essential parts.[66] Industries in Indonesia had been established under the pressure of military need, not with the aim of commercial success. After the war, the economic justification for wartime Japanese manufacturing was often questionable.[67] While occupation gave some Indonesian administrators experience in supervising industry, it did little to create entrepreneurs.[68]

By 1947 in Singapore, 'many of the mushroom industries of the occupation folded up in the face of competition with imported goods which were both better and cheaper'.[69] The Japanese occupation did not leave a legacy of industrialization; Singapore's industrial success dates from the late 1960s, and is not explained by World War II experience.

Wartime administrations created a second legacy, that of economic controls, through abundant Japanese examples of the use of government power over the economy to institute state direction, monopoly and administered pricing. In Thailand, the military government became increasingly involved in the economy during the war, while after it other Southeast Asian governments drew on the Japanese occupation model to varying degrees. Some countries continued, or soon adopted, the Japanese example of extensive military involvement in the economy and implemented repressive economic policies reminiscent of wartime Japanese administrations.

65 Marr, *Vietnam: state, war*, p. 638, n. 4; Brocheux, 'Economy of war', pp. 314, 317, 326.

66 MNA, 1/9 Village industries, Lt. Gen GOC in-c Twelfth Army to HQ ALFSEA, August 1945.

67 Department of Economic Affairs, Batavia, 'Industries', pp. 21, 24 and 'Economic prospects of the Indonesian islands', p. 6; Fruin, *Het economisch*, p. 45.

68 Sutter, *Indonesianisasi*, pp. 267, 271.

69 Malaya, *Malaya, a report on the 1947 census*, p. 35.

Burma, Southeast Asia's most laissez-faire pre-war economy but highly controlled after the war, was one instance of the role of the Japanese occupation in helping to shift economic policy towards an interventionism unacceptable under pre-war colonial rule.[70] Even before the end of the war, Burma's 1944 New Order Plan argued that 'the Burmese Government must have the widest scope and facilities ... in devising a war-time civilian economic structure to undertake, organize and control, either partly or completely according to requirements, all activities relating to [the Burmese people's basic material] necessities'.[71] Although the returning British administration introduced greater state control and established a rice marketing board, the independent Burmese government soon nationalized much of the economy and assumed a central role in it.[72]

The third economic legacy was the path that post-war Southeast Asian industrialization had to take. Import substitution for goods like textiles and basic manufactures was an obvious choice due to high pre-war consumption of these goods and simple production technologies. However, for all industrialization, uncompetitive real exchange rates made import substitution the only realistic option. Cost considerations ruled out manufacturing for export. Wartime inflation in Southeast Asia far exceeded world inflation and left post-war internal price and wage structures at least some five to six times higher than pre-war levels. Nevertheless, Southeast Asian governments typically re-established official exchange rates at pre-war parities rather than devaluing to offset wartime inflation and create the competitive real exchange rates required for manufacturing for export.[73]

Conclusion

Japan's use of war as an instrument of policy was badly misconceived, its protestations of 'an Asia for the Asians' were without credibility and its wartime empire lacked cohesion. The Southeast Asian constituent of empire was assembled in a chaotic few months and disintegrated in a little over three years. Despite this short time, efforts by Japan to further Asian nationalism and the sudden Japanese military collapse in August 1945 led to sweeping political

[70] Owen, 'Economic and social change', pp. 143–44.

[71] Burma, *Burma's New Order Plan*, p. 36.

[72] Tinker, *Union of Burma*, p. 255.

[73] Golay, *Philippines*, pp. 117–18; United States, Department of State, *Economic survey mission to the Philippines*, pp. 12–14, 18; Manarungsan, *Economic development*, p. 189; Ingram, *Economic change*, pp. 165–67; Yang, *Multiple exchange rate system*, pp. 26–33, 134; Malayan Union, *Report on the British military administration*, pp. 36–37, 44; Donnison, *British military administration*, p. 238; Department of Economic Affairs, Batavia, 'Economic data ... 1948', pp. 19–22.

change in Burma, Indonesia and Vietnam, and revolution in the last two. Without the Japanese occupation and power vacuums after Japan's surrender, the balance in Southeast Asian decolonization between continuity and change might well have tipped towards the former.[74] As it was, war and occupation gave rise to a Southeast Asia sufficiently different in ideologies and economic outlook that the following chapters treat the two groups of Southeast Asian countries separately. Part III deals with the inward-looking countries and Part IV with outward-looking Southeast Asia.

[74] Cf. Benda, 'Structure', p. 134; Marr, *Vietnam 1945*, pp. 150–51.

PART III

The Southeast Asian Socialist Experiment

Part III Introduction and Themes

The five economies, three in Indochina, Burma and Indonesia, which comprised Southeast Asia's post-World War II communist or socialist experiments, shared seven prominent features. These provide themes that run throughout this part of the book. Despite an overtly capitalist ideology, South Vietnam (formally the Republic of Vietnam) is also considered with the socialist group because of Vietnam's 1975 unification, and because its economy was similar in major respects to those of its Indochinese counterparts of North Vietnam (formally the Democratic Republic of Vietnam), Cambodia and Laos.

One commonality was that the socialist countries began the 1950s with the lowest per capita incomes in Southeast Asia, little industry and limited human capital. All these characteristics afforded a weak base from which to develop and told heavily against any of the countries soon building socialist, industrial economies. Over the next nearly four decades, policy decisions, disunity and insurgency or war further prejudiced the chances of any of the countries for sustained growth.

In 1950, per capita income in all the countries attempting various versions of socialism was less than 2011 US$1,500. Taken together, their per capita incomes averaged US$885, just two-fifths of the average of US$2,266 for the countries that turned outwards after World War II. Between 1950 and 1990, the countries that began in the socialist group grew slowly, except for Indonesia from the 1970s. In 1990, all in the group had per capita incomes of less than 2011 US$1,650. That compared with a 1990 average for the outward-looking economies of Thailand, Malaysia, Singapore and the Philippines of 2011 US$6,355 excluding Singapore, and US$10,433 with its inclusion.

Indonesia is analysed with the socialist group because, until 1966, it attempted to create a version, and adopted a rhetoric, of socialism. Soon after this attempt was abandoned, Indonesia began to grow more rapidly. Similarly, excepting Burma (Myanmar), accelerated growth started for others in the socialist group from the late 1980s, after they turned towards the world economy and away from earlier socialist doctrines. Vietnam, Cambodia and Laos grew at a pace similar to that at which the three most successful outward-looking countries of Singapore, Malaysia and Thailand had already been growing since the later 1960s or early 1970s. Within the socialist group, Burma is an exception to turning outwards and adopting more market-friendly policies. Its economic orientation has been variable and uncertain; data for it became unreliable well before 1990.

Taking Vietnam as a whole, the countries had, as a second common aspect, the strongest nationalisms and Southeast Asia's most adverse reactions to their colonial experiences. Partly reflective of that, and partly as a reaction to the narrowness of pre-war economies, they shared a determination to develop economically. For all countries that meant industrialization.

In the socialist economies, industrial strategy characteristically relied on import substitution and trade protection, and so an inward orientation. North Vietnam attempted closely to follow the Soviet heavy industry model. Soviet industrialization success also exercised a strong influence on Burma and Indonesia. South Vietnam, though seemingly looking economically outward, was similar to North Vietnam in economic narrowness because of a strong inwards bias towards the United States and dependence on it for most manufactures.

Third, every government, not least South Vietnam's, neglected agriculture; all pursued discriminatory policies that damaged it. In the six economies, per capita agricultural output generally remained lower than before World War II; for three decades or more after 1945, production of the chief pre-war agricultural staples stagnated or, typically, fell. Decline was disastrous for development and industrialization, since agriculture makes an indispensable contribution to industry through providing a source of raw materials, a market for industrial goods and finance, accumulated through agricultural surpluses, which can be invested directly, taxed or earn foreign exchange. Marxist theory emphasizes agricultural collectivization as the means to increase mobilization of these surpluses. Vietnam, in the North and then after 1975 in the South, as well as Cambodia and Laos looked to collectives to transfer agricultural surplus from the countryside to finance state investment. The failure of collectives in Vietnam, Cambodia and Laos to yield the expected investable surpluses was instrumental to the three economies turning outwards in the later 1980s and 1990s.

Being recipients of high foreign assistance was a further, fourth, feature that the socialist countries and South Vietnam shared. In 1955, after the end of the First Indochina War, both North and South Vietnam needed extensive reconstruction, lacked capital, suffered from corruption and depended on foreign aid and military assistance from major powers.[1] Aid donors, aligned according to the Cold War sides, split between capitalism and communism. South Vietnam was propped up by the United States, as well as by a number of Western countries, although they made much smaller contributions than America did. The

[1] Shabad, 'Economic developments', pp. 38–41, 45; Thien, 'Economic development', pp. 56–58.

Soviet Union, and to a lesser extent China and countries in the Soviet bloc, supported North Vietnam. American aid extended – for similar political and strategic reasons arising from the Second Indochina War – to Laos and Cambodia. Aid lasted until 1975, when in both countries communist governments gained power. Burma and Indonesia were never funded by aid to the same extent as the Indochinese economies, but foreign assistance was substantial enough to make this a feature of socialist Southeast Asia.

Fifth, all the countries had to deal with protracted periods of war or internal rebellion. Conflict engulfed all of Indochina for much of the period from 1946 to 1975. Since independence, Burma's military has struggled with, at different times, various insurgencies, while Indonesia devoted substantial budgetary resources to countering Outer Island separatist movements. Cambodian governments, except during the Pol Pot government, fought Khmer Rouge revolutionaries for most of the period between 1960 and 1990. For every country, more or less constant conflict drained resources and told against economic development.

Military dictatorships or army-dominated governments have been the rule throughout communist and socialist Southeast Asia. War and insurgencies contributed to strengthening the military and its intertwining with civilian leaders. For long periods, most countries were led by men who owed their role as leaders to an ascendancy during World War II: Ne Win, Sukarno, Sihanouk and Ho Chi Minh. The military in post-war socialist Southeast Asia was largely unchallengeable because it was the most organized group and the sole one backed by armed force. In South Vietnam, the importance of the American army and a large Vietnamese one paralleled the military's political centrality in the other countries.

In all six economies, weak pre-war entrepreneurship among indigenous groups constitutes a sixth common pattern. South Vietnam apart, all sought to create local – meaning ethnically non-Chinese, non-Indian or non-European – entrepreneurs and gave these individuals, or their state-enterprise substitutes, preferential treatment. Discrimination against, and often expulsion of, groups not regarded as indigenous, or frequent violence against them, was repeated in all five societies and also in southern Vietnam after unification with the North. Recurrent, too, was the failure of indigenous entrepreneurs to deliver industrialization and modernization but, instead, using their favoured positions to engage in rent-seeking. In the non-communist countries of Burma and Indonesia, state industry became a substitute for private entrepreneurship.

In North Vietnam, as the communists took control soon after World War II, and then in the south after the country's unification, state directed and dominated industry was always the rule, in line with orthodox Marxism-Leninism. Burma and Indonesia arrived at a large state industrial sector in stages. Although Burma had substantial state enterprise after independence, following a 1962 military coup this extended throughout the economy. In Indonesia, widespread nationalization became necessary after the 1958 expropriation of Dutch enterprise.

Governments in the six economies heavily supported inefficient, overwhelmingly import-substitution state industry, had stagnant agricultural sectors and maintained weak tax bases due to continued reliance on taxing agricultural export staples, now in decline. A result in all the economies, and a seventh feature, was large budget deficits financed partly by foreign aid, but often mainly by monetary expansion. This, together with weak productive capacity, led to a pattern of high, often runaway, inflation punctuated by periodic demonetizations.

Part III of the book divides into three chapters. The first (Chapter 10) explores the mixtures of nationalist, socialist and communist motivations which shaped the economies of the two Vietnams, Cambodia and Laos and also evaluates their economic policies and performance. Chapter 11 examines a similar range of issues for Burma and Indonesia. In Chapter 12, finance for the socialist regimes as well as for South Vietnam and change in plural societies in these countries are considered. There follows a separate Conclusion to Part III which evaluates common features and failings of the Southeast Asian socialist experiment and its economies.

10

The Indochinese Economies: Classical Marxian Socialism and Extreme Communism

In Indochina, Marxist regimes, the focus of this chapter, gained ascendancy at different times and varied in doctrinaire orientation. As a result of the First Indochina War of 1946–54 and the April 1954 Geneva Accords, Vietnam split into two countries divided at the 17th parallel: the Democratic Republic of Vietnam in the North and the capitalist Republic of Vietnam in the South. During the Second Indochina War (1954–75), the United States supported South Vietnam militarily and economically. The Soviet bloc and China similarly aided North Vietnam. Following the defeat of American and South Vietnamese forces in April 1975, Vietnam became a single country. North Vietnam, and as unified Vietnam after 1975, instigated rigid, Soviet-style orthodox Marxism until the late 1980s.

Cambodia and Laos, Indochina's other constituents, gained independence in 1953. During the Second Indochina War, they remained, as mere pawns, in orbit around the United States until America's 1975 withdrawal from Indochina. Between 1975 and 1978, Cambodia, under Pol Pot, practised an extreme vision of pure communism. From 1975, Laos, now under Vietnamese influence, followed a textbook Marxism. Beginning in 1979, after Vietnam's invasion on Christmas Day 1978 and subsequent occupation, Cambodia became a more conventional Marxist state. In neither country, however, was Marxism followed with quite the same singleness of purpose or durable conviction as in Vietnam, or with any more economic success than Vietnam had over four decades of inflexible socialism.

Indochina's economies adhered to the Marxist development model to varying degrees but were all strongly influenced by it.[1] The model has two sectors, and divides the economy between agriculture and industry. The industrial sector grows faster than the agricultural, and heavy industry, through receiving investment priority, more quickly than light. Agriculture is fundamental to the development of industry. Agricultural output yields the surplus needed to finance industrialization and allow the transfer of labour to the industrial sector. The surplus comes through land reform and the formation of agricultural

[1] Marx, *Capital*, vol. 2, part 3, chs. 18–21.

collectives. Their establishment generates production gains through economies of scale and centralized management and enables the state easily to requisition the gains. Although state surplus appropriation temporarily depresses peasant living standards, in the longer term these rise as the economy grows and more consumer goods become available. A command economy and planning create efficiency.

Successful Marxist development towards rapid, industrial-based growth requires four key conditions to be met. These should be borne in mind throughout the chapter's analysis of the Indochinese economies. First, there has to be an already relatively well-developed economy with a significant industrial sector and capacity to absorb technology. Second, agriculture must yield a surplus and the state appropriate it to finance industrialization. Third, industrial gestation periods need to be short, ideally of around a year as assumed by Marx in his 'reproduction schema'. Fourth, even though investment in heavy industry outruns light, the establishment of comparatively efficient light industry is essential to supply goods to the rest of the economy.[2]

The chapter first analyses South Vietnam. It then turns to North Vietnam and Vietnam as a whole after its re-unification. The final two sections of the chapter look at Cambodia and Laos, both before and after the 1975 advent of socialist governments.

South Vietnam

South Vietnam started as a society and economy reliant on external aid and became increasingly so. After the 1954 Geneva Accords and French military withdrawal from Indochina, massive American aid set a pattern that supported and shaped almost all aspects of South Vietnam's economy and society. South Vietnam's dependent economy is best understood by tracing the intertwining of its political and war histories, American military decisions, resulting aid and the country's economic development.

South Vietnam Politics and Aid

Soon after the Geneva Accords, Ngo Dinh Diem was appointed prime minister of South Vietnam, but even then, some observers regarded it as a non-viable state: 'Largely through the obstinate insistence of our own [US] State Department the inept and chaotic Ngo Dinh Diem remains in power. But anarchy, rather than Diem, governs ... Experts are betting that South Vietnam will fall of its own corrupt weight.'[3] The regime did not, however, fall immediately.

2 Cf. Erlich, 'Development strategy', pp. 238–46.

3 C. L. Sulzberger, 'Liberation in reverse – who is rolling back whom?' *New York Times*, 8 December 1954.

A 1955 referendum resulted in Ngo Dinh Diem becoming the first president of the Republic of Vietnam. For the next 20 years, South Vietnam's survival depended on the United States. Economic and political reliance operated in parallel and reinforced each other.

By 1955, the United States had assumed 90 per cent of the economic responsibility for maintaining a South Vietnamese military force of some 250,000. In 1955 and 1956, United States aid amounted to over half a billion dollars, and between 1955 and 1960 gross aid to South Vietnam averaged some 22 per cent of its GNP.[4] The economy was weak, and American aid created a major disincentive to self-reliance and development. A confidential 1959 Bank of England assessment found that the United States funded three-quarters of the South's foreign exchange resources for current payments, and an even higher proportion of the national budget. The South Vietnam regime was 'contentedly puffing at the opium pipe of American aid'.[5] 'Lavish aid' did not, however, promote development, and in 1961 South Vietnam was 'the protype of a dependent economy [and] becoming a permanent mendicant'.[6]

During the 20 years of South Vietnam's existence, from 1955 to 1975, its economy never became self-sustaining. Nor did any of its governments ever gain political legitimacy. Successive administrations had two main objectives: to avoid the war effort collapsing and to contain inflation. The first failed with the fall of Saigon on 30 April 1975, while the second, although preventing runaway inflation, only partially succeeded. By 1974, prices were 26 times higher than they had been in 1956.

One estimate is that between 1950 and 1975 the United States spent US$112 billion on all forms of assistance to South Vietnam, including aid originally given to the French.[7] By the mid-1950s, the United States, driven by a fight against communism in Asia, had already extended large amounts of economic aid and military assistance (together referred to here as aid) to South Vietnam. Through much of the Second Indochina War, American subventions ballooned (Table 10.1).

Recent scholarship has drawn attention to some positive aspects of the Ngo Dinh Diem regime. By most accounts, however, between 1955 and Diem's assassination in 1963 by US-supported military officers, Diem left, as well as a dysfunctional economy, a 'toxic legacy' of social and religious fragmentation along with a 'noxious' political one.[8] Between 1963 and 1965, five Vietnamese administrations followed Diem's assassination, and political collapse seemed likely. Finally, in 1965 General Nguyen Van Thieu took power in a coup.

4 Hammer, 'Progress report', pp. 230–31; Dacy, *Foreign aid*, p. 3.
5 BE, OV98/2 K. B. Gibson, 'Enclosure to despatch no. 71 (E)', 20 November 1959, p. 18.
6 Taylor, 'Lavish aid', p. 256.
7 Donnell, 'South Vietnam in 1975', p. 11.
8 Fear, 'Ambiguous legacy', pp. 10, 46, 54–56; Catton, *Diem's final failure*, p. 210.

Table 10.1 *United States aid and net real resource transfers to South Vietnam, 1955–75 (million US$)*

(a) United States economic and military assistance

	Economic aid	Military assistance	Total
1955	322.4		322.4
1956	210.0	176.5	386.5
1957	282.2	119.8	402.0
1958	189.0	79.3	268.3
1959	207.4	52.4	259.8
1960	181.8	72.7	254.5
1961	152.0	71.0	223.0
1962	156.0	237.2	393.2
1963	195.9	275.9	471.8
1964	230.6	190.9	421.5
1965	290.3	318.6	608.9
1966	793.9	686.2	1,480.1
1967	666.6	662.5	1,329.1
1968	651.1	1,243.4	1,894.5
1969	560.5	1,534.0	2,094.5
1970	655.4	1,577.3	2,232.7
1971	778.0	1,945.6	2,723.6
1972	587.7	2,602.6	3,190.3
1973	531.2	3,349.4	3,880.6
1974	657.4	941.9	1,599.3
1975	240.9	625.1	866.0

(b) Real net resources transferred

	Real net resources	Real income support	Real net resources % of GNP
1956	150.6	–	16.9
1957	191.5	–	21.2
1958	171.7	–	17.5
1959	143.8	–	13.4
1960	148.8	–	13.4
1961	194.4	–	17.5
1962	217.4	–	18.1
1963	209.7	–	17.0
1964	226.2	176.4	16.8
1965	248.9	301.9	16.9
1966	456.7	792.5	30.9
1967	519.5	498.0	34.5

Table 10.1 (*cont.*)

(b) Real net resources transferred

	Real net resources	Real income support	Real net resources % of GNP
1968	380.8	529.2	26.2
1969	544.8	491.5	36.3
1970	516.5	541.5	32.3
1971	462.5	685.8	28.2
1972	377.2	423.6	23.0
1973	279.8	284.0	17.0
1974	249.0	238.7	15.1

Notes: 1. US economic aid and military assistance is for fiscal years. 2. Net resources transferred are the deficit in the current account of the balance of payments. 3. Income support is essentially gross dollars transferred and includes various US aid programmes, direct dollar support and US piastre purchases. 4. Real net resources transferred measures the real value of aid deflated by the price of imports to Vietnam. Real transfers as a percentage of South Vietnam's GNP declined after 1969 mainly because the price of Vietnamese imports more than doubled between 1969 and 1974 and not because of a fall in the nominal value of aid.
Source: Dacy, *Foreign aid*, pp. 106, 200, 206.

Dramatic increases in the US presence in Vietnam and aid quickly followed the American Congress's August 1964 Gulf of Tonkin Resolution, which gave US President Lyndon Johnson broad, though ill-defined, authority for war in Vietnam. American Marines first landed in Vietnam in March 1965. By April 1969, the United States had 543,000 troops in Vietnam, while South Vietnam's military numbered 1 million. Between 1965 and 1969, American military assistance increased almost fivefold and total aid over threefold. From 1966 to 1970, real resources transferred to South Vietnam amounted to about a third of its GNP and reached 36.3 per cent in 1969. Beginning in 1970, however, the amount of real net resources transferred fell sharply, mainly because of a rise in the price of Vietnamese imports. The fall was the major reason for sluggishness in the economy in the late years of the war (Table 10.1).[9] Aid stabilized the Vietnamese economy, paid for imports far in excess of exports and slowed rates of inflation to acceptable levels. Although none of these things conferred political legitimacy on Thieu, elected president in 1967, they all made important contributions to preventing general unrest.

[9] Dacy, *Foreign aid*, pp. 205–6.

North Vietnam's 1968 Tet Offensive was not an American military defeat, but it turned United States public opinion strongly against war in Indochina. Under US President Richard Nixon's 1969 policy of 'Vietnamization', American troops progressively withdrew from Vietnam. Although a major North Vietnamese invasion in March 1972 was only partially countered by South Vietnamese troops and intense American bombing of the North, the attack on the South did not alter a United States policy of withdrawal. By the end of 1972, even before the signing of the January 1973 Paris Peace Accords, all but 25,000 US soldiers had left Vietnam. Aid remained high through 1973, but from 1971 its real value in terms of resource transfers began to drop markedly. By 1974, transfers to South Vietnam were half their 1970 level. One reason for the fall was that high inflation cut into the real value of US economic aid. More important was that with the withdrawal of US troops, America lost interest in unrestrained financial support for South Vietnam (Table 10.1). The loss of aid and decreased presence of American personnel pushed the South Vietnamese economy into a prolonged recession, although at that time US Secretary of State Henry Kissinger thought 'the Vietnam economic picture … one of the most encouraging aspects of our efforts in Southeast Asia' and other American officials considered the economy near 'takeoff'.[10]

Land Ownership and Redistribution

In 1945 in the Mekong Delta region of the south of Vietnam, about 6,500 landowners, including 500 French citizens, owned about 1.5 million hectares of a total cultivated area of 2.8 million hectares.[11] Figures for the delta in 1955 are not strictly comparable to those for 1945 but indicate a still strongly skewed distribution, with some 15 per cent of owners having 75 per cent of cropland.[12]

Until 1954, the communist Viet Minh controlled most of the South except the cities and used this dominance to redistribute land or force rent reductions through intimidation, arrest or assassination. After 1955, the Viet Cong (guerrillas operating in the South and supported by North Vietnam) adopted similar tactics to implement tenant-centred land reform in areas of the South they controlled.[13] Towards the end of the decade, the South Vietnam government, as it regained areas in the South, returned land to owners of record.

Between 1955 and 1970, the land reform policy of South Vietnam's government was expropriation with compensation. Expropriations totalled approximately 452,000 hectares and distributions 267,000 hectares.[14]

[10] Quoted in Dacy, *Foreign aid*, p. 71.
[11] Bredo et al., *Land reform*, p. 3; Nguyen, *Economic development*, p. 4.
[12] Dacy, *Foreign aid*, p. 111; Nguyen, *Economic development*, p. 4.
[13] Sansom, *Economics*, pp. 55–61; Bredo, 'Agrarian reform', pp. 746–48.
[14] Dacy, *Foreign aid*, p. 112.

South Vietnam began land redistribution in earnest in 1970. The 'Land to the Tiller' programme – a strategy strongly pushed, and largely financed, by the United States – was regarded as fundamental to Vietnamization. By the time of South Vietnam's defeat in 1975, the land title to some 1.2 million hectares had been distributed to nearly 1 million poor or landless farmers. Estimated land still cultivated by tenants was only about 300,000 hectares. The United States financed over three-quarters of compensation to landowners. There was, however, a substantial element of expropriation: just 20 per cent of compensation was in cash and the rest in government bonds yielding a 10 per cent return but a large negative real interest rate due to delayed payment schedules.[15] Land redistribution in the South was so sweeping that it had been essentially accomplished. After Vietnam's unification, this enabled the government to emphasize 'coordinating socialist transformation with socialist building' rather than land-rent reform.[16]

South Vietnam Economic Development and Foreign Aid

For South Vietnam, the First Indochina War created a legacy of developmental disadvantages. Eight years of war badly damaged infrastructure. Vietnam's 1954 partition resulted in a flow from north to south of mainly Catholic refugees. About half of the migrants went to Saigon, creating a major problem of urban unemployment and underemployment.[17] Large parts of the countryside were controlled by between about 5,000 to perhaps 12,000 Viet Cong guerrillas (the National Liberation Front).[18] The American military and South Vietnamese soldiers only slowly reclaimed Viet Cong areas. Starting in 1959, the government attempted to counter the Viet Cong presence in rural areas through forcible resettlement of their inhabitants in so-called agrovilles. These were classified into two groups. One consisted of suspect 'Viet Cong' families, which were kept under close surveillance in an effort to accomplish pacification and encourage development, while the other group comprised families known to support the government.[19]

During the Second Indochina War, United States aid, regarded as essential to the South's existence and American geo-political goals, made economic development difficult, and perhaps impossible. Between 1956 and 1974, GNP at constant prices grew at an annual rate of 3.5 per cent (Table 10.2). Per capita income increased at about 1.4 per cent. Growth, however, depended mainly on aid and the expansion of public administration and defence, which increased

15 Dacy, *Foreign aid*, pp. 15, 113.
16 Nguyen, *Economic development*, p. 161.
17 Dacy, *Foreign aid*, pp. 3, 6.
18 Hendry, 'Economic development', p. 4.
19 Zasloff, 'Rural resettlement', pp. 328–29.

Table 10.2 *South Vietnam GNP, 1955–74 (billion piastres)*

	GNP current prices	GNP constant 1960 prices
1955	63.6	–
1956	68.7	65.4
1957	67.0	66.5
1958	71.3	72.2
1959	80.1	79.1
1960	81.8	81.8
1961	84.5	81.8
1962	93.8	88.2
1963	100.3	90.5
1964	114.5	98.8
1965	144.8	108.0
1966	236.2	108.5
1967	356.7	110.7
1968	385.3	105.8
1969	557.6	110.2
1970	804.4	117.5
1971	979.9	120.7
1972	1,102.0	120.4
1973	1,551.0	120.8
1974	2,229.0	121.5

Source: Dacy, *Foreign aid*, p. 40.

from 16.0 per cent of Net Domestic Product in 1960 to 35.3 per cent by 1969 and 38.1 per cent in 1972. After the Tet Offensive, the government together with the South Vietnamese army absorbed half of male manpower. That eradicated an earlier unemployment problem, but it resurfaced with America's 1970s military run-down. When aid decreased, the economy stagnated, notably in the 1970s (Table 10.2).[20]

Between 1955 and 1975, South Vietnam exported little, and after 1965 almost nothing. From 1966 to 1972, exports were between 2 per cent and 6 per cent of imports (Table 10.3). Aid paid for imported American consumer goods and rice as well as financing a third to half of the government budget deficit. Imports provided the goods to prevent inflation from skyrocketing. South Vietnam became divorced from the international economy; almost all trade was with the United States. For a country with such a large trade deficit as South Vietnam's, the exchange rate is arbitrary but, in practice, it was grossly overvalued. Imports

[20] Dacy, *Foreign aid*, pp. xvi, 41, 59, 70, 212.

Table 10.3 *South Vietnam exports, imports and trade deficit, 1954–74*

	Exports US$ m	Imports US$ m	Exports as % imports
1954	50.6	235.0	21.5
1955	69.2	231.6	29.9
1956	45.1	191.5	23.6
1957	80.5	246.6	32.6
1958	55.2	208.8	26.4
1959	75.1	198.7	37.8
1960	84.5	210.9	40.1
1961	69.8	231.9	30.1
1962	56.0	230.9	24.3
1963	76.7	238.1	32.2
1964	48.5	245.8	19.7
1965	35.5	297.0	12.0
1966	27.6	460.0	6.0
1967	16.4	547.4	3.0
1968	11.7	473.9	2.5
1969	11.9	652.5	1.8
1970	11.5	502.3	2.3
1971	12.4	598.1	2.1
1972	15.6	571.0	2.7
1973	58.0	562.4	10.3
1974	84.9	659.9	12.9

Notes: 1. Imports are commercial imports and exclude public aid, Japanese reparations, French loans and other US and unidentified items. 2. Percentages differ somewhat from those in Dacy, *Foreign aid*, p. 83.
Source: Dacy, *Foreign aid*, p. 106.

of US manufactures together with South Vietnamese government insistence on an overvalued exchange rate discouraged local industrialization. Instead of local industry, South Vietnam relied on imports. Individuals favoured by Vietnamese politicians, and so given access to buy US dollars to pay for imports, realized large rents and became wealthy. Manufacturing accounted for 11.7 per cent of Net Domestic Product in 1960, but only 8.9 per cent by 1972. Local industry, mainly oriented towards Saigon consumers and items tied by natural protection to the home market, employed 2 per cent to 3 per cent of the workforce.[21]

[21] Dacy, *Foreign aid*, p. 81.

The United States imported rice to keep its price low and prevent unrest, especially in the cities, which would threaten the government. The south of Vietnam, historically a major rice producer, still ranked at the beginning of the 1960s as among the world's largest. But imported rice, exchange rate overvaluation and an unstable countryside discouraged production by Vietnamese farmers. South Vietnamese per capita rice output, although appreciably above subsistence levels, stayed more or less unchanged. Nor did non-rice staples, chiefly manioc and sweet potatoes, increase much and remained unimportant compared to rice (Table 10.4). By 1964, South Vietnam exported only a small amount of rice, and after the mid-1960s, rice exports declined to almost nothing.[22] Rubber became the main agricultural export, while South Vietnamese farmers, faced with unattractive exchange rates and artificially low prices, fed some of their rice to hogs.

North Vietnam and Vietnam after Unification

After Partition in 1954, the aim of the new North Vietnamese government was to build a socialism that was closely modelled on the Soviet Union and realized through agricultural collectivization and the development of heavy industry. A near identical strategy was implemented in re-unified Vietnam after 1975. Industrialization was to be financed by agriculture. Agricultural collectivization did not, however, result in the output surpluses needed for industry.[23] Lacking these surpluses, or agricultural exports as an adequate source of foreign exchange, Vietnamese industrialization relied heavily on foreign aid. Moreover, industrialization soon became cripplingly skewed towards heavy industry and was massively inefficient.

War, first with the United States and after 1975 with Cambodia and then with China, disrupted the Vietnamese economy, drained resources and cut into economic growth. Although for years Communist Party leaders blamed economic failure on these conflicts rather than their development model, by the late 1970s it was apparent that Soviet-style socialism had delivered neither 'catch-up' growth nor improved living standards for the great mass of Vietnamese. Vietnam's government had little choice but to start a process of reform.

Starting Point, Economic Structure and Development

In 1955, North Vietnam began its transition to socialism from a weak position. The First Indochina War caused the abandonment of rice fields, destroyed hydraulic systems irrigating 320,000 hectares and badly disrupted rail and river

22 CIA, 'Rice situation in South Vietnam', p. 9.

23 The term 'agricultural surplus' is used loosely; for a discussion of its possible meanings, see Ellman, 'Did the agricultural surplus', pp. 850–58.

Table 10.4 *South Vietnam rice and staple production, 1956–73*

	Rice (000 tons)	Corn (000 tons)	Mungo (mung beans) (000 tons)	Manioc (000 tons)	Sweet potatoes (000 tons)	Non-rice staples (000 tons)	All staples (000 tons)	Population (000 persons)	Rice per capita (kg)	All staples per capita (kg)
1956	3,412	31	5	126	104	266	3,678	12,737	243.0	262.0
1957	3,192	30	5	149	142	326	3,518	13,077	221.4	244.1
1958	4,235	29	6	163	137	335	4,570	13,426	286.2	308.8
1959	5,092	26	6	181	203	416	5,508	13,785	335.1	362.5
1960	4,955	27	7	220	221	475	5,430	14,153	317.6	348.1
1961	4,607	32	8	255	236	531	5,138	14,530	287.6	320.8
1962	5,205	38	10	313	273	634	5,839	14,918	316.5	355.1
1963	5,237	37	11	389	300	737	5,974	15,317	310.2	353.8
1964	5,185	46	12	289	301	648	5,833	15,715	299.3	336.7
1965	4,822	44	12	236	278	570	5,392	16,124	271.3	303.4
1966	4,336	35	14	290	246	585	4,921	16,543	237.8	269.9
1967	4,688	33	20	262	254	569	5,257	16,973	250.6	281.0
1968	4,366	32	13	260	235	540	4,906	17,414	227.4	255.6
1969	5,115	31	12	233	226	502	5,617	17,867	259.7	285.2
1970	5,715	31	11	216	220	478	6,193	18,332	282.8	306.5
1971	6,100	34	13	270	230	547	6,647	18,809	294.2	320.6
1972	5,900	42	14	247	241	544	6,444	19,373	276.3	301.8
1973	7,165	–	–	–	–	–	–	19,945	325.9	–

Source: Dacy, *Foreign aid*, pp. 99–100.

transport. Only Soviet and Chinese food aid averted famine in 1954–55. Nearly 93 per cent of a population of some 13.5 million was in agriculture; handicrafts accounted for 71 per cent of industrial output. Modern industry consisted of seven enterprises, accounted for 1.5 per cent of material output and employed only a few thousand workers. Following Partition, about 1 million people left for South Vietnam, around 7 per cent of the North's inhabitants. Moreover, the exodus included most of those with the highest human capital and skills that would be critical in rebuilding and transforming the economy.[24]

Gross Material Product (GMP) in Marxian economic systems is defined as the product of social labour, and during an accounting period measures newly created product (national income), material inputs and depreciation. GMP excludes substantial parts of the service sector, leaving industry and agriculture as the main economic sectors but including in these transport services. A material product means a physical good; although a painting, for example, is tangible, it is omitted from GMP as not being a product of social labour.[25]

Table 10.5 uses agriculture and industry as representative of GMP to show trends in the North Vietnamese economy. Between 1955 and 1970, three broad phases characterize the economy. The first is rapid recovery until 1960, and a second slower growth through 1965. A third began in 1966, after the escalation of the Second Indochina War, and was marked by economic contraction. Over the same 15-year period, population grew at an annual rate of 3.2 per cent, reaching 19.5 million in 1966 and 21.8 million by 1970. Per capita output increased in most years until 1965 but then declined substantially, as GMP fell and population continued to increase (Table 10.5).

After 1955 and into the 1970s, the North Vietnamese remained desperately poor, with an annual income (in 1959 prices) of no more than roughly US$78, and generally less (Table 10.5).[26] From 1960 onwards, agricultural output rose only marginally. Most gains in GMP were in industry and handicrafts, especially the former. From 1955 to 1965, industry expanded, at 1959 prices, at a rate of some 24 per cent annually, before falling back, seriously hampered by American bombing and, to avoid this, industrial decentralization of major factories to the provinces (Table 10.5). During the post-1965 phase of the war, nearly half the male labour force was mobilized for military-related activities.[27]

Shares by sector of GMP and of national income tell a broadly similar story. Each indicates the Communist Party's emphasis on industry, although this is more pronounced for GMP than national income (Table 10.6). Industry accounted for well over two-fifths of GMP by 1971, while the industrial sector rose from 16.0 per cent of national income in 1957 to 28.3 per cent by 1971. Between 1957 and 1971, the contribution of agriculture to GMP shrank from

[24] Nguyen, *Economic development*, pp. 32, 41–42, 47, 64; Vickerman, 'Note', p. 224; Beresford, *Vietnam*, p. 125.

[25] Becker, *National income accounting*, pp. 71–78.

[26] Nguyen, *Economic development*, pp. 98, 151.

[27] Beresford, *National unification*, pp. 166–68; Nguyen, *Economic development*, pp. 149, 151.

Table 10.5 *North Vietnam gross material product, 1955–70 (1959 prices)*

(a) Dong aggregates, population and output per capita

	Total GMP dong m	Agriculture dong m	Industry dong m	Handicrafts dong m	Population m	Per capita output dong
1955	1,882	1,565	317	225	13.5	139.4
1956	2,470	1,843	627	366	14.0	176.4
1957	2,759	1,894	865	496	14.5	190.3
1958	3,214	2,201	1,013	527	15.0	214.3
1959	3,695	2,384	1,311	596	15.5	238.4
1960	3,517	2,046	1,471	630	15.9	221.2
1961	3,896	2,225	1,671	679	16.5	236.1
1962	4,451	2,349	2,102	729	17.1	260.3
1963	4,570	2,309	2,261	747	17.7	258.2
1964	5,017	2,406	2,611	783	18.3	274.2
1965	5,213	2,507	2,706	812	18.9	275.8
1966	4,651	2,487	2,164	649	19.5	238.5
1967	4,198	2,467	1,731	519	20.0	209.9
1968	3,885	2,500	1,385	416	20.6	188.6
1969	4,073	2,605	1,468	440	21.2	192.1
1970	4,593	2,714	1,879	564	21.8	210.7

(b) 1959 = 100

	Total GMP	Agriculture	Industry	Handicrafts	Population m	Per capita output
1955	50.9	65.6	24.2	37.8	87.1	58.5
1956	66.8	77.3	47.8	61.4	90.3	74.0
1957	74.7	79.4	66.0	83.2	93.5	79.8
1958	87.0	92.3	77.3	88.4	96.8	89.9
1959	100.0	100.0	100.0	100.0	100.0	100.0
1960	95.2	85.8	112.2	105.7	102.6	92.8
1961	105.4	93.3	127.5	113.9	106.5	99.0
1962	120.5	98.5	160.3	122.3	110.3	109.2
1963	123.7	96.9	172.5	125.3	114.2	108.3
1964	135.8	100.9	199.2	131.4	118.1	115.0
1965	141.1	105.2	206.4	136.2	121.9	115.7
1966	125.9	104.3	165.1	108.9	125.8	100.1
1967	113.6	103.5	132.0	87.1	129.0	88.1
1968	105.1	104.9	105.6	69.8	132.9	79.1
1969	110.2	109.3	112.0	73.8	136.8	80.6
1970	124.3	113.8	143.3	94.6	140.6	88.4

Note: For 1955–60 GMP is in 1956 prices but because of strict price control this makes no appreciable difference.
Source: Nguyen, *Economic development*, p. 98.

Table 10.6 *North Vietnam gross material product and national income structure, 1957–71 (%)*

(a) Gross material product	1957	1960	1965	1968	1971
Agriculture	41.3	34.1	29.9	32.2	30.5
Industry and handicrafts	24.3	33.5	40.5	37.9	43.9
Construction	7.3	9.6	10.8	10.6	11.6
Transport and communications	2.4	2.7	2.6	3.3	3.3
Commerce and services	15.6	13.1	10.3	9.8	5.6
Other	9.1	7.0	5.9	6.2	5.1
Total	100.0	100.0	100.0	100.0	100.0
(b) National income	**1957**	**1960**	**1965**	**1968**	**1971**
Agriculture	44.4	42.3	39.8	43.9	42.1
Industry	16.0	18.2	23.1	19.9	28.3
Construction	3.4	4.7	6.8	6.4	7.9
Transport and communications	2.3	2.8	2.5	2.4	3.0
Commerce and services	20.8	20.5	17.3	16.4	8.9
Other	13.1	11.5	10.5	11.0	9.8
Total	100.0	100.0	100.0	100.0	100.0

Note: For national income, agriculture includes forestry and industry includes handicrafts.
Source: Nguyen, *Economic development*, p. 104.

two-fifths to less than a third, but for national income remained relatively unchanged at over two-fifths. Gains in industry came chiefly at the expense of a sharp contraction in commerce and services. That sector declined as a share of national income from a fifth in 1957 to 8.9 per cent in 1971, while GMP dropped from 15.6 per cent to just 5.6 per cent. The falls were the reverse of the usual pattern in capitalist economies of a growing importance of services in the development process (Table 10.6). The falling share reflected both the officially recorded status of services as an unproductive sector and an extension of state monopoly over trade.

The main change in the structure of employment was a drop in the proportion of the workforce in agriculture from over four-fifths in 1960 to slightly less than two-thirds by 1975 (Table 10.7). Even at that level, however, Vietnam remained an overwhelmingly agrarian economy and an unambiguously little-developed one. Tellingly, a decrease in workers in agriculture by 1968 was not offset by increases in agricultural labour productivity to provide the higher

Table 10.7 *North Vietnam employment structure, 1960–75 (%)*

	1960	1965	1975
Agriculture	83.0	78.6	64.7
Industry	7.0	8.3	10.6
Construction	1.7	3.3	7.5
Transport and communications	1.2	1.7	2.2
Trade	3.0	2.3	3.1
Total material production	96.6	94.2	89.9
Non-material production	3.4	5.8	10.7

Notes: 1. Agriculture includes forestry. 2. Categories may not add to total material production because of a small number of people in other industries.
Source: Vickerman, 'Note', p. 230.

rural per capita incomes or the surpluses earmarked for investment in industry. The preponderance of workers in agriculture, the lack of much change in its output and, discussed below, a decrease in per capita food production all point to the depth of poverty in North Vietnam. So, too, does its high and increasing dependence on food aid. Although industrial employment rose from 7.0 per cent of the workforce in 1960 to 10.6 per cent by 1975, this did relatively little to absorb the shift in workers out of industry. The single largest employment-creating sector was non-material production, meaning in particular health and education, both of which improved considerably.[28]

Post-1975 Vietnam faced a major problem in the welding together of two economies which sharply differed in developmental levels and economic ideologies. In 1975, North Vietnam had a per capita income of about half that in the South (US$250 compared to US$125 in the North) and consumption was 'a bare subsistence level'.[29] Rather than gaining a substantial southern industrial base, the new government inherited a collection of light, consumer-oriented industries, mainly located around Saigon, along with high urban unemployment and a population opposed to Soviet-style socialism.

Nevertheless, the government pressed full speed ahead towards socialist construction. It was, just as in the North before 1975, to be realized through central planning and the investment of peasant-created agricultural

[28] Beresford, *National unification*, pp. 163–65 and *Vietnam*, pp. 147–48; Vickerman, 'Note', pp. 227–29.
[29] Kimura, 'Vietnam', pp. 1045, 1040.

Table 10.8 *Vietnam population and per capita income, 1975–85*

	Population million	Per capita income 1970 constant prices (1975 = 100)	Per capita income 1982 constant prices (1975 = 100)	Per capita income US$
1975	48.7	100.0	100.0	98
1976	49.8	114.6	114.6	101
1977	50.9	116.9	116.0	101
1978	52.0	119.6	119.6	100
1979	53.1	119.1	119.1	97
1980	54.3	113.4	121.6	91
1981	55.5	122.3	127.9	94
1982	56.8	132.2	136.6	99
1983	58.1	136.1	143.7	–
1984	59.5	143.6	152.0	–
1985	60.9	–	–	–

Sources: Kimura, 'Vietnam', pp. 1041, 1043; World Bank, *World development indicators, 2020*.

surpluses in heavy industry. The 1976–80 Five-Year Plan for North Vietnam became, with some appropriate revisions, the Second Five-Year Plan for all of Vietnam.[30]

The decision to accelerate a transition to socialism and adopt for Vietnam the North Vietnam economic model meant the imposition on the South of rigid controls, austerity and worsening living standards, partly because of a draining away of resources to support the North. A dash for socialism in the South was, as the Party later acknowledged, a serious mistake. Per capita income in Vietnam, after at first increasing, remained static until 1980, although it subsequently rose appreciably (Table 10.8). Even so, the country still ranked as among the world's very poorest nations.[31] Despite the rise in per capita income beginning in 1981, real wages and living standards fell and there was considerable malnourishment. Rice rations in Saigon had to be supplemented with sweet potatoes and manioc. Many pre-school children were malnourished. Hanoi had frequent blackouts. Monthly salaries of fixed income earners, including high-ranking officials, covered no more than a quarter of the budget of even thrifty individuals. Even those people had to raise poultry or pigs, sell gifts sent from abroad or engage in illegal trading to survive. In the

[30] Nguyen, *Economic development*, pp. 174–75, 189.
[31] Kimuma, 'Vietnam', p. 1040.

North, about 3 million peasants annually faced food shortages during the several months between the two rice harvests.[32]

Vietnam Economic Model

After independence in 1955, North Vietnam implemented a command economy reliant on planning, agricultural collectivization, industrialization and administered pricing. Formal economic planning began with the Three-Year Plan for 1958–61 and the Five-Year Plan for 1961–65. Development strategy followed the classical Marxian model and echoed the Soviet Union's approach between the two world wars.

Collectivization was fundamental to the Vietnamese development model. Prior to the formation of collectives, land reform was a basic first step. Land redistribution, beginning in 1945 and continuing through 1956, closely copied the Maoist redistributive concept, had Chinese advisors and aimed for 'the liquidation of the land-owing class and the establishment of the Proletarian dictatorship in the countryside'.[33] By 1956, 810,000 hectares, or about 37 per cent of cultivable land, had been distributed to 2.1 million families (9.5 million peasants) at an average of 0.4 hectares per family.[34]

Enforcement was violent. Land reform cadres, following Chinese policy, were ordered 'to find at all costs "four to five per cent" of landlord households in every commune' and not to worry about committing leftist excesses. At least 15,000 people were murdered and, partly because there were not always enough landlords available, middle peasants (someone who lives solely by tilling his land without exploiting others), as well as poor peasants and even agricultural labourers, were mistakenly executed. In 1955, the Party regarded land reform as too moderate, but later recognized the excesses of 'leftist errors' and an element of 'infantile leftism'.[35]

Agricultural Collectivization in North and South Vietnam

After the completion of land reform, the North Vietnam government regarded collectivization as the next stage of a strategy 'to solve the question of food' and 'win the battle of rice'.[36] Orthodox Marxism teaches that collectivization unlocks the productive potential of agriculture. Scale economies realized through collectives yield a larger agricultural surplus, as does centralized management to

[32] Vo, *Vietnam's economic policy*, pp. 106, 160–69, 229; Kimura, 'Vietnam', pp. 1040–46; Beresford, *Vietnam*, p. 168; Nguyen, *Economic development*, p. 189.

[33] Ngyuen, *Economic development*, p. 72.

[34] Ngyuen, *Economic development*, pp. 56–57.

[35] Vo, *Vietnam's economic policy*, pp. 2–7; Holcombe, *Mass mobilization*, pp. 259–80.

[36] Ngyuen, *Economic development*, p. 126.

purchase inputs, make decisions and market output. Centralization, which can check peasant consumption, allowing a rise in living standards for poor and middle peasants, comes only through cooperatives.

Vietnam, and later Cambodia and Laos, adopted the Maoist collectivization model, which emphasizes, in contrast to the importance of capital in the Soviet model, that gains arise from the combined labour efforts of previously isolated farmers and group enthusiasm. Machines are unnecessary and cooperatives can occur 'without funds, without carts, without oxen'.[37] Part of the model's attractiveness, apart from the sanction of its Maoist origins, was the shortage of capital and the difficulty of using machines on tiny holdings. But, the Mao model notwithstanding, capital in the form of oxen, carts, water pumps and tractors clearly boosts productivity.

North Vietnam began to implement cooperativization in 1955. It became official policy in 1959 and by then determined implementation was well underway. For the next 27 years, until the beginning of liberalization in 1986, cooperatives, first in the North and then in the South after 1975, were central to Vietnamese economic failure. Food availability stagnated or declined and living standards fell.

The North moved towards complete collectivization in three stages, starting with work exchange teams, then low-order cooperatives and finally high-order cooperatives. Farmers in work exchange teams pool land, labour and other resources to participate, either seasonally or permanently, in joint projects. Seasonal teams join together at specific times such as planting or harvesting, while those in permanent teams still cultivate their own land. Payment for their work in the cooperative is part of the crop and according to work days and work points. Members of low-order cooperatives receive a share of the crop according to the amount of land contributed. High-order cooperatives eliminate land payment; members are paid only for work supplied and on entering the cooperative, aged 16, contribute farm tools, animals, 'share money' and whatever land they have. To create a 'subsidiary household economy', cooperative members are allocated 5 per cent of cooperative land, the so-called '5 per cent soil'. The cooperative has the other 95 per cent.[38]

In the North, land reform and cooperatives met with open revolt in 1956 in Nghe An in North Annam. Dissent was countered by the execution or, mainly, deportation of some 6,000 peasants to labour camps.[39] Much of resistance was, however, passive, and in 1960, 86 per cent of northern peasant families were in cooperatives, almost all low-order. By 1971, the proportion had risen to nearly

37 Quoted in Pryor, *Red and green*, p. 54 from Mao Tse-tung, 'On the collectivization of agriculture' [1955] in Mao Tse-tung, *The writings of Mao Tse-tung, 1949–1976*, vol. 1, *September 1949–December 1955*.

38 Ngyuen, *Economic development*, pp. 57–59; Woodside, *Community and revolution*, pp. 252, 256; White, 'Alternative approaches', p. 142.

39 Gittinger, 'Communist land policy', pp. 119–20; Fall, *Two Vietnams*, p. 157.

96 per cent of families in 20,000 cooperatives, most of which were officially considered to be high-order, if not always such in reality.[40]

After 1975 in the South, the government immediately moved to transform agriculture from small peasant holdings to large-scale cooperatives. The intentions were the same as they had been in the North; to effect socialist transformation and to appropriate agricultural surplus, which would be used to develop heavy industry. Because of the Viet Cong's 1960s land reform campaigns in 'liberated areas' and South Vietnam's 1970s 'Land to the Tiller' programme, land redistribution was not a major issue. There was only some re-adjustment of land holding, which meant taking land from upper middle peasants, rich peasants and rural capitalists to reallocate to landless or poor peasants and give them the means to participate in the collective economy. After an initial collectivization stage of organizing mutual aid groups, the intention was to shift towards higher collectivization forms. At first, these were to be transitional units of 30 to 50 hectares with the means of production owned by the cooperative, distribution according to labour and rents paid for land and machines. Ultimately, the South would have full agricultural cooperatives of 200 to 300 hectares.[41]

In southern Vietnam's Mekong Delta, peasant opposition to cooperatives was considerable for the same reasons as in the North: a lack of incentives and the cost of supporting non-working officials. Patterns of land and property ownership were an additional barrier to acceptance: 70 per cent of peasants were middle peasants and owned 60 per cent of farm equipment and 90 per cent of draught animals.[42] These individuals lacked an incentive to surrender ownership to cooperatives. Reflective of this reality, in 1985 in the delta, no more than a quarter of peasant households had joined cooperatives. For southern farmers, whether in cooperatives or not, state agricultural pricing added a major disincentive to produce output for sale to the state, because it turned the internal terms of trade against the rural sector and in favour of industry to extract surplus. Farm production was further checked by shortages and the low quality of items like hot water flasks, bicycles, canned milk and fabrics, which were desired by peasants and would act as inducement goods to exchange for agricultural products. Furthermore, cooperatives bore social levies of contributions to welfare funds and production costs. The latter included supporting, fully or partially, large numbers of Party cadres and their families. A village of no more than a thousand people might have 50 or 100 cadres and the more successful a village was in raising production the greater their number in the village's governing structure.[43]

40 Ngyuen, *Economic development*, pp. 57–59.
41 Vo, *Vietnam's economic policy*, pp. 71–72.
42 Ngo Vinh Long, 'Cooperativization', p. 169; Kerkvliet, 'Village-state relations', pp. 404–6; Vo, *Vietnam's economic policy*, p. 79.
43 Ngo Vinh Long, 'Cooperativization', pp. 167–68.

Production Assessment of Cooperatives

Cooperative agriculture, lacking peasant support and so trapped in low productivity, failed to mobilize large investable surpluses or raise rural living standards. Between 1955 and 1975 in North Vietnam, annual per capita staple production, almost all of which consisted of rice, fell markedly, declining at an average rate of 1.1 per cent annually. By 1973/75, output had dropped to an annual 245 kilograms per capita, equivalent to 672 grams a day or, if distributed equally, about 2,410 calories per person (Figure 10.1). Between 1976 and 1986, the production of rice and all staples increased, boosted by the Mekong Delta's contribution and in response to pricing reforms. The output of both staples and paddy rose on a per capita basis by about a quarter (Figure 10.2).

The first of two main reasons for cooperative economic failure was that because of the Party's fixation on heavy industry, agriculture received relatively small budget allocations and inadequate attention.[44] Agricultural mechanization, such as small motors for pumping water, husking and threshing, mechanical threshers and rice husking machinery, dramatically raises agricultural productivity. However, in North Vietnam mechanization did not start until 1965, and in 1972 only just over half of cooperatives had small machines.[45] In the South after 1975, rather than investing in tractors and other farm equipment, the government tried to collectivize machinery, causing peasants to neglect or sabotage it. In 1983, southern collectives and cooperatives had only 3,200 tractors although that comprised 84 per cent of all tractors still in operation.[46]

Second, and even more important than agricultural investment, economic incentives were lacking. Peasant agriculture is efficient because labour is applied until its marginal product is zero, so long as this is consistent with a willingness to expend effort and peasants are likely to make this expenditure for tangible benefits. State-administered prices, mandated deliveries and the absence of a direct link between work and rewards caused peasants to withhold property and effort from cooperatives and instead cultivate family plots. In the North before joining cooperatives, many peasants tried to sell draught animals, and even cut down their fruit trees. As cooperative members, peasants adopted a 'one foot in, one foot out' approach of contributing as little work as possible. Average daily working hours provided to cooperatives might be only four or five. At times of high labour stress, like harvesting, labour was hard to mobilize, while those who worked did so with low efficiency. The government tinkered with incentives to try to alter work patterns, but these do not appear to have changed much between 1965 and 1975, since most peasant income came from their own plots. In 1975, the 5 per cent of land allocated to family plots generated 54.3 per cent of peasant income and cooperative land;

44 Vo, *Vietnam's economic policy*, pp. 30–34, 85, 144–45, 169, 194, 245.
45 Ngyuen, *Economic development*, p. 124.
46 Ngo Vinh Long, 'Cooperativization', p. 167.

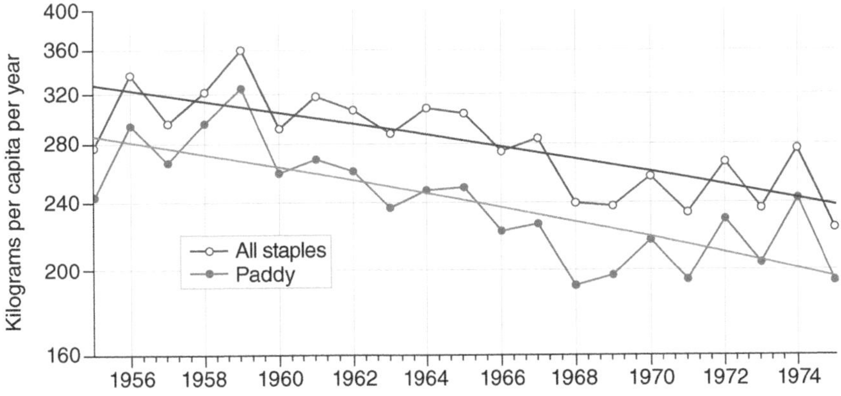

Figure 10.1 North Vietnam all staples and paddy production, 1955–75
Sources: Kerkvliet, *Power*, pp. 246–47; Population is from Nguyen, *Economic development*, p. 98.

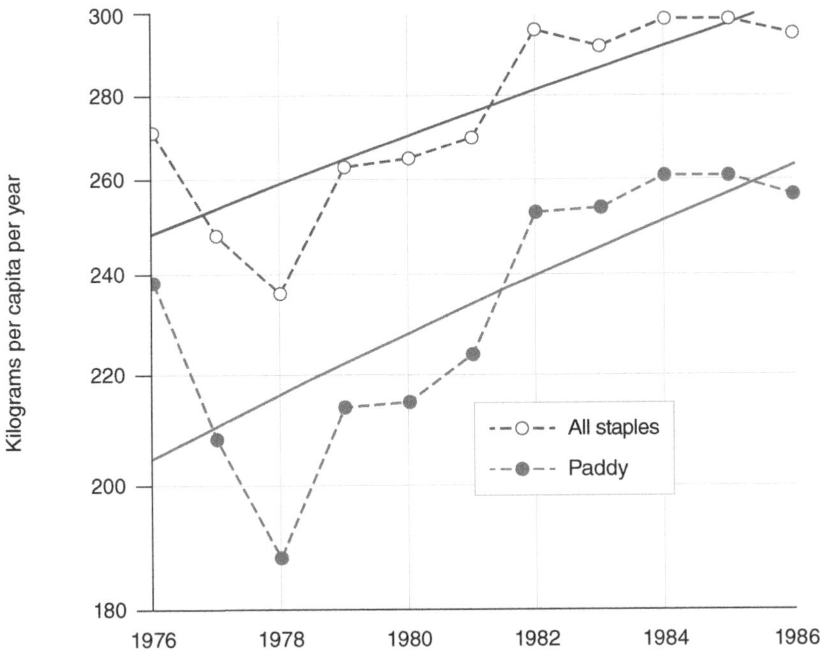

Figure 10.2 Vietnam all staples and paddy production, 1976–86
Source: Vo, *Vietnam's economic policy*, pp. 83, 138, 196.

the other 95 per cent of cultivation, just 34.6 per cent. Private plots, in 1983, had yields twice those of cooperatives and furnished a third to half of foodstuffs consumed by members and over 90 per cent of their consumption of pork, chicken, vegetables and fruits.[47] Many cooperative families in the Red River Delta who had received oxen or water buffalo to breed on a contractual basis did not look after them responsibly, since they did not own the cattle. The result was an endemic cattle shortage, which undermined the economy.[48] In the first half of the 1980s, reforms to offer peasants more production incentives, many based on a contract system, did not add sufficiently to output to be counted a success. During the latter part of the decade, agriculture was de-collectivized.[49]

Application of Vietnam Economic Model, Model Assessment and Foreign Aid

To transform the economy after Vietnam's division, government in the North moved quickly to replace private enterprise with cooperatives and state stores. In 1955, private merchants accounted for 72 per cent of wholesale trade and 80 per cent of retail trade but in 1957 for 47 per cent and 60 per cent of these categories respectively. The transformation was almost complete by 1960: the state sector controlled 91 per cent of retail trade and all foreign trade. After 1965, decentralization due to US bombing forced a sharp reversal away from the socialist sector in domestic commerce, although not in transport, where the state enterprise share was still over four-fifths of the total. By 1975, however, North Vietnam's two main economic sectors were the state-owned economy and the collective economy; the private economy was negligible.[50]

In Vietnam's socialist regime, heavy industry was classed as Group A (Department I in Marx's 'reproduction schema' in volume 2 of *Capital*) and meant producer goods. Specifically, these included machinery, metallurgy, chemicals, minerals and construction products. North Vietnamese planners placed particular emphasis on electricity generation, coal, iron and steel and machine tools. Light industry, Group B and Department II, comprised principally consumer goods such as textiles, paper and food products.

Until 1975 and for much of the following decade in the unified Vietnam, planners rigidly followed the orthodox Soviet approach of prioritizing investment and, especially, investment in heavy industry. Between 1955/57 and 1969/71, investment in industry rose from under a third to two-fifths of total investment, while within the industrial sector the share of investment in heavy industry grew at the expense of light industry and to three-quarters of resources allocated to industry (Table 10.9). Handicrafts appear as a separate category in official North Vietnamese statistics, perhaps originally because the industrial sector was so small. However, the separation of handicrafts from light

47 Vo, *Vietnam's economic policy*, pp. 15–18, 131–32.
48 Woodside, *Community and revolution*, p. 232.
49 Werner, 'Socialist development'.
50 Ngyuen, *Economic development*, pp. 64–66, 158.

Table 10.9 *North Vietnam and Vietnam investment allocation, 1955/57–1985*

	Shares of industrial investment %		Shares of total investment %		
	A: heavy industry	B: light industry	All industry	A: heavy industry	B: light industry
North Vietnam					
1955/57	66	34	31	20	11
1958/60	67	33	46	31	15
1961/64	78	22	53	41	12
1965/68	82	18	33	27	6
1969/71	76	24	40	30	10
Vietnam					
1976	67	33			
1979	67	33			
1980	73	27			
1981	84	16	42	35	7
1982	85	15	53	45	8
1983	80	20	40	32	8
1984	74	26	34	25	9
1985	75	25	31	22	7

Note: For 1985, investment shares for heavy and light industry may be approximate because the share of investment in the two categories does not add to industrial investment as a share of total investment.
Sources: Nguyen, *Economic development*, p. 142; Vo, *Vietnam's economic policy*, pp. 86, 144.

and heavy industry has considerable relevance in understanding why North Vietnamese development strategy was unsuccessful. Handicrafts were fundamental in providing incentives for the mass of the peasantry, since consumer manufactures were in short supply and available supplies did not penetrate far beyond cities. Handicrafts and light industry more generally would have had the further advantage of being labour using and so in keeping with Vietnam's factor endowment of abundant labour.

Both handicrafts and consumer goods were, however, viewed as having a quite limited role in Vietnam's development.[51] From 1955 to 1973, heavy industrial output increased 18-fold compared to half as much for light industry and a quarter as much for handicrafts (Table 10.10). Emphasis on heavy industry and a

[51] Vickerman, 'Note', p. 227; Gough, 'Economy: interview with Nguyen', p. 378.

Table 10.10 *North Vietnam industrial production, 1955–75*

(a) Dong m, 1959 prices

	A: heavy industry	B: light industry	Total industry	Handicrafts
1955	86	231	317	225
1956	180	447	627	370
1957	190	644	834	489
1958	258	755	1,013	527
1959	425	886	1,311	603
1960	503	968	1,471	633
1962	788	1,313	2,101	735
1963	893	1,367	2,260	746
1964	1,044	1,567	2,611	783
1965	1,217	1,634	2,851	754
1966	1,278	1,493	2,771	786
1967	1,053	1,352	2,405	734
1968	1,149	1,399	2,548	696
1971	1,445	2,037	3,482	830
1972	1,245	1,841	3,086	814
1973	1,539	2,134	3,673	979
1975	–	–	4,940	–

(b) Index 1955 = 100

	A: heavy industry	B: light industry	Total industry	Handicrafts
1955	100.0	100.0	100.0	100.0
1956	209.3	193.5	197.8	164.4
1957	220.9	278.8	263.1	217.3
1958	300.0	326.8	319.6	234.2
1959	494.2	383.5	413.6	268.0
1960	584.9	419.0	464.0	281.3
1962	916.3	568.4	662.8	326.7
1963	1,038.4	591.8	712.9	331.6
1964	1,214.0	678.4	823.7	348.0
1965	1,415.1	707.4	899.4	335.1
1966	1,486.0	646.3	874.1	349.3
1967	1,224.4	585.3	758.7	326.2
1968	1,336.0	605.6	803.8	309.3
1971	1,680.2	881.8	1,098.4	368.9
1972	1,447.7	797.0	973.5	361.8
1973	1,789.5	923.8	1,158.7	435.1
1975	–	–	1,558.4	–

Source: Nguyen, *Economic development*, p. 140.

Table 10.11 *North Vietnam consumer goods share of imports, 1955–75 (%)*

Year	%
1955	54.6
1956	32.2
1957	32.6
1958	24.7
1959	16.0
1960	12.7
1964	22.2
1974	32.2
1975	30.3

Source: Vickerman, 'Note', p. 229.

lack of home production starved Vietnamese consumers of basic goods. Nor did imports do much to alleviate shortages. Consumer goods as a proportion of total imports fell dramatically between 1955 and 1964, from 54.6 per cent to 22.2 per cent, although by 1975 they had recovered somewhat to 30.3 per cent (Table 10.11).

The government in post-1975 Vietnam adopted the same investment policy as that previously followed in the North: the view that socialism required heavy industry. Until 1984, industry received a share of total investment similar to that which it had been accorded by the North Vietnamese government. Even when investment in industry fell, heavy industry was still granted the lion's share. Between 1976 and 1985, it took from two-thirds to four-fifths of industrial investment (Table 10.9).

Without question, war created major barriers to Vietnam's development. But since none of the four conditions for successful Marxist development, set out in the chapter's introduction, were met, it seems unlikely that the model adopted by Vietnam would ever have succeeded. The first condition of a base of existing development was not met, since North Vietnam was, in 1955, a peasant, technologically backwards economy. In 1975, this lack of development remained largely true of Vietnam.

Second, agricultural collectivization did not yield surpluses to finance industrialization. Between 1960 and 1975 in the North, collectivization failed even to add enough to the output of staple foods to keep pace with population increase. Rather than the intended accumulation, the state had to rely on food aid and to pay peasants high prices to obtain grain for re-sale to urban workers at highly subsidized prices. These subsidies drained the state budget.[52]

[52] Beresford, *Vietnam*, pp. 134, 140, 168–69.

After 1975, the attempt to introduce agricultural collectivization in the South found little acceptance. In 1982, just 10 per cent of southern peasants had joined cooperatives, and only 30 per cent were members of mutual aid teams, the initial stage in forming collectives.[53] Although with the addition of agriculture in the Mekong Delta per capita output of staple foods in Vietnam increased, output still fell far short of the surpluses needed to finance industry.

In North Vietnam, the constraint that agriculture imposed on industry was overcome only through foreign aid, almost all from the Soviet Union and China. Aid largely financed North Vietnam's industrialization. Most aid went towards heavy industry. Little attention was paid to agriculture before 1965. Between the 1965 start of intense US bombing and near the 1975 end of the war, 'rural areas were left basically to fend for themselves'. Rural dwellers apparently lived at a near minimum subsistence level of consumption, while urbanites relied largely on imported rice and consumer goods from China.[54]

Data on foreign aid were kept secret but its importance to the North Vietnamese economy is obvious. From 1960 to 1964, the contribution of aid to total budgetary revenues rose from a fifth to two-fifths. Between 1966 and 1975, aid comprised over half to two-thirds of budgetary revenues and from 1976 to 1980 a third to two-fifths (Table 10.12). Vietnam acquired an 'import mentality', a belief that foreign aid would cover any shortage of foreign exchange.[55]

Estimates of absolute amounts of aid vary but suggest a total of nearly US$1 billion from 1955 to 1965. Aid increased greatly due to the escalation of the war, and between 1965 and 1975 may have amounted to non-military aid of US$1.8 billion from the USSR and US$1.5 billion from China. These figures are, however, conjectural because of a lack of data on Chinese food aid. From 1955 to 1975, Soviet military aid was said to be between US$6 billion and US$10 billion and eight to 14 times greater than from China. Non-military aid was mainly in the form of loans and consisted chiefly of capital goods, and before long also intermediate goods needed because of the establishment of industry.

An absence of domestic output of many intermediate inputs meant that they had to come from abroad as Vietnamese heavy industry expanded, a familiar pattern in import-substituting regimes. From 1960 to 1964, the means of production, including intermediate goods, comprised more than 90 per cent of aid; nearly all the rest of aid came as services rather than consumer goods. In 1978, China ended all aid to Vietnam, but during the Second Five-Year Plan of 1976–80, Soviet assistance amounted to US$1.45 billion. Aid lessened after 1981 and was chiefly in the form of loans rather than grants.[56] Decades of aid loans

[53] Gough, 'Economy: interview with Nguyen', p. 377.

[54] Beresford, *National unification*, pp. 134, 163, 164.

[55] Spoor, 'Finance', p. 355 and see Vo, *Vietnam's economic policy*, pp. 42–43.

[56] Vo, *Vietnam's economic policy*, pp. 38–44, 98–102, 154–57; Fforde, 'Economic aspects', pp. 194–95; Beresford, *National unification*, pp. 173–74, 197.

Table 10.12 *North Vietnam and Vietnam revenue and aid as percentages of budgetary expenditure, 1960–80*

	Internal revenues	Foreign aid	Total
1960	77.6	22.4	100.0
1961	76.9	23.1	100.0
1962	74.1	25.9	100.0
1963	73.5	26.5	100.0
1964	78.5	21.5	100.0
1965	57.7	42.3	100.0
1966	39.0	61.0	100.0
1967	33.4	66.6	100.0
1968	31.1	68.9	100.0
1969	31.5	68.5	100.0
1970	32.4	67.6	100.0
1971	36.0	64.0	100.0
1972	39.7	60.3	100.0
1973	40.1	59.9	100.0
1974	39.4	60.6	100.0
1975	45.1	54.9	100.0
1976	55.2	44.8	100.0
1977	65.5	34.5	100.0
1978	68.0	32.0	100.0
1979	59.2	40.8	100.0
1980	59.4	40.6	100.0

Source: Vo, *Vietnam's economic policy*, pp. 40, 101.

left Vietnam heavily indebted to the Soviet Union and, lacking other means of repayment, during the 1980s thousands of workers were sent there to earn Eastern Bloc currency.[57]

In regard to the third and fourth conditions for socialist industrial-based economic development (short industrial gestation periods and the establishment of comparatively efficient light industry), heavy industry both in the North and in unified Vietnam, rather than developing as planners anticipated, had long gestation periods, was notoriously inefficient, became a drain on resources and turned into an enclave. Industry was hampered by shortages of raw materials and spare parts. By the early 1970s, many industries operated at half of capacity or less. Underutilization contributed to high-cost structures.

[57] Esterline, 'Vietnam in 1987', p. 91.

These led to a dependence on state subsidies, funded through budget deficits which added to inflation. Shoddy products were the general rule, as was corruption everywhere including within the Party; the theft of state property for sale on the black market; and state-enterprise reliance on the black market for inputs. Worker indifference, absenteeism and moonlighting due to low, and for urban workers below subsistence, wages were major problems.

The development strategy followed by Vietnam might have seemed to accord with the concept of a 'big push'. But as formulated by Rosenstein-Rodan, the push depended on supply creating its own demand through the simultaneous establishment of a number of light, labour-intensive, consumer-oriented industries like shoe and textile manufacture. Workers in one industry would demand the output of their own and of other industries. Industrial development would provide most wage goods and, through expanding the domestic market, allow the realization of scale economies. The Rosenstein-Rodan argument excluded producer goods such as steel, chemicals and petrochemicals on the grounds of comparative disadvantage.[58] By contrast to Rosenstein-Rodan's concept of a 'big push', Vietnamese heavy industry did not realize scale economies and had few linkages to other sectors of the economy; most consumer goods and raw materials had to be imported from China.[59]

Vietnam developed as a shortage economy. Shortages become chronic if, as in Vietnam, administered prices bear little, if any, relation to supply and demand. Furthermore, the standard of Vietnamese-made consumption items and inputs for agriculture were often so low that they were hardly worth having. Manufactured goods in Vietnam might not work at all and were shunned in favour of imported Chinese goods. Shortages and poor quality gave peasants little incentive to expand agricultural production or sell output. From the early 1960s onwards, as was explained to a visiting academic, 'we have had a virtual absence of industrial machinery for agriculture, and also not enough for light industry, so our cities didn't have much to sell to the countryside. As a result, the peasants were not keen to sell to the city folk.'[60] Without foreign aid, the absence of agricultural surplus would have constrained North Vietnamese industry. At the same time, a lack of consumer goods – the inducement goods historically fundamental to the expansion of peasant production in Southeast Asia – constrained agriculture.[61]

By the late 1970s, it was apparent to most, but not admitted by all those in the Party, that North Vietnam's economy had stagnated and that the promised improvement in living standards had not materialized. Reform began

58 Rosenstein-Rodan, 'Problems', pp. 202–11.

59 Nguyen, *Economic development*, p. 150; Beresford, *National unification*, pp. 181–83, 207, 217 and *Vietnam*, pp. 141, 143, 172; Vo, *Vietnam's economic policy*, pp. 147–49.

60 Gough, 'Economy: interview with Nguyen', p. 378.

61 Vickerman, 'Note', pp. 224–34.

in 1979 with decisions that opened the way to a series of piecemeal adaptations, more use of a price system and movement towards the market. These changes did not, however, achieve the hoped-for results. A decisive shift finally occurred after the Politburo meeting at the end of August 1986. By then, all senior Party leaders agreed with the slogan 'renewal or death' (*doi moi hay la chet*), although disagreeing about the speed of reform. Even after the start of reforms, however, the 'price scissors' were widened to try to extract more surplus from farmers.[62]

Vietnam's post-1975 development strategy was poorly suited to a hardly developed, labour-abundant agricultural economy. By the late 1970s, arable land per farm worker was just 0.46 of a hectare (compared to 1.0 in India and 48 in the United States). Unemployment in the mid-1980s was estimated to be at least 15 per cent and possibly 20 per cent, and there was high underemployment.[63] These considerations and rapid population growth pointed to the appropriateness of a labour-intensive, export-oriented economic strategy. Although prior to the late 1980s the advantages of this strategy began to be recognized, it was not fully embraced.[64] However, examples of rapid growth elsewhere in Southeast Asia, especially Singapore, could not be ignored and soon led to Vietnam's full participation in the global economy and state capitalism combined with Communist Party authoritarian rule (Chapter 15).

Cambodia

Independence to 1975

Norodom Sihanouk (later Prince Sihanouk) was king during Cambodia's World War II Vichy regime and was instrumental in securing Cambodian independence in 1953. From 1955 to 1970, Sihanouk had a monopoly of political power in Cambodia, a hold which did much to set the stage for the country's split into factions, subsequent political chaos and the ascendancy of the Khmer Rouge.[65] The United States backed the governments of Prince Sihanouk and, after a March 1970 coup, continued support for the rightist regime of Marshal Lon Nol, formerly prime minister in the Sihanouk government. Lon Nol abolished the monarchy and renamed the Kingdom of Cambodia the Khmer Republic. Although taking power with a vow to end corruption, Lon Nol's government was deeply corrupt and sustained only by American aid, given in conjunction with the Second Indochina War. Soon after Lon Nol took power, the United States renewed its bombing raids in Cambodia. By 1975, the country had suffered from heavy American bombing.

62 Vo, *Vietnam's economic policy*, pp. 181–98.
63 Kimura, 'Vietnam', pp. 1045, 1048–49.
64 Beresford, *National unification*, pp. 191, 237–38.
65 Chandler, *History*, pp. 227–32.

Democratic Kampuchea

Under Pol Pot and his Khmer Rouge, the popular name for members of the Communist Party of Kampuchea, Cambodia engineered an extreme communist state and modern economic history's most unrealistic economy. Change began in April 1975, after Pol Pot's revolutionary army, in total only some 60,000 men, entered Phnom Penh and overthrew the Lon Nol regime. The reign of Pol Pot ended soon after 25 December 1978, when Vietnam invaded Cambodia, and within two weeks established the pro-Vietnamese People's Republic of Kampuchea. Vietnam occupied the country for the next 10 years.

The long-term goals of the Pol Pot government did not appear so different from those elsewhere in Southeast Asia: Cambodia would, from an agricultural base, build a modern industrial economy. By 1978, Pol Pot had plans for a steel mill, which was already partly under construction.[66] But the road Cambodia mapped out towards modernization was intensely radical, a vision of the ultimate outcome of communism.

One of the regime's chief economic architects, Khieu Samphan, had believed, since his 1950s student days in Paris as a member of a leftist Khmer student intellectual group, that contact with the world economy had impoverished Cambodia.[67] In pursuit of national independence, the Pol Pot government extended the logic of this dependency theory argument to its outermost limits. Under communism, Cambodia would return to a 'pure and authentic' past and gain genuine national independence.[68] Autarky became near total, well beyond anything during the World War II Japanese occupation. The government aimed to reconstruct Cambodia from 'ground zero'. Peasants and the revolutionary army were seen as the sole untainted classes; agriculture was the base from which Cambodia would be reconstructed. Schools were closed and people with skills and education killed. The National Library in Phnom Penh became an abattoir. Money and markets were abolished, as was private land. Foreign trade was virtually eliminated, although some barter persisted in border areas, and a few essential goods continued to be imported or obtained through Chinese aid. Self-sufficient and strictly supervised, communes were to yield the agricultural surplus that would enable Cambodia to develop, entirely through its own efforts and independently from the international economy.

Agricultural Collectives

Cambodia between 1975 and 1978 was the most radical of the Indochinese economies in immediately implementing full collectivization. Some 85 per cent

[66] Twining, 'Economy', pp. 136–37.
[67] Jackson, 'Intellectual origins', pp. 245–46.
[68] Twining, 'Economy', p. 125.

of Cambodians already worked in agriculture, and within days the cities were emptied and their inhabitants forced to join cooperatives. Communes or state farms were given ownership of all land, and personal plots outlawed.[69]

Collectivization has political as well as economic motives. The politics of control was especially important to the Cambodian goal of entirely remaking society. City dwellers transported to cooperatives were allowed to own only a bowl and spoon, which, if not already in their possession, had to be fashioned from a piece of wood. Those from rural villages who had earlier joined the Khmer Rouge were permitted to keep some original personal possessions until these wore out, but not to replace them. Meals were in communal dining rooms, food rationed by overseers, usually Party cadres, and accommodation strictly separated into dormitories for men, women and children. The clothing ration was one new set a year. Replacement footwear had to be fashioned from old tyres to make Mao sandals. Initially, cooperatives consisted of some 150 to 200 people but later grew to around 2,000.

A cooperative is typically based on a mix of material and moral incentives. Material incentives depend on some degree of relating work effort or output to reward. Negative incentives include coercion and punishment; positive ones can come through a greater role in deciding working conditions and decision-making, and from work competitions and formal recognition of diligent or superior work effort such as the Soviet Union's Stakhanovite movement.

Cambodia, alone among Marxist countries, based its production system entirely on negative moral incentives. Workers were assigned a quota, but payment of food and clothing bore no relationship to the work required to fulfil the quota. When the assigned work was finished a worker could stop. There were no rewards for extra work, but if a job was not completed, no matter how many hours it took, punishment such as food deprivation or death was exacted.[70]

Those farming Cambodian cooperatives never knew how much they produced. Grain was taken away every day or two by oxcart or truck. Surpluses could not, however, have been very large, judging by meagre rations and widespread malnutrition. Nor, during the less than a decade before their eventual demise following the removal of Pol Pot, do Cambodian cooperatives appear to have been successful in increasing output that would yield surpluses and finance for industrialization.

Economic Assessment

From 1975 to 1979, the death toll in Cambodia was probably between 1.7 million and 1.9 million people, amounting to over a fifth to just under a quarter

69 Twining, 'Economy', provides the description of cooperatives on which these paragraphs are based.

70 Pryor, *Red and green*, pp. 181–90; Chandler, *Tragedy*, pp. 269–71.

of the population. Cambodian economic data are highly suspect. Extrapolated GDP data presented in the Maddison Project for Pol Pot's Cambodia estimate a 39.6 per cent rise in per capita income between 1975 and 1978 to 2011 US$1,292. It is hard, however, to believe that, under Pol Pot, GDP per capita, already low in 1975, did not in fact contract sharply, possibly by even as much as half. Somewhat more realistically than Maddison, United Nations data show that per capita income fell from 2015 US$342 in 1975 to 2015 US$315 in 1978 and did not regain the 1978 level until 1987. An increase in Cambodian human capital (based on years of schooling and returns to education) during the Pol Pot years, shown by the Penn World Table, also seems unlikely.[71] Clearly, any GDP per capita drop under Pol Pot fell disproportionately on different sections of the population, since the closure of the cities greatly affected their former residents and the urban professional classes and businessmen. Urbanites were, if not murdered, now discriminated against in the countryside in food distribution as well as having no income. By contrast, peasants in traditional areas suffered a smaller cut in income and living standards.

During the three years of Pol Pot, nutrition and mortality statistics are a more telling indicator of welfare than income. For many people, per capita daily calorie intake appears to have been extremely low, with not much in the way of vegetables, fats or protein and for lengthy stretches sharp downturns in food availability. By early 1977, at least half the population was in a very weak condition, reducing work capacity and so the harvest. Population fell from 7.4 million in April 1975 to an estimated 5.8 million at the end of the regime in 1978, a decline that would have caused GDP per capita to rise supposing that GDP had actually remained unchanged after 1975.

Most of the population loss of about 1.6 million is accounted for by murder in Cambodia's 'killing fields', but hundreds of thousands of people also died as a result of malnutrition and disease.[72] The Pol Pot regime took a heavy toll on Cambodia in income, human capital formation and social dislocation. All these, further compounded by the legacy of war in Indochina, made it unrealistic to expect much development in an already undeveloped Cambodia until at least the second part of the 1980s.

Laos

Independence to 1975

The 1954 Geneva Accords partitioned Laos between the Royal Lao government and the Pathet Lao (Lao Nation), the latter with roots in World War II and the Indochinese communist movement. Three years of negotiation finally

[71] Penn World Table, version 10.0.
[72] Twining, 'Economy', p. 150.

overcame the country's de facto division. Political unity did not, however, last. Like the other constituents of France's administrative division of Indochina, the post-World War II history of Laos was marked by conflict and near continuous intervention by external powers.[73]

In 1958, Laos, as it began to be drawn into the Indochina War, was poor, undeveloped and over large areas still a traditional peasant economy. The politics of the next 17 years did nothing to improve Laotian chances for development. Apart from a brief period, Laos did not have a government that unified the entire country. Unification happened only after the success of a communist revolution, shortly before the 1975 fall of Saigon.

By 1958, the United States, anxious to avoid a neutral Laos and instead to align it with America in the Vietnam War, began to build up the Royal Lao Army. Laos decisively split between its United States-underwritten government and the Pathet Lao, backed by China and North Vietnam. The government and Royal Lao Army controlled the west of Laos and the Pathet Lao the north; in the east, North Vietnam controlled the Ho Chi Minh trail which it maintained with some 25,000 Vietnamese troops. During the Second Indochina War, the United States bombed the North Vietnam-dominated area of Laos, even more heavily than it had Japan in World War II. As part of a Laotian civil war, America also conducted from 1960 to 1975 in northern Laos a 'secret war'. In this war, America funnelled materiel to an army led by Vang Pao and comprising minority hill people, mainly the Hmong and the Mien, together with Thai 'volunteers'.

In Laos, the United States established, through its Agency for International Development based in Vientiane (Viang Chan), an administration that paralleled the Laotian government. The Laos economy depended on American aid. By 1964, imports to Laos exceeded its exports by 30 times. American funds and the Laotian printing of money financed both this trade gap and the Laos government. Aid created an urban consumer economy, mainly around Vientiane, although little industry. Development around Vientiane gave some of Laos an air of prosperity but hardly changed living standards for the mass of Lao. Corruption was rife; Vientiane had the world's largest legal opium den.[74]

Revolution occurred in Laos largely as an outcome of the war in Indochina. In 1975 after the communist Pathet Lao gained power, Laos offered especially infertile ground on which to build a socialist economy or develop economically. The country was poor and did not have high education levels, a strong industrial base or an ethnically united polity. In 1960, although the first three years of school were compulsory, only around a third of some 300,000 eligible children had been enrolled in school. About a fifth of those attending school completed all six years of primary education and of these only 7,500 went on

[73] Stuart-Fox, *History of Laos*, pp. 59–89.
[74] Stuart-Fox, *History of Laos*, pp. 130–33, 149.

to secondary schooling.[75] When figures first become available in 1970, GDP per capita was 2015 US$390, above Burma and Vietnam but under a quarter of income in Malaysia.[76] The population of 2.1 million in 1960, and 3.3 million in 1980, divided between perhaps 60 ethnic groups. Of all Laotians possibly 40 per cent were ethnic Lao. The Lao Loum (lowland Lao who inhabited the western Mekong valley region) were the population's largest component. A mountainous terrain covering 80 per cent of the country, weak infrastructure and an overwhelmingly rural population, at least 85 per cent of the total and spread thinly over much of Laos, further hindered economic integration. Road density was low and major communications routes were along rivers running down from the mountains. For at least part of the year, many people, cut off from normal communications, lived in near economic autarky.[77]

The Pathet Lao

After the Pathet Lao took power in 1975, Laos became a client of Vietnam and looked to the Soviet Union as the main source of aid. The Lao People's Revolutionary Party created a single party state, excluding individuals and minority ethnic groups it did not want. The country's new leaders 'had virtually no experience in government. Orthodox Marxists, they followed textbook teaching to centralize buying, selling and production decisions as a state function.'[78] A flood of refugees to Thailand further prejudiced development because it included the Lao Loum bourgeoise, eliminating 90 per cent of the educated class. Restrictions on capitalists and class enemies resulted in an exodus of merchants, and for those who remained in the country curtailed trade in rice and livestock. When no socialist trading organization was immediately established to replace merchants, peasants reverted to self-sufficiency, handlooms were reassembled under houses and urbanites were urged to grow their own food.[79]

Agricultural Collectives

Unlike in Vietnam and Cambodia, land redistribution did not precede the Laotian government's launch of collectivization in 1978–79, although some spontaneous 'land reform' occurred in Laotian peasant communities after the revolution.[80] Cooperatives were seen as a way rapidly to increase agricultural

[75] LeBar and Suddard, eds., *Laos*, pp. 77–78.
[76] United Nations, 'Gross domestic product'.
[77] Evans, *Lao peasants*, p. xii.
[78] 'Laos shakes free of textbook Marxism', *Financial Times*, 25 November 1987.
[79] Evans, *Lao peasants*, pp. 66–67, 83–84 and '"Rich peasants"', p. 233; Brown and Zasloff, 'Laos 1976', p. 110.
[80] Evans, '"Rich peasants"', p. 233.

productivity through the application of science and technology and a reorganization of labour, including an absorption of surpluses.[81] However, the state lacked the apparatus to enforce collectives or extract surpluses and perhaps partly because of this, as well as due to widespread peasant resentment against cooperatives, Laos adopted a voluntary model, Lenin's 'civilized cooperatives'.[82]

The formation of cooperatives was through 'moral persuasion' rather than force. Members could resign and take their land to return to private production, a decision that cooperatives were powerless to prevent. A number of large landowners joined cooperatives as the best way to protect their land, and some enrolled on the government promise of investment in technology, especially tractors. These were scarce in Laos and their availability would have considerably raised productivity. Others resisted cooperatives by destroying crops or slaughtering cattle to prevent them becoming communal property.[83] For landless and poorer rural dwellers, cooperatives had the attraction of pooling resources and sharing output. Soon, however, disputes arose over the appropriate division of output between those who contributed land and capital and others supplying only labour. Moreover, government investment, including scientific inputs and a delivery of machinery, did not materialize. Without investment and therefore higher productivity, which was impossible except perhaps through labour reorganization, cooperatives became a way to redistribute income from rich to poor. While the latter continued to support cooperatives, many landowners either left with their land or, alternatively, ejected the landless.

The government suspended its cooperative drive in mid-1979. A weakening by 1983–84 of government institutional support for agricultural cooperatives was followed in 1988 by a reformulation of the entire cooperative strategy together with de facto state recognition of the failure of agricultural cooperatives and acceptance of a peasantry of private landholders. The Lao People's Democratic Republic adopted an evolutionary approach to rural agrarian change, with trading cooperatives becoming the primary link to the countryside.

In the later 1980s, as Laos began to liberalize the economy and turn outwards, it was still little developed or industrialized, with a per capita income of 2015 US$605 in 1986. That was, however, well above levels in Vietnam and Cambodia and three times Burma's.[84] By 1992, the Laotian constitution no longer mentioned socialism.[85]

[81] Discussion of cooperatives in Laos is based on Evans, *Lao peasants*.
[82] Lenin, 'On cooperation'.
[83] Stuart-Fox, *History of Laos*, pp. 179–80.
[84] United Nations, Statistics Division, 'Per capita GDP at current prices'.
[85] Owen, ed., *Modern Southeast Asia*, p. 495.

Conclusion

Inflexibility characterized the socialist regime in North Vietnam and the regimes in Cambodia and Laos after 1975. Substantial industrialization, and certainly a widely based transition to heavy industry, were probably never possible in the short space of time envisaged. The available bases on which the three Indochinese economies could build were too lacking in infrastructure and human capital. In Vietnam, planners overlooked the development logic of a factor endowment of an abundance of labour and a scarcity of capital. For all three economies, ignoring the roles of incentives and prices stopped agriculture from making its crucial contributions to development. The absence of this input from agriculture and poor policy choices undermined the chance for development that, as discussed in the concluding part of the book, agricultural growth and more appropriate industrial strategies might have created.

11

Burma and Indonesia: Socialism Their Own Ways

What Burma and Indonesia thought of as socialism was quite different from Vietnam's conception. Neither country set out, except in the broad sense of social democracy, to implement socialism. But, when they did, it was quite distinctive in each, although in both mixed with a large dose of nationalism, nationalization of foreign enterprise and frustration at the hitherto slow pace of economic development.

For Burma and Indonesia foreign aid was not always as important as for the Indochinese economies, but both countries exemplified the other features of socialist Southeast Asian economies identified in the Introduction to Part III. Burma is the focus of the chapter's first section and Indonesia the second.

Burma

In 1950/52, Burma's per capita income was at the bottom of a group of countries which themselves badly trailed the rest of Southeast Asia. Nevertheless, Burma's leadership, and, encouraged by their leaders, also the masses, believed that once free of British domination, Burma would become a wealthy country.[1] Perhaps that belief was based on Burma's resources of rice, teak and some oil, as well as a feeling of being free of colonial exploitation. Certainly, these resources have been central to a myth, perpetuated by foreigners, that newly independent Burma began as a wealthy country with bright prospects.[2]

In common with the rest of socialist Southeast Asia, instability created by war and insurrection plagued Burma from independence onwards. Although by the 1950s the central government had established control of much of Burma, its rule has never extended to the entire country. Three results of simultaneous insurrection by various factions and minority ethnic groups have been to disrupt the economy, drain the budget in favour of defence spending and bolster the power of the army, making military rule more likely.

[1] Walinsky, *Burma*, p. 63.

[2] See, for example, *The Times*, 'Editorial', 2 April 2012; Thant Myint-U, 'What to do about Burma'.

Four additional features of socialist Southeast Asia – a neglect of agriculture, a weak indigenous entrepreneurial inheritance, an emphasis on industrialization and a heavy reliance on finance through money creation – are intertwined throughout Burma's post-war economic history. Each one has impacted on, and often reinforced, the other three. The strongly adverse Burman reaction to colonialism, lack of a pre-war Burmese entrepreneurial presence and economic deprivations related to World War II largely explain why post-war Burma followed a strategy of socialism, Burmanization (Burman ownership of the economy and promotion of Burman culture) and industrialization through nationalization. For substantial periods after the establishment of military rule from 1962, Burma isolated itself from foreign influences and interests. In the late 1980s, after an announced ending of socialism, a move towards liberalization measures marked a change in Burma. The departure was, however, partial and temporary and never fully opened the economy. Nor did it end military dictatorship. A professed mission to save Burma from capitalism provided the army with a justification for its rule since 1962. The military government was highly economically and socially destructive and left Burma as Southeast Asia's poorest country.

Civilian Government, 1948–58

Following independence in 1948, Burma was a mixed economy and intended to establish a democratic, socialist, non-aligned state. U Nu, elected prime minister, was charismatic, popular, devoutly Buddhist and a decent person but administratively inept and politically indecisive.[3] Nu's Anti-Fascist People's Freedom League remained in power until 1958, when officially he asked (but possibly was told to ask by General Ne Win, who was prominent in Burma's World War II army) that the military temporarily take charge to stabilize the country due to its fractious politics and prepare for fresh parliamentary elections. Surprisingly, in 1960 the army relinquished power. In the resulting parliamentary elections, Nu won a landslide victory. He remained prime minister until an army coup in October 1962 re-installed a military government, again headed by Ne Win.

Due to World War II legacies of destruction, dislocation and insurgency, independent Burma began from an economic position worse than in 1937/38. Three aims guided economic policy: socialism, industrialization and Burmanization. Industrialization was seen as 'the high road to socialism, modernity and development'.[4] Having its own industry would prevent Burma from ever again experiencing the shortages of World War II. Because of a perceived lack of entrepreneurs, industrialization would be realized through

[3] Walinsky, 'Rise and fall', pp. 272–74.

[4] Walinsky, *Economic development*, p. 495 and see p. 299.

nationalization. Its extension over major parts of the economy would create Burmanization which was consistent with a socialist aim of equity.

During the 1950s, the economy recovered only slowly and incompletely. For most of the decade, GDP remained well below its 1937/38 level, regaining it only in 1958/59. More tellingly, per capita consumption in 1959/60 was considerably lower than at the end of the 1930s. The population's widely held expectation that upon independence Burma would become a wealthy country was always unrealistic, but probably not to the extent that in the 1950s the economy fell short of expectations.

As it always had, the economy depended heavily on rice exports. These accounted for about three-quarters of total exports. During the 1950s, however, paddy production remained below 1937/38 output. Total exports were also less than before the war, when account is taken of a post-war price level three times that prior to the war (Table 11.1). The drop in rice output mainly explains lower total exports. The export fall reflected population growth requiring more rice for home consumption, gross mismanagement that caused rice stocks to accumulate until unsaleable but also contraction in other export sectors like teak, for which exports at the outset of the 1960s were two-thirds their pre-war level.

Continued insurgency also partly accounts for the decline in rice exports and no more than partial economic recovery in the 1950s. Upon independence, the government inherited a 'tumbled house', needing immediate restoration to avoid total collapse. Repair was difficult, however, since for two years little of the country outside Rangoon was under government control.[5] During the 1950s, two communist groups, the Red Flags (Trotskyites) and the White Flags (Stalinists), waged guerrilla war against the government. So, too, did the People's Volunteer Organization (a left-wing militia with World War II arms), remnants of the Nationalist Chinese KMT, the Karen National Defence Organization, which demanded an independent state, and, at various times, several other ethnic groups. The total number of insurgents was not large, perhaps 30,000, but countering them required at least 15 times as many government troops. Rebels interdicted parts of export areas. The delta, teak forests in the north and Burma's oilfields were either outside government control or plagued by guerrilla banditry, demands for tax payments from the local inhabitants and destruction of their crops. All transport links were disrupted; every mile of railway line beyond the Rangoon suburbs was liable to insurgent attack.[6]

Policies are, however, a more important explanation than insurgency for the 1950s economic performance. Burma's economy was not the classic, centrally planned socialism of Vietnam. A 1948 Two-Year Plan, not implemented

[5] Furnivall, 'Twilight', p. 162.

[6] Tinker, *Union of Burma*, pp. 34–61, 295–96; Trager, 'Failure of U Nu', p. 326.

Table 11.1 *Burma economic indicators, 1938/39–1961/62*

	1938/39	1947/48	1949/50	1951/52	1952/53	1953/54	1954/55	1955/56	1956/57	1957/58	1958/59	1959/60	1960/61	1961/62
GDP 1938/39 = 100 constant prices	100	72	61	74	79	82	87	90	97	105	113	112	112	121
Population 000	16.1	17.6	18.0	19.8	20.1	20.4	20.7	21.1	21.4	21.7	22.1	22.5	22.8	23.2
Population 1938 = 100	100	109	111	123	124	126	128	130	132	135	137	139	141	144
Consumption per capita	100	84	63	68	72	72	72	72	87	81	84	89	94	86
Agricultural production 1937–41 = 100	100	77	65	75	84	79	79	81	93	82	95	100	97	98
Paddy production million tons	8.05	5.54	4.69	5.25	5.74	5.53	5.71	5.78	6.36	5.49	6.49	6.92	6.74	6.62
Total exports million crores	48	74	66	110	130	107	112	117	118	89	99	117	100	127
Rice % total exports	46.7	78.5	87.7	73.6	78.5	78.5	75.4	75.0	75.8	74.5	72.3	70.7	66.4	67.3
Rice prices £ sterling	–	–	–	–	60	50	42	36	34	32	33	33	–	–
Rice prices 1952/53 = 100	–	–	–	–	100	83	70	60	57	53	55	54	–	–
CPI Rangoon 1938 = 100	100	303	353	320	313	298	310	331	351	338	300	338	–	–

Notes: 1. One ton = 2,240 lbs. 2. The price for 1938/39 in 'CPI Rangoon' is the price level for 1941 and probably overstates prices for 1938/39. 3. Rice prices are the government to government price for small mills special, 42 per cent broken.

Sources: Burma, *Economic survey, 1963*, pp. 5, 9, 15, 65; Walinsky, *Economic development*, pp. 372, 660–61; Maddison Project Database, version 2020.

until 1951 due to insurgency, emphasized a commitment to socialism, but was a sketchy 55-page list of targets including 13 new groups of industries.[7] The 1952 *Pyidawtha* (meaning happy and prosperous people) Conference adopted an elaborate and ambitious Eight-Year Plan (the *Pyidawtha* Plan), formulated by an American consulting firm, Knappen Tippetts Abbett. Post-war world food shortages and the 1950–52 Korean war boom had created high rice prices, and their continuation was a central assumption of planning. Rice and other primary commodity export earnings were to finance industrialization and development. The State Agricultural Marketing Board, established along with a timber marketing board by the post-war British colonial administration, would capture export earnings for the state to invest in industry. State monopoly power to buy rice at low prices and sell at high was thought to guarantee a large investable surplus. Industrialization would favour heavy industry to include 'the erection of the inevitable steel mill' and leave Burma no longer a 'colonial economy'.[8]

After 1953, falling rice prices undermined the financial plans for the new Burma economy, and the Eight-Year Plan was abandoned halfway through the decade. During the later 1950s, the price of rice declined to a little over half of its 1952/53 level (Table 11.1). Consistent with a rejection of colonialism and foreign interests, Burma intended to finance development domestically. That proved largely possible through the first half of the 1950s, when State Agricultural Marketing Board receipts financed about four-fifths of capital expenditure. However, during the second part of the decade the government – faced with the fall in rice prices, little increase in rice output after 1954 and losses incurred by nationalized industries – had to turn to foreign aid to pay for about half of capital spending and money creation to finance most of the rest. The government lacked the administrative machinery to collect taxes and was disinclined to tax in ways harmful to the *ludu* (common man or masses).[9]

Despite the post-1953 collapse in world rice prices, the government refused to clear mounting and rotting stocks by lowering the price at which it sold the grain. Instead, it negotiated several barter arrangements, mostly with Eastern Bloc countries. Barter, however, proved a 'dismal failure', because reciprocal deliveries happened at inconvenient or irregular times and were often goods assigned inflated prices and of low quality.[10]

Joint ventures might have afforded an acceptable way to Burmanize the economy, but the threat of nationalization discouraged foreign investors, and the sole significant industrial investment by a foreign company was a Unilever soap factory.[11] By 1952, most firms owned by foreign nationals had

7 Burma, *Two-year plan*, pp. 23–26.
8 Trager, *Building a welfare state*, p. 22.
9 Walinsky, *Economic development*, pp. 410–11, 418–23, 429; Tin Maung Maung Than, *State dominance*, pp. 77, 81.
10 Allen, 'Burma's clearing account agreements', p. 148.
11 Tin Maung Maung Than, *State dominance*, p. 89.

been nationalized and private trade and industries operated under direct government control.[12] Pawnshops, previously mostly operated by Chinese, were nationalized.

All nationalized industries accumulated losses. One main reason for this was a lack of qualified administrators, skilled manpower and state capacity, all essential for a successful socialist economy because of the central economic role of government. Other reasons were project selection which, despite limited resources, favoured heavy, capital-intensive industries; their reliance on imported intermediate inputs; a small domestic market; and costs above world prices.

Important components of the initial industrialization programme, in addition to the steel mill, were jute, sugar and weaving mills and a pharmaceuticals plant capable of supplying Burma's needs, this last a pet project of U Nu and partly motivated by his recollections of the World War II shortages of drugs and medical supplies. The plant, financed through budgetary spending and built by a large British pharmaceutical manufacturer, produced a fortified yeast tablet at a cost (mostly in foreign exchange) almost the same as imported, and much-preferred, vitamins. Government agencies were to distribute the yeast tablets free to schools, but the distribution network failed and some 135 million tablets soon backed up at the plant.[13]

Despite the crucial role given to agricultural revenue in Burma's development planning, agriculture was largely taken for granted and received little investment; Burma remained an economy of small peasant cultivators using traditional methods. The agricultural sector had 45 tractors in 1953 and just 243 by 1961.[14] The Two-Year Plan identified 'an imperative need for State credit in agriculture' but various rural credit programmes became bankrupt and failed.[15] The risk of nationalization deterred private rice millers from maintaining and modernizing their mills.[16]

Although intended, agricultural collectivization never happened. The 1948 Land Nationalization Act aimed to redistribute some 9 million acres of agricultural land to landless farmers on a one-yoke (8.4 acres) basis but redistribution was implemented in only one area of Lower Burma.[17] A *Pyidawtha* Conference in 1954 outlined a land nationalization programme, and between 1953/54 and 1957/58, 1.5 million acres were redistributed out of a total of 3.4 million nationalized acres. Redistribution was, however, corrupt and acted as a drag on production, because land allocation was not necessarily in economically efficient parcels and because tenants on larger holdings lost tenancy rights. Confusion

12 Mya Maung, 'Burmese Way', p. 535.
13 Walinsky, *Economic development*, pp. 299–315, 345, 453–54, 480.
14 Myat Thein, *Economic development*, p. 35.
15 Burma, *Two-year plan*, p. 11.
16 Walinsky, *Economic development*, pp. 283–85, 492.
17 Walinsky, *Economic development*, pp. 99–100; Tun Thet, 'Outline', pp. 63–64.

over title and delays in establishing it discouraged land maintenance such as work on bunds and dykes.[18]

State Agricultural Marketing Board policies created waste and inefficiency and, even more important, ignored the centrality of incentives for rice cultivators to increase production. Rice purchasing prices, which were fixed in 1948 at Board buying stations throughout Burma, remained unchanged through 1961. Buying station prices increasingly fell far below market levels and ignored transport, storage and interest costs. In a free market, it took four to six months to clear the rice crop, but, since constant prices offered no incentive to hold rice stocks, clearage happened almost immediately, causing wastage and deterioration due to storage problems of rain, theft and mixing of different grades. Regions that grew rice for local consumption now sold to state buying centres which shipped rice to seaports. Rice then had to be shipped back to these regions to prevent food shortages.[19]

At the same time as using low rice purchasing prices to tax peasants, they, along with other consumers, were taxed through import quotas for which licences were issued. Burmese nationals received most of the licences as part of Burmanization and to exclude Indian traders. Burma echoed a common Southeast Asian experience in trying to promote indigenous entrepreneurship: Burmese re-sold nearly all their licences to Indian or European firms, taking a profit on the sale but leaving the composition of the import trade almost unchanged.[20]

Origins of Army Dominance

A weak Burmese business community and factionalized political sector left the military as the only strong and cohesive group in Burma; neither politicians nor business ever offered an effective counterweight. Army dominance in Burma's economy and society had its roots in World War II and the 1950s. When the British returned to Burma they found, as a British Military Administration report observed in August 1945, the Patriotic Burmese Forces (successor to the Burma National Army, led by its elite and dominated by Burmans) 'the sole effective political organization in the country' and strong enough to impose its will on all other political groups.[21] Subsequently, army dominance only grew. In the 1950s, civilian government could counter insurgency only through reliance on the army.

18 Walinsky, *Economic development*, pp. 293–94, 492.

19 Myint, 'Economic theory', pp. 485–86; Allen, 'Burma's clearing account agreements', p. 149; Myat Thein, *Economic development*, pp. 33–36.

20 Tinker, *Union of Burma*, pp. 258–60; Walinsky, *Economic development*, pp. 424–25, 502.

21 BNA 1/5 86 British Military Administration Report, August 1945 (dated 29 September 1945), p. 8.

Table 11.2 *Burma, Indonesia and other Southeast Asia military spending as a percentage of total health and education expenditure, 1960 and 1990*

	1960	1990
Burma	241	222
Indonesia	207	49
Malaysia	48	38
Philippines	44	41
Thailand	96	71

Source: Myat Thein, *Economic development*, p. 118.

For current and capital budgetary provision, the military had 'a first claim – and a heavy one – on resources'.[22] Military spending, in 1960 and still in 1990, as a percentage of combined educational and health expenditure was about five times as much as in Malaysia and the Philippines (Table 11.2). During the army's 1958 to 1960 caretaker regime, the scope of its Defence Services Institute, originally a sort of military Post Exchange store, greatly expanded. Through the Institute, the army took over some 30 commercial and manufacturing enterprises and embarked on a number of others. High-ranking military officers, although lacking experience or economic technique, headed all these businesses. The army quickly became, and thereafter remained, 'the largest and the most powerful business organization' in Burma. The complex of army-controlled business ventures promised 'a vast reservoir of future well-paid jobs for military personnel, their relatives and their friends'.[23]

The Ne Win Government, 1958–60, and the Return of U Nu

Ne Win's 1958 assumption of the prime ministership and his 18-month, essentially military, rule was authoritarian and had fascist overtones. The government stabilized the economy, introduced a degree of efficiency, countered insurgency and imposed social order, cleaning up Rangoon and clearing it of an influx of squatters.[24] By the time of the 1960 parliamentary elections, the Ne Win government was strongly disliked by Burmese. In the elections, U Nu won an overwhelming victory. During Nu's tenure, the army became increasingly

22 Walinsky, 'Role of the military', pp. 312–13.
23 Walinsky, *Economic development*, p. 261.
24 Butwell and von der Mehden, '1960 election', p. 154.

dissatisfied with the economy and a deterioration in public life as well as security conditions. These last, according to U Nu, 'were bad but comparatively not so bad as things were in 1949–1950'.[25] When told on 2 March 1962 that the army had seized power, Nu first remarked, 'So? What am I supposed to do?'[26] Nu immediately began four-and-a-half years of military detention and Burma moved inexorably towards becoming a one-party, army-run state.

The Burmese Way to Socialism, 1962–88

The military-dominated Revolutionary Council headed by Ne Win took power in March 1962 'to safeguard socialist development' and the next month set out its Burmese Way to Socialism. The declaration broke decisively with parliamentary democracy, acknowledging it as a desirable ideal but arguing that only Council rule would promote socialism.[27] By 1969, when Nu made his first of a number of unsuccessful comeback attempts to lead a political groundswell and restore democratic rule, the economy had been grossly mismanaged. Living standards had fallen except for the military; famine conditions had obtained in 1967, accompanied by riots over the lack of essential food; political parties had been banned; and the security situation had worsened.[28] This state of affairs still described Burma two decades later, in 1988, when civilian and military personnel were urged to grow their own food, and violent riots – partly in response to a sweeping demonetization – lasted for months in Yangon (Rangoon) and other major cities.[29] In the wake of the disorder, a group of army officers staged a coup and forced Ne Win to resign.

Post-1962 revolutionary Burma shared with Vietnam a similar approach to development and encountered a like set of problems. Development strategy depended on the forcible extraction of an agricultural surplus to invest in import-substitution industrialization. But the Burmese type of socialism was quite distinct from Vietnam's. It was not a classic socialism of central planning and agricultural collectivization. If anything, however, the Ne Win regime, although strongly opposed to communism, adopted aspects of Marxist doctrine more dogmatically than Vietnam and, for as long as possible, combined these with self-imposed isolation from the outside world and a near autarkic economy as necessary for Burmanization and self-reliance.

Burmese socialism became an extreme version of socialism in one country. Only a few foreigners were allowed to enter the country and only a few Burmese

25 *The Guardian*, 1 April 1961 quoted in Trager, 'Failure of U Nu', p. 317.
26 Nu, *Saturday's son*, p. 343.
27 Trager, 'Failure of U Nu', p. 323.
28 Butwell, 'U Nu's second comeback try', pp. 869, 873; 'U Nu still willing to lead after four decades', *Financial Times*, 12 September 1988; Brown, *Burma's economy*, p. 146.
29 Steinberg, *Burma*, p. 137.

to leave. Burma, renamed in January 1974 the Socialist Republic of the Union of Burma, nationalized most of the economy and implemented administered prices. The government closely adhered to these policies long after soaring inflation and a ubiquitous black market showed them as entirely unrealistic.

Increasingly, and before long almost wholly, the Ne Win government, although always claiming to be socialist, was run for the benefit of a military elite. By the 1970s, Burma's numerous insurgency groups and considerable internal political unrest threatened Ne Win's regime. At least some of the insurgents were armed with advanced American weapons from the Indochina War. Ne Win managed, however, to remain firmly in power, because of control over the army and because of the vacuum left by the absence of any other well-organized set of interests.[30]

While the military (*Tatmadaw*) claimed to be protecting socialism and Burmanization, the true rationale for its rule, and so the main explanation for Burma's dysfunctional economic and social system, was the naked self-interest of an army elite determined to maintain privilege in an otherwise poor and undeveloped economy. The military grew into a state within a state and became a self-perpetuating elite. It controlled banking and most larger enterprises, and had its own special shops, health care and private education. Goods could be bought from military stores, stocked with items otherwise unavailable except at black market prices. These goods could be profitably sold by those in the army with access to the stores to the non-military population.[31]

Economic Strategy, Nationalization and Drugs Trade

Official data for Burma are notoriously unreliable and misleading, because of government reporting in administered, rather than the more realistic black market, prices, because of an official desire to present data in a favourable light and because of weak statistical collection. It is clear, however, that, as in 1931 and 1962, Burma at the end of the 1980s remained a largely agricultural economy and that almost all exports were primary commodities. Rice, forest products and minerals and gems accounted for almost three-quarters of exports. In both 1931 and 1988, agriculture employed about two-thirds of the workforce and processing and manufacturing under 10 per cent. Four-fifths of agricultural holdings were household-based units farming less than five hectares. In 1990, agriculture's contribution to GDP of just under half appears to have been greater than in 1962, with the agricultural share growing at the expense of industry, including manufacturing, and services. That suggests that between 1962 and 1990, much of a near doubling of population was accommodated in rural areas rather than migrating to informal urban service sector work (Table 11.3).

[30] Badgley, 'Union of Burma', p. 156.

[31] Myat Thein, *Economic development*, p. 80; Steinberg, *Burma*, pp. 24–25, 74–76.

Table 11.3 *Burma GDP and employment structure, 1931–90*

(a) GDP at current market prices %	1962	1975	1985	1990
Agriculture	32.1	36.5	48.2	48.5
Industry	21.9	14.0	13.1	13.1
(Manufacturing only)	15.2	10.4	9.9	9.0
Services	46.0	49.5	38.7	38.4
Total	100.0	100.0	100.0	100.0
(b) Employment structure		**1931**	**1987/88**	
Agriculture, fishing, forestry and mining		70.2	65.7	
Processing and manufacturing		9.1	8.7	
Transport, communications and construction		5.1	5.0	
Trade		9.0	9.8	
Social services and administration		4.7	6.7	
Others		1.9	4.1	
Total		100.0	100.0	

Sources: Myat Thein, *Economic development*, p. 87; Tin Maung Maung Than, *State dominance*, p. 287.

Table 11.4 derives from government data converted to US dollars at official, not black market, exchange rates, and indicates some rise in GDP per capita from the early 1960s to the end of the 1980s. Less subject to doubt were marked improvements in life expectancy, infant mortality, school enrolment and literacy due to social spending and the international diffusion of medical technologies. However, all, except literacy, remained poor by international standards. In 1989, Burma ranked 106th of 160 on the Human Development Index. The government successfully claimed United Nations least-developed status in 1987, enabling it to obtain foreign aid on more favourable terms.

The strategy to mobilize an agricultural surplus continued to be implemented by mandating rice deliveries to a state buyer, the State Agricultural Marketing Board (renamed several times), and generally paying farmers a third, but sometimes as much as a half, of world prices (Table 11.5). Low internal rice prices, as well as being maintained to maximize surpluses, had the further objective of protecting real wages to prevent urban unrest.[32] Taxing rice through differential pricing was the main fiscal basis of the state and Burma's chief source

[32] Myat Thein, *Economic development*, pp. 91–92.

Table 11.4 *Burma economic and social indicators, 1963–89*

	1963	1975	1989
GDP per capita constant US$	154.6	160.2	181.2
Population 000	23.2	30.6	40.7
Life expectancy: male	41.4	47.9	53.3
Life expectancy: female	47.2	54.1	59.9
Infant mortality (per 1,000 live births)	123.0	108.3	83.4
Primary school enrolment rates: male	–	61.5	–
Primary school enrolment rates: female	–	56.2	–
Literacy aged 15 and above %	57	71	80
Human development rank (of 160)	–	–	106

Notes and Sources: For per capita GDP, population, enrolment rates and life expectancy, infant mortality and enrolment rates are from World Bank, *World development report, 2022.* Enrolment rates are for the per cent of primary school-aged children in school and for 1974. Source: World Bank, *World development report, 2022.* For infant mortality, the 1963 figure is for 1968. The HDI rank is for 1990. Source: UNDP, *Human development report*, 1990, p. 16. Southeast Asian countries below Myanmar in 1990 were Laos (128) and Cambodia (140). Singapore was 37, Malaysia 52 and Thailand 66. The Human Development Index measures education, life expectancy and per capita income. Literacy is from Myat Thien, *Economic development*, p. 114 and refers to 1961, 1973 and 1986.

of foreign exchange; the government had neither the administrative machinery nor the inclination effectively to tax non-agricultural parts of the economy. Rice production did not, however, create the anticipated surplus because, as population expanded, yields did not rise appreciably beyond the levels of the late 1950s. Output grew relatively slowly until the later 1970s when there was more use of high-yielding varieties (Table 11.6). One reason for slow growth was a neglect of agriculture and lack of investment in it. At the end of the 1980s, most Burmese farmers used traditional techniques and Burma had 10,900 tractors compared to 142,700 in Thailand.[33]

A more important explanation than technology for low exportable agricultural surpluses was a lack of incentives to grow rice due to low state prices paid for stipulated quota deliveries of paddy and restrictions on imports, creating a paucity of consumer goods in exchange for rice. Farmers responded to a declining terms of trade between paddy and manufactured goods in two ways. One was not to sell to the state marketing board; the other to withdraw towards

[33] Khin Maung Kyi et al., *Economic development*, p. 29.

Table 11.5 *Burma rice and paddy prices, 1962–87 (kyat per ton)*

	Procurement				Retail		
	Government	Free market	Export	Gov't procurement as % export price	Free market	Government	Free market as % government price
1962/63	149	166	443	33.6	378	222	170.3
1963/64	149	159	447	33.3	395	222	177.9
1964/65	149	155	472	31.6	357	229	155.9
1965/66	149	147	484	30.8	499	229	217.9
1966/67	163	165	521	31.3	1,400	251	557.8
1967/68	172	209	578	29.8	1,300	265	490.6
1968/69	172	528	703	24.5	900	265	339.6
1969/70	172	244	667	25.8	568	311	182.6
1970/71	172	281	465	37.0	628	311	201.9
1971/72	172	538	419	41.1	1,038	311	333.8
1972/73	204	582	512	39.8	1,109	427	259.7
1973/74	431	729	826	52.2	1,344	640	210.0
1974/75	431	744	1,609	26.8	1,368	710	192.7
1975/76	431	679	1,756	24.5	1,283	804	159.6
1976/77	431	579	1,157	37.3	1,123	870	129.1
1977/78	431	732	1,373	31.4	1,368	894	153.0
1978/79	446	1,132	1,439	31.0	1,674	935	179.0
1979/80	446	1,211	1,494	29.9	1,176	935	125.8
1980/81	472	1,253	1,506	31.3	1,647	935	176.1

(*continued*)

Table 11.5 (*cont.*)

	Procurement				Retail		
	Government	Free market	Export	Gov't procurement as % export price	Free market	Government	Free market as % government price
1981/82	472	1,833	2,350	20.1	1,289	894	144.2
1982/83	472	1,986	2,510	18.8	1,500	894	167.8
1983/84	472	2,291	1,770	26.7	1,834	894	205.1
1984/85	472	2,444	1,577	29.9	2,022	894	226.2
1985/86	472	2,521	1,317	35.8	2,126	894	237.8
1986/87	472	2,597	1,421	33.2	2,139	894	239.3
1987/88	472	2,879	820	57.6	5,747	894	642.8

Sources: Union of Burma, Ministry of Planning and Finance, *Report to the Pyithu Hluttaw*; Myat Thein, *Economic development*, p. 92.

Table 11.6 *Burma rice sown area and production, 1937–85*

	Sown area m hectares	Production m tons	Population 000 persons	Yield tons per hectare	Production tons per capita	Production grams per capita per day
1937	5.053	6.892	15,925	1.364	0.433	1,186
1938	5.011	5.744	16,145	1.146	0.356	975
1939	5.031	7.942	16,368	1.579	0.485	1,329
1940	5.066	6.894	16,594	1.361	0.415	1,138
1941	4.988	7.738	16,824	1.551	0.460	1,260
1942	4.329	5.752	16,727	1.329	0.344	942
1943	3.090	3.053	16,908	0.988	0.181	495
1944	2.631	2.545	17,090	0.967	0.149	408
1945	2.629	2.677	17,272	1.018	0.155	425
1946	3.201	3.844	17,454	1.201	0.220	603
1947	3.479	5.440	17,636	1.564	0.308	845
1948	3.965	5.164	17,818	1.302	0.290	794
1949	3.649	4.581	18,000	1.255	0.255	697
1950	3.703	5.403	19,488	1.459	0.277	760
1951	3.828	5.601	19,788	1.463	0.283	775
1952	4.016	5.842	20,093	1.455	0.291	797
1953	4.034	5.579	20,403	1.383	0.273	749
1954	3.975	5.561	20,722	1.399	0.268	735
1955	4.051	6.025	21,050	1.487	0.286	784
1956	4.077	6.282	21,387	1.541	0.294	805
1957	3.896	5.423	21,734	1.392	0.250	684
1958	4.087	6.882	22,090	1.684	0.312	854
1959	4.200	7.183	22,459	1.710	0.320	876
1960	4.217	7.085	22,839	1.680	0.310	850
1961	4.597	6.798	23,232	1.479	0.293	802
1962	4.837	7.550	23,638	1.561	0.319	875
1963	5.049	7.667	24,057	1.519	0.319	873
1964	5.109	8.373	24,490	1.639	0.342	937
1965	5.014	7.929	24,937	1.581	0.318	871
1966	4.989	8.531	25,399	1.710	0.336	920
1967	4.934	7.646	25,876	1.550	0.295	810
1968	5.019	7.896	26,368	1.573	0.299	820
1969	4.955	7.859	26,874	1.586	0.292	801
1970	4.975	8.033	27,393	1.615	0.293	803
1971	4.977	8.046	27,926	1.617	0.288	789
1972	4.862	7.240	28,474	1.489	0.254	697

(*continued*)

Table 11.6 (*cont.*)

	Sown area m hectares	Production m tons	Population 000 persons	Yield tons per hectare	Production tons per capita	Production grams per capita per day
1973	5.089	8.466	29,235	1.664	0.290	793
1974	5.177	8.448	29,799	1.632	0.284	777
1975	5.204	9.062	30,335	1.741	0.299	818
1976	5.077	9.172	30,872	1.807	0.297	814
1977	5.136	9.313	31,408	1.813	0.297	812
1978	5.243	10.362	31,863	1.976	0.325	891
1979	5.026	10.283	32,405	2.046	0.317	869
1980	5.127	13.107	33,061	2.556	0.396	1,086
1981	4.921	13.923	33,669	2.829	0.414	1,133
1982	4.882	14.146	34,306	2.898	0.412	1,130
1983	4.831	14.165	34,980	2.932	0.405	1,109
1984	4.917	14.255	35,671	2.899	0.400	1,095
1985	4.902	14.317	36,346	2.921	0.394	1,079

Source: Khin Win, *Century of rice improvement.*

subsistence farming, as they had during World War II.[34] Population growth and rice sold on the black market further eroded the surplus in state hands. Between 1961/62 and 1987/88, the exported rice surplus fell by 74 per cent, from 1.7 million tons to less than half a million tons a year (Table 11.7). Burma did not approach pre-World War II levels of rice production of grams per capita per day until the 1980s (Table 11.6).

Comprehensive nationalization began soon after 1962 and rapidly extended throughout the economy, until by the mid-1970s it included all but agriculture, small business, some retail trade and road and river transport. Most of the key military leaders were 'as simple-minded in their knowledge of socialism, as they were about most other areas of knowledge; and since they were by profession activists the decision to nationalize fully must have been a tempting one to make'.[35] Marketing and distribution, including wholesale and retail stores, warehouses and consumers' cooperatives, became a state monopoly selling at prices set by the government and organized as the People's Stores Corporation. By 1964, 3,000 wholesale and retail shops had replaced Burma's previously 12,000 private wholesale shops, 120,000 retail shops and

[34] Stifel, 'Economics', p. 815; Mya Maung, 'Burmese Way', pp. 546–47.
[35] Walinsky, 'Role of the military', pp. 322–23.

Table 11.7 *Burma rice production, surplus for export and consumption, 1961/62–1987/88 (000 tons)*

	1961/62	1974/75	1977/78	1987/88
Production	3,871	4,857	5,408	13,721
Surplus exported	1,676	165	562	431
Domestic consumption	2,254	4,643	4,791	13,289
Exports + consumption	3,930	4,808	5,353	13,720

Note: Exports and consumption do not exactly sum to production.
Sources: Union of Burma, Ministry of Planning and Finance, *Report to the Pyithu Hluttaw*; Myat Thein, *Economic development*, p. 96.

4,000 cooperatives.[36] Military officers and members of the Burma Socialist Programme Party knew, according to the Chairman of the Revolutionary Council, 'only how to wage war'. Nevertheless, these men directed the nation's trade and industry and implemented a rationing system of quotas and price controls for all goods and services.[37]

One result of comprehensive government controls was to end any Indian and Chinese participation in the economy; another was a breakdown in the distribution system, creating acute shortages of rice, other basic foodstuffs and consumer goods. In 1967, in response to the shortage of rice, the government allowed its purchase directly from farmers to reduce spreading panic in the cities. Rice sellers set up pavement shops at transport terminals.[38] Most goods were rationed, and if a desirable item was said to have appeared in a state store, long queues built up outside it.[39]

Under military rule, the number of industries rapidly increased. Part of the expansion was towards light, primarily consumer-oriented industries like food and beverages and wearing apparel, but a much greater increase was in industries manufacturing construction and industrial materials, this latter reflecting a desire for heavy industrialization (Table 11.8). Many of the new enterprises were, as in the 1950s, only 'packaging industries' and heavily dependent on imported materials and capital goods, rendering their value added low and foreign exchange dependence high. Shortages of foreign exchange constrained industry by starving it of raw materials, new equipment and spare parts.[40]

36 Kyaw Yin Hlaing, 'Reconsidering', p. 19.
37 Mya Maung, 'Burmese Way', p. 541.
38 Stifel, 'Economics', pp. 804–6.
39 Kyaw Yin Hlaing, 'Reconsidering', p. 16.
40 Khin Maung Kyi et al., *Economic development*, pp. 63–65.

Table 11.8 *Burma industrial enterprises by type, 1962 and 1974*

	1962		1974	
	No.	%	No.	%
Food and beverages	89	53.3	163	21.8
Wearing apparel	9	5.4	58	7.8
Personal and household goods	2	1.2	30	4.0
Housing and construction materials	11	6.6	106	14.2
Industrial materials	40	24.0	357	47.8
Printing	16	9.6	33	4.4
Total	167	100.0	747	100.0

Source: Tin Maung Maung Than, *State dominance*, p. 125.

An even more serious problem was that industries were typically poorly managed, usually operated at as little as a third of capacity and suffered from poor work effort and lax worker discipline. Rice was subsidized, but notwithstanding subsidies, real wages were low and declining, which exacerbated already poor workforce management and eroded work incentives. State enterprises had little incentive to raise output, improve quality or reduce wastage, since they operated on a soft budget constraint of being automatically granted credit if investment was carried out according to an approved plan. In 1975/76, enterprise reforms to commercialize state enterprises and a bonus scheme for employees did not raise efficiency or productivity. A scheme to reward model employees with the status of 'socialist worker' was soon met with indifference.[41]

In 1973, a deteriorating economy and low foreign exchange earnings forced Burma to abandon its isolationist, self-reliance strategy. In turning somewhat towards the outside world, the government began to accept foreign aid, mainly from international agencies and as concessional loans from Japan. In 1966, the trade balance turned decisively negative, and thereafter the gap between exports and imports widened. During the later 1970s, and even more in the 1980s, Burma relied chiefly on aid to finance continuous budget and trade deficits and also state-enterprise capital expenditure, much of which consisted of imports of capital and intermediate goods. Aid was not, however, productively used, and only just enough to sustain Burma's international financial position. Foreign reserves dwindled to almost nothing and, as Burma's external debt mounted, by the later 1980s aid became harder to obtain.[42]

41 Tin Maung Maung Than, *State dominance*, pp. 129, 141–42, 186–88, 270, 273; Tun Wai, 'Myanmar', pp. 197–98; Khin Maung Kyi et al., *Economic development*, p. 61.

42 Tin Maung Maung Than, *State dominance*, pp. 204, 210–11, 265; Tun Wai, 'Myanmar', pp. 187, 194–97, 199; Mya Maung, 'Burma's economic performance', pp. 517–19.

Controls on prices and imports, together with inadequate local production, created a large black market and drugs trade. The latter had a long history. After World War II, some of the KMT, supported by the CIA, sold opium grown in Burma's northern Shan States to equip their army in hopes of someday invading China. A number of Burma's many insurgent groups financed themselves through a large cross-border trade with Thailand and China in both black market consumer goods and narcotics. The latter made Burma a major world centre for the trade in heroin and, later, methamphetamines.

The state, unable effectively to counter what the US government branded as Burma's 'narco-armies', turned to its advantage their trade in drugs and became dependent on it. State banks accepted deposits from drug lords who then could use the money to purchase property or for construction projects, including state-awarded ones. By the 1990s, the Directory of Myanmar Chamber of Commerce read like a who's who of the drugs trade.[43] The government exercised its power to capture some of the drug money and used it to build up the army. Additionally, the drugs trade supplemented military salaries through bribes. Peaceful co-existence with drug barons eased fiscal pressure on the government and helped it to counter problems of urban dissent and rural insurgency. During the 1990s, more than a dozen rebel armies, but not including the Karen National Union, made peace with the government. However, this internal armistice proved only temporary.[44]

Following serious and prolonged urban riots, which were met with brutal repression, a 'counterfeit coup' in July 1988 overthrew Ne Win by forcing his resignation. The Burmese Way to Socialism was abandoned, the Burma Socialist Programme Party dissolved, and a market-oriented policy officially adopted in March 1989. The coup has been termed 'counterfeit' because the same people who had surrounded Ne Win remained in power.[45] Economic reform made Burma more like other Southeast Asian countries in attracting foreign investment, beginning to vent surplus labour and giving scope for the rise of the 'crony class' of businessmen. Reform was, however, partial and internal politics did not change. The army perpetuated and built on its privilege, dominating all levels of government, civil administration and commerce.

Indonesia

Economic Structure

Between independence in 1949 and 1966, Indonesia, under its particular version of socialism, remained poor and little industrialized. GDP per capita at best

[43] Meehan, 'Insurgency and state building', pp. 381, 396 and see p. 401 for the reference to narco-armies.

[44] Lintner, 'Drugs and economic growth', pp. 171, 186–89.

[45] Mya Maung, 'Burma's economic performance', p. 503.

Table 11.9 *Indonesia GDP per capita and population, 1930–76*

	GDP per capita	Population distribution (m persons)			Urban/rural divide (%)			
					Java & Madura		Outer Islands	
	2011 US$	Java & Madura	Outer Islands	Total	Rural	Urban	Rural	Urban
1930	1,704	41.7	18.9	60.6				
1938	1,655							
1950	1,280							
1951	1,356							
1956	1,533							
1961	1,690	63.0	34.0	97.0	84.4	15.6	86.7	13.3
1966	1,535							
1971	1,946	76.1	43.1	119.0	82.0	18.0	83.5	16.5
1976	2,536	83.0	48.8	131.8	81.8	18.2	82.4	17.6

Sources: Maddison Project Database, version 2020; Wing and Nasution, 'Indonesian economic policies', p. 54.

regained its 1938 level and was well below this in 1966 (Table 11.9). Geographical splits and their accompanying cultural, religious and social differences had an importance for Indonesia even more pronounced than elsewhere in Southeast Asia. They were, at least arguably, more basic than economic considerations during the late 1950s Outer Island rebellions against the Javanese centre of concentrated government and political power.[46] Development was hindered by centralization and a lack of good public administration and communication with the Outer Islands which could take days or weeks.[47]

In 1961, about two-thirds of Indonesians crowded into Java, 60 miles (100 km) wide and 661 miles (1,064 km) long with average population densities of 477 persons per square kilometre and in some districts over 1,000, while the remainder of the population spread out across the Archipelago's Outer Islands.[48] Both in Java and the Outer Islands, over four-fifths of Indonesians were rural dwellers and the economy predominantly agricultural (Table 11.9 and 11.10).

Agriculture accounted for over half to almost three-fifths of national income, and two-thirds of this agricultural contribution came from peasant food crops.

46 Glassburner, 'Role of economic interest', p. 178; Pluvier, *Confrontations*, pp. 32–33.
47 Paauw, 'From colonial to guided', pp. 243–45.
48 Pelzer, 'Physical', p. 13.

Table 11.10 *Indonesia distribution of national income, 1953–69*

	1953	1957	1965	1969
Agriculture: total	57.0	52.6	58.7	49.3
Agriculture: peasant food crops	36.2	35.5	35.8	30.3
Agriculture: peasant export crops	7.9	6.7	9.1	7.3
Agriculture: estate crops	4.5	3.4	3.6	2.5
Agriculture: other	9.5	9.6	10.2	9.2
Industry	12.0	14.7	11.9	17.2
Services	23.1	23.1	25.8	28.5
Government	7.9	10.2	3.6	5.0

Notes: 1. Other agriculture includes livestock, forestry and fishery.
2. Components of agriculture do not add to total agriculture because of deductions for export duties and statistical tax. For 1957, components of national income do not add to 100 in the source.
Source: Wing and Nasution, 'Indonesian economic policies', p. 50.

Peasant production contributed more than estate output to exports. The smaller share for estates was partly because the dislocation of Japanese occupation persisted, and because by 1957 squatters occupied almost a third of estate land in Java and Sumatra.[49] Outside the plantation sector, large land holdings were the exception: some 90 per cent of farmers cultivated under one hectare and most less than half a hectare.[50]

In 1961, agriculture employed even higher shares of the workforce than in 1930, almost 70 per cent in Java and Madura and over 80 per cent in the Outer Islands. Manufacturing centred in Java but engaged just 7.8 per cent of workers and consisted mainly of handicrafts and light consumer goods industries like food processing (Tables 11.10 and 11.11).[51] While unemployment was low, a 1961 labour survey estimated rural underemployment in Java and Madura as a third of the labour force.[52]

Political Realities

Sukarno, the charismatic World War II leader, served as president through a series of unstable 1950s governments. For the mass of Indonesians, he had the

[49] Feith, *Decline*, p. 570.

[50] Mears, 'Indonesia', pp. 427–28.

[51] Paauw, 'From colonial to guided', pp. 177, 179, 182.

[52] Hawkins, 'Job inflation', pp. 267–68; Indonesia, Department of Labour, *Report on the labour force sample survey.*

Table 11.11 *Indonesia employment structure, 1930–76 (% and millions)*

	(a) Indonesia				(b) Java and Madura				(c) Outer Islands			
	1930	1961	1971	1976	1930	1961	1971	1976	1930	1961	1971	1976
Agriculture	68.8	73.6	66.2	62.0	64.3	69.4	61.4	58.7	79.5	81.6	75.4	68.4
Manufacturing	10.6	7.8	9.9	10.1	11.6	9.1	11.4	11.3	8.3	5.2	6.9	7.9
Trade and services	20.6	18.6	23.9	27.9	24.1	21.4	27.2	30.0	12.2	13.2	17.7	23.6
Total	100.0	100.0	100.0	100.0	100.0	99.9	100.0	100.0	100.0	100.0	100.0	99.9
No. (millions)	20.9	34.8	44.1	51.0	14.4	22.7	28.8	33.2	6.2	12.1	15.3	17.8

Note: The numbers employed in Java and Madura and the Outer Islands do not add to the total in the source and the table in the source does not add to 100.0 for Outer Islands, 1976.

Source: Dapice, 'Overview of the Indonesian economy', p. 9.

status of a god king, but was neither adept at nor interested in economic matters. From 1959, now openly acknowledging an administrative role, Sukarno also became prime minister until, amid economic chaos, he was toppled by an army coup in 1966. A power centre himself, Sukarno adroitly played three further centres off against each other: the PKI (Indonesian Communist Party), the army and the Outer Islands. The communists, with about 20 per cent of the vote, were strong in the densely populated areas of rural Java, while the army, as an outcome of World War II, had an elaborate grassroots organization, and had prestige as a founder of the state. In Java, the military was part of a strong army–Muslim alliance against the communists.[53] Sukarno, lacking a mass party of his own, made overtures to the communists but to maintain his position needed the support of the army, which was institutionally opposed to communism. The Outer Islands, the third main power centre, accounted for over four-fifths of Indonesia's exports and so had, as well as their own histories and cultural orientations, economic interests different from Java's, where manufacturing was centred and which consumed most imports.

Economic Plans and Socialism

Indonesian socialism, in its meaning and impact on the economy, varied markedly before and after 1957. Like Burma, Indonesia at first adopted a comparatively gradualist approach to the economy, but beginning in 1957 veered to a radical, nationalistic and strongly anti-capitalistic stance. Even after 1957, however, central planning in the sense of Soviet, Eastern European or Vietnamese economies was unimportant.

Two main objectives of a 1951 Urgency Economic Plan were to use state-supplied finance to build an Indonesian entrepreneurial class and develop industry at all levels. For Indonesia's 1945 generation, industrialization, including heavy industry, was synonymous with development.[54] Indonesia aimed to establish, as well as textile factories, 61 power plants and an iron and steel works. Results, however, were disappointing: 'Freely distributing economic resources – physical capital, credit or special privileges of various sorts – had little immediate effect on output or the structure of the economy.'[55] By 1952, developmental expenditures put pressure on the budget and began to cause economic destabilization.

Under the *Benteng* policy destabilization increased. The policy, initiated by a 1953–55 government, aimed to create indigenous entrepreneurs by restricting for many goods import licences to Indonesians and excluding applications

[53] Higgins, *Indonesia: crisis*, p. 11 and *Indonesia's economic stabilization*, pp. 96–100; Feith, *Decline*, pp. 601–2.

[54] Woo and Nasution, 'Indonesian economic policies', p. 22.

[55] Paauw, 'From colonial to guided', p. 217.

from Chinese. As it had in Burma, restriction led to a burgeoning of Indonesian 'briefcase' importers, a briefcase their only office and obtaining import licences and foreign exchange for Chinese their sole functions. Only a few hundred Indonesians conducted any real business, and these appear to have been primarily Sumatrans.[56] Many of the new Indonesian banks were no more than 'get rich quick' organizations. The banks benefited from the difference between low government and high market interest rates and spent heavily on prestige items like furniture, cars and mountain bungalows 'for the staff'.[57]

The Five-Year Plan of 1956 (approved 1958), devised by a team of foreign experts, persisted in the effort to foster a middle class of Indonesian entrepreneurs and industrialists. The plan set out priorities for public sector expenditure but had a laissez-faire quality and made almost no attempt to regulate the private sector. In 1957, radical Indonesians gained political ascendancy over the so-called pragmatists, causing the Five-Year Plan to be discarded and by 1959 virtually abandoned.

Beginning in 1957, Sukarno – frustrated by a succession of governments and lack of economic progress but fascinated by revolution and anxious to keep its spirit alive – directed the abandonment of constitutional democracy and a move to a radical socialism. The approach would be, in Sukarno's terminology, Socialism *à la* Indonesia and would incorporate, he announced in August 1959 on Independence Day, a Guided Economy and Guided Democracy, the latter with roots in Japan's Greater East Asia Co-Prosperity Sphere as a regime of paternalistic guidance.[58]

Indonesian socialism amounted to an attempt to reconcile a modern economic order with a traditional society, and had two distinguishing features. One, a continuation of pre-1957 policy, was 'Indonesianisation' to end economic dominance by foreign, especially Dutch, enterprise and Indonesia's Chinese and Indian minorities; the other, a 'collectivist', village-like organization of the economy on a basis of mutual assistance (*gotong rojong*) to perform some village agricultural tasks. As well as rejecting parliamentary democracy, socialism would reject individualism, private self-interest and a profit motive.[59] In a June 1959 speech, Sukarno explained that a 'transfer of power from white [Dutch] and yellow [Japanese] hands to brown [Indonesian] hands' was not enough, if the economic system 'remained capitalistic and not socialistic as it should be'.[60] After wholesale nationalization in 1959, Indonesian socialism

[56] Higgins, *Indonesia: crisis*, pp. 91, 107; Mackie, 'Indonesian economy', pp. 47–48; Lindblad, *Bridges*, pp. 130–35; Corden and Mackie, 'Development', p. 55.
[57] Feith, *Decline*, p. 565.
[58] Benda, 'Democracy', pp. 450–53.
[59] Humphrey, 'Indonesia's national plan', p. 20; Pauker, 'Indonesia's eight-year development plan', pp. 120–22; Mackie, 'Indonesian economy', pp. 44–45.
[60] Quoted in Higgins, *Economic development*, p. 703.

could also be defined as meaning state ownership of the means of production and the incorporation of a nationalistic approach as well as the rhetoric of socialistic egalitarianism. Socialism *à la* Indonesia lacked, however, the realities of egalitarianism and, more important, a strong central government able to finance its plans through taxation.[61]

An Eight-Year Overall Development Plan (1960), commissioned by Sukarno, was drawn up entirely by political figures. The plan consisted of a 17-volume, 5,100-page shopping list of projects, divided into categories A and B, but was vague on financing these. Finance relied partly on foreigners to invest in natural resource industry, but there was no provision for finance for all the projects, except possibly through foreign aid. An obvious financial resource would have been foreign exchange earnings based on the pre-war export economy. The government was, however, little interested in revenue via this trade option or in modernizing and developing the agricultural export sector. No agency had responsibility for administering the overall plan which, according to Sukarno himself, was 'rich in fantasy'.[62]

Economic Influences

There were three major influences on the Indonesian economy: trade taxes, inflation and pressure to export capital.[63] All three were important, but after 1957 their importance intensified, because of internal rebellion and political decisions on external relations. Sukarno, as head of an authoritarian government after constitutional democracy had been extinguished, was chiefly responsible for making political judgements. They resulted in an economic crisis leading to his downfall.

The Indonesian tax structure remained essentially the same as in 1939, and relied heavily on taxing trade. Taxes on imports and exports accounted for half of total revenue; income tax was almost non-existent and other direct taxes remained relatively unimportant.[64] Trade continued to depend substantially on traditional agricultural exports but, apart from rubber and petroleum, these did not recover to 1938 levels. After the early 1950s Korean war boom ended, rubber prices fell sharply, and from 1951 to 1959 total export value dropped from 22.4 per cent to 4.7 per cent of GDP. Between the early 1950s and 1966, only petroleum exports increased much in volume. The traditional export of sugar remained much lower than before World War II and rubber exports stagnated at their early 1950s level. Limited progress was made towards self-sufficiency,

[61] Booth, *Economic change*, pp. 201–3.

[62] Grant, *Indonesia*, p. 114; Mackie, *Problems*, p. 27 and see Mackie, 'Indonesian economy', pp. 50–52.

[63] Corden and Mackie, 'Development', p. 37.

[64] Mackie, *Problems*, p. 55; Corden and Mackie, 'Development', pp. 37–39.

Table 11.12 *Indonesia exports and imports, 1951–60*

	Exports current rupiah bn	GDP current rupiah bn	Exports % of GDP	Rice imports 000 kg	Textile imports 000 kg
1951	14.8	66.0	22.4	–	–
1952	10.7	81.6	13.1	765,808	94,292
1953	9.6	86.6	11.1	371,500	156,192
1954	9.9	94.6	10.5	261,063	129,861
1955	10.8	125.1	8.6	127,784	146,834
1956	10.6	145.2	7.3	763,175	157,694
1957	11.0	171.0	6.4	563,438	134,030
1958	9.2	180.2	5.1	681,465	95,664
1959	9.9	210.1	4.7	604,154	97,849
1960	–	–	–	961,987	137,015

Source: Paauw, 'From colonial to guided', pp. 183, 201.

and continued large imports of the two main wage goods of rice and textiles added to pressure on the government budget (Tables 11.12 and 11.13).

From 1952, the budget was continuously in deficit. These deficits, financed largely by printing money, were the principal cause of inflation, the second of the three main influences on the economy. Until 1957, budget deficits and inflation remained relatively modest in most years. Beginning in 1962, however, deficits as a percentage of gross expenditure increased markedly as money supply expanded and high inflation took hold, reaching 62 per cent in 1965 (Table 11.14). Even before then and increasingly thereafter, the government tried to control the budget deficit through tariffs, quantitative import licencing, delays in granting licences, surcharges, import prepayments and a complex of an ever more comprehensive system of subsidies and taxes. This last operated through a multiple exchange system. Trade restrictions, along with inflation, created the third influence by setting up pressure to export capital. Exporting or repatriating capital from Indonesia was prohibited, causing exporters to manipulate the trade system to find ways to send funds out of the country.

Export taxes and an exchange rate which valued the rupiah at multiples of from three to as much as 10 to 12 times black market rates discriminated massively against the Outer Islands, as the source of most exports, and in favour of Java, as the main consumer of imports. Along with heavily taxing exports, Indonesia's overvalued exchange rates undermined an incentive to produce exports and, instead, created incentives to circumvent legal channels or withdraw from the market. By the later 1950s, Outer Island farmers

Table 11.13 *Indonesia agricultural and mining production, 1938–69*

	Paddy million kg	Rubber million kg	Sugar million kg	Tin in ore billion kg	Crude petroleum billion kg
1938	–	302.9	1.071	0.019	–
1951	11,968	0.219	0.428	0.031	8.093
1952	12,773	0.299	0.458	0.036	8.523
1953	14,064	0.309	0.620	0.034	10.261
1954	15,061	0.288	0.718	0.036	10.813
1955	14,432	0.267	0.852	0.034	11.818
1956	14,619	0.266	0.786	0.031	12.820
1957	14,677	0.258	0.828	0.028	15.559
1958	15,344	0.245	0.771	0.024	16.310
1959	15,950	0.228	0.855	0.022	18.721
1960	16,860	0.219	0.678	0.023	20.606
1961	15,900	0.231	0.643	0.019	21.287
1962	17,111	0.218	0.592	0.017	22.747
1963	15,276	0.218	0.664	0.013	22.231
1964	16,192	0.234	0.655	0.016	26.851
1965	17,072	0.228	0.775	0.015	27.955
1966	17,960	0.217	0.612	0.013	26.778
1967	17,398	0.205	0.666	0.013	25.311
1968	20,032	0.215	0.603	0.017	34.946
1969	20,464	0.223	0.625	0.017	43.086

Note: For 1938, data are for exports.
Sources: Indonesia, *Statistical pocketbook of Indonesia 1941*, pp. 79, 80, 86; Wing and Nasution, 'Indonesian economic policies', pp. 52–53.

began to shift towards subsistence production.[65] Taxes on imports encouraged under-declaration, smuggling and barter trade in Outer Island rubber sent to Singapore.[66] The budget deficit worsened as the need to limit it increased and trade restrictions multiplied.

Political and Economic Crises

Each of three crises required considerable government expenditure, destabilized the economy, added to the budget deficit, reduced exports and

[65] Paauw, 'From colonial to guided', p. 194; Mackie, 'Indonesian economy', p. 63.
[66] Huff, *Economic growth*, pp. 280–81.

Table 11.14 *Indonesia government budget, 1950–70 (billion rupiah)*

	Gross revenue	Gross expenditure	Budget surplus or deficit (–)	Deficit or surplus as % of expenditure
1950	7.0	8.7	–1.7	–19.5
1951	11.8	10.6	1.2	11.3
1952	12.3	15.0	–2.7	–18.0
1953	13.6	15.7	–2.1	–13.4
1954	12.5	15.4	–2.9	–18.8
1955	14.2	16.3	–2.1	–12.9
1956	19.2	20.8	–1.6	–7.7
1957	20.6	25.6	–5.0	–19.5
1958	25.3	35.5	–10.2	–28.7
1959	30.5	44.3	–13.8	–31.2
1960	49.8	58.3	–8.5	–14.6
1961	62.2	88.5	–26.3	–29.7
1962	75.0	122.1	–47.1	–38.6
1963	161.0	329.8	–168.8	–51.2
1964	282.1	681.3	–399.2	–58.6
1965	960.8	2,526.3	–1,565.6	–62.0
1966	13.1	29.4	–16.3	–55.4
1967	60.2	87.6	–27.35	–31.2
1968	149.8	185.3	–35.5	–19.2
1969	45.9	58.6	–12.7	–21.7
1969/70	251.6	342.7	–91.1	–26.6

Note: Numbers in the first two columns are affected by remonetization and inflation.
Source: Wing and Nasution, 'Indonesian economic policies', p. 39.

strengthened the position of the military. The first crisis dated from December 1956, when army colonels in command of Sumatra and Sulawesi (Celebes) military districts began to defect from central government authority and establish autonomous military governments. A Muslim–Christian alliance, the Outer Island insurgency supported itself partly by smuggling cocoa and rubber, obtained arms through Singapore and had covert military help from the United States. The rebels sought greater regional autonomy and more of the royalties from Sumatran oil fields; they opposed communism and President Sukarno.

Jakarta tolerated rebellion through 1957, but in March 1958 intervened militarily after a revolutionary government, the Pemerintahan Revolusioner Republik Indonesia, declared itself and set up headquarters in Sumatra. The central government, aided militarily by the Soviet Union, soon crushed the brunt of the rebellion. However, the conflict continued until 1961, largely as a guerrilla action. Greater reliance on the army increased its power and raised its status to Indonesia's most privileged group, as well as necessitating more military spending, the latter badly draining reserves.[67]

In 1949, when Indonesia became independent, West Irian (two peninsulas of western New Guinea renamed Irian Jaya and after 2002 West Papua) remained a Dutch colony. Sukarno regarded the liberation of West Irian as essential to 'completing the revolution'.[68] After the United Nations, in 1957, supported the Netherlands and voted against opening negotiations on transferring West Irian to Indonesia, Sukarno oversaw two linked actions. Together they inaugurated the second crisis, which overlapped with the first and made an even larger contribution to the budget deficit than the first.[69]

One measure instituted by Sukarno, and the first of two Indonesian Confrontations, was to invade West Irian. Invasion required substantial spending on the military and expanded the budget deficit. By 1962, when Indonesia eventually took control of West Irian, government revenue was just three-fifths of spending (Table 11.14). The gap was largely financed by monetary expansion.

The other measure, initiated by Sukarno on the grounds that it was needed to end any colonial presence and so complete the revolution, was to retaliate against the Netherlands over West Irian by seizing, in late 1957 and 1958, Dutch-owned property and expelling 50,000 Dutch nationals. Confiscation extended to some 500 estates, the KPM shipping line, three banks and mining and manufacturing firms, some US$2 billion of Dutch assets and 700 enterprises in all. The suddenness and scope of seizures and expulsions left Indonesia no realistic alternative to nationalization of most enterprises, because of a lack of Indonesian technicians, administrative staff and managers to operate the firms and unwillingness to countenance a continued local Chinese and Indian business presence.[70]

By February 1959, nationalization had been completed. Army officers, although without managerial experience, were often put in charge of nationalized enterprises, further bolstering the power of the military as well as giving army members scope for lucrative jobs, contracts, bribes and appropriating for themselves formerly Dutch residential properties. One result of nationalization was the associated military gain in material well-being. Another outcome, aided by now high inflation, was more glaring social inequality through the creation of a 'new rich'.[71]

67 Feith and Lev, 'End of Indonesian rebellion', pp. 32–46; Feith, *Decline*, pp. 586–90; Doeppers, 'Incident', pp. 182–95; Kahin, 'In memoriam', pp. 101–5; Pluvier, *Confrontations*, pp. 49–57.

68 Higgins, *Indonesia: crisis*, pp. 117–18.

69 Mackie, *Problems*, pp. 30, 32.

70 Lindblad, *Bridges*, pp. 180–205; Glassburner, 'Economic policy-making', p. 130; Mackie, 'Indonesian economy', pp. 50–52; Paauw, 'From colonial to guided', p. 180.

71 Mackie, *Problems*, p. 63.

Nationalization swelled government budgetary spending, because state enterprises almost always operated at well below capacity, lost money and were automatically state supported under Indonesia's system of socialist finance. State industry suffered from insufficient supplies and rampant corruption, found difficulty in financing imports of intermediate and capital goods and lacked skilled labour and trained managers. The seizure of KPM and resulting loss of 78 per cent of inter-island shipping severely impacted communications. Just prior to nationalization the company had directed most of its vessels to Singapore, subsequently selling some to a Singapore Chinese shipowner and redeploying others outside Indonesia.[72]

Late in 1959 with the completion of nationalization and to make the economy more indigenous, the government issued an order prohibiting aliens, meaning Chinese without Indonesian citizenship, from engaging in retail trade in rural Indonesia. Areas permitted to Chinese were 85 cities and towns in Java and 120 outside it. The restrictions on Chinese were a response to demands by some groups for discrimination against them, and the failure of granting special privileges to Indonesians to yield any substantial increase in Indonesian business, instead leading to the creation of dummy enterprises. After the retail trade ban, some 102,000 Chinese left Indonesia for China.

In an attempt to alleviate considerable economic disruption following the ban, the government established a system of retail cooperatives. These and indigenous enterprises were, however, far too weak to replace a complex Chinese network established to market crops and distribute manufactured goods, and, in time, some Chinese were tacitly allowed to return to business. Government cooperatives, known as *sandang pangan* (clothing and food) stores, had lower standards than Chinese distribution, sold at fixed prices higher than before the ban and operated on a ration card system. Although *sandang pangans* soon appeared in Java, they did so only in 1961 in the Outer Islands, leading to rationing, long queues and a rapid exhaustion of stocks. Government policy to set prices and control output spawned a vast new bureaucracy of state enterprise to distribute goods. Following the takeover of the Dutch 'Big Five' trading firms as part of nationalization and the law against alien retail trade, government companies held 80 per cent of the import trade and had greater monopoly power than the Dutch had ever enjoyed.[73]

After the 1962 transfer of West Irian to Indonesia, Sukarno, buoyed by this success, initiated a new, second Confrontation, this time to 'Crush Malaysia' (*Ganjang Malaysia*). This new campaign was launched the day after the 9 July

[72] Lindblad, *Bridges*, pp. 191–92; Feith, *Decline*, pp. 577–78; Thomas and Glassburner, 'Abrogation, take-over', pp. 166–77; Paauw, 'From colonial to guided', pp. 160, 196.

[73] Somers, *Peranakan Chinese*, pp. 24–28; Coppel, *Indonesian Chinese*, pp. 37–38; Pluvier, *Confrontations*, pp. 70–71; Thomas and Glassburner, 'Abrogation, take-over', pp. 175–76; Mackie, *Problems*, p. 24 and 'Indonesian economy', p. 48.

1963 signing of the Malaysia agreement to unite Malaya, Singapore, North Borneo and Sarawak as a single country. The Malaysian Confrontation was presented as necessary to counter a neo-colonialist plot to create Malaysia and so maintain British influence in the region. Important reasons for the Confrontation were, however, Sukarno's love of the romance of revolutionary diplomacy and to preserve the strength of the army. Additional motives were to distract attention from the contrast between increasingly dire Indonesian economic circumstances and Malaysia's prosperity; strong anti-Chinese feeling in Indonesia; and, prompted by a neighbouring large Chinese population, fear of a Chinese communist fifth column in Singapore and Malaysia.[74]

Singapore, Indonesia's single biggest export market, had long been a source of resentment to many Indonesians. They viewed it as a middleman exploiter which functioned through Chinese merchants, moneylenders and usurers. Beginning in September 1963, the Indonesian government boycotted Malaysia, especially Singapore, and took over British and American enterprises in Indonesia, although not the Anglo-Dutch firm Unilever. Jakarta also reached accommodation with Shell, Caltex and Stanvac (Standard Vacuum Oil Company), which together accounted for a quarter of export revenue.[75] Indonesian troops landed on the Malay Peninsula, and briefly invaded Sarawak in British Borneo; gangs of youths ransacked and set fire to the British Embassy in Jakarta.

Yet more military spending on the Confrontation with Malaysia further reduced government revenue and expanded yet further the budget deficit (Table 11.14). So too did more economic disruption and the replacement of legal trade to Malaysia by the extensive smuggling of Outer Island produce to the Straits ports of Singapore and Penang. Foreign assistance would have helped to fill the resulting revenue gap and alleviate budgetary pressures. Previously, these had been eased by aid from America, the Soviet Union and several other countries. However, the United States, a large donor from 1950 to 1961, cut off assistance in response to Confrontation.[76]

Sukarno's vision of struggle, confrontation and revolution, rooted in his and Indonesia's experiences of the 1920s and 1930s and the Japanese occupation, 'offered no real prospect of permanent stability ... resolution could only come, in the end, through cataclysm'.[77] By 1966, when Confrontation with Malaysia ended, Indonesia had gone through a failed 1965 coup against Sukarno; a successful army coup in 1966 motivated partly by Sukarno's increasing favouritism towards Indonesia's communists; the mass killing of some million persons

[74] Pluvier, *Confrontations*, pp. 69–75.

[75] Grant, *Indonesia*, pp. 194–99; Lindblad, *Bridges*, pp. 12, 24, 172.

[76] Paauw, *Financing economic development*, pp. 345–54; Lindblad, *Bridges*, pp. 204–6; Legge, *Sukarno*, pp. 363, 369; Grant, *Indonesia*, pp. 109–14, 194–97.

[77] Legge, *Sukarno*, p. 383.

said to be communists; and hyperinflation.[78] Suharto (Soeharto) replaced Sukarno as president in March 1967. Socialism, as envisaged by Sukarno, ended and Indonesia embarked on a new era: the 'New Order' and a more outwards-looking, trade- and development-oriented economy.

Conclusion

In both Burma and Indonesia, by the late 1950s the economy disappointed the optimistic expectations that had existed at the time of independence. The attempted solution of state ownership seemed the only route to rapid development and to indigenous entrepreneurial participation. However, state corporations suffered from the legacy of a lack of trained personnel, further compounded by widespread corruption. They were generally poorly managed; typically became a drain on the state budget; and, although justified partly on grounds of indigenization, were often in economic activities inappropriate to the current stage of economic development.

In each country, a fundamental fiscal barrier to socialism was a poorly developed, inadequate tax system. Governments were too weak to tax effectively and shied away from taxation for fear of creating urban unrest. Instead, they looked to tax agriculture through prices and restrictive regulations. State pricing decisions destroyed incentives for agriculturalists to produce, and so cut off the main source of export earnings and government revenue. Available economic surplus, said to have been drained off by colonialism, fell far short of that anticipated at the outset of independence.

Armies in the two countries were able to wield considerable power because they built on an inheritance from World War II, during which they had gained strength and numbers as an organized armed force; because of leading roles in independence struggles; and because governments depended on the army to counter insurgency. Sukarno, in the absence of his own political power base, courted the Indonesian army, which he needed to continuously 'refresh' revolution. From 1966 onwards, Indonesia pulled itself back from annihilation, but in Burma, the army chose to intensify its autocracy and create a tenacious fiefdom of privilege at the expense of the economy and the great bulk of the Burmese population.

[78] Feith, 'President Soekarno', pp. 977–80.

12

Socialist Finance and Plural Societies

Two prominent aspects of Southeast Asian socialist regimes were their experiences of high inflation and rejection of maintaining plural societies. The first part of this chapter on finance examines the institutions of socialist finance permissive of high inflation and the responses to it. A second part looks at socialist Southeast Asia's reactions to plural societies and their large Chinese and Indian minorities.

Finance

High inflation dogged financial systems in socialist Southeast Asia and undermined attempts at price control. Unless inflation can be kept within manageable levels, as in South Vietnam and Laos, through continuous injections of external funding, three responses are possible. One, adopted in post-1917 Russia, is to make a virtue of hyperinflation: it would, according to a view attributed by Keynes to Lenin, effectively destroy capitalism.[1] No Southeast Asian country took that tack. A second possibility is reform and an end to the unrestrained printing of money. Lasting reform is likely to mean a movement away from centralist, or state-run finance, towards a capitalist, debt-asset system of financial intermediation. That happened in Indonesia only after the coup against Sukarno, and in the Indochinese economies not until the late 1980s. The third possibility – adhered to in Burma – is denial.

Institutions of Socialist Finance

In classical socialism, the entire banking system is state owned. Banks consist of a central bank and a few specialized banks to oversee, for example, investment, foreign trade and saving. Because central and commercial banking functions are not separate, one can speak, as Lenin envisaged, of a monobank. Banks have no interest in profits; they are simply a branch of the bureaucracy and carry out its will. Credit policy, as in socialist Southeast Asia, passively follows the requirements of production and commerce; state enterprises are

1 Fetter, 'Lenin', p. 78.

not responsible for their financial success and tend to depend on subsidies.[2] The survival of firms depends not on the market but government bureaucratic decisions reached, in part, through bargaining between authorities and firms' managers. These negotiations and weak price responsiveness allow state firms a 'soft' budget constraint. Softness contributes, in turn, to a passive role for money: the central bank's distribution of cash and credit adjusts to the directives of decision-makers.[3]

Even before independence, North Vietnam began to implement classic Marxist socialist finance and established, in 1951, the Democratic Republic of Vietnam State Bank as a supplier of credit and issuer of money. In 1954, and again after re-unification in 1975, all financial institutions were nationalized and merged with the State Bank. An investment and development bank (1958) and a foreign trade bank (1963) operated as special departments of the State Bank, creating a one-tier banking system until 1989.[4]

In post-1948 Burma, the approach to finance was at first moderate. The 1948 to 1952 Burma Currency Board, operationally similar to pre-war currency boards and administered from Chelsea SW3 in London, hardly betokened radicalism.[5] In 1952, when Burma's Parliament established the Union Bank as the central bank, it stipulated as reserves 25 per cent of the amount of currency in circulation plus bank deposits to guard against excessive currency issue.[6] 'Despite their Socialist convictions', Walinsky explains, 'the basic attitude of the Burmese leaders toward finance was at the outset essentially conservative. The years of high rice prices [until 1954] and budgetary surpluses confirmed their adherence to the concept of balanced budgets and the repugnance they felt for deficit financing.'[7]

The shift to a Marxian concept of finance began after the 1962 military coup, adoption of the Burmese Way to Socialism and nationalization of all Burma's main economic sectors except agriculture. Early in 1963 all banks were nationalized and in 1967 merged into a Lenin-esque monolithic bank, the People's Bank of the Union of Burma, to act as a central bank and with specialized divisions for commercial loans, foreign trade, agriculture and insurance. Just three sources of finance existed outside this monobank: Trade Corporation No. 1, the cooperative societies and private moneylenders.[8] In 1976, the People's Bank was split into a central bank, the Union of Burma Bank, and three separate banks – one each for the domestic economy, agriculture and foreign

[2] Beresford, *Vietnam*, pp. 168–70 and *National unification*, p. 207; Spoor, 'Finance', p. 351.
[3] Kornai, *Socialist system*, pp. 131–48.
[4] Kousted et al., *Monobank*, pp. 8–10.
[5] Burma, *Report of the Burma Currency Board*, 1947/8–1951/2.
[6] Maung Maung, 'Central banking', pp. 1–2.
[7] Walinsky, *Economic development*, p. 409.
[8] Emery, *Financial institutions*, pp. 7–9.

trade – and a new insurance corporation. The objective was to make the economy's bank, the Myanmar Economic Bank, semi-autonomous and able to grant credit according to commercial guidelines. In practice, however, inclusion in the annual budget of a state-enterprise investment programme remained sufficient to justify a loan, irrespective of the firm's financial viability.[9]

In 1953, Indonesia's pre-war Java Bank was set up as a central bank with a legal reserve requirement of 20 per cent of bank notes, balances on current account and other demand liabilities. However, by 1954 the reserve constraint was suspended, and before long abolished. Indonesian government spending, in complete contrast to its pre-war currency board system, became entirely independent of the level of reserves.[10]

In reaction to a perceived lack of capital for industrial undertakings and to encourage indigenous entrepreneurship, Indonesia established a development bank, Bank Industri Negara, specifically as a source of long-term finance for new industry. The bank mobilized few if any new savings. Rather, it relied heavily, and probably almost entirely, on government financing. Profits in enterprises in which Bank Industri Negara invested were small, as were its bond sales. In the 1950s, Indonesian government finance shifted resources to priority sectors, but these flows added little, if anything, to real output.[11]

The 1957 Indonesian seizure of Dutch estates was paralleled in the financial sector by the 1958 nationalization of all Dutch banks.[12] By 1959, Indonesia had abandoned any pretence of an independent central bank, and its financial system took on all the features of classical socialist finance.[13] Between 1960 and 1965, government management was extended and consolidated to create a single 'monster bank' divided into five units. Often, only relatively small bureaucratic factions and power groups determined to which state enterprises resources would be channelled.[14] The Bank of Indonesia became predominantly a payment agency for the government.[15] During the last two years of the Sukarno regime, Indonesia's banks became directly dependent on central bank finance.[16] Monetary policy became fiscal policy: state finance attempted to shift resources to priority sectors and use inflation as a means of taxation.[17]

9 Tun Wai, 'Myanmar', p. 168; Myat Thein, *Economic development*, pp. 25–26.

10 Higgins and Hollinger, 'Central banking', pp. 58, 75–76; Higgins, *Indonesia's economic stabilization*, pp. 36–38 and *Indonesia: crisis*, p. 95.

11 Hensley, 'Development banks', pp. 401–9; Higgins, *Indonesia's economic stabilization*, p. 93.

12 Bevan et al., *Political economy*, p. 213; Woo et al., *Macroeconomic policies*, p. 113.

13 Higgins and Hollinger, 'Central banking', p. 77.

14 Woo et al., *Macroeconomic policies*, p. 13; Arndt, 'Banking', pp. 362–67; Bevan et al., *Political economy*, p. 410.

15 Cole and Slade, *Building*, p. 37.

16 Arndt, 'Banking', p. 378.

17 Grenville, 'Monetary policy', pp. 114–15.

Budget Deficits, Money and Inflation

North Vietnam incurred budget deficits mainly to finance government investment in heavy industry, credit extension to state trading corporations and subsidized food for state workers. Deficits were partly met by foreign aid but substantially by 'a rather uncontrolled growth of the money supply'.[18] Structurally, North Vietnam had little capacity to produce consumer goods, and collectivized agriculture failed to yield an anticipated surplus of cheap, abundant food. As a result, monetary expansion created demand, which consistently outdistanced the domestic availability of consumer goods and services and imports of them. Initially, imports alleviated some of a growing tension between the demand and supply of consumer goods and raw materials, but that balance did not survive the shift towards more and more imported capital goods in the (largely unsuccessful) attempt to build heavy industry. Administered prices prevented open inflation, but suppressed inflation was considerable and shortages, queues, rationing and black markets became endemic. By the late 1950s, North Vietnam could be described as an institutionalized shortage economy and as having a 'continuing goods famine'.[19] Black markets, ubiquitous and often resorted to by state enterprise, eliminated only some of North Vietnam's monetary overhang.

In the 1950s, Burma's government also prioritized financing state industry, but the consequences of this for the budget deficit, an accompanying increase in money supply and creation of excess demand, could to some extent be offset by liberalizing imports and selling foreign exchange to the private sector.[20] Beginning in 1963, state enterprises operated under a 'soft budget constraint'.[21] Monetary policy became mainly financing large state-enterprise deficits. Although receipts from a profits tax on these enterprises peaked at almost half of total tax revenue in 1969/70, they fell to less than two-fifths in 1972/73.[22]

Prices under the socialist system were fixed, and as shortages grew Burma became an extreme example of repressed inflation, with a two-tier structure of an official and a black market. By the 1980s, the black market was estimated to be at least half as large as the legal economy, and was perhaps three or four times its size.[23] Black market exchange rates per US dollar were already nine

[18] Spoor, 'Finance', p. 354.

[19] Beresford, *Vietnam*, p. 168 and see Spoor, 'Finance', pp. 348, 354; Vo, *Vietnam's economic policy*, p. 45.

[20] Myat Thein, *Economic development*, pp. 25–26; Tin Maung Maung Than, *State dominance*, pp. 82–83; Walinsky, *Economic development*, p. 415.

[21] Tin Maung Maung Than, *State dominance*, p. 133.

[22] Tin Maung Maung Than, *State dominance*, pp. 78, 83, 133, 193, 198; Tun Wai, 'Myanmar', pp. 178–80, 196.

[23] Myat Thein, *Economic development*, p. 77; Mya Maung, 'Burma's economic performance', p. 520.

Table 12.1 *Myanmar official and black market exchange rates, 1988–96 (kyat to US$)*

	Official rate	Black market rate	Ratio black market to official
1988	5.00	45	9.0
1989	5.80	60	10.3
1990	6.62	80	12.1
1991	6.20	122	19.7
1992	6.30	110	17.5
1993	6.10	117	19.2
1994	6.10	110	18.0
1995	5.90	120	20.3
1996	5.90	148	25.1

Source: Mya Maung, 'Burma's economic performance', p. 516.

times the official rate in 1988 and thereafter the disparity grew (Table 12.1). The black market, by 1970 popularly known as 'Corporation 24', became a way of life on which everyone depended. Consumers obtained from the *hmaung-kho* (literally 'taking refuge in the dark') a whole range of products including rice; government officials and military officers sold goods to the market which they had bought at their special shops.[24]

Throughout almost all the 1950s, Indonesia had continuous inflation, putting pressure on the balance of payments which the authorities responded to with trade controls and multiple exchange rates. Inflation quickly eroded gains from two formal devaluations and various informal ones. Nevertheless, until 1961, confidence in the currency was well maintained. Inflation lagged well behind increases in money supply, M1, and annual price increases remained at Latin American levels. Beginning in 1961, however, budget deficits worsened and monetary expansion gained pace. Money supply, M1, doubled or more every year, owing both to budget deficits created by Indonesia's Confrontations and Sukarno's grand projects, including national monuments, the great mosque, luxury hotels, the Sarinah department store, conferences and other expenditures apparently for less official purposes.[25] Between 1963 and 1965, the construction of national monuments accounted for a rise in government investment spending to over 30 per cent of government expenditure.[26] Confidence in the currency evaporated and, as circulation velocity rose, price

[24] Steinberg, *Burma*, p. 163.
[25] Arndt, 'Banking', p. 67.
[26] Woo et al., *Macroeconomic policies*, p. 28.

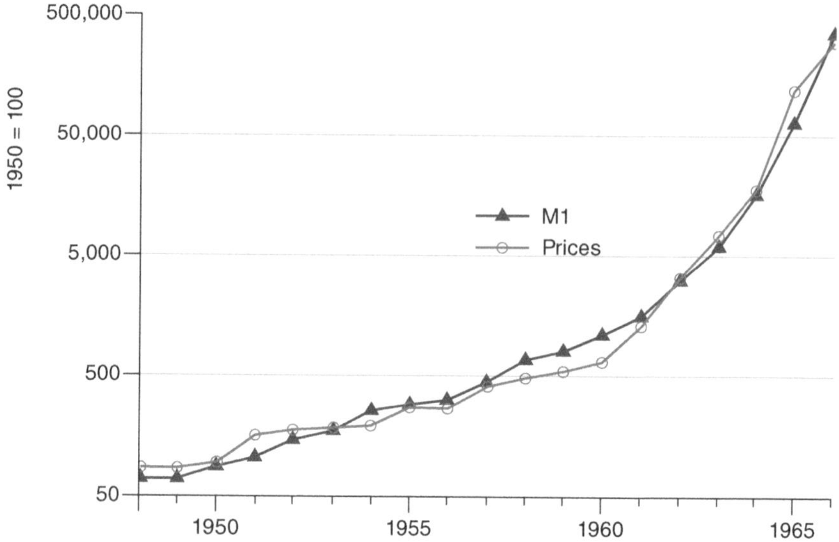

Figure 12.1 Indonesia money supply and prices, 1948–March 1966
Source: Arndt, 'Banking', pp. 51, 59.

rises outdistanced monetary expansion. By March 1966, Indonesia had genuine hyperinflation, with price increases of more than 40 per cent a month; prices increased from an index number of 100 in 1950 to 298,235 in March 1966 (Figure 12.1 and Table 12.2).

Responses to Shortages and High Inflation

There are three possible ways for governments to counter shortages – like those characteristic of socialist Southeast Asia as well as South Vietnam – which arise because monetary expansion creates a demand for goods in excess of supply.[27] One is to change relative prices to equilibrate demand and supply. Prices in socialist Southeast Asia had, however, no more than limited flexibility, partly because of the desire to avoid lowering the living standards of state workers and partly because of the possibility of social unrest in response to falling real wages.

Extensive use was made of a second option, as described in Chapters 10 and 11: that of rationing, both formal and informal through queues; place of work as a criterion for rations; limits on quantities that could be sold to individuals; and waiting times for goods to appear. Typically, rationing worked in favour

[27] Ellman, *Socialist planning*, pp. 301–15 discusses shortages and alternatives to dealing with them.

Table 12.2 *Indonesia money supply and prices, 1938–66*

	Currency rupiah bn	Demand deposits rupiah bn	M1	M1 1950 = 100	Prices 1954 = 100	Prices 1950 = 100	% increase in M1	% increase in prices
1938 March	0.24	0.18	0.42	9.7	–	–	–	–
1947 Dec.	1.27	1.23	2.50	58.0	–	–	–	–
1948	1.64	1.37	3.01	69.8	44.0	86.3	20.4	–
1949	1.75	1.56	3.31	76.8	42.0	82.4	10.0	–4.5
1950	2.58	1.73	4.31	100.0	51.0	100.0	30.2	21.4
1951	3.33	1.71	5.04	116.9	84.0	164.7	16.9	64.7
1952	4.35	2.25	6.60	153.1	89.0	174.5	31.0	6.0
1953	5.21	2.27	7.48	173.5	94.0	184.3	13.3	5.6
1954	7.47	3.64	11.11	257.8	100.0	196.1	48.5	6.4
1955	8.65	3.59	12.24	284.0	135.0	264.7	10.2	35.0
1956	9.35	4.02	13.37	310.2	133.0	260.8	9.2	–1.5
1957	14.1	4.82	18.92	439.0	206.0	403.9	41.5	54.9
1958	19.9	9.49	29.39	681.9	243.0	476.5	55.3	18.0
1959	26.4	8.5	34.9	809.7	275.0	539.2	18.7	13.2
1960	34.1	13.8	47.9	1,111.4	330.0	647.1	37.2	20.0
1961	48.5	19.1	67.6	1,568.4	644.0	1,262.7	41.1	95.2
1962	102.9	33.0	135.9	3,153.1	1,648.0	3,231.4	101.0	155.9
1963	175.5	87.9	263.4	6,111.4	3,770.0	7,392.2	93.8	128.8
1964	451.9	251.2	703.1	16,313.2	8,870.0	17,392.2	166.9	135.3
1965	1,966.6	808.8	2,775.4	64,394.4	61,400.0	120,392.2	294.7	592.2
1966 March	4,221.8	11,004.50	15,226.	353,278.4	152,100.0	298,235.3	448.6	147.7
1966 May	6,106.5	11,000.20	17,106.7	396,907.2	–	–	12.3	–

Source: Arndt, 'Banking', pp. 51, 59.

of state workers and urban areas. Rations were almost always insufficient for a reasonable standard of living, and necessitated recipients taking second or even third jobs. Rationing had the disadvantages of adversely affecting labour productivity through separating performance and reward, as well as the demoralizing effect of black markets.

Monetary reform is a third option. Purchasing power can be drained by confiscating cash and bank deposits through declaring old money no longer legal tender or exchanging it, often in only small amounts, for new money at unfavourable rates. However, demonetization works for only short periods unless, following it, either the supply of goods increases sufficiently to match demand or the monetary expansion that gave rise to the demand ceases. Demonetizations that were only briefly effective were the usual Southeast Asian experience.

In February 1959, monetary reform in North Vietnam introduced a new dong equal to 1,000 old dong and set an upper limit of 2,000 new dong as eligible for exchange. The demonetization took some 40 million dong out of the economy. Nevertheless, monetary expansion continued after 1959 at an even more rapid rate, and by 1963 inflationary pressures intensified.[28]

The introduction of a new currency in May 1978, not long after Vietnam's re-unification, combined demonetization with a campaign to eliminate a 'comprador bourgeoisie', especially Cholon's Chinese merchants, thought to have large cash holdings and to by-pass official state trade channels. A strict limit was placed on the amount of cash exchangeable for new banknotes, and anything above that amount was put in savings accounts which were frozen. Accounts could be accessed only after application to the authorities.[29]

Demonetization was again necessary by the mid-1980s but, in combination with price reform and large wage rises between 1985 and 1986, it proved disastrous. One new dong exchanged for 10 old dong and strictly limited quantities of currency could be converted. At the same time, state employees began to be paid in money rather than heavily subsidized rationed commodities, and wages were approximately doubled. A freeing of the market and money far in excess of the availability of goods set off an inflationary spiral which reached an annual rate of 1,000 per cent. Scarcities and malnourishment became widespread and large-scale famine threatened because farmers, in response to rapid inflation, hedged against it by keeping rice back.[30]

In 1990, as Vietnam began to liberalize under *doi moi*, it moved to a two-tier banking system. The former commercial functions of the State Bank were

[28] Spoor, 'Finance', pp. 348–49.

[29] Vo, *Vietnam's economic policy*, pp. 90–91; Beresford, *Vietnam*, p. 168.

[30] Ellman, *Socialist finance*, p. 310; Barbara Crossette, 'Hanoi, citing famine fears, seeks emergency aid', *New York Times*, 15 May 1988; UPI Archives, Paul Wedel, 'Shortage threatens famine in Vietnam', 5 June 1988; Keith B. Richburg, 'Near famine in '88, Vietnam now exports rice', *Washington Post*, 19 April 1990; Beresford, *Vietnam*, pp. 168–69.

transferred to banks which included two existing ones and new industrial and agricultural banks. These banks had autonomy to operate as commercial banks and open foreign branches and representative offices.[31]

Burma demonetized in 1964, in 1985 and again in 1987. Because of an ever-present threat of demonetization, saving accounts served as a form of quasi-money. Business people kept deposits in savings accounts, withdrawing cash only as needed. They usually withdrew deposits on Mondays but redeposited these withdrawals on Fridays, because of the expectation of demonetization announcements on weekends and not wanting to be caught holding large amounts of cash.[32] The 1964 demonetization, which took a quarter of the currency out of circulation, was aimed at domestic and foreign capitalist 'exploiters' who were thought to be operating against the Revolutionary Council. However, a government promise to exclude 'honest savers' enabled those regarded as responsible for exploitation to avoid surrendering notes through their use of agents.[33] Demonetization in 1985 again involved taking a quarter of the currency out of circulation. Although the demonetization was said to be to expropriate tax evaders and black marketeers, a legal provision to recompense innocent individuals offered a loophole that the target groups successfully utilized.[34]

The 1987 demonetization, the most drastic yet, invalidated 56 per cent of the money supply. Poor people were seriously affected, but the only compensation was an extra month's remuneration for pensioners and government employees. Through wiping out the savings of a large part of the population, demonetization created a widespread desperation among the population, set off prolonged and violent riots and led to the military coup that replaced Ne Win.[35] The new government immediately resumed printing large quantities of money.[36] Although the 1987 demonetization reduced the 1988 money supply by two-fifths, by 1989 it had returned to the level of 1987 (Table 12.3). Between 1988 and 1995, Burma's money supply rose 70-fold, although government data show just a fivefold increase in prices.[37] By 1996, the black market rate for the kyat per US$ had risen to 25 times the official rate (Table 12.1).

A series of Indonesian demonetizations partly explain the tendency for Indonesians to hold cash in their homes and not banks.[38] The first 'monetary purge', literally a 'monetary cut', occurred in 1950 to eliminate the overhang of

31 Klump and Gottwald, 'Financial sector reform', p. 280.
32 Tun Wai, 'Myanmar', p. 196; Steinberg, *Burma*, p. 5.
33 Mya Maung, 'Burmese Way', p. 542; Stifel, 'Economics', p. 809.
34 Tin Maung Maung Than, *State dominance*, p. 193.
35 'Riots over kyats' and 'Ne Win's new way', *Far Eastern Economic Review*, 17 September 1987.
36 Turnell, *Fiery dragons*, pp. 237–39, 252–54.
37 Khin Maung Kyi et al., *Economic development*, p. 117.
38 Mackie, *Problems*, p. 75.

Table 12.3 *Burma money supply, 1979–90 (million kyat)*

	Money	Quasi-money	Money + quasi-money
1979	6,897	1,111	8,008
1980	7,919	1,675	9,594
1981	8,909	2,277	11,186
1982	9,921	3,172	13,093
1983	10,644	4,065	14,709
1984	12,171	4,971	17,142
1985	13,655	6,004	19,659
1986	13,265	6,808	20,073
1987	18,276	7,777	26,053
1988	10,770	8,444	19,214
1989	18,097	7,660	25,757
1990 March	25,300	9,721	35,021
1990 Sept.	30,066	10,899	40,965
1990 Dec.	32,329	11,406	43,735

Source: Tun Wai, 'Myanmar', table A15 and p. 193.

a large volume of government notes of about Rp. 6 billion and Dutch *Nica* or 'Red' money of Rp. 3.3 billion issued as legal tender in any territory under the control of the Netherlands prior to independence.[39] *Nica* money and Java Bank notes above Rp. 2.50 were to be cut in half, the right-hand side exchangeable for 3 per cent government bonds, the left-hand side for new Java Bank notes. Half of time and demand deposits over Rp. 400 were to be exchanged for government bonds redeemable in instalments over 40 years. By 1952, however, money supply was more than double its 1949 level due to finance for the budget deficit and inflation accompanying the Korean war boom. During the remainder of the 1950s, money supply M1 rose at rates of from a little under 10 per cent a year to over 50 per cent (Table 12.2).

The second monetary purge in 1959 decreased rupiah in circulation from Rp. 34 billion to Rp. 21 billion by reducing the value of bank notes of Rp. 500 and Rp. 1,000 by a factor of 10 and freezing 90 per cent of bank deposits of Rp. 25,000 or more. The rupiah was also devalued by almost 300 per cent and trade taxes increased. Prices stayed relatively stable for only a short while, however, because of the growing budget deficit. A May 1963 IMF stabilization

[39] For descriptions of the 'monetary purges', see Woo and Nasution, 'Indonesian economic policies', pp. 41–43; Mackie, *Problems*, p. 29; Glassburner, 'Economic policy-making', pp. 122–23.

programme, meant to attract foreign aid, was undermined by a widening budget deficit due to the Malaysian Confrontation and resulting military expenditure. A third, 1965, 'monetary purge' was followed by more lasting reform after Indonesian political upheaval and the coup against Sukarno.

South Vietnam and Laos

South Vietnam and Laos were not exceptions to the Southeast Asian pattern of monetary expansion, but inflation was kept under control when the two countries had United States support. Persistently high inflation did not escalate, because the main objective of United States aid was to avoid high inflation for fear that it would destabilize the American-supported regimes and cause populations to shun or rise against them. In each country, American aid was not intended to promote development but to prevent rampant or runaway inflation by financing a substantial part of the budget deficit and most, or even all, of trade deficits. Since taxation fell well short of covering large budget deficits, governments financed this chiefly by printing money.

Between 1955 and 1975, South Vietnamese money supply, M1, rose by a factor of 27.4, and while price rises tracked this increase for much of the period, they lagged it (Figure 12.2). Until the First Indochina War's escalation in 1964, price rises had remained moderate at no more than about 6 per cent a year. Subsequently, budgetary support provided by aid was chiefly responsible for maintaining inflation measured by the wholesale price index from 1965 through 1973 at an annual rate of 26.5 per cent. Devaluation would have been an option to deal with a grossly overvalued piastre, but the South Vietnamese government resisted this, because it would have hurt privileged groups and reduced the piastre value of aid. Finally, in 1974, prices began decisively to outdistance money supply, when foreign aid, 'the glue that held Vietnam together', dropped.[40]

In Laos between 1954 and 1961, inflation was modest and gradual, but started to become a problem soon after the August 1959 installation of the new, United States-backed government and consequent devaluation of the Laotian kip to a free market level.[41] After a suspension of American aid due to internal Laotian political upheavals, inflation increased to annual rates of 91 per cent during 1962 and 98 per cent in 1963 due to internal political turbulence.[42] By then, government revenues were a fraction of expenditure, about two-thirds of which went towards the military and police. Additionally, Laos ran large trade deficits. Laotian peasants were not taxed because of the danger that taxes would lead to

[40] Dacy, *Foreign aid*, pp. 134–35, 211 and see pp. 33–34, 174–78.

[41] This section on Laos draws on Stuart-Fox, *History of Laos*, pp. 105, 130, 162, 172, 182.

[42] Joel, 'Foreign Exchange Operations Fund', pp. 137–38.

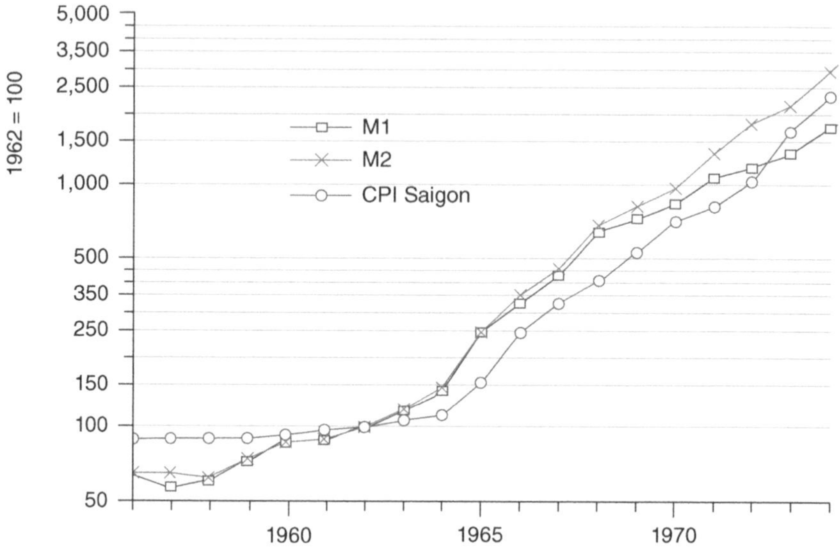

Figure 12.2 South Vietnam end of year money supply and first quarter prices, 1956–74
Source: Dacy, *Foreign aid*, pp. 150–51.

their supporting the Pathet Lao, while the Laotians formulating government policy did not want to tax themselves.[43]

To limit chronic budget shortfalls, provide for military needs, prevent devaluation and keep inflation low enough to ensure political stability, international donors, principally the United States, established two aid schemes. One was commodity import programmes which had the twin objectives of supplying Laos with essential goods and, through sales of these to the government, requiring local currency withdrawals. The other, the Foreign Exchange Operations Fund, set up at the beginning of 1964, sold dollars to the government in exchange for kip to furnish the government with foreign exchange and at the same time reduce the quantity of money in circulation. Commodity aid had the advantage of countering inflationary pressure by increasing the supply of goods, but the range of goods was restricted by American law and most aid came through Fund purchases of the kip.[44]

After the 1975 revolution and an abrupt cessation of American aid, the kip fell by 80 per cent. Soviet Union aid was insufficient to make up for the loss of American support and, faced with inflation of 400 per cent a year in 1976, the government fixed the price of basic commodities, including rice, and restricted

[43] Brown and Zasloff, 'Laos 1977', p. 170; Joel, 'Foreign Exchange Operations Fund', p. 137.
[44] Joel, 'Foreign Exchange Operations Fund', pp. 141, 143, 148–49.

the movement of food and goods.[45] That and the June 1976 devaluation of the kip and its replacement by a 'liberation kip' helped to restrict inflation to 50 per cent during 1977. Finally, in 1979, as part of reforms signalled by the suspension of the cooperativization programme, the 'liberation kip' was replaced by the 'National Bank kip' at a rate of 100 to 1, a demonetization that devalued the currency to about its black market level.[46]

The Plural Society under Socialism

After World War II, Southeast Asia's pre-war plural societies evolved in three different ways. One was some recognizable version of pluralism as part of a political-economic social bargain (Malaysia and Singapore); a second, assimilation, greater than in Malaysia and Singapore, through marriage into the more numerous, indigenous group but, after marriage and citizenship, a large role for the non-indigenous group as entrepreneurs (Thailand and the Philippines). The first two patterns are discussed in later chapters. In a third pattern, characteristic of communist and socialist Southeast Asia, minority groups, which had been a main component of the pre-war commercial structure, were legislated against and forced to leave or expelled.

Pre-war plural societies survived the Southeast Asian socialist experiment in a diminished state. In Vietnam and Burma, no longer with the large pre-World War II Chinese or Indian presence, the structure of plural societies altered more towards other ethnic and minority groups. The composition of the principal cities also changed, since Chinese and Indians had disproportionately resided in them. Minority discrimination and periodic expulsions or even massacres of Chinese and Indian minorities had roots in their importance in the region's pre-war commercial structure compared to indigenous majorities, which felt exploited and held back unfairly. Authoritarian rule encouraged these popular perceptions of unfairness, partly owing to nationalism, partly for political gain and partly to divert attention from economic failings after independence. Moreover, regimes had the power to expel minorities.

In pre-World War II plural societies, Chinese and Indians had remained separate from majority indigenous groups and retained their own languages, cultural preferences and economic characteristics. This separation remained in socialist Southeast Asia, because of historical inertia, discriminatory policies of governments and divergent preferences and behaviours between minority and majority groups. Slow growth and labour surpluses made it unnecessary for majority groups to hire from minorities, which would have helped to break down barriers.

45 Brown and Zasloff, 'Laos 1977', p. 170.
46 Brown and Zasloff, 'Laos 1979', p. 108.

Indochina

In socialist Indochina, the elimination of class enemies, capitalists and 'compradors' destroyed the pre-war business structure and replaced it with state enterprise. President Diem had disliked South Vietnam's Chinese mercantile and industrial community. Nevertheless, southern Chinese business, able to draw on links with Southeast and East Asian Chinese, thrived. The Chinese developed a close relationship with the US military, through supplying many of its needs, as well as with the Saigon administration and military through valuable gifts, offering shares in industrial and banking firms and giving lavish entertainment.

Southern Chinese business, although facing difficulty after Vietnam's 1975 re-unification, continued to operate, partly owing to the corruptibility of many communist cadres. In March 1978, however, as part of reforms to establish socialism firmly, the government launched a campaign against private business. Much of this business was Chinese-owned and centred in Cholon, regarded as the strong capitalist heart beating inside socialist Vietnam and where half of Vietnam's ethnic Chinese lived. At the apex of Chinese business were figures such as the rice king, coffee king, fabric king, gasoline king, scrap-iron king, agro-machine king and wheat flour king. An extensive and close-knit network of large and smaller Chinese traders operated under these kings.[47]

The 1978 reforms allowed small traders, of whatever ethnic heritage, to stay in business until alternative employment was found for them, but only if they dealt in non-state-controlled goods. Armed guards were placed on traders' warehouses until the government completed inventories and took goods. Demonetization in 1978, allowing the conversion of no more than small amounts of old currency, further expropriated traders. In 1979–80, Chinese homes were reduced to shambles by Public Security Bureau officials and then looted continuously by bands of thieves who, eventually, reduced the houses to nothing more than their frames.[48] Government reforms were instrumental in the 1978 and 1979 exodus of 'boat people'. During 1978–79 alone, it was estimated that some 420,000 people, many of whom were Chinese, left Vietnam.

A main objective of the 1978 reforms was to eliminate Cholon's large Chinese-owned trading companies which before World War II, and still in 1978, controlled the Mekong Delta rice trade. The government aimed to strengthen socialism by preventing the Cholon trading companies from undermining the state's grain purchase policy and to bolster the cooperative system by increasing agricultural surpluses and bringing more of it under state control. Reform drove Mekong Delta trading companies out of business and often out of Vietnam.

47 Turley, 'Urban transformation', p. 615.
48 Stern, 'Overseas Chinese', p. 523.

The 1978 extension of state-sector economic dominance to the south largely eliminated the largest merchants in Vietnam's Chinese business community, and, with them, key components of Vietnam's pre-war mercantile structure and plural society. Increased state control was, however, economically counter-productive. Rice procurement fell and grain and other goods nominally under state control were diverted to the black market. Delta farmers, unable to secure essential inputs and paid low government prices, concentrated on feeding their families.[49]

Pre-war and independent Cambodia, although marked by enmity for Vietnamese who arrived in substantial numbers during French colonial rule, did not have the same anti-Chinese feeling as often found elsewhere in Southeast Asia. There had not been, as in many countries, great waves of Chinese immigration accompanying European rule, and, more important, Cambodia's abundance of good, rain-fed land limited Chinese–Khmer competition and conflict. Because irrigation was unnecessary, few Khmer could accumulate enough land wealth to enter commerce and land availability enabled most peasants to be owner-occupiers. A lack of conflict facilitated the emergence of a Cambodian elite through intermarriage between wealthy Chinese business families and those of the Cambodian aristocracy.[50] In Cambodia under Pol Pot, however, anyone suspected of being bourgeois and not a peasant, which included the pre-1975 commercially dominant Chinese community, was murdered.[51]

Laos traced a path not unlike Vietnam's. After the revolution, nationalization, socialization and the threat of imprisonment drove prominent Laotian families as well as the predominantly Chinese business and entrepreneurial class to seek refuge in other countries. Many of these refugees were Lao-Chinese whose families had been living in Laos for generations. The educated middle class, however, stayed in Laos, believing (wrongly) that there would be national reconciliation on the precepts of Buddhism.[52]

Burma

The plural society in Burma was already under severe pressure during colonial rule, and the anarchy during the Japanese occupation intensified ethnic conflict. Major sources of Burmese grievance against Indians were the undercutting of wages by Indian labour; Chettiar 1930s foreclosures on much of Irrawaddy Delta rice land; and dominance of the tier of Indian traders and merchants who

49 Beresford, *National unification*, pp. 114–15 and *Vietnam*, pp. 153–54; Vo, *Vietnam's economic policy*, pp. 66–71, 89–90; Thrift and Forbes, *Price*, p. 134; Stern, 'Overseas Chinese', pp. 528–31.

50 Willmott, *Chinese in Cambodia*; Fisher, 'Review: Willmott', pp. 368–71.

51 On Cambodia's pre-World War II Chinese business community, see Willmott, *Chinese in Cambodia*, pp. 44–64.

52 Stuart-Fox, *History of Laos*, p. 162.

operated below the European apex of colonial commercial structures. In the late stages of colonial rule, and encouraged by Burmese politicians, Indians suffered from discriminatory legislation, immigration restrictions and pogroms. Although in colonial Burma Indians might have assimilated, Burmese attitudes would have made this difficult. Further barriers to assimilation were Indian arguments for closer ties with India, a continuation of British rule and separate representation in the 1937 Legislative Assembly.

During the Japanese occupation, the mass exodus of some 500,000 Indians ended a large part of the Indian presence in Burma, since most evacuees never returned. Pre-war Rangoon was over half Indian; in 1953, the proportion was less than a fifth. Nationalization under the Burmese Way to Socialism substantially eliminated the remaining Indian component in Burmese society as well as part of the Chinese one. During 1963 and 1964, in response to government anti-Indian policies, Indians began, as at the outset of World War II, to walk across the border to India; special ships organized by India's government arrived to repatriate Indians. The government deported Indians; most were squeezed out economically. In July 1964, the *New York Times* reported that 100,000 Indian nationals had departed by air and sea. Departing Indians were stripped of their possessions in Burma and, on departure, of everything they carried – bank accounts, jewellery, clothing and cooking utensils. Another estimate puts departures by 1965 at 300,000. According to India's foreign minister, Chinese had not left to the same extent as Indians, because most refused to go to the People's Republic of China and Nationalist China refused to take them. After 1965, the majority of Indians remaining in Burma were small farmers who had taken Burmese citizenship.[53]

Indonesia

Chinese society in Indonesia was, as throughout the region, but most notably in Malaya and Singapore, complex. It broadly divided into two groups. *Totok* Chinese were, strictly, those foreign born but the term generally applied to a group who were descendants of immigrants and primarily oriented towards China. *Peranakans* were locally rooted and ranged along a spectrum of cultural assimilation. In the Outer Islands, *Totoks* easily outnumbered *Peranakans* but in Java the reverse was true. *Totoks* overwhelmingly engaged in business, while the *Peranakans* showed a preference for the professions and employment in large enterprises. They were also the group more likely to hold Indonesian citizenship, referred to as WNI Chinese, and to be Christians, an outcome of having attended

[53] Holmes, 'Burmese domestic policy', pp. 191–92; 'Uprooted Indian traders reach Indian "home"; nationalization drive expels many who have never seen ancestral land', *New York Times*, 24 July 1964; Badgley, 'Burma's zealot wungyis', p. 55; and see Chakravarti, *Indian minority in Burma*.

Catholic or Protestant schools. Despite the cultural and orientational complexities of Indonesia's some 2.3 to 2.6 million Chinese, indigenous Indonesians do not seem to have perceived these distinctions. Instead, they lumped together all Chinese, assigning them a common (unflattering) set of characteristics and viewing them as immune to change: 'Once a Chinese, always a Chinese.'[54]

An underlying resentment among most indigenous Indonesians against Chinese had roots in a feeling of victimization created by Dutch colonial policies, and in the 1950s was fed by a combination of envy and an inferiority complex. Indigenous Indonesians derided Chinese dedication to business but resented and envied their wealth and power. Economic considerations lay at the base of much of indigenous Indonesia's historic antipathy towards the Chinese.[55] After independence, anti-Chinese feeling was, if anything, exacerbated by the extension of the wealth and power of Chinese enterprise, which filled spaces formerly occupied by the Dutch and gained at the expense of indigenous Indonesian business. Furthermore, the allegiance of Chinese came into question, because about 400,000 Indonesian-born Chinese rejected Indonesian nationality when it was offered to them in 1949–51.[56]

Beginning in 1964, the citizenship status of Chinese became a major issue following the introduction in Parliament of a draft law which would have sharply restricted the number of Chinese allowed to become Indonesian citizens. The citizenship question greatly raised political consciousness among Chinese and led to the formation of *Baperki* in 1964, Indonesia's largest Chinese political organization. By the early 1960s, when the citizenship issue was finally resolved through a treaty with China, Indonesian Chinese faced severe cultural and economic discrimination.[57]

In 1957, the authorities extended more control over Chinese-medium schools, arguing its necessity to safeguard Indonesian national interests. The military authorities, acting under martial law, made it illegal for Indonesian citizens to attend alien schools without special permission. At the end of 1957, there were 2,000 Chinese-medium schools in Indonesia with 425,000 students of whom 250,000 were Indonesian citizens, but by July 1958, just 850 schools remained and all their 150,000 students were alien Chinese. The 1958 Outer Island rebellion further reduced the number of Chinese schools, because a strong Islamic element among the rebels opposed a Chinese presence. After the regulation of Chinese schools, Chinese students wanting further education went to China or Taiwan.

54 Skinner, 'Chinese minority', pp. 104–12.

55 Woo and Nasution, 'Indonesian economic policies', p. 65; 'Population and manpower', in Glassburner, ed., *Economy of Indonesia*, p. 181; Skinner, 'Chinese minority', pp. 104–12; Somers, *Peranakan Chinese*, p. 55.

56 Skinner, 'Chinese minority', pp. 110–11; Mackie, 'Preliminary survey', pp. 9–15.

57 Coppel, *Indonesian Chinese*, pp. 36–39.

Economic measures against the Chinese were laws or regulations aimed only at aliens. One example was a 1957 head tax on aliens at varying rates for household heads, wives and children. For a typical family, the tax totalled well above Indonesian per capita income. The principal instance of economic discrimination, discussed above, was the 1959 ban on aliens engaging in retail trade in rural areas, which caused some 100,000 Chinese to emigrate. The army supervised the removal of alien traders and disposal of their assets.[58]

During the first half of the 1960s, the decline of constitutional democracy and rise of army power isolated the Chinese. Few checks on anti-Sinitic politics existed, except insofar as Sukarno could impose them. He was able to stop open advocacy of anti-Chinese measures, but covert harassment and discrimination continued.[59] From the 1960s onwards, the Chinese issue periodically flared up – as in the riots of May 1963 and anti-Chinese violence of 1996 to 1999 in conjunction with the Asian financial crisis – with the sacking of shops and massacre of Indonesian Chinese.[60]

Following the 1965 upheaval and coup against Sukarno, left-wing organizations, including the Indonesian Communist Party (PKI) and *Baperki*, were banned and Chinese schools closed for three years.[61] During this time, the entire Chinese community was subject to attacks due to a tendency to identify them with the PKI and Beijing. Nevertheless, and despite the 1959 mass Chinese exodus and ongoing tensions, Chinese retained a major business and entrepreneurial presence in Indonesia, partly through assimilation and partly through returning to the country or emigrating to it.

The plural society that largely arose under colonial rule created a development and social choice for independent Southeast Asia. Outward-looking Southeast Asia determined in favour of development and so to a degree of tolerance for its Chinese and Indian minorities as well as for European business. An important reason for this decision was to be able to make use of the entrepreneurial skills of non-indigenous populations in furthering growth and development.

Conclusion

All of the socialist economies and South Vietnam printed money to finance large budget deficits as well as negative trade balances and to maintain

[58] Bernard Kalb, 'Indonesia begins alien trade ban; Peiping envoy fails in effort to halt decree aimed at Chinese merchants', *New York Times*, 1 January 1960; Coppel, *Indonesian Chinese*, pp. 37–38; Paauw, 'From colonial to guided', pp. 210–11; Skinner, 'Chinese minority', pp. 114–15.

[59] Skinner, 'Chinese minority', pp. 114–15.

[60] Somers, *Peranakan Chinese*, pp. 45–47.

[61] Suryadinata, 'Indonesian Chinese education', pp. 67–70.

overvalued exchange rates. High inflation, open and suppressed, shortages and black markets resulted. The initial response was always to try to restore balance through some form of trade controls. An increase in tax proceeds was never seriously attempted either through direct taxation or by emphasizing the development of traditional primary-exporting sectors which, owing to trade taxes, were historically the main source of revenue.

In socialist Southeast Asia, monetary policy became fiscal policy: state finance attempted to use inflation to tax sectors with contracts fixed in monetary terms or not easily changeable and to shift resources from them to priority sectors.[62] At some point, however, government revenue from the inflation tax falls. If governments try, as those in Southeast Asia did, to make up for this by printing ever greater quantities of money, the public's willingness to hold real balances declines. A consequent increase in money's velocity of circulation leads to higher inflation and, if exacerbated by further monetary expansion, to hyperinflation, as happened in Indonesia.

Before the late 1980s, Vietnam was so committed to Soviet socialism that financial alternatives to it were not considered for decades. A logical alternative, and the one to which Vietnam eventually turned, was a state-directed finance similar to that also adopted in China. Vietnam, for ideological reasons, always planned for a purely state solution and it left no place for private enterprise or the Chinese and Europeans who before World War II had almost exclusively organized it.

After independence, Burma and Indonesia set out to institute some form of democratic socialism in which the private financial sector would play an important role. That was never consistent with the desire for indigenous business to become important within a few years. When this strategy of indigenization did not yield quick results, Burmese and Indonesian governments considered that they had little option but to turn to state ownership. The consequent need to finance the inefficiencies of state ownership led to chronic inflation.

Indonesia turned, before long, to a more liberal finance, a choice that it should have made at the outset. Burma, however, persisted with, and made worse, the encompassing and stifling state finance into which it fell. In both countries, the legacy of minority local commercial dominance, deep-seated attitudes and imperatives of indigenization soon ruled out a social tolerance and societal change which might eventually have led to an assimilation incorporating minority business skills.

The varieties of socialism instituted in Southeast Asia failed disastrously as systems of finance and in the preservation of peaceful societies where minorities were protected. Given their pre-World War II histories, it seems unlikely that early post-war Burma and Indonesia would have adopted the Vietnamese

[62] Grenville, 'Monetary policy', pp. 114–15.

option of state-directed finance. If so, a more successful approach to establishing workable post-World War II financial systems might have been to persist with some mixture of state and private finance along with government regulation. That choice would have been consistent with some form of democratic socialism. If that had been managed, it might also have taken greater account of the rights of groups that were components of pre-war plural societies in both countries.

Conclusion Part III

The economic systems that are examined in this part of the book differed enormously. They ranged from Vietnam's classic Soviet central planning to an extreme pure communism in Pol Pot's Cambodia. Socialism in Burma and Indonesia meant a nationalist rejection of colonialism and capitalism and seemed to offer modernity. When this, and the implied industrialization, proved difficult, socialism came to be defined by nationalism and comprehensive nationalization. After failures of indigenous entrepreneurship, state ownership appeared to offer the only route to modernity consistent with rejecting capitalism. Cambodia, after Pol Pot, and Laos arrived at communist regimes only briefly and by the historical accidents of a geography adjacent to Vietnam and its 1975 military victory.

World War II's legacy weighed heavily on Vietnam, Burma and Indonesia. War and revolution entrenched a regime in Vietnam that for four decades dogmatically adhered to a strict Marxist, Soviet socialism, while the living standards of the great mass of the population stagnated or fell. In Burma and Indonesia, the war and Japanese occupation created leaders who, although charismatic, were unfit to govern. Burma's U Nu was unable to act decisively and disappeared for long periods on Buddhist retreat, while Ne Win determined on a socialism about which he knew almost nothing and which was entirely inappropriate. In Indonesia, Sukarno, anxious continually to re-create the heady experience of revolution, led his country down a path of self-destruction. None of these leaders understood much about economics and cared even less. Indonesia came back from annihilation from 1966, but in Burma the army, once in power and with the self-interest of maintaining privilege, entrenched its dominance.

In Vietnam, Burma and Indonesia, World War II, the Japanese occupation, independence and a re-ordering of society or revolution all worked together. These changes broke down social and status barriers, gave rise to an anticipation of modern sector employment and raised expectations that after independence the economy would produce a rapidly expanding volume of goods. In countries that turned to socialism, their colonial histories, together with war and occupation, were instrumental in the creation of anti-Western, anti-colonialist leaders rather than the pro-Western leadership that after independence remained in charge of Thailand, Malaya and the Philippines.[1] The new leaders of Burma and Indonesia always considered that some form of socialism would offer the answer to achieving rapid material progress, but began searching for this mainly with socialist rhetoric.

For the five Southeast Asian countries that looked to become successful socialist economies and societies, the region's lowest per capita incomes made any transition towards socialism difficult and war or insurrections further complicated matters. Government policies that emphasized industrialization and generally heavy industry, but failed adequately to recognize the role of agriculture and its interdependence with industry in the development process, probably ensured that a successful transition to a strong socialist economy was impossible. Moreover, and crucially for development, all the Southeast Asian socialist systems ignored the centrality of positive material incentives to increasing output.

Cooperatives in Pol Pot's Cambodia implemented only negative incentives, while the other Indochinese economies dismissed the microeconomic rationality of peasant farmers and peasant decision-making, undermining the possibility of anticipated surpluses. Peasants almost immediately recognized that collectivization did not serve their own or their families' economic self-interest, and so withheld effort and resources from cooperatives to concentrate, instead, on cultivating their own plots. Without state compulsion to remain in cooperatives, better-off Laotian farmers soon left them. Governments dismantled collectives when, finally, they accepted that collectivization was a brake on development, creating neither a large surplus for industry nor higher peasant incomes and living standards. Burma and Indonesia never tried land reform or agricultural cooperatives. Meaningful land redistribution was effectively impossible in land-starved Java and little more than spoken of in Burma. Neither country invested adequately in agriculture nor did either, as additions to weak taxation capacity, seriously attempt to develop more advanced tax systems than those in place before World War II.

In all countries and including South Vietnam, despite differing socialisms, common development strategies bred a like pattern of economic problems. All attempted to build an advanced industrial economy on a largely peasant economy and to do so without adequate finance, administrative resources or infrastructure. An emphasis on heavy industry, together with a neglect of agriculture and inability to establish modern tax systems as the main possible sources of state revenue, led to large budget deficits and negative trade balances, giving rise to trade restrictions, necessitating largely unrestrained money creation and leaving foreign aid as a principal means of settling international obligations.

The lack of adequate domestic productive capacity, and the resort to printing money to finance deficits that had largely been generated by inefficient

[1] Feith, *Decline*, pp. 603–4.

state industry, resulted in chronically high or runaway inflations in socialist Southeast Asia and South Vietnam. Inflation was only temporarily remedied by demonetization, although South Vietnam avoided this because of American aid. Large numbers of those in minority groups were forced out of the socialist countries because of a reaction against pre-World War II capitalist commercial structures, the major roles in commerce of Chinese and Indians and the failures of indigenous entrepreneurship. Throughout Indochina, the elimination of class enemies, capitalists and 'compradors' destroyed pre-war business structures and led to their replacement with state enterprise. Members of the business and entrepreneurial classes, mostly ethnic Chinese, were either murdered or sought refuge in other countries. There were mass evacuations of Indians from Burma and Chinese from Indonesia. Forced removals of prominent groups in Southeast Asia's plural societies considerably changed the ethnic composition of Burma and Vietnam, although relatively little permanent change occurred in Indonesia, since many Chinese stayed in the country and others who had left returned.

The pre-1945 origins of independence movements in Southeast Asia were nationalist, but the newly independent countries, discussed in this part of the book, progressively turned leftwards, Vietnam apart. The Vietnamese leadership had always had clear socialist goals. After independence, as Burma and Indonesia became more radical, they increasingly employed socialism as a development ideology. Socialism looked attractive not just because it was not capitalism but because it promised the rationality of science. As a system, socialism emphasized the realization of progress, attainment of development, use of planning and achievement of communal goals. It stressed 'a rational society in which people extend helping hands to one another because they value highly the process of industrialization through community effort'.[2] Beginning in 1975, the leaders of Laos and Cambodia were similarly attracted by these qualities of socialism and took to extremes its ideals.

By the late 1980s, disappointment with the various forms of socialism was universal throughout socialist Southeast Asia, although for its own ends, the Burmese government hung onto claims to be socialist. A central reason for the failure of Southeast Asian versions of socialism was that the importance of comparative advantage and prices as incentives was ignored. An emphasis on heavy industry was inappropriate for agrarian, substantially peasant societies. Instead, stress should have been placed on developing agriculture and agricultural exports.

Vietnam, in particular, should have looked for ways to take advantage of a factor endowment of abundant labour. Import-substitution policies should have concentrated on industries with relatively simple technologies and sufficient domestic demand for home production to realize available scale

[2] Apter, 'Ideology and discontent', p. 23.

economies. In 1950, the same opportunities for exporting manufactures that obtained by the beginning of the 1970s did not exist. Even so, industrial export opportunities in agricultural processing and light, labour-intensive industries should have been sought out and used to advantage. Policies like those suggested, along with a recognition of the importance of prices and incentives, are the strategies recently used by Southeast Asian countries in promoting rapid growth. Socialist Southeast Asia would have done better to institute a similar economic policy framework from the 1950s onwards while still pursuing the social democratic goals of poverty alleviation and societal justice.

PART IV

Outward-looking Southeast Asia

13

Malaysia and Thailand: Land Abundance and Technology

This chapter is largely one of close comparisons. From the 1950s to 1990, both Malaysia and Thailand were outstanding examples of rapid export-led growth; both stand out as export-led trade and development success stories; and both remained good examples of dualism with modern sectors and large, poor rural populations. Each country drew on abundant land to take advantage of the opportunity to extend pre-World War II vent-for-surplus agricultural growth, Malaysia through rubber and palm oil, Thailand through rice and an expanding contribution from other commodity exports.

Although both countries greatly increased agricultural output from the 1950s onwards, they diverged sharply in how they achieved this. Malaysia quickly adopted new techniques to produce and market rubber and palm oil, and the growth of these exports relied substantially on technical progress. Thai agriculture grew chiefly through extending the cultivated area.

Agriculture continued to be an important constituent of the two countries' growth stories and a major component of foreign exchange earnings. Revenue from agricultural exports enabled the Malaysian and Thai governments to invest in development, maintain financial stability and avoid more than relatively small budget or current account balance-of-payments deficits. Agriculture could not, however, provide sufficient employment in either country for large flows of new job seekers created by population increase at much faster rates than before 1940. The problem became ever more pressing as land extension moved towards its physical limits.

Malaysia and Thailand responded, as recommended by development economists at the time and followed by most developing countries, with programmes of import-substitution industrialization. These fell short of meeting the requirement for employment and were instrumental in the creation of local rent-seeking elites. During the 1970s, the two countries, encouraged by the examples of Singapore and the three Asian Newly Industrialized Countries (NICs) of South Korea, Taiwan and Hong Kong, combined import substitution with a strategy of manufacturing for export and incentives to attract foreign investors. These were principally multinationals in search of cheap labour, especially to assemble electronics and electrical products. Production by the multinational (MNEs) arrivals added greatly to exports and created jobs but, initially, the enterprises retained aspects of being enclave clusters. The chapter's first section deals with Malaysia and the second with Thailand.

Malaysia

On the eve of World War II, Malaya was wealthy by Southeast Asian standards and had grown faster than its Southeast Asian neighbours. Nevertheless, a reliance on vent-for-surplus exports had failed, except briefly in the 1920s, to deliver 'catch-up' growth. Between 1947 and independence in 1957, Malaya's economy remained much the same structurally as it had been before the war. Independent Malaya, like its regional neighbours, needed to find new paths to development, since surplus land – until the 1930s a principal means of absorbing population increase – would eventually be exhausted. Moreover, by the 1960s Malaysia, like Singapore, had among the world's highest population growth rates.[1]

This section discusses how Malaysia came into being and its separation from Singapore and how, for the three decades after independence, it developed to rank among the world's foremost developing country success stories. Helped by the good fortune of rich natural resources, the economy grew simultaneously on multiple fronts to escape the growth constraints of vent-for-surplus agriculture. At the same time as yields on existing land rose through land-saving technology, cultivated area also increased and agriculture became more diversified. Malaysia also industrialized, at first through limited import substitution and, beginning in 1968, through manufacturing for export. Impressive growth was not, however, accompanied by a more balanced distribution of either economic activity or income between the three main ethnic groups. By the late 1960s, the need to resolve these issues blighted Malaysia's remarkable growth record, and a main feature of government policy became the search for ways to achieve equality while maintaining rapid growth.

Political Origins

After the end of World War II and during a 15 August to 3 September 1945 power vacuum prior to re-occupation by the British, inter-ethnic conflicts between Malays and Chinese descended into chaos, described as 'near-anarchy'.[2] As the Japanese army retreated to the cities, the Malayan Communist Party/Malayan People's Anti-Japanese Army (a World War II guerrilla army dominated by ethnic Chinese) took control of some 70 per cent of smaller towns and villages as well as large parts of the peninsula. Chinese reprisals against Malays accused of collaboration were severe. Malays retaliated savagely. Fighting ceased after

1 Malaysia, *First Malaysia plan*, p. 41.
2 Jones, *Japan's new order*, p. 390.

the British return, but soon resumed with increased intensity and lasted until March 1946, by which time the Malayan People's Anti-Japanese Army had been 'defeated militarily' by the Malays. Their emergence as clear winners in the inter-ethnic conflict was fundamental in shaping the history of modern Malaya and the course of its plural society.[3]

Britain planned to form, and rule as a single entity, a Malayan Union consisting of the nine Malay states, together with Penang and Malacca, but not Singapore, which was to become a separate Crown Colony. The Malayan Union foundered almost immediately. Malays considered that their political power had been insufficiently recognized in visualizing the Union and expressed opposition to it through civil disobedience and refusal to participate in the process of government.[4] Revised proposals for a Federation of Malaya, under British control and again consisting of the Malay states plus Penang and Malacca but excluding Singapore, were accepted. The Federation came into being in February 1948. British abandonment of the Malayan Union and its replacement by the Federation of Malaya marked 'a crucial turning point in Malaya's nation-building history'.[5] Throughout the Federation's existence, British Commonwealth forces fought the guerrilla (mainly Chinese) units of the Malayan National Liberation Army, the successor to the Malayan People's Anti-Japanese Army. The war, known as the Malayan Emergency (1948–60) by the British and as the Anti-British National Liberation War by their opponents, was bloody. Many of the World War II guerrilla strongholds served likewise for the Liberation Army and became the Emergency's principal battlegrounds.[6] When the Emergency formally ended in 1960, British/Malay forces had subdued the communists. Well before that, however, Malaya had gained independence.

Lee Kuan Yew foreshadowed subsequent Federation–Singapore friction by embroidering on an exchange between Abdul Razak (key in the mission to secure Malayan independence and later prime minister) and Sir John Martin, the chief British civil servant in charge of negotiations for Malayan independence. Razak asked when he arrived in London in January 1956 to negotiate: 'Are you going to make things difficult for us?' and Martin replied: 'No, we are going to give it [independence] to you on a golden platter.'[7] In August/September 1963, with the inauguration of Malaysia hanging in the balance, Lee upped the ante by sneering at Malaya's easy route to independence and

[3] Cheah, *Red star*, p. 296.

[4] MacMichael, *Report on a mission to Malaya*. On Colonial Office plans for the Malayan Union, see NA, CO273/675/7, 'Future policy in Malaya'. Possible British options for charting Malaya's post-war political configuration are discussed in NA, CO273/677/11, Sir Shenton Thomas, 'Memorandum on post-war Malaya', 29 February 1944.

[5] Cheah, *Red star*, p. xiii and see pp. xiii–xiv and 'Sino-Malay conflicts', pp. 108–11; Harper, *End*, pp. 49–51.

[6] Harper, *End*, pp. 49–50.

[7] The exchange is quoted in Shaw, *Tun Razak*, p. 106.

(woundingly) saying 'Indonesia had fought for independence whereas some countries, which he [Lee] did not name, had been handed freedom on a silver platter by British royalty.'[8] Nevertheless, the creation of Malaysia proceeded, and Singapore joined the Federation in 1963, along with the former British Borneo states of Sabah and Sarawak. Predominantly *Bumiputera* (indigenous or 'sons of the soil' peoples including Malays) populations in the two Borneo states offset Singapore's mostly Chinese demographic to preserve Malaysia as majority Malay. However, the union lasted only until 1965, when Singapore was expelled and set its own course as a city state.

After Singapore left Malaysia, the country consisted of peninsular Malaysia, where over four-fifths of Malaysians lived, and the two states of Sabah and Sarawak with about 8 per cent and 10 per cent of the population respectively. Peninsular Malaysia divided ethnically between Malays and other indigenous peoples, Chinese, Indians and a small number of Europeans and Eurasians. Malays, along with other indigenous groups, made up over half of peninsular Malaysians, Chinese about a third and Indians some 10 per cent.

Malaysia's traditional areas, the east coast and northern states, had disproportionately large Malay settlement; most Chinese and Indians lived in the tin and rubber belt along the west coast and especially in the cities and larger towns. Sabah and Sarawak were each approximately two-thirds *Bumiputera*, but Sarawak was a third Chinese and Sabah just over a fifth. The text and tables that follow refer to Malaysia unless peninsular Malaysia is indicated.

Economic Growth, 1957–87

Between 1960 and 1987, the Malaysian economy ranked among the world's foremost developing country success stories of growth and stability. During the 1960s, real per capita income in 2011 US$ grew at an annual rate of 3.1 per cent. The decade's close was punctuated in the most brutal of ways by the 13 May 1969 communal riots, which ultimately led to a 1971 New Economic Policy to give Malays a greater share in the economy. The policy probably reduced growth, in effect trading it in favour of equality among ethnic groups, but from 1970 to 1980 Malaysian real per capita income still increased at an annual rate of 5.8 per cent. Growth turned negative between 1984 and 1987 due to an attempt to develop capital-intensive import-substitution industry. Nevertheless, from 1960 to 1987, despite a doubling of population to 16 million, per capita income almost trebled (Table 13.1).

Throughout the period, growth was export-led. The Malaysian ratio of exports to GDP was historically extremely high, and from 1960 to 1987

[8] 'Threat to abandon the Malaysia project', *The Times*, London, 9 September 1963. I owe this and the preceding reference to Tony Stockwell.

Table 13.1 *Malaysia economic and social indicators, 1960–87*

	1960	1970	1980	1985	1987
GDP per capita constant 2011 US$	2,439	3,314	5,829	6,626	6,723
GDP per capita constant 2015 US$	1,235	1,748	3,026	3,437	3,456
GDP constant 2015 US$ bn	10.1	18.9	41.8	53.6	57.1
Population 000	8,156	10,804	13,798	15,599	16,522
Exports/GDP	53.1	45.6	57.5	54.9	62.9
Life expectancy: male	59	63	66	68	68
Life expectancy: female	61	66	70	72	72
Infant mortality (per 1,000 live births)	68	43	25	19	17
Primary school enrolment rates: male	91	–	–	–	–
Primary school enrolment rates: female	83	–	–	–	–
Literacy aged 15 and above %	–	–	70	–	83
Gini coefficient	0.42	0.50	0.51	0.48	0.47
Human development rank (of 130)	–	–	–	–	85

Notes and Sources: 1. Per capita GDP 2011 US$ are from the Maddison Project Database, 2020 and per capita GDP constant 2015 US$ from World Bank, *World development indicators, 2020*. In 1950, Malaysian GDP per capita in 2011 US$ was 2,485. Other data are from the World Bank unless indicated otherwise below. 2. The 1987 literacy rate is the figure for 1991. 3. Gini coefficients are for 1957–58, 1970, 1979 and 1984 and from Bruton, *Sri Lanka and Malaysia*, p. 215. 4. Human development data are for 1990. The Human Development Index is 0.80 out of a possible maximum of 1.0 and for 1990. The rank of 130 countries is in ascending order and places Malaysia as having high human development. In comparison to Malaysia's 85, Indonesia ranked 54, the Philippines 65, Thailand 78 and Singapore 96. United Nations, *Human Development Report, 1990*, p. 111.

increased further, rising from over 50 per cent in 1960 to more than 60 per cent by 1987. Export ratios were boosted by the discovery of additional primary commodity staples, notably petroleum, relatively high commodity prices and from the mid-1970s by substantial manufactured exports. Fundamental to swift Malaysian growth were moderate government policies, an outward-oriented economic stance, and – the events of 13 May 1969 notwithstanding – internal political and social stability.

Social gains accompanied growth, although these were far from evenly distributed, since the social and economic aspects of a dual economy, geographical dualism and plural society had not been eradicated. Overall, life expectancy increased appreciably to an average of 70 years and, more striking, infant mortality dropped sharply from 68 per 1,000 live births in 1968 to 17 by 1987. Death rates fell from 10.5 per 1,000 in 1960 to 5.1 per 1,000 by 1987 and over the same period birth rates from 42.7 to 29.2, and so to levels and a balance similar to developed countries. Among developing countries, primary school enrolment rates in 1960 were already high, so that by the later 1980s over four-fifths of the population aged 15 and over was literate. Inequality can increase quickly in a rapidly growing economy, but in Malaysia was not too marked. The Gini coefficient, 0.42 in 1960, reached 0.51 in 1980, but then fell back to 0.47 by 1987, suggesting weak support for the Kuznets hypothesis that income distribution worsens in the early stages of growth but then improves. According to the United Nations, at the close of the 1980s, Malaysia ranked – alone in Southeast Asia along with Singapore – as a country of high human development (Table 13.1).

The composition of exports changed fundamentally, both because of additional primary commodity staples and because of the development of a large export-oriented manufacturing industry. Although the long-term prospects for rubber and tin looked dim, demand for both commodities continued to rise moderately, and export revenue was maintained through increased rubber production. In 1960, rubber and tin accounted for 69 per cent of Malaysian exports. Between 1960 and 1987, while the value of primary exports rose sevenfold, the contribution of rubber and tin to total exports dropped to 11 per cent compared to 34 per cent for the other primary commodity staples. Manufactures contributed 45 per cent of the export total, the same as the primary commodity sector (Table 13.2).

A succession of resource-intensive exports, notably palm oil and petroleum, accords with the staples theory.[9] Additional primary commodity staples, along with continued contributions from rubber and tin, were crucial in supporting the transition to a new post-war economy. Primary commodity staples added importantly to exports, and provided a base of foreign exchange earnings as well as employing a large share of the labour force. For most of the years between 1957 and 1987, Malaysia had current account surpluses, and even when there were deficits these were not large. Able to tap a reliable inflow of foreign exchange and owing to moderate import-substitution policies, Malaysia avoided the balance-of-payments problems and stop-go policies that create a pressure to turn inwards typical of many newly independent developing countries.

Fundamental structural alteration accompanied the change in export composition. In 1960, the primary sector still comprised over two-fifths of GDP, but by 1987 contributed under a third. Over the same period, the manufacturing share rose from 8.7 per cent to 22.5 per cent of GDP. The gain in manufacturing was at the expense of services, agriculture and mining. In 1960, Malaysia was still unambiguously a little-developed economy with over three-fifths of

[9] Watkins, 'Staple theory'; Caves, '"Vent-for-surplus"' and 'Export-led growth'.

Table 13.2 *Malaysia export composition, 1960–87 (million ringgit)*

	1960	1965	1970	1975	1980	1987
Rubber						
Value	2,001	1,462	1,724	2,026	4,618	3,915
% of total exports	55	39	34	22	16	9
Tin						
Value	508	872	1,054	1,206	2,505	839
% of total exports	14	23	20	13	9	2
Palm oil						
Value	61	107	264	264	2,515	3,263
% of total exports	2	3	5	3	9	7
Sawn timber						
Value	75	–	206	–	1,178	1,770
% of total exports	2	–	4	–	4	4
Sawlogs						
Value	119	87	644	1,111	2,616	4,286
% of total exports	3	2	12	12	9	9
Petroleum						
Value	147	87	203	853	6,709	6,290
% of total exports	4	2	4	9	24	14
Manufactures						
Value	–	227	612	1,661	6,270	20,344
% of total exports	–	6	12	18	22	45
Other						
Value	722	941	456	2,110	1,761	4,428
% of total exports	20	25	9	23	6	10
Total	3,633	3,783	5,163	9,231	28,172	45,135

Notes: Data in Table 13.1 suggest that exports in 1980 were 30,676 million ringgit, not 28,172 million ringgit as shown in this table. There is no obvious explanation for the discrepancy since population data from Bruton and the World Bank are the same for 1980.
Sources: Bruton, *Sri Lanka and Malaysia*, p. 393; Jomo, *Growth*, pp. 54–55.

the labour force in the primary sector. By 1985, this had fallen to a third and manufacturing, which engaged just 6.4 per cent of workers in 1960, provided 15.3 per cent of employment. Between 1960 and 1985, the greatest disparity in the structures of GDP and employment was in services. Their contribution to GDP shrank markedly, but rose from a quarter of employed workers to

Table 13.3 *Malaysia GDP by sector, 1960–87*

(a) Million ringgit 1970 prices

	1960	1970	1980	1985	1987
Agriculture and mining	2,501	4,575	9,155	11,261	12,326
Manufacturing	497	1,650	5,572	7,084	8,526
Construction, utilities, transport, communications	457	1,285	3,274	4,891	4,518
Services	2,268	4,342	9,141	13,314	12,926
Import duties less imputed bank charges		456	743	467	−328
GDP	5,723	12,308	27,885	37,019	37,968

(b) %

	1960	1970	1980	1985	1987
Agriculture and mining	43.7	37.2	32.8	30.4	32.5
Manufacturing	8.7	13.4	20.0	19.1	22.5
Construction, utilities, transport, communications	8.0	10.4	11.7	13.2	11.9
Services	39.6	35.3	32.8	36.0	34.0
Import duties less imputed bank charges	0.0	3.7	2.7	1.3	−0.9
GDP	100.0	100.0	100.0	100.0	100.0

Source: Jomo, *Growth*, pp. 40–41.

two-fifths. An increase in hard or rest-of-the-economy-pulled services partly explains the rise but it was also because new jobs lagged labour force growth and people moved into 'soft' or labour-supply-pushed services. The rise in the unemployment rate from 6.0 per cent in 1960 to 7.6 per cent in 1985 as well as widespread underemployment throughout these years tell a story of abundant labour (Tables 13.3 and 13.4). Worryingly, and relevant for future Malaysian development, despite the expansion of manufacturing, it showed no evidence of increases in either labour or factor productivity.[10]

Bargain and Equity

Continuance of a plural society in an independent Malaya required, after the British departure, the re-establishment of a balance between ethnic groups which was acceptable to all, and on which the maintenance of any plural

[10] Bruton, *Sri Lanka and Malaysia*, pp. 221, 341.

Table 13.4 *Malaysia employment by sector, 1960–85*

(a) 000 persons

	1960	1970	1980	1985
Agriculture and mining	1,304	2,003	1,991	1,783
Manufacturing	136	448	755	836
Construction, utilities, transport, communications	155	365	511	663
Services	515	1,204	1,559	2,188
Total employed	2,110	4,020	4,816	5,470
Unemployment rate	6.0	7.8	5.7	7.6

(b) %

	1960	1970	1980	1985
Agriculture and mining	61.8	49.8	41.3	32.6
Manufacturing	6.4	11.1	15.7	15.3
Construction, utilities, transport, communications	7.3	9.1	10.6	12.1
Services	24.4	30.0	32.4	40.0
Total employed	100.0	100.0	100.0	100.0

Source: Jomo, *Growth*, p. 79.

society depends. Achievement of that equilibrium in Malaya entailed overcoming Malay misgivings about being overwhelmed by non-Malays, largely the Chinese who were over a third of the population and, along with Europeans, dominated the economy. The 'Bargain of 1957', much of it formally incorporated in the Malayan constitution, accommodated – though in the event only temporarily – the peaceful continuance of a plural society by recognizing the special position of the Malays as Malaya's indigenous (*Bumiputera*) people. The constitution specified Malay as the national language and Islam as the state religion. The institutions and symbols of the state were Malay or British. Considerable amounts of land were reserved for the exclusive use of the Malays – as Britain had done since the 1913 Malay Reservations Enactment – to allow a traditional mode of living which, still at the beginning of the 1980s, made Malaysia's major towns 'foreign ground to most rural Malays'.[11] In exchange, non-Malays were given automatic citizenship if born after Independence Day 1957, and otherwise had alternative accessible paths to citizenship. There was a guarantee of the private use of non-Malay languages and English as an official

[11] Bailey, *Sociology*, p. 11.

Table 13.5 *Malaysia population by historic economic function, state and ethnic group, 1957 (% of population)*

	% of population				
Tin and rubber belt					
Johore	48.0	42.4	7.7	1.9	927
Perak	39.7	44.2	14.9	1.2	1,221
Malacca	49.1	41.5	8.1	1.3	291
Negri Sembilan	41.5	41.2	15.1	2.2	365
Penang	28.8	57.2	12.2	1.8	572
Selangor	28.8	48.2	20.1	2.9	1,013
Traditional Malaya					
Kedah	67.7	20.5	9.7	2.1	702
Perlis	78.4	17.4	1.8	2.4	91
Kelantan	91.6	5.7	1.2	1.5	506
Terengganu	92.1	6.6	1.1	0.2	278
Pahang	57.2	34.6	7.0	1.2	313
Avg. Federation of Malaya	49.8	37.2	11.3	1.7	6,279

Source: Malaya, *Population census, 1957: Final report*, pp. 3–4.

language for 10 years. Crucially, while the bargain agreed the primacy of Malay political power, it tacitly recognized Chinese economic dominance as well as sizeable economic inequality.

Tables 13.5 and 13.6 divide peninsular Malaysia into the tin and rubber belt along the west coast encompassing Perak and extending southwards, and the traditional areas of Kelantan, Terengganu and Pahang on the east coast together with the extreme northwest states of Perlis and Kedah. In 1957, traditional Malaya was overwhelmingly inhabited by Malays, who reached population shares of over 90 per cent in Terengganu and Kelantan. Chinese and Indians predominated in tin and rubber areas and together outnumbered Malays living in these parts of Malaysia.

Poverty in Malaysia had strong ethnic and geographical dimensions. Both reflected Malaya's pre-World War II history and development as a dual economy: that Malay household incomes were far less than those of Chinese and Indians, and below the average for peninsular Malaya; and that household incomes in urban Malaysia, where Chinese disproportionately lived, far exceeded those of rural dwellers, and for the larger cities especially so. The poor concentrated in rural areas, lived principally outside the historic tin and rubber belt and were, by some margin, disproportionately Malays. The other

Table 13.6 *Malaysia income and poverty by historic economic function, state and ethnic group, 1970*

	Malay	Chinese	Indian	Others	All communities	Incidence of household poverty
	Mean monthly income ringgit					
(a) Historic economic function						
Tin and rubber belt						
Johore	33	55	51	210	44	29.0
Perak	32	62	41	299	47	43.0
Malacca	35	64	51	77	49	32.4
Negri Sembilan	33	80	59	854	53	33.0
Penang	37	59	59	341	54	
Selangor	57	89	73	369	78	22.9
Traditional Malaya						
Kedah	28	54	38	36	35	61.0
Perlis	26	40	16	10	26	59.8
Kelantan	25	86	88	24	28	67.1
Terengganu	29	95	59	294	32	60.3
Pahang	40	77	74	50	53	38.9
Avg. Peninsular Malaya	34	68	57	183	50	39.6
(b) Urban and rural						
Metropolitan cities	77	92	92	328	92	
Towns	50	70	56	122	62	
Rural areas	30	55	44	124	38	

Notes: 1. 'Others' are based on small samples and not necessarily representative. 2. Although the tin and rubber belt began in southern Kedah, the majority of it can be regarded as 'traditional' in the 1930s. 3. Metropolitan cities are defined as a population of 75,000 or more and towns as from 10,000 to 74,999. 4. The incidence of poverty is for 1976, for households and defined as households in poverty divided by the total number of households.
Sources: Anand, *Inequality and poverty*, pp. 94–95, 98; Bruton, *Sri Lanka and Malaysia*, p. 398.

group, much smaller than the Malays, with egregious poverty were Chinese whom the British had forcibly moved to 'new villages' constructed to counter communism during the Malayan Emergency. Chinese as a whole, however, were the wealthiest Asian group and some distance ahead of Indians.

In the 20 years after independence, the gap between Malay and Chinese household income in peninsular Malaysia widened. That was partly because between 1957 and 1970 cultivated land area increased at 2.0 per cent a year but population grew at 2.7 per cent, and because large numbers of Malays remained in rural areas. In 1970, the incidence of household poverty in traditional Malaysia was roughly twice that in the tin and rubber states. Similarly, the mean income of Malay households in traditional areas was about half that of Chinese resident in the tin and rubber belt, as well as significantly below Indian income. While Chinese household incomes were twice Malay in 1957, by 1976 the difference was two-and-a-half times. There was a strong correlation between poverty and the low-productivity occupations of being a paddy farmer, coconut grower, rubber smallholder or fisherman. Malays concentrated in these activities, which were the mainstays of employment in traditional areas.

By the standard of countries with similar per capita incomes, a move to cities in Malaysia was small, a retardation that the expansion in land availability may have encouraged.[12] Although between 1970 and 1984 poverty incidence in the traditional land-based Malay employments fell considerably, the decline was less than in urban areas where, by the mid-1980s, poverty had been almost eradicated (Table 13.7). Like income, land was unequally distributed in Malaysia. In 1970, corporations, principally foreign, owned 70 per cent of estate acreage. Insofar as Asians owned estates, Chinese estate ownership was twice Malay (Table 13.8).

Riot and Turning Point

No one knows how many people died as an outcome of four days of savage race riots that broke out in Kuala Lumpur on 13 May 1969, but fatalities totalled many more than the official figure of 196. Language rights had been a source of tension since Malayan independence, and during the 1969 General Election ethnic appeals were made by almost all opposition parties.[13] Tensions boiled over immediately after the election results severely reduced the parliamentary majority of the Alliance Party (later Barisan Nasional), a political coalition of the main and moderate Malay, Chinese and Indian parties. After an inflammatory Malay rally three days after the election at the residence of the Chief Minister of Selangor, Malays attacked Chinese in central Kuala Lumpur.[14]

12 Bruton, *Sri Lanka and Malaysia*, p. 239.

13 Snider, 'Race', pp. 1071–72.

14 Shaplen, 'Letter from Malaysia', pp. 114–16; Milne, '"National ideology" and nation building', p. 565; Tilman, 'Malaysia', pp. 906–07; Thomas, *My story*, pp. 28–30.

Table 13.7 *Malaysia poverty incidence by rural, urban and occupation, 1970–84 (% of households in poverty)*

(a) Rural and urban	1970	1976	1984
Rural	58.7	47.8	24.7
Urban	21.3	17.9	8.2
Total	49.3	39.6	18.4
(b) Rural poverty by occupation	**1970**	**1976**	**1984**
Rubber smallholders	64.7	58.2	43.4
Paddy farmers	88.1	80.3	57.7
Estate workers	40.0	–	19.7
Fishermen	73.2	62.7	27.7
Coconut smallholders	52.8	64.0	46.9
Other agriculture	89.0	52.1	34.2
Other industries	35.2	27.3	10.0
(c) Urban poverty by occupation	**1970**	**1976**	**1984**
Agriculture	–	40.2	23.8
Mining	33.3	10.1	3.4
Manufacturing	23.5	17.1	8.5
Construction	30.2	17.7	6.1
Transport and utilities	30.9	17.1	3.6
Trade and services	18.1	13.9	4.6
Other	–	22.4	17.1

Sources: Bruton, *Sri Lanka and Malaysia*, p. 399; Malaysia, *Fourth Malaysia plan, 1981–85*, p. 86.

Economic factors may not have been wholly responsible for the rioting, but were important. 'Whatever their proximate causes', the riots 'owed their origin to inadequate efforts to redress socio-economic imbalances.'[15] These included great income inequality, the frustration of Malays with their financial disadvantage, a perceived lack of Malay access to better jobs and the greater number of urban Malays, now able to feel directly the realities of ethnic imbalances. It was clear to all communities that the 'Bargain of 1957' was no longer acceptable; there had to be more equality effected through a new political contract.

15 Malaysia, *Third Malaysia plan*, p. 6.

Table 13.8 *Malaysia measures of wealth and land inequality, 1957–76*

(a) Ratios of Chinese to Malay incomes

	Per household	Per person
1957/58	2.16	1.74
1967/68	2.32	2.00
1970	2.25	1.84
1973/74	2.21	2.03
1976	2.49	–

(b) Ownership of estate acreage, 1970

	Corporations		Others		Total	
	000 acres	% of total	000 acres	% of total	000 acres	% of total
Malay	5.0	0.3	349.3	47.1	354.3	14.1
Chinese	457.0	25.9	243.3	32.8	700.3	27.9
Indian	4.9	0.3	74.8	10.1	79.7	3.2
Other Malaysians	48.1	2.7	13.2	1.8	61.3	2.4
Government	–	0.0	17.0	2.3	17.0	0.7
Foreign	1,249.6	70.8	44.0	5.9	1,293.6	51.6
Total	1,764.6	100.0	741.6	100.0	2,506.2	100.0

Source: Snodgrass, *Inequality*, pp. 82, 97.

The 1969 General Election was the 'culmination and termination' of the politics underlying the Federation of Malaya, a 'turning point for Malaysian political development'.[16] It followed from this that the 1971 New Economic Policy, formulated by the National Operations Council set up in response to the election results and their aftermath, marked a 'genuine new departure for Malayan development policy', another 'turning point' in post-independence Malaysian history.[17] The New Economic Policy (NEP) set an agenda that offered opportunities for the Malay elite but threatened the status of Chinese and Indians.

16 Rudner, 'Malaysian general election', pp. 17–20.

17 The first quote is from Snodgrass, *Inequality*, p. 60, the second from Bruton, *Sri Lanka and Malaysia*, p. 266.

Table 13.9 *Malaysia agricultural production, 1960–85*

	Agricultural production 1960 = 100	Rice production 000 metric tons	Rice kilograms per hectare	Rubber 000 metric tons	Palm oil 000 metric tons
1960	100	–	–	696	92
1965	124	1,058	2,567	852	149
1970	170	1,429	2,723	1,215	402
1975	227	1,718	2,937	1,417	1,135
1980	270	2,129	2,698	1,600	2,575
1985	316	1,953	2,977	1,469	4,130

Source: Bruton, *Sri Lanka and Malaysia*, p. 395.

Agriculture

Expansion onto new land, technical change and the replacement of rubber with oil palm combined to account for the strong role that agriculture played in Malaysian growth. Between 1960 and 1973, agricultural production doubled and in 1985 was over three times as much as after independence (Table 13.9). Reflecting continuous productivity increase, by 1985 the agricultural ratio of employment (32 per cent of the labour force) to output (30 per cent of GDP) was 1.1 compared to 0.8 (15 per cent of employment and 19 per cent of GDP) for manufacturing (Tables 13.3 and 13.4). Agriculture's contribution to GDP increased fivefold from 1960 to 1987. At the end of this period, the agricultural sector still accounted for a third of national income, despite growing more slowly than manufacturing and declining relatively as a share of national income (Table 13.3).

Although rubber was a lagging sector, between 1960 and 1985 rubber output more than doubled. Because the productive life of a rubber tree is 25 to 30 years, by the 1950s extensive re-planting was needed to prevent rubber exports from declining. Technical change, effected especially through the innovative work of the Rubber Research Institute, raised productivity, notably on estates, through the use of high-yielding varieties of seeds and clones. Improved methods of tapping, collecting latex and grading and packaging as technically specified rubber in block form, again due substantially to the Rubber Research Institute, also increased yields, reduced contamination and kept natural rubber competitive with synthetic rubber. By 1965, Malaysia's was the world's most efficient natural rubber industry.[18]

[18] Malaysia, *First Malaysia plan*, p. 43.

Table 13.10 *Peninsular Malaysia estate and smallholder rubber planted area and yields, 1950–73 (lbs per acre)*

	Estates yield per planted area	Smallholdings yield per planted area	Smallholdings % of estates yield
1950–1954	389	365	93.8
1955–1959	420	359	85.5
1960–1964	516	305	59.1
1965–1969	689	379	55.0
1970–1973	972	543	55.9

Source: Snodgrass, *Inequality*, p. 176.

Over 90 per cent of estate rubber land had been re-planted with high-yielding trees by 1971, but just 63 per cent of smallholdings.[19] Although smallholder planting was encouraged, as encapsulated in the official slogan 'Replant or Die', it was hindered by the loss of income for those with only a few acres of land until new trees matured, as well as by tenancy, sharecropping arrangements and poor access to credit. In the mid-1960s, for many smallholders, government re-planting grants were insufficient to overcome these barriers to replacing older trees.[20] Between 1960 and 1973, smallholder yields were slightly more than half of estate mainly because trees were often near the end of their useful life and an average smallholding size of just 3.3 acres allowed less efficient smallholder than estate collection methods (Table 13.10). Over a similar period, value added per smallholder was about a third of that on estates.[21]

Palm oil gave Malaysia a new, swiftly growing export. The advantages of oil palm compared to rubber of higher returns per acre, a maturation period of three years, not seven, lower labour requirements and a buoyant market encouraged palm oil production. Estates switched from rubber to oil palm and its acreage further increased through the opening of new land. The incorporation of high-yielding seeds and clones in new plantings maximized production.

The two main aspects of government-directed rural development were land expansion and a paddy programme. The aim of both programmes was to alleviate Malay poverty through making land available to the poor, chosen on a points system, and establishing more productive, better organized farms. Both initiatives anticipated, especially until the 1970s, that Malays would remain

19 Malaysia, *Second Malaysia plan*, pp. 12–13.

20 Malaysia, *First Malaysia plan*, p. 99; Fisk, 'Productivity and income', pp. 19–22; Ho, 'Land settlement projects', p. 4.

21 Bruton, *Sri Lanka and Malaysia*, p. 239.

on the land. The Federal Land Development Authority (FELDA), operational in 1956, was the most important, and most successful, of several federal and state authorities established to increase cultivated land.[22] Under FELDA, contractors, nearly all Chinese, cleared land for settlers, virtually all Malays, for allocation in small plots to grow rubber or oil palm. By 1971, FELDA schemes had spread throughout peninsular Malaya but concentrated in its middle and south and largely excluded Kelantan, Terengganu and Perak. During the 1960s, FELDA developed some 300,000 acres of land and between 1971 and 1980 a further 923,000 acres (Figures 13.1 and 13.2).[23] Despite this opening and improvement of substantial amounts of land, FELDA and other programmes benefited a relatively small number of families.[24] Two-thirds of rubber smallholdings were Malay-owned, and poverty among them, although falling considerably during the 1970s, remained high (Table 13.7).

Peninsular Malaya's lack of large, flat, naturally watered areas made paddy growing difficult and, despite arguments dating back decades for Malayan food self-sufficiency, rice was never, in comparison to world prices, grown economically. Help for paddy farmers concentrated on investing heavily in drainage and irrigation and the maintenance of a guaranteed minimum price for rice above world prices. During the 1970s, some half a million acres of paddy land were provided with improved irrigation, most of which made possible double cropping. Yields increased by 50 to 90 per cent in areas with major irrigation projects, but for the peninsula as a whole rice yields changed little between 1960 and 1985 (Table 13.9).

Although by 1975 Malaysian rice output reached some 90 per cent of domestic consumption, that level of production depended on a system of subsidies, tariffs and taxes. The government required rice importers to purchase, at a guaranteed minimum price, an amount of domestic rice equal to their imports. Importers could recover the loss on expensive (and poor quality) domestic rice by selling imported rice at the same high guaranteed minimum price, in effect a tariff on rice and so a subsidy to producers and tax on consumers.[25] The poverty incidence of paddy farmers, near universal in 1970, fell to three-quarters in 1976 and, despite irrigation schemes and guaranteed prices, was still well over half in the mid-1980s (Table 13.7). The main explanations for poverty were the fragmentation of paddy holdings, lack of double cropping and tenancy problems.

[22] For detailed descriptions and evaluations of FELDA programs, see Ho, 'Land settlement projects', pp. 1–15; Wikkramatileke, 'State aided rural land colonization', pp. 377–403 and 'Federal land development', pp. 62–86.

[23] Malaysia, *Third Malaysia plan*, p. 270; Snodgrass, *Inequality*, pp. 177–78.

[24] Bruton, *Sri Lanka and Malaysia*, p. 278.

[25] Brown, 'Rice price stabilization', pp. 171–72.

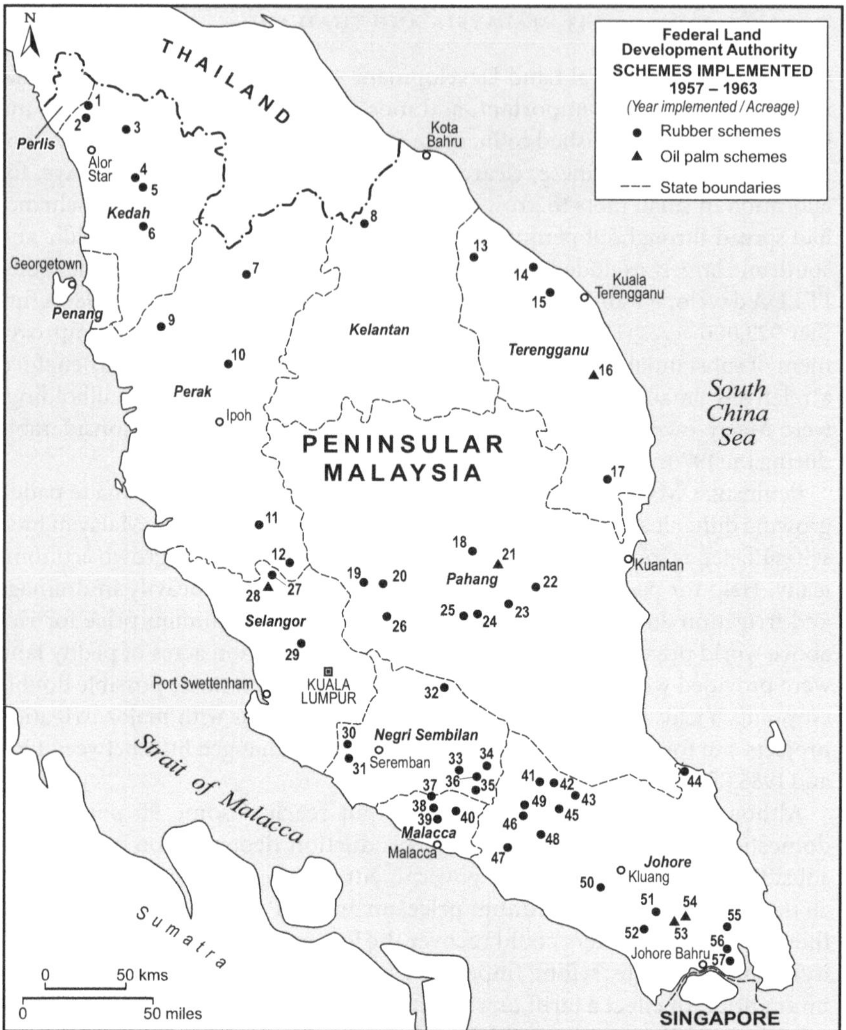

SCHEMES IMPLEMENTED 1957 – 1963
(Year implemented / Acreage)

1. Batu Lapan *1958/1,118*
2. Guar Napai *1959/1,914*
3. Bukit Tembaga *1959/1,988*
4. Sungei Tiang *1959/4,800*
5. Lubok Merbau *1963/3,698*
6. Teloi Kanan *1962/1896*
7. Bersia *961/3,526*
8. Ayer Lanas *1957/4,200*
9. Ijok *1960/5,159*
10. Lasah *1962/4,076*
11. Sungei Klah *1961/5,580*
12. Sungei Behrang *1963/3,750*
13. Tenang Besut *1962/2,587*
14. Chalok *1958/5,000*
15. Belara *1962/2,331*
16. Jerangau *1962/8,734*
17. Sebrong Tayor *1962/2,211*
18. Sungei Tekam *1961/3,938*
19. Bilut Valley *1959/5,111*
20. Klau Valley *1962/6,006*
21. Ulu Jempol *1962/7,000*
22. Kampong New Zealand *1960/2,636*
23. Bukit Tajau *1963/3,914*
24. Kampong Awah *1960/4,062*
25. Sungei Nerek *1963/4,171*
26. Sungei Sertik *1963/4,169*
27. Gedangsa *1960/7,055*
28. Sungei Dusun *1962/7,989*
29. Sungei Bliaya *1961/3,987*
30. K.L.B.J *1960/5,535*
31. Sendayan *1960/5,672*
32. Sungei Lui *1961/1,773*
33. Bukit Rokan *1961/6,391*
34. Pasir Besar *1962/5,987*
35. Bukit Jalor *1963/5,441*
36. Sungei Kemelah *1963/5,067*
37. Hutan Percha *1960/3,200*
38. Kampong Menggong *1952/1,086*
39. Machap *1959/1,336*
40. Kemendore *1958/4,237*
41. Medoi *1961/2,770*
42. Kemelah *1961/3,545*
43. Tenang *1960/3,548*
44. Endau *1959/2,394*
45. Chemplak *1962/4,075*
46. Bukit Serampang *1960/3,768*
47. Parit Haji Idris *1960/253*
48. Lenga *1961/2,510*
49. Bukit Serampang Utura *1963/2,986*
50. Ayer Hitam *1960/3,195*
51. Teck Wah Heng *1961/2,683*
52. Bukit Batu *1962/2,988*
53. Kulai *1960/7,960*
54. Pasir Raja *1962/4,377*
55. Pasak *1962/3,344*
56. Sungei Tiram *1960/577*
57. Kong Kong *1960/3,740*

Figure 13.1 Malaysia Federal Land Development Authority schemes, 1957–63
Source: Wikkramatileke, 'Federal land development', p. 64.

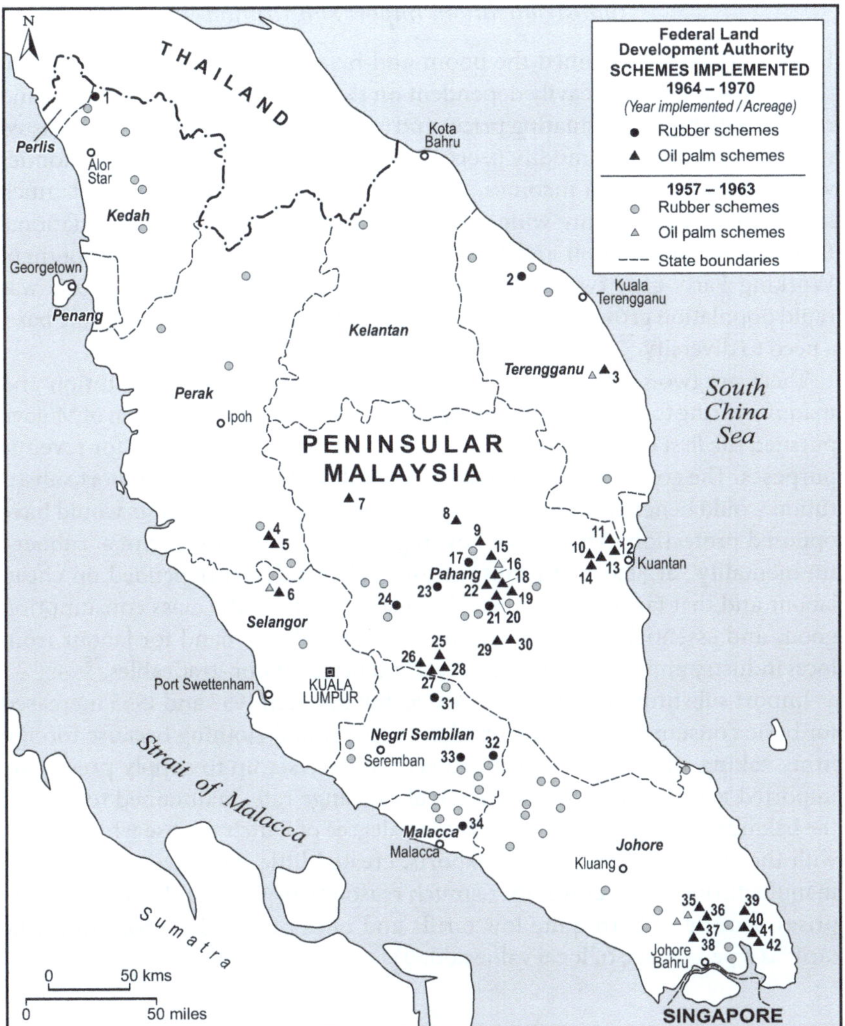

SCHEMES IMPLEMENTED 1964 – 1970
(Year implemented / Acreage)

1. Laka Tamin *1970/???*			32. Palong *1970/???*
2. Chalok Barat *1970/6,400*	12. Bukit Goh *1967/8,754*	22. Jengka III *1967/5,138*	33. Bukit Rokan Utura *1970/???*
3. Bukit Bading *1964/6,300*	13. Sungei Panching Timor *1969/2,740*	23. Jenderak *1970/???*	34. Bukit Senggeh *1970/???*
4. Trolak Utura *1968/4,900*	14. Sungei Panching Selatan *1967/3,500*	24. Sungei Semantan Utura *1970/???*	35. Sungei Sayong *1965/5,310*
5. Trolak Selatan *1968/3,390*	15. Jengka I *1966/6,186*	25. Bukit Puchong *1967/5,333*	36. Bukit Besar *1964/4,970*
6. Sungei Tengi *1967/7,000*	16. Jengka II *1966/5,177*	26. Chemonoi *1968/6,435*	37. Bukit Ramun *1965/4,050*
7. Sungei Koyan *1968/5,567*	17. Jengka VIII *1970/4,510*	27. Sungei Kemahal *1967/6,200*	38. Utura Tebrau *1964/7,100*
8. Padang Piol *1967/8,664*	18. Jengka IV *1967/4,475*	28. Bukit Mendi *1967/6,740*	39. Bukit Apino *1970/???*
9. Sungei Tekam Utura *1967/5,314*	19. Jengka V *1968/4,589*	29. Kepayang *1968/5,610*	40. Ayer Tawar III *1970/???*
10. Sungei Panching Utura *1967/3,500*	20. Jengka VI *1968/4,354*	30. Mayan *1970/???*	41. Ayer Tawar II *1969/7,256*
11. Bukit Kuantan *1969/4,900*	21. Jengka VII *1970/4,147*	31. Pasoh *1970/???*	42. Ayer Tawar I *1968/5,629*

Figure 13.2 Malaysia Federal Land Development Authority schemes, 1964–70
Source: Wikkramatileke, 'Federal land development', p. 65.

Industrialization: Import Substitution

In 1957, Malaya's remained the boom-and-bust economy that it had been in the inter-war period, heavily dependent on two primary commodities, tin and rubber, with highly fluctuating prices and uncertain futures. Industry consisted mostly of primary commodity processing and, in contrast to many economies with similar per capita incomes, manufacturing productivity was not much higher than the economy-wide average.[26] Major reports by the International Bank for Reconstruction and Development and the Industrial Development Working Party gave two reasons that Malaya should industrialize. One was rapid population growth; the other, in light of Malaya's narrow economic base, a need to diversify.[27]

There are two routes to industrial diversification: import substitution and manufacturing for export. After independence in 1957, the Federation of Malaya pursued the first of these paths, but tariffs were modest and chiefly for revenue purposes. The government, dominated by Malays, believed that import substitution would benefit the Chinese and, furthermore, estate interests would have opposed protection. An estate lobby, regarded as representative of a 'rubber–tin mentality', argued that profits in the rubber industry depended on cheap labour and that tariffs would raise the cost of wage goods (mass consumption goods and essential goods) as well as increasing the demand for labour from local industry and so bid up wage levels and prices of non-tradeables.[28]

Import substitution was not extensive, but between 1957 and 1965 increased for basic consumer goods like textiles, footwear and clothing because foreign firms, taking advantage of tariff protection, were set up to supply previously imported goods. An uncompetitive real exchange rate, maintained to protect the balance of payments, gave Malaysia a degree of Dutch disease which, along with the strength of traditional exports, created little incentive to move into manufacturing. Neither was there much reason to begin manufacturing enterprises because of both quite low tariffs and rates of effective protection (the tariff as a percentage of local value added).[29]

New Economic Policy

The Second Malaysia Plan (1971–75) set out the NEP to correct economic imbalance, emphasize national unity, eventually eradicate poverty and eliminate the

[26] Bruton, *Sri Lanka and Malaysia*, p. 191.

[27] International Bank for Reconstruction and Development, *Economic development*; Singapore, 'An industrial development programme'.

[28] Wheelwright, *Industrialization*, p. 97 and 'Reflections', pp. 71–72; Power, 'Structure of protection', pp. 207–09.

[29] Malaysia, *Second Malaysia plan*, pp. 147–49; Bruton, *Sri Lanka and Malaysia*, pp. 337–41; Power, 'Structure of protection', pp. 210–17; Rabenau, 'Trade policies', pp. 27–35.

association between ethnic group and economic function. The actual strategy was growth with redistributive equity, but the goals were ambitious. Within 20 years, Malays and other indigenous peoples 'will manage and own at least 30 per cent of the total commercial and industrial activities in all categories and scales of operation'.[30]

Malays, given the history of Malaysia and level of inequality, could never have reached these goals in two decades through private Malay enterprise.[31] During the 1970s, assistance to Malay entrepreneurs under the NEP did not generally result in viable enterprises, due to a lack of managerial and financial skills, poor project selection and, possibly, too much protection. Malaysia repeated the Burmese and Indonesian experiences of 'Ali-Baba' enterprises in which a Malay frontman contributed his name, a government licence and influence, but a Chinese (the Baba) ran the business.[32] To achieve the NEP goals, the state became 'bureaucratic entrepreneurs'.[33] It established state-owned and controlled enterprises and financial institutions as well as purchasing, or partly expropriating, these from Chinese and foreign firms. The state businesses would be held in trust for Malays until they were in a position to acquire equity in these companies from their own savings.[34]

Between 1971/75 and 1981/85, public sector investment as a share of GDP more than doubled to 17.6 per cent, but dropped during the later 1980s as the state divested itself of ownership in favour of private Malay ownership (Table 13.11). By 1988, the share of *Bumiputera* capital may have reached around the 30 per cent target.[35] State ownership, special privileges for a relatively small group of Malays and a convergence of business and political power created, by the late 1970s and into the 1980s, a strong group of *Bumiputera* rent-seekers (Chapter 15). These individuals, having grown rich and powerful from NEP policies, became important defenders of them.[36]

Industrialization: Exporting Manufactures

The export of manufactures affords the second industrialization option. In 1968, after passing the Investment Incentive Act, Malaysia, influenced by Singapore's success, moved decisively to add export orientation to import substitution as a means of industrialization. The Act offered tax holidays to pioneer enterprises and investment credits to non-pioneer firms and aimed

30 Malaysia, *Second Malaysia plan*, pp. 41–42 and see p. 1.
31 Golay, 'Malaya', p. 369.
32 Bruton, *Sri Lanka and Malaysia*, pp. 294–95.
33 Milne, 'Politics', p. 249.
34 Malaysia, *Fourth Malaysia plan*, p. 53; Malaysia, *Mid-term review of the second Malaysia plan*, pp. 14, 84–85.
35 Jomo, *Growth*, pp. 157–60.
36 Bruton, *Sri Lanka and Malaysia*, pp. 298, 351; Jomo, *Growth*, pp. 154–56.

Table 13.11 *Malaysia consumption and investment and savings, 1956/60–1986/88 (% GDP)*

	1956/60	1961/65	1966/70	1971/75	1976/80	1981/85	1986/88
Consumption: total	*79.2*	*82.4*	*79.9*	*77.3*	*69.9*	*72.8*	*77.0*
Consumption: private	64.5	66.8	63.0	59.9	53.3	55.1	49.0
Consumption: public	14.7	15.6	16.9	17.4	16.6	17.7	28.0
Investment: total	*12.6*	*16.8*	*17.0*	*25.7*	*27.2*	*35.7*	*25.8*
Investment: private	9.9	9.5	11.0	17.8	17.3	18.1	15.0
Investment: public	2.7	7.3	6.0	7.9	9.9	17.6	10.8
Gross national savings	*16.6*	*15.3*	*18.0*	*22.0*	*29.8*	*27.1*	*31.5*

Note: Data are for GNP by expenditure category.
Source: Jomo, *Growth*, p. 47.

to attract foreign investors. Malaysia welcomed foreign investment to create employment and boost exports. An additional attraction was that because Malays had not assumed a role in modern industry, foreign enterprise counterbalanced Chinese business and limited its opportunities for industrial investment.[37]

Table 13.3 reflects the impact of Malaysia's establishment of an export-oriented manufacturing sector. In 1960, agriculture and mining accounted for five times as much GDP as manufacturing (shares of 43.7 per cent and 8.7 per cent respectively) but by 1980, this gap had narrowed considerably. A high proportion of manufactured exports depended on foreign investment and originated from the 12 export processing zones established from 1971 onwards as part of the Investment Incentive Act. The zones were, however, an enclave, an appendage and not indigenous, because they had few linkages to the rest of the economy. Net exports were a third of gross exports.[38] Exports from the zones, which consisted chiefly of electronics and textiles, were created almost entirely through labour. The main benefit of the zones was employment. Low inflation contributed to downwards pressure on wages which, along with good infrastructure, a stable economy and welcoming government, made Malaysia an attractive location for the manufacture of labour-intensive goods.[39]

[37] Bruton, *Sri Lanka and Malaysia*, pp. 255–59.
[38] Jomo, *Growth*, p. 66.
[39] Bruton, *Sri Lanka and Malaysia*, pp. 263, 297, 313–14, 366.

'Look East' and Heavy Industry

At the end of the 1970s, Malaysia did not have the heavy industry often regarded as a proof of development, and its GDP per capita had fallen further behind Japan's. Mahathir Mohamad, since his late 1970s tenure as Minister of Trade and Industry, had favoured heavy industrialization and a Japanese developmental state model. In 1981, as prime minister, he implemented these ideas, urging Malaysia to look 'Look East'.

An attempt was made to copy Japan, including the Japanese work ethic. The Heavy Industries Corporation of Malaysia was established to oversee a drive for growth and deepen industrialization. Initiatives included iron and steel mills and the manufacture of the Proton car. However, most of these industries were inefficient at world prices, and required a shift towards infant industry protection and subsidies that was costly. The policy to 'Look East', together with a sharp deterioration in the terms of trade for primary commodities, soon created sizeable balance-of-payments deficits. From 1985 to 1987, GDP per capita (in 2011 US$) fell slightly below its 1984 level, a growth disruption that caused much of the programme to be abandoned. Beginning in 1987, Malaysia, though still drawing on natural resource exports, but saddled with an inefficient state sector, even more fully embraced an export-oriented, labour-intensive, foreign-investment-dependent model. The economy started to grow at impressive rates, although still relying mainly on greater factor inputs of capital and labour and not an increase in their productivity.

Plural Society

Two possible alternatives to the plural society are to force minorities from the country, as happened in Burma, Indonesia and Vietnam, or, as suggested by Geertz, an 'integrative revolution'. In this, over time and with economic growth, people assume new roles which become more important to them than communal identification.[40] Society moves away from a horizontal or parallel structure of classes, for which the defining characteristic is race or ethnic group, and to a vertical class structure in which all groups occupy all class levels.

A third possibility, adopted in Malaysia at independence, was to bargain over ethnic equity and design a political system that reached a balance sufficiently acceptable to all ethnic groups to maintain a social equilibrium.[41] Malaysia tried to achieve this balance, since it was apparent to everyone that ethnic, cultural and lifestyle attitudes were so different that integration was not possible. The 'Bargain of 1957' was one attempt to satisfy the demands of an equity, agreed

[40] Geertz, 'Integrative revolution', pp. 105–57.

[41] Bruton, *Sri Lanka and Malaysia*, pp. 351–54 illuminatingly discusses Malaysia's plural society.

among the ethnic groups as 'fair', which was necessary to contain, in Geertzian terminology, primordial loyalties and to promote a stable plural society.[42]

The NEP, although inherently discriminatory in giving Malays the balance of political power, was a further attempt. However, since the Policy's 1971 implementation, discrimination against Malaysian Chinese and Indians socially, educationally and economically reached such an extent that many had voted with their feet, and many of those who remained were resentful. Special rights and privileges based on ethnicity threaten the social stability of pluralism, because they undermine a plural society, as defined by Furnivall, in which different groups, although not mixing, live in amity (Chapters 15 and 18).[43]

Thailand

Like Malaysia, Thailand was well off by Southeast Asian standards, and for some time after World War II grew mainly through vent-for-surplus exports. Pre-war Thailand was much less industrialized than Malaysia but, like it, remained much the same structurally in the late 1950s as it had been in 1940. Although the Kingdom successfully diversified its economy by extending production to new crops and away from a near total dependence on rice and, to a lesser extent, tin and rubber, industrialization was even more imperative than for Malaysia, since relatively little technological improvement in agriculture made land especially pressing as a medium-term growth constraint. By the mid-1980s, after a limited import-substitution phase, Thailand, as Malaysia, looked to increasing manufactured exports to provide employment for a population that had grown quite rapidly during the 1950s and early 1960s.

During the post-World War II decades, despite a history of military coups, government in Thailand remained surprisingly stable, and the economy benefited. Stability was explained partly by a deferential Thai respect for authority and the king, partly by rapid growth and perhaps partly because an overwhelmingly large and scattered rural population told against organized protest. This section considers the evolution of the Thai economy between 1950 and the late 1980s, by which time an expansion of manufactured exports was driving unprecedentedly swift growth.

Economic Growth

By 1951, GDP again exceeded its 1938 level, and from 1951 to 1960 increased in 2011 US$ at an annual rate of 2.7 per cent. Thailand's economy recovered rapidly from the aftermath of World War II because its rice economy, unlike

[42] Geertz, 'Integrative revolution', p. 135.

[43] Bruton, *Sri Lanka and Malaysia* makes this last point and see his illuminating discussion of Malaysia's plural society, pp. 351–56.

Burma's and Indochina's, quickly returned to pre-war production levels, enabling Thailand to benefit from an international rice shortage, the Korean war boom and high rice prices until the mid-1950s. Between 1947 and 1960, however, population growth, at 3.5 per cent annually, was among the highest in the world and much faster than historically. Population increase was due to a renewed confidence among Thai after a wartime decline in birth rates, improved health services, including programmes to combat malaria as well as smallpox and cholera, and a continued normalization of the sex ratio among the Chinese immigrant population. From 1951 to 1960, population increase limited GDP per capita growth to just 2.2 per cent a year according to Ingram's 1962 base-weighted index and 2.7 per cent using the deflated 2011 US$ of Maddison (Table 13.12 and 13.13).[44]

Until 1979, agriculture was the leading sector in post-war growth, giving way to manufacturing only in the 1980s. Even then, most Thai had farming as their principal occupation. In the 1950s, rice accounted for around half of exports and a further fifth came from rubber (Table 13.14). During the 1960s and 1970s, although Thailand remained largely a rice economy, agriculture's leading-sector status increasingly depended on a diversification of crops.

By the mid-1960s, as population growth slowed, it was easily outstripped by continued swift GDP expansion. Between 1960 and 1990, while population grew at an annual rate of 2.4 per cent a year, from 1960 to 1980 GDP per capita grew by 4.4 per cent a year, and between 1980 and 1990 by 6.1 per cent annually – a secular boom that stands in sharp contrast to Thailand's near stagnant per capita income from the 1890s until World War II.

Infrastructure Development

From 1950 and into the 1970s, heavy investment in infrastructure of roads, ports, electric power, telecommunications and irrigation projects contributed significantly to higher GDP and, more important, created a foundation for continued growth. Between 1951 and 1970, transport and communication's share of GDP more than doubled to 6.5 per cent of national income and construction nearly doubled to reach 5.3 per cent of national income (Table 13.15). Both sectors were buoyed by road and irrigation projects and, furthermore, by infrastructure formation associated with urbanization, mainly in Bangkok where the population grew from 1.4 million in 1950 to 3.1 million by 1970 and 4.0 million a decade later.

To finance infrastructure, Thailand relied substantially on United States aid programmes which, at that time, were motivated by a fear of regional communism and the ongoing conflict in Indochina. America essentially became the economic ally that during World War II Prime Minister Phibun had hoped

[44] Ingram, *Economic change*, p. 222.

Table 13.12 *Thailand economic and social indicators, 1951–90*

	1951	1960	1970	1980	1985	1987	1990
GDP per capita 1962 prices baht	1,743	2,121	3,239	–	–	–	–
GDP per capita 2011 prices US$	1,353	1,718	2,700	4,071	4,862	5,453	7,385
GDP per capita constant 2015 US$	–	581	945	1,428	1,695	1,890	2,547
GDP constant 2015 US$ bn	–	15.1	34.9	67.7	88.2	101.9	144.0
Population 000	21,669	27,397	36,885	47,374	52,027	53,946	56,558
Exports/GDP	14.8	11.7	14.1	18.1	20.5	24.9	30.9
Life expectancy: male	–	52	57	62	65	66	67
Life expectancy: female	–	57	62	67	71	72	73
Infant mortality (per 1,000 live births)	–	101	71	47	38	35	30
Primary school enrolment rates %: male	–	–	79	–	–	–	–
Primary school enrolment rates %: female	–	–	72	–	–	–	–
Literacy aged 15 and above %	–	71	–	84	–	–	–
Gini coefficient	–	0.47	–	0.66	–	–	–
Human development rank (of 130)	–	–	–	–	–	–	78

Notes and Sources: 1. GDP per capita 1962 prices baht is from Ingram, *Economic change*, p. 222; GDP per capita 2011 US$ from the Maddison Project Database, 2020; and GDP per capita constant 2015 US$ from World Bank, *World development indicators, 2020*. 2. For 1951, data for exports/GDP are for 1952 and from Ingram, *Economic change*, p. 335 and IBRD, *Public development program*, p. 263. 3. The 1947 census recorded population as 17,443, indicating a 1947 to 1960 annual population growth rate of 3.5 per cent. 4. The 1960 literacy rate is from Ingram, *Economic change*, p. 278. The 1980 literacy rate is the figure for that year. 5. Thailand, *Statistical Yearbook, 1954/55* gives the 1952 infant mortality rate as 63. 6. Gini coefficients are for 1962/63 and 1981 using income unit household per capita income, weighted by family size and from Warr, *Thai economy*, p. 415. World Bank figures beginning in 1981 are estimates and appreciably lower. 7. Primary school enrolment rates are for 1972. 8. Human development data are for 1990. The index ranks 130 countries in ascending order and placed Thailand as somewhat below high human development. In comparison to Thailand's 78, Malaysia ranked 85, Indonesia 54, the Philippines 65 and Singapore 96. United Nations, *Human Development Report, 1990*, p. 111.

Table 13.13 *Thailand and world rice exports, 1934/38–1952 (000 metric tons of milled rice)*

	Thailand	Burma	Indochina	World	Thailand % of world exports
1934/38	1,388	3,070	1,320	9,650	14.4
1950	1,508	1,198	115	4,250	35.5
1952	1,413	1,261	230	5,000	28.3

Source: Yang, *Multiple exchange rate system*, p. 161.

Table 13.14 *Thailand main commodity exports, 1938/39–1991*

(a) Four main commodity exports

	Total merchandise exports current prices	Four exports as a % of total exports				Total % share four exports
	million baht	Rice	Tin	Rubber	Teak	
1938/39	204	48.6	15.4	12.6	3.3	79.9
1950	3,473	48.1	7.4	20.9	4.1	80.6
1952	4,619	56.9	4.8	21.8	2.1	85.7
1955	7,120	44.0	6.2	25.3	3.7	79.2
1958	6,447	46.0	4.0	20.6	3.7	74.3
1960	6,942	29.8	6.2	29.9	4.1	70.1
1963	9,676	35.4	7.7	19.7	1.4	64.1
1967	14,166	32.8	12.9	11.1	1.4	58.2
1969	14,722	20.0	11.3	18.1	1.1	50.5

(b) Share of paddy and rubber in agricultural crop contribution to GDP

	Paddy % GDP	Rubber % GDP	GDP m baht 1988 prices
1961/66	53.6	4.5	276,868
1967/71	48.0	5.1	444,506
1972/76	41.8	5.6	602,876
1977/81	37.1	5.9	868,077
1982/86	35.8	6.5	1,136,544
1987/91	31.1	9.8	1,748,767

Note: Percentages of paddy and rubber are for GDP at 1972 prices.
Sources: Yang, *Multiple exchange rate system*, pp. 154, 156; Ingram, *Economic change*, p. 312; Dixon, *Thai economy*, p. 149; Thailand, National Statistical Office, *National income of Thailand*, 1996.

Table 13.15 *Thailand percentage of GDP by economic sector, 1951–88*

	1951	1955	1960	1970	1980	1985	1988
Agriculture	50.1	42.0	39.8	27.0	20.6	19.9	16.9
Mining and quarrying	1.9	1.6	1.1	2.9	2.6	2.5	2.4
Manufacturing	10.3	11.8	12.6	16.0	21.7	20.7	23.0
Construction	2.9	4.0	4.6	5.3	4.5	4.2	4.0
Electricity and water	0.1	0.2	0.4	1.0	2.0	2.5	2.8
Transport and communication	3.1	5.1	7.5	6.5	6.7	7.2	7.4
Wholesale and retail trade	18.0	19.6	15.2	17.4	16.9	16.3	17.0
Banking, insurance and real estate	0.4	1.4	1.9	2.5	2.8	3.0	3.6
Ownership of dwellings	3.7	3.0	2.8	5.6	4.8	4.4	4.1
Public administration and defence	2.8	4.8	4.6	4.4	5.2	5.4	4.8
Services	6.7	6.5	9.6	11.5	12.2	13.9	14.0
Total	100.0	100.0	100.0	100.0	100.0	100.0	100.0

Sources: 1951–60: Ingram, *Economic change*, p. 234; 1970–88: Tambunlertchai, 'Manufacturing', p. 179.

Japan could be. A number of projects drew on finance from the International Bank for Reconstruction and Development (World Bank). These included railway rehabilitation, development of the Port of Bangkok and the Chao Phraya River dam at Chainat some 120 miles north of Bangkok (Figure 13.3). Traditionally, the irrigation of rice was by diversion channels but by the mid-1950s the limits of this had been reached. Through regulating the flow of water and its storage in the dry season, the Chao Phraya project distributed water to an area of 4,500 square miles, opening a large area of land for cultivation.[45]

Roads were the single most important infrastructural development. Before World War II, Thailand had few roads, and beyond central Bangkok few motor vehicles. Beyond Bangkok, road transport relied chiefly on bullock caravans.[46] By 1945, existing roads had fallen into such disrepair that for the next three years road rehabilitation and improvement took all the efforts of the Highways Department.[47] In 1949, there were just 760 kilometres of paved national highways, but this rose, partly through the paving of gravel and laterite roads, to over 5,000 kilometres by 1965 and 7,822 kilometres in 1969. Table 13.16 and Figure 13.3 show the still fragmentary road network in 1955, and how roads

[45] Ungphakorn, 'Thailand', pp. 155, 162; Riggs, *Thailand*, p. 353.

[46] Dobby, *Southeast Asia*, p. 285; Ouyyanont, 'Bangkok', p. 101; Stamp, 'Siam', p. 218.

[47] Kingdom of Thailand, *Report of the financial adviser 1941–1950*, p. 46.

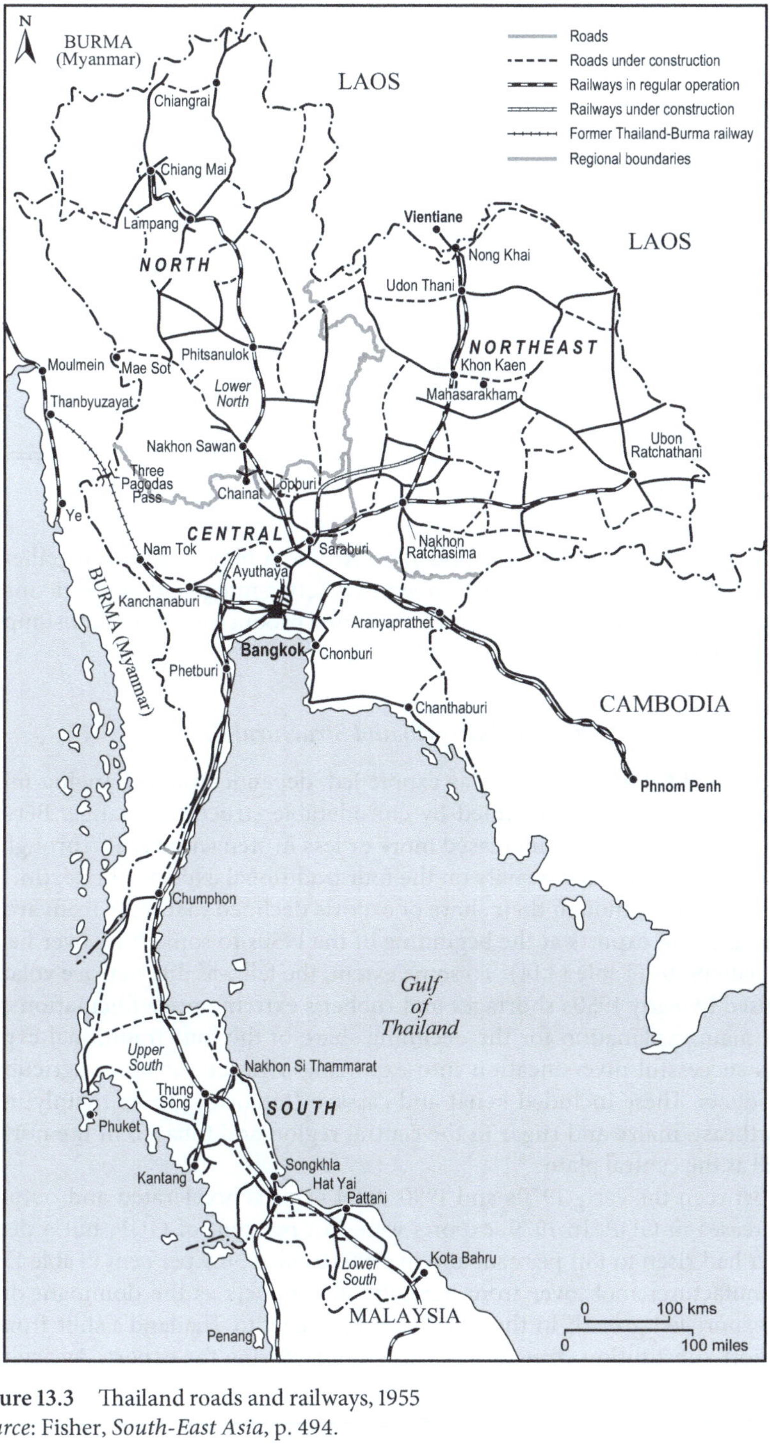

Figure 13.3 Thailand roads and railways, 1955
Source: Fisher, *South-East Asia*, p. 494.

Table 13.16 *Thailand highways, 1949–69 (kilometres)*

	National highways		Provincial highways		Total	
	Paved	Gravel and laterite	Paved	Gravel and laterite	Paved	Gravel and laterite
1949	760				760	5,030
1957	2,129	5,797				
1960	2,972	5,387	151	1,967	3,123	7,354
1965	5,046	4,314	405	2,203	5,451	6,517
1967	5,506	4,010	581	3,312	6,087	7,322
1969	7,822	2,146				

Source: Ingram, *Economic change*, p. 277.

built after the war and those under construction helped to knit together the Kingdom. New road construction led to a better-integrated domestic market and encouraged the production of agricultural products for home consumption and export.

Export-led Growth and Structural Change

Post-World War II growth was export-led, depended on a changing mix of exports and was accompanied by considerable structural change. Between 1952 and 1970, exports increased more or less in step with GDP. Through the 1960s, Thailand relied heavily on the four traditional exports of rice, tin, rubber and teak, although their share of exports declined markedly from around four-fifths of exports at the beginning of the 1950s to something over half by the late 1960s (Table 13.14). To some extent, the fall was due to price volatility caused by early 1950s shortages and rubber's extreme price fluctuations, but the main explanation for the declining share of the four traditional exports was successful diversification into exporting a variety of other agricultural products. These included kenaf and cassava (tapioca), grown mainly in the northeast, maize and sugar in the central region and tobacco in the north as well as the central plain.[48]

Between the early 1970s and 1990, total exports accelerated and outpaced increases in GDP. In 1970, exports were 14.1 per cent of GDP, but a decade later had risen to 18.1 per cent and in 1990 stood at 30.9 per cent (Table 13.12). Manufactures took over from agricultural products as the dominant driver in export-led growth in the 1980s, owing largely to Thailand's shift from an import-substitution strategy towards manufacturing for export. Agricultural

[48] Silcock, *Economic development of Thai agriculture*, pp. 53–55.

exports continued to increase, but low-wage manufactures, mainly electronics and electrical goods and textiles, fuelled the post-1980 increase in exports as a share of GDP and unprecedentedly rapid rates of growth. By 1983, when Seagate set up in Thailand, it occupied a lower-skill, lower-cost niche in a regional electronics production network organized through Singapore.

Structural change was most apparent in the changing composition of national income (Table 13.15). Agriculture's share of GDP fell continuously, dropping from half in 1951 to a little over a quarter by 1970 and 16.9 per cent in 1988. Over the four decades, however, agricultural output continuously increased and for much of the period bore out a seeming paradox that the faster agriculture grows, the faster its relative share declines. The rise in manufacturing from 10.3 per cent of GDP in 1951 to 12.6 per cent by 1960 casts some doubt on the assertion that modern development in Thailand dates from 1958.[49] Although a clear 1958 increase in GDP is apparent, a basis for this growth must have been created earlier after World War II when Thailand, under Phibun, began to invest in import-substituting industrialization and infrastructure. That investment afforded a foundation on which the governments of first Sarit Thanarat and then Thanom Kittikachorn built from 1958 to 1973. Both regimes were anti-communist, pro-American military dictatorships, marked by massive corruption, and both were considerably helped economically by the Indochina War. Because of it, the United States gave large amounts of aid, which substantially contributed to the maintenance of financial stability and continued infrastructure development.[50]

During the 1950s, manufacturing gained in prominence, mainly due to government efforts, continuing from the 1930s but now enhanced, to launch import-substitution industries and move Thailand away from its extreme pre-war dependence on rice, tin, rubber and teak. In 1948, Phibun, who had been prime minister until 1944, returned to power. He began to champion the establishment, generally as government ventures, of many of the same import-substitution industries that Thailand, in response to wartime shortages, had attempted, with little success, to develop during the Japanese occupation: sugar refining, textiles, paper, glass and the manufacture of gunny bags for rice transport. These early post-war industrial projects were plagued by high cost structures, inefficiency and rent-seeking, and were a drain on the state budget. Many of them were soon abandoned, partly in response to the recommendation of a 1959 World Bank mission advisory report, which advocated less state support for industry and greater emphasis on infrastructure investment.[51]

Between 1960 and 1990, the tariff structure remained typical of developing countries. Nominal tariffs were moderate. But effective rates of protection

[49] Muscat, *Fifth tiger*, p. 47 on modern growth but cf. his comments p. 85.

[50] Nuechterlein, 'Thailand', pp. 842–50; Stifel, 'Technocrats', pp. 1186–87, 1191–93.

[51] International Bank for Reconstruction and Development, *Public development program*, pp. 96–97; Anamwathana, *Thailand's economy*, pp. 97–107; Silcock, 'Promotion', p. 263; Suehiro, *Capital accumulation*, p. 179.

Table 13.17 *Thailand effective protection of manufacturing by trade-oriented groups, 1969–87 (%)*

	1969	1974	1984	1987
Export group	−43	−35	2	4
Import-competing group excluding tyres and tubes	54	63	21	39
Import-competing group including tyres and tubes	648	–	–	–
Non-import-competing group excluding cigarettes and soft drinks	187	77	53	55
Non-import-competing group including cigarettes and soft drinks	–	812	–	–

Source: Warr, 'Thai economy', p. 41.

(the percentage by which the tax effected by tariffs raises (or lowers) local value added and so actually protects (or not) domestic activities) were biased against export industries and favourable to home manufacturers. Thai exports tended to be labour intensive and included agri-based industries such as rice milling, frozen seafood and most rubber products like gloves as well as garment and footwear manufacture. By contrast, effective protection, in heavily taxing imported manufactures, favoured the domestic manufacturing sector, both import-competing (imports over 10 per cent of total consumption and net import positive) and non-import-competing (all goods not in the export or import-competing groups). Beverages, tobacco, ceramic and glass products, tyres and tubes and fabricated metals enjoyed especially high protection (Table 13.17).[52] The structure worked against some of Thailand's largest and most successful industrial export-oriented groups, and created a shelter generating large rents for Thai business groups and multinationals which concentrated on producing for the home market.

After World War II, and still at the beginning of the 1990s, although the large majority of Thai remained in agriculture, principally as rice growers, the increase in GDP was accompanied by change in the structure of employment (Table 13.18). The proportion of the workforce in agriculture fell continuously from 84.8 per cent in 1947 to almost two-thirds in 1990 and three-fifths in 1994. Increased employment shares were split more or less evenly between the other two main sectors of industry and services. Industrial employment rose from a miniscule 3.0 per cent of workers in 1947 to 14.2 per cent by 1990 and, over the same period, services from about an eighth of employment to over a fifth.

[52] Warr, 'Thai economy', pp. 39–42; Tambunlertchai, 'Manufacturing', pp. 140–41.

Table 13.18 *Thailand structure of employment, 1947–94*

(a) Persons millions	1947	1960	1970	1980	1990	1994
Agriculture	7.63	11.42	13.29	18.32	19.25	19.70
Industry	0.27	0.58	0.97	2.01	4.31	5.10
Services	1.09	1.87	2.50	5.15	6.78	7.58
Total	8.99	13.87	16.76	25.48	30.34	32.38
(b) %						
Agriculture	84.8	82.3	79.3	71.9	63.5	60.8
Industry	3.0	4.2	5.8	7.9	14.2	15.8
Services	12.2	13.5	14.9	20.2	22.3	23.4
Total	100.0	100.0	100.0	100.0	100.0	100.0

Sources: Yang, *Multiple exchange rate system*, p. 151; Dixon, *Thai economy*, p. 12.

Despite some movement of labour out of agriculture, the agricultural share of the workforce remained exceptionally high, and remarkably so for a country with Thailand's gains in national income and income levels. The Thai ratios, shown in Table 13.19, panel a, of agricultural employment to agricultural GDP of 0.28 at the beginning of the 1980s, and 0.18 in the early 1990s, were easily the lowest of any major country in Asia, and probably the world.[53]

Because of Thailand's abundance of productive land, farm incomes were not abnormally low by Asian standards (Table 13.19, panel b). Nevertheless, using mid-1980s data, division of sectoral populations by sectoral fractions of GDP for a number of Asian countries shows a ratio for Thailand's non-agricultural to agricultural GDP per capita of 12.0. By both this measure and the ones in Table 13.19, panel a, Thailand's agricultural–non-agricultural dualism was an Asian outlier.

Both sets of ratios in Table 13.19 emphasize an apparently great difference in productivity between Thai agriculture and the rest of the economy. The ratios, as well as comparison with Malaysia, indicate a lack of agricultural technological change in Thailand and the possibility of profitably transferring labour out of agriculture. Transfer could, for example, have been from low-productivity rice cultivation in some parts of Thailand like the northeast, which were outside the main growing area of the central plain (Figure 13.4).[54]

[53] Dixon, *Thai economy*, p. 19.

[54] Warr and Nijathaworn, 'Thai economic performance', p. 68.

Table 13.19 *Asia ratios of agricultural employment and agricultural GDP, 1980–93*

(a) Ratio of agricultural GDP to agricultural employment

	1980	1993
Thailand	0.28	0.18
Burma	0.90	0.89
Malaysia	1.00	0.73
Indonesia	0.46	0.40
Philippines	0.42	0.54
China	0.50	0.58
India	0.47	0.46
Pakistan	0.56	0.48
Bangladesh	0.63	0.45
Sri Lanka	0.51	0.52
South Korea	0.44	0.50

(b) GDP per capita and ratio of non-agricultural to agricultural real GDP per capita, 1985

	2011 US$	Non-agric. to agric. GDP per capita
Thailand	4,862	12.0
Burma	1,506	1.2
Malaysia	6,626	3.2
Indonesia	3,143	4.2
Philippines	3,135	2.9
China	2,619	5.8
India	1,720	5.2
Pakistan	2,230	3.7
Bangladesh	925	3.0
Sri Lanka	3,484	3.1
South Korea	8,859	3.5
Nepal	1,194	8.1

Sources: panel a: Dixon, *Thai economy*, p. 19; panel b: Lewis and Kapur, 'Updating country study', p. 1372; Maddison Project Database, 2020.

The high share of the Thai labour force in agriculture is partly explained by four considerations. Taken together, these would appreciably modify, but not entirely reverse, a conclusion of extreme dualism in Thailand. One is a slower

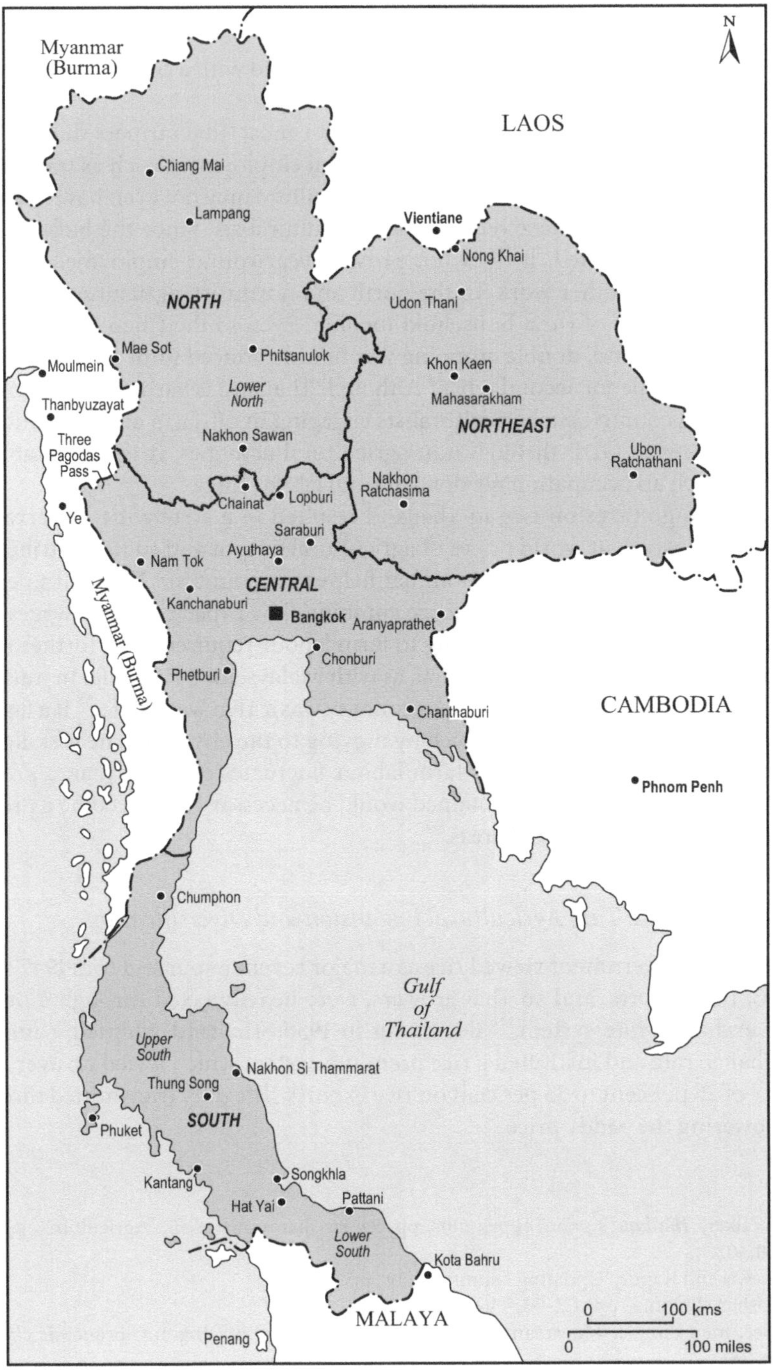

Figure 13.4 Thailand regional divisions
Sources: Donner, *Five faces*, p. 78; Ferrara, *Political development*, frontispiece; Mike Montesano, personal communication.

decline in agriculture in countries such as Thailand with a comparative advantage in exporting agricultural products.

A second, and major, consideration is that most Thai farmers did not rely on agriculture alone but had non-agricultural employment such as trade, construction or government employment. Agriculture may not even have been the main occupation of those recorded as agriculturalists. Since the bulk of Thai agriculture is rain-fed, it does not provide year-round employment, giving ample scope for other work. In the north and northeast, agriculture accounts for less than half of rural household income. Even in the Chao Phraya Delta in central Thailand, double cropping was not introduced until the 1970s, leaving farmers time for second jobs.[55] Although Thailand is hardly unique among developing countries in agriculturalists engaging in off-farm employment and contributing to GDP through non-agricultural activities, it is remarkable in having such an occupationally divided rural labour force.[56]

Third, high taxes on rice in Thailand resulted in a systematic undervaluation of the worth at world prices of agricultural output and so its contribution to GDP.[57] The fourth explanation that helps to account for Thailand's persistently large agricultural labour force combines low expected urban wages and the need for flexibility in adjusting to farm labour requirements, further reinforced by a preference of many Thai, as with Malays, for a rural life. In much of Thailand outside Bangkok, the rice economy was a Thai way of life.[58] If a farmer cannot improve his position much by moving to the city unless he is skilled in some way, and if the need for farm labour fluctuates over the year, a greater urban wage premium than obtained would be necessary to overcome a preference for remaining in rural areas.[59]

Rice Tax, Agricultural Expansion and Diversification

Thailand's government viewed rice as a major revenue source. From 1947 until 1955, rice exports, and so Thai growers, were heavily taxed through a multiple exchange rate system.[60] Beginning in 1956, Thailand adopted a unitary exchange rate and instituted a rice premium system which levied on average a duty of 25 per cent to 35 per cent on rice exports. The duty transmitted directly to lowering the paddy price.

[55] Walker, *Thailand's political peasants*, pp. 59–85; Siamwalla et al., 'Agriculture', pp. 85, 91, 102.
[56] Lewis and Kapur, 'Updating country study', pp. 1372–73.
[57] Usher, 'Income', pp. 431–33, 436–39.
[58] See, for example, Moerman, *Agricultural change*, pp. 9–10; Ingram, *Economic change*, p. 257.
[59] Usher, 'Income', pp. 440–41; Bertrand and Squire, 'Relevance', pp. 487–91, 506–08.
[60] Corden and Mackie, 'Development'.

Multiple exchange rates and the rice premium had three important effects. One was that multiple exchange rate profits accrued to the Bank of Thailand, enabling foreign reserves wiped out by World War II to be quickly restored and Thailand to return to its pre-war conservative fiscal and monetary policies and low inflation. The rice premium continued this currency conduit to the government and became an important source of its revenue and support for Thailand's cautious fiscal stance. Second, the tax on rice increased the attractiveness of cultivating non-rice crops and encouraged agricultural diversification. The third effect was to keep domestic rice prices low, which subsidized urban areas at the expense of peasant growers and further centralized power in Bangkok. Wartime inflation had badly eroded civil service wages and after the war the government's 'cheap rice' policy became a way to raise real wages without altering nominal pay.[61]

Surplus land in Thailand did not end until the late 1970s, and the economy used this resource to extend pre-World War II vent-for-surplus growth.[62] Although post-war Malaysia also tapped unexploited land, Thai agricultural growth differed from Malaysian in relying largely on bringing more land under cultivation. Between 1950 and 1988, as forest land was cleared and claimed for agriculture, farm holding land trebled from 8 million to 24 million hectares. Over the period, paddy land doubled to 11.9 million hectares, and in 1988 comprised half of farm holding land. Increases in other agricultural cultivation were even more rapid: an eightfold rise in land under field crops and a fourfold one in tree crops, both reflections of agricultural diversification (Table 13.20).

Land extension was not matched by similarly paced agricultural technical progress. Before World War II, Thai agriculture employed virtually no machinery. By the later 1960s, however, there had been a modest technological revolution through the use of fertilizers and machinery. Even so, still only about half of land planted in annual crops was tilled by tractors. In most provinces agricultural research stations had been set up, but their impact was slight.[63]

Rice yields in Thailand reflected a lack of technological progress. In 1979/81, Thai yields were only slightly higher than before World War II, and between 1959/61 and 1991/93 rose by just 57.1 per cent, more slowly than in any other Southeast Asian country except Malaysia and Cambodia and far below the region's post-war pace setters (Table 13.21).

There were three important reasons why there was so little technological improvement in Thai rice yields compared to other Southeast Asian countries. One was that artificially low rice prices discouraged farmer investment in technical improvements. Technological change was further suppressed by among

61 Siamwalla, 'History', pp. 236–37.

62 Siamwalla et al., 'Agriculture', p. 97.

63 Motooka, 'Conditions governing agricultural development', pp. 439–40; Ingram, *Economic change*, pp. 271–75, 279; Bertrand and Squire, 'Relevance', p. 495.

Table 13.20 *Thailand land utilization, 1950–88 (million hectares)*

	1950	1955	1960	1965	1970	1975	1980	1982	1984	1986	1988
Forest land	31.71	29.73	28.19	26.23	23.27	20.92	16.55	15.58	15.15	14.66	14.38
Farm holding land	8.27	9.03	10.00	12.76	15.04	17.95	19.04	19.77	20.05	20.78	23.65
Farm holding land: paddy land	5.40	5.77	6.20	6.64	9.37	11.40	11.77	11.72	11.83	11.88	11.87
Farm holding land: field crops	0.73	0.76	1.11	1.98	2.25	3.19	4.12	4.69	4.81	5.13	5.72
Farm holding land: tree crops	0.77	0.83	0.93	1.54	1.46	1.67	1.78	1.90	1.93	2.23	3.13

Source: Siamwalla et al., 'Agriculture', p. 90.

Table 13.21 *Southeast Asia comparative rice yields, 1931/40–1991/93 (metric tons/hectare)*

	1931/40	1959/61	1969/71	1979/81	1991/93	% increase 1959/61–1991/93
Thailand	1.6	1.4	1.9	1.8	2.2	57.1
Malaysia	1.1	2.0	2.4	2.8	3.1	55.0
Indonesia	1.1	1.7	2.3	3.3	4.4	158.8
Burma	1.4	1.7	1.7	2.7	2.9	70.6
Vietnam	–	2.0	2.1	2.8	3.3	65.0
Cambodia	–	1.1	1.4	1.0	1.3	18.2
Laos	–	0.8	1.3	1.4	2.4	200.0
Philippines	1.1	1.2	1.6	2.2	2.8	133.3

Sources: For 1931/40, data are from Barker et al., *Rice economy*, p. 47. Data for 1959/61–1991/93 are from Dixon, *Thai economy*, p. 156.

the highest fertilizer prices relative to rice prices in Asia.[64] Second, some of the expansion of rice cultivation until 1975 involved a movement onto poorer quality land which reduced average yields. The third reason was that raising yields

[64] Warr and Nijathaworn, 'Thai economic performance', pp. 68–69; Usher, 'Income', p. 437.

was not pressing so long as surplus cultivable land was available. A reflection of this land availability and cultivation of less good land was that until the 1970s cultivated land per agricultural worker increased.[65]

Poverty and Geographical Income Disparity

Thailand, in common with its Southeast Asian neighbours, was marked by an inheritance of pre-World War II regionalization and a dual economy. Figure 13.4 shows the four main geographical divisions of the country: the north, northeast, central and south. In the Central Region, Bangkok and its vicinities could be regarded as a fifth region, since it contained by far Thailand's largest city and easily the greatest concentration of wealth.

The persistence, as in Malaysia, of large differences in the incidence of poverty was one aspect of entrenched regional differences in Thailand. These reflected history, geographical endowments, economic activity and perhaps attitudes. A further contributory factor to regionalization was Thailand's antiquated, regressive tax structure, heavily reliant on indirect taxes and biased against rural areas. Between 1975/76 and 1988, the income level considered to be a poverty threshold approximately doubled, and the incidence of poverty fell by a third from 30.0 per cent to 21.2 per cent (Table 13.22). That suggests that economic growth made the vast majority of Thai much better off in terms of income. From 1960 to 1990, life expectancy and infant mortality improved dramatically; in 1990, Thailand ranked as just below having high human development. Between the 1960s and the 1980s, however, quite marked income disparities emerged. Gini coefficients of 0.47 in 1966 but 0.66 in 1980 indicate that as Thailand grew economically and became a wealthier society it also became a much more unequal one (Table 13.12).

Between 1975/76 and 1988, the benefits of growth did not spread evenly and differences in poverty incidence and the speed of its eradication were considerable (Table 13.22). In Bangkok, poverty was always by far the Kingdom's lowest, and between 1975/76 and 1988 also fell the fastest, more than halving from 7.8 per cent to 3.5 per cent of the population, despite a continuous large influx of newcomers to the metropolis. Likewise, over this period poverty in municipal areas decreased by half to 6.1 per cent in 1988. Bangkok had only about a tenth, and municipal areas less than a fifth, of the poverty in the northeast. The latter was saddled with the geographical disadvantages of a historic lack of development, remoteness, poor access to transport or to a port and extreme variability of rainfall.[66]

[65] Siamwalla et al., 'Agriculture', p. 88; International Bank for Reconstruction and Development, *Public development program*.

[66] Dixon, 'Development, regional disparity', pp. 211–17, 222–23.

Table 13.22 *Thailand poverty incidence and economic growth, 1975/76–1988*

	1975/76	1981	1986	1988
Poverty lines (baht per capita per year constant prices)				
Urban	2,961	5,151	5,834	6,203
Rural	1,981	3,454	3,823	4,076
Poverty incidence				
By community type				
Municipal areas	12.5	7.5	5.9	6.1
Sanitary areas	14.8	13.5	18.6	12.2
Villages	36.2	27.3	35.8	26.3
By region %				
North	33.2	21.5	25.5	19.9
Northeast	44.9	35.9	48.2	34.6
Central	13.0	13.6	15.6	12.9
South	30.7	20.4	27.2	19.4
Bangkok and vicinities	7.8	3.9	3.5	3.5
Whole Kingdom	30.0	23.0	29.5	21.2
Avg. % real GDP per capita growth over preceding period				
% per year	2.9	4.8	3.6	9.3

Notes and Sources: For 1975/76 GDP per capita growth is for 1970–75. Per capita income is from Maddison Project Database, 2020. Other data are from Warr, 'Thai economy', p. 73.

The size and persistence of disparities throughout Thailand point to three things. One is that more government attention to enhancing rural productivity would likely have made Thailand a more equitable society.[67] Second, modernization of the tax structure and redress of its bias against rural areas would probably have reduced income differences and poverty incidence. The third observation is the puzzle, discussed earlier, of why there was not more interregional migration than apparently occurred, even allowing for an understatement of migration due to the household registration system in Thailand, which counts people where they are registered rather than where they live.

The Plural Society, 'Bureaucratic Capitalism' and Public Enterprise

In most Southeast Asian plural societies, extreme tension arose from the domination of Asian business by non-indigenous Chinese or Indians and the

[67] Lewis and Kapur, 'Updating country study', pp. 1373–75.

entrepreneurial aspirations of majority indigenous populations. Thailand, however, lacked – and increasingly so as Chinese assimilated into Thai culture – this same tension. Although in Thailand, as elsewhere in Southeast Asia, the post-World War II resentment of non-indigenous Asian business success was present, the Thai accommodated, and appreciably diffused, this in two ways. Together, these considerably resolved conflict in favour of cooperation and acceptance. One, sometimes described as 'bureaucratic capitalism', encompassed much of non-foreign enterprise, and was an opportunist marriage between the Thai elite and Chinese entrepreneurs. The other consisted of a proliferation of state-owned enterprises run by a Thai elite and for its benefit. This section discusses these two systems in turn.

Bureaucratic capitalism describes the establishment in domestic manufacturing, trade and finance of a strong private–government–military business relationship, and was the outcome of Thailand as a bureaucratic state, a Thai-ification of business implemented by Thai politicians beginning in the 1930s and Thai ethnic-Chinese business dominance. Although bureaucratic capitalism emerged in embryonic form before World War II and its roots were in Thai economic nationalism, anti-Chinese feeling and emphasis on import-substitution industrialization, it did not develop fully until World War II.

In Thailand, as in Malaysia for Malays, the Thai indigenous, majority group engaged very little in business. Non-foreign, meaning essentially non-European, business was dominated by ethnic-Chinese Thai, a community which, by the 1950s, was far in the minority in Thailand but hard to quantify due to assimilation, intermarriage and differing degrees of 'Chineseness'. Historically, about half of ethnic Chinese lived in Bangkok. Still in the 1960s in the capital and elsewhere, Chinese 'aliens' or their direct descendants carried out almost all non-foreign economic activity except rice farming and some state ventures.[68] Thai, however, held nearly all political power.

Even after bureaucratic capitalist arrangements became pervasive, they involved only a few individuals, made up on one side of a small group of influential Thai politicians and military officers. On the other side were ethnic-Chinese Thai businessmen. Together, they controlled a large number of private or state-sponsored companies, as distinct from state-owned or public enterprises, and benefited financially from this control as directors, entrepreneurs, salaried employees, shareholders or from other payments such as bonuses.

From 1948 onwards, Thai politicians and military officers who gained power with the return of Phibun as prime minister increasingly played on anti-ethnic Chinese economic feeling and emphasized the 'Thai economy for the Thai people'.[69] It was, however, 'the nationalism of an *élite* group which sees

[68] Ayal, 'Private enterprise', pp. 6–7.

[69] See, for example, Suehiro, *Capital accumulation*, p. 138; Anamwathana, *Thailand's economy*, pp. 108–15.

the economic interest of the Thai people largely in terms of its own economic self interest'.[70] Using this nationalism and their political dominance, the Thai elite enacted, or threatened to promulgate, laws or controls that would severely restrict or even curtail Chinese business. By the early 1950s, these measures, or the threat of them, extended to every level of Chinese enterprise.

The ethnic-Chinese business response was effectively the only one possible, other than leaving Thailand. Chinese entrepreneurs effected formal business alliances, either through incorporating Thai officials on boards of directors or beginning new enterprises with them. Business groups, which formed around cliques of influential Thai, were organized around banks, placing them at the heart of bureaucratic capitalism. A symbiotic government–military–private business–finance relationship quickly emerged. Thai in the government bureaucracy or military conferred 'protection' – licences, contracts or other privileges and perhaps capital – and ethnic-Chinese Thai offered entrepreneurship as well as possibly capital. Cooperation greatly accelerated after a 1951 coup when its perpetrators needed enhancement of their power and prestige.

Bureaucratic capitalism was a product of those with business power in search of political influence and political power in search of legitimate wealth and business control. The result was further to concentrate Thai and Chinese influence and wealth and strengthen the dominance of Bangkok.[71] Within the Thai political and military elite, competition between rival cliques – for example those grouped around Phibun, military leader Sarit Thanarat, the clique led by Field Marshal Phin Chunhawan and police director general Phao Siyanon or around promoters of the 1932 Thai revolution – and shifting alliances of individuals between cliques intensified the need for members of cliques to reinforce political power with business power. For Chinese entrepreneurs, the instability of cliques made it prudent to diversify risk through maintaining an alliance with more than one of them.[72]

By mid-1953, Thailand's bureaucratic capitalism was, by international standards, extreme both in its ubiquity and in its widespread acceptance among Thai as a natural order. Almost no major business operated without a combination of Chinese management and the close involvement of Thai military and/or political figures who benefited financially. Union occurred through existing commercial and financial enterprises inviting top government officials onto their boards of directors; through Chinese supplying capital and Thai officials protection; or through Chinese Thai citizens joining semi-official Thai enterprises as managers. For instance, in 1953, the Bangkok Bank, a Chinese

[70] Silcock, 'Promotion', p. 258.

[71] Skinner, *Leadership and power*, pp. 186–99; Suehiro, *Capital accumulation*, pp. 169–72, 367.

[72] Ayal, 'Some crucial issues', p. 158; Riggs, *Thailand*, pp. 270–97; Wilson, *Politics in Thailand*, pp. 177–80.

enterprise established in 1944, was re-organized with the Minister of Economic Affairs as chairman, a Thai general as vice-chairman and a board including two Thai brigadier-generals who were also deputy ministers, as well as a Thai police lieutenant-colonel. Even the hyper-nationalistic Thai veterans corporations were managed by Chinese.[73] Based on 107 companies' records of board membership, between 1952 and 1957 the boards of 42 companies had three or more cabinet politicians, 25 had two and 40 one.[74]

In the post-war decades, public enterprise, defined as 50 per cent or more government ownership, occupied an important and growing role in the Thai economy and its modernization. In the 1950s, there were some 60 public enterprises, but by 1989 this had increased to 76. The 76 had revenues and recurrent expenditures, each equal to a fifth of GDP. Many public enterprises provided essential infrastructure, such as utilities, ports, the railway and mass transit, and had natural monopoly aspects in all or part of their businesses. Others, especially those prominent in the 1950s, traced their roots to import-substitution industries started by Phibun. These included, in 1959, sugar and paper mills, the manufacture of gunny bags from locally grown kenaf and the production of pharmaceuticals, paper and tobacco products. Although by the 1980s most of these post-war industries were no longer in public ownership, a jute mill in the northeast, the tobacco monopoly and sugar refining still were.[75]

Public enterprise, like bureaucratic capitalism, helped to meet the demands of the Thai elite for a stake in business, because it was run by high-ranking politicians and military officers who benefited financially – most transparently through salaries, directors' fees and bonuses – from their engagement as executive managers. Typically, in the 1950s and still in the 1980s, competence and relevant experience had little or no role in determining executive appointments. Instead, these depended on political influence. Factory managers did not generally remedy the lack of executive-level commercial and industrial competence. Historically, the perception was that anyone with a university degree could run any enterprise despite having no training. Managers had limited power to dismiss poorly performing workers or reduce overmanning.

The monopoly position of most public enterprises enabled the sector as a whole to generate a substantial surplus. The majority of enterprises, however, lost money, and the public sector was considered a by-word for inefficiency. No mechanism to evaluate performance or profitability of public enterprises existed. Thai public enterprise was a drain on the government budget, entailed acceptance of managerial ineptitude, lacked accountability and implied

[73] Skinner, *Leadership and power*, pp. 191–99.

[74] Riggs, *Thailand*, pp. 255–64.

[75] International Bank for Reconstruction and Development, *Public development program*, pp. 90–93; Dhiratayakinant, 'Public enterprises', pp. 265–69; Silcock, 'Promotion', pp. 260, 262–63; Suehiro, *Capital accumulation*, pp. 128–30, 138–40, 276.

widespread resignation to the status quo.[76] In all these respects, it paralleled its counterparts in socialist Vietnam and Burma (Chapters 10 and 11).

Conclusion

Between the end of World War II and the late 1970s, Malaysia and Thailand remained heavily dependent on vent-for-surplus, staples economies. After 1950, both countries successfully postponed a realization of the limitations of this growth partly by bringing more land under cultivation and developing their range of agricultural exports, Malaysia through palm oil and Thailand through a range of upland crops. Malaysia had, furthermore, the good fortune of finding, in petroleum, a major new staple. In Thailand, the outstanding feature of vent-for-surplus growth was its heavy dependence on land extension, while Malaysia relied to a much greater extent on technical progress in rubber and palm oil production.

Developing countries have often run into problems with an import-substitution strategy because, after its initial apparent success, there is an increasing need for imports of intermediate and capital goods to support a cluster of highly protected, inefficient industries. The increased need for imports typically leads to balance-of-payments deficits and, to correct these, frequent recourse to stop-go policies. The Philippines, for example, encountered these problems, but Malaysia, Singapore and Thailand did not. There were two reasons for this. One was that continued high commodity exports, and in Thailand also tourism, afforded sufficient foreign exchange to support the balance of payments. The Malaysian and Thai current accounts recorded small surpluses or at most tiny deficits. The other was that import-substitution phases were brief and moderate. Both countries soon complemented an import strategy with an export-oriented manufacturing one which yielded adequate foreign exchange.

Comparative advantage remained good to Malaysia and Thailand. Still in the 1980s, as land surplus disappeared and comparative advantage shifted towards labour- not land-intensive production, Malaysia and Thailand could draw on abundant natural resources to produce commodities for which world demand held up well: rubber, palm oil, petroleum and rice. During the 1980s, both countries increasingly recognized their shifting comparative advantage. In each country, export-led growth accelerated through the establishment of industries mainly organized by multinationals which were attracted by an abundance of low-cost labour to manufacture electronics and electrical parts and components for onwards shipment as part of global supply chains. By the 1990s, a

[76] Dhiratayakinant, 'Public enterprises', pp. 285–88; International Bank for Reconstruction and Development, *Public development program*, pp. 90–93; Riggs, *Thailand*, pp. 304–10; Suehiro, *Capital accumulation*, p. 150.

pressing question in regard to these industries became whether Malaysia and Thailand should, or could, pursue, through dynamic comparative advantage, an attempt to move from a dependence on low-skill, low-wage labour towards more skilled, higher value added production.

While not discounting luck as a (perhaps underrated) factor in economic growth, the experience of the two countries has three main lessons. One is that for small countries, like those in Southeast Asia, trade is the best hope for an engine of growth; a second, the importance of policies that maximize this growth option. As population expanded and outran the possibilities of agriculture and import substitution, Malaysia and Thailand used an emerging comparative advantage of abundant labour to perpetuate trade as a growth engine through the export of low-wage manufactures. The third lesson is a caveat: that before long labour, like land by the late 1970s, runs up against the limits of finiteness. Technology, not trade, is the true engine of growth, a theme to which the book returns in Part V.

14

The Philippines and Singapore: Lagging Country and Successful City State

These countries are paired for their contrasts. Among Southeast Asia's outward-looking countries, the Philippines ranks as the outstanding failure; Singapore stands out by some margin as the Southeast Asian success story. It has served from the late 1960s onwards as an economic model for emulation by other countries in the region and beyond. Southeast Asia's 'sick man' is a description so often applied to the post-World War II Philippines that it has become a cliché.

Singapore is tiny. A city state and mostly municipality, it is less than half the size of London. Only 30 miles long and 17 miles wide, the length of Singapore island is walkable in a day. For the less ambulatory, all of Singapore can easily be reached by public transport. The Philippines, by contrast, sprawls over an archipelago of 7,000 islands and a rugged terrain, making air transport a usual mode of travel.

Singapore's sole natural resource is a location unrivalled in Asia for being central in Southeast Asia and astride the world air, shipping and other communications networks. Unlike the Philippines' main natural endowment of agricultural land, Singapore's location is not an exhaustible resource. In the Philippines, the land frontier had closed by the 1960s but Singapore's location continues to be built on advantageously, and the island has continued to benefit from exogenous global forces during successive waves of world development.

Development in Singapore owed much to an efficient, non-corrupt government, the sole one in Southeast Asia. That partly resulted from the luck of good leadership. But it was also due to Singapore's smallness, which made it easy for leaders to impose a semi-authoritarian government to enforce tight control and keep citizens under close surveillance. Singapore was, and remains, a place where wealthy Asians lodge their assets.

Historically, the Philippines, analysed in the first section of the chapter, suffered from endemic corruption. In 1970, Emery observed that 'The Philippines has probably had more financial scandals or financial institutions in distress than any other Southeast Asian country';[1] a reputation only subsequently enhanced by

[1] Emery, *Financial institutions*, p. 482.

further balance-of-payments crises, capital flight and rampant crony capitalism during the 20-year regime of President Ferdinand Marcos. Singapore's government played a major role in directing development, the prototype of a developmental state. The Manila central government, not infrequently, acted to the benefit of its elected officials and their associates. It had a history of responding more to special interests and lobbyists than to the mass of Filipinos. Many or even most Philippine provinces had local bosses with their own interests.

In crucial respects, Singapore, the subject of the chapter's second section, is not comparable to other Southeast Asian nations. Most obviously, in addition to considerations such as size, state efficiency and unrivalled Asian location, Singapore lacks, apart from some market gardening, an agricultural sector. To grow and develop, Singapore did not have to solve the fundamental problem in other Southeast Asian countries of the need to modernize agriculture and raise its productivity. Industry and services, both with potentially much higher growth rates than agriculture, set the limits of Singapore's pace of development. In exchange for its exports, Singapore could draw on a perfectly elastic world supply of food. Development in the Philippines struggled with a large, low-productivity agricultural sector which contributed little to the economy from rural industrialization or services.

Singapore soon recognized that industrialization through import substitution would not provide sufficient jobs for its swiftly growing population, nor would it find enough demand in its small home market to make viable many import-substitution industries. In response, Singapore turned quickly, as one of the four Asian NICs, to manufacturing for export. The Philippines, by contrast, stuck for years with import-substitution policies, implemented through exchange controls and high tariffs. Within a decade of independence, import substitution had created a strong lobby of rent-seeking Filipino manufacturing interests. When the Philippines embraced manufactured exports as a route to development, this was only latterly and somewhat half-heartedly. Singapore and the Philippines were, however, similar in that in both countries manufacturing for export depended heavily on foreign multinationals.

The Philippines

Macroeconomic and Social Trends

Between 1950 and 1990, GDP per capita doubled and population trebled, implying annual growth rates of 1.8 per cent and 2.9 per cent respectively (Table 14.1). Rapid income gains concentrated between 1950 and 1959 during first-stage import substitution, when the manufacturing sector expanded at over 10 per cent annually and GDP at 7.0 per cent annually, although GDP per capita at 3.8 per cent a year (Table 14.2). Subsequently, macroeconomic crises and continued rapid population growth checked further equally large income increases.

Table 14.1 *Philippines economic and social indicators, 1950–90*

	1950	1959	1966	1972	1982	1986	1990
GDP per capita 2011 prices US$	1,706	2,393	2,636	2,954	3,859	3,218	3,433
GDP per capita constant 2015 US$	–	1,193	1,327	1,487	1,924	1,576	1,730
GDP constant 2015 US$ bn	–	31.3	42.3	56.4	96.2	87.9	107.1
Population 000	21,131	27,685	34,304	40,850	53,557	59,186	65,088
Fertility rate (children born per woman)	–	7.1	6.7	6.0	5.0	4.6	4.3
Exports/GDP	–	10.2	13.7	10.5	13.0	15.4	17.1
Workers' remittances % of exports	–	–	–	–	24.8	23.4	20.6
Consumer price index	–	1.1	1.5	2.5	9.3	19.2	28.6
Real wages: agricultural 1962 = 100	–	–	93.6	74.3	65.0	70.7	–
Real wages: urban unskilled 1962 = 100	–	–	96.1	88.9	45.1	25.7	–
Real wages: urban skilled 1962 = 100	–	–	89.1	75.2	45.5	27.8	–
Life expectancy: male	–	59	61	61	61	62	63
Life expectancy: female	–	63	65	66	67	68	70
Infant mortality (per 1,000 live births)	–	66	58	55	52	48	40
Primary school enrolment rates %: male	–	–	–	–	94	97	–
Primary school enrolment rates %: female	–	–	–	–	94	98	–
Literacy aged 15 and above %	–	–	–	–	83	94	93
Gini coefficient: urban	–	0.49	0.53	0.50	–	0.47	0.49
Gini coefficient: rural	–	0.38	0.42	0.47	–	0.40	0.42
Human development rank (of 130)	–	–	–	–	–	–	65

Notes and Sources: 1. Per capita GDP 2011 US$ are from the Maddison Project Database, 2020; and GDP per capita constant 2015 US$ from World Bank, *World development indicators, 2020*. Other data are from the World Bank unless indicated otherwise below. For 1959, data are for 1960 and from the World Bank. 2. Population data are from Maddison Project Database 2020 and for 1959.

Table 14.1 (*cont.*)

3. Literacy rates are 1980 for 1982, 1985 for 1986 and 1989 for 1990. 4. Gini coefficients are for 1971, 1985 and 1991 and from Vos and Yap, *Philippine economy*, p. 24. 5. Workers' remittances as a percentage of exports are from Vos and Yap, *Philippine economy*, p. 55. 6. Real wages are from Boyce, *Philippines*, pp. 26, 28. 7. Gini coefficients for 1956 and 1966 are from Berry, 'Income', p. 316 and relate to 1956 and 1965 respectively. 8. Human development data are for 1990. The index ranks 130 countries in ascending order and placed Thailand as somewhat below high human development. In comparison to the Philippines' 65, Malaysia ranked 85, Indonesia 54, Thailand 78 and Singapore 96. United Nations, *Human Development Report, 1990*, p. 111.

Table 14.2 *Philippines economic sector and GDP per capita growth rates, 1950–90 (% annual growth)*

	Agriculture	Industry	Manufacturing	Services	GDP
1950–1959	5.6	8.2	10.7	7.2	7.0
1959–1968	4.2	5.1	5.5	4.7	4.7
1968–1982	3.5	6.9	5.4	5.1	5.3
1982–1990	0.9	-0.5	0.7	3.1	1.2
1950–1990	3.6	5.3	5.6	5.1	4.7

Source: Hooley, 'American economic policy', pp. 481–82.

The gloomy 1971 prognosis of Power and Sicat that population growth, then 3.5 per cent a year, 'will inevitably subvert all attempts at successful development' partly accounted for Philippine development failures. Continued high natural increase, as well as curbing per capita income gains, added to a persistent labour surplus condition, and resulted in unemployment and downwards pressure on real wages.[2] Although the fertility rate, which averaged 7.1 children per woman in 1960, subsequently fell, even in 1990 it remained high at 4.3 births (Table 14.1). While from 1959 to 1982 GDP grew at close to 5.0 per cent annually, population increase of about 2.9 per cent a year meant that GDP per capita advanced by only 2.1 per cent.

A shift in the structure of both GDP and employment away from agriculture and towards industry and services, although progressive, was limited (Tables 14.3 and 14.4). In 1990, 45 per cent of workers were still in the agricultural sector, producing a little over a fifth of GDP compared to a quarter from

[2] Power and Sicat, *Philippines*, p. 126.

Table 14.3 *Philippines GDP by economic sector, 1950–90*

(a) 1985 pesos millions	1950	1959	1966	1972	1982	1986	1990
Agriculture, fishing, forestry	39.3	63.9	84.9	106.0	149.6	145.7	160.7
Manufacturing	20.6	51.4	71.8	104.9	174.3	146.5	183.9
Other industry	12.2	15.3	20.6	28.0	90.6	58.7	71.6
Services	41.9	78.7	108.5	142.6	238.9	240.5	304.4
Total	114.0	209.4	285.9	381.5	653.5	591.4	720.7
(b) %	**1950**	**1959**	**1966**	**1972**	**1982**	**1986**	**1990**
Agriculture, fishing, forestry	34.5	30.5	29.7	27.8	22.9	24.6	22.3
Manufacturing	18.1	24.5	25.1	27.5	26.7	24.8	25.5
Other industry	10.7	7.3	7.2	7.3	13.9	9.9	9.9
Services	36.8	37.6	38.0	37.4	36.6	40.7	42.2
Total	100.0	100.0	100.0	100.0	100.0	100.0	100.0

Source: Hooley, 'American economic policy', pp. 480–82.

manufacturing. Much of agriculture remained traditional and low productivity. Between 1950 and 1990, the decline in agriculture from over a third of GDP to about a fifth is mainly explained by increases in the shares of manufacturing and services. By 1966, manufacturing's contribution to output had already reached a quarter in conjunction with import-substitution industrialization, but thereafter rose only marginally. Manufacturing absorbed relatively little labour, because the import-substitution strategy pursued by the Philippines favoured capital-intensive, low employment-creating industrialization. From 1966 to 1990, a rise in service employment by 11.6 percentage points but only a 4.2-point increase in the services addition to GDP partly reflects a push of labour into urban informal services as the only available employment.[3]

In 1990, the Philippines ranked 65th in human development, halfway between the world's least- and most-developed countries (Table 14.1). Its ranking was buoyed by comparatively high educational provision but held back, as were other social indicators, by the slow augmentation in GDP per capita. Educational provision was a positive inheritance from American colonialism, and after independence most Filipinos had at least primary level education and were literate. Gains in longevity came slowly, however, and between 1959 and 1990, life expectancy rose only four years for males to reach age 63, although it

[3] Vos and Yap, *Philippine economy*, pp. 16–17; Boyce, *Philippines*, pp. 19–22.

Table 14.4 *Philippines employment by economic sector, 1962–90*

(a) 000 persons	1962	1966	1972	1982	1986	1990
Agriculture, fishing, forestry	5,898	6,290	6,863	8,920	10,289	9,981
Manufacturing	1,052	1,229	1,323	1,741	1,905	2,236
Mining	40	26	36	74	150	129
Construction	236	283	432	604	629	968
Services	2,378	3,109	3,927	6,031	7,623	8,883
Total	9,603	10,937	12,582	17,371	20,595	22,196
(b) %	**1962**	**1966**	**1972**	**1982**	**1986**	**1990**
Agriculture, fishing, forestry	61.4	57.5	54.5	51.3	50.0	45.0
Manufacturing	11.0	11.2	10.5	10.0	9.2	10.1
Mining	0.4	0.2	0.3	0.4	0.7	0.6
Construction	2.5	2.6	3.4	3.5	3.1	4.4
Services	24.8	28.4	31.2	34.7	37.0	40.0
Total	100.0	100.0	100.0	100.0	100.0	100.0

Source: Philippines, *Statistical yearbook of the Philippines*, 1976, pp. 54–55, *1989*, pp. 11/8–9, 11/12–15, *1992*, p. 11/3.

increased more for females, from 63 to 70. After 1959, infant mortality fell continuously from 66 per 1,000 live births, but in 1990 was still worryingly high at 40 infant deaths per 1,000. Measured by Gini coefficients, the Philippines was an unequal society and especially so in urban areas (Table 14.1). However, a Gini measure fails fully to reflect pervasive inequality and throughout the four decades beginning in the 1950s, telling aspects of an unequal society were a large and growing mass of landless rural workers, high absolute poverty and a strong urban bias.

Chronology of Crises

The Philippines' post-World War II history was one of crises which began soon after the war. A late 1940s run-down of foreign reserves and a balance-of-payments crisis pushed the Philippines into a system of import restrictions and exchange controls, which strongly favoured import substitution and created an influential lobby of manufacturing interests. By 1959, the waning of a first, easy phase of import substitution and the growing foreign exchange requirements of home manufacturers for production inputs led to balance-of-payments problems. From 1960 to 1962, the authorities responded to continuing, severe balance-of-payments pressure and egregious rent-seeking by phasing out exchange controls and floating the peso. It quickly fell below a historic 1903 rate of 2 pesos to the dollar, and in 1965 was pegged at 3.90 pesos.

In 1972, the balance of payments was again in difficulty, this time because, beginning in 1966 under the newly elected President Ferdinand Marcos, the government financed growth through foreign borrowing. Unsustainable debt forced an early 1973 devaluation to 6.4 pesos to US$1. A decade of high foreign borrowing from 1973 to 1982, accompanied by massive capital flight, ended in a 1983 to 1985 contraction in GDP and another payments crisis. Economic instability contributed to the February 1986 overthrow of Marcos's 20-year reign in the so-called People Power Revolution. In 1990, the chapter's end year, per capita income remained 11.0 per cent below its 1982 peak (Table 14.1), and did not again match that level until 1997.

Rapid Growth and Decline: World War II to 1966

The Philippines began the post-war years handicapped by extreme devastation from the Japanese occupation and a badly overvalued exchange rate, but with the seeming advantage of high foreign reserves. In 1946, Philippine manufacturing production was 21 per cent of its typical pre-war level and agricultural output 58 per cent of that before the war.[4] The United States Congress made rehabilitation assistance conditional on acceptance, by the now independent Philippines government, of a 1946 Trade Act. The Act maintained American trade preferences and, importantly, specified retention of the historic exchange rate of 2 pesos to US$1, despite wartime inflation two-and-a-half times higher than in the United States, by far the Philippines' main trading partner. While the retention of pre-war exchange parity protected the dollar value of American investment in the Philippines, it considerably overvalued the peso. In so doing, the maintenance of parity ensured that Philippine goods were internationally uncompetitive.[5]

At the end of 1945, Philippine foreign exchange reserves peaked after the transfer from the United States of sugar- and coconut oil-processing excise taxes and various currency reserve funds.[6] Subsequently, the Philippines had large foreign exchange earnings from invisibles, mainly US military expenditures, pension payments and war-damage benefits. During the later 1940s, however, reserves were quickly run down by large trade deficits, which arose

[4] United States, *Economic survey mission to the Philippines*, p. 6.

[5] Power and Sicat, *Philippines*, pp. 31–34; United States, *Economic survey mission to the Philippines*, pp. 12–18: Golay, 'Philippine trade act', pp. 54–55 and 'Commercial policy', pp. 578–79.

[6] Golay, *Philippines*, p. 76.

because exports were constrained by a still incapacitated economy but imports were high due to post-war reconstruction and pent-up consumer demand, the latter further encouraged by exchange rate overvaluation of perhaps twice the peso's true worth.[7] By 1949, Philippine reserves had dropped to a quarter of their 1945 level and the first balance-of-payments crisis occurred.

The immediate, almost knee-jerk, reaction to the 1949 crisis and capital flight was to impose exchange controls and restrict imports. Throughout the 1950s, these responses evolved into ever more complex sets of restrictions, and created vested interests.[8] Development policy became twofold. One strand was that primary exports would be replaced as the leading sector by industrialization, at first incentivized by controls on imports of consumption goods along with foreign exchange at bargain prices, but later, as policy evolved, by high nominal, and much higher effective, tariff protection. The other strand was that the traditional agricultural component of a dualistic economic structure, comprising about 70 per cent of cultivated land, would make the nation self-sufficient in basic foodstuffs, especially rice and maize.[9] It seemed self-evident that growth depended on promoting the economy's 'fastest growing sectors' and this meant import-substitution industry, since 'these sectors are probably not to be found among the export sectors'.[10]

Owing to slight pre-war industrialization and wartime devastation, the Philippines had considerable scope for manufacturing 'catch-up' growth.[11] Attracted by this opportunity for industrialization and by manufacturing profits of about twice those in agriculture, resources flowed from it and towards industry. During most of the 1950s, the manufacturing component of industry, and the industrial sector more generally, expanded extremely rapidly (Table 14.2).

The World War II Japanese occupation and 1950s government-engineered incentives for import substitution provided a basis for two strong Filipino (as contrasted with ethnic-Chinese Filipinos) entrepreneurial responses. In the 1940s, a number of emergent Filipino industrial entrepreneurs were originally artisans but during the war had operated as buy and sell traders (dealers in second-hand and black market goods) and after 1945 sold American war surplus. Using profits from these activities and responsive to post-war shortages, the new 'craftsmen-entrepreneurs' started as manufacturers, typically on a small scale requiring initial capital of perhaps US$25,000.

During the 1950s, a further broad grouping of manufacturing entrepreneurs arose, this time as a product of government import controls and dollar

7 Emery, 'Successful Philippine decontrol', p. 275.
8 Power and Sicat, *Philippines*, pp. 33–34; Castro, 'Central bank', pp. 38–39.
9 Hooley and Ruttan, 'Philippines', p. 238.
10 Legarda, 'Foreign exchange decontrol', p. 25.
11 Baldwin, *Foreign trade regimes*, pp. 122, 149.

Table 14.5 *Philippines percentage changes in industrial production, 1950–65 (% change from previous year)*

Year	%
1950	20.7
1951	17.3
1952	5.3
1953	13.0
1954	12.4
1955	12.6
1956	15.7
1957	8.0
1958	7.7
1959	8.3
1960	3.2
1961	6.6
1962	5.7
1963	6.4
1964	8.3
1965	2.0

Source: Power, 'Import substitution', p. 190.

allocations for imports. These 'merchant-entrepreneurs' generally engaged in industries requiring large initial amounts of capital of around 1 million dollars and usually already had operated as merchants.[12] While no doubt attracted by the chance for monopoly profits in import-substitution industries, they were also concerned, as merchants, to avoid a squeeze on their import businesses due to government restrictions. For the merchant-entrepreneurs, a fundamental skill was lobbying to secure for themselves favourable government treatment in establishing import-substitution industries. Their success in securing licences and foreign exchange at preferential rates and associated profits gave rise to a new entrepreneurial elite. A strong body of Philippine industrialists now paralleled a pre-war elite of sugar planters and millers as a second influential lobby.

By the later 1950s, most of easy import substitution had been realized and industrial production, which from 1950 to 1956 had recorded annual growth of 12 per cent to 21 per cent in all but one year, slowed markedly (Table 14.5).

[12] The terms for entrepreneurs are attributable to Carroll, 'Filipino entrepreneurship', pp. 109, 123–26 and this paragraph is based on his article and book *Filipino manufacturing entrepreneur*.

Import composition became increasingly capital-intensive, a trend that had been encouraged by cheap foreign exchange, minimum wage legislation and a shift from finished goods to raw materials, semi-manufactures and capital goods. Many of these goods had to be imported and tended to use more foreign exchange than they saved. Philippine import substitution soon ran up against the well-known problem that continued industrialization requires more, and more capital-intensive, inputs and becomes import-dependent, unless local manufacturing can either break into export markets or extend production backwards to materials, intermediate goods and equipment.[13] However, industry in the Philippines – uncompetitive at international prices – failed to export and, furthermore, established few backwards linkages. Local production replaced, for example, imports of refrigerators and air conditioners, but their manufacture required imported sheet steel, compressors and other machinery.[14]

Nor were primary commodity exports able to provide the foreign exchange earnings to support increasingly import-dependent industrialization, by the 1950s backed by a powerful lobby. During the 1950s, agriculture, which had been sidelined by Philippine planners and lacked the good fortune of the emergence of any major new staple, grew more slowly than industry and at about half the rate of manufacturing. The lagging agricultural sector constrained industrial expansion through a lack of foreign exchange and wage goods as well as through a restricted internal market (Table 14.2).[15]

Between 1959 and 1972, exports continued to depend largely on primary commodities, and the export share of GDP remained small at a little over 10 per cent. In the early 1970s, traditional exports consisting of five main export groups – sugar, coconut products, abaca, logs and lumber and copper – accounted for four-fifths or more of total exports (Table 14.6).[16] Among the traditional exports, only sugar production, through the adoption of higher-yielding cane, improved technically and had considerable value added by processing. Other of the main exports yielded below their potential foreign exchange earnings, which could have been increased through more processing prior to export and the export of resource-intensive manufactured goods. Until the mid-1960s, coconut products mostly left the Philippines as low-value copra, not higher-value coconut oil, and the export of logs and lumber to Taiwan enabled the latter to become the world's largest exporter of plywood. Copper was exported as concentrates.

The second, 1959, Philippines balance-of-payments crisis increased pressure for reform as, too, did widespread and rampant rent-seeking and

[13] Power, 'Import substitution', pp. 169–70, 192; Sicat, *Historical and current perspective*, pp. 14–17.

[14] de Dios et al., 'Martial law', p. 5.

[15] International Labour Organization, *Sharing*, pp. 15–18, 26–30.

[16] Baldwin, *Foreign trade regimes*, pp. 8–9.

Table 14.6 *Philippines export composition by categories, 1972–87*

	Total exports million US$	Exports % GDP	Traditional exports % of exports	Other agricultural % of exports	Non-traditional manufactures % of exports	Traditional exports quantity 1972 = 100
1972	1,106	13.1	82.3	7.7	8.6	100.0
1975	2,294	14.5	72.7	7.7	17.9	88.0
1978	3,422	14.2	56.8	8.7	31.4	99.7
1980	5,788	16.4	51.1	8.3	36.4	99.6
1982	5,021	12.6	38.5	8.5	48.9	90.0
1984	5,391	16.7	29.9	7.8	58.2	60.9
1985	4,629	14.1	25.8	9.1	61.7	59.5
1986	4,842	15.6	22.6	8.4	61.7	80.7
1987	5,720	16.5	23.8	12.4	63.7	71.7

Notes: Traditional exports consist of coconut products, sugar products, forest products and minerals. A sharp 1987 drop in coconut prices helps to explain the fall that year in traditional exports as a percentage of total exports but a large increase in volume. The main constituents of non-traditional manufactures are electrical equipment and components and garments.
Source: Dohner and Intal, 'Marcos legacy', p. 454.

government favouritism, which had grown up around a plethora of import and exchange controls. As an example, under a 1955 barter law allowing 'no-dollar imports', manufacturers (as well as others) could import goods duty free, including intermediate and capital goods, provided the importer generated foreign exchange earnings equivalent in value to the cost of the imports. A black market in barter rights quickly developed and a large new, foreign exchange-earning export trade in rice bran invoiced to Hong Kong appeared. Hong Kong, however, recorded no imports of rice bran, all Philippine consignments apparently having been lost at sea.[17]

In April 1960, the Philippines began a programme of decontrol phased over two years. Imports were regulated through the Central Bank and a multiple exchange rate system, which soon became a 'major source of graft and corruption'.[18] Regulation effectively devalued the peso but was complicated by as many as eight different rates. These increased scope for favouritism and corruption by giving varying discounts on foreign exchange and allowing the sale

17 Castro, 'Philippine export development', p. 194.

18 Power and Sicat, *Philippines*, p. 92 and see Golay, *Philippines*, pp. 140–62; Baldwin, *Foreign trade regimes*, pp. 50–53.

of some exports at a free market rate. By mid-1962, exchange controls were mostly abolished. The peso immediately dropped from 2 pesos to the dollar to 3.90, but was not officially devalued until late 1965.

After decontrol, high protection continued, now effected through a tariff law enacted in 1957. The tariff structure perpetuated an earlier import-substitution bias towards non-essential goods by generally affording them the highest protection and discouraged backwards integration of Philippines manufacturing.[19] Philippines import-substitution policy further accentuated a strong urban bias, inherited from before World War II, through foreign exchange, credit and tax incentives for manufacturers, who were largely based in Manila.[20] Protected consumer goods industries concentrated around Manila. It became an '"import enclave"' which 'instead of linking backward to other regions of the economy … links on the supply side to the rest of the world. Even on the demand side, the market for many of the consumption goods depends on the free-spending new urban classes that were created by the new industrialization itself.'[21]

The higher peso price for the dollar changed relative prices to the advantage of commercial and exportable crops, and land use shifted towards these and away from food crops. The resulting higher food prices added to inflation and cut real wages substantially, making consumers the main losers from decontrol. Despite the liberalization of decontrol, local manufacturing remained profitable. The sector was still sheltered against imports, and was even more protected for goods that did not compete with imports.[22] In 1965, effective protection for non-import-competing goods averaged 83 per cent and 183 per cent for sugar, a level of protection for the latter explained by sugar's strong lobby of growers and millers. By contrast, exports, excluding sugar, had the disadvantage of 19 per cent negative effective protection, making them more expensive than the imported product (Table 14.7). Decontrol decelerated manufacturing production. The manufacturing sector had grown at an annual rate over 10 per cent from 1950 to 1959, but from 1959 to 1968 still expanded at 5.5 per cent annually (Table 14.2).

Marcos and Debt-fuelled Growth

In 1965, Ferdinand Marcos's election to the presidency, a position he occupied for the next 20 years, began an era marked by rapid but unsustainable debt-fuelled growth; a precipitous fall in real wages; brutal repression; a

[19] Power and Sicat, *Philippines*, pp. 35, 42.
[20] Ranis, 'Marcos's economic legacy', p. 118 and 'Two memoranda', p. 212.
[21] Power and Sicat, *Philippines*, p. 106.
[22] Treadgold and Hooley, 'Decontrol and redirection', pp. 116–28.

Table 14.7 *Philippines average rates of protection for manufacturing, 1965 (% of protection)*

	Nominal protection	Effective protection
Exports excluding sugar	−8	−19
Sugar	35	183
Import-competing	30	59
Non-import-competing	26	83
All manufacturing	2	48
Except exports	28	71

Source: Power, 'Protection in the Philippines', p. 278.

power base built on personal, predominantly regional, relationships within the Philippines; the military and favouritism; corruption on a scale not previously practised; a declaration of martial law stretching from 1972 to 1981 after which Marcos ruled by decree; and economic collapse during the regime's final four years. Finally, the United States, long supporters of Marcos, concluded that a tide of popular protest and the challenge of Corazon Aquino – widow of Benigno, assassinated by the regime – rendered a continued Marcos presidency untenable. In February 1986, the Americans airlifted Marcos and his family from Manila to Hawaii.[23]

The inaugural Marcos regime immediately instituted a policy 'of massive credit relaxation' to accelerate economic development, cutting the basic rediscount rate and reducing bank reserve requirements.[24] Central Bank credit available to the commercial banks expanded threefold between December 1965 and July 1966, and the Development Bank of the Philippines began refinancing programmes which aimed fully to restore the economy's productive capacity. The government emphasized rural development and spent heavily on infrastructure to try to raise agricultural growth rates which, it was argued, would increase traditional exports and cut food imports to provide more foreign exchange for imports of raw materials and capital goods. Furthermore, the production of additional wage goods for the industrial sector would support import substitution by expanding the market for domestic manufactures.

The green revolution – based on high-yielding rice strains requiring large inputs of water and fertilizer – was the main rural development success. By the

[23] The events are told in detail in Shaplen, 'From Marcos to Aquino – I' and 'From Marcos to Aquino – II'.
[24] Dohner and Intal, 'Marcos legacy', p. 382.

1969 election, the government could run on the slogan 'Marcos means more rice'.[25] Between 1962/64 and 1983/85, a doubling of both rice yields and output enabled the Philippines to limit imports of rice – the staple Filipino foodstuff – or even avoid them entirely, and still feed its growing population. From 1963 to 1984, rice output grew at an annual rate of 3.4 per cent and population at 2.8 per cent.[26] Even so, the Philippines 'green revolution' fell short of reaching the high yields that would have been possible with better access to credit to finance fertilizer and water inputs. Significant increases in the output of the non-traditional crops of bananas, pineapples, mangoes and coffee added to available foreign exchange but were far from sufficient to support the strategy of relying on commodity export earnings to support import-substitution industrialization.

Until the 1960s, the Philippines land frontier remained open and migration, mainly to Mindanao, offered a safety valve for the growing pressures of population increase, landlessness, widespread tenancy and serious rural poverty.[27] For some time, land reform had seemed a way to alleviate these problems and limit rural–urban migration. Although Marcos made considerable efforts to effect 'Land to the Tiller' programmes, these, ultimately, did relatively little to redistribute land in rice and corn areas and nothing outside them.[28] A further rural development strategy was to offer subsidized credit through government-sponsored agencies. From the 1950s through the 1970s, these government lending programmes proved, as throughout Southeast Asia, impractical and repeatedly failed. Poor monitoring of lending and a general borrower perception that loans were 'free' loans which did not require repayment caused the schemes to become bankrupt and the government to tire of putting money into them.[29]

Hoped-for rapid agricultural growth, on a scale equivalent to the 5.6 per cent annually during the 1950s, did not materialize. Between 1968 and 1982, agriculture grew at an annual rate of 3.5 per cent (Table 14.2). By mid-1967, a slow expansion of traditional exports relative to more ambitious credit creation, foreign borrowing and import-substitution policies forced a reintroduction of exchange controls. Continued deficit spending for development and rapid monetary growth associated with the 1969 presidential election caused debt to mount, and by 1970 resulted in another balance-of-payments crisis, the third since World War II. In response and under pressure from an IMF

[25] Abueva, 'Philippines', p. 58.

[26] Boyce, *Philippines*, pp. 63–64, based on *Statistical yearbook of the Philippines 1976*, pp. 134–64 and *Philippine statistical yearbook 1986*, pp. 266–75.

[27] Hooley and Ruttan, 'Philippines', p. 249; Barker, 'Barriers', p. 141; Dohner and Intal, 'Marcos legacy', pp. 376, 574.

[28] Lindsey and Ranis, *Evidence to the Subcommittee*, p. 125; Kerkvliet, 'Land reform', pp. 290–97; Hainsworth, 'Economic growth', pp. 22–23.

[29] Cristina, 'Credit', pp. 210–25; Esguerra, 'Assessment', pp. 168–91; Floro and Yotopoulos, *Informal credit markets*.

structural adjustment programme, the Philippines floated the peso. It quickly fell in value and during the early 1970s 6.4 pesos were required to buy 1 dollar.

After the 1970 balance-of-payments crisis, the Philippines shifted from a 1960s strategy of natural resources export-driven growth towards 'debt-driven growth'.[30] Outstanding Philippines external debt, which between 1962 to 1970 had risen three-and-a-half times, increased a further 15-fold from 1970 to 1982 to US$24.2 billion, and by 1986 reached US$28.9 billion (85 per cent of GDP and six times greater than merchandise exports).[31] From 1970 to 1982, aided by capital inflows to finance balance-of-payments deficits and a government once again spending beyond its means, real Philippines GDP grew at 5.4 per cent annually, although population increase of 2.8 per cent a year restricted per capita growth to 2.6 per cent.

Through the 1970s, the Philippines continued to emphasize import substitution with its by then entrenched interests but added to this a second industrial strategy of promoting low-wage manufactured exports. Fiscal incentives were a main tool of both policies. Import substitution now stressed a need for industrial deepening through developing the production of domestic intermediate and capital goods. Incentives were extended to copper smelting and refining, chemicals as well as synthetic fibres, and, beginning in the mid-1970s, to the producers of automobiles, trucks, motorcycles and consumer electronics. For these final goods, a Progressive Manufacturing Program supported the use of local intermediate inputs by progressively reducing the amount of foreign exchange available for their import. To compensate for restricted foreign exchange available to firms, they were given protection from foreign competition as well as from new domestic entrants. Despite the small domestic Philippine market, five automobile and nine truck manufacturers joined the programme. Influenced, like Malaysia, by successful capital-intensive Korean heavy industrialization, the Philippines government tried to copy this strategy. A 1979 initiative of Major Industrial Projects included diesel engine manufacturing and coconut-based chemicals. The first five of the industrial projects – financed almost entirely by foreign loans – created few jobs and at a cost of half a million dollars for each new worker.[32]

Sharp falls in urban skilled and unskilled real wages, which between 1969 and 1980 more than halved, provided a basis for an expansion of manufactured exports (Figure 14.1). The Industrial Incentives Act, 1967, and the Export Incentives Act, 1970, together with amendments to both, offered subsidies to attract manufacturers, chiefly foreign multinationals. More important to these enterprises, however, was that under the acts the Philippines set up export

[30] Ranis, 'Brief reflections', p. 33.

[31] Boyce, *Philippines*, p. 258. Data are from the Philippines government for 1962 and the World Bank for 1970 to 1986.

[32] Dohner and Intal, 'Marcos legacy', pp. 405–08, 445.

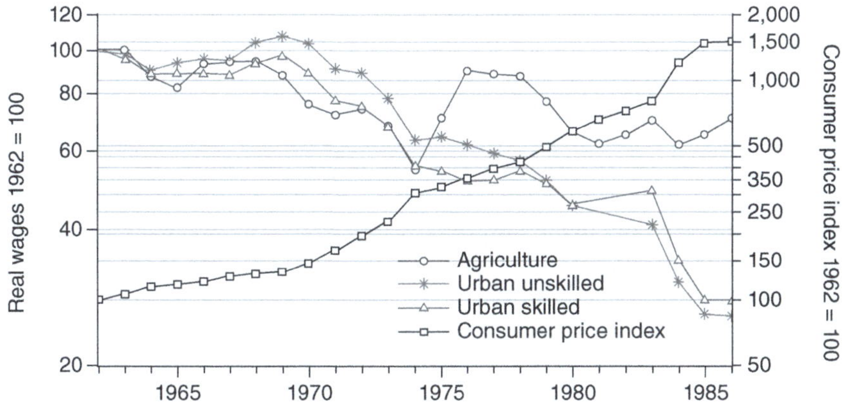

Figure 14.1 Philippines prices and real wages, 1962–86
Source: Boyce, *Philippines*, pp. 26, 28, 38.

processing zones and bonded warehouses which allowed importers to buy inputs at world prices.[33]

After 1972, export composition shifted rapidly from primary commodities towards manufactures (Table 14.6). Two factors explain the shift. First, the volume of traditional primary exports initially stagnated and, after 1982, dropped markedly, due to taxation of the sector and the production disincentive of peso depreciation. Second, non-traditional exports, predominantly electronics components and garments produced in export processing zones, grew from almost nothing in 1972 to become a significant component of manufacturing export value.

Non-traditional manufactures rose from 8.6 per cent of total exports in 1972 to nearly half a decade later and three-fifths by 1986 (Table 14.6). Over the same 1972 to 1986 period, however, manufacturing declined slightly as a share of both GDP and employment (Tables 14.3 and 14.4). Although owing to the new manufacturing industries exports as a proportion of GDP increased from 10.5 per cent in 1972 to 15.4 per cent in 1986, this rise did not accurately reflect the impact of manufactured exports on the Philippines economy. For both electronics and electrical components and garments, local value added was low. Bonded warehouses and export processing zones, the sites of most electronics and garment assembly, functioned as enclaves with few linkages to the rest of the economy other than employment.[34] While Taiwan and Korea used export processing zones to ease the transition from import substitution to

[33] Alburo and Shepherd, 'Trade liberalization experience', pp. 42–44; Dohner and Intal, 'Marcos legacy', pp. 453–57.

[34] Alburo and Shepherd, 'Trade liberalization experience', p. 67; Boyce, *Philippines*, p. 255; Vos and Yap, *Philippine economy*, pp. 18–19.

a more broadly based non-traditional export orientation, that did not happen in the Philippines.[35]

Exports of electronics and electrical products and garments offered a useful source of employment but these and other low-wage export industries could absorb no more than some of the surplus labour. Filipinos were forced to go abroad to find work and foreign job markets became 'a vent for labour pressures [and social tensions] that would otherwise be dangerously building up'.[36] By the 1980s, Filipino workers ranked as a major export, their remittances home equalling from a fifth to a quarter of the value of goods exports (Table 14.1).

Marcos, Rent-seeking and Debt

Marcos and his regime raised rent-seeking in the Philippines to a new level. 'Crony capitalism' describes the distribution, to an inner circle of cronies, of exclusive privileges consisting of some combination of rent-generating monopoly ownership, contracts, credit and government financial guarantees. By the 1980s, Marcos's cronies, and most of all Marcos himself, ended up owning a large share of the Philippine economy. The accumulation of wealth in this way – Filipinos termed it 'salivating capitalism' – was fundamental to the consolidation of political power by Marcos, and to elevating his family from being outside to becoming part of a Philippine elite of large landowners and industrialists.

Much greater government involvement in the economy and, integrally associated with this state expansion, Marcos's distribution of patronage began after the declaration of martial law in 1972. Between 1970–72 and 1978, government investment in the economy – much of it financed by foreign capital – increased from 1.6 per cent to 7.2 per cent of GDP, amounting to 30 per cent of domestic capital formation. State corporations in energy, agricultural infrastructure and transport undertook a large share of the investment. Public sector expansion, especially in construction, enabled Marcos to dispense patronage – through the award of contracts and access to credit and foreign exchange – and so enrich his close associates, as well as himself. Further to secure his rule, Marcos expanded the army from about 60,000 in 1972 to over 250,000 by 1975, appointed army officers to the boards of state-owned corporations and filled the higher ranks with officers from his home province of Ilocos Norte.

Under martial law, government creation of monopolies in many major industries gave rise to rents that rewarded Marcos's associates. Monopolized industries included gambling, shipping, flour imports and the monopsony

35 Ranis, 'Brief reflections', p. 31.

36 Mangahas, 'What happened', p. 132 and see International Labour Organization, *Sharing*, pp. 11–13.

buying of sugar and coconuts. The government effected the transfer of assets – through forced sale, foreclosure or the grant of equity in enterprises – from enemies or rivals of Marcos to his cronies. Even Procter and Gamble, Lever Brothers and Cargill were required to sell their coconut mills to UNICOM, a Philippines multinational.[37]

1980s Crisis and Collapse

Easy access to petrodollars and crony capitalism reinforced each other in creating the two underlying causes of a build-up of debt that resulted in a 1983 Philippines balance-of-payments crisis. The availability of petrodollars accelerated public sector investment and so also opportunities to create and distribute the rents fundamental to an accompanying rise of cronyism. At the same time, international commercial banks seeking outlets for petrodollars lent on a large scale for private projects. Often, these loans required 'little justification beyond the existence of government guarantees'. Almost inevitably, a number of projects, leveraged with the credit available to cronies, failed and had to be taken over or bailed out by the government or, more often, public corporations or financial institutions. At the end of the Marcos era, nearly 90 per cent of the assets of the Development Bank of the Philippines and over half of those of the Philippine National Bank were non-performing, a total of US$7 billion.[38]

By the 1980s, debt had deepened because a share of the capital inflows during the 1970s and early 1980s – substantial, but difficult reliably to quantify – had left the Philippines as capital flight, known locally as 'dollar sailing'. Filipino 'sailers' included corporations, government officials including Marcos, his cronies, currency traders and the professional class. Marcos's 1972 declaration of martial law 'frightened every Filipino who had anything to lose. [E]very successful businessman, lawyer, accountant, doctor, and dentist … has some form of cash or assets which he began to squirrel abroad.'[39] One estimate is that, without capital flight between 1973 and 1986, Philippines debt would have been 60 per cent instead of 98 per cent of GDP.[40] Hard currency exited through false invoicing of exports and imports, kickbacks, inter-bank transfers and as US dollars exchanged for pesos on Manila's black market in the Chinese financial district of Binondo.[41]

In 1981, after the lifting of martial law, serious political instability accelerated capital flight. At the same time, the current account deficit widened

37 Dohner and Intal, 'Marcos legacy', pp. 469–76; de Dios et al., 'Martial law', pp. 23–25.
38 Dohner and Intal, 'Marcos legacy', p. 570.
39 Shaplen, 'From Marcos to Aquino – II', p. 61.
40 de Dios et al., 'Martial law', p. 18.
41 Boyce, *Philippines*, pp. 282–85.

sharply owing to the second oil price shock, the terms of trade worsened and world interest rates rose, this last particularly crippling, since in 1980 almost half of Philippines debt was short term or at floating interest rates. In the 1980s, the Central Bank ran down reserves to finance a growing current account deficit.[42] The budget deficit, which had not been large, increased from ₱3.4 billion in 1980 to ₱12.2 billion the next year and ₱14.4 billion in 1982 (4.3 per cent of GDP). Foreign borrowing financed half the deficit in 1981 but only a third in 1982 as it became more difficult to borrow from abroad. Two-thirds of domestic financing came through money creation, which contributed to rising inflation and falls in real wages.[43] Finance was also made available by the IMF, which, starting in 1980, extended the first of 10 structural adjustment loans with accompanying reform packages as a condition for continued financial support.

After the assassination of Aquino in August 1983, confidence in the Marcos administration and economy completely evaporated and yet more capital left the Philippines.[44] It was, however, merely the denouement of an unsustainable economy. From late 1982, international lenders had begun to withdraw. By late 1983, a rapid exhaustion of Philippine reserves had occurred over the previous year, and interest payments on Philippines debt exceeded new capital inflows.[45] The balance-of-payments crisis during the second half of 1983 was the worst in Philippine history.

In October 1983, the Philippines declared the first of a series of 90-day debt moratoriums. The peso, which had already fallen from ₱9 to ₱11 to the dollar in June 1983, was further devalued to ₱14 in October. However, the black market rate was ₱30, and to stabilize the peso to help meet IMF targets, the government intervened by operating the 'Binondo Central Bank' from early 1984 to February 1986. The National Intelligence and Security Authority rounded up Binondo's best-known Chinese black marketeers and struck a deal – the alternative to which was punishment – that so long as the Chinese bought and sold foreign exchange at government-dictated rates they could keep the dealing profits. At the end of 1984 the peso, when floated as part of an IMF adjustment package, declined to ₱20 per dollar.[46]

Structural adjustment, although judged successful in its aims of stabilizing the economy, exacted high economic and social costs in economic contraction, unemployment and falls in real wages. Urban areas were particularly affected. Prices rose 50 per cent between 1983 and 1984 and a further 23 per cent the next

[42] Dohner and Intal, 'Marcos legacy', pp. 519–21; Lindsey, 'Economic crisis', pp. 1193–94; de Dios et al., 'Martial law', pp. 13–14.

[43] Remolona and Lamberte, 'Financial reforms', pp. 31–33.

[44] Chris Sherwell, 'Why confidence drained away', *Financial Times*, 19 September 1984.

[45] Boyce, *Philippines*, p. 283.

[46] Dohner and Intal, 'Marcos legacy', pp. 525–27; Boyce, *Philippines*, pp. 257–58.

year. In 1962, daily agricultural wages without meals (41 1986 pesos) were less than half urban unskilled wages (90 1986 pesos) and a third of urban skilled wages (121 1986 pesos). Due to the precipitate urban falls, in 1986 the gap between agricultural and urban unskilled wages (in 1986 pesos) had been reversed to ₱29 and ₱23 respectively and agricultural wages at ₱29 were not too far adrift of urban skilled wages (₱35). In 1986, real urban unskilled wages were less than a quarter and skilled wages under a third of their 1970 levels (Figure 14.1).

Poverty measurement is ill-defined in the Philippines and sensitive to assumptions as well as the choice of deflators. It is clear, however, that between the 1950s and 1990s, extensive poverty remained a persistent aspect of the Philippines. High Philippines absolute poverty, defined as the inability to meet nutritional requirements, was partly explained by the large proportion of the population in low-productivity agriculture. Throughout the post-war decades, using the headcount method (the percentage of the population living below the poverty line), around half to as many as three-quarters of Filipinos in the rural areas of the Visayas and Bicol were poor.[47]

During the 1983 through 1986 debt crisis, poverty almost certainly increased as inflation cut into real wages. Although affecting rural areas, the crisis particularly impacted urban areas through extremely high unemployment and sharp falls in living standards.[48] These drops, along with famine in Negros, probably encouraged political change and the People Power Revolution. The latter ended the Marcos presidency and led to his replacement by Corazon Aquino.

GDP per capita began to rise again in 1986 but did not recover to its 1978 level until 1990. Political instability paralleled the depressed economy. A succession of coups, the most serious and well-coordinated attempt by part of the army in December 1989, were launched against the Aquino regime. Her Fifth Philippine Republic survived, however, and in 1992 she was followed as president by her defence minister Fidel Ramos.

Nationalism, Pluralism and Import and Retail Trades

In the Philippines, Chinese were a tiny proportion of the population – at most 1 per cent in 1939 and concentrated in Manila – but, as throughout most of Southeast Asia, they were major importers and dominant as retail traders.[49] Along with many indigenous Southeast Asians, Filipinos shared a bias against 'middlemen' which translated into anti-Chinese feeling. 'Filipinization' of the

[47] Boyce, *Philippines*, pp. 33–37; Mangahas, 'What happened', pp. 133–34, 139–40; Hainsworth, 'Economic growth', pp. 22–24.

[48] For example, Lindsey, 'Economic crisis', pp. 1199–200.

[49] Wong, *Chinese*, pp. 4–5.

economy preoccupied a Constitutional Convention, set up under the provisions of the 1934 Philippines Independence Act, and in the post-independence period became a 'dominant objective of Philippine economic policy'.[50]

Initial measures to secure greater Filipino economic participation focused on the import and retail trades. The focus was partly because these trades were an obvious source of historic Filipino anti-Chinese feeling; and partly because, in the 1946 Philippine Trade Act, the United States pre-empted anti-foreign legislation by forcing the Philippines to accept parity with non-citizens in natural resource extraction and public utilities (rescinded only after the 1974 Laurel–Langley Agreement).

Immediately after World War II, Philippine government corporations and administrations directly imported relief and rehabilitation supplies and, through allocating these to Filipino firms, ensured greater Filipino participation in both the import and retail trades. Within two years, however, government imports were limited to flour as normal commercial channels for other goods were re-established, and the opportunity to favour Filipino firms was largely lost. In 1948, alien (American and Chinese) firms handled some three-quarters of imports.

Beginning at the end of 1948 and throughout the 1950s, import controls, foreign exchange allocations and quotas provided a new means to increase the Filipino role as importers. The first exchange control order specified a 20 per cent allocation of imports to 'new importers' and a raft of legislation and executive orders which followed raised allocations to Filipinos. Controls subsidized Filipino importers, because they raised the peso selling price of imported goods relative to their import cost.[51] Between 1948 and 1957, the number of Filipino importers increased from several hundred to over 3,000. Official data show a more than doubling of the Filipino share of imports to 54 per cent, accompanied largely by a drop in the Chinese share from 39 per cent to only 14 per cent. The data are, however, illusory, since a proportion, which is unknown, of the new Filipino 'importers' were only licence holders and sold their import rights to Chinese.[52]

Greater 'Filipinization' of the retail trade after 1948 proved even more difficult to achieve than for imports. Importers apparently passed on little of the subsidies obtained through controls to retailers. Although the thrust of government policy to nationalize retail trade became to subsidize Filipino retailers, various subsidy schemes proved ineffective and at the close of the 1950s Filipinos still had not replaced alien retailers.

[50] Golay, *Philippines*, p. 317.
[51] Golay, *Philippines*, pp. 317–30.
[52] Hartendorp, *History of industry*, pp. 678–79.

Singapore

In 1960, Singapore remained, as it historically was, essentially a staple port. The economy depended on providing handling, shipping and merchant services for rubber, tin and palm oil from a surrounding Southeast Asian hinterland and in return channelling to the region food and manufactured goods, the former mainly from Southeast Asia and the latter from the West and Japan. Between 1947 and 1957, population grew at 4.4 per cent annually, said to be the highest in the world.[53] Natural increase accounted for almost all this growth; less than a fifth was due to net immigration and migration.[54] Singapore had some breathing space before population increase began to translate into rapid labour force growth, but by the early 1960s there was a need, exacerbated by already substantial unemployment and high underemployment, to create, somehow, jobs for large flows of youths seeking employment. As Goh Keng Swee, Singapore's finance minister when it became part of Malaysia in 1963 and again for the 1965 Republic, later recalled: the most that a new labour force entrant could hope for was work as a bus driver and for that you had to know someone.[55]

After the People's Action Party (PAP), led by Lee Kuan Yew, won the 1959 general election, it 'committed to a programme of industrialisation' which, based on import substitution, appeared the best, perhaps the only, industrialization and job creation option.[56] Malaya as well as much of Indonesia offered possible markets where imports might be replaced by goods manufactured in Singapore.

Until independence in 1965, Singapore focused on developing through expanding import-substitution industry. When, however, Singapore split from Malaysia in 1965, the chance of a long-term, protected Malaysian market evaporated. Moreover, the 1967 British pull-out East of Suez and closure of the British naval base on the north of the island compounded Singapore's job creation difficulties. The closure threw large numbers of Singaporeans out of work and in 1966 unemployment reached 8.9 per cent. This section tells how Singapore, starting decisively by 1967, turned outwards to the international economy, took advantage of emerging trends in it to manufacture for export and, through a strong government, developed remarkably rapidly. Real GDP per capita increased by six-and-a-half times between 1960 and 1990, a rise accompanied, before long, by full employment, low inflation, high saving and rising real wages (Table 14.8).

53 Singapore, *Development plan, 1961–1964*, p. 1.

54 Singapore Legislative Assembly, *Report of the Committee on Minimum Standards of Livelihood*, pp. 2, 5, 55; International Labour Organization, *Report to the Government of Singapore on social security measures*, p. 66.

55 Goh Keng Swee, Interview with the author, 17 August 1989.

56 Singapore, *Annual report of the Division of Commerce and Industry*, p. 19.

Table 14.8 *Singapore economic and social indicators, 1947–90*

	1947	1960	1965	1970	1980	1990
GDP per capita 2011 prices US$	3,572	3,464	3,991	6,650	13,601	22,666
GDP per capita constant 2015 US$	–	3,610	4,212	6,993	13,944	23,256
GDP constant 2015 US$ bn	–	5.9	7.9	14.5	33.7	70.9
Population m	1.0	1.6	1.9	2.1	2.4	3.0
Population: Chinese %	77.8	75.4	–	76.2	76.9	74.7
Population: Indians %	7.7	9.0	–	7.0	6.4	7.6
Population: Malays %	12.1	13.6	–	15.0	14.6	13.5
GDP deflator 1985 prices 1960 = 100	–	100.0	104.9	112.2	204.7	261.6
Manufactured exports/GDP	–	34.2	31.6	22.8	73.8	108.5
Life expectancy	–	65	–	68	72	74
Life expectancy: male	–	62	–	65	70	73
Life expectancy: female	–	69	–	72	74	78
Infant mortality (per 1,000 live births)	87	35	–	14	12	7
% of age group in primary education	–	111	–	111	107	110
% of age group in secondary education	–	32	–	53	55	69
% of age group in tertiary education	–	6	–	8	8	n.a.
Literacy aged 10 and above %	37.4	52.3	–	72.2	83.0	90.1
Population per physician	–	2,300	–	1,400	1,150	840
Real average monthly earnings Singapore dollars (S$): all workers	–	–	–	–	813	1,465
Real average monthly earnings S$: manufacturing	–	–	–	–	676	1,278
Human development rank (of 130)	–	–	–	–	–	96

Notes and Sources: 1. GDP per capita 2011 US$ are from the Maddison Project Database, 2020; and GDP per capita constant 2015 US$ from World Bank, *World development indicators, 2020*. For 1947, GDP per capita is the 1950 figure. Other data are from Huff, *Economic growth*, pp. 412 (GDP deflator), 386–87, 412 (manufactured exports/GDP), 328 (real average earnings) and 352 (population, life expectancy (except male and female)); infant mortality, education, literacy and population per physician are from the World Bank, *World development indicators, 2020*. For 1947, infant mortality is from Singapore, *Annual report on the registration of births and deaths, 1940–1947*, pp. 4, 9. 2. Percentages of Chinese, Indians and Malays in the population are for the census years 1947, 1957, 1970, 1980 and 1990. 3. Before World War II, only about half of children aged 6–12 attended school; in 1947, the proportion still had not reached two-thirds. IBRD, *Economic development of Malaya*, pp. 120–21, 364; Mackenzie, *Economic and commercial conditions in Malaya*, p. 17. 4. Human development data are for 1990. The index ranks 130 countries in ascending order and placed Thailand as somewhat below high human development. In comparison to Singapore's 96, Malaysia ranked 85, Thailand 78, Indonesia 54 and the Philippines 65. United Nations, *Human Development Report, 1990*, p. 111.

By 1960, Singapore had already made large social gains, and further advances, if not greater equality, accompanied post-1960 growth. Between 1947 and 1960, infant mortality fell by 60 per cent, and literacy rates rose sharply to over half of the population aged 10 and over. By 1990, literacy, reflecting a new post-World War II policy to provide free, universal primary education, reached 90 per cent. In 1960, life expectancy of 65 years was high by developing country standards, and over the next three decades climbed further partly due to large increases in real wages and the number of physicians in the population. By 1990, Singapore unambiguously ranked as a developed country.

Singapore's development strategy was to emphasize growth, to spend on long-term investment, not short-term consumption, and to leave to one side redistributional concerns.[57] Available evidence indicates that in the mid-1960s Singapore had a rather unequal personal income distribution, 0.50 as measured by the Gini coefficient. Although studies conflict, the coefficient may have improved to about 0.44 by 1975; if so, it then worsened to the upper 40s by the mid-1980s.[58] However, the 1990 census showed a household income distribution over all ethnic groups of 0.43.[59] The tendency for more equal income distribution on a household than a personal basis suggested by some studies was consistent with Singapore's high female participation rates; by 1980, 55.1 per cent of households had more than one person working,[60] and in 1990, 40 per cent of married couples had both husband and wife working.[61]

Swift Growth and Change

Between 1960 and 1990, trade was, again, the engine for Singapore's rapid growth. But three changes set these decades apart from earlier twentieth-century development. First, economic development ceased to depend on the traditional staples as the economy diversified, initially through manufactures and then through financial and business services. By 1970, manufacturing had become a leading sector. Three years later, it ended Singapore's labour surplus condition, and with it a dual economy for Singaporeans, so that 1973 may be dated as a turning point in economic development.

The second change was that growth stemmed from a new set of entrepreneurs: public (i.e. government) enterprises and, even more, multinational

57 Singapore, *Development plan 1961–64*, pp. 6, 18; Singapore, *Parliamentary debates*, 24 (13 December 1965), cols. 52, 69 (budget statement); Lee, *Social revolution*, p. 6.

58 Rao and Ramakrishnan, 'Economic growth, structural change', pp. 92–122; Lee Sheng-Yi, 'Income distribution', pp. 71–98; Lim, *Policy options*, pp. 398–403.

59 Lau Kak En, *Singapore census of population, 1990, Households and housing* [statistical release 2], p. 10.

60 Khoo Chian Kim, *Census of population 1980 Singapore*, pp. 123, 130.

61 Lau Kak En, *Singapore census of population, 1990, Households and housing* [statistical release 2], p. 15.

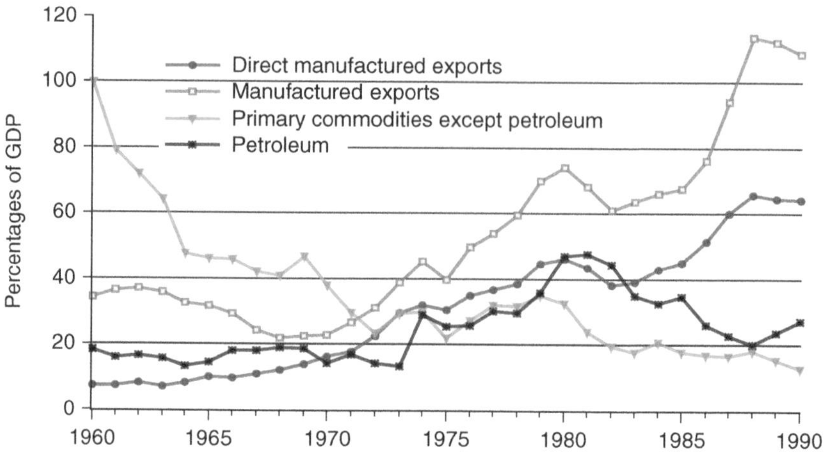

Figure 14.2 Singapore main export groups as percentages of GDP, 1960–90
Sources: Singapore, *Singapore trade statistics*, 1956–90; Singapore, *Report on the census of industrial production*, 1960/61–1990.

enterprises. By 1990, agency houses had, with a few exceptions, disappeared; local Chinese entrepreneurs, although still found especially in primary commodity exports, took a back seat. Third, an activist government committed to development guided economic transformation. Planning, begun with the report of a United Nations team in 1961, lay behind Singapore's growth.[62]

Five main features of Singapore's economic development from 1960 to 1990 can be discerned. One is sustained, exceptionally high growth rates of output. Between 1960 and 1990, real GDP per capita in 2011 US$ increased swiftly, doubling between 1960 and 1970 and again between 1970 and 1980 and rising by two-thirds between 1980 and 1990. Over the period, GDP per capita grew at 6.5 per cent per annum (Table 14.8).

Second, the structure of trade changed. After 1970, although Singapore remained a major world exporter of rubber and primary commodities as well as developing into a large oil refining centre, it grew decisively away from a staple port and towards the export of Singapore-made manufactures. In 1960, primary commodity exports (measured against GDP) were equivalent to 99 per cent of GDP and non-petroleum direct manufactured exports (goods not simply re-exported) were just 7 per cent. Direct manufactured exports stood at 12.7 per cent of GDP in 1966 but increased to almost half in 1979 and nearly two-thirds by 1990 (Figure 14.2).

Between 1960 and 1990, manufacturing grew at a real rate of over 12 per cent annually and direct manufactured exports even faster at more than 16 per cent.

[62] United Nations, *Proposed industrialization programme*.

Table 14.9 *Singapore real annual average manufacturing growth rates excluding petroleum, 1960–90 (%)*

	1960–90	1960–67	1967–73	1973–90	1973–80	1980–90	1986–90
Direct exports	16.2	10.4	31.8	10.8	12.8	11.4	16.5
Output	12.3	12.0	22.7	9.0	10.7	9.1	15.6
Value added	12.8	12.2	26.7	8.7	10.3	8.6	12.7

Source: Huff, *Economic growth*, p. 318.

Table 14.10 *Singapore GDP by industrial sector, 1960–90 (1985 market prices, %)*

	1960	1967	1970	1973	1980	1990
Agriculture	3.6	2.8	2.2	1.7	1.1	0.3
Quarrying	0.2	0.2	0.2	0.2	0.2	0.1
Manufacturing	16.6	20.5	24.8	28.4	29.5	29.0
Electricity, gas, water	1.7	2.0	1.9	1.9	2.0	2.1
Construction	5.3	8.6	9.5	8.1	7.1	5.3
Commerce	24.6	23.6	22.0	20.9	18.9	17.6
Transport and communications	8.8	6.9	7.3	8.5	12.0	14.2
Financial and business services	14.0	15.5	16.9	17.6	20.5	26.2
Public administration, community, social and personal services	19.6	17.8	14.9	13.3	11.6	10.4
Total	100.0	100.0	100.0	100.0	100.0	100.0
GDP at 1985 market prices (S$m)	5,059	8,283	12,172	17,274	28,833	57,049

Note: Totals may not add up to 100.0 per cent because GDP is less imputed bank service charges and plus import duties.
Source: Huff, *Economic growth*, p. 303.

After the 1967 decision by Singapore to turn outwards, annual growth rates were swiftest from 1967 to 1973 (22.7 per cent for manufacturing output and 31.8 per cent for direct manufactured exports), but for most sub-periods from 1960 to 1990 the growth of each of the categories of output, exports and value added was double-digit. Although manufacturing value added increased at somewhat slower rates than output, its continuous growth shows how in the process of expanding manufactured exports Singapore also moved towards more sophisticated production (Table 14.9).

Third, economic growth was accompanied by fundamental structural transformation (Tables 14.10 and 14.11). Two principal changes occurred. The share

Table 14.11 *Singapore employment by industrial sector, 1947–90*

	1947	1957	1970	1980	1990
(a) Persons 000					
Agriculture	29.1	32.7	22.5	17.0	5.1
Quarrying	1.2	1.6	2.2	1.1	0.8
Manufacturing	58.9	74.2	143.1	324.1	447.4
Electricity, gas, water	0.8	4.0	7.6	8.5	6.7
Construction	9.4	24.6	43.1	72.3	122.1
Commerce	75.4	114.3	152.9	229.8	337.5
Transport and communications	53.0	50.3	79.0	119.9	146.6
Financial and business services	7.6	21.7	23.1	79.4	167.2
Public administration, community, social and personal services	110.4	146.3	177.0	224.6	303.5
Unclassified	11.8	2.1	0.4	0.4	0.0
Total	357.5	471.9	650.9	1,077.1	1,537.0
(b) %					
Agriculture	8.1	6.9	3.5	1.6	0.3
Quarrying	0.4	0.3	0.3	0.1	0.1
Manufacturing	16.5	15.7	22.0	30.1	29.1
Electricity, gas, water	0.2	1.0	1.2	0.8	0.4
Construction	2.6	5.2	6.6	6.7	7.9
Commerce	21.1	24.2	23.5	21.3	22.0
Transport and communications	14.8	10.7	12.1	11.1	9.5
Financial and business services	2.1	4.6	3.5	7.4	10.9
Public administration, community, social and personal services	30.9	31.0	27.2	20.9	19.8
Unclassified	3.3	0.4	0.1	0.0	0.0
Total	100.0	100.0	100.0	100.0	100.0

Source: Huff, *Economic growth*, pp. 410–11.

of manufacturing in total output increased rapidly, from 16.6 per cent in 1960 and from 20.5 per cent in 1967 to 28.4 per cent by 1973. In 1990, manufacturing contributed 29.0 per cent of GDP and accounted for 29.1 per cent of employment. The other structural change was the altered composition of the tertiary sector. Between 1960 and 1990, services (commerce, finance and business and public administration) accounted for over half of GDP, but the sector's composition shifted away from commerce and public administration and towards finance and business services, which by 1990 accounted for over a quarter of

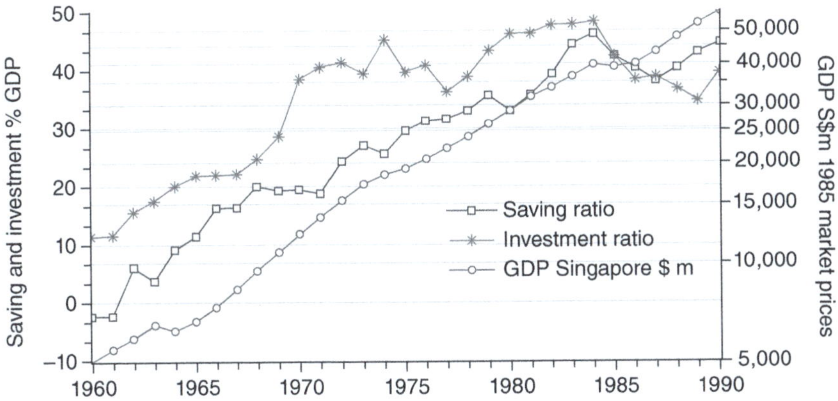

Figure 14.3 Singapore GDP, saving ratio and investment ratio, 1960–90
Source: World Bank, *World development indicators, 2022.*

national income. The shift reflected the absorption of workers from labour-supply-pushed services like hawking and into manufacturing and the development of Singapore as a centre for international services.

In Singapore, a high proportion of services were internationally tradeable. The main diversification, and greatest growth, in tradeable services came through the Republic's development as an international financial centre. After 1978, financial and business services emerged as an engine of growth, and over the next 12 years were the economy's fastest growing sector. By 1990, financial and business services provided 26.2 per cent of GDP, or almost as much as manufacturing, but, reflecting the capital-intensive, high-productivity nature of many traded services, made up just 10.9 per cent of employment, a third of that in manufacturing. The successful expansion of financial and business services represented the most important part of development planning to establish Singapore as a centre for what government planners termed 'brain services' – occupations with a high human capital content and typically dependent on substantial inputs of formal education.[63]

Fourth, high saving and investment characterized Singapore's economic development. An urban economy and international services centre like Singapore required heavy infrastructural investment. The PAP government raised the savings ratio by enforcing state-directed abstinence from consumption. The savings ratio, still under 10 per cent in 1964, reached 27 per cent in 1973, over 30 per cent by 1976, and averaged over 40 per cent from 1983 (Figure 14.3).

[63] Hon Sui Sen, *Economic pattern in the 1970s*, pp. 19–23; Singapore, Ministry of Trade and Industry, *Development plan for the eighties*, pp. 9–13; Singapore, *Report of the Economic Committee, Singapore economy: new directions*, pp. 139–43, 177–92.

The investment ratio also increased sharply, and from 1970 was sustained at high levels, with gross capital formation usually over 40 per cent of GDP (Figure 14.3). In the 1970s, Singapore – partly through government use of employee pension funds to finance planned state investment – saved enough to finance almost two-thirds, and by the 1980s virtually the whole, of its capital formation. However, the process of capital accumulation was more complex than suggested by this apparently increasing reliance on domestic savings, since throughout the post-1966 period, direct foreign investment made a growing contribution to capital formation.

Fifth, Singapore's post-1959 development occurred with low inflation, remarkable for an economy already chronically short of labour by the late 1970s. For 18 of the 30 years from 1961 to 1990, the GDP deflator was 2.6 per cent or less, and exceeded 5 per cent in only seven years, despite high world inflation and Singapore's very open economy. The annual inflation rate averaged below 2 per cent in every decade except the 1970s.

Multinationals and Government

The means by which Singapore achieved its rapid post-1966 manufacturing development are summed up in the explanation that 'we imported entrepreneurs in the form of multinational corporations and the government itself became an entrepreneur in a big way'.[64] Strong government intervention was required for the injection into Singapore's economy of multinationals and public enterprise. Together they afforded the two types of 'entrepreneurial substitute' possible, and obviated any need for the PAP government to look to the Chinese-educated and China-oriented Chinese who had traditionally been Singapore's entrepreneurs.

Manufacturing production depended heavily – and increasingly – on exports (Table 14.11). Foreign firms were almost wholly responsible for manufactured exports and by 1975 dominated the manufacturing sector as a whole. In 1990, wholly and majority foreign-owned firms accounted for three-quarters of manufactured output and 86 per cent of direct exports. Linkages created by foreign firms were largely to other foreign-owned firms. Since multinationals organized the marketing of the goods they made, Singapore sidestepped the difficulty for a developing country of breaking into world markets.

Electronics and electrical goods became by far the largest single source of manufacturing employment and output. By the beginning of the 1970s, Singapore had the lion's share of offshore assembly activities of the United States and European semiconductor industries. Singapore's trade in integrated circuits emerged between 1980 and 1984 and in disk drives from 1986 to 1990.

[64] Goh Keng Swee, interview with the author, 17 August 1989.

By the late 1980s, the Republic accounted for over half of global production of disk drives. Shipment of electronics and electrical goods to the United States again made America Singapore's principal export market.

By 1988/90, multinationals' production decisions had created a new regional division of labour, based on skill differences, differential factor prices, especially for labour, and superior communications facilities in Singapore. As well as manufacturing products itself, Singapore often had a services rather than a manufacturing role in regional production; the Republic's exports of electronics goods might therefore have a high import content and low domestic value added. For example, electronics components could be imported to Singapore for re-shipment to Malaysia for assembly, and after completion of work there imported again by Singapore, perhaps as a finished good like a television set, for checking and warehousing, before export to a final destination.[65]

Export-oriented manufacturing provided a solution to Singapore's need to create jobs. Manufacturing employment stood at 74,000 in 1957, but by 1970 had nearly doubled and by 1980 approached doubling again (Table 14.11). Between 1967 and 1973, when manufacturing growth was at its most rapid, jobs in the production of electronics and electrical goods and in textiles and garments accounted for about half of the rise in employment. Although the labour force continued to grow rapidly, unemployment fell from 8.9 per cent in 1966 to 4.5 per cent in 1973, the latter effectively constituting full employment (Tables 14.12 and 14.13).

The government set up, as its agent, the Economic Development Board (EDB), to be 'the spearhead for industrialization by direct participation in industry and providing necessary infrastructure'.[66] Coordination through the EDB was basic to the new export drive, and in 1968 its success spawned additional development-oriented institutions: the Board's largest industrial estate, at Jurong, came under the management of the Jurong Town Corporation, and the financial arm of the EDB became the Development Bank of Singapore.

Internationally Competitive Wages

Until the mid-1960s, despite underemployment and growing unemployment in Singapore, a historical problem of internationally uncompetitive wages persisted: Singapore was 'a high cost producer by Asian standards',[67] with wage costs '20–30 per cent too high for world markets'.[68] After the 1965 split with

[65] Singapore, Ministry of Trade and Industry, *Economic survey 1987*, pp. 35–36, *1990*, pp. 89–90, 96–97, *1991*, pp. 79–80.

[66] Singapore, Economic Planning Unit, Prime Minister's Office, *First development plan 1961–1964: review of progress*, p. 37.

[67] Singapore, 'An industrial development programme', p. 7.

[68] United Nations, *Proposed industrialization programme*, p. 115.

Table 14.12 *Singapore labour force growth, 1947–90*

(a) Persons 000

	Total	Male	Female
1947	357.5	310.5	47.1
1957	480.3	393.8	86.5
1970	726.7	539.2	187.5
1980	1,116.0	730.6	385.4
1990	1,562.8	934.3	628.5

(b) Annual average growth rate

	Total	Male	Female
1947–1957	3.0	2.4	6.3
1957–1970	3.2	2.4	6.1
1970–1980	4.4	3.1	7.5
1980–1990	3.4	2.5	5.0
1947–1990	3.5	2.6	6.2

Source: Huff, *Economic growth*, p. 293.

Table 14.13 *Singapore unemployment rates, 1957–90 (%)*

Year	%
1957	4.9
1966	8.9
1968	7.3
1970	6.0
1972	4.7
1973	4.5
1974	3.9
1980	3.3
1984	2.7
1986	6.5
1988	3.3
1990	1.7

Source: Huff, *Economic growth*, p. 291.

Table 14.14 *Singapore, United States, Japan and Asian NICs hourly compensation costs for production workers in manufacturing, 1975–90 (current US$ and index United States = 100)*

	1975		1980		1987		1990	
	$	Index	$	Index	$	Index	$	Index
United States	6.36	100	9.87	100	13.52	100	14.88	100
Japan	3.05	48	5.61	57	10.83	80	12.64	85
Singapore	0.84	13	1.49	15	2.31	17	3.78	25
South Korea	0.33	5	0.97	10	1.65	12	3.82	26
Taiwan	0.40	6	1.00	10	2.26	17	3.95	27
Hong Kong	0.76	12	1.51	15	2.09	15	3.20	22
Asian NICs	0.50	8	1.15	12	2.06	15	3.75	25

Notes: 1. Hourly compensation includes all direct payments to workers before any payroll deductions and employer expenditures for legally required insurance programmes and contractual and private benefit plans. Compensation may also be adjusted upwards to include taxes on payrolls or employment or downwards to reflect subsidies and so reflect labour costs. 2. Asian NICs refers to a US-trade weighted average level for Singapore, South Korea, Taiwan and Hong Kong.
Source: US Department of Labor, *International comparisons, 1991*, pp. 5, 6, 12–14.

Malaysia, the problem of high wage levels had to be solved if Singapore were to embark on export-oriented industrialization. The necessary adjustment in Singapore's labour market might eventually have come through market forces.

It was, however, government that decisively effected adjustment and, moreover, then enforced internationally competitive wages. Government control of the labour market was embodied in legislation: two measures, the Employment Act and the Industrial Relations (Amendment) Act of 1968, 'de-politicised the labour movement, established de facto government control over unions [and] transferred bargaining power from workers to employers'.[69] Few work stoppages occurred after 1967; they had been virtually eliminated by 1977. Singapore's total of two work stoppages, involving 159 workers in the 13 years 1978–90, cannot have reflected a free labour market.

By 1969, for comparable job classifications in key electrical and electronics assembly industries, hourly compensation costs in Singapore were less than one-eleventh of the United States level, and below those in South Korea, Taiwan and Hong Kong. Productivity in Singapore was equal to that in these

[69] Lim and Pang, *Trade, employment*, p. 11.

three countries, and at least as high as in the United States.[70] Low-wage but productive, reliable labour secured through government intervention was fundamental in accounting for the decision of multinationals to locate in Singapore for component and assembly electronics work as part of vertically integrated international manufacturing. In addition to wage levels, distance costs and government influences help to explain multinationals' locational decisions; on both counts, supply response effected through government made Singapore attractive to multinationals. Its geographical position cut distance costs, while the government's provision of good communications infrastructure made an important contribution by minimizing the time and expense of shipment to and from the island.[71]

Government influences – political risk as perceived by multinationals, fiscal incentives offered by the host country and facility of business operation – worked strongly in Singapore's favour. Political stability and social quiescence greatly reduced the danger of interruption to multinational production, especially important for component manufacture and intra-firm trade. Singapore offered generous fiscal incentives, including tax holidays and reductions, and 100 per cent foreign ownership of equity. Planning in Singapore, which made available ready-to-move-into industrial sites, attracted multinationals, as did the efficient and honest government and government bureaucracy. The quality of its government placed Singapore apart from the rest of Southeast Asia and stands in stark contrast to the Philippines as described earlier in the chapter. In 1973, 'Texas Instruments simply got browned off with red tape in Taiwan and revamped its investment plans to centre on Singapore – the company was in operation only 50 days after the investment decision was made'.[72]

Inflation

In 1972 the government inaugurated the National Wages Council, a tripartite body which published guidelines for pay increases. Without this, full employment would almost certainly have set up strong inflationary wage pressure and internationally uncompetitive pay rises, driving multinationals elsewhere. Although not officially mandatory, these guidelines were closely observed. The government controlled unions; more than this, a measure of its power was that, in the absence of statutory or other overt enforcement mechanisms

[70] Leong, *Wage levels*, pp. 2–7, 13–19, 25; United States Tariff Commission, *Economic factors*, pp. A-90, 166–73.

[71] Helleiner, 'Manufactured exports', pp. 35–41; Sharpston, *International sub-contracting*, pp. 111–18.

[72] 'Drive for foreign investment becomes increasingly selective', *Financial Times*, Singapore survey, 1 October 1973.

to limit wage payments by foreign multinationals, they did not bid up wages, despite incentives to do so due to labour scarcity and Singapore's attractiveness as a location. Increases in real wages averaged just 1.7 per cent from 1973 to 1978.[73] Then, boosted initially by a three-year wage correction policy decreed by Singapore planners, real average monthly earnings for all workers doubled by 1990 to reach S$1,465.[74] The government measured its success in containing labour costs against the average for the Asian NICs. Although in 1975 Singapore wages were significantly above this average, by 1990 they matched it exactly (Table 14.14).

During the later 1970s and 1980s, planning in Singapore, which emphasized technical education and industrial training for workers, drew in multinationals.[75] Electronics multinationals tended to move to Singapore at earlier stages of product development or for specialized, niche work. By the 1980s, virtually every international electronics producer was represented in Singapore, and workers were more likely to make a finished product than only components. Higher skills and the use of more capital contributed to raising value added per manufacturing worker in Singapore and allowed real wages to rise.[76]

Government Enterprise

The Singapore government began, as non-statutory undertakings, a range of enterprises that the colonial administration would have considered outside the scope of government, including Singapore International Airlines (SIA), Neptune Orient Lines (an international shipping line) and International Trading Company (Intraco). The main non-statutory public enterprises, often themselves with subsidiaries and associated companies, were owned through three government holding companies. Government companies were estimated to number 490 in 1983, including the subsidiaries of statutory boards. Singapore's state-owned enterprises remained notable for efficient and effective management, and the vast majority of them appear to have run at a profit or at least broken even.[77] But reflecting a philosophy that private enterprise would provide the main force for growth, the state-owned enterprise sector was never large by developing country standards, and in 1985 probably accounted for no more than 10 per cent of GDP.

[73] 'An interim report of the deliberations of the Economic Committee', Singapore, Ministry of Trade and Industry, *Economic survey of Singapore 1985*, p. 20.

[74] Singapore, Ministry of Labour, *Yearbook of labour statistics, 1990*, p. 23.

[75] Singapore, *Parliamentary debates* 35, 1 (1 March 1976) (budget statement), cols. 27–28.

[76] For discussion of the growing use of skilled labour, see Sandilands and Tan Ling-Hui, 'Comparative advantage', pp. 34–56.

[77] Low, 'Public enterprises in Singapore', pp. 253–87; Krause, 'Hong Kong and Singapore', pp. s62–s64.

Government-enforced Saving Rates

The driving force in Singapore's saving process was public sector savings – the current surplus in the consolidated accounts of the public sector. These savings increased from less than a quarter of national savings in 1974 to three-fifths by 1984.[78] Public sector savings consisted of the government's budget surplus, together with the surpluses realized by statutory boards. Statutory boards were harnessed by the PAP government for economic development. The boards often had 'substantial commercial operations' and their monopoly power, either legislated or natural, enabled the government to realize large profits to create public sector savings so long as reasonable commercial efficiency was maintained.[79] Seven main boards – the Housing and Development Board, Jurong Town Corporation, Public Utilities Board, Port of Singapore Authority, Urban Redevelopment Authority, Telecommunication Authority of Singapore and Sentosa Development Corporation – were central in determining public sector savings.

The private sector's contribution to Singapore's high saving rate was largely due to saving forced by the government through a social security scheme – the Central Provident Fund (CPF). The CPF increased the domestic saving rate because (unusually among developing countries) it operated on the provident fund principle: on retirement, individuals were paid benefits determined by total past contributions from themselves and their employers plus interest, rather than payments being made to retirees from the contributions of those still working. Collection was effected through withholding at source employers' and employees' contributions to the CPF, typically in equal shares and based on an employee's wages.

The CPF grew rapidly and, helped by full employment and growing wage employment, widened to encompass the large majority of Singapore workers by 1973. There was also a deepening of the CPF as total contributions were put up to 50 per cent of employees' wages by 1984, and as real wages rose. After 1974, public sector and CPF saving progressively reduced the importance of voluntary private sector saving. The contribution of voluntary private savings fell from almost three-fifths of national savings in 1974 to less than one-quarter by 1983.

Through borrowing from the CPF at below market interest rates, the government obtained a cheap, non-inflationary source of finance and relied extensively on it to provide infrastructure and public goods. At the same time, in its public sector mobilization of finance by the extraction of saving through monopoly power, Singapore operated a state-directed capitalism which, in

[78] For discussion of public sector saving, see Lim, *Policy options*, pp. 215–31.

[79] Singapore, *Report of the public sector divestment committee*, p. 61, and see pp. 19–20, 43–49.

Gurley and Shaw's terminology, was a technology of finance resembling socialist central planning more than private free market capitalism. Public sector savings, like those of the CPF, were put at the government's disposal.[80]

Public compliance in saving through the CPF was strengthened by the expectation of low inflation, which would protect the real value of savings. At the same time, the rapid gains in real wages and spread of home ownership to almost all Singaporean households induced acceptance of government wage control. A 'virtuous circle' of macroeconomic policy was thereby completed: low inflation, with consequent real exchange rate competitiveness, and extensive infrastructure helped to ensure continued foreign capital inflows giving access to multinational technology and marketing, which made real wage gains possible. Furthermore, these gains were largely guaranteed, since Singapore citizens wishing to work were almost assured of a job. The job security of Singapore nationals was, in part, underwritten through hosting up to 200,000 foreign workers by the mid-1970s who could be sent home, and so bore much of the risk of unemployment in an economic downturn. In 1985, when growth turned negative due to falls in foreign demand for electronics and ship repair as well as a contraction in domestic demand, there was a net reduction of 96,000 jobs. However, over three-fifths of those affected were foreign workers.[81] These workers thus came to fulfil a function of labour force flexibility similar to that of recently arrived immigrants from South China before World War II.

Domestic capital resources were mobilized for economic development when the government used its control over savings for investment in projects such as housing and infrastructure. The government also required a compulsory contribution from employers to a Skills Development Fund, which was used as part of a programme to train workers for higher technology jobs and develop human capital.[82] Infrastructure provided under government auspices was the most modern and efficient possible, including port, airport, telecommunications, roads and a mass rapid transit system. For business in Singapore, the effect was to provide a subsidy which reduced expenses of operating within the Republic as well as of reaching world markets.

Singapore's high investment could increasingly have been domestically financed. Indeed, by the late 1980s national savings exceeded gross capital formation, reflected in a current account surplus on the balance of payments. But it was generally accepted that the government invested a high proportion of Singapore's public savings abroad in equities and bonds, real estate and short-term assets. In effect, through this government investment abroad, Singapore exchanged an outflow of national savings for an inflow into the

80 Cf. Gurley and Shaw, 'Financial structure', p. 262.

81 Singapore, Ministry of Trade and Industry, *Economic survey 1985*, p. 4; Wilson, 'Monetary policy', p. 11.

82 Lim Chong Yah, 'The NWC as I see it', p. 53; Hu, *Budget statement* (Singapore), p. 6.

domestic economy of private foreign capital, which brought with it technology and assured access to markets. The exchange explains a part of what might otherwise seem a paradox: that high saving largely relied on the public sector but high investment came chiefly from the private sector.

Planning and Government Intervention

The leaders of independent Singapore began with a general belief in the effectiveness of planning but had no definite idea of the course it should follow. A coherent, clearly defined development strategy, essential to any shade of planning, emerged from the later 1960s as political leaders and planners increasingly perceived the strength of the world economy's new flows of trade and foreign investment. As part of the same process, Singapore's leaders found control over strategic domestic markets and institutions the most effective way to respond to opportunities in the world economy in order to meet the main planning objectives of providing jobs, absorbing surplus labour and achieving rapid economic growth.[83] There was no ideological commitment to free enterprise as such: 'The government has to be the planner and the mobilizer of the economic effort' but 'the free enterprise system, correctly nurtured and adroitly handled, can serve as a powerful and versatile instrument of economic growth'.[84]

Interventionism in Singapore's post-1959 development was organized around government directives, and so had considerably more force than indicative planning. Evaluation of development plans and planning objectives is complicated by the fact that, like most government matters in Singapore, described even in the 1990s as a 'corporate state that is mainly run by PAP technocrats', key documents were kept secret.[85] It is clear, however, that planning for manufacturing development in Singapore never involved detailed blueprints, because of the priority accorded to reaction to the international market, the impossibility of predicting its course and the need for flexibility to ensure a quick and competitive response. Yet there were requirements common to all industries – good infrastructure and a cheap, disciplined and trained labour force – and these were made prime objectives which were then systematically met.

Singapore planners, helped by intelligence from EDB overseas offices, closely monitored the world market, and initiatives were undertaken to attract desirable industries. For example, the potential of electronics was spotted on a 1966 ministerial visit to Taiwan.[86] The EDB targeted manufacturing activities,

[83] Goh Keng Swee, interview with the author, 17 August 1989.
[84] Goh Keng Swee, *The Asian*, 20 August 1972.
[85] Shee Poon Kim, 'Singapore in 1991', p. 119.
[86] C. C. Wee, 'Export – Singapore's new road to prosperity', *Singapore Trade and Industry* (August 1966), p. 54; Goh Keng Swee, 'MNCs brought jobs and sparked change', *Straits Times Weekly*, 29 August 1992.

in that the Board looked for industries beneficial to Singapore – on criteria like value added, skill content and capital intensity – which were likely to be attracted to the Republic, enquired as to the necessary incentives including tax concessions and then provided them.[87] But in manufacturing, the aims remained general; Singapore planners' approach to the international economy contrasted with the targeted protectionism and idea of 'picking winners' practised in Japan, South Korea and Taiwan. Rather, in keeping with a tiny domestic economy, Singapore adhered to free trade and tried to be attractive to a range of activities through supply-oriented policies, an approach later likened to backing all the horses in a race.[88] In the public sector, largely responsible for infrastructural development, rolling five-year plans operated. The Ministry of Finance was responsible for the broad orchestration of policies until the formation of the Ministry of Trade and Industry in 1979; institutions such as the EDB and Jurong Town Corporation organized planning in their specialized areas.

Singapore planning featured the concentration of decision-making in a few hands, also observed elsewhere in East Asia.[89] In Singapore's 'top-down' approach, at the summit the planning system was described as 'a high degree of good and eclectic steersmanship'.[90] This approach economized on entrepreneurial talent and helped to ensure loyalty to the government and further its tight control. The PAP leadership achieved effective implementation of plans and policies through the lower levels of bureaucracy by a willingness to pay government officials substantially more than the private sector and by an emphasis on individual accountability.[91]

Services Development and Government

In the development of financial and business services, a more precise planning strategy prevailed than for manufacturing. It was set out in the 1972 budget speech, strengthened in the *Economic development plan for the eighties* (1981) and further elaborated later that decade in *The Singapore economy: new directions* (1986). Significantly, this more targeted approach to planning reflected Singapore's greater market power in attracting financial services based on 'natural' comparative advantage – that is, when a free, competitive market prevails. Location on the world's main east–west communications network and the existing presence in the Republic of a critical mass of international financial

[87] Singapore, Economic Development Board, *Yearbook 1991/92*, pp. 26–27.

[88] Goh, 'MNCs brought jobs'. See also Singapore, Economic Planning Committee, *Strategic economic plan*, p. 68.

[89] Mason et al., *Economic and social modernization*, pp. 257, 493; Wade, *Governing the market*, pp. 195–227, particularly p. 217.

[90] Low, 'Singapore economy in 1987', p. 259.

[91] Chew Soon Beng, *Small firms in Singapore*, pp. 222–23.

institutions, ancillary services and infrastructure gave Singapore more freedom to 'pick winners' in financial services than in manufacturing. Starting in the later 1960s, the rapid expansion of international financial intermediation emphasized and widened Singapore's locational advantages. For offshore dealings, the island linked the Atlantic, Middle East and Pacific regions, which in the 1970s enabled Singapore to become a funding centre, acting as an entrepôt between deposit centres like Bahrain in a region of surplus funds and arranging centres like Hong Kong near ultimate borrowers.[92] Because Singapore bridged the time zone gap between the New York/London and Hong Kong/Tokyo markets, it could emerge as a leading foreign exchange dealing centre with the initiation of 24-hour international trading. By the 1990s, Singapore was the fourth-largest foreign exchange market after London, New York and Tokyo.[93]

Financial services would not have become an engine of growth in Singapore's economy in the absence of an activist government. One aspect of the government's contribution to the development of financial and business services was the provision of frequently overlooked public goods – the maintenance of honest markets, an environment conducive to easy operation and the stability of the Singapore dollar. In a sense, these public goods were no more than the British colonial government had supplied. But that would be to understate the real achievement of the PAP government, since such public goods were dissipated in other parts of Asia.

The separation from Malaysia (and in 1973 the full split between the Singapore and Malaysian currencies) allowed the Singapore government freedom of action to initiate policies promoting financial development.[94] In 1968, the Singapore government, in consultation with international banks, spotted the possibility of an Asian dollar market, similar to that for Eurodollars and in which US dollar funds in Asia could be pooled and loaned. The government immediately reacted by abolishing a withholding tax of 45 per cent on interest paid to non-residents for deposits made by Asian Currency Units (ACU) – any banking unit operating in the Singapore Asian Dollar Market – and quickly followed this with a variety of other measures targeted at establishing the market.[95] Singapore's activist government policy 'stole the march on Hong Kong', where the authorities lacked a similar development commitment. Although Hong Kong subsequently moved to establish a dollar market, by then a first-mover advantage made impossible a successful challenge to the Republic.[96]

92 Dematte, 'International financial intermediation', p. 101; John B. Caoutte, 'Time zones and the arranging centres', *Euromoney* (July 1978), pp. 48–54.
93 Singapore, Ministry of Trade and Industry, *Economic survey 1992*, p. 66.
94 Singapore, Monetary Authority of Singapore, *Annual report 1971*, pp. 23–28.
95 Hodjera, 'Asian currency market', pp. 224–25.
96 Jao, 'Hong Kong's future', pp. 44–45 and 'Rise of Hong Kong', pp. 692–93.

In the 1970s the Singapore government aggressively built on Singapore's comparative advantage in financial and business services through introducing financial innovations. Together, the Development Bank of Singapore and the Monetary Authority of Singapore, established in 1971 as a quasi-central bank, became strong and responsive institutions which the government could use in its strategy to develop Singapore as the 'Zurich of the East'.[97] The growth of the Asian Dollar Market showed how, in pursuit of a target, the government, characteristically moved, initially through 'permissive' legislation, to attract a new financial activity by reducing transaction costs through measures to lower taxes and facilitate the ease of setting up and operation for foreign firms.[98] But when the market proved unresponsive, the government was willing to take the lead through the government-owned Development Bank of Singapore and the Asian Dollar Bond Market, which the Singapore government started by floating US dollar-denominated bonds. As the private sector, after initial hesitation, embarked on similar initiatives, the Asian Dollar and Bond Markets – with their respectively short- and longer-term maturities – introduced significant market specialization and complementarity in Singapore's offshore banking system.[99] The Asian Dollar Market remained the more important of the two, and after reaching US$54.4 billion by 1980, grew to US$390.4 billion in 1990, a growth rate of 21.8 per cent.[100]

The establishment of Singapore as a '"financial supermarket", offering the widest range of financial services'[101] was central to the *Economic development plan for the eighties*; during that decade, every budget statement contained new measures to promote financial innovation. A complementary thrust of government policy which aimed at attracting international financial institutions to Singapore was demonstrably successful. From 1981 to 1990, while there remained 13 Singapore local banks offering a full range of banking services, the number of foreign banks rose from 86 to 128, and merchant banks from 39 to 68. By 1990, there were 199 ACU, since virtually all banks and merchant banks dealt in Asian dollars.[102]

Singapore's ever-growing cluster of financial institutions created opportunities for specialization and scale economies for these institutions, and so

97 'Singapore dollar shows its strength' and 'Growing sophistication in the financial community', *Financial Times*, Singapore Survey, 1 October 1973.

98 For example, see Singapore, *Parliamentary debates* 39, 10 (5 March 1980) (budget statement), cols. 628–31.

99 Hon Sui Sen, *Economic pattern in the 1970s*, p. 16; Singapore, *Parliamentary debates* 32, 10 (26 February 1973) (budget statement), col. 460; Lee Sheng-Yi, 'Developing Asian financial centres', pp. 212–15.

100 Singapore, Monetary Authority of Singapore, *Annual report 1990/91*, p. 92.

101 Singapore, Ministry of Trade and Industry, *Economic development plan for the eighties*, pp. 10–11.

102 Singapore, Monetary Authority of Singapore, *Annual report 1990/91*, p. 81.

reinforced government efforts towards broadening and deepening financial services in the Republic. In association with the Monetary Authority of Singapore, the government targeted specific financial instruments and institutions and strongly encouraged them with fiscal incentives. These were instrumental in establishing a new futures and options market, organized through the Singapore International Monetary Exchange (SIMEX). It offered a variety of contracts – with Eurodollar futures the most popular – and operated on a 24-hour mutual-offset basis with the Chicago Mercantile Exchange. By the later 1980s, as the government had planned, merchant banking had taken off in Singapore, and it was increasingly a centre for fund management.[103]

By 1990, Singaporeans had benefited considerably from the city's growth as a financial centre and consequent expansion of employment in financial and business services (Table 14.10). As the main component of brain services targeted by the government, financial and business services provided high-quality jobs, reflected in wages considerably above the average in Singapore. Brain services, as had been the planning intention, helped Singapore to move away from a dependence on cheap labour and towards higher value added, human capital-intensive jobs.[104]

Why Did the Singapore Government Succeed?

Government interventionism in Singapore successfully adapted the domestic economy to changes in the international economy, and showed that it might be necessary – not merely possible – to use 'dictatorial' means to allow the 'free market' to work. Since developing country governments are typically interventionist, but often with poor results, why did interventionism succeed in Singapore?

Part of the answer was Singapore's substantial 'transformation capacity', indicated by its responsiveness to global change throughout its twentieth-century development. But the 'quality of intervention' mattered. It rested on four, interrelated, factors: government autonomy from local interest groups; stability, both initial and perpetuated by a favourable sequencing of events; material gains for the bulk of the population which, together with a perceived likelihood of stability, promoted government control without harsh repression; and the ability, good economic judgement and policy choices of individuals in charge of the government.

[103] For example, see Singapore, Ministry of Trade and Industry, *Economic survey 1990*, pp. 8, 69–70; Singapore, Monetary Authority of Singapore, *Annual report 1990/91*, pp. 29, 33, *1991/92*, p. 40.

[104] Singapore, Statistics Division, Ministry of Labour, 'Wages and earnings in the financial sector, 1979–1982', *Singapore Statistical News* 6, 2 (1983), pp. 1–6; Singapore, Ministry of Trade and Industry, *Economic survey 1985*, p. 12; Singapore, Report of the Economic Committee, *Singapore economy: new directions*, pp. 32, 171, 181, 219–21.

The first of the four factors – the autonomy of government – allowed an all-out systematic commitment to economic development, which was a different, altogether rarer, thing than the proclaimed allegiance to a goal of development usual in Southeast Asia. Government identification with, and capture by, particular interest groups – a lack of autonomy – is often the rock on which a determined, sustained drive to development founders. Singapore had such interest groups in a local entrepreneurial class deriving from its Chinese-educated, China-oriented majority as well as a similarly oriented trade union movement.

The political achievement of Lee Kuan Yew's PAP in the 1959 elections and afterwards was to gain the backing of the majority of the Chinese population. That enabled him to neutralize, with a carefully judged combination of repression and merit-oriented policies, his political opponents and gain widespread endorsement, if not a mass popular following. The government's decision to rely for economic development on multinationals and state-owned enterprises allowed Singapore's local business elite largely to be excluded from the decision-making process. Businessmen could not decide policy, 'nor can they exert pressure on wide government'.[105]

The second and third factors – a sequencing to produce stability and material gains – which accounted for the quality of intervention can be considered together. Historical evolution produced in Singapore a sequencing that gave rise to stable government, competent administration and strong, efficient institutions, variables with great explanatory power in accounting for economic growth, as development economics stresses.[106] From 1959 to 1966, the Singapore government laid the basis, through the EDB, for development-oriented institutions. After 1966, these institutions – the EDB, Development Bank of Singapore and Jurong Town Corporation – could be directed towards export-oriented industrialization. Reliance on the same, small group of men to serve as directors for these and other state undertakings gave continuity and flexibility to Singapore's development effort.[107] At the same time, the government took control of the mass media. A former government minister elaborated on press freedom: 'How many Singaporeans really want free speech anyway? They want orderliness, a decent living.'[108] Both of the latter were achieved and visible corruption, endemic in many developing countries, was absent in Singapore under Lee Kuan Yew. Although the Singapore strategy

105 Lee Sheng-Yi, 'Business elites in Singapore', p. 50.

106 Reynolds, 'Spread of economic growth', p. 976; Roundtable Discussion, 'Development strategies: the roles of the state and the private sector', World Bank, *Proceedings of the World Bank Annual Conference on Development Economics 1990*, comment by N. Stern, p. 435.

107 The same was true in South Korea: Mason et al., *Economic and social modernization*, p. 493.

108 S. Rajaratnam, former Foreign Minister, quoted in Buruma, *God's dust*, p. 143.

worked, it was risky: control by a few people lends itself to corruption and in the longer term, after a rise in living standards, free speech becomes of greater importance to any society.

The obvious economic progress – in the appearance of Singapore, housing and gains in real wages – contributed to the PAP's acceptance by voters and Singapore's one-party elected Parliament. But the government took no chances: 'Opponents of the government have been relentlessly harried and it takes courage for a professional person to stand openly against the PAP.'[109] No more than mild criticism of the government was tolerated. A law lecturer at the National University observed of the Singapore judiciary: 'It is absolutely futile for people to talk about challenging executive decisions in court. If it is not legal, the government will make it legal, and it will make it legal retrospectively.'[110]

Fourth, the calibre of Singapore's post-1959 political leadership cannot be doubted. Distinguishing features of these men were their personal integrity and a high level of formal education with, more specifically, often extensive training in economics. The contrast with leaders like U Nu, Sukarno and Marcos is apparent.

The Singapore elite remained essentially the same, small group of leaders who dominated politics between independence in 1959 and Lee Kuan Yew's 1990 retirement, by then as the world's longest-serving prime minister. Singapore combined the good luck of favourable developments in the global economy and the good fortune of having a leadership which took advantage of the developments.

Chinese City, Plural Society and Meritocracy

As a Chinese city surrounded by a Malay world, and in view of anti-Chinese feeling throughout Southeast Asia, Singapore's PAP leadership was especially concerned to maintain a society in which all ethnic groups existed amicably. For a city state like Singapore to flourish, it requires well-disposed neighbours, internal peace and stability. Inter-ethnic conflict or external hostility could undermine the Republic's very existence.

The Singapore approach to its plural society was to try to create a national identity inclusive of all ethnic groups; emphasize the idea of equality of opportunity; base advancement on merit; and enforce through social engineering a break-up of ethnic residential localization. A child's failure to do well in exams translated into a severe career disadvantage. Under the Singapore policy of merit judged on a competitive basis, Malays lagged behind other groups in

[109] 'A fresh style in Singapore' (editorial), *Financial Times*, 28 August 1991.
[110] 'Stand up and be quoted', *Straits Times Weekly*, 13 July 1991.

income, in the proportion of students attending university and, most important, in integration into Singaporean society.[111]

PAP government policy pushed, shaped and almost certainly hurried the social and demographic transformation of Singapore's inter-war plural society. As the 1970 census remarked: 'the main motivating factor of population movement in Singapore today is the planned programme of the Government'.[112] After the establishment of the Housing and Development Board in 1960, the government acted systematically to end residential localization as well as potential political or special interests based on ethnic (including Chinese dialect) groups. From the 1960s onwards the previously well-defined concentrations of Chinese ethnic groups, Malays and Indians continuously disappeared consequent on a deliberate government resettlement programme and, by 1990, near universal public housing. Social engineering could be extended to virtually all Singaporeans through an educational approach that made English the first language in all schools and, for Chinese, a 'speak Mandarin' campaign. Even by 1970, there had begun 'a gradual shift from the traditional type of economic activities largely associated with specific ethnic groups'.[113]

Summary

Singapore's development relied on a combination of external free trade and strong internal economic control. Beginning in 1959, Singapore increasingly became a government-directed society, popularly known as Singapore Inc. After 1965, the fundamental departure in Singapore was not, as often argued, the adoption of free trade, which was always a basic Singapore tenet, but decisions to intervene decisively in the labour market, to force Singaporeans to save and whenever necessary to take active steps to ensure the presence of the conditions for economic growth.

Milton Friedman remarked that Lee Kuan Yew was a 'benevolent dictator', and drew the lesson that 'it is possible to combine a free private market economic system with a dictatorial political system'.[114] But the lesson is more subtle: that Singapore successfully combined authoritarian interventionism at home and *international* free trade. In Southeast Asia, Vietnam, after *doi moi*, came closest to copying this strategy. Above all, the genius of Singapore's interventionist government – and so ultimately its quality – was to recognize the importance of vigorous policies to take advantage of free international trade but

[111] 'PM pledges to back plans to aid Malays', *Straits Times*, 21 July 1990; Lau Kak En, *Singapore census of population, 1990, Households and housing* [statistical release 2], p. 7 and *Economic characteristics* [statistical release 4], p. 16.

[112] Arumainathan, *Report on the census of population 1970*, vol. I, p. 246.

[113] Arumainathan, *Report on the census of population 1970*, vol. I, p. 188, and see p. 201.

[114] Friedman, 'Welfare state syllogism', pp. 12–13.

avoid interference with it. The Singapore development strategy, facilitated by a comparative ease of management through being a small island, had important elements of a command system that directed and encouraged private enterprise towards market opportunities arising in the international economy – itself increasingly shaped by multinational enterprise. The Singapore economy depended on the three export sectors of primary commodities, manufactures and services. Through free trade, Singapore maximized, for each of these sectors, its geographical advantage of location.

An important caveat to Singapore's development was its heavy dependence on the mobilization of more labour and more capital. At the end of the 1980s, manufacturing still depended on multinationals for technology; little research and development was undertaken in Singapore. Larger factor inputs – not, as usual in industrial countries, technical progress, so-called total factor productivity – could be shown almost entirely to account for Singapore's expansion of manufacturing output.[115] The Republic's leaders perceived as a serious problem the apparent lack of technological progress, and by the 1990s embarked on a concerted effort to incorporate technical progress in the economy.

Conclusion

The Philippines and Singapore were similar in being essentially private enterprise economic systems, but otherwise contrasts dominated. Perhaps above all, Singapore believed in market solutions, and, in reaching these, the fundamental importance of the price mechanism, while Philippine authorities distrusted the market. Unlike the Philippine approach of intervention to replace the market, Singapore did not hesitate to intervene to make it work and realize planning objectives. If possible, the strategy was to work through incentives but, if necessary, through employing near dictatorial methods as, for example, in controlling trade unions to ensure that the price of labour was internationally competitive. In the Philippines, a lack of faith in the possibilities of the market and a reliance instead on exchange controls, regulation of imports and patch-up solutions was, Sicat concludes, 'the most powerful explanation for the culmination of problems that the economy has encountered'.[116]

Singapore began, as part of Malaya and then Malaysia, to try to solve its employment problem with an import-substitution industrial strategy but, after independence in 1965, turned decisively outwards to rely on job creation by multinationals manufacturing for export. The government aggressively searched for low-wage manufactures that the Republic could competitively

[115] Tsao, 'Growth without productivity', pp. 25–38; Krause et al., *Singapore economy reconsidered*, pp. 14–17; Young, 'Tale of two cities', pp. 36–38, 45.

[116] Sicat, *Historical and current perspective*, p. 6 and see pp. 4 and 40.

produce. By contrast, the Philippines fostered, and then nurtured, an enclave of high-cost, low-employment industries unable to sell outside a small, protected domestic market. These industries made at most a dent in reducing a growing surplus of labour. Taxation and forced savings from a fully employed workforce helped Singapore to finance infrastructure and remain a model of fiscal responsibility, but for lengthy periods this latter eluded the Philippines government. Never able to live within its means, by the mid-1980s the Philippines had gone through four balance-of-payments crises.

The Philippines neglected agriculture in favour of an emphasis on industrialization. A lagging agricultural sector continually held back the Philippine economy. Agriculture failed to furnish a large enough export base to provide needed foreign exchange or to develop sufficiently to hold more labour in rural employment after the exhaustion of surplus land. By contrast, Singapore, as a city state, did not have to solve the problem of agricultural development. Instead, the Republic could draw freely on unlimited food supplies at world prices. Nor was the premature rural–urban migration of the Philippines a problem: Singapore could regulate worker inflows, obtaining labour as needed from its poorer neighbours. Freed of these difficulties, and at the same time with the good luck of both a growing world demand for cheap labour to produce manufactured exports and a high-quality leadership, Singapore's economy grew at a rate at which industry can expand and, latterly, found a further dynamic growth source when it increasingly turned towards international services.

PART V

Export-oriented Southeast Asia

Trade, Industrialization and Development in the Late Twentieth and Twenty-first Centuries

15

Exports, Industrialization and Rapid Growth

In Part V, the book once more adopts the macro approach of Part I. It focuses on patterns of trade and growth in Southeast Asia as a whole from the late 1960s when, during a new phase of globalization, trade again fuelled growth, as it had during post-1870 globalization. Trade again depended on demand which mainly originated in the West. And trade again was facilitated by inventions in communications technology – shipping, air and container transport and the internet – made in the West. These inventions linked Southeast Asia ever closer to the global economy, creating new export opportunities for Southeast Asian goods.

With labour supplies less elastic in the United States and Western Europe, multinational enterprises began to search for sources of cheap labour to produce manufactures for developed country markets. After the 1985 Plaza Accord forced the yen's revaluation, Japanese manufacturers, a number of whom had already gained a Southeast Asian foothold in the 1960s and 1970s, also accelerated their search for low-cost labour. At the same time, swift post-World War II population growth, which made the region more like thickly populated Asia, altered Southeast Asian comparative advantage in favour of labour-intensive production. Countries in the region had the chance to utilize the abundant labour which had become their principal factor endowment and to industrialize. When labour could not be exported through embodiment in goods sent abroad, workers physically exported themselves through migration.

The opportunities for growth and industrialization based on labour-intensive manufacturing were, compared to 1870s to 1929 globalization, enhanced. While agriculture, the source of nearly all pre-World War II exports, grows at most by 3 per cent a year, industry can grow by 8 per cent to 10 per cent annually, or more. These are 'catch-up' growth rates. As Southeast Asian countries turned towards export orientation based on manufactures, the result, Myanmar apart, was radical economic transformation. Starting in the 1970s, most Southeast Asian countries could answer 'yes' to the fundamental economic question: Did countries grow fast enough to change the structure of the economy and improve standards of living for most people?

How those in Southeast Asia responded to the chance to industrialize and the consequent effect on the region's economies and peoples is the focus of this and the next chapter. The chapter's first section assesses patterns of Southeast Asian growth and compares the 1930s slump and late 1990s Asian financial crisis. Beginning in the 1970s, the region shifted towards quite rapid growth. The second section analyses this post-1970 growth in terms of a Southeast Asian development model and outlines its main components. Attention is drawn to differences in the timing of the shift to more rapid growth between the countries that looked outward after World War II and their inward-looking counterparts. A third section delineates the split of Southeast Asia into migrant-receiving and migrant-sending countries. In its fourth section, the chapter considers how different countries experienced export-led growth based on new staples of electronics and electrical products, scientific and photographic equipment and garments and footwear.

Patterns of Growth

Population and Comparative Advantage

In 1950, Southeast Asia was still predominantly a region of lightly peopled countries. Only Java and northern Vietnam were densely populated. Indonesia, because of Java, accounted for 45 per cent of Southeast Asia's population; all other countries had no more than 25 million people, and a number far less (Table 15.1).

Between 1950 and 1970, Southeast Asia's population grew by over 100 million. Larger populations pressed on land availability and increases could not be accommodated in the pre-World War II primary commodity-based vent-for-surplus economy or through import substitution. The region's comparative advantage had shifted away from the export of land-intensive products towards labour-intensive ones. The shift was initially most apparent in Singapore, with secure access to almost no land after separation from Malaysia and where from 1950 to 1970 population increased at an annual rate of 3.6 per cent (Table 15.1). Altered comparative advantage was, however, evident throughout the region, as was the need to provide jobs for expanding populations.

After 1970, as population continued to increase, the region's new comparative advantage became ever more obvious. From 1950 to 1990, Southeast Asia's population expanded by over 250 million and then added another nearly 250 million between 1990 and 2022 despite a slower growth rate. Over the period 1950 to 2022, the population of most Southeast Asian countries grew at 2.0 per cent or more annually. That compared to annual world population growth of slightly less than 2.0 per cent over the same period. By 2022, Southeast Asia's population was over 680 million in contrast to some 180 million in 1950 (Table 15.1).

Table 15.1 *Southeast Asia growth of population, 1950–2022*

(a) Population, 000 persons

	1950	1966	1970	1990	2010	2022
Malaysia	6,434	9,900	10,910	17,507	27,682	32,956
Singapore	1,022	1,934	2,075	3,047	5,140	5,750
Thailand	20,042	33,036	37,091	55,197	65,650	68,457
Philippines	21,131	34,304	38,604	65,088	98,601	121,234
Indonesia	82,612	108,103	117,338	179,323	240,372	273,409
Vietnam	25,348	38,378	42,577	67,283	89,604	103,574
Cambodia	4,471	6,780	7,396	9,345	14,418	16,514
Laos	1,886	2,619	2,845	4,210	6,368	7,666
Myanmar	19,488	25,399	27,393	39,243	50,285	56,210
Total population	182,433	260,454	286,228	440,243	598,120	685,771

(b) Annual growth rates %

	1950–2022	1950–1970	1970–1990	1990–2010	1990–2022	2010–2022
Malaysia	2.3	2.7	2.4	2.3	2.9	1.5
Singapore	2.4	3.6	1.9	2.6	2.9	0.9
Thailand	1.7	3.1	2.0	0.9	1.0	0.3
Philippines	2.5	3.1	2.6	2.1	2.9	1.7
Indonesia	1.7	1.8	2.1	1.5	1.9	1.1
Vietnam	2.0	2.6	2.3	1.4	2.0	1.2
Cambodia	1.8	2.5	1.2	2.2	2.6	1.1
Laos	2.0	2.1	2.0	2.1	2.8	1.6
Myanmar	1.5	1.7	1.8	1.2	1.6	0.9
Total	1.9	2.3	2.2	1.5	2.0	1.1

Source: Maddison Project Database, 2023.

GDP Growth, Exports and Early and Later Industrializers

The chapter uses two sets of GDP data. The first, in 2011 US$, links with pre-1950 data used earlier in the book to enable Table 15.2 to make clear how much the pace of post-1950 growth differed from earlier expansion. The second set is available starting only in 1960 and is expressed in 2015 US$. Unlike the first data set, it has the advantages of continuing beyond 2022 and of comparability with other data in this chapter which are also in 2015 US$.

Table 15.2 *Southeast Asia GDP per capita, 1950–2022*

(a) GDP per capita 2011 US$

	1950	1966	1970	1985	1990	1996	2007	2018	2022
Malaysia	2,485	2,942	3,314	6,626	8,179	12,669	17,210	25,176	26,629
Singapore	3,572	4,317	6,650	16,611	27,515	32,724	51,844	74,518	80,320
Thailand	1,302	2,251	2,700	4,862	7,385	10,458	12,695	16,610	16,421
Philippines	1,706	2,636	2,812	3,135	3,502	3,791	5,173	8,235	8,371
Indonesia	1,280	1,535	1,882	3,143	4,007	5,851	7,157	11,768	12,802
Vietnam	1,049	1,369	1,172	1,471	1,634	2,323	4,037	6,842	8,050
Cambodia	768	1,116	1,031	1,540	1,404	1,451	2,423	3,692	3,944
Laos	697	818	850	1,382	1,481	1,900	3,389	6,455	7,168
Myanmar	631	925	1,023	1,506	1,253	1,469	3,543	5,803	5,177

(b) Annual growth rates %

	1950–2022	1950–1966	1966–1970	1950–1970	1950–1990	1966–1996	1996–2007	2007–2018	2018–2022
Malaysia	3.3	1.1	3.0	1.4	3.0	5.0	2.8	3.5	1.4
Singapore	4.4	1.2	11.4	3.2	5.2	7.0	4.3	3.4	1.9
Thailand	3.6	3.5	4.7	3.7	4.4	5.3	1.8	2.5	−0.3
Philippines	2.2	2.8	1.6	2.5	1.8	1.2	2.9	4.3	0.4
Indonesia	3.2	1.1	5.2	1.9	2.9	4.6	1.8	4.6	2.1
Vietnam	2.9	1.7	−3.8	0.6	1.1	1.8	5.2	4.9	4.1
Cambodia	2.3	2.4	−2.0	1.5	1.5	0.9	4.8	3.9	1.7
Laos	3.3	1.0	1.0	1.0	1.9	2.8	5.4	6.0	2.7
Myanmar	3.0	2.4	2.5	2.4	1.7	1.6	8.3	4.6	−2.8

Source: Maddison Project Database, 2023.

Although both the inward- and outward-looking countries began the 1950s with low GDP per capita, they started from markedly different levels (Table 15.2). In 1950, GDP per capita in the outward-looking countries ranged from 2011 US$1,302 in Thailand to US$3,572 in Singapore. GDP per capita in inward-looking Southeast Asia was as little as US$631 in Burma, US$697 in Laos and US$1,280 in Indonesia.

Between 1950 and 1970, real incomes in the outward-looking countries, buoyed by primary commodity exports and import-substitution industrialization, approximately doubled, except in Malaysia where GDP per capita rose by about a third. Singapore's GDP per capita increased by more than half from 1966 to 1970, after it turned outward to export following the split with Malaysia. Growth in the inward-looking countries was much slower than in the outward-looking ones. From 1950 to 1990, GDP per capita only about doubled in Burma and Laos but was still short of doubling in Vietnam and Cambodia. Indonesia was the inward-looking exception. Soon after the fall of Sukarno in 1966 and stagnation under socialism, Indonesia grew at a much faster pace as it opened towards the global economy. From 1950 to 1990, Indonesian GDP per capita rose more than threefold to somewhat over US$4,000.

Singapore first turned outwards to export manufactures in the late 1960s, marking the beginning of a new phase in the history of Southeast Asian growth. During the 1970s, other Southeast Asian countries started to follow Singapore's example, and by the 1990s most did. Between 1966 and 2007, real GDP per capita increased nearly sixfold in Malaysia and Thailand and by 12 times in Singapore. Indonesia grew not far from fivefold. GDP per capita tripled in Vietnam and rose by four times in Laos. Two exceptions to such swift growth were Cambodia and the Philippines. Cambodian growth did not get underway until the later 1990s, but thereafter was quite rapid. For much of the period after 1960, the Philippines grew more slowly than elsewhere in Southeast Asia, held back by a continuing overemphasis on import substitution, political instability, recession during the later 1980s and rent-seeking politicians, among whom Marcos and his cronies were the most conspicuous example (Table 15.2).

Figures 15.1 to 15.7 show annual data for GDP per capita and exports for periods ranging from 1960 to 2023. Within the growth swings shown in the boxes accompanying the figures, one can highlight episodes of even decade-long annual per capita hyper-growth rates of 5 per cent or 6 per cent or more. Bouts of rapid growth ultimately spread throughout most of Southeast Asia, but the region's inward- and outward-looking countries contrasted sharply in the timing of these growth spurts. Among the outward-looking countries, Singapore, Malaysia and Thailand, as well as growing the fastest, had the most pronounced growth surges (Figures 15.1a to 15.3a). Until the 1997 Asian financial crisis, growth in Malaysia, Singapore and Thailand was broken only briefly in Malaysia during 1984 to 1987 by the 'Look East' emphasis on heavy industry, and over a similar period in Singapore by mild recession. Real

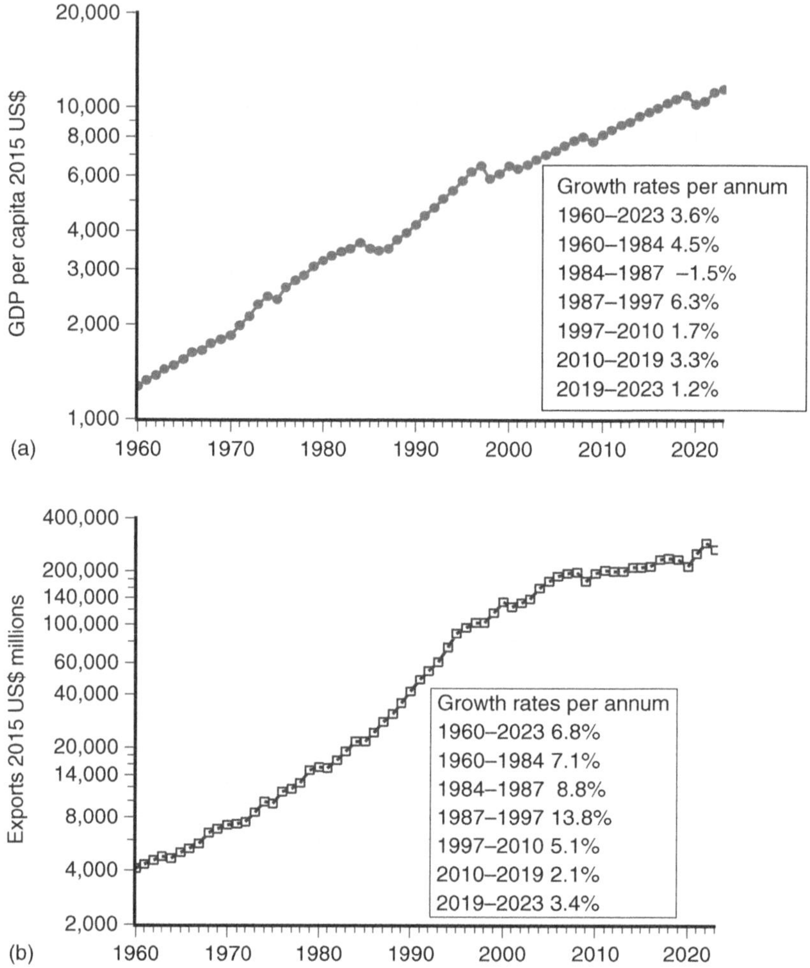

Figure 15.1 Malaysia growth periods of GDP per capita and exports, 1960–2023. (a) Malaysia growth periods of GDP per capita, 1960–2023. (b) Malaysia exports of goods and services, 1960–2023
Source: World Bank, *World development indicators, 2025.*

GDP per capita in Singapore increased at 6.7 per cent annually from 1960 to 1984 and 5.6 per cent between 1987 and 1997. Malaysia and Thailand, copying Singapore's example as the electronics and electrical goods industries spread in Southeast Asia, had their periods of most rapid GDP per capita growth later than Singapore's, beginning in the later 1980s. Malaysia and Thailand each grew at 6.3 per cent annually from 1987 to 1997. After the Asian financial crisis, however, the growth of GDP per capita in all three countries slowed markedly,

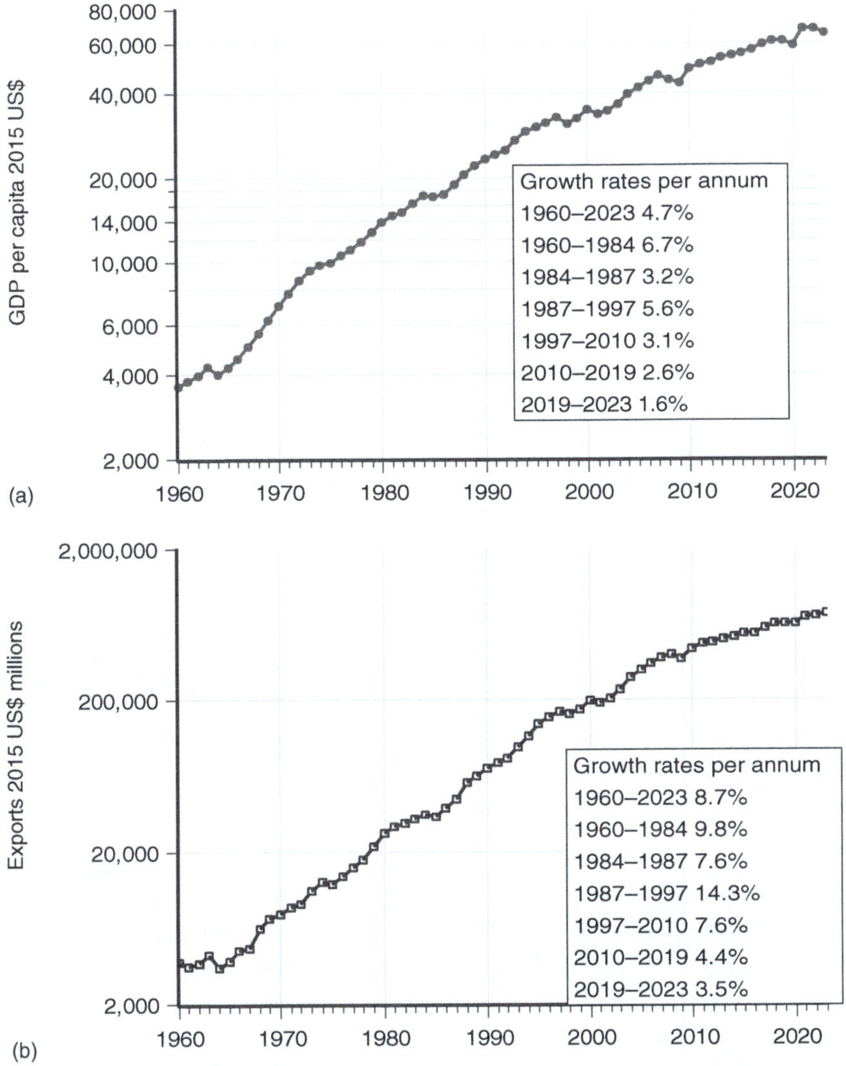

Figure 15.2 Singapore growth periods of GDP per capita and exports, 1960–2023. (a) Singapore growth periods of GDP per capita, 1960–2023. (b) Singapore exports of goods and services, 1960–2023
Source: World Bank, *World development indicators, 2025.*

and from 2010 to 2019 was 3.3 per cent in Malaysia, 2.7 per cent in Thailand and 2.6 per cent in Singapore. During 2019 to 2023, the Covid pandemic and associated disruption further slowed growth and turned it negative in Thailand.

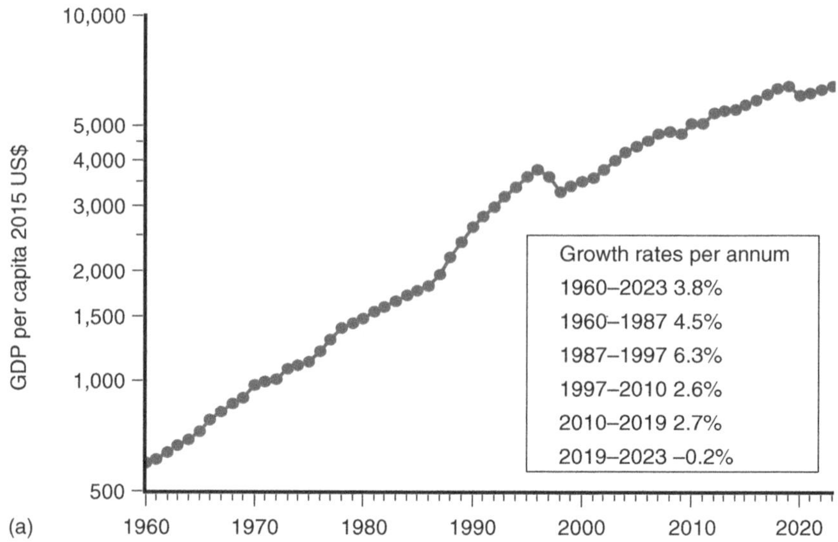

(a)

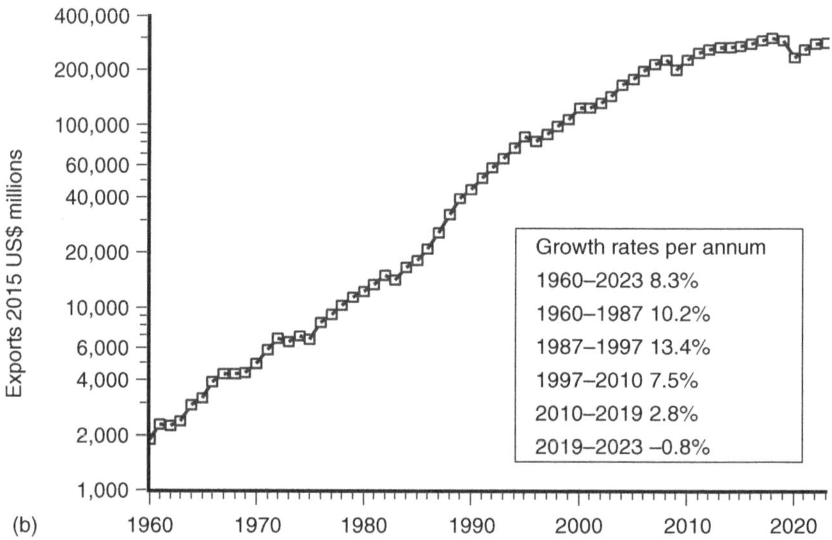

(b)

Figure 15.3 Thailand growth periods of GDP per capita and exports, 1960–2023. (a) Thailand growth periods of GDP per capita, 1960–2023. (b) Thailand exports of goods and services, 1960–2023

Source: World Bank, *World development indicators, 2025.*

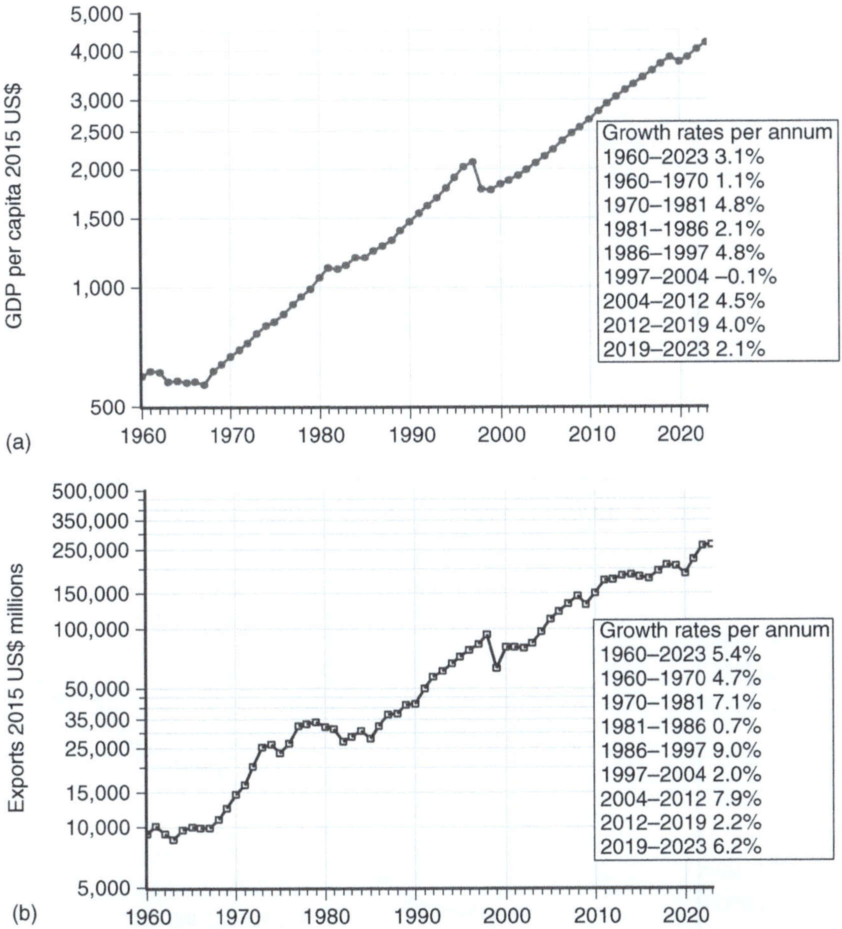

Figure 15.4 Indonesia growth periods of GDP per capita and exports, 1960–2023. (a) Indonesia growth periods of GDP per capita, 1960–2023. (b) Indonesia exports of goods and services, 1960–2023
Source: World Bank, *World development indicators, 2025.*

In an outward and inward categorization as originally defined by Myint, Indonesia and the Philippines are growth outliers: beginning in 1970, Indonesia (Figure 15.4a) grew more rapidly than the Philippines (Figure 15.5a), although neither matched the rapidity of expansion in Malaysia, Singapore and Thailand.[1]

[1] Myint, 'Inward- and outward-looking countries of Southeast Asia'.

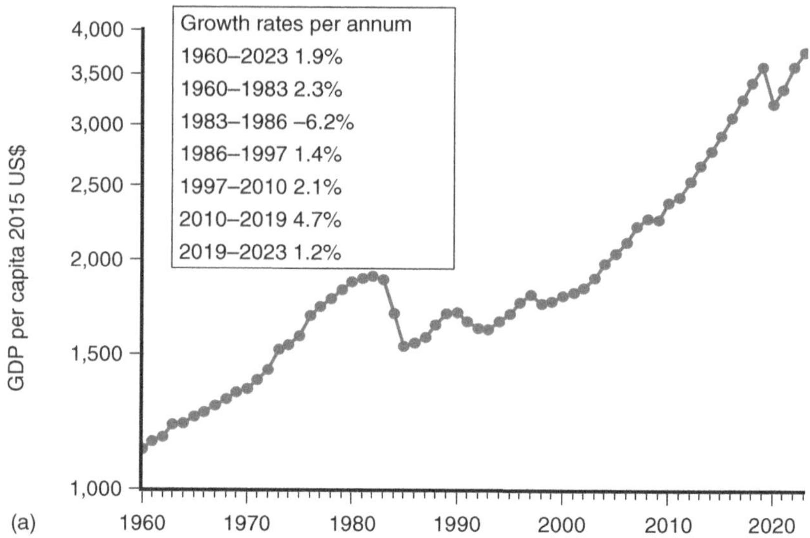

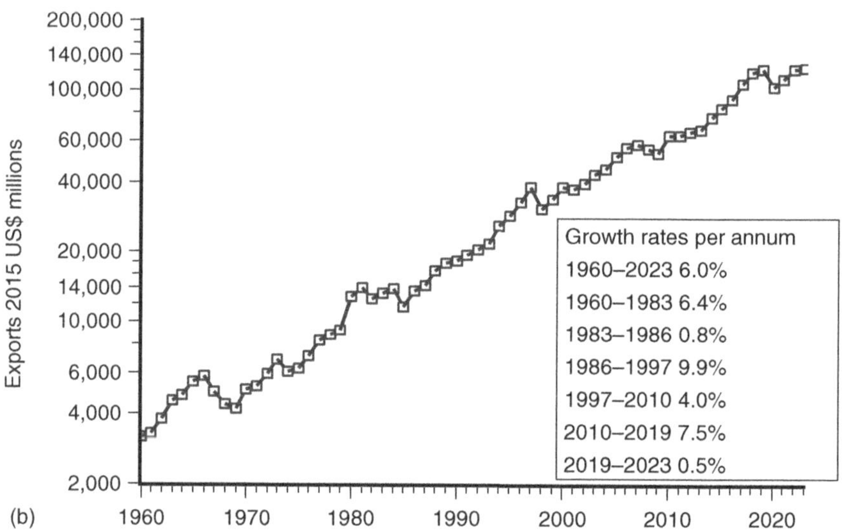

Figure 15.5 Philippine growth periods of GDP per capita and exports, 1960–2023. (a) Philippine growth periods of GDP per capita, 1960–2023. (b) Philippine exports of goods and services, 1960–2023
Source: World Bank, *World development indicators, 2025.*

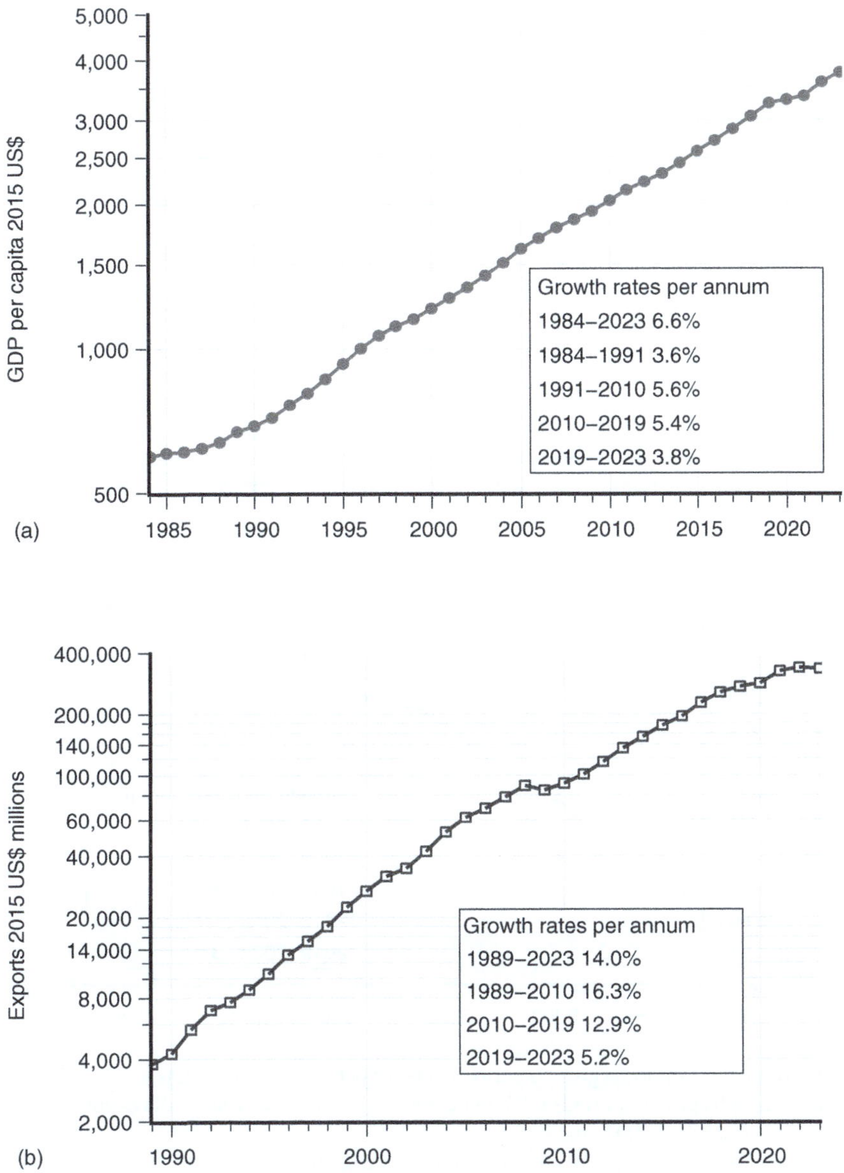

Figure 15.6 Vietnam growth periods of GDP per capita and exports, 1984–2023. (a) Vietnam growth periods of GDP per capita, 1984–2023. (b) Vietnam exports of goods and services, 1989–2023
Source: World Bank, *World development indicators, 2025.*

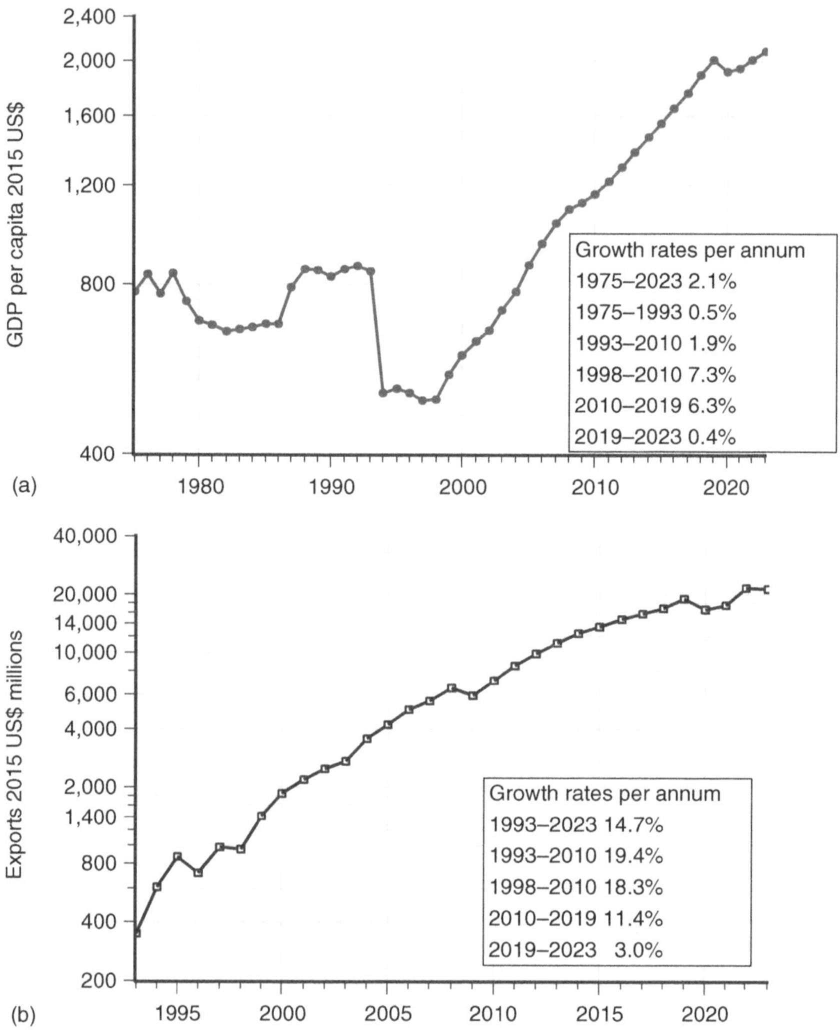

Figure 15.7 Cambodia growth periods of GDP per capita and exports, 1975–2023. (a) Cambodia growth periods GDP per capita, 1975–2023. (b) Cambodia exports of goods and services, 1993–2023
Source: World Bank, *World development indicators, 2025.*

Following the replacement of Sukarno by Suharto, Indonesia, although reclassified by Myint in 1984 as outward-looking, never shifted decisively towards this orientation, even though the post-1966 Indonesian policy regime can be regarded as 'broadly open'. Indonesia did not, however, embrace globalization except in the late 1960s and between 1986 and 1997.[2] For most of its post-1970 history, the Indonesian economy has principally relied on exporting energy and other resource-intensive commodities, manufacturing and providing services for the domestic market.[3]

Until the 1990s, the Philippines, although also identified by Myint as outward-oriented, fits uneasily in this categorization, because it continued partly to favour its inward stance of 1950s import substitution.[4] A confusion of the outward and inward economic categories arises to some extent because these groupings can be defined in terms of political orientations. The Philippines was traditionally closely allied with the West, especially the United States, and in that sense was 'outwards'. By contrast, even after Sukarno, governments in Indonesia along with much of its population have distrusted openness and Western involvement and favoured nationalism.[5]

Swift growth in the three Indochinese economies began only during the 1990s, but then recorded growth rates similar to earlier ones for Singapore, Malaysia and Thailand. Between 1991 and 2010, Vietnam's real GDP per capita grew at 5.6 per cent per annum and Cambodia's at 7.3 per cent from 1998 to 2007 (Figures 15.6a and 15.7a). Growth continued almost unbroken until the 2019 onset of the Covid pandemic, though the pandemic only somewhat checked expansion in Vietnam, but much more in Cambodia.

Rapid Southeast Asian growth was export-led – a rate of export growth higher than that of GDP. In Singapore, exports of goods and services grew at an annual rate of 8.7 per cent between 1960 and 2023 and 14.3 per cent at their peak from 1987 to 1997. Malaysian export growth, at first relying heavily on traditional staple commodities, averaged 7.1 per cent annually from 1960 to 1984 as manufactures gained momentum, then 13.8 per cent for the 10 years beginning in 1987. Exports from Thailand increased at a yearly average of 8.3 per cent between 1960 and 2023. When the Thai economy boomed from 1987 to 1996, exports grew at 13.4 per cent. After *doi moi*, Vietnam's exports expanded at a remarkable 16.3 per cent from 1989 to 2010, followed by growth of 12.9 per cent from 2010 to 2019 (Figures 15.1b to 15.3b and 15.6b).

Indonesia (Figure 15.4b) benefited from being a large exporter of oil, gas, palm oil, coal and timber as well as other primary commodities. Commodity exports, including an oil boom from 1973 to 1981, have, however, punctuated Indonesian GDP and exports with marked economic fluctuations. Indonesian exports increased at 7.1 per cent annually between 1970 and 1981 after recovery from the Sukarno years, and at 9.0 per cent from 1986 to 1997, during Indonesia's one prolonged period of outward orientation. From 1960 to 2023,

2 Hill and Pane, 'Indonesia and the global economy', p. 266 and see p. 290.

3 Hill, 'Asia's third giant', p. 471.

4 Myint, 'Inward- and outward-looking countries revisited: Indonesia'.

5 Damuri and Pangestu, 'Who is afraid', pp. 114–17.

Indonesian export growth of 5.4 per cent annually compares with GDP per capita increase of 3.1 per cent.

Philippine export expansion was 6.0 per cent from 1960 to 2023, and 9.9 per cent between 1986 and 1997 when the economy turned more outwards. The Philippines did not, however, come close to equalling the GDP per capita growth record of the other outward-looking countries. From 2010 to 2019, after years of a weak economy, GDP per capita growth in the Philippines was 4.7 per cent a year. Although electronics exports often involved simple assembly tasks with little value added locally, the commendable 2010 to 2019 GDP per capita increase reflected export growth of 7.5 per cent, partly due to services exports and notably back-office services (Figures 15.4b and 15.5b). Cambodian exports, nearly all garments and footwear, rose from a very low base to annual increases of 18.3 per cent from 1998 to 2010 and 11.4 per cent between 2010 and 2019, but from 2019 to 2023, along with GDP per capita, contracted sharply (Figure 15.7b).

Downturns: 1930s Slump, Asian Financial Crisis and Covid Pandemic

Table 15.3 compares the impact on GDP per capita of Southeast Asia's two main downturns – the 1930s slump and the 1997 Asian financial crisis – during the 150 years covered in this book. The slump, originating in the United States and then spreading throughout the world, was wholly exogenous to Southeast Asia, but the crisis was not. It had roots in Thailand. Thai companies and banks assumed large, short-term US dollar-denominated debt during the exuberance of 1987 to 1997 rapid export-led growth with the seeming safety of a pegged currency. Overborrowing made difficult the repayment of earlier loans, and this became impossible after the unpegging of the Thai baht from the dollar. A twin banking and balance-of-payments crisis developed. The Thai baht was forced off its peg in the summer of 1997 and by October had lost a quarter of its value.

In response to crisis in Thailand, financial contagion spread to Malaysia, Indonesia and the Philippines. Confidence in regional currencies, economies and financial systems evaporated. Most Southeast Asian currencies plummeted, capital flowed outwards and economic activity slumped.[6] In 1998, GDP per capita in Indonesia, which was even more badly affected than Thailand, dropped 14.5 per cent. Loans from international agencies, China and the United States together with reforms to Southeast Asian financial regulation ended the crisis.

The 1930s depression was much the worse of the two downturns, because its impact on GDP per capita was more protracted and because per capita incomes were comparatively low, leaving little room for cuts in consumption.

6 Miller and Luangaram, 'Financial crisis', p. 78.

Table 15.3 *Southeast Asia downturns: 1930s slump and Asian financial crisis*

	(a) 1930s slump			(b) Asian financial crisis	
	Last year before slump	Years for GDP per capita to regain pre-slump level		Last year before crisis	Years for GDP per capita to regain pre-crisis level
Malaysia	1929	41	Malaysia	1997	3
Singapore	1929	6	Singapore	1997	2
Thailand	1929	9	Thailand	1997	5
Philippines	1929	8	Philippines	1997	3
Indonesia	1930	10	Indonesia	1997	7
Vietnam	–	–	Vietnam	1997	0
Cambodia	–	–	Cambodia	1997	0
Laos	–	–	Laos	1997	0

Source: Maddison Project Database, 2023.

In Malaysia, it took four decades to regain the income level of 1929, because of a heavy dependence on rubber exports and then the disruption of World War II. Elsewhere in Southeast Asia, recovery times ranged from seven to 11 years, the latter for Indonesia.

In comparison to the slump, the Asian financial crisis was less serious. It did not halt continuous growth in the three Indochinese economies. Singapore recovered to its pre-crisis GDP per capita in two years and Malaysia and the Philippines in three. Thailand's recovery took five years but only it and Indonesia, which did not return to its pre-crisis income for seven years, rivalled the impact of the 1930s depression on Southeast Asia.

The 2019 to 2022 Covid pandemic, and the resulting dislocation of global trade and supply chains, precipitated the most recent, although one of the less severe, of the downturns affecting Southeast Asia. However, the pandemic's effect on world trade once again demonstrated a central argument of the book: the importance to Southeast Asian growth of globalization and its accompanying unhindered flows of trade. During the pandemic, in all of Southeast Asia, the levels of exports and GDP per capita fell, although by 2023, except in Thailand, both had recovered to at least their 2019 levels. Between 2019 and 2023, the rates of growth of GDP per capita were lower than during 2010 to 2019, and dropped the most in countries (Thailand, Cambodia, the Philippines and Vietnam) where export growth was most seriously affected. Drops in exports and growth were particularly striking in Vietnam and Cambodia, because until 2019 both economies had been expanding swiftly. Between 2010 and 2019, Vietnam's exports grew at 12.9 per cent annually and its GDP per capita at 5.4 per cent, but from 2019 to 2023 these rates decreased to 5.2 per cent and 3.8 per cent respectively. In Cambodia, the falls were even sharper: average annual growth for exports dropped from 11.4 per cent in 2010 to 2019 to 3.0 per cent between 2019 and 2023, while the comparison for GDP per capita was 6.3 per cent during 2010 to 2019 but 0.4 per cent from 2019 to 2023 (Figures 15.6 and 15.7).

In 2025/26, a threatened drift towards protectionism could mean an end to globalization. If so, the evidence of the pandemic suggests that it would probably also impede the post-1970 Southeast Asian model of rapid export-led development. However, as argued in Chapter 18, a retreat from globalization would not entirely halt all Southeast Asian growth and continued advance in the region.

Export-led Growth

Beginning in 1970, two experiences of export-led growth in Southeast Asia are apparent (Figure 15.8a). These mirror, and are at least partly responsible for, the region's contrasting growth patterns. In Thailand, Malaysia, Indonesia and the Philippines – the early followers of Singapore's success – exports as a share of GDP grew rapidly after 1970, peaking in Malaysia at as much as 121 per cent of GDP in 1999 and 71 per cent in Thailand in 2008. An increase in exports relative to GDP was due to a drop in GDP, not higher exports. In the early industrializers by 2011, or even before, exports as a proportion of GDP began to decline sharply, tracing over the last half-century a broadly inverted U-shaped pattern. Recent falls in high levels of export dependence suggest that trade, as well as being a primary growth engine for over 30 years, needs also to promote growth and diversification in the wider domestic economy, enabling Southeast Asian countries to grow away from an earlier vent-for-surplus pattern, even if at a cost of slower growth.

By contrast, in the late industrializers of Vietnam, Cambodia and Laos, exports began to increase swiftly only after the late 1980s ending of Soviet-influenced socialism. Able to vent labour through exports, export growth in the Indochinese countries continued to outpace GDP, most spectacularly in Vietnam, where by 1997 the value of exports was more than 100 per cent of national income (Figure 15.8b). Throughout Southeast Asia, a feature of periods of hyper-growth was the mobilization of labour. Workers were drawn from agriculture to industry, pulled from low- to higher-value services, and more women joined the labour force.

High growth depended on a remarkable change in the composition of Southeast Asian exports. The change made much of the region look, if to some extent superficially, more like a developed country in moving towards exporting manufactures rather than primary commodities. As late as 1974/76, Southeast Asia, Singapore apart, still mainly depended on primary commodity

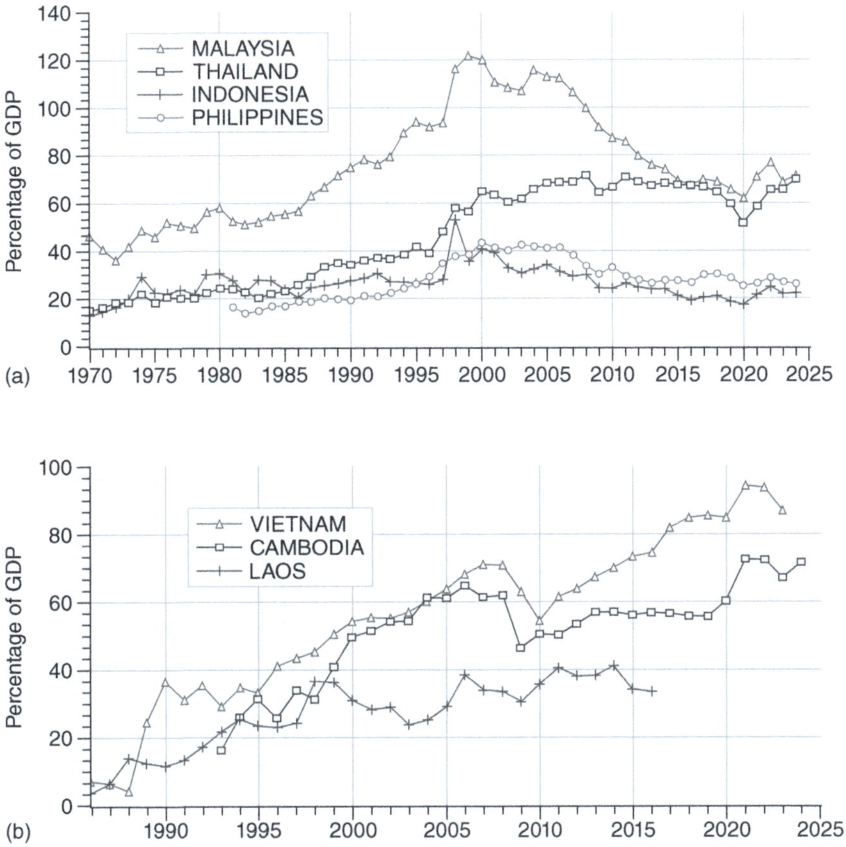

Figure 15.8 Southeast Asia early and late industrializers: exports as a percentage of GDP, 1970–2024. (a) Southeast Asia early industrializers: exports as a percentage of GDP, 1970–2024. (b) Southeast Asia late industrializers: exports as a percentage of GDP, 1986–2024
Source: World Bank, *World development indicators, 2025.*

exports. By 1995/97 in Malaysia, Singapore, Thailand and the Philippines, manufactures accounted for between over two-thirds and four-fifths of merchandise exports. Exceptions to such large shares of manufactured exports were Indonesia, able to export large amounts of oil, gas, coal and palm oil (a continuation of a tradition of Outer Island vent-for-surplus production), and Vietnam, also with major energy exports as well as having important agricultural exports. Most exports went to high-income countries, although Singapore slightly blurs the picture as a high-income recipient of exports from elsewhere in the region and also as an exporter to the rest of (low-income) Southeast Asia (Table 15.4).

Table 15.4 *Southeast Asia and United States exports and export composition and direction, 1960–2023*

(a) Southeast Asia exports of goods and services as a % of GDP

	Malaysia	Singapore	Thailand	Philippines	Indonesia	Vietnam	Cambodia	Laos	Myanmar	United States
1960	64.5	162.9	16.1	11.9	11.5	–	13.9	–	–	5.0
1964/66	44.3	122.9	17.3	19.3	10.1	–	11.4	–	–	5.0
1974/76	48.8	145.4	20.1	21.8	24.6	–	–	–	–	8.1
1984/86	55.3	152.6	23.6	24.8	22.9	6.6	–	3.5	–	7.2
1995/97	93.0	175.7	42.9	41.9	26.7	38.9	30.1	23.3	–	10.8
2008/10	84.6	177.6	66.3	26.5	22.9	64.7	44.9	26.8	–	11.1
2017/19	66.7	180.8	66.3	31.2	20.3	109.9	65.7	–	24.4	12.4
2022/23	72.7	183.8	65.4	27.5	23.1	89.9	69.5	–	–	11.3

(b) Manufactures as a % of merchandise exports

	Malaysia	Singapore	Thailand	Philippines	Indonesia	Vietnam	Cambodia	Laos	Myanmar	United States
1962	–	26.2	2.1	4.6	0.3	–	1.6	9.4	0.9	62.9
1964/66	5.2	29.8	2.1	5.8	0.0	–	0.6	4.4	0.5	62.0
1974/76	15.1	42.0	15.0	12.2	1.1	–	–	1.4	4.4	65.6
1984/86	30.3	53.6	38.4	27.4	14.1	–	–	–	–	69.7
1995/97	75.7	83.9	72.0	70.6	48.1	44.1	–	–	–	78.7
2008/10	63.1	70.7	72.2	73.6	38.4	59.3	95.6	–	26.0	68.4
2017/19	68.6	79.8	78.4	88.8	46.1	71.2	68.3	18.9	39.7	67.5
2022/23	67.5	73.5	72.7	79.4	43.7	85.4	87.2	27.6	44.4	55.0

(c) Merchandise exports to high-income countries as a % of merchandise exports

	Malaysia	Singapore	Thailand	Philippines	Indonesia	Vietnam	Cambodia	Laos	Myanmar	United States
1960	–	57.8	81.6	95.2	86.7	74.4	80.6	–	28.1	66.3
1964/66	–	–	69.3	98.2	77.8	–	58.8	–	32.2	67.1
1974/76	85.2	62.0	78.8	93.1	95.7	–	–	–	45.8	67.8
1984/86	83.8	61.1	77.5	89.3	94.3	48.5	48.2	–	45.8	72.9
1994/96	82.8	61.5	78.5	88.5	82.6	72.8	43.2	13.4	48.5	71.5
2008/10	66.1	50.5	60.5	78.2	65.0	69.7	93.2	21.2	32.2	63.4
2017/19	59.4	50.2	54.1	75.4	54.3	64.8	78.8	13.0	30.1	59.9
2022/23	61.3	50.1	56.1	71.5	43.7	68.2	75.8	13.3	41.5	60.6

Source: World Bank, *World development indicators, 2025.*

Southeast Asian Development Model

A Southeast Asian development model was basic to rapid growth everywhere in the region except Myanmar and Indonesia, the latter due to its continued heavy dependence on natural resource exports and government hesitancy, other than from 1986 to 1997, to look to global production networks. The model has three main components additional to manufacturing for export. One is dependence on multinational enterprises to provide capital and technology; and a second, closely related to the first, high foreign capital inflows. Third, Southeast Asian industrialization relied initially on labour-intensive processes that allowed the venting of unemployed or underemployed workers. The reliance often persisted, so that as available supplies of domestic labour dried up, the most successful industrializers, instead of moving to more skill-intensive production, turned towards importing migrant labour from other Southeast Asian countries. High domestic savings and capital formation, discussed in the next chapter, were both a product of this industrialization and made it possible.

Multinationals, Global Value Chains and New Staples

The Southeast Asian attachment to multinationals could be likened, as Lee Kuan Yew observed of Singaporean growth, to hitching a ride on an escalator. It was powered by the expansion of world trade in electronics and electrical goods, scientific and medical devices and garments and footwear. The manufacture of electronics and electrical goods and scientific and medical devices typically involved making, assembling or testing only their components and parts while garments and footwear were generally final products. Most of the trade in all these categories of goods depended on global value chains organized by multinationals as the lead enterprises.

In Southeast Asia for electronics and electrical goods, these lead multinationals were organizations like Apple, Dell, Samsung and Motorola. They generally sourced through intermediaries which for electronics and electrical goods were contractors, themselves multinationals and with interests not just in most of Southeast Asia but worldwide. Because of specific production technologies and the close links between lead enterprises and contractors, these value chain networks were sometimes termed producer-driven. For garments and footwear, the lead enterprises and distributors were brand manufacturers such as Nike, Adidas and Calvin Klein or retailers like Walmart and Target. These value chains could be described as buyer-driven, because both brand manufacturers and retailers frequently relied on global sourcing companies to link them to producers and so, unlike lead multinationals in electronics and electrical goods production, operated in Southeast Asia through predominantly arm's-length relationships.[7]

[7] Athukorala and Hill, *Revisiting globalization*, pp. 8–10.

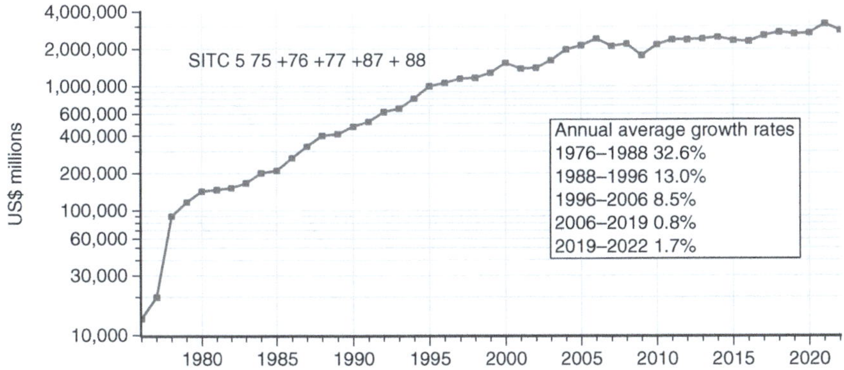

Figure 15.9 World exports of electronic and electrical products, 1976–2022

Notes: SITC 7 is Machinery and transport equipment. Its main components in Southeast Asian electronic and electrical goods exports are SITC 75 Office machines and automatic data-processing machines, SITC 76 Telecommunications and sound-recording and reproducing apparatus and equipment and SITC 77 Electrical machinery, apparatus and appliances, n.e.s., and electrical parts thereof. Important at the three-digit level is SITC 776 Television picture tubes, cathode-ray (including video monitor cathode-ray tubes). SITC 87 is Professional, scientific and controlling instruments and apparatus, n.e.s. and SITC 88 is Photographic apparatus, equipment and supplies and optical goods, n.e.s.; watches and clocks.

Source: I owe these data to Prema-Chandra Athukorala, who compiled it from the World Integrated Trade Solution (WITS) database of the World Bank.

Machinery and transport equipment (Standard International Trade Classification (SITC) 7), which encompassed the electronics and electrical goods and components and scientific and medical devices (SITC 75, 76, 77, 87 and 88), was at the heart of Southeast Asian globalization-dependent, export-led growth. Between 1976 and 1988, world exports of SITC 75 (office and data-processing machines), 76 (telecommunications and recording apparatus), 77 (electric machinery, apparatus and appliances), 87 (scientific and controlling instruments) and 88 (photographic equipment and optical goods) grew at an annual rate of 32.6 per cent and from 1988 to 1996 at 13.0 per cent (Figure 15.9). The early industrializing economies of Singapore, Malaysia and Thailand rode the boom in these goods. For the higher-income Southeast Asian countries, garments and footwear manufacture was never as important as the production of electronics and electrical goods, and as wages rose made up an increasingly small share of exports. Garments and footwear were the main exports for low-income, low-wage countries, principally Cambodia, Laos and, until the 2010s, Vietnam.

Export-oriented manufacturing in Southeast Asia typically meant joining global value chains – a sequence of production leading to the sale of a final

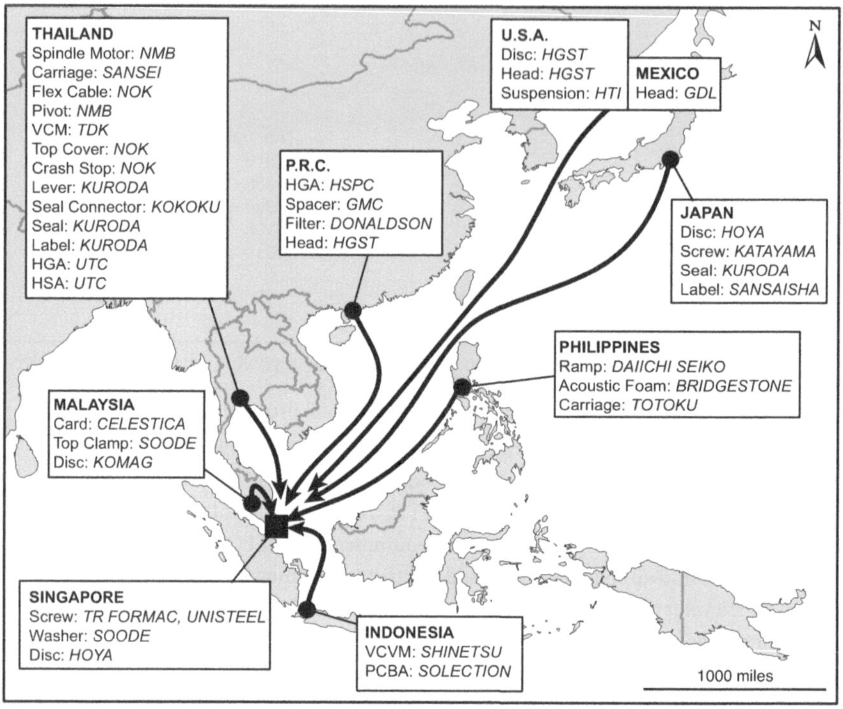

Figure 15.10 Singapore component sources for hard disk drive assembly, 2011
Source: Hiratsuka, *Production networks*, p. 21.

product and generally involving a number of different countries and firms. Plugging into global value chains entailed becoming part of an international putting out system based on specialization and a division of labour according to its differential costs. In Southeast Asia, suitably low wage levels were fundamental to becoming part of global value chains.

The fabrication of components, component assembly into final products and work in stages of the production of garments all incorporated inputs sourced from multiple locations. Most were Southeast Asian or Asian but included North American, Mexican and European. The production chain might be long and could go through several stages, a process of regional specialization and integration that maximized the venting of labour. Southeast Asian countries traded among themselves and, according to labour costs and skills, specialized in specific stages of the production process. In intra-Southeast Asian trade, a component or input might be exported after the performance of one production stage and, following the end of a second, be re-imported for a further production stage. The break-up of production into geographically separate stages meant that components even for a particular stage could come from multiple suppliers. Widespread outsourcing to reduce costs considerably increased the length, complexity and geographical diversity of value chains. In 2011, a hard disk drive assembler in Singapore or Thailand was sourcing up to 50 separate parts from suppliers in around 10 countries (Figure 15.10).

The nearby clustering of many interdependent industries within a country or in neighbouring Southeast Asian countries limited transport costs. Good regional communications networks, low transport costs, efficient services to link fragmented production processes and a lack of trade barriers within the Association of Southeast Asian Nations (ASEAN) allowed goods to be delivered from one Southeast Asian factory to another within 24 hours, facilitating regional specialization and permitting ever finer divisions of labour. Import content tended to be high and value added low, both for component production and assembly operations.

Once a country was incorporated in value chains, multinationals, usually through their contractors or sourcing companies, oversaw production and assured access to overseas markets by arranging the export of output. Multinationals typically specified products, or often components of them, and design. Technology for the manufacture of electronics and electrical goods as well as scientific and medical devices was predominately located outside Southeast Asia. Initially, all that Southeast Asian countries needed to do, at a minimum, was furnish land for production and a labour force including technicians, engineers and mid-level managers. The challenge to countries in the region was to assume more of the production process and move towards higher value-added, more skill-intensive activities.

For Southeast Asian countries, a main benefit, certainly at first, of becoming part of a global division of labour organized by multinationals was employment creation. In Southeast Asia, however, electronics manufacture created for some countries major backward linkages to ancillary local engineering firms and suppliers and forward linkages to packaging, transport and other services.[8] Both linkages and upgrading depended on the provision of suitably skilled workers and birth of new, local firms.

Within a value chain, product and process upgrading meant increasing the number of product lines and for electronics and electrical goods was essentially a widening of production. Deepening involved functional upgrading of moving up a global value chain to higher value-added activities. These decisively pushed a country towards development. Among Southeast Asian countries, functional upgrading occurred mainly in Singapore.

Export specialization in electronics, electrical, scientific and medical device parts and components and/or garments and footwear soon occupied a prominence in Southeast Asian trade sufficient to allow these goods to be considered

[8] See, for example, Choy, 'Singapore's changing economic model', p. 131.

the region's new staples. Because along a value chain the contributions of labour and skill inputs varied, wage levels largely determined regional production patterns and so the relative importance of the new staples to different countries. For the higher-wage countries of Singapore, Malaysia and Thailand, electronics products became a major staple, assuming a corresponding importance in the exports of these countries.

Garment and footwear manufacture predominated in Cambodia and Laos and along with electronics contributed to Indonesian growth. Both Cambodia and Laos relied heavily on female labour working at wages substantially below China's. Accordingly, China outsourced unskilled repetitive parts of garment production to the two Southeast Asian countries. Vietnam and the Philippines relied on all of the new staples but increasingly moved towards electronics and electrical goods and away from garment and footwear exports. The Philippines shift was especially pronounced after the Multi-Fibre Arrangement ended in 1994.

Table 15.5 shows the great importance, Indonesia apart, to Southeast Asian manufacturing of the fabrication of electronics, electrical, scientific and medical device parts and components and goods from 1988 to 2022. Manufactures usually accounted for about half to four-fifths of non-oil exports, and electronics and electrical goods and scientific and medical devices parts and components and goods were a mainstay of the trade in manufactured exports. Crucially, foreign investment-driven growth hinged not just on exporting cheap Southeast Asian labour embodied in goods sent abroad but also on sharply falling global and regional transport costs, reductions of trade barriers, a country's ability to offer a suitable range of services associated with production and advances in production technology. Appropriate infrastructure, including transport, roads, ports, airports and power supplies – along with at least basic education – were fundamental permissive components of Southeast Asian industrialization.

The contiguous countries of Singapore, Malaysia and Thailand were easily and cheaply accessible to one another by good transport networks and so able to maximize inter-country specialization within different parts of, typically, regionally integrated production processes. The three countries formed a regional core of electronics and electrical parts and components manufacture, relying on these for most exported manufactures. By the end of the 1990s, the Philippines, after its establishment of export processing zones, became a second Southeast Asian centre for parts and components production, and without these would have had slight manufactured exports. In Vietnam over just 12 years beginning in 2010, a parts and components industry expanded at breakneck speed to account for half of manufactures exported. Manufacturing was more diversified in Indonesia and never depended more than marginally on electronics. Indonesian industry, in contrast to its smaller Southeast Asian neighbours, traditionally looked chiefly towards the domestic market.

Table 15.5 *Southeast Asia total exports, non-oil exports, manufactured exports and electronics and electrical goods and scientific and medical device exports as a percentage of manufactured exports, 1988–2022 (US$ millions and %)*

(a) Malaysia	1988	1996	2000	2006	2010	2019	2022
Total exports	11,697	88,630	115,293	191,402	195,193	333,858	23,569
Non-oil exports	9,342	82,061	108,215	173,881	167,077	304,757	71,107
Manufactured exports	3,014	68,506	96,345	140,012	108,800	135,973	126,600
Manufactures as % of non-oil exports	32.3	83.5	89.0	80.5	65.1	44.6	74.0
SITC 75, 76, 77 and SITC 87 and 88	1,617	48,659	75,339	104,258	63,355	73,185	74,220
SITC 75, 76, 77, 87 and 88 as % of manufactures	53.6	71.0	78.2	74.5	58.2	53.8	58.6

(b) Singapore	1988	1996	2000	2006	2010	2019	2022
Total exports	12,593	88,437	89,694	139,618	125,633	255,158	133,874
Non-oil exports	10,077	78,113	88,855	137,298	123,330	251,157	128,690
Manufactured exports	8,711	72,751	82,866	127,003	104,014	116,351	101,879
Manufactures as % of non-oil exports	86.5	93.1	93.3	92.5	84.3	46.3	79.2
SITC 75, 76, 77 and SITC 87 and 88	5,379	56,150	61,895	77,356	38,506	39,418	33,297
SITC 75, 76, 77, 87 and 88 as % of manufactures	61.7	77.2	74.7	60.9	37.0	33.9	32.7

(*continued*)

Table 15.5 (*cont.*)

(c) Thailand	1988	1996	2000	2006	2010	2019	2022
Total exports	8,280	56,084	71,376	136,893	185,847	136,893	230,872
Non-oil exports	8,279	55,570	70,588	134,598	184,091	134,598	230,216
Manufactured exports	3,666	40,458	55,760	106,570	136,176	106,570	170,987
Manufactures as % of non-oil exports	44.3	72.8	79.0	79.2	74.0	79.2	74.3
SITC 75, 76, 77 and SITC 87 and 88	583	20,830	27,534	49,799	51,157	65,400	71,281
SITC 75, 76, 77, 87 and 88 as % of manufactures	15.9	51.5	49.4	46.7	37.6	61.4	41.7

(d) Indonesia	1988	1996	2000	2006	2010	2019	2022
Total exports	14,026	50,928	63,453	118,370	171,405	199,573	237,951
Non-oil exports	6,873	37,188	48,361	90,971	127,459	161,166	180,787
Manufactured exports	2,598	24,597	34,639	52,931	62,652	88,278	99,678
Manufactures as % of non-oil exports	37.8	66.1	71.6	58.2	49.2	54.8	55.1
SITC 75, 76, 77 and SITC 87 and 88	49	4,006	8,678	15,877	15,572	15,186	13,654
SITC 75, 76, 77, 87 and 88 as % of manufactures	1.9	16.3	25.1	30.0	24.9	17.2	13.7

(e) Philippines	1988	1996	2000	2006	2010	2019	2022
Total exports	4,444	23,737	46,508	71,494	54,590	94,358	65,188
Non-oil exports	4,372	23,393	46,415	70,815	53,545	93,386	64,431
Manufactured exports	1,756	19,243	41,718	56,811	32,155	47,630	41,660
Manufactures as % of non-oil exports	40.2	82.3	89.9	80.2	60.1	51.0	64.7
SITC 75, 76, 77 and SITC 87 and 88	662	13,794	35,025	47,196	21,628	34,037	28,931
SITC 75, 76, 77, 87 and 88 as % of manufactures	37.7	71.7	84.0	83.1	67.3	71.5	69.4

(f) Vietnam	1988	1996	2000	2006	2010	2019	2022
Total exports	315	7,250	14,059	42,378	73,092	325,195	342,777
Non-oil exports	255	5,746	10,412	33,127	65,917	322,678	341,280
Manufactured exports	19	3,402	7,171	24,491	49,510	214,320	297,862
Manufactures as % of non-oil exports	7.5	59.2	68.9	73.9	75.1	66.4	87.3
SITC 75, 76, 77 and SITC 87 and 88	–	164	747	3,374	8,200	87,970	147,264
SITC 75, 76, 77, 87 and 88 as % of manufactures	–	4.8	10.4	13.8	16.6	41.0	49.4

Notes: The data are based on SITC revision 3. The one-digit SITC 7 group is Machinery and transport equipment. Its main components in Southeast Asian electronic and electrical goods exports are SITC 75 Office machines and automatic data-processing machines, SITC 76 Telecommunications and sound-recording and reproducing apparatus and equipment and SITC 77 Electrical machinery, apparatus and appliances, n.e.s., and electrical parts thereof (including nonelectrical counterparts, n.e.s., of electrical household-type equipment). Important at the three-digit level is SITC 776 Television picture tubes, cathode-ray (including video monitor cathode-ray tubes). SITC 87 is Professional, scientific and controlling instruments and apparatus, n.e.s. and SITC 88 is Photographic apparatus, equipment and supplies and optical goods, n.e.s.; watches and clocks.
Source: I owe these data to Prema-Chandra Athukorala who compiled it from the World Integrated Trade Solution (WITS) database of the World Bank.

Electronics and electrical parts and components had, as fragmentation theory outlines, strong growth potential due to high income elasticities of demand, and were divisible into many specialized manufacturing processes at several locations according to varying labour intensity of production and wage costs.[9] Scope for countries to move from unskilled activities to more skilled and capital-intensive ones allowed the possibility of factor endowments evolving and comparative advantage shifting towards higher value-added production. Investment in education and skills facilitated a shift towards more skilled jobs. These jobs helped to explain rising wages in some countries and, through linkages and spillover effects, promoted a move away from an earlier heavy reliance on the venting of cheap labour and towards a broader domestic economic development.

The global electronics industry divided into three tiers: lead firms, contract manufacturers/tier 1 suppliers and component manufacturers. The three divisions of global value chains approximately corresponded to the scope to add value along a chain. Lead firms were the multinationals that researched, invented, branded and marketed products (for example, Apple, Lenovo, Dell and Samsung). Contract manufacturers/tier 1 suppliers, of which the Taiwanese firm Foxconn was the largest, were also usually multinationals. They produced final goods according to the specifications of lead firms and in doing so provided electronics manufacturing services such as the purchase of components, final assembly and possibly also design. As well as Foxconn, other large contract manufacturers in Southeast Asia were Flex, Jabil Circuit, Celestica and Sanmina-SCI. Flex, formerly Flextronics and headquartered in Austin, Texas, had 12 facilities in Malaysia, a presence built up with major tax incentives. At the bottom of the tiers were numerous component manufacturers. These firms had relatively little market power and generally sold to contract manufacturers which fulfilled production contracts for lead firms.[10]

Moving up a value chain towards higher value-added activities through functional upgrading required abundant human capital with a mix of university graduate and postgraduate degrees as well as appropriate skills. Even given these, functional upgrading was difficult for Southeast Asian countries because of a clear industrial separation of functions between research and design, manufacturing and assembly of final products and fabrication. This industry modularity was reinforced by the usual practice of lead firms to undertake higher value-added activities at corporate headquarters or design centres.

[9] Feenstra, 'Integration of trade', pp. 31–33, 42–47; Jones, 'Production fragmentation', pp. 348–50, 353–54.

[10] Sturgeon and Kawakami, 'Global value chains' (2011), pp. 124–29 and 'Global value chains' (2010), pp. 10–20; Frederick and Gereffi, *Philippines*, pp. v–vi, 10–42; Raj-Reichert, 'Global value chains', pp. 701–02, 707–09.

South Korea and China established lead electronics firms but Southeast Asian countries did not.[11]

In Southeast Asia, participation in global electronics value chains was mainly confined to component manufacture and assembly. Only Singapore consistently and continuously advanced along global value chains. The Republic moved from the assembly of transistor radios in the 1960s, to consumer electronics during the 1970s, and to the manufacture of computer equipment by the 1980s.[12]

The head offices of many tier 1 suppliers and contract manufacturers were in Taiwan or the United States, but some were in Singapore, including Venture and Beyonics. Singapore exhibited functional upgrading in wafer fabrication; the provision of a large share of the world's hard disk media; and the design and marketing of semiconductors. In this last example of functional upgrading, Singapore followed the fabless foundry model, so called because chips were designed but not fabricated. Fabrication was outsourced to cheaper, lower value-added locations in the supply chain along with the assembly, testing and packaging of semiconductors.[13] Progression along value chains and the Republic's impressive expansion as a provider of financial and other high value-added services helped to account for its high wages and high per capita incomes.[14]

Foreign Investment

When moving into Southeast Asia, multinationals brought with them the capital and equipment needed to establish production. Table 15.6 sets out UNCTAD data for the net stock of foreign direct investment in Southeast Asia, defined as stocks of investment inflows minus outflows. Although an annual inflow figure has sometimes been taken by scholars as representing foreign direct investment in Singapore, it considerably overstates the addition to net stocks in the Republic as well as doing so to a lesser extent for some other Southeast Asian countries.[15]

Malaysia and Thailand in particular became large investors abroad, but Singapore stood out as the Southeast Asian country that, as an investor,

[11] Sturgeon and Kawakami, 'Global value chains' (2011), pp. 124–29 and 'Global value chains' (2010), pp. 10–20; Frederick and Gereffi, *Philippines*, pp. v–vi, 10–42; Raj-Reichert, 'Global value chains', pp. 701–02, 707–09; Hobday and Rush, 'Upgrading the technological capabilities', pp. 1338–41, 1345–46.

[12] Choy, 'Singapore's changing economic model', p. 133.

[13] Bown and Wang, *Semiconductors*, pp. 2, 8, 14; Sturgeon and Kawakami, 'Global value chains' (2010), pp. 18–20.

[14] Sturgeon and Kawakami, 'Global value chains' (2010), pp. 18–20.

[15] For example, Lim and Pang, 'Rethinking'.

Table 15.6 *Southeast Asia net stock of foreign direct investment, 1980–2024 (stock of inwards investment minus stock outwards)*

(a) FDI stock millions of dollars	1980	1985	1997	2007	2013	2020	2024
Malaysia	4,755	6,014	24,553	18,573	10,709	44,832	83,537
Singapore	−1,605	5,208	34,115	100,141	339,772	634,699	1,056,752
Thailand	968	1,983	11,058	78,724	126,853	116,225	125,127
Philippines	1,084	2,430	6,893	13,379	19,356	39,227	54,795
Indonesia	10,274	24,922	59,402	37,530	214,274	152,270	181,055
Vietnam	7	38	11,019	40,235	68,511	165,398	235,526
Cambodia	–	–	925	3,537	8,934	35,716	50,925
Laos	2	2	426	1,160	2,795	10,804	15,298
Myanmar	5	5	1,099	5,433	14,171	35,960	41,043
Total Southeast Asia	15,490	40,602	149,490	298,712	805,375	1,235,131	1,844,058

(b) FDI/GDP %	1980	1985	1997	2007	2013	2020	2024
Malaysia	19.4	19.3	24.6	9.6	3.3	13.3	19.8
Singapore	−13.5	27.2	34.1	55.3	110.5	186.7	193.1
Thailand	3.0	5.1	7.4	29.9	30.2	23.2	23.8
Philippines	2.9	7.0	7.3	8.6	6.8	10.9	11.9

Indonesia	14.2	29.2	27.5	8.7	23.5	14.4	13.0
Vietnam	–	0.3	41.0	52.0	40.0	61.0	49.4
Cambodia	–	–	26.9	40.9	58.7	138.4	109.9
Laos	–	0.1	24.4	27.5	23.3	56.5	92.7
Myanmar	0.5	0.4	19.5	34.8	23.4	45.0	55.4

(c) FDI stock US$ per capita	1980	1985	1997	2007	2013	2020	2024
Malaysia	345	386	1,139	695	363	1,385	2,349
Singapore	–665	1,904	8,987	21,824	62,931	111,629	175,050
Thailand	20	38	182	1,190	1,862	1,665	1,746
Philippines	23	45	94	150	196	358	473
Indonesia	70	151	293	162	851	557	639
Vietnam	nil	1	143	471	755	1,699	2,332
Cambodia	nil	nil	82	259	595	2,136	2,887
Laos	1	1	84	195	427	1,485	1,969
Myanmar	nil	nil	24	109	273	661	753

Sources: UNCTAD, *World investment report, 1999*, pp. 491–92, *2014*, p. 210, *2021*, pp. 253–54, *2025*, pp. 258–59; World Bank, *World development indicators, 2025* for GDP and population.

assumed one of the Kuznets characteristics of modern economic growth in reaching out to the region and beyond.[16] In 1992, the Singapore government began an initiative, backed by fiscal incentives, tax concessions and finance, for Singapore's economy to have a 'second wing' of local business setting up enterprises throughout Asia. These included investment in the Singapore–Johor–Riau Islands Growth Triangle and industrial parks in China, Vietnam and India, all modelled on the Jurong Industrial Estate.[17] In 2023, Singapore's stock of direct investment abroad was reported as US$1,188 billion.[18]

While for Singapore, judging on the basis of UNCTAD data for yearly investment flows compared to the Republic's annual gross capital formation, a net figure for the addition of annual investment flows to stocks seems plausible for some years, for others it probably exceeds the actual addition to the stock of investment. No one can doubt that Singapore, described as an island with wall-to-wall multinationals, received large amounts of foreign direct investment. But the true amount is not known.

A possible reason for overstatement of Singapore investment stocks is double counting due to Singapore's role as an international financial centre. 'Double counting' occurred if special purpose entities in Singapore, such as holding companies or regional headquarters, channelled funds abroad to other special purpose entities which then returned the funds to Singapore as foreign direct investment, so-called round tripping.[19] Although UNCTAD data for 2020 showing that Singapore received 4.4 per cent (and an even higher share in 2024) of the world total stock of net foreign direct investment probably exaggerate the actual investment stock in the Republic, it suggests Singapore's importance as a wealth management centre with financial instruments that may be recorded as foreign direct investment but were not in fact used for that purpose. Furthermore, the apparently large investment stock points to a continuation, and probably enhancement, of Singapore's historic role as a conduit and manager for foreign direct investment in other Southeast Asian countries. Some of what seems to be foreign investment may also in fact be money laundering, since already large financial flows and a proliferation of family financial offices make Singapore attractive for these operations.[20]

Three other large net foreign direct investment recipients in the region were Thailand, Malaysia and Vietnam. Net foreign direct investment to the three was still small in the first half of the 1980s, but from 1997 to 2024 rose enormously. However, the spectacular increase in net capital inflows to Vietnam far outdistanced investment in Thailand and Malaysia. Between 1997 and 2024, net

[16] Kuznets, 'Modern economic growth', p. 248.

[17] Choy, 'Singapore's changing economic model', pp. 125–26, 133–34.

[18] Singapore, *Economic survey, 2024*, p. 11.

[19] Patterson et al., 'Key concepts'.

[20] Owen Walker, 'Singapore battles dirty money from scam farms', *Financial Times*, 16 November 2025.

capital inflows to Southeast Asia excluding Singapore increased nearly seven times. As labour costs in Singapore rose, many electronics firms either migrated to or set up initially in Thailand, Malaysia and Vietnam, boosting foreign direct investment in these countries. Although Indonesia had sizeable investment inflows, these partly reflected its large population and resource base.

Both the net stock of foreign direct investment as a proportion of GDP and net stocks of foreign direct investment per capita afford further gauges of the importance to countries of the Southeast Asian development model. Although investment as a share of GDP fell in Malaysia after 1997 and in Thailand after 2007, it rose sharply in Cambodia as that country joined Vietnam to form part of Southeast Asia's development model. Between 2007 and 2024 in Cambodia, a 14-fold rise in net foreign investment, taking it to well over 100 per cent of GDP, was substantially due to large inflows of capital from China. Cambodia was known to be a 'Chinese satellite state' and the upsurge in investment reflected China's Belt and Road Initiative, the opening of special Cambodian export zones and its extremely liberal investment climate, which granted 100 per cent foreign ownership of enterprises.[21] Like Cambodia, tiny Laos was a target for infrastructure investment from neighbouring China.[22]

In Southeast Asia except Singapore, stocks of foreign investment per capita remained small. Taking the 2020 figure for Singapore's foreign investment stock as a reasonable approximation of actual foreign investment that stayed in Singapore, the Republic had accumulated an astonishing stock of US$112,000 per capita. Growth in Singapore – which has depended heavily on these large additions of capital and inflows of migrant labour – can be understood in the context of the Solow model.[23] That model explains growth as a function of capital inputs, so long as labour is available to use the capital, and of technical progress. This last is key (and so a cause of worry to Singapore officials) because diminishing returns to capital imply that sustainable growth can be realized only through technical progress, which growth accounting has typically found relatively unimportant in the Republic.

Labour and Wages

Productive labour at low cost was essential to attracting multinationals. Singapore, reacting to Western and Japanese multinationals scanning the world for the cheap, reliable labour no longer available in the West, led the way in Southeast Asian countries making themselves attractive to multinationals.

[21] A. Anantha Lakshmi, 'Cambodia looks to reduce reliance on China amid US trade war', *Financial Times*, 14 January 2026.

[22] See, for example, 'Rail link draws Laos further into Beijing's orbit', *Financial Times*, 31 October 2019; Menon and Warr, 'Lao economy', pp. 70–72; Bird and Hill, 'Tiny, land-locked, indebted', pp. 118–23, 129.

[23] Solow, 'Contribution', pp. 66–84.

These enterprises initially favoured Singapore as a location for electronics production, because, above all, it could, after rapid post-World War II population increase, supply abundant, compliant and reasonably educated labour.

Still in the 2010s in most of Southeast Asia, wages remained far lower than in developed countries, and well below those in China. Female wages were universally less than male, often significantly so (Table 15.7). Partly because of cheapness and labour docility, women became a major part of the Southeast Asian labour force, both in electronics production and, even more, in the garment and shoe industries. In venting labour, Southeast Asia could draw on unemployed or underemployed urban workers, a pool swelled by high post-World War II birth rates as well as premature rural–urban migration; the transfer of underemployed labour from agriculture to industry; and women joining the labour force for the first time. Although previously unemployed workers afforded a pure Smithian vent-for-surplus gain, most of trade gains came from labour reallocation.

Migrant Labour

Differential development and wage levels, as well as continued population increase, combined to divide Southeast Asia into migrant-sending and -receiving countries (Table 15.8). Trade and migration are substitutes. The Philippines, Indonesia, Vietnam, Cambodia, Laos and Myanmar all relied substantially on migration as a way of exporting labour, since venting opportunities in export industries were insufficient to absorb surplus labour.[24]

Singapore alone was always a net recipient of migrants, but after the 1970s this increased enormously as the Republic brought in low-cost labour and recruited skilled migrants. By 2002, both Thailand and Malaysia, including their electronics industries, were also dependent on large inwards migration for supplies of cheap labour. In Malaysia, most foreign workers were low-skilled and engaged in basic services, agriculture and manufacturing. Between 1990 and 2005 in Malaysia, foreign workers accounted for over a third of the increase in labour supply and more than 98 per cent were low-skilled migrant contract workers.[25] Downwards pressure on wages due to large migrant inflows was partly responsible for the reluctance of large numbers of Malaysians and Thai to take low-skilled and low-paid jobs, choosing instead to remain in the countryside and semi-rural areas.

Both Malaysia and Thailand were large recipients of illegal migration. In 2017, official reports estimated that Malaysia had some three million legal

[24] On these economies as labour surplus, see, for example, Anas et al., 'Indonesian economy', pp. 250–51; World Bank, *Middle class in the Philippines*, p. xii. In the 1990s, Indonesia needed to create 2.4 million jobs annually; Woo et al., *Macroeconomic policies*, p. 6.

[25] Malaysia, National Economic Advisory Council, *New economic model*, p. 50.

Table 15.7 *Southeast Asia, China and Japan wages, 2010–20*

(a) Avg. monthly wages, 2014 US$

Singapore	3,731
Malaysia	682
Thailand	408
Philippines	216
Indonesia	165
Vietnam	212
Cambodia	121
Laos	119
China	685
Japan	3,111

(b) Monthly minimum wages in the garment industry, 2015 US$

	For unskilled workers	Lowest relevant rate for unskilled workers
China	297	155
Philippines	269	150
Malaysia	253	225
Indonesia	247	92
Thailand	237	n.a.
Vietnam	145	100
Cambodia	128	n.a.
Sri Lanka	n.a.	66

(c) Avg. monthly earnings in manufacturing, US$

	Total	Male	Female
Singapore 2020	3,541	3,857	2,910
Malaysia 2020	605	646	536
Thailand 2020	464	496	427
Indonesia 2015	124	137	102
Philippines 2020	278	285	266
Vietnam 2020	308	334	287
Cambodia 2019	252	259	249
Laos 2017	222	267	178
Myanmar 2020	171	180	163

Notes and Sources: panel a: International Labour Organization, Regional Office for Asia and the Pacific, *Wages, productivity and labour share in China*, p. 2; panel b: International Labour Organization, *Employment, wages and working conditions*, p. 12; panel c: Average monthly earnings of employees by sex and economic activity; International Labour Organization, www.ilo.org/data.

Table 15.8 *Southeast Asia migration inflows and outflows, 1962–2017 (000 persons; negative numbers are net migrant outflows, positive numbers net inflows)*

	Malaysia	Singapore	Thailand	Philippines	Indonesia	Vietnam	Cambodia	Laos	Myanmar
1962	–58.6	0.4	0.0	–218.1	450.0	0.0	0.0	0.1	0.0
1972	–135.3	5.9	395.6	–375.1	508.3	0.0	–125.0	0.0	0.0
1977	–5.4	14.3	287.2	–476.6	378.7	–858.9	–85.0	–198.8	0.0
1992	292.4	297.8	–607.5	–698.9	–35.4	–394.2	409.4	–60.6	–713.7
2002	671.5	92.8	373.7	–1,244.4	–1,149.7	–651.0	–35.2	–148.1	–1,208.1
2007	761.9	721.3	59.0	–1,548.1	–1,333.7	–800.0	–296.0	–110.3	–1,336.9
2012	250.0	317.0	167.3	–834.6	–454.4	–400.0	–150.0	–112.3	–528.2
2017	250.0	135.1	97.2	–335.8	–494.8	–400.0	–150.0	–73.5	–816.6

Note: Migrant outflows from Cambodia in 1972 and 1977 reflect the uncertainties of the Second Indochina War and then the Pol Pot regime, and the 1992 figure a return of population after earlier political and social disruption.
Source: World Bank, *World development indicators, 2020.*

foreign workers, most of whom came from Indonesia and Bangladesh. There were additionally in Malaysia a World Bank estimated 1.5 million irregular (essentially illegal) foreign workers. Other estimates put the figure as high as 4 million.[26] The foreign workforce in Malaysia, according to the World Bank estimate, was about 15 per cent of the total labour force, but the percentage could be higher, depending on the true number of irregular workers. In 2018, Thailand had a non-Thai resident population of 4.9 million, mostly from Cambodia, Laos, Myanmar and Vietnam, which comprised 10 per cent of the labour force.[27]

Singapore's government, already heavily committed to large inflows of immigrant labour, announced, in a 2013 White Paper, its intention of yet further increasing the admission of immigrants, setting a target of an average population increase of 100,000 annually until 2030, creating a population of some 6.5 to 6.9 million.[28] All the main reasons for the policy involved the long-standing and successful PAP bargain with the electorate: that it would, in large numbers, continue electorally to support the Party so long as the PAP continued to deliver growth and a rising standard of living.[29] By 2013, however, growth was threatened by a birth rate of then 1.19 (0.97 in 2023 and 1.26 in 2025) for Singapore citizens; by a failure substantially to increase total factor productivity, leaving continued growth mainly reliant on ever greater inputs of labour and capital; by, at least in the government's view, insufficient skills among Singapore citizens to keep growth going; and by the inevitable slowing of growth as the economy matured.

Increased immigration satisfied, at least in the short to medium term, the government's growth agenda because it involved both skilled and unskilled immigrants. The former, many from China or Malaysian ethnic Chinese and often professionals, were offered a chance of permanent residence and in time citizenship. They made up for the low Singapore birth rate and, by turning the city into 'New Asia's hub for innovation and creative enterprise', compensated for a perceived lack of sufficient skills among Singaporeans.[30] Unskilled immigrants, principally from poor Asian countries, furnished labour inputs required for growth and, through downwards pressure on wages for services and construction near the bottom of the labour market, boosted the standard of living of Singapore's middle class vital to PAP electoral support.

26 World Bank, *Who is keeping score?*, pp. viii–ix, 45. Irregular workers are defined as illegal entrants, persons not authorized to work although legal entrants, overstayers and refugees and asylum seekers who seek employment.

27 United Nations, *Thailand: migration report*, p. xi.

28 Singapore, *Population white paper*.

29 On this 'social contract' with voters, see, for example, Huff, 'Singapore's economic development: four lessons', p. 44; Lim, 'Fifty years of development', p. 5.

30 Singapore, *Report of the Economic Strategies Committee*, p. 67.

The White Paper immediately brought opposition, even protest, from many Singapore citizens because of overcrowding, pressure on services and housing prices. The feeling existed that new arrivals, although with permanent residence status (545,000 in 2024), were not true Singaporeans and that, by living in enclaves and not learning English, they did not wish to integrate.[31] In 2013 Singapore's population was 5.39 million but by 2024 had risen to 6.04 million. Of this total, 3.31 million were citizens in 2013 and 3.64 million in 2024, implying that at least half the population increase was due to labour inflows. These help to explain continued unease among Singapore citizens over immigration. At the low end of the labour market, immigrant workers drove down wages for poorer Singaporeans, while at the top end immigration increased competition for jobs and likely crowded out some citizens.

In the migrant-sending countries, remittances contributed significantly to GDP. By the later 2010s, remittances were 3 to 4 per cent of GDP in Myanmar, over 6 per cent in Vietnam and 10 per cent in the Philippines. In 2020 in the Philippines, emigrants amounted to 5.2 per cent of the population compared to Vietnam's 3.1 per cent and Indonesia's 1.7 per cent.[32] Most Southeast Asian migrants left the region, often for the United States or for work in construction or domestic service in the Middle East. However, many went to Southeast Asia's three migrant-receiving countries of Singapore, Malaysia and Thailand, establishing their own enclaves of living, eating and entertainment areas.

Country Experience

Singapore, Malaysia, Thailand: an Electronics Core

Early export-led industrialization in Singapore centred on the production of semiconductors. National Semiconductor began operations in 1968 and Texas Instruments opened a Singapore plant the next year. Together, and functioning as so-called 'anchor firms', they helped to attract, through external economies and agglomeration effects, other electronics firms: Tandon in 1971 and Hewlett Packard in 1972. In addition to the availability of cheap labour, electronics firms clustered in Singapore because of its generous tax and many other incentives; the city's location on the world's main east–west transport route, giving low-cost access by air to world markets; an integrated regional transport network; a safe and stable environment; widespread familiarity with English (important for American firms); and, before long, the appearance of local

[31] Jeremy Grant, 'Medal win at 2012 games stokes debate on Singapore's migrants', *Financial Times*, 10 August 2012; Yahoo! News, '4,000 turn up at Speakers' Corner for population White Paper protest', 16 February 2013, https://sg.news.yahoo.com/huge-turnout-at-speakers--corner-for-population-white-paper-protest-101051153.html?guccounter=1.

[32] United Nations, *World migration report, 2024*, p. 124.

precision engineering and other support firms, this last attracting multinationals through a so-called supplier access effect.

Job creation for unemployed and underemployed Singaporean workers was at first facilitated by the labour-intensive and unskilled nature of many manufacturing jobs in the electronics and textile and garment industries. As Goh Keng Swee observed, 'The electronic components we make in Singapore probably require less skill than that required by barbers or cooks, consisting mostly of repetitive manual operations.'[33] Still in 1975, manufacturing hourly compensation (total employer) costs in Singapore were 13 per cent of those in the United States. Output per hour was probably higher, and involved mainly electronics and electrical products, notably integrated circuits (or chips) consisting of thousands or even millions of various components fabricated onto a wafer made of silicon.

The fall in unemployment from 8.9 per cent in 1966 to 4.5 per cent in 1973 represented a turning point from labour surplus to labour scarcity and signified the end of the dual economy for Singapore citizens, though not for what later became a vast migrant workforce. Despite the end of labour surplus, wages remained low and competitive, because the government managed labour supply (Chapter 14). By the early 1970s, Singapore had established an industrial base for electronics and, perhaps more important, a reputation of reliability along with a welcoming, subsidy-rich environment for multinationals.

Drawn by Singapore's existing electronics industry, Seagate began to manufacture in Singapore in 1982. Initially, Seagate used its Singapore factory to burn and test magnetic circuit boards and assemble magnetic circuit arms, but in 1983 built a second Singapore factory to assemble disk drives. Two years previously, Apple and Digital Equipment Corporation, both large users of disk drives, had opened in Singapore. Between the early 1980s and mid-1990s, most of the world's other disk drive manufacturers followed Seagate to Singapore, attracted by a fast ramp-up of production due to a large local pool of engineers, the provision of factory sites by the Economic Development Board, numerous government subsidies and an environment of local supporting industries. These last, as linkages developed, numbered some 100. Seagate and IBM made Singapore the centre for their high-end disk production owing to its combination of engineering capabilities unmatched in Southeast Asia and low production costs (Table 14.14).[34] Between 1986 and 1996, Singapore accounted for half of world disk drive production. At the same time, however, Singapore's continual active promotion of the provision and export of international services accounted for a considerable share of the Republic's growth.

Before long, Malaysia, Thailand and the Philippines, aware of rapid growth in their city state neighbour, started to copy Singapore's outward-looking,

[33] Goh, *Decade* (budget speech, 1970), p. 27.

[34] McKendrick et al., *Silicon Valley*, pp. 161–68.

multinational-dependent, cheap-labour, subsidy-driven manufacturing export model which revolved largely around electronics products. Electronics and electrical production began in Penang in the late 1960s, soon after its start in Singapore. In the 1970s under the Second Malaysia Plan of 1971–75 (an improvement on the Investment Incentives Act, 1968), Malaysia established Free Trade Zones to attract multinationals which were relocating low-wage electronics and electrical operations from more developed countries including Singapore. In addition, the Second Plan offered government incentives such as pioneer status giving tax advantages to promoted industries, investment tax credits and tax holidays.[35] Job creation was a main focus of the Plan, since in 1970 unemployment was around 8 per cent and the number of job seekers joining the labour force was rapidly increasing. The aim in Malaysia, as elsewhere in Southeast Asia, was to create jobs such that 'Unemployment and underemployment will then cease to be factors tying down large numbers of Malaysians to poverty.'[36]

During the 1970s, an initial wave of electronics multinationals setting up in Malaysia included Texas Instruments, Intel, Motorola and Hewlett Packard. By 1980, 25 electronics factories operated in four Free Trade Zones in Penang, and Malaysia was the world's largest exporter of semiconductors.[37] During the 1980s, Japanese, Korean and Taiwanese multinationals were attracted to Malaysia, because currency appreciation after the 1985 Plaza Accord raised wages in their home countries. In 2005, Malaysia had some 200 multinational electronics firms employing 110,000 workers and 350 downstream firms with employment of 25,000.[38]

Between the end of the 1990s and 2014, some firms in Malaysia, supported by government grants, began chip and wafer fabrication, but functional upgrading remained slow, constrained by a chronic lack of human capital and poor technological environment.[39] Semiconductor production comprised three-fifths of the Malaysian electronics and electrical industry, and Malaysia was the world's sixth largest chip exporter, positions on which the Malaysia 2030 industrial plan of 2023 looked to build. The goal was functionally to upgrade by establishing more advanced semiconductor design capabilities and attracting a leading firm in wafer fabrication.[40]

During the 1970s and 1980s, Thailand became an assembly hub for semiconductors. Earlier experience in electronics production and its abundance of managers and engineers helped Thailand, like Malaysia, to establish clusters for

[35] Malaysia, *Second Malaysia Plan, 1971–1976*, pp. 91, 149–58.

[36] Malaysia, *Second Malaysia Plan, 1971–1976*, p. 5 and see p. 15.

[37] Hutchinson, '"Developmental" states', p. 228; Raj-Reichert, 'Global value chains', p. 702.

[38] Hutchinson, '"Developmental" states', p. 224.

[39] Rasiah, 'Industrial policy experience', pp. 134–40; Edgington and Hayter, 'In situ upgrading', pp. 227, 248–50.

[40] Malaysia, Ministry of Investment, Trade and Industry, *New industrial master plan 2030*, pp. 49–72.

the production of hard disk drives. While both countries continued to manufacture and test semiconductors, the disk drive industry became particularly important to Thailand but less so to Malaysia. Thailand's semiconductor industry found difficulty in upgrading from downstream activities like assembly and testing to upstream industry, and in 2015 semiconductors accounted for just a quarter of Thailand's electronics and electrical exports. Only around 3 per cent of over 2,000 firms in the Thai electronics industry were in semiconductor-related activities.[41]

In the spread of disk drive industries to Thailand and Malaysia, Singapore functioned as a centre – a sort of 'anchor country' – from which an integrated Southeast Asian regional production network developed. For manufacturers, inter-country production in disk manufacture was strongly complementary not competitive. Rising wages in Singapore were the most important reason for the industry's relocation of labour-intensive production away from Singapore and for the use of Singapore for skilled operations and as a regional headquarters. Even so, Singapore wages were low enough and its labour sufficiently skilled that Singapore remained an important electronics manufacturing centre. In 2025, Singapore manufactured 10 per cent of the world's chips, a fifth of electronic equipment and 80 per cent of DNA chips. These involved implanting millions of DNA strands on a glass or silicon surface to produce chips able to sequence DNA.[42]

When, in 1983, Seagate set up its first Thailand factory near Bangkok, wage costs were half of Singapore's. Through much of the 1980s, the Thai government guarded competitiveness by holding minimum wages below inflation. In Bangkok, Seagate could respond flexibly to the disk drive industry's extreme volatility and competitiveness, since it was 'able to get 10,000 workers very quickly' and could call workers in the 'middle of the night to meet special orders'.[43] By 1999, Seagate employed 35,000 workers in Thailand.[44]

It took five years after the arrival of Seagate for another disk drive manufacturer to set up in Thailand, but subsequently drive manufacturers flooded into Bangkok and nearby areas like Ayutthaya. IBM came in 1991 and, as it and other firms arrived, external economies and agglomeration economies strengthened. Thailand became a leading producer of motors and disk drive head-related products and, in the process, ever more embedded in the Southeast Asian production network. By the early 2000s, Thailand had 35 disk drive factories and was second only to Singapore as the world's largest manufacturer of drives. Soon, it surpassed Singapore.[45] Disk drives were a leading sector in Thailand

[41] Intarakumnerd et al., 'Global production networks', pp. 2, 11.
[42] Wong, *Onward together*, p. 20.
[43] McKendrick et al., *Silicon Valley*, p. 190.
[44] Hobday and Rush, 'Upgrading technological capabilities', p. 1348.
[45] UNCTAD, *Case study of electronics industry*, pp. 1, 17; Intarakumnerd and Jutarosaga, 'Evolution', pp. 276–77.

and a main factor in its extremely rapid export expansion between 1987 and 2010. Although after 2010 drives remained important to the Thai economy, they became a 'sunset product' because of the move to storage in the cloud.

Despite a well-established electronics industry, disk drive assembly in Malaysia began only in 1988, partly because it was previously discouraged by Prime Minister Mahathir's 1980s 'Look East' strategy for heavy industrialization. After 1988, a Penang disk drive cluster grew rapidly. Maxtor was typical in its reasons for moving to Penang as an extension of Singapore operations. Rising land and labour costs in Singapore created savings for Maxtor that allowed it to recoup in six months the cost of investing in Penang. The alertness of, and subsidies from, the Penang Development Corporation created first-mover advantages that helped to ensure that disk drive production was located chiefly in Penang, not neighbouring Perak.[46]

For Thailand and Malaysian disk drive manufacturers, the regional specialization, fragmentation and just-in-time delivery characteristic of electronics production was facilitated by a combination of nearness to Singapore, good road and air transport connections to it as well as to each other and ASEAN free trade beginning in 1992. Proximity reduced the cost of managerial oversight, since one manager could travel between countries in at most a few hours. All Southeast Asian governments used subsidies to attract electronics firms to their countries. When subsidies expired, they were generally renewed, especially if firms could claim to be now engaging in some new aspect of production. Externalities and agglomeration effects further added to the attractiveness of establishing plants in Malaysia and Thailand, because, as more drive manufacturers opened, suppliers followed them and because the pool of managers, engineers and trained workers widened.

Seagate's operations in Thailand concentrated in or around Bangkok but as labour there became less elastic and wages rose, Seagate pioneered an assembly facility in Khorat in northeast Thailand. Although continuing to deepen its operations in Penang, Seagate also opened in Ipoh in response to the availability of a large pool of workers and low land prices. Similarly, when Penang became relatively costly as a production site, disk drive manufacturers moved low-end assembly to Indonesia and the Philippines.

While industrialization in Thailand centred on a large electronics sector, automobile production for export became increasingly important. The Thai auto industry illustrates the advantage of integrating into a global value chain, and contrasts sharply with Malaysia's experience. The latter's strategy was to rely on near total import substitution to produce Proton (from 1983) and later Perodua (from 1992) automobiles behind high tariff protection. Although Malaysia continued to manufacture cars, the reliance on import substitution

[46] McKendrick et al., *Silicon Valley*, p. 190.

proved uneconomic and, in terms of economic cost, the industry failed badly because of a limited domestic market and a high dependence on imported inputs. By contrast, Thailand's automotive industry, forced to turn outwards by the 1997 Asian financial crisis, joined largely Japanese-organized supply and assembly chains. Thailand became the world's largest manufacturer, or perhaps more accurately assembler, of light pickup trucks and a major exporter of them – the 'Detroit of the East'.[47]

Philippines: Halting Progress

As the electronics industry spread across Southeast Asia, the Philippines, attractive for its low wages and a population with many English speakers, was an early competitor to Malaysia in the production of electronics components and electrical goods. However, the Philippines, undermined by the instability of the Marcos years and the 1980s economic downturn, did not emerge as a Southeast Asian centre for disk drive production until the 1990s.[48] Although a small mechanical-parts cluster had developed, the breakthrough came only in 1995, when three Japanese disk drive final assemblers moved to Manila. A number of Japanese first- and second-tier suppliers followed this lead, as did Singapore and Malaysian suppliers. By the end of the 1990s, Manila was another Southeast Asian disk drive cluster.[49]

Subsequently, however, the benefits for the Philippines of its participation in global electronics value chains were disappointing, especially after the 2007 world financial crisis and despite the establishment of export processing zones. Electronics production in the Philippines was mostly labour intensive, depended disproportionately on female labour and consisted chiefly of component manufacture, assembly and testing. Main competitors to the Philippines were Malaysia, Thailand and Vietnam, all of which outdistanced it in advancement along a value chain range of products and in establishing backward and forward linkages. Intel left the Philippines in 2009, apparently at least partly because of a move to Vietnam. While Malaysia and Thailand hosted some contract/tier 1 suppliers, the Philippines had predominantly tier 3 capabilities, as did Laos and Myanmar.[50]

In the mid-2010s, the Philippines contributed just 1 per cent of world exports of electronics and electrical goods. Final product production consisted mainly of low-value items like office and storage equipment and computer peripherals. Backward linkages were weak and value added low, since raw materials comprised some 80 per cent of costs and were mostly imported. Although scope to

[47] Warr and Kohpaiboon, 'Thailand's automotive manufacturing corridor'.

[48] McKendrick et al., *Silicon Valley*, p. 189; Rasiah, 'Industrial policy experience', p. 132.

[49] Hiratsuka, *Production networks*, pp. 13–15.

[50] Frederick and Gereffi, *Philippines*, p. 27.

progress up global chains was apparent, advancement was held back by a poor education system and the migration of engineers overseas. In the absence of a vibrant, labour-using manufacturing sector, most surplus Philippine labour remained in agriculture, and became part of a poorly remunerated service sector or migrated abroad.[51]

Indochinese Economies: the Latecomers

Vietnamese manufacturing for export, aided by a US–Vietnam bilateral trade agreement, at first relied substantially on garments and footwear. By 2019, Vietnam ranked as the world's second largest exporter of footwear. Both garments and footwear contributed importantly to employment as new, labour-intensive staples. In 2023, the garment industry employed some 3.3 million workers, of whom three-quarters were female, and footwear manufacture a further 1.5 million.[52]

During the 2010s, the rapid rise of a Vietnamese electronics industry eclipsed garments and footwear as Vietnam's leading staple. In 2009, Samsung opened a mobile phone manufacturing plant in Bac Ninh province in northern Vietnam, and ranked, in the mid-2020s, as the country's largest electronics investor and exporter. However, the breakthrough occurred in 2006 when Intel announced an investment of a billion dollars to establish, in Saigon Hi-Tech Park, its biggest chip-making plant outside the United States. A Vietnamese returning from Silicon Valley was instrumental in Intel's decision to invest in Vietnam, and a similar California connection was also key in other electronics firms locating outside Ho Chi Minh City in Saigon Hi-Tech Park or one of several other industrial parks.[53] One example is Global Equipment Services, headquartered in Santa Carla, California and also with operations in India and Japan, which manufactured machines to produce chips according to the specifications of clients.[54] A US–China trade war during the first Trump presidential administration boosted the Vietnamese electronics industry. By 2019, although Vietnam had many electronics firms, most engaged principally in simple electronics and mobile phone assembly.[55]

51 Frederick and Gereffi, *Philippines*, pp. 42–69; World Bank, *Middle class in the Philippines*, pp. xii, 59–60.

52 International Labour Organization, 'Empowering women'; Oanh et al., 'Participation', p. 84.

53 Klingler-Vidra and Wade, 'Science and technology policies', p. 725; Van Can and Dang, 'Challenges', pp. 258–59.

54 Interview with Manager, Global Equipment Services Vietnam, Saigon Hi-Tech Park, 27 November 2015.

55 Rasiah, 'Expansion and slowdown', pp. 124–25; Rasiah and Yun, 'Industrializing Southeast Asia', p. 113.

Industrialization in Cambodia began to take off in the 1990s and in Laos after 2000. Both countries depended heavily on the CMT (cut, make and trim) trade in garments. Although Cambodia diversified into simple electronics and automobile parts, in 2018, the so-called GTF (garments, textiles and footwear) sector accounted for 74 per cent of Cambodian exports, with garments contributing 66 per cent and footwear the remaining 8 per cent. Often international buyers, not multinationals, sourced garments for developed country firms, but for footwear, multinationals including Nike, Adidas and Asics were key players in both Cambodia and Vietnam.

Raw materials for footwear manufacture in the Indochinese economies came from as many as 12 different countries. Most labour in the manufacture of footwear, as also for garments, was female and salaried. In Southeast Asia's output of garments and footwear, productivity, wages and value added were all low. China and Taiwan were large foreign investors in Southeast Asian garment and footwear factories, but the United States and the European Union the chief markets.[56]

Apart from its main attraction of low wages, foreign export firms were drawn to Cambodia by: the concession of 100 per cent foreign ownership, Cambodia's 1999 accession to the ASEAN free trade area, the Generalized System of Preferences privileges (for garments and footwear), favourable tariff treatment for imports and the establishment of special export zones. These last afforded, as well as tax incentives, infrastructure provision and a range of services. The Southern Economic Corridor, promoted by the Asian Development Bank and dating from 1998, linked Cambodia to the Greater Mekong Subregion (substantial areas of Thailand, Vietnam and Laos). Many firms wanted this access, and to secure it located in metropolitan Phnom Penh or border regions such as Koh Kong province.[57]

Indonesia: an Exception

Indonesia – remarkably and (rather unexpectedly) successful after 1966 – conformed to the Southeast Asian development model for only a decade, and otherwise hardly at all. The decade of export-led growth from 1986 to the 1997 Asian financial crisis was Indonesia's most spectacular interlude for its rapidity. During the remaining four decades, Indonesia swung between boom, bust and recovery, and relied for growth mainly on a uniquely Indonesian mixture of exporting primary commodity staples – chiefly oil, gas, coal and wood products – state-dominated heavy industry and services.

[56] International Labour Organization, *Footwear sector – new opportunities*, pp. 2–13, *Wages and productivity in the garment sector*, pp. 2–7, *Opportunities for a just transition*, pp. 11–16 and *Employment, wages and working conditions*, pp. 9–10, 13, 20; Rasiah, 'Garment manufacturing', pp. 150–61.

[57] Kuroiwa, '"Thailand-plus-one"', pp. 34–36.

During the 1950s and even into the 1960s, Indonesia remained poor and overwhelmingly rural. In 1965, GDP per capita, while above the poorest African countries, was much less than Nigeria's and well below Ghana's.[58] The economy was heavily reliant on highly labour-intensive technology, imported industrial inputs and outdated plant and equipment. Textile manufacture was predominantly either a cottage, handloom industry or used machinery left over from the 1930s Dutch attempts at industrialization.

After the chaos of the Sukarno years, recovery and rehabilitation of the Indonesian economy under the 'New Order' of Suharto did not occur until 1970. That year, Indonesia decisively exceeded its pre-1966 peak per capita income. Between 1970 and 1981, growth was rapid, and depended, above all, on an oil boom beginning in 1973 under the aegis of the OPEC cartel. In the summer of 1973, the benchmark price of West Texas Intermediate crude oil was US$26 a barrel. Prices then rose vertically to US$69 a barrel in January 1974, and reached a peak of US$155 in April 1980, although by March 1986 they had collapsed to US$30. By the start of the 1980s, oil and gas accounted for about three-quarters of merchandise exports and two-thirds of government revenue.[59] Growth also came from increased manufacturing capacity in response to pent-up consumer demand, more efficient mineral production and a construction boom.

The oil boom shifted the terms of trade massively in Indonesia's favour. Gross Domestic Income (GDI) takes account of the terms of trade to reflect an economy's effective purchasing power. From 1973 to 1974, and again between 1976 and 1981, GDI sharply diverged from GDP. At its peaks in 1974 and from 1979 to 1981, GDI growth was almost three times that of GDP.[60] More important, both GDP and GDI growth rates obscure the long-term impact on Indonesia of the boom in financing fundamental change.

Indonesia lost some of the oil windfall to unproductive uses. These included B. J. Habibie's ambitious and costly investments under the Strategic Industries Board, the national car project controlled by President Suharto's youngest son and the many projects undertaken by Pertamina, the giant state-owned oil monopoly company. Pertamina, until a 1975 default when it was unable to roll over a short-term loan, became 'an unofficial and largely unsupervised development agency'. Its conglomerate complex included a tanker fleet, filling stations, a steel plant, several office buildings, a data-processing centre, a tourist resort, a fertilizer factory, an airline and a number of rice plantations.[61] But by no means all the oil revenue was dissipated. In contrast to nearly all of the other 17 suddenly oil-rich countries, Indonesia successfully navigated boom and bust, both in following prudent macroeconomic policies and investing

[58] World Bank, *World development indicators, 2025.*

[59] Hill, 'Indonesia's industrial policy', p. 151.

[60] Hill, *Indonesian economy*, pp. 11–13, 27.

[61] Woo et al., *Macroeconomic policies*, p. 4 for the quote and p. 32.

productively. The latter provided much of the groundwork for the subsequent swift growth.

Indonesia used part of the oil windfall to invest in agriculture and take advantage of the opportunity the green revolution offered. New oil wealth funded rural development and an accelerated spread of high-yielding varieties of rice through dramatic increases in expenditure on their two complementary inputs: fertilizer (through subsidies) and irrigation infrastructure. At the same time, price support for rice was raised. By the end of the boom, Indonesia, compared to other newly oil-rich countries, had been particularly successful in raising food output per capita.[62] The government recycled oil revenues into state enterprise and a range of heavy industries which strengthened manufacturing capacity and fed directly into domestic demand for manufactures. During the Sukarno era, physical infrastructure was neglected but oil revenue financed spectacular increases in transport and communications.[63]

Export-led growth from 1986 to 1997 had the same ingredients as elsewhere in Southeast Asia: low wages, the organization of multinationals and a liberal trading environment. This last occurred in stages. The end of the oil boom encouraged policymakers in Indonesia, which has historically moved between nationalism and pragmatism, briefly towards the latter and to adopt an outward orientation. Reform was, however, only partial during an interlude from 1983 to 1985 of devaluation, recession and reappraisal. The decisive breakthrough to liberalization occurred in 1986 with a large real effective devaluation, sweeping reforms to trade policy, the financial system and fiscal and monetary policies.[64]

Wages in Java, where export-led growth centred, were no higher than elsewhere in Indonesia and, crucially, below both the minimum wage and market level. Internationally competitive wages and a large pool of unskilled and semi-skilled workers in a country where the government 'struggles to create enough decent jobs' exactly suited labour-intensive manufacturing.[65] Indonesia was helped, too, because by the later 1980s other Southeast Asian countries were shedding excessively labour-intensive jobs and because of preferential access to developed country markets under the Multi-Fibre Arrangement.

Between 1986 and 1997, garments, woven fabrics and footwear accounted for the bulk of exported manufactures. Although foreign investment in garment production was slight, foreign partners were essential in linking Indonesia to world markets. Smaller firms participated in the export boom but, as elsewhere

62 Gelb, *Oil windfalls*, pp. 89–91.

63 Hill, *Indonesian economy*, pp. 3, 8, 134–38, 157–58, 169, 182, 202–03 and 'Indonesia's industrial policy', pp. 160–62.

64 Kuncoro, 'Trends in manufacturing', pp. 182, 191; Hill, 'Indonesia's industrial policy', p. 154.

65 Hill and Negara, 'Setting the scene', p. 5 and see Hill, 'Myths', p. 264.

in Southeast Asia, a high proportion of exports went through international and domestic subcontracting networks involving larger firms.[66]

The manufacture of electrical goods and electronics in Indonesia, as in the rest of Southeast Asia, depended on multinationals but Indonesian participation in both industries was always small by Southeast Asian standards. Fairchild and National Semiconductor set up assembly plants in the early 1970s, but closed them in 1986 due to a slump in world demand for semiconductors. During the export boom, electronics production gained ground, but in 1993 still accounted for only a small share of labour-intensive manufactured exports.[67]

The economy did not recover to its pre-Asian financial crisis 1997 GDP per capita until 2004, and subsequent growth was markedly below earlier levels. Indonesia was traditionally ambivalent towards openness and international cooperation and tended towards a growing protectionism.[68] Various levels of bureaucracy operated a labyrinthine regulatory system of so many layers and such complexity and arbitrariness that it became 'notorious among international investors'.[69] Exports were disappointing both in terms of value added and job creation and, partly owing to this, attempts to accelerate growth and achieve a developed country income by 2045 were uncertain of success.[70] A more outwards orientation offered a possible route to raising growth rates, but still in the early 2020s 'very little has been gained by entering global value chains'.[71]

In the mid-2010s, exports comprised only some 10 per cent of manufactured output. About a third of exported manufactures were food products, of which crude palm oil and palm oil products – primary commodity staples and bulked or processed locally – dominated, followed, as a distant second, by *kretek* cigarettes. Electronics accounted for some 10 per cent of manufacturing value added but this showed little growth. Manufacturing, heavily dependent on domestic demand, dragged down GDP growth. Natural resource-based products, notably palm oil, coal and wood products, and services accounted for much of growth. During the 2010s, natural resources, as part of a secular boom, comprised as much as over three-fifths of merchandise exports.[72] Services, chiefly

66 Hill, *Indonesian economy*, pp. 169, 172.

67 Hill, 'Indonesia's industrial policy', pp. 152–54, 172.

68 Anas and Narjoko, 'International cooperation', pp. 309–12; Hill and Pane, 'Indonesia and the global economy', pp. 284–87.

69 Surianta and Patunru, 'Repositioning Indonesia', p. 126.

70 Hill, 'Challenge for Jokowi 2.0'.

71 Kuncoro, 'Trends', p. 205 and see Anas et al., 'Indonesian economy', pp. 264–68; Surianta and Patunru, 'Repositioning Indonesia', p. 124; A. Anantha Lakshmi and Diana Mariska, 'Why a commodities boom is not lifting Indonesia's economy', *Financial Times*, 21 August 2025.

72 Shrestha and Coxhead, 'Can Indonesia secure', pp. 8–9.

tourism and trade, afforded the main source of employment growth but were not internationally competitive.[73]

Indonesia has often been compared with Nigeria, another windfall petroleum economy in 1973. In several respects, the comparison is unfair: Indonesia had much slower population growth and could draw on many more natural resources than the African economy. Natural resource rents helped Indonesia to maintain a large, inefficient state-owned sector as well as to finance endemic corruption and postpone reform and yet achieve more or less continuous expansion and greatly better the welfare of its people. Even so, the contrast between Indonesia and Nigeria is, for example, apparent in the legacy of twice Nigerian President Muhammadu Buhari. His regimes were 'economically ruinous. He closed land borders to drive up agricultural production and manufacturing but ended by starving industries and shutting in entrepreneurs. Dollar trading became the hottest rentier gig in town as the value of the naira plummeted.'[74] Policy, governance, economic management matter. Indonesian comparative superiority in these is fundamental in explaining why in 1965 Nigeria's GDP per capita income was two-and-a-half times more than Indonesia's but in 2024 less than three-fifths Indonesian income.[75]

Myanmar: Uncertain Future

The uncertainties in regard to Myanmar and their political roots are indicated elsewhere in the book. It seemed to some during brief periods when Myanmar partially liberalized and began to look outwards that it would follow the Southeast Asian development model, perhaps with features similar to Indonesia's from 1986 to 1997. Myanmar embarked on the assembly of imported fabrics as garments for a time during the mid-1990s and again after 2012. Clothing manufacture based on cheap, predominantly female labour raised growth and created jobs, especially in the suburbs of Yangon where most of this manufacturing centred. However, informed observers point to the unreliability of Myanmar statistics. Consequently, these are reported but not discussed.

Conclusion

During large parts of the half-century or so beginning in the late 1960s, Southeast Asia grew rapidly and trade was once more the engine of growth. Economic development ceased to depend on primary commodity staples as

[73] Anas and Wikapuspita, 'Indonesia's services sector', pp. 209–12, 217.

[74] Ayisha Osori, 'As Buhari prepares to depart, Nigeria is in desperate need of serious reform', *Financial Times*, 8 May 2023.

[75] World Bank, *World development indicators, 2025.*

economies diversified through manufactures and services. Manufacturing made a sufficient impact on most Southeast Asian economies to be regarded as a leading sector. Growth in the region depended heavily on the emergence of new sets of staples and new entrepreneurs in the form of multinationals.

Manufacturing for export did not, however, universally end labour surpluses or eliminate dual economies. Despite large electronics sectors, wages and terms of employment in these and other modern sector activities were often not high or attractive enough to draw low-productivity labour from traditional pursuits. While the production of electronics parts and components, garments and footwear enabled the export of a substantial share of available labour in these forms, this venting was limited by world demand, the pool of available domestic labour willing to migrate at existing wages, low-wage competition from outside the region and insufficient skills or infrastructure. A number of countries exported surplus labour not embodied in manufactures but as migrants who went abroad for employment.

16

Correlates of Growth: Savings, Capital Accumulation and Social Progress

Trade and growth facilitated a shift beginning in the late 1960s towards high saving and capital accumulation. Both of these, in turn, promoted growth: a virtuous circle from growth to saving and, via capital accumulation, back to growth. Most saving was private not government saving, and as per capita incomes increased and poverty declined, it became possible for greater proportions of Southeast Asians to exercise the high saving preference characteristic of the region. Foreign capital inflows and private saving were complementary. In some countries, saving was augmented by mandatory government saving schemes. A spread of political and economic stability, the latter represented by relatively low inflation rates, over much of the region further encouraged high saving.

The chapter's first section looks at savings and capital accumulation and a second at structural change and value added. In the second section, the chapter compares value added in the three main sectors of Southeast Asia's economies and makes the point that agricultural productivity, despite improvements, remained far lower than in industry. Enquiry into this 'agricultural productivity gap' for a range of developing countries indicates that it persisted little changed through a variety of measures, suggesting a misallocation of workers across sectors.[1]

Rapid growth was accompanied by marked improvements in infant mortality, life expectancy and measures of education as well as reductions in poverty, the subjects of the third section. A fourth section evaluates educational provision in Southeast Asia, considers its appropriateness for development and identifies a tendency for governments to prioritize quantity at the expense of quality. The last section concludes and looks forward to the book's final two chapters on urbanization and an assessment of development in Southeast Asia.

Savings and Capital Accumulation

For Lewis, and many others dating back to Adam Smith, capital accumulation is central to economic development. Fundamental to this accumulation is the

[1] Gollin et al., 'Agricultural productivity gap'.

problem of how a little-developed economy converts from saving and investing 4 or 5 per cent of national income to saving 12 or 15 per cent. The answer given by Lewis is that a fraction of the population, perhaps 10 per cent, starts, for whatever reason, to save more from their incomes.[2]

In the 1960s, Malaysia and Thailand, as over 20 per cent savers, already exceeded Lewis's 15 per cent saving threshold but all other countries were below it. Beginning in the 1970s, however, all of Southeast Asia raised levels of saving and capital accumulation as a percentage of GDP far beyond anything that Lewis had imagined. Throughout the region, savings and capital accumulation routinely reached 25 per cent of national income, and in some countries over 40 per cent. Saving in Singapore was even higher. The bulk of saving was private, except in Singapore where public and government-enforced saving dominated (Chapter 14). Public saving accounted for only roughly a sixth of total savings in the region as a whole, although in Singapore, and to a lesser extent Malaysia, mandatory government schemes for private saving probably forced these levels above what they would otherwise have been.

Part of the explanation for high Southeast Asian saving was, as elsewhere in Asia, a strong preference of individuals to save. They were probably encouraged towards this behaviour by a lack of comprehensive welfare schemes in Southeast Asian countries and by the region's history of political uncertainty. The other part of the explanation – different from anything Lewis envisaged and applicable to countries that adopted the Southeast Asian development model – was that Southeast Asia turned to global multinational enterprise and oriented towards their foreign investment and exporting the goods they produced.

Multinationals, as well as enabling the region to draw on the knowledge and skills bound up with capital accumulation, boosted saving rates, and with this promoted capital accumulation, in three ways. One was that jobs in production organized by multinationals and the ancillary employment created by them both raised per capita incomes and widened the domestic saving base considerably in excess of Lewis's 10 per cent of the population from whom saving was likely to come. Second, export-led growth and saving have been shown to be positively related. A one percentage point increase in the degree of export orientation was associated with a 0.03 per cent increase in the long-run saving rate as well as adding to growth and so saving. Third, foreign investment and private domestic savings were complementary not competitive.[3]

As well as contrasting patterns of GDP per capita growth, different savings and capital formation histories obtained for the region's early and later industrializers (Figures 16.1 and 16.2). Among the early industrializers of Malaysia, Singapore and Thailand for most of 1960 to 2024, gross saving rates and gross

[2] Lewis, 'Economic development', pp. 155–57.

[3] Athukorala and Suanin, 'Saving transition', pp. 1220–23.

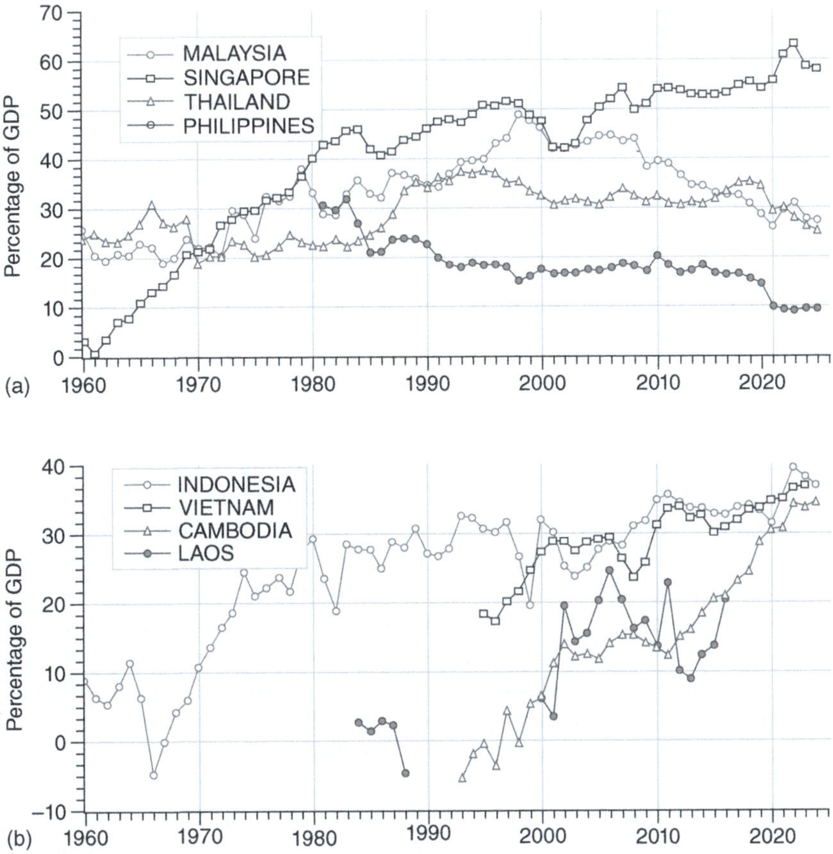

Figure 16.1 Southeast Asia gross saving rates of early and late industrializers, 1960–2024. (a) Malaysia, Singapore, Thailand and the Philippines gross saving rates, 1960–2024. (b) Indonesia, Vietnam, Cambodia and Laos gross saving rates, 1960–2024
Source: World Bank, *World development indicators, 2025.*

capital formation moved broadly similarly. In 1960 in Malaysia and Thailand, savings were already at, or above, Lewis's 12 per cent target, but in Singapore they were 3 per cent of GDP. Saving in Singapore in 1961 fell to 0.7 per cent, checked during the early 1960s by political instability and uncertainty leading up to union with, and in 1965 separation from, Malaysia as well as by high young age dependency (Figure 16.1). By the early 1970s in Malaysia, Singapore and Thailand, the saving rate grew rapidly, reaching more than 40 per cent by the 1997 Asian financial crisis. After it, savings turned downwards except in Singapore, which cemented its place as the world's 'stellar saver'. In most years from 2007 to 2024, Singapore savings remained above 50 per cent of GDP and in 2022 peaked at an astonishing 63 per cent (Figure 16.1).

After 1960 in the early industrializers of Malaysia, Singapore and Thailand, gross capital formation rose sharply, able to draw during most of 1970 to 2024 on high savings. By 1960, capital formation was already around 12 to 15 per cent of GDP and reached high points just before the Asian financial crisis. Subsequently, however, capital formation dropped more than saving rates. The highs were 47 per cent in Singapore in 1984, 44 per cent in Malaysia in 1995 and 43 per cent in Thailand in 1995. After 2000, capital formation in the three countries averaged 25 per cent.

The Philippines had a different trajectory than the other outward-looking countries of Malaysia, Singapore and Thailand. Between 1960 and 1969, the saving rate in the Philippines averaged 0.0 per cent.[4] Subsequently, the saving rate rose to an average of 32 per cent in 1981/83 but then declined, held back by the serious recession of the immediate post-Marcos years (Chapter 14). Capital formation in the Philippines climbed to as much as 28 per cent in 1983 before falling sharply due to the economic collapse beginning at the end of that year. From 2008 to 2024, capital formation averaged 23 per cent of GDP.

Singapore has important similarities to a state socialist economy in the government's control over a proportion of savings and promotion of a high rate of investment. Under state socialism, the determination of an optimal share of savings in national income is a policy choice and the possibility of wasteful overinvestment a danger. Although in Singapore reliance on foreign investment limited the state's scope to determine an optimal investment share, as early as the mid-1980s whether the government enforced 'oversaving' became a prominent issue.[5] Critics of the government maintained that such high saving was inefficient because of a misallocation of resources; a failure to maximize utility due to an unnecessary sacrifice of current consumption; and, as often in Soviet socialist eastern Europe, a serious risk of negative returns at savings levels above about 35 per cent.[6]

In Singapore by 2012 to 2024, saving rates of over 50 per cent but capital formation of about half that lent force to criticisms of oversaving. Such high saving was possibly explained by a legacy of Singapore governmental 'psychological uncertainty' dating from the political uncertainty of the 1960s.[7] The attitude was probably also founded in Singapore's circumstances as a tiny, predominantly ethnically Chinese populated, island alien to the rest of Southeast Asia, making the Republic vulnerable to the region's potential instability.

[4] Athukorala and Suanin, 'Saving transition', p. 1214.

[5] Lim, *Policy options*, pp. 37, 234–35; Koh, 'Saving, investment and entrepreneurship', pp. 85–86.

[6] Ellman, *Socialist planning*, pp. 141–42; Kalecki, 'Outline of a method', pp. 214–15, 221; Horvat, 'Optimum rate', pp. 572–76; Sen, 'On optimising', pp. 484–86; Eckstein, 'Capital theory', pp. 92–95.

[7] Pang and Lim, 'Labor, productivity and Singapore's development', pp. 2–3.

Data for the later industrializers are mostly patchy or non-existent until these economies abandoned socialism and began to turn outwards, Indonesia after 1965 and Vietnam, Cambodia and Laos in the late 1980s and 1990s. Under socialism, saving rates were low or even negative. Saving, along with growth, increased rapidly as the countries opened to the global economy. In Indonesia, savings rose from zero during the last year of Sukarno in 1965 to 29 per cent by 1980, and thereafter normally fluctuated near or above that level. During the 1990s, savings in Vietnam, Cambodia and Laos also traced a path of steep ascent analogous to the earlier one in Indonesia, but one not interrupted by the 1997 Asian financial crisis. In Vietnam after 2010, savings stayed above 30 per cent and in 2022 and 2023 rose to 37 per cent. Savings in Cambodia were over 30 per cent from 2020 onwards and in Laos reached 20 per cent in 2016.

After 1965 in Indonesia and during the 1990s in Vietnam, Cambodia and Laos, the higher saving rates that accompanied growth facilitated capital formation, which rose broadly in line with savings. In 2014, gross capital formation was 30 per cent or over in all four economies (Figures 16.1 and 16.2).

Four considerations help to explain for early and later industrializers the contrasting patterns of saving and capital formation in Southeast Asia. One is the impact of the Asian financial crisis. While the crisis appears for the early industrializers to mark a turning point, it did not for their later industrializing counterparts, suggesting a need to look further for contributing factors. Among these are exports, growth rates and changing dependency ratios. The importance of exports to growth in Southeast Asia's small, trade-dependent economies runs throughout this book, and after about 2000, as exports as a share of GDP declined, so too did growth rates. Annual growth in GDP per capita, which after 2010 averaged just 2 to 3 per cent, gave less scope, even at these countries' high-income levels, for saving than afforded by growth of 5 per cent to 6 per cent or more during the 1980s and 1990s. At the same time, except in the Philippines, increasing old age dependency, dating from around the Asian financial crisis, cut into saving rates through encouraging dissaving, apart from Singapore where saving depended heavily on government decisions. By contrast, after 2000 in the late industrializers exports and growth remained high and old age dependency low (Figure 16.3). The Philippines was an exception to these patterns, behaving as an early industrializer for saving and capital formation but turning into a later industrializer for age dependency.

Structural Change and Sector Value Added

In the little more than two decades between 1972/74 and 1995/97, manufacturing for export, and the expanding domestic markets it helped to promote, transformed the structure of GDP in most of Southeast Asia's economies from predominantly agricultural to industrial. In 1995/97, industry, defined as

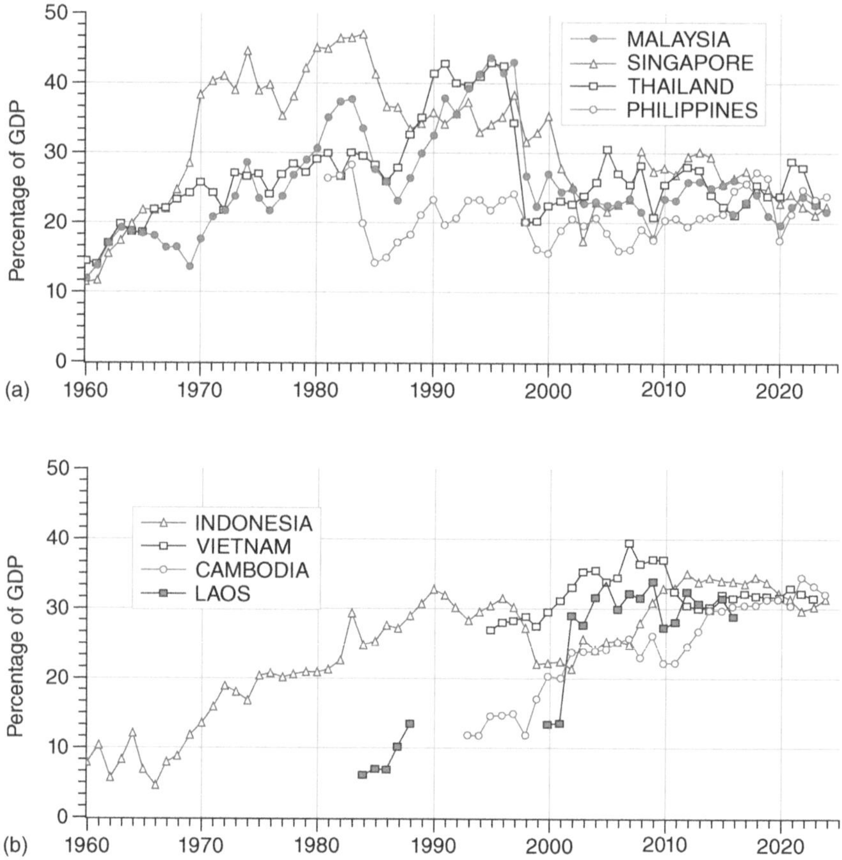

Figure 16.2 Southeast Asia gross capital formation of early and late industrializers, 1960–2024. (a) Malaysia, Singapore, Thailand and the Philippines gross capital formation, 1960–2024. (b) Indonesia, Vietnam, Cambodia and Laos gross capital formation, 1960–2024
Source: World Bank, *World development indicators, 2025.*

manufacturing, construction and utilities, contributed from about a third to more than two-fifths of GDP everywhere in Southeast Asia except Cambodia and Laos (and probably Myanmar). However, by 2006/08 the industrial sector in these two countries made up a quarter of GDP and, at least according to available data, a fifth in Myanmar (Table 16.1).

The structure of employment changed less than that of GDP. Most Southeast Asian countries retained the hallmarks of less developed economies, because Southeast Asia's export-led industrialization left large quantities of labour in agriculture and low-productivity services. The region still needed to complete development, either along the path of manufacturing for export it had followed

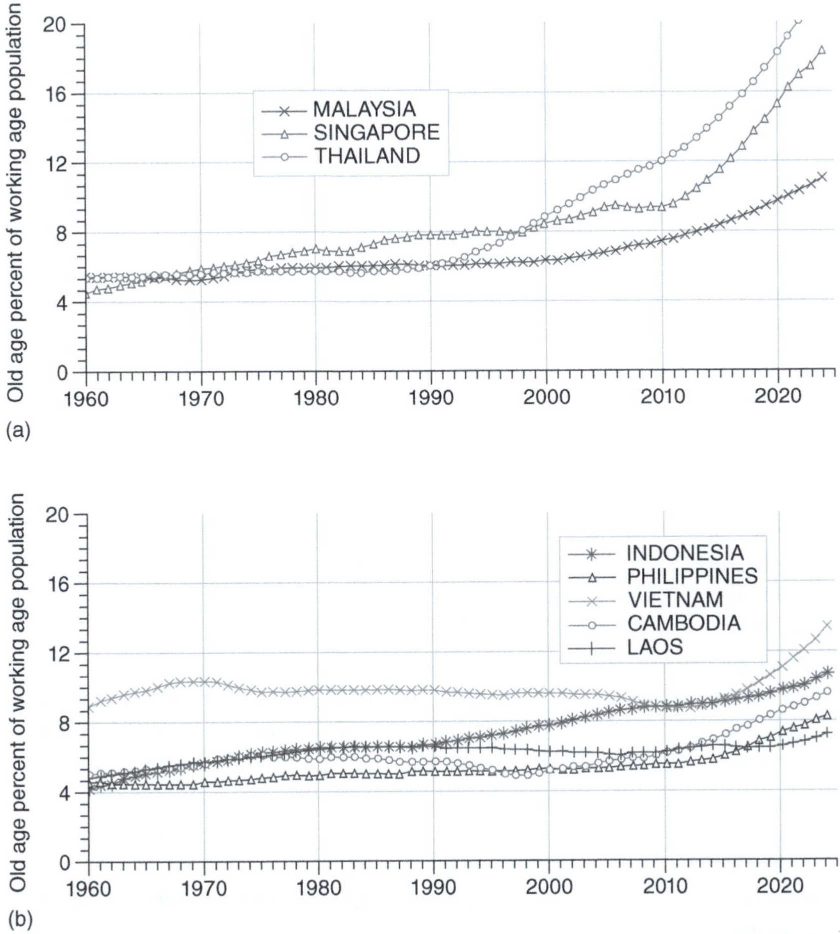

Figure 16.3 Southeast Asia old age dependency ratios of early and late industrializers, 1960–2024. (a) Southeast Asia early industrializers' old age dependency ratios, 1960–2024. (b) Southeast Asia late industrializers' old age dependency ratios, 1960–2024
Source: World Bank, *World development indicators, 2025.*

since the 1970s or, if this proved unviable, through some modifications to development strategy (Table 16.2).

Between 2000 and 2023, three main features of employment structure stand out. One was a shift from agriculture and mining towards manufacturing and services, varying in timing according to when industrialization occurred. By 2000, manufacturing employment in the early industrializers was already at or near its maximum of 15 to 25 per cent of employment but just 10 per cent in the Philippines. Between 2000 and 2023 in Singapore and Malaysia, the manufacturing share declined markedly, giving way to services and echoing drops in manufactured exports as proportions of GDP (Table 16.2).

Table 16.1 *Southeast Asia sectoral distribution of GDP, 1960–2022/23*

	1960	1972/74	1984/86	1995/97	2006/08	2016/18	2022/23
Malaysia							
Agriculture	43.7	30.9	20.3	11.9	9.5	8.7	6.4
Industry	24.7	36.4	39.2	43.2	43.7	36.4	36.3
Services	31.6	32.7	40.5	44.9	46.7	54.9	57.3
Singapore							
Agriculture	3.9	2.1	0.9	0.2	0.0	0.0	0.0
Industry	21.2	34.8	35.7	33.6	29.5	26.0	26.9
Services	74.9	63.1	63.3	66.2	70.4	74.0	73.1
Thailand							
Agriculture	36.4	26.9	16.3	9.1	9.6	8.3	8.5
Industry	18.5	26.7	32.3	37.2	39.5	35.3	32.6
Services	45.0	46.5	51.4	53.7	50.9	56.4	58.9
Philippines							
Agriculture	26.9	30.2	24.4	20.4	12.7	9.5	8.1
Industry	31.3	35.2	35.9	32.1	33.1	30.7	29.6
Services	41.8	34.6	39.7	47.5	54.2	59.8	62.3
Indonesia							
Agriculture			23.8	16.6	13.7	13.1	12.5
Industry			37.0	43.2	47.3	39.5	39.3
Services			41.1	40.2	39.0	43.6	48.2
Vietnam							
Agriculture			39.1	26.9	19.3	19.6	12.7
Industry			28.1	30.2	38.0	31.7	39.5
Services			32.8	42.9	42.7	48.7	47.8
Cambodia							
Agriculture				48.0	33.2	23.4	15.1
Industry				16.0	26.3	30.9	45.9
Services				36.0	40.5	39.7	39.0
Laos							
Agriculture				53.9	35.4	19.6	16.8
Industry				20.5	27.7	31.7	37.6
Services				25.6	36.9	48.7	45.6
Myanmar							
Agriculture					42.5	24.5	19.3
Industry					20.8	34.5	42.5
Services					36.7	41.0	38.2

Table 16.1 (*cont.*)

Notes: 1. Data are for value added by each of the three sectors as a percentage of their total value added but do not take account of taxes and subsidies. 2. For Malaysia, Singapore, Laos and Vietnam 2016/18 data are for 2014/16. 3. For Indonesia 1984/86 and 2016/18 data do not add to 100 in the source.
Source: World Bank, *World development indicators*, 2017, 2022 and 2025.

During just two decades after 2000, in the late industrializers of Vietnam and Cambodia the relative importance of employment in agriculture and manufacturing shifted dramatically as part of the move towards exporting manufactures. In Vietnam, agriculture as a share of employment dropped from two-thirds to a little over a quarter; manufacturing more than doubled from 10.3 per cent to 23.4 per cent. At the same time, Vietnam became a major exporter of rice, coffee, pepper and cashew nuts, demonstrating, like Malaysia with palm oil, how agricultural exports can be maintained alongside the export of manufactures to support an economy.

In all countries, services were a large gainer, increasing by between 10 and 17 percentage points in the space of just over two decades. Throughout Southeast Asia, service sectors were, however, in 2023 still a much smaller share of employment than in developed countries, apart from Singapore where, as a city, services would account for the bulk of employment. In Cambodia, the manufacturing share of employment rose from 7.0 per cent in 2000 to 17.0 per cent in 2023, but the recorded fall in the share of agricultural employment, from nearly three-quarters in 2011 to nearly a third by 2023, is not credible. In 2024, despite substantial movement to Phnom Penh for mainly very low-productivity soft service jobs, the urban population was still only a quarter of Cambodia's total population.

A second feature was that employment in agriculture, except in Singapore and Malaysia, remained high. Less than a quarter of Filipinos worked in agriculture but elsewhere in Southeast Asia, Malaysia and Singapore apart, the proportion was 27 per cent or more and far higher than in a typical developed country. In Malaysia in 2000, and even more by 2023, the agricultural sector had largely been rationalized and productivity increased, although a substantial contingent of poor, mainly Malay, small cultivators remained.

The third main aspect of employment structure was a large increase in its services component, since manufacturing expansion fell well short of absorbing the declining agricultural shares. Part of increased proportions in services is explained by service jobs created by manufacturing and the higher incomes accompanying its growth. However, substantial informal sectors and slum populations in urban Southeast Asia show that soft or labour-supply-pushed services in fact absorbed a considerable proportion of those moving from agriculture.

Table 16.2 *Southeast Asia employment by sector, 2000–23 (% and 000 persons)*

(a) Malaysia	2000	2006	2011	2016	2023
Employed population	9,269	10,275	12,352	14,164	15,392
Agriculture and mining	17.0	15.0	12.1	12.0	10.6
Manufacturing	23.5	20.3	18.2	16.9	16.8
Transport, const, utilities	13.4	14.8	15.2	14.4	13.3
Services	46.1	49.9	54.5	56.7	59.3
Total	100.0	100.0	100.0	100.0	100.0
(b) Singapore	**2000**	**2006**	**2011**	**2016**	**2023**
Employed population	2,095	2,506	3,150	3,570	3,840
(of which residents)	1,483	1,797	1,999	2,165	2,352
Agriculture and mining	0.2	0.2	0.2	0.1	0.1
Manufacturing	19.5	16.8	14.6	10.5	9.0
Transport, const, utilities	17.0	16.0	15.5	14.2	13.9
Services	63.3	67.0	69.6	75.2	77.0
Total	100.0	100.0	100.0	100.0	100.0
(c) Thailand	**2000**	**2006**	**2011**	**2016**	**2023**
Employed population	31,293	35,686	37,953	37,693	39,912
Agriculture and mining	44.3	39.9	33.0	31.3	30.3
Manufacturing	14.9	15.4	15.8	16.7	15.7
Transport, const, utilities	8.2	9.3	9.3	10.0	9.8
Services	32.6	35.4	41.9	42.0	44.2
Total	100.0	100.0	100.0	100.0	100.0
(d) Philippines	**2000**	**2006**	**2011**	**2016**	**2023**
Employed population	27,453	32,636	37,192	40,998	46,890
Agriculture and mining	37.4	36.2	33.6	27.5	23.6
Manufacturing	10.0	9.4	8.3	8.3	8.0
Transport, const, utilities	13.1	13.1	13.5	16.0	16.6
Services	39.5	41.3	44.7	48.1	51.8
Total	100.0	100.0	100.0	100.0	100.0
(e) Indonesia	**2000**	**2006**	**2011**	**2016**	**2023**
Employed population	89,838	95,457	107,416	118,412	139,852
Agriculture and mining	47.0	42.2	37.7	31.8	29.4
Manufacturing	13.3	12.2	13.8	12.9	13.8
Transport, const, utilities	9.3	10.9	10.9	10.9	11.6
Services	30.4	34.6	37.6	44.4	45.2
Total	100.0	100.0	100.0	100.0	100.0

Table 16.2 (*cont.*)

(f) Vietnam	2000	2006	2011	2016	2023
Employed population	37,600	43,980	50,500	53,300	51,300
Agriculture and mining	65.1	56.3	49.1	42.0	27.3
Manufacturing	10.3	13.9	13.9	16.9	23.4
Transport, const, utilities	5.9	8.3	9.5	10.9	13.6
Services	18.6	21.6	27.3	30.4	35.7
Total	100.0	100.0	100.0	100.0	100.0
(g) Cambodia	**2000**	**2006**	**2011**	**2016**	**2023**
Employed population	5,275	5,275	7,247	–	8,967
Agriculture and mining	73.8	73.8	72.0	–	36.0
Manufacturing	7.0	7.0	8.8	–	17.0
Transport, const, utilities	–	–	–	–	14.3
Services	–	–	–	–	32.8
Total	–	–	–	–	100.0

Notes: 1. For 2023, Malaysia and the Philippines data are for 2022 and for Cambodia for 2021. 2. Data for Myanmar and Laos are too sparse and too unreliable to be worth reporting.
Source: Asian Development Bank, *Key indicators*, 2024.

Proportions of employment in the main sectors of the Southeast Asian economies and their contributions to GDP and total value added in the economy were quite different. Differences point to the scope for rapid growth due to labour transfer between sectors and, related to this, the low productivity of workers in some sectors. Agriculture absorbed much more labour than its workers contributed to GDP; manufacturing added considerably more to GDP than its share of employment. In 2023 in most of Southeast Asia, agriculture's share of GDP was only roughly a third to half its employment share, although in Thailand this proportion was just over a quarter. The large disparity in Thailand may be partly because, as discussed in Chapter 13, many workers were enumerated in agriculture but engaged in off-farm work for several months of the year. In Malaysia, unlike elsewhere in Southeast Asia, there was a fairly close correspondence between how much agriculture added to GDP and the proportion of workers in the agricultural sector.

Data for 1990 to 2023 for value added per worker help in understanding Southeast Asian growth through the transfer of labour from low-productivity agriculture to manufacturing, industry and services (Table 16.3). Value

Table 16.3 *Southeast Asia value added per worker in agriculture, industry and services, 1991–2023 (2015 US$)*

(a) Agriculture

	1991	1996	2010	2019	2023
Malaysia	11,919	11,644	13,356	15,821	15,229
Singapore	10,217	9,039	6,060	24,298	35,954
Thailand	2,003	1,461	2,328	3,103	3,295
Philippines	1,779	1,856	2,470	3,520	3,272
Indonesia	1,526	1,705	2,172	3,529	3,668
Vietnam	610	712	1,229	2,025	2,427
Cambodia	–	643	1,003	1,360	1,500
Laos	–	–	1,273	1,429	1,250
Myanmar	–	–	1,095	1,313	1,282

(b) Industry

	1991	1996	2010	2019	2023
Malaysia	18,103	24,777	27,380	30,350	30,111
Singapore	38,173	55,652	109,254	171,744	198,631
Thailand	11,981	12,010	16,787	17,194	16,892
Philippines	9,909	10,173	12,287	14,468	14,008
Indonesia	9,412	11,625	13,205	13,661	14,691
Vietnam	4,320	6,100	5,419	7,059	7,823
Cambodia	–	3,652	3,392	5,563	5,865
Laos	–	–	12,114	22,200	26,503
Myanmar	–	–	3,777	7,966	6,696

(c) Services

	1991	1996	2010	2019	2023
Malaysia	7,734	11,596	15,771	19,976	21,109
Singapore	51,338	59,662	75,409	85,338	90,800
Thailand	13,118	13,275	10,994	14,666	13,926
Philippines	6,228	6,102	6,801	9,284	9,165
Indonesia	3,707	4,567	5,747	7,221	8,042
Vietnam	4,107	6,100	4,848	6,724	8,290
Cambodia	–	2,605	2,877	4,004	3,715
Laos	–	–	–	9,877	10,162
Myanmar	–	–	2,045	3,775	3,127

Note: For Thailand, 1991 data for industry and services are for 1993.
Source: World Bank, *World development indicators, 2025.*

added per worker in agriculture was typically between a fifth and a third of that in industry, although in Malaysia, due to an efficient plantation sector, it reached a half. In Laos, too, the ratio of agriculture to industry was around two-fifths, mainly due to low industrial productivity. The Cambodian ratio was around a tenth because of a combination of traditional peasant agriculture and capital-intensive, high-productivity infrastructure projects like hydroelectricity.

Between 1990 and 2023, although agricultural productivity rose continuously from its starting points, it remained low except in Malaysia, where in 2023 value added per worker was 2015 US$15,229. Elsewhere, except for Singapore's miniscule agricultural sector, in 2023 agricultural productivity was a fraction of Malaysia's, ranging from as little as 2015 US$1,250 in Laos to US$3,668 in Indonesia. From 1991 to 2023, a Malaysian rise of over a quarter in agricultural value added per worker reflects the efficiency of its large estate sector and the dissemination of technical knowledge by agricultural extension services, including to smallholders. In most of Southeast Asia, in both agriculture and industry value added per worker rose significantly, indicating a transition towards higher growth through gains in labour productivity in all sectors as well as through labour movement between sectors.

Value added in services was well above agriculture, reflecting low agricultural productivity in most of Southeast Asia, but distinctly less than in industry. An exception was Vietnam where in 2023 services value added exceeded industrial. Although soft, labour-supply-pushed services figured prominently in labour surplus Vietnam, the importance of other services in Vietnamese development and relatively unproductive industries such as garment and footwear manufacture combined to account for the higher service value added.

Social Trends and Poverty

Three considerations devalue GDP per capita as a good indicator of social welfare. One is that it ignores distributional considerations, and a second that many Southeast Asian countries have high levels of inequality, not just within populations but also between city and countryside as well as between ethnic groups. Third, these inequalities were often perpetuated by policies that favoured growth over equity. Nevertheless, in Southeast Asia, as is apparent from Figures 16.4 and 16.5, the rank order of both life expectancy and infant mortality were closely correlated with GDP per capita.

Two features of the figures are evident. One is continuous, generally unbroken, improvement in both life expectancy and infant mortality. The other is that for each measure, considerable differences exist between the initially outward-looking countries of Malaysia, Singapore, Thailand and the Philippines and the early post-World War II inward-looking ones of Indonesia, Vietnam, Cambodia, Laos and Myanmar.

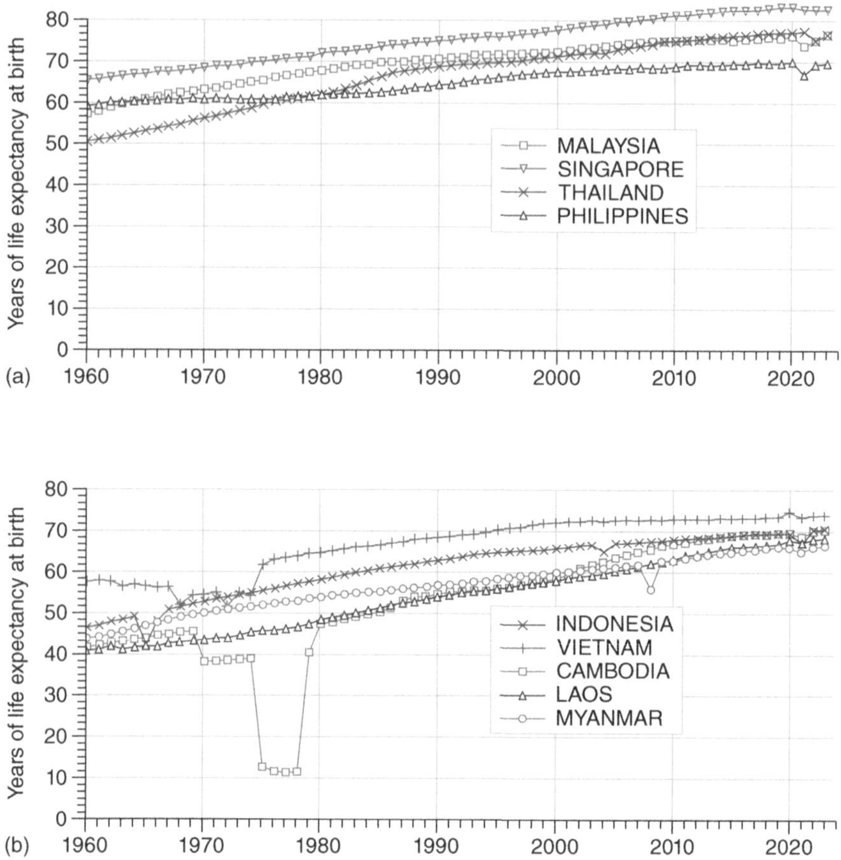

Figure 16.4 Southeast Asia life expectancy early and late industrializers, 1960–2024.
(a) Malaysia, Singapore, Thailand and the Philippines life expectancy, 1960–2024.
(b) Indonesia, Vietnam, Cambodia, Laos and Myanmar life expectancy, 1960–2024
Source: World Bank, *World development indicators, 2025.*

For life expectancy, a gap between the population unweighted averages for the four outward-looking countries and their five inward-looking counterparts was 12 years in 1960 but by 2023 the difference had narrowed to six years, reflecting the new phase of growth in most of Southeast Asia and the rapidity with which medical and health technologies were diffused. Within the outward-looking group of countries, life expectancy in 1960 in Thailand lagged well behind others in the group. However, in both Thailand and Malaysia in the later 1970s and 1980s notably rapid improvements in longevity occurred as these two countries became more export-oriented and GDP per capita rose. The Philippines made its swiftest gains during the 1990s, when it also moved towards an export economy. Life expectancy among the inward-looking countries was dragged down

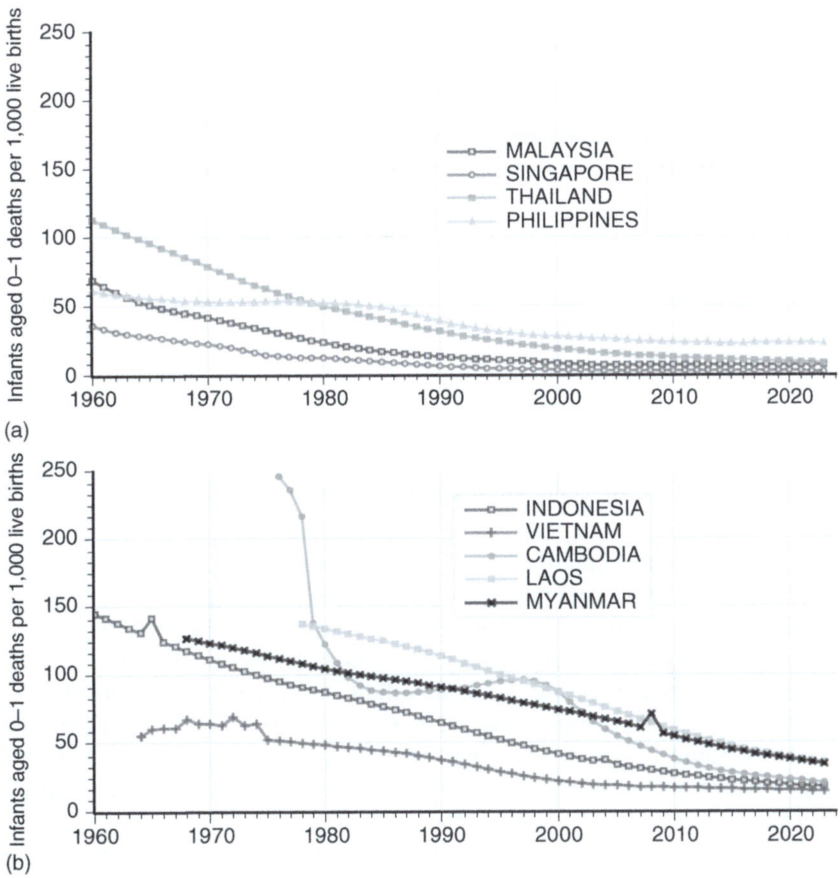

Figure 16.5 Southeast Asia infant mortality early and late industrializers, 1960–2023. (a) Malaysia, Singapore, Thailand and the Philippines infant mortality, 1960–2023. (b) Indonesia, Vietnam, Cambodia, Laos and Myanmar infant mortality, 1960–2023
Source: World Bank, *World development indicators, 2025.*

during the 1970s in Vietnam by war and in Cambodia by the murderous Pol Pot regime. In 1977, Cambodian longevity fell to just 11 years.

Taking 1960 to 2023 as a whole, within both the inward and outward groups improvements in life expectancy were more pronounced among countries that in 1960 trailed others in their respective groups. Between 1960 and 2023, the difference between the worst and best of the inward-looking group narrowed from 17 to 8 years. A similar convergence did not occur among the outward-looking countries. That was partly because Singapore is entirely a city, and people usually live longer in urban than in rural areas, which in the other countries were major components of their populations (Figure 16.4).

Table 16.4 *Southeast Asia poverty headcount for household income of US$8.30 (2021 PPP) per day, 1987–2023 (% of population)*

	1987	1997	2007	2015	2023
Malaysia	43	30	25	6	3
Thailand	78	59	37	17	10
Philippines	87	78	73	66	59
Indonesia	99	97	93	82	70
Laos	–	96	90	75	–
Vietnam	–	90	79	30	22
Myanmar	–	–	–	83	–

Note: Figures may be two years either side of the year shown. For Laos, the 2015 figure is for 2018.
Source: World Bank, *World development indicators, 2025.*

Infant mortality is an important constituent of life expectancy and especially sensitive to sanitation and the availability of clean drinking water. In 1980, both the inward- and outward-looking groups displayed even larger differences in infant mortality than life expectancy. The 1980 difference between the best and worst of the inward countries was 85 infant deaths per 1,000 live births and for the outward 40 deaths. Over the four decades 1980 to 2023, both groups recorded rapid progress. The outward-looking countries converged around a population unweighted average of 10 deaths per 1,000 live births and the inward-looking ones 24 deaths (Figure 16.5).

Poverty is difficult to compare between countries because each uses national measures, and these differ between countries as well as over time for individual countries. Table 16.4 allows some comparison for the region as a whole and points to three main conclusions. One is that between 1987 and 2023 average household incomes rose rapidly. In 1987, the overwhelming majority of Southeast Asians had household incomes of under US$8.30 (2021 Purchasing Power Parity or PPP) per day, but by 2023 far fewer did. In 2023, three-quarters of Vietnamese, 90 per cent of Thai and almost all Malaysians were above US$8.30, approximately a threshold below which the World Bank regards as being economically insecure.[8]

Second, in 2023 earnings dispersion remained substantial, indicating considerable scope for a regional division of labour based on labour cost. In the Philippines, Laos, Indonesia and Myanmar in 2015 and (judging from incomplete data) still in 2023, most households had per capita incomes of less than

[8] Cf. World Bank, *Riding the wave*, pp. 11, 51.

Table 16.5 *Southeast Asia child labour as measure of exploitative employment, 2015 (% employed children aged 15 and under)*

	%	World rank
Thailand	8.3	64
Philippines	11.1	74
Indonesia	6.9	60
Vietnam	6.9	60
Cambodia	18.3	87
Laos	10.1	72

Note: The lower the world rank the lower the percentage of employed children. Japan had 1.0 per cent of children employed and a rank of 3. In Nepal 33.9 per cent of children were employed, giving a rank of 117.
Source: World Economic Forum, *Human capital report, 2015*, pp. 95, 155, 181, 241, 280, 303.

2021 PPP $8.30. Third, in a number of countries the high shares of earnings of less than $8.30 suggest a lack of semi-skilled manufacturing jobs and that labour surpluses were present. These circumstances help to account for the large migrant outflows from such areas to higher earnings ones.

Table 16.5 is revealing of both poverty and income distribution, since being poor is a principal cause of child labour. The high incidence in Cambodia and Laos of child labour is, if striking, perhaps unsurprising because the two countries were the most affected by the Second Indochina War and had among Southeast Asia's lowest per capita incomes as well as large agricultural sectors to which children are often expected to contribute their labour. More unexpected – but telling of quite skewed income distributions and a concentration of wealth in the capital cities – was the high incidence of child labour in the comparatively wealthy Philippines and Thailand, even allowing for the latter's abnormally high share of employment in agriculture.

Educational Expansion and Development

Education Measures

It is frequently argued that colonial governments underinvested in education and did not prioritize the right kind of education, usually meaning technical education. The first aspect of educational provision, but not often the second, changed radically once countries gained independence: all governments greatly expanded the availability of education. Reasons for the expansion included the view that a supply of educated persons would promote development through investment in human capital; pressure to satisfy rising popular expectations of providing universal education; and as a response to the pressure of parents for their children to have a middle-class job.

Tables 16.6, 16.7 and 16.8 indicate the results of this educational expansion for adult literacy and primary as well as lower secondary education. By 1980, 70 per cent or more of populations were literate except in Indonesia, and probably in Cambodia and Laos. In 2022, literacy was above 90 per cent except in Cambodia, Laos and Myanmar where it was in the 80s (Table 16.6).

Data for populations aged 25 and over with a primary education show that in 1980 this was not the norm except in Singapore, and even there just 55 per cent of people were educated to primary standard (Table 16.7). The table points to two things. One is legacies of patchy colonial education; pre-World War II immigrant populations which arrived without schooling and too late in life for any but the possibility of adult education; and World War II when under the Japanese schools effectively closed. The other is that widespread education was not necessary to get underway the kind of labour-intensive growth like Southeast Asia's. However, Southeast Asian countries used some of the gains from trade to invest in education. By 2023, most Southeast Asians aged

Table 16.6 *Southeast Asia adult literacy, 1980–2022 (% of population aged 15 and over)*

	1980	1990	1997	2007	2013	2022
Malaysia	70	83	89	93	–	95
Singapore	83	89	93	–	97	98
Thailand	88	–	93	96	–	91
Philippines	83	94	93	95	96	98
Indonesia	67	82	–	92	95	96
Vietnam	84	88	90	94	–	96
Cambodia	–	–	67	77	78	85
Laos	–	–	–	–	58	88
Myanmar	79	–	90	–	–	89

Notes: 1. Figures may deviate from the date shown by two years or, in a few instances, by three years. 2. For Cambodia, the 2021 figure is 72 per cent. For Laos, the 2013 figure is for 2011. The 2015 percentage for Laos is 85 per cent.
Source: World Bank, *World development indicators, 2025.*

Table 16.7 *Southeast Asia population aged 25 and over with at least primary education, 1980–2023 (%)*

	1980	2010	2016	2023
Malaysia	42	91	94	95
Singapore	55	84	86	79
Thailand	12	61	66	75
Philippines	57	82	84	86
Indonesia	27	73	80	84
Vietnam	71	79	85	87
Cambodia	–	49	56	43
Laos	–	69	57	74
Myanmar	–	–	55	87

Notes: Figures are as reported but suggest, in some instances, that country criteria may have changed between years. Dates for data may vary by as much as three years from the year shown in the table.
Source: World Bank, *World development indicators, 2025.*

Table 16.8 *Southeast Asia population aged 25 and over with at least lower secondary education, 1980–2023 (%)*

	1980	1990	2010	2023
Malaysia	21	–	68	81
Singapore	38	51	76	85
Thailand	10	–	39	54
Philippines	34	46	67	62
Indonesia	10	19	45	57
Vietnam	–	13	54	66
Cambodia	–	–	30	22
Laos	–	–	34	40
Myanmar	17	–	–	43

Notes: Figures are as reported but suggest, in some instances, that country criteria may have changed between years. Dates for data may vary by as much as three years from the year shown in the table. For Myanmar for 2023 data are for 2019. The 2020 figure for Myanmar is 78.
Source: World Bank, *World development indicators, 2025.*

25 and over had at least a lower secondary (and so basic) education except in Cambodia, Laos and Myanmar (Table 16.8).

The expansion of secondary education puts pressure on university systems to expand, both as an outlet for youth unable to find jobs and to accommodate the desire of many more people for a middle-class job for which a university degree is necessary. After World War II, university education changed from a few, selective institutions, typically modelled on their counterparts in the ruling colonial power, towards favouring a proliferation of universities and mass attendance. Throughout the region, university administrators had barely repaired the damage of World War II 'when they found themselves swamped with a growing tide of students, swollen three- or four-fold within a decade, with thousands more knocking at their doors'.[9] In 1961, Thailand had 15,000 students enrolled in a total of five universities; but by 1972, partly reflecting a 'modernizing' behest of American advisers and pressure from Thai technocrats, there were 100,000 students enrolled in 17 universities.[10] Supply-driven university expansion may, however, result in a top-heavy educational system in which resources are disproportionately allocated to tertiary education. In the 1980s, education was the largest single item in the Malaysian government budget, and half of this expenditure was on tertiary education, which involved only 4 per cent of the relevant age group.[11]

If an economy is not growing quickly enough to create a demand sufficient to absorb the products of supply-driven university expansion, inappropriately employed graduates as well as a surplus of unemployed or underemployed graduates and technicians result. The Philippines and Singapore were contrasting examples. In 2022 in the Philippines, the 18 per cent of the population aged 25 and over with university or equivalent qualifications compared with 36 per cent in Singapore and 38 per cent in the United States (Table 16.9). University expansion in the Philippines, however attractive as a consumption good as well as a public good, considerably exceeded the economy's absorptive capacity, forcing many of those with university degrees or technical training to migrate abroad to find work, often as domestic servants. In the Philippines, the figure of about 121,000 individuals with a doctorate was also likely in excess of domestic employment opportunities. By contrast, rapid growth in Singapore's economy enabled it to absorb, and gain from, its high proportion of university graduates. Yet by the mid-2020s even Singapore displayed clear signs of a labour market oversupplied with graduates both in the inability, after six months, of some 12 per cent of new degree holders to find employment and the disappointment of others with the work they found.[12]

9 Myint, 'Universities of Southeast Asia', p. 118.

10 Anderson, 'Withdrawal symptoms', p. 1.

11 Jomo, 'Whither Malaysia's new economic policy?', p. 475.

12 'Graduates should stay "calm", with early data showing better employment rates: Tan See Leng', *Business Times* (Singapore), 10 July 2025.

Table 16.9 *Southeast Asia population aged 25 and over with at least university or equivalent qualification, 2022 (%)*

Country	%
Malaysia	15
Singapore	36
Thailand	17
Philippines	18
Indonesia	9
Vietnam	12
Laos	5
Myanmar	9
United States	38

Source: World Bank, *World development indicators, 2025.*

Education and Development

Beneficial and necessary as educational expansion can be, it has not served Southeast Asian economic development well. Government response to the pressures for more education was typically an overemphasis on widening education to ensure its greater accessibility but with insufficient attention both to educational deepening through the quality of instruction and the demand for skilled personnel. Skills are particularly needed if export industries are to shift to higher value-added activities as supplies of cheap labour become exhausted. Often, educational quality in Southeast Asia was compromised by a failure of students to reach a standard of competence in the international language of English. In some countries, notably Malaysia, standards were lowered by an emphasis in schooling on religious instruction at the expense of literacy and numeracy; and by ethnic quotas for students as well as for staff appointments.

Educational widening, low-grade education and industrial skill shortages in export industries were features of both the Thai and Malaysian economies. Initially, much of widening in Thailand was through two universities set up in the 1970s with unlimited entry. The universities were established in response to the popular clamour for education to obtain a 'good' job, symptomatic of 'diploma disease'.[13] In 2007, Thailand had 74 universities but by 2020 this had grown to 155 universities, consisting of 26 autonomous universities, 10 public

[13] Dore, 'Diploma disease revisited', pp. 55–61.

universities, 72 private universities and 47 Rajabhat (public universities originally founded as teacher training colleges) and Rajamangala (technology institutions elevated to university status) universities.[14]

In Malaysia from the late 1980s, there was a rapid expansion in both public and private higher education institutions. In 2014, public sector higher education in Malaysia had expanded to include 20 universities classified as research institutions, 33 polytechnics, 91 community colleges and 14 higher institution centres of excellence.[15] By the 2020s, Malaysia had some 160 public universities, polytechnics and community colleges.

The Malaysian government also liberalized higher education to allow private providers. By 2020, Malaysia had about 435 private colleges and universities. These included international branch campuses of foreign universities, such as Nottingham University (UK) and Monash University (Australia). In 1996, the Private Higher Educational Institutions Act allowed the use of English as the medium of instruction in twinning programmes and branch campuses of foreign universities. In a country hungry for education, enrolment in private higher education institutes exceeded that in public institutions. Malay students predominated at public institutions, which were mostly Malay-medium, while non-Malay students were in the majority at private institutions, many of which were English-medium.[16]

In neither Thailand nor Malaysia did impressive educational enlargement produce a workforce well suited to development, partly because of the emphasis on quantity, partly due to the 'wrong kind' of education and partly owing to relatively few university–industry links.[17] Thai education, as in Malaysia and Myanmar with similar legacies of a British system, remained largely academic not vocational, and chiefly in the social sciences and humanities. From at least the 1990s, Thai universities and vocational schools proved unable to supply firms with enough capable engineers and workers. Development in Thailand was held back by resulting persistent skill shortages and labour market mismatches, especially in manufacturing.[18]

In Malaysia, an official enquiry concluded that critical to an explanation of sluggish growth was an inability to participate in the knowledge economy and a 'lack of appropriately skilled human capital'.[19] The enquiry found that in 2007, 80 per cent of the Malaysian workforce had received education up to only the secondary level (the *Sijil Pelajaran Malaysia*, equivalent to the English O level (General

14 Intarakumnerd and Jutarosaga, 'Evolution', p. 267.

15 Selvaratnam, 'Malaysia's higher education', p. 210.

16 Shah, *Striving*, pp. 131–34; Hawati, 'Malaysian higher education', p. 13.

17 Intarakumnerd and Jutarosaga, 'Evolution', pp. 266–73, 279; Rattanakhamfu, 'Comment on "Evolution"', pp. 283–84.

18 Khoman, 'Education policy', pp. 326, 341; Doner, *Politics*, pp. 48–49; Brimble and Doner, 'University–industry linkages', pp. 1022, 1027; Dixon, *Thai economy*, pp. 243, 268; Intarakumnerd et al., 'Global production networks', p. 22.

19 Malaysia, National Economic Advisory Council, *New economic model*, p. 44.

Certificate of Education)), while the share of skilled workers employed across Malaysian industries had declined.[20] Subsequently, both the Eleventh (2016–20) and Twelfth (2021–25) Malaysia Plans stressed the need to build human capital and improve its relevance for the labour market. Although the percentage of skilled manufacturing workers appears to have increased, the gains were modest.

Judged by international standards, educational progress in Malaysia has not been encouraging. The Programme for International Student Assessment (PISA) 2018 Malaysian test results were well below levels associated with a country with a per capita income as high as Malaysia's. In 2022, PISA scores were even below those of 2018. It afforded little comfort that relative to their per capita incomes, schooling in Thailand and Indonesia ranked worse than Malaysia's.[21] Malaysian universities, as reported in the *Times Higher Education* world university rankings, have historically come far down the list.[22] In 2025, the best university in Malaysia fell into the 201 to 250 ranking in the *Times Higher Education* list.

Education in Malaysia was compromised by language policy. After the implementation of the New Economic Policy in the 1970s, Malays and other *Bumiputera* gained preferential university entry, and beginning in 1983 Malay was the language of instruction for the entire public education system. While Malays, especially in rural areas, benefited from the new language policy, and it could be defended on grounds of national unity, Malay as the principal language of instruction told against economic development in two fundamental respects. One was largely to cut off Malaysian public education from global technological discourse. Prominent among Malay students was:

> the inability or unwillingness of many to deal with English. Opportunities were lost to function in English which is currently the global language of research, publication, scientific discourse and electronic communication and a tool for increasing mobility. Students regurgitated lecture notes, reluctant to refer to English-language texts, journals and sources of reference ... Unless political measures support the widespread use of English, the engagement of young Malaysians in global knowledge creation will continue to be limited.[23]

Competition in university staffing was essentially limited to Malays. They held almost all university senior management, administrative and academic positions.[24]

[20] Malaysia, National Economic Advisory Council, *New economic model*, pp. 5–6.

[21] World Bank, *PISA 2018*, pp. 30, 38; Tham and Chong, 'Transforming Malaysia's higher education', pp. 243–44; Lee, 'Comment on "Transforming Malaysia's higher education"', p. 262.

[22] Selvaratnam, 'Malaysia's higher education', p. 199.

[23] Mukherjee and Wong, 'National University of Singapore'. p. 135; see also Selvaratnam, 'Malaysia's higher education', p. 206.

[24] Selvaratnam, 'Malaysia's higher education', p. 203.

A second main effect of Malaysian language policy was a large outflow of human capital among Chinese and Indians. The 2010 National Economic Advisory Council concluded that 'We are not developing talent and what we have is leaving. The human capital situation in Malaysia is reaching a critical stage [and] outward migration of skilled Malaysians is rising rapidly.'[25] Malaysian Chinese students went, if possible, to universities in other countries, and because many never returned there was a brain drain.[26]

Analysis of education in Indonesia and the Philippines tells an all too familiar Southeast Asian story. By international measures, primary and secondary schooling ranked poorly and this extended to the tertiary level. In the mid-2010s, none of Indonesia's universities appeared in the *Times Higher Education* top 800.[27] For Indonesia, educational weakness was summed up as: 'the learning process still relies heavily on recitation and replication of textbook content, while neglecting critical and creative thinking, communication and language skills and logic. Mathematics, one of the fundamentals of logical thinking, is still taught as a memorized subject.' The quality of teachers was such that 'conceptual mistakes made at the primary level are often repeated at higher levels from one generation of students to another'.[28] Although from the end of the 2000s the government spent at least 20 per cent of the budget on education, increased spending was not followed by improved education and so a boost to human capital.[29]

Educational quality in the Philippines was almost universally poor. Public schools, attended by the great bulk of children, suffered from acute overcrowding, 'disastrously falling standards' and low attainment in sciences and math.[30] Low education standards are partly attributable to the stunting from which two to three of every 10 children in the Philippines suffer and which impairs cognition and educational performance.[31] Among randomly tested 15-year-olds in 2018, PISA results for the Philippines were the lowest out of the 79 countries. They were the lowest in reading literacy and second from bottom in science and math. The possibility of learning, according to a 2017 study, was severely impaired by half of primary and secondary school teachers being unable to answer half of the questions on the content of their subjects.[32] Employers

25 Malaysia, National Economic Advisory Council, *New economic model*, p. 6 and see p. 54.

26 'Malaysia takes Nvidia AI chip smuggling claims to China seriously', *Malay Mail*, 7 February 2024.

27 Anas and Wikapuspita, 'Indonesia's services sector', pp. 233–34.

28 Kuncoro, 'Trends', p. 206.

29 Resosudarmo and Abdurohman, 'Is being stuck', pp. 157–58; Negara and Ramayandi, 'Laying the foundations', pp. 15–17; Selvaratnam, 'Malaysia's higher education', p. 204.

30 Rocamora, 'From regime crisis', p. 37; and see Villamil, 'Education', p. 165; Wallace, 'Investment climate', pp. 196–97.

31 Ulep, 'Future of children', p. 1.

32 World Bank, *Middle class in the Philippines*, pp. 72–75 and *PISA 2018*, pp. 30, 38.

'have difficulty in finding workers with the fundamental skills needed to keep pace with technological changes and modern labor market needs'.[33]

In the Philippines, despite bilingual education aims of competence in both Filipino and English, no more than a fraction of students had mastered English. As in Malaysia, this cut off many students from international discourse, even though the IT industry, especially important to the growing Philippines service sector, demanded English-language capability. Both fluency in English and IT skills were vital, since services were a key developmental constituent, and an important part of this sector was the role of the Philippines as 'the world's call centre capital'.[34]

Part of the reason for the poor quality of schooling in the Philippines was a top-heavy education system in which expenditure was disproportionately diverted to fund universities. Government spending was, however, 'not buying quality tertiary education'. The expenditure supported educational widening, not deepening. The Philippines had 110 state universities/colleges and 77 local ones as well as some 1,600 private higher education institutions. However, only three Philippines universities ranked in the world's top 500 and all three were far down the rankings.[35]

Few Southeast Asian universities were internationally recognized, as were the University of Rangoon before World War II and the University of Malaya in the 1950s and early 1960s. Standards in most of the region's universities were generally regarded as being low and as having markedly declined. Singapore was the exception. In 2024, the National University of Singapore came third and Nanyang Technological University fourth in the *Times Higher Education* ranking of universities in Asia. No other Southeast Asian university ranked in the top 50.[36]

The National University of Singapore stood apart from low Southeast Asian university standards partly due to its strong emphasis on being 'international'. Education in Singapore emphasized technical training and as a result had an abundance of technically qualified engineers and scientists. These personnel enabled Singapore to become an Asian centre for medical and other services as well as training Singaporean engineers who worked all over Asia. And yet the Singapore manufacturing sector remained short of being the world leader that some industries in South Korea and Taiwan became. This suggests that education is not the whole key to promoting the development of manufacturing, and that other important factors such as market size, access to technology, marketing networks, brand names and entrepreneurship loom large.

33 World Bank, *Middle class in the Philippines*, p. xiv.
34 The description comes from the subtitle of Sallaz, *Lives on the line*.
35 Villamil, 'Education', p. 156 and see pp. 167–69.
36 *Times Higher Education*, 'Asia university rankings 2024'.

Conclusion

Southeast Asia's post-World War II development emphasizes the importance to growth of industrialization, saving, capital accumulation, labour mobilization and, at least for Singapore, state activism. These, A. K. Sen pointed out, are the themes of 'traditional development economics'.[37] As part of the same growth process, Southeast Asia made great strides in achieving some of the other aspects of development, conceptualized by Sen as expanding the economic freedoms of longevity, literacy and access to education.[38]

After 1950, school attendance, literacy, numeracy, infant mortality and life expectancy all improved markedly. Economic insecurity, defined as a per capita household income of under 2021 PPP US$8.30 a day, was not eradicated but became far less prevalent. Most Southeast Asian countries had enviable records of post-1970 growth and social progress. Nevertheless, all except Malaysia retained quite sizeable agricultural sectors in which for decades value added per worker increased relatively slowly and remained low. A number of countries exported large amounts of labour. Most had dual economies and substantial slum populations. These facts suggest that the Southeast Asian development model was incomplete. Slowing post-2010 growth in the early industrializers tended, by the mid-2020s, to confirm this conclusion. All of these issues are taken up in the next chapter on urbanization and in the concluding one, which assesses the course of Southeast Asian development.

37 Sen, 'Development: which way now?', pp. 745–53.

38 Sen, *Development as freedom*, pp. 3, 40–41, 91, 144.

17

Urbanization since 1950: Industrialization and Agglomeration

After World War II, Southeast Asia, still overwhelmingly rural in 1950, urbanized on an unprecedented scale as part of the region's radical transformation effected by globalization and industrialization. It required from the 1870s until World War II for the population of even some of the six largest Southeast Asian cities – Rangoon (Yangon), Bangkok, Singapore (for all of Malaya), Jakarta, Manila and Saigon-Cholon (Ho Chi Minh City) – to reach around 1 million. By 1975, the number of million cities had increased to nine. All but three had populations of 2 million or more. In 2018, Southeast Asia had 30 cities of a million or more. These included the six main cities of 1950 plus Kuala Lumpur. All seven were mega-cities of 5 million to over 10 million.

Among developing countries, Southeast Asia is exceptional in its post-World War II rapid economic growth and industrialization. The chapter's main purpose is to link this development and the expansion of the region's largest cities. I argue from a perspective of evolutionary geography that Southeast Asia's main cities – established on the basis of 'first nature' locational advantage as optimal sites for port 'gateways' to link Southeast Asia to world markets – remained dominant after World War II through self-reinforcing centripetal forces.[1]

Three main components have contributed to a localization and agglomeration process. One was that domestic and global investors identified the region's main cities – one, or at most two, in each country – as advantageous locations for investment in services, import-substitution industry and export-oriented industrialization. During Southeast Asia's phase of import substitution, centripetal forces pulled populations and production into urban agglomerations, because of their transport and communication facilities, large consumer markets, abundant labour supply and external economies. These same forces operated again when the region's countries turned outwards to export manufactures. In Southeast Asia, contrary to the literature, globalization and trade

[1] See, for example, Krugman, 'First nature, second nature', pp. 129–44 and 'History and industry location', pp. 80–83; Fujita and Mori, 'Role of ports', pp. 93–120.

liberalization often strengthened, not weakened, the centripetal forces that concentrated industry in or quite near the main urban centres.[2]

Second, governments tended to invest disproportionally in the dominant urban centre as the seat of political power and a main showcase of development. Access to government and urban amenities and opportunities drew industry and people including lobbyists to the largest cities. Third, rural–urban migration, if frequently only into underemployment and the informal sector, swelled Southeast Asia's principal cities. Migration created the diseconomies of congestion and over-urbanization. However, this and other migration also added to market size and labour supply.

An initial section of the chapter deals with Southeast Asia's near continuous post-World War II regional urbanization. The second section analyses patterns of the growth of the region's main cities and explains the use of data. A third section examines the effect of globalization and industrialization in concentrating industry in the region's principal cities. Partly owing to this concentration, as shown in the fourth section, the cities that were primate before World War II retained this status. The fifth section considers the socialist countries of Vietnam and Cambodia, and argues that despite differences in political systems, urbanization followed much the same patterns as in capitalist Southeast Asia. A brief exception was the Cambodia of Pol Pot and the Khmer Rouge, who determined to reverse urbanization to build a true Maoist socialism. The still high proportions of most Southeast Asian urban populations who in the mid-2020s lived in slum and squatter areas are the subject of the sixth section, which is followed by a conclusion.

Regional Urbanization

In 1960, just 40 million Southeast Asians – less than 19 per cent of the region's 213 million inhabitants – resided in cities. Somewhat over a quarter of Malaysians and 30 per cent of Filipinos were urban dwellers. In other countries, only between a fifth to as little as 8 per cent of populations could be classed as urban (Table 17.1).

The urban share of most Southeast Asian populations rose continuously from 1960 to 2024, the main exceptions being Cambodia, where in the later 1970s the urban population dropped sharply due to the Khmer Rouge's strategy of emptying the cities, and the Philippines, where the level remained broadly stable after 1990 (Table 17.1). From 1960 to 1990, urbanization in the Philippines, notable for its urban bias, was high relative to a GDP per capita in 1990 of 2015 US$1,730 (Table 17.1). However, thereafter, despite further substantial increases in income, the proportion of the population that was urban

2 Krugman and Elizondo, 'Trade policy', pp. 137–50; Krugman, 'Urban concentration', pp. 7–8.

Table 17.1 *Southeast Asia urban population and as a percentage of total population, 1960–2024*

	Myanmar	Thailand	Malaysia	Singapore	Indonesia	Philippines	Vietnam	Cambodia	Laos
(a) Urban population millions									
1960	4.2	5.4	2.2	1.6	12.8	8.0	4.8	0.6	0.2
1975	7.3	10.1	4.6	2.3	25.2	14.7	9.2	0.3	0.3
1990	10.4	16.6	9.0	3.0	55.5	29.1	13.8	1.4	0.7
2000	12.6	19.8	14.4	4.0	88.8	36.0	19.5	2.3	1.2
2010	14.2	30.1	20.3	5.1	122.9	43.7	26.6	2.9	1.9
2018	16.0	35.7	25.0	5.6	149.4	51.3	34.6	3.8	2.5
2020	16.5	36.8	26.1	5.7	155.7	53.1	36.6	4.1	2.7
2024	17.7	38.9	28.2	6.0	167.8	56.3	40.6	4.6	3.0
(b) Urban % total population									
1960	19.2	19.7	26.6	100.0	14.6	30.3	14.7	10.3	7.9
1975	23.9	23.8	37.7	100.0	19.3	35.6	18.8	4.5	11.1
1990	25.2	29.4	49.8	100.0	30.6	47.0	20.3	15.5	15.4
2000	27.0	31.4	62.0	100.0	42.0	46.1	24.4	18.6	22.0
2010	28.9	43.9	70.9	100.0	49.9	45.3	30.4	20.3	30.1
2018	30.6	49.9	76.0	100.0	55.3	46.9	35.9	23.4	35.0
2020	31.1	51.4	77.2	100.0	56.6	47.4	37.3	24.2	36.3
2024	32.5	54.3	79.2	100.0	59.2	48.6	40.2	26.0	39.8
2024 GDP per capita 2015 US$	1,158	6,573	11,868	67,707	4,368	3,925	4,018	2,184	2,724

Source: World Bank, *World development indicators, 2025.*

changed little. The slowdown in urbanization reflected high rural compared to urban birth rates and the unattractiveness of migration to cities, where unemployment and underemployment was high, and in the 1990s half or more of inhabitants lived in slums.

From 1960 to 2024, while Southeast Asia's population increased at an annual rate of 1.9 per cent, its urban component grew at 3.5 per cent, equivalent to doubling about every two decades. Malaysia's urban population rose 13-fold, as did Indonesia's. However, even in 2024, urbanization in Southeast Asia remained comparatively low because of the region's differential industrialization and development levels. Although over half of Southeast Asians, or 363 million of a total of 693 million, dwelt in cities, that overall proportion is misleading because Indonesia was relatively urbanized and more than two-fifths of Southeast Asians were Indonesians. Singapore apart, Malaysia was easily the most urbanized country, with four-fifths of inhabitants living in cities. More than half of Thai and 59 per cent of Indonesians were urban residents, but in other countries the populations were heavily rural. While the urban share in the Philippines was 49 per cent, it was as little as a quarter in Cambodia and between 33 and 40 per cent in Myanmar, Vietnam and Laos. The low urban shares in these last four countries correlated with their low per capita incomes (Table 17.1).

From 1960 to 2024, as urban systems matured, the share of urban population in most of the region's main cities fell as smaller cities expanded faster (Table 17.2). Improved internal transport partly explains the fall. Increased trade consequent on turning outwards to export may, as some of the literature suggests, also have contributed to a decentralizing effect but manufacturing continued to concentrate in the main cities or on their fringes.[3]

The largest drop in the proportion of urban population in a country's main city was in Indonesia. Jakarta contained 20.9 per cent of urban Indonesians in 1960 and 19.1 per cent in 1975, but by 2024 just 6.8 per cent. In 1975, in addition to Jakarta and Surabaya, Bandung was the only Indonesian city of over 1 million. By 2018, while Jakarta stood out in size, Indonesia, reflective of being an archipelago with several large islands, had moved towards a more balanced urban pattern. As well as the three large cities, in 2018 Indonesia had 13 further cities whose populations clustered in a range of between just over 1 million to a little over 3 million. Million cities included Outer Island ones like Bandar Lampung, Makassar and Pekanbaru, which in 1975 were under half a million (Figure 17.1). Sharp drops in main city shares also occurred in Cambodia and Laos, where Phnom Penh and Vientiane surrendered some of their previous overwhelming dominance in urban hierarchies (Table 17.2).

[3] Ades and Glaeser, 'Trade and circuses', pp. 195–227.

Table 17.2 *Southeast Asia population in largest city as a percentage of urban population, 1960–2024*

	Myanmar	Thailand	Malaysia	Indonesia	Philippines	Vietnam	Cambodia	Laos
1960	38.1	39.9	15.8	20.9	28.6	29.2	66.1	45.0
1975	29.4	38.2	14.4	19.1	34.1	25.5	29.7	55.3
1990	27.9	35.4	23.4	14.7	27.4	22.1	44.1	43.0
2000	28.3	32.4	29.1	9.4	27.7	22.5	50.8	37.8
2010	30.0	28.1	29.0	8.0	27.9	23.1	52.4	32.3
2018	31.4	29.3	31.6	7.1	27.0	23.7	51.4	26.9
2020	31.5	29.4	32.0	7.0	26.8	23.7	51.3	25.9
2024	32.3	28.9	31.3	6.8	26.5	23.6	51.2	24.4

Source: World Bank, *World development indicators, 2025.*

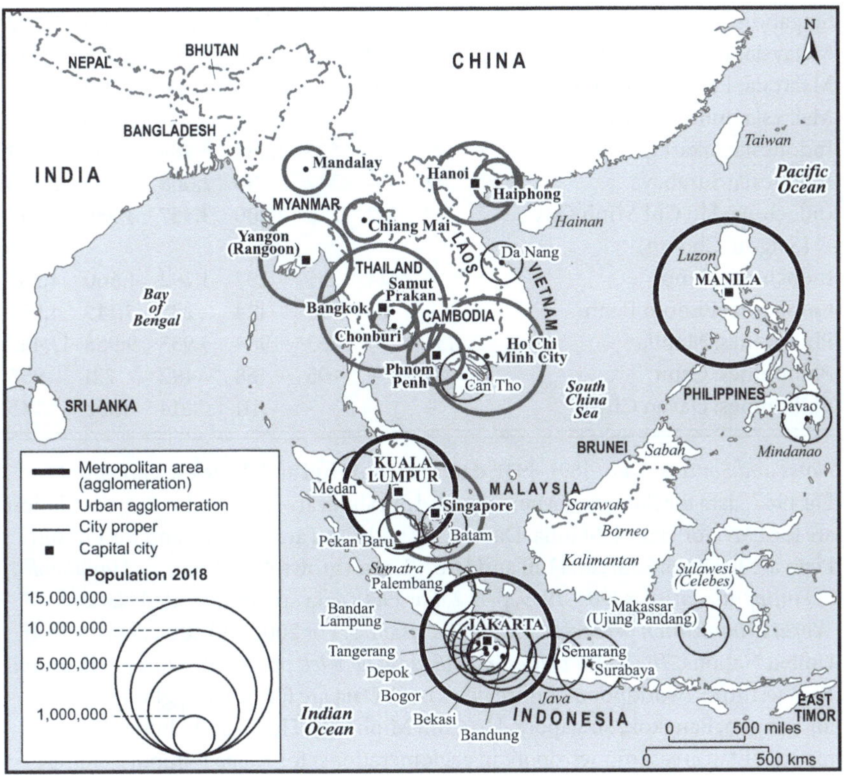

Figure 17.1 Southeast Asia million cities, 2018
Source: United Nations, *World's cities in 2018 – data booklet*, pp. 20–21.

Main City Growth

In modern history, urbanization and industrialization typically go together. Yet this became true of Southeast Asia only from the beginning of the 1950s. Before World War II, the region's main cities had relatively little industry. A largely services and commercial role explains why by World War II or soon after even the region's largest cities had populations of no more than about 1 million (Table 17.3). After the War, Southeast Asian countries gained independence

Table 17.3 *Southeast Asia population of main cities, 1891–2018 (000 persons)*

	1891	1911	1931	1947	1980	2000	2018
Burma: Yangon (Rangoon)	180	293	400	613	2,378	3,573	5,182
Burma: Mandalay	189	138	148	186	499	874	1,374
Thailand: Bangkok (Krung Thep)	100	130	400	890	4,723	6,395	10,156
Thailand: Chiang Mai	–	–	–	38	103	407	1,135
Singapore	154	260	446	941	2,415	3,914	5,792
Malaysia: Kuala Lumpur	19	47	111	176	921	4,176	7,564
Malaysia: Penang (George Town)	52	101	149	189	251	181	–
Malaysia: Johor Bahru	–	–	–	47	247	630	983
Indonesia: Jakarta	127	–	533	1,264	5,984	8,390	10,517
Indonesia: Surabaya	118	–	342	715	2,008	2,611	2,903
Indochina: Ho Chi Minh City (Saigon-Cholon)	81	182	256	1,200	3,457	4,389	8,145
Indochina: Hanoi	–	114	135	237	1,292	1,660	4,283
Cambodia: Phnom Penh	–	62	96	124	238	1,149	1,952
Philippines: Manila	154	234	463	984	5,955	9,958	13,482
Philippines: Cebu	–	–	95	168	492	721	956
Philippines: Davao City	–	–	–	111	614	1,152	1,745

Notes and Sources: 1. For 1891–1931, data are from Huff and Angeles, 'Globalization'. For 1947, data for Rangoon, Mandalay and Surabaya are for 1950; for Saigon-Cholon are for 1949, for Hanoi, Manila, Davao City and Cebu are for 1948; and for Phnom Penh are for 1946. Sources: Huff and Huff, 'Urban growth', Philippines, *Handbook of Philippine statistics 1903–1959*, p. 8. 2. For 1980, data are from United Nations, *World urbanization prospects: the 2007 revision*. 3. For 2000 and 2018, data are from United Nations, *The world's cities in 2018: data booklet*, pp. 20–21; *World Population Review*: https://worldpopulationreview.com/. Data are for urban agglomerations for Yangon, Bangkok, Singapore, Ho Chin Minh City, Hanoi and Phnom Penh but metropolitan areas (or metropolitan agglomerations) for Kuala Lumpur, Jakarta and Manila. Data used in the text for Hanoi for 1952 through 1975 are from Turley, 'Urbanization', p. 379.

and industrialization became a priority. New industrial ventures concentrated in the region's main cities. Industry drove urbanization, and urban concentrations attracted industry because they were foci for the country's transport and communications infrastructure, because they possessed thick labour markets and because they had the largest and most affluent concentration of consumers.

The main cities afforded the country's greatest abundance of skilled labour and supplies of power and water as well as the principal market for manufactured goods for local markets. Investors, however wrongly in the aggregate, perceived the main cities as, on balance, affording positive external economies unavailable in smaller urban areas. A clustering of industry to realize external economies – to overcome through nearness, in Hirschman's phrase, the 'frictions of space' – brought yet more industrial activities as well as associated services.[4] Industry and services created jobs and these drew in labour, although often well beyond what new employment opportunities merited. In Southeast Asia, globalization, industrialization and urbanization strongly reinforced one another and largely by-passed less populated, poorer areas. As during the region's pre-1940 growth and the shaping of dual economies, Southeast Asian growth was again not balanced but starkly skewed towards imbalance.

Data

Beginning in the later 1950s, the geography of the region's main cities started to change fundamentally as they spread beyond their early post-World War II administrative boundaries to encompass surrounding urban development and become, according to varying descriptions, successively, conurbations, urban agglomerations, mega-cities, mega-urban regions, metropolitan areas (or agglomerations) and even megalopolises. Knowing to which of the many definitions data refer is not always easy, and the standardization of data across countries is difficult. To facilitate cross-country comparison, this study utilizes United Nations terminology and data rather than national statistics.

The chapter uses 'urban agglomeration' to mean a 'population contained within the contours of a contiguous territory inhabited at urban levels of residential density', and regards this as synonymous with the term 'city' and as defining a city's boundaries. A mega-city sometimes denotes a city with a population of 10 million or more but here the cut-off is taken as 5 million, a level for which in 2018 all of Southeast Asia's main cities qualified except in Cambodia and Laos. A 'metropolitan area' or 'metropolitan agglomeration', also sometimes described as a mega-urban region or even simply as a city, 'comprises an

[4] Krugman, 'Urban concentration', pp. 7–8; Hirschman, *Strategy*, p. 197 and see Rosenthal and Strange, 'How close', pp. 27–49 on the importance of often quite near proximity.

urban agglomeration and surrounding areas at a lower settlement density with strong economic and social linkages to the city'.[5] The fewest people live in a city proper, an urban agglomeration is larger and a metropolitan area larger still. To be a megalopolis, a settlement must have over 10 million people, as by 2018 Manila, Bangkok and Jakarta did.

For 1980 to 2018, the data in Table 17.3 show the populations in the area of each city as it was defined at the particular time. Because of changes in the boundaries of Southeast Asian cities, the data in Table 17.3 are not comparable over more than short periods for any given, initial area of a 'city'. For any particular city area, populations may be approximately comparable between 1950 and 1975, when data are generally for a core city or its administrative boundaries. Populations may also be compared for 2000 and 2018, since by then data are for either urban or metropolitan areas and consistent for one of these descriptions for individual countries but not between them. For these last two dates, data in Table 17.3 are for urban agglomerations for Yangon, Bangkok, Singapore, Ho Chin Minh City, Hanoi and Phnom Penh but metropolitan areas for Kuala Lumpur, Jakarta and Manila. Singapore's size is understated, since nearby parts of Malaysia and Indonesia were part of the Singaporean economy as constituents of a Growth Triangle, established in partnership with Malaysia and Indonesia and extending from southern Malaysia to encompass Johor Bahru, Singapore and some small Indonesian islands.

Table 17.4 shows for Bangkok, Jakarta and Manila, with populations by 2000 of 10 million to over 20 million, a pattern of a relatively small, densely populated urban core surrounded by much more extensive areas of less densely peopled but faster growing zones, an inner zone and an even larger outer one. The core, which roughly corresponds to the city proper of 1960, contains at most about half of the population of an urban or metropolitan area. If urban populations are taken to include a surrounding region drawn into a city's orbit through a degree of economic and social interconnectedness (that is: a metropolitan area as defined by the United Nations), populations may far exceed those for a continuously built-up city. For example, if Bangkok means the area governed by the Bangkok Metropolitan Area (BMA), its 2018 population was a little over 10 million but more than twice that number lived in the Bangkok Metropolitan Region (BMR), which includes Bangkok's spillover into five surrounding provinces.[6] Table 17.4 provides three examples of urban growth through expansion. By the 1990s, the core of Jakarta constituted only 12 per cent of its land area. Similar figures for Bangkok were 11 per cent and for Manila 5 per cent. In 2000, the core

[5] United Nations, Department of Economic and Social Affairs, Population Division, *World urbanization prospects, 2018*, p. 5 and see United Nations, *World's cities in 2018; data booklet*, p. 1.

[6] Forbes, *Asian metropolis*, pp. 47–48.

Table 17.4 *Southeast Asia area and population distribution mega-urban regions, 1990 and 2000*

(a) Bangkok	Area sq. km	Population millions 1990	Population millions 2000	Annual growth 1990–2000
Core	876	5.4	5.9	0.8
Inner zone	1,907	1.6	2.4	4.1
Outer zone	4,465	1.6	2.2	3.1
Totals area/population	7,248	8.6	10.4	1.9
(b) Jakarta	Area sq. km	Population millions 1990	Population millions 2000	Annual growth 1990–2000
Core	662	8.2	8.3	0.2
Inner zone	2,374	5.4	9.4	5.7
Outer zone	3,139	3.4	3.4	-0.1
Totals area/population	6,175	17.1	21.2	2.1
(c) Manila	Area sq. km	Population millions 1990	Population millions 2000	Annual growth 1990–2000
Core	633	7.9	9.9	2.3
Inner zone	3,105	4.2	6.4	4.3
Outer zone	8,323	3.8	5.4	3.5
Totals area/population	12,061	15.9	21.6	3.1

Notes: The source uses data for mega-urban regions which differ from urban and metropolitan agglomerations as defined by the United Nations and in Table 17.3.
Source: Rimmer and Dick, *City in Southeast Asia*, p. 89.

areas of these cities held at most somewhat over half of their populations. The majority of those in Jakarta and Manila inhabited the inner and outer zones beyond the core.[7]

Patterns of Main City Expansion

In 1950, despite World War II expansion, Southeast Asia's main cities remained compact around a central core of businesses and settlement. As Singapore

[7] In 2025, the UN adopted the Degree of Urbanization methodology which defines a city as 'any contiguous geographical area with a population density of at least 1,500 inhabitants per square kilometre and a population of at least 50,000'. Using this definition, Jakarta, at 42 million, is the world's largest city and Manilla has a population of 25 million. United Nations, *The world's cities in 2025: data booklet*, pp. 3, 12.

grew, in 1947 large numbers of additional inhabitants continued to cluster around its central core of settlement, creating a densely packed mass of population on either side of the Singapore River. By 1947, 680,000 of Singapore's total population of 941,000 lived in the 20,000 acres that comprised Singapore Municipality and within the Municipality some 300,000 people crowded into just 1,000 acres. In large blocks of houses, often back-to-back, densities reached 1,000 or more to the acre.[8]

Southeast Asia's main cities could be described as 'colonial' in the sense that these cities developed under colonial rule and functioned as centres of commercial export economies, the seat of local political decisions, administration and legal and insurance services as well as being a nexus of transport.[9] In 1959, Bangkok was a 'flat city made watery in appearance by the many transportation canals … vertical punctuations are achieved chiefly by the pagodas, temples, occasional modern buildings (mostly 4–5 floors in height), smokestacks and radio T.V. towers … for the majority of the people, the journey to work is very short or non-existent'.[10] When Malaysia became independent in 1957, Kuala Lumpur remained a relatively small city of 316,000. Malaysia's new capital and largest city was still a 'Chinese town with a colonial overlay'.[11] Beginning in the 1960s, buildings of over 10 storeys started to appear in the central business area. Modern offices were displacing shop-houses, a single office building often taking the space of several shop-houses.[12]

For Southeast Asia's principal cities, the usual urban growth pattern was the formation of conurbations established through urbanization spreading outwards from a central area along dominant ribbon roads axial to main roads leading into and out of the city. Development along these ribbons reproduced on a small scale the businesses of the centre, served surrounding residential areas and acted as 'neighbourhood' shopping centres. A conurbation formed as new housing estates appeared adjacent to ribbon roads and were incorporated into the city as it further extended to include surrounding villages and towns.

Subsequently, the city, now with high-rise office buildings and banks appearing as principal features of the city centre, grew yet more to encompass surrounding towns and infrastructure. With this typically urban sprawl, in essentially centrifugal patterns across an expanding web of decreasingly proximate terrain, came economic and social diversification across that space. Rising land values and the need for more and cheaper space pushed industry out of city centres to surrounding fringe areas. Through repeating the process, the once colonial city of modest size became an urban agglomeration or extended

[8] Singapore, *Report of the Housing Committee Singapore 1947*, pp. 1–2.
[9] McGee, *Southeast Asian city*, pp. 55–64.
[10] Quoted in Falkus, 'Bangkok', p. 163.
[11] Rimmer and Dick, *City in Southeast Asia*, p. 62.
[12] Sendut, 'Structure of Kuala Lumpur', p. 135.

its reach to encompass a metropolitan area, as for example Kuala Lumpur by the twenty-first century. Either an urban agglomeration or a metropolitan area might have a population of several million or more.

Kuala Lumpur and Singapore

Figure 17.2 shows the street pattern of central Kuala Lumpur in 1965. By then, the beginnings of a conurbation were apparent as the city's municipal boundary expanded outwards in all directions. Kuala Lumpur extended to the north and south through ribbons of building along Pudu Road and Jalan Tuanku Abdul Rahman and to the east and west to envelop rubber estates and abandoned tin-mining land, both re-developed as housing estates. The cheapness of disused tin-mining land encouraged lateral extension. As early as the later 1970s, it seemed clear that Kuala Lumpur would eventually stretch along corridors of some 30 miles over the Klang Valley to form its 2022 metropolitan area and include Port Klang (Figure 17.3).

Petaling Jaya, established in 1953 12 kilometres from Kuala Lumpur, was the first of Malaysia's new towns. The original plan was that Petaling Jaya would serve as an overspill for some of the (by then large) population in Kuala Lumpur's squatter and overcrowded areas.[13] However, Petaling Jaya developed as a middle-class suburb. So, too, did a large number of other new towns, all satellites to Kuala Lumpur, built soon after Petaling Jaya. In the mid-1970s, Petaling Jaya was among peninsular Malaysia's most industrialized towns. Shah Alam, a new town planned in the mid-1960s and well established a decade later, facilitated a formative urban corridor between Kuala Lumpur and Port Klang, formerly Port Swettenham. More than a fifth of the town's 7,539-acre site was originally an industrial area. Shah Alam became a main location for import-substitution industry such as food processing, pharmaceuticals and automobile assembly which centred on the Kuala Lumpur market.[14] Similarly, other new towns, because of their proximity to Kuala Lumpur, typically provided industrial zones, as well as housing, shopping and leisure (Figure 17.2).[15]

In 1963, following the extension of Kuala Lumpur's boundaries, the city encompassed Malay rural villages, Chinese 'new villages' and segregated squatter areas, totalling some 100,000 people, or about a quarter of the 'urban' population.[16] Subsequently, the Malaysian capital continued to increase its size by expanding to incorporate other urban or quasi-urban areas over a substantial

[13] Concannon, 'New town in Malaya', pp. 41–43.

[14] Lee, 'Emerging urban trends', p. 364.

[15] Aiken and Leigh, 'Malaysia's emerging conurbation', pp. 549–54; Sendut, 'Structure of Kuala Lumpur', pp. 136–38.

[16] Rimmer and Dick, *City in Southeast Asia*, p. 62.

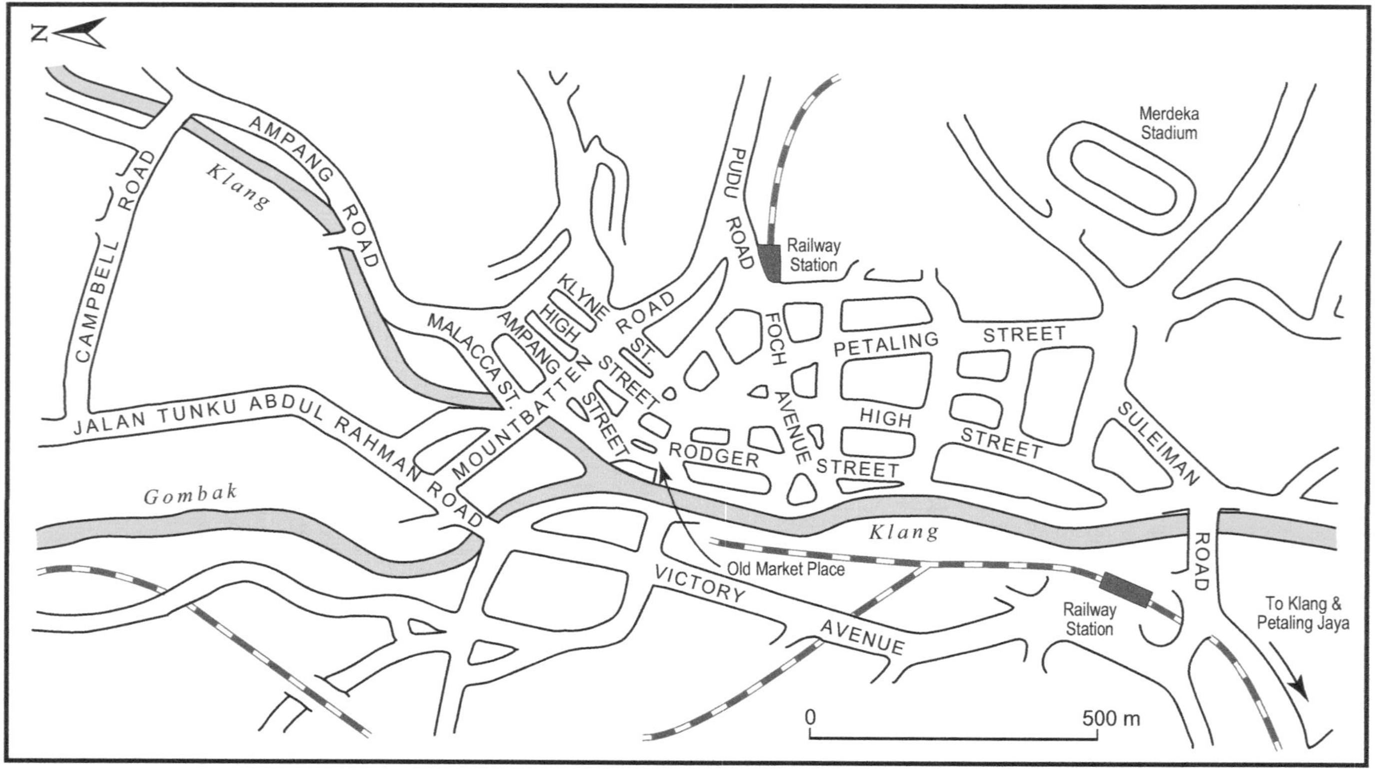

Figure 17.2 Central Kuala Lumpur street pattern, 1965
Source: Sendut, 'Structure of Kuala Lumpur', p. 131.

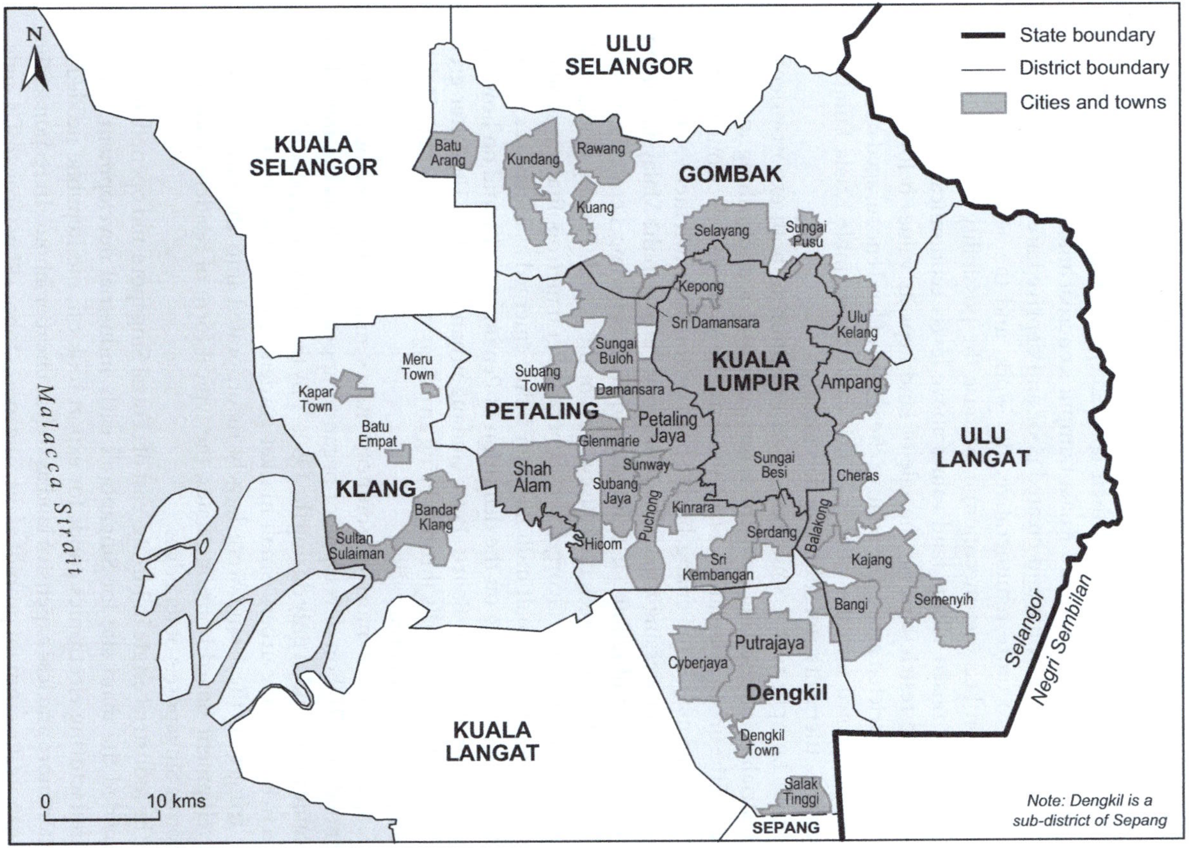

Figure 17.3 Kuala Lumpur metropolitan area (Klang Valley), 2020
Source: Malaysia, *MyCensus* 2020.

part of the country's wealthiest region, leaving other large Malaysian cities well behind as urban rivals.

Kuala Lumpur's growth integrated many villages designated by the Malay Reserve Enactment of 1913 as Malay reservations. The Act was intended to preserve the Malay lifestyle of traditional subsistence and cash crop activities by preventing Malays from selling their land except to other Malays. Yet for the villages, reservation land and Kuala Lumpur's encroachment undermined an earlier Malay way of life and created poor and deprived areas. Villagers were drawn away to more remunerative, city work, and the acquisition of land for cultivation became uneconomic, because the possibility of future urban development raised village land values above levels economical for farming. However, the restrictions on the sale of land kept its values below those in nearby unrestricted areas. The relative cheapness of land encouraged non-local Malays to crowd into the villages, which came to resemble Kuala Lumpur's squatter settlements, not suburban development.[17]

Kuala Lumpur was a Southeast Asian exception to both export-oriented industrialization locating near the largest city and a diminishing main city share of the urban population. From the start, the Malaysian electronics industry clustered mainly in Penang, having been originally drawn there by the creation of export processing zones. The position of Penang in the Malaysian urban hierarchy was ambiguous. If defined to include Seberang Perai, the former Province Wellesley, across the causeway from the island, Penang would rank second in Malaysia as a Georgetown–Seberang Perai metropolitan agglomeration of over one and a half million. Johor Bahru emerged as Malaysia's second or third city, depending on the definition of Penang as a city and on how one accounts for the Johor Bahru–Pasir Gudang urban corridor. The latter grew from a low base, primarily through being an extension across the Strait of Johor of Singapore's industrialization.

Singapore, unlike most of Southeast Asia's main cities, was a carefully planned city. Ribbon development began to appear as early as the 1890s but became pronounced only during the 1950s.[18] By the 1980s, Singapore island was effectively entirely urban. Small market gardens and fishing villages around the fringes of the island were largely incorporated into the city. Housing Development Board housing estates, the typical form of residence, stretched towards Singapore's outer edges.

The industrial estate in Jurong, east of central Singapore and opened in 1968, provided the main site for Singapore's early industrial development, but as manufacturing electronics goods for export took off, the Republic needed to obtain more and less expensive land as well as cheaper labour. In response, the Singapore government promoted the Singapore–Johor–Riau Growth Triangle.

[17] Brookfield et al., *City in the village*, pp. 96–110.
[18] Dick and Rimmer, *Cities, transport*, pp. 297–98.

The development, although across water, was analogous to the centrifugal pattern of expansion of other Southeast Asian cities. By 2018, Johor Bahru, as a component of the triangle, had about a million people, but this was no more than a seventh of Kuala Lumpur's population.

Bangkok

Bangkok, Jakarta and Manila all traced paths of early post-World War II expansion similar to Kuala Lumpur's and Singapore's. In the 1960s and 1970s, Bangkok's extension into the surrounding region swiftly added population. Although a proportion of those in the areas incorporated into Metropolitan Bangkok must have migrated from rural Thailand, the city's outwards thrust may have accounted for as much, or perhaps even more, of its growth as rural–urban migration. Initially, industrial and commercial areas developed along arterial roads and, from these spearheads, settlement filled in and widened. Bangkok absorbed Thonburi to its west in 1972 and subsequently included in its metropolitan area a large number of centres that had been physically and economically separate. As the city spread into adjacent provinces, paddy fields, orchards, vegetable gardens and former canals were built on and became part of Metropolitan Bangkok.

The Eastern Seaboard Project began in 1981 and over the next decade made the three provinces of Chachoengsao, Chonburi and Rayong, along the inner eastern coast of the Gulf of Thailand, part of the BMR, extending its reach along a 200-kilometre belt. Originally, the Project involved the construction of two deep-sea ports, at Laem Chabang in Chonburi province and at Map Ta Phut in Rayong province, as well as industrial estates around the ports and a petrochemical complex for natural gas discovered in the Gulf of Thailand in the 1970s. At first and despite government provision of infrastructure, development was slow, but it rapidly gained pace during Thailand's boom of the late 1980s and 1990s. Development spread along a ribbon of the Pattaya Road, subsuming the surrounding countryside into housing projects, retail complexes and some 30 industrial estates. As the boom gained force, many of the estates were developed by the private sector. Initially, electronics industries clustered in Chonburi province but during the late 1990s the industry spread inland in Chonburi and Rayong provinces.[19]

In 2018, the United Nations recorded Bangkok as having some 10 million inhabitants, although a wider definition of the city would considerably increase this number (Tables 17.3 and 17.4). Functioning as a hub for world air routes and with a cosmopolitan air, Bangkok was Southeast Asia's nearest rival to Singapore. The latter, in just three decades after 1960, was transformed, under

[19] Mieno, 'Eastern seaboard development plan', pp. 87–102; United Nations, *Population growth: Bangkok*, p. 15; Phongpaichit and Baker, *Thailand's boom*, pp. 8–9, 88.

government direction, into a genuinely global city. Bangkok lacked, however, Singapore's locational advantages, communications infrastructure, shipping links and business and financial networks, all unmatched in Asia except in Hong Kong.

As Bangkok grew, chiefly in response to largely uncontrolled market forces, by the later 1980s it became probably the world's most congested city. Congestion was greatly worsened by Bangkok's historical reliance on water transport on the river and canals, and an urban pattern of many narrow streets which originated as private lanes leading to houses. Unplanned development over this earlier transport network left modern Bangkok with about a quarter as much urban space devoted to roads as is usual in cities.

Jakarta

Crowded onto a low-lying site, Jakarta's rise to mega-city status depended chiefly on drawing surrounding areas into its orbit. The 2018 population of Jakarta exceeded 10 million but was over 20 million for the Jakarta Metropolitan Region and 42 million in 2025 using the Degree of Urbanization methodology. Known as Jabotabek, the region incorporates the city of Jakarta, six further administrative units, three municipalities and three districts. The extension of Jakarta's reach to constitute a metropolitan area replaced large amounts of rice cultivation with urban sprawl, but between this sprawl and the remaining agricultural land were substantial urban areas and populations. Although counted as part of Jabotabek, considerable areas of it could be classed as semi-rural or rural.

The name Jabotabek derives from a fusion of Jakarta and Botabek, this last denoting the three districts of Bogor, Tangerang and Bekasi around Jakarta (Figure 17.4). Toll roads linking Jakarta to the three districts as well as Cikampek provided corridors for the expansion of population industry. These links, through reducing development costs outside Jakarta, encouraged housing construction, the establishment of new towns and the outwards movement of industry. Bekasi, as a part of the Jakarta urban agglomeration, is notable for its industrial core, as is Tangsel (South Tangerang) on the western border of Jakarta, although it leaned more toward tech and services.[20]

Manila

Manila city – compact in 1950 around Manila Bay and in 2018 still with a population of less than 2 million – expanded into Metro Manila (the National Capital Region) in a centrifugal pattern but as hubs around the Epifanio de Los Santos Avenue ring road built in the late 1960s. Already in the 1950s,

[20] Rimmer and Dick, *City in Southeast Asia*, pp. 95, 98.

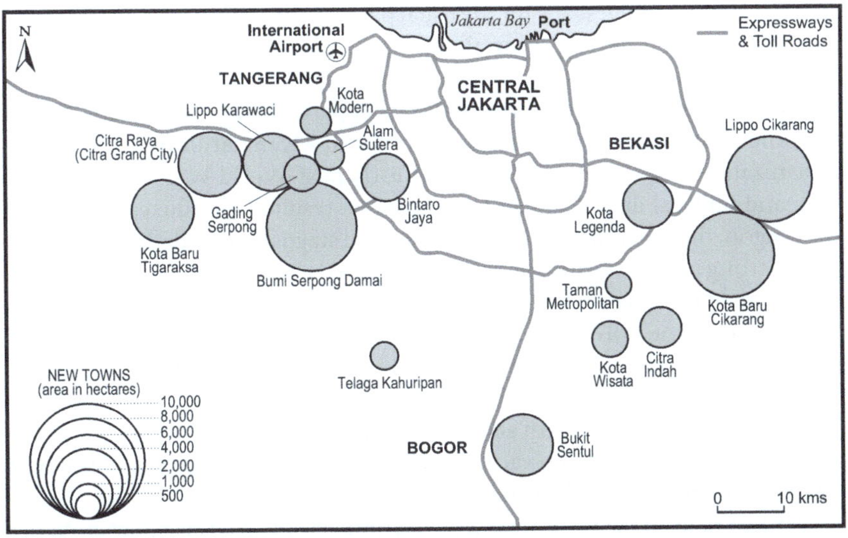

Figure 17.4 Jabotabek (Jakarta Metropolitan Region)
Source: Dick and Rimmer, *Cities, transport*, p. 285.

Quezon City, north of the ring road, had become the designated location for government offices, but a combination of rivalry between leading families and official bureaucracy choked off the city's growth.[21] Instead of this government area attracting Philippine business, private developers built Makati to the southeast of the city core on a 900-hectare site which had been part of an old hacienda. Makati replaced Binondo, in the heart of the city, as the main business district. Most multinationals set up in the high-rise offices in Makati, and it was also a focus of entertainment, culture and expensive residences. By 2018, Metro Manila, also designated a Philippines administrative region, encompassed 16 cities and municipalities and had a population of 13.5 million. It ranked seventeenth among the world's most populous urban areas and was the sole Southeast Asian urban agglomeration or metropolitan area in the top 25.[22]

Yangon

The post-World War II expansion of Yangon (Rangoon) differed from other main Southeast Asian cities due to both geographic and economic factors. Although Yangon expanded outwards as elsewhere in Southeast Asia,

[21] The history is traced in Pante, *Capital city*.

[22] Dick and Rimmer, *Cities, transport*, pp. 267–70; United Nations, Department of Economic and Social Affairs, Population Division, *World urbanization prospects, 2018*, p. 77.

geography limited the scope for the usual pattern of Southeast Asian early-stage growth of ribbon development along radial roads. The city's expansion was restricted to the south and west by the Hline (Hlaing) and Rangoon Rivers and to the east and west by creeks, rivers and swamps. Economically, decades of civil war and slow or negative economic advance in Myanmar impacted Yangon's urbanization in two ways. One was that early post-World War II rural stagnation and internal displacement due to conflict resulted in influxes of squatters to Yangon; the other that industrialization and stagnant growth did not give the same strong impetus to urbanization as occurred elsewhere in Southeast Asia.

Hemmed in by natural barriers for much of the post-1950 period as Yangon was, the construction of satellite towns beyond its geographical constraints was a major force in urban growth. During the insurrections of 1948 to 1951, rural migrants left a moribund and civil war-torn countryside to flood into Yangon in search of safety. In an already badly overcrowded city, migrants created squatter settlements on vacant land, bombed-out areas, pavements next to main roads and along railway lines.

For fear of losing votes, the elected government of U Nu was reluctant to deal with an endemic and worsening squatter problem, but this became a priority for Ne Win's 1962 caretaker military administration as part of a programme to clean up Yangon. The military regime built three satellite towns and moved almost a third of Yangon's inhabitants to them. After 1988, three more satellite towns were constructed. They were meant to house squatters displaced from Yangon partly by fires and partly compulsorily by civil servants implementing a resettlement policy. Resettlement also served the political expediency of a place outside the centre to remove squatters after their active participation in the political turmoil of 1988.[23]

The government ordered urban squatters listed for relocation to dismantle their houses, pack their possessions and at a specified time to move to satellite towns. Squatters were transported to the towns, usually after evening curfew, by army truck. Satellite towns were rudimentary. They had little or no provision for water, no sewers or solid waste disposal systems and no official communications or transport services. Nor were those relocated given title to land in the satellite towns.[24]

Although the original central business district remained economically important, by the 1990s Yangon extended to encompass some 33 townships and cover over four times its 1958 area, some of which was officially classified as 'rural' but in reality part of Yangon.[25] Despite this extension and a Myanmar population of over 50 million, in 2018 Yangon was the smallest of Southeast Asia's main cities, partly because Myanmar was heavily agricultural and partly

[23] Nwe, 'Yangon', pp. 95–110; Naing Oo, 'Urbanization', pp. 242–43, 250–51.

[24] Naing Oo, 'Urbanization', p. 256; Forbes, *Asian metropolis*, pp. 90–92.

[25] Myanmar, *Population and housing census, 2014: migration and urbanization*, p. ixv; Nwe, 'Yangon', p. 95.

because industrialization gave less impetus to growth than in other of Southeast Asia's main cities. For most of the post-1950 decades, a bias towards capital-intensive industry limited industrial job opportunities.

There was, however, as elsewhere in Southeast Asia, an increased impetus to urbanization when, in the late 1990s, Myanmar began to manufacture for export. The 2014 census found that North Yangon was Myanmar's most important destination of internal migrants because of the attraction, mainly for female workers, of employment in garment manufacturing. Similarly, four industrial zones established around Mandalay pulled migrants to them.[26]

After 1965 and until about 2010, rural–urban migration was not a main factor in Yangon's population growth. Yangon lacked the attraction for migrants of a leading industrial sector with substantial employment absorptive capacity. From 1973 to 1983, the city's growth relied chiefly on natural increase. Cityward migration was discouraged by higher urban than rural unemployment, a greater capacity of the countryside than the city to absorb labour after the introduction of high-yielding rice in 1978 and the lack of services in Yangon's squatter settlements.[27]

Beginning in 2010, migration regained its pre-1965 importance in Yangon's growth for two reasons. One was the possibility of employment in garment manufacture; the other a low urban birth rate. By the time of the 2014 census, Yangon's fertility level was 1.85, and migration accounted for 81 per cent of the city's growth.[28]

A building boom in the 1990s, when Myanmar looked outwards, changed Yangon somewhat from the city beloved by some tourists for its near non-existent post-World War II modernization. Nevertheless, and despite the construction of some hotels, shopping centres, condominiums near the centre and industrial estates on the city's fringe, in 2022 large parts of Yangon, especially its central area, remained run down or had become derelict. Some 58 per cent of the city's residents lived in slum and squatter areas and 64 per cent in substandard accommodation (nearly all constructed of wood and bamboo or bamboo and thatch). These magnitudes of poor housing were easily the largest of any of Southeast Asia's main cities.[29]

Globalization and Industrialization

Globalization and industrialization, which brought inflows of foreign investment in Southeast Asian industry, became major forces in the expansion of all Southeast Asia's main cities and even to some extent of Yangon. The economic

[26] Myanmar, *Population and housing census, 2014: population dynamics*, p. 22.

[27] Naing Oo, 'Urbanization', pp. 244, 246–49, 253, 257; Nwe, 'Yangon', pp. 103–10; Myanmar, *Population and housing census, 2014: migration and urbanization*, p. 5.

[28] Myanmar, *Population and housing census, 2014: migration and urbanization*, p. 142.

[29] Naing Oo, 'Urbanization', p. 255.

dominance of main cities was strengthened by the electronics and electrical industries and garment manufacture, as well as continued industrialization consequent on import substitution, because all these activities were pulled to earlier economic development and often were labour intensive with attendant employment creation. In Southeast Asia's main cities, people were drawn to the jobs that industry offered, and with industrialization came the linkages of additional work in associated and secondary industrial development, construction and services, all of which stimulated further cityward migration. These multiplier effects likely outweighed the jobs directly attributable to industrial employment.

Malaysian import-substitution industries had concentrated industry in the new towns around Kuala Lumpur like Petaling Jaya, because of access to its market, transport infrastructure and labour force.[30] The growth of Metropolitan Kuala Lumpur has been described as 'superinduced': the outcome of growth-oriented 'active strategies to attract foreign investments', although, as discussed below, the city's growth owed much to Prime Minister Mahathir's determination to make the extended metropolitan area a showpiece of Malaysian development.[31] By 2025, the Kuala Lumpur metropolitan agglomeration, although with 30 per cent of Malaysia's population, was expected to account for two-fifths of its GDP.[32] Although Penang's growth gained momentum as a centre for the electronics industry, the city was nevertheless easily outpaced in size by expansion in the Kuala Lumpur–Klang Valley mega-urban region.

From the start of its determined establishment in 1949, import-substitution industry in the Philippines clustered in and around Manila, because the city and its immediate hinterland offered the principal market for consumer goods and best access to imported components (Chapter 14). During the 1960s and 1970s, the Philippines tried to use investment incentives to balance regional development. The government banned new industries in Metro Manila, established export processing zones elsewhere in the country and promoted an integrated development of rural areas and urban growth centres. All these measures proved ineffective. By the early 2000s, Metro Manila produced over half of Philippines GDP.[33] Market forces dominated: most new industries insisted on locating in central Luzon and specifically within the National Capital Region.[34]

From the mid-1970s to mid-1990s, the National Capital Region accounted for half of both manufacturing value added and employment. Most of the rest of Philippines industry was in central Luzon and Southern Tagalog. The far north and south of Luzon, the Eastern Visayas and Central and Western Mindanao had little modern sector industrialization and appeared to have stagnated. Despite

30 Dick and Rimmer, *Cities, transport*, pp. 327–29.
31 Lee, 'Challenges', p. 323.
32 Yasin et al., 'Urbanization and growth', p. 7.
33 Balisacan et al., 'Spatial disparities', p. 169.
34 Ocampo, 'Metro Manila mega-region', p. 289.

the development of electronics production in Cebu in the Central Visayas, after the Philippines turned outwards to manufacture for export, this industrialization and the government's creation of export zones increased the spatial concentration of industry in Luzon and especially around Manila. At the end of the 1990s, virtually all exports from the zones came from Luzon.[35]

Land use in Manila followed a usual Southeast Asian pattern driven by rising land prices and industry's space requirements. Beginning in the 1990s, manufacturing industries began to move out of Metro Manila. Industrial estates grew up in the borders of the metro area, and then, in the 2000s, along the fringes in Cavite, Batangas and Laguna. The once-industrial estates near the centre of the city gave way to high-rise residential and commercial buildings and mixed-use high-density enclaves.[36]

The story in Jakarta echoed that of the region's other main cities. In Jakarta's transformation 'the driving force was national industrialization which was highly concentrated around the outskirts of Jakarta'.[37] Import substitution, much more than manufacturing for export, drove Jakarta's growth because Indonesia turned resolutely outward for only a decade from the late 1980s to 1996. By the time that Indonesia began to manufacture for export, industry was already located principally in Jakarta and its immediately adjacent *kabupaten* (administrative districts) together with Bogor (Botabek). These areas produced 31 per cent of Indonesia's industrial output (excluding oil and gas) of medium and large firms. Manufacturing was highly concentrated in the industrial clusters that surround Jakarta.[38] Foreign investment and industry centred on Jakarta, notably for consumer durables and modern product industries. Electrical equipment became a significant industry as, too, did cement and glass products and automobile assembly, this last chiefly for the domestic market.

Surabaya in East Java offered Indonesia's only serious industrial rival to Jakarta but came a distant second. Domestic and foreign investors shunned central Java because it lacked a historic industrial base and the attraction of 'Jakarta's economic dynamism (and access to powerful decision-makers)'. Surabaya was attractive as the other Indonesian industrial centre because of a 'concentration of mass markets, skilled labour and entrepreneurship'.[39]

Already in 1970, 80 per cent of Thailand's industrial output concentrated around Bangkok.[40] Subsequent growth built on that base. In Bangkok after the 1985 Plaza Accord, inwards Japanese investment in labour-intensive industry propelled Thailand's most rapid decade of growth from 1987 to 1997 (Figure 15.3)

35 Hill, 'Industry', pp. 243–46.

36 World Bank, *Philippines urbanization review*, p. 14.

37 Dick and Rimmer, *Cities, transport*, p. 283.

38 Kimura and Chen, 'Value chain connectivity', pp. 173–74, 184.

39 Hill, 'Indonesia's industrial transformation', p. 104 and see pp. 106, 120; Dharmapatni and Firman, 'Problems and challenges', p. 301.

40 Falkus, 'Bangkok', p. 162.

and set in motion a secondary boom in finance, insurance and real estate, transforming the city's skyline through the addition of the 94-storey Baiyoke II Tower and a number of other high-rise buildings.[41] Inwards foreign investment and industrialization along with the latter's associated services strengthened the role of the BMA as 'a powerful growth engine that propels the whole [Thai] economy forward'.[42]

Despite government policies to spread industrialization more widely, electronics production and other new industry continued to locate in clusters along corridors in a radius of 80 kilometres from Bangkok.[43] Much of Thailand's economy concentrated in Bangkok and its vicinities, which in 2009 accounted for about half of the country's GDP.[44] Because investors repeatedly chose to locate in Bangkok and five neighbouring provinces (Metropolitan Bangkok), the region became an 'industrial enclave' with stronger links to the international economy than the hinterland.[45] An extensive network of roads and other infrastructure defined the corridors spreading outwards from Bangkok and afforded the electronics industry rapid communication with Singapore. The pull of the Eastern Seaboard, which forms part of the metropolitan industrial area including the heavy industry complex of Rayong, was greatly increased by the government's development of the new deep-sea port of Laem Chabang in 2001 and Suvarnabhumi international airport in 2006.[46]

Primate Cities

By 1940, the pattern of Southeast Asia's main cities – based initially on a geography of spatial nodality for transport and then confirmed by second nature advantages of population and built environment – had been firmly established. World War II strengthened this pattern: in 1950, all of Southeast Asia's main cities were also primate cities. Between 1950 and 2018, every main Southeast Asian city except Hanoi retained primate status, measured against the second largest city (Table 17.5).

Within Southeast Asia, however, two contrasting patterns appeared. One was that by 2018, for Manila, Bangkok and Yangon, primacy declined as urban systems filled in and the diseconomies associated with the largest urban areas stimulated, to at least some extent, the growth of their second city counterparts. Nevertheless, the gaps between first and second cities remained quite large.

41 Dick and Rimmer, *Cities, transport*, p. 309.
42 Krongkaew, 'Changing urban system', p. 287.
43 Kaothien, 'Regional and urbanisation policy', pp. 1028–30; United Nations, *Population growth: Bangkok*, pp. 17–20.
44 Wisaweisuan, 'Spatial disparities', p. 185.
45 Dick and Rimmer, *Cities, transport*, p. 309 and see United Nations, *Population growth: Bangkok*, p. 12; Kaothien, 'Bangkok metropolitan region', p. 329.
46 Rimmer and Dick, *City in Southeast Asia*, p. 95.

Table 17.5 *Southeast Asia main cities and centralization, 1950–2018 (population 000 and ratio of the first to second largest city)*

	1950		1975		2000		2018		2000–2018
	Pop. 000	Ratio 1st to 2nd city	Pop. 000	Ratio 1st to 2nd city	Pop. 000	Ratio 1st to 2nd city	Pop. 000	Ratio 1st to 2nd city	Growth rate largest city %
Burma									
Yangon (Rangoon)	1,302	7.8	2,151	4.9	3,573	4.2	5,157	3.8	2.1
Mandalay	167		442		847		1,374		2.7
Naypyidaw	12		37		117		500		8.0
Thailand									
Bangkok (Krung Thep)	1,360	20.6	3,842	41.3	6,395	9.7	10,156	8.9	2.6
Chiang Mai	66		93		407		1,135		5.9
Samut Prakan					656		1,272		3.7
Malaysia									
Kuala Lumpur	208	4.4	645	3.5	4,176	6.6	7,564	7.7	3.4
Johor Bahru	47		183		630		983		2.5
Klang	42		148		631				
Penang									
Singapore									
Singapore	1,016		2,236		3,914		5,792		2.2
Indonesia									
Jakarta	1,452	2.1	4,813	2.8	8,390	3.2	10,517	3.6	1.3
Surabaya	679		1,736		2,611		2,903		0.6

(continued)

Table 17.5 (*cont.*)

	1950		1975		2000		2018		2000–2018
	Pop. 000	Ratio 1st to 2nd city	Pop. 000	Ratio 1st to 2nd city	Pop. 000	Ratio 1st to 2nd city	Pop. 000	Ratio 1st to 2nd city	Growth rate largest city %
Vietnam									
Ho Chi Minh City (Saigon)	1,123	4.0	2,808	1.5	4,621	1.2	8,145	1.9	3.2
Hanoi	280		1,884		3,752		4,283		0.7
Philippines									
Manila	1,544	8.7	4,999	10.2	9,958	8.6	13,482	7.7	1.7
Cebu	178		415		721		956		1.6
Davao	124		488		1,152		1,745		2.3

Notes: Data are strictly comparable between 2000 and 2018 only because by 2000 all of the largest cities had gained population through becoming metropolitan or urban agglomerations.
Sources: United Nations, *World urbanization prospects, 2007 revision* and *World's cities in 2018: data booklet*, pp. 20–21.

In Thailand, Samut Prakan and Chonburi were part of Bangkok's metropolitan area, and the Kingdom's genuine second city could be regarded as Chiang Mai in the north. Despite Chiang Mai's rapid growth as a centre for tourism and education, Bangkok remained in 2018 almost nine times larger. Between 2000 and 2018, Davao, the leading city on Mindanao and the second largest urban area in the Philippines, grew faster than Manila but was still only about an eighth of its size.

Margins by which Yangon was a primate city increased through the 1953, 1973 and 1983 censuses.[47] However, this changed partly due to the 2005 move to Naypyidaw to make the central Myanmar city on the southern edge of the Dry Zone the country's new administrative capital. In 2018, Naypyidaw, heavily reliant on inwards migration of civil servants and service providers, ranked third among cities in Myanmar and had about two-fifths as many people as Mandalay. The latter was, in turn, at 1.2 million, about a quarter of Yangon's size.[48]

The second pattern of increasing primacy was evident in Kuala Lumpur, the difference between Jakarta and Surabaya as well as, for much of 1960 to 2018, the gap between Ho Chi Minh City and Hanoi. In the growth of all three larger cities, as often in developing countries, political power and disproportionate government spending through investment in infrastructure and prestige projects was fundamental.[49] Centralizing effects operated through both an expansion of government and the importance of the largest city, especially if also a capital, as a place where political favours were dispensed and things got done. The assumption of enhanced administrative and political roles for Jakarta and Kuala Lumpur as capital cities in newly independent countries drew in population. The same was true of Hanoi after Vietnamese re-unification in 1975.

Kuala Lumpur grew between 1960 and 2018 at a rate implying a doubling in size about every 13 years. Such rapid expansion can only be explained by political decisions. After Malaysian independence in 1957, Kuala Lumpur was the centre of the new government and it promoted the city's development and its Malay character as a matter of policy. Independence in 1957 was followed by an infusion of provincial Malays who joined either government administrative and security services or the informal sector. Nevertheless, Malays, although 49 per cent of the Malaysian population, still comprised only 15.9 per cent of the city's inhabitants (Table 17.6).

Even in 1975, Kuala Lumpur remained a city of just 645,000. Although no longer, as in 1957, dwarfed by Singapore – a provincial, poor relation to its southern neighbour – neither was Kuala Lumpur the size that might be expected of the capital of a prosperous nation and Southeast Asia's most

47 Naing Oo, 'Urbanization', p. 252

48 Myanmar, *Population and housing census, 2014: population dynamics*, pp. xii, 19 gave population figures of 5.21 million persons in Yangon, 1.22 million in Mandalay and 1.16 million in Naypyidaw (Nay Pyi Taw) Government Territory.

49 Ades and Glaeser, 'Trade and circuses'; Davis and Henderson, 'Evidence'.

Table 17.6 *Kuala Lumpur and nearby areas ethnic composition of the population of Malaysian citizens, 1957–2022*

	Chinese %	Indians %	Malays and other *Bumiputera* %	Others %	Total %	No. 000
1957	62.8	15.9	15.9	5.4	100.0	477
1980	51.9	14.3	32.8	1.0	100.0	977
2000	43.5	11.4	43.6	1.5	100.0	1,287
2022	41.1	10.0	48.2	0.7	100.0	1,778

Note: The 2022 data are estimates.
Sources: Malaya, *Population census of the Federation of Malaya. Report no. 2, State of Selangor*, p. 3; Malaysia, *General report of the population census, 1980*, vol. 2, pp. 226–27; Malaysia, *Population and housing census, 2000*, p. 47; Malaysia, Department of Statistics, *Current population estimates*, p. 74.

urbanized country. In some respects, Singapore, as it had historically, still functioned as Malaysia's capital city.[50]

After the May 1969 riots, the Malaysian government, with its New Economic Policy, took the early steps that were to lead towards developing Kuala Lumpur 'as a capital of world standing' and to acquire a more Malay personality. In 1990, Prime Minister Mahathir determined that Kuala Lumpur – under the New Development Policy, Vision 2000 – would be transformed into a global city-region to rank alongside Singapore.[51] The latter had become an international city and at least approached the goal set by Lee Kuan Yew of being the New York of the East. Although Kuala Lumpur, in 2000, was well short of Singapore's international role and ambience, the city, as a metropolitan area, was now somewhat more populous than its rival to the south.

Between the 1990s and early 2000s, the government systematically planned and reshaped Kuala Lumpur with a range of mega-projects and the infrastructure, notably super-highways, to accommodate a spreading, road-based metropolitan area. As late as 1989, Kuala Lumpur had just two motorways and expressways. Their number increased to 20 in 2010 and 26 by 2019, facilitating rapid urbanization but also unattractive urban sprawl.[52]

Four projects were especially spectacular, modern high-rise equivalents of the world's great cathedrals. One was the Kuala Lumpur City Centre, which

50 Sendut, 'Structure of Kuala Lumpur', pp. 128–29: Rimmer and Dick, *City in Southeast Asia*, p. 62; Aiken and Leigh, 'Malaysia's emerging conurbation', p. 548.
51 Rimmer and Dick, *City in Southeast Asia*, pp. 72–75.
52 Yasin et al., 'Urbanization and growth', pp. 9–10.

included the Petronas Twin Towers, completed in 2003 and then the world's two tallest buildings; and a second the oversized Kuala Lumpur International Airport and 'Airport City' incorporating two new towns. The third was the 50-kilometre Multimedia Super Corridor inaugurated in 1996 (in its IT2000 plan Singapore anticipated its own multimedia concentration) to accommodate high-tech activities.

Fourth, Putrajaya, a 10,000-acre 'garden city', served as an imposing new administrative capital and incorporated one of the world's only grand pink mosques and acres of parkland. Putrajaya, like the other three mega-projects, stood as a monument to the ambitions of Prime Minister Mahathir, Malay culture and the economic advance of Malaysia. In 2018, the metropolitan agglomeration of Kuala Lumpur considerably exceeded Singapore in population, although the inclusion of some of the population in Johor Bahru and Riau as part of growth generated by Singapore would narrow the size differential (Table 17.5).

By 2000, the ethnic composition of the inner parts of Kuala Lumpur had changed from being a Chinese city to one that was equally Malay and Chinese (Table 17.6). In 2022, Kuala Lumpur, now a predominantly Malay city, approximately accorded with Malaysia's overall ethnic balance, continuing a trend apparent after independence and intended by the government. Kuala Lumpur and the surrounding area (excluding non-citizens) was 48.2 per cent Malay, 41.1 per cent Chinese and 10.0 per cent Indian (Table 17.6). The composition of the Klang Valley was similar. In both instances, if non-citizens are included, they would account for some 9.0 per cent of the population.[53]

Under Sukarno, the shift in Indonesia to the status of a unitary state increased Jakarta's population (and its attractiveness for import-substitution industry) through a greater concentration of governmental activities, and the construction of modernizing symbols including the Sarinah department store, a luxury hotel and national monument (Chapter 11). The New Order of Suharto implemented yet further centralization, adding to a concentration of power and inflows of lobbyists and others. Java dominated Indonesia, and in this key Indonesian agglomeration 'Greater Jakarta has assumed ever greater prominence'.[54]

Between 1950 and 1975, Hanoi, as the capital for most of the period of the socialist Democratic Republic of Vietnam, grew at an annual rate of 7.9 per cent, the fastest growth of the main cities in Southeast Asia. After 1975, Hanoi, now the capital of a unified Vietnam, expanded more rapidly than Ho Chi Minh City, and in 2000 had closed the size gap to approaching parity between the two urban agglomerations. Subsequently, however, as Vietnam turned outwards to export, Ho Chi Minh City's historic industrial and commercial dominance told, and in 2018, as a Zipfian distribution posits, the southern city was nearly twice the size of Hanoi.

53 Malaysia, *My Census 2020*.
54 Hill et al., 'Economic geography', p. 132.

Socialist Urbanization

The strategy of socialist countries has often been to economize on the costs of urbanization by blocking or otherwise discouraging migration and directing industry away from major urban centres.[55] Of the five countries discussed in this book as having aspects of socialism, only the Cambodian Pol Pot regime can be regarded as a strict adherent to a doctrine of tight limitations on urbanization although, as in so much else, an extreme one. Otherwise, urbanization in declared socialist countries traced a similar path to the rest of Southeast Asia. The Pol Pot regime officially regarded Cambodia's city inhabitants as class enemies. Myanmar and Indonesia under Sukarno did not consistently enforce strong anti-urbanization policies, and Laos did so mainly as a by-product of driving much of its city-dwelling middle class into exile (Chapter 10). None of these three countries are considered in this sub-section, which first looks at Vietnam and then Cambodia.

Vietnam, although concerned until the late 1980s to follow Soviet Marxism, adopted a pragmatic approach to urbanization. The North Vietnamese leadership recognized that 'building socialism' depended on industrialization and that required cities. Vo Nguyen Giap explained: 'The crucial front in our country cannot be the city but our Party does not underestimate the role of the city'.[56] Vietnam implemented strict de-urbanization policies only when it needed to disperse industry and population in the face of American bombing and after re-unification to deal with a refugee problem in cities in the south.

Ideology did little to restrain urban growth in Hanoi after 1943. Urban growth depended mainly on migration, and this was as rapid as anywhere in Southeast Asia, or more so.[57] Between the census years of 1943 and 1974, Hanoi grew from 120,000 to 1,378,000, an annual increase of 7.2 per cent.[58] An enlargement of Hanoi's boundaries in 1961 added some 233,000 to the city. If the increase of 233,000 is subtracted from the 1974 population, growth from 1943 to 1974 was 6.6 per cent annually compared to 1.8 per cent for the country as a whole.[59]

Short-term fluctuations in Hanoi's urbanization were violent and the product of the two Indochina wars.[60] Starting in mid-December 1946, two months of fighting in Hanoi destroyed all essential services and most industry. By 1948–49, perhaps only 10,000 people remained in the city. From the outset of the 1950s, people, including large numbers not previously resident in Hanoi,

[55] Thrift and Forbes, *Price*, p. 29.
[56] Quoted in Thrift and Forbes, *Price*, p. 88 and see Turley, 'Urbanization', pp. 374–77 and 'Urban transformation', p. 624.
[57] Nguyen, 'Urbanization processes', p. 353.
[58] Turley, 'Urbanization', p. 379. A United Nations estimate puts the 1975 population at 1.9 million, Table 17.5.
[59] Turley, 'Urbanization', p. 379.
[60] This paragraph is based on Turley, 'Urbanization'.

began to flood into the city, because occupation by the French Expeditionary Force assured a plentiful food supply and relative safety compared to the Red River Delta, which was subject to ongoing French pacification efforts. In 1952, Hanoi's population, at 217,000, far exceeded its 1943 level and by 1954 had climbed to 400,000.

After the defeat of the French at Dien Bien Phu, their subsequent withdrawal from North Vietnam and the 1954 Geneva Accords, planning the economy in Hanoi took on an added relevance. The 1958–60 Three-Year Plan aimed to transform Hanoi from a 'colonial consumption centre into a producing city' and create industrial sites throughout the city. These sites and some new industrial towns and settlements stimulated Vietnamese urbanization, increasing industry as a share of urban employment from under a fifth in 1955 to 27.6 per cent by 1965.[61] In Hanoi, the establishment of industry and the annexation of outlying areas raised the city's population to 900,000 in 1961. After the United States began bombing in 1966 in Operation Rolling Thunder, Hanoi's population fell by between a third and a half due to evacuation.

Following a temporary halt in bombing in November 1968, people began to come back to Hanoi, but the government discouraged return, and in 1970 the population was 200,000 less than in 1961. In April 1972, when the United States again started bombing Hanoi, it had some 1.2 million people. The authorities, able to draw on the experience of the later 1960s, were successful in speedily and thoroughly evacuating the population. After the 1973 Paris Peace Accords ended the bombing, both former residents and newcomers, ignoring official instructions to remain in the countryside, streamed into Hanoi. Its estimated almost 1.4 million inhabitants in 1974 (the United Nations estimate for 1975 is 1.9 million) created, for the first time, a refugee problem which was worsened by a shortage of housing due to bombing and problems of food supply.

By the last year of the Second Indochina War, some two-fifths of South Vietnam's population lived in Saigon and other southern cities, especially the medium-sized ones of Da Nang, Cam Ranh and Qui Nhon. During the later years of the Second Indochina War, large numbers of people sought refuge in Saigon and its population swelled to 3.5 million and possibly 4.5 million. The city was home to half a million Chinese, 1.5 million slum dwellers and a huge war wreckage of orphaned children, drug addicts and prostitutes.[62]

In the south of Vietnam after re-unification in 1976, two government policies had major effects on urbanization. One was to resettle in the countryside a large share of those in Saigon as well as other southern cities; the other an elimination of the 'comprador bourgeoisie', which drove large numbers of people, including many Chinese, abroad (Chapter 10).

[61] Nguyen, 'Urbanization processes', p. 353.

[62] Turley, 'Urban transformation', pp. 616–17, 622; McCoy, 'Tale of three cities', pp. 37–38; Jones, 'Population trends', p. 791.

Relocation to the countryside of many of those in Ho Chi Minh City and other urban areas was a matter of necessity, since the sustainability of their large populations had depended on an American presence. Although wartime urbanization gave way to government removal and de-urbanization, the latter was less than planners anticipated. By December 1976, between 700,000 and 1 million people had left Ho Chi Minh City for rural areas, either voluntarily or under duress. Under the Second Five-Year Plan of 1976–80, 1.5 million (well short of a target of 4 million) people were relocated both within the south and from north to south. However, large numbers of people drifted back to Ho Chi Minh City and in 1980, its population stood at 3.5 million.[63]

After taking power in Cambodia in April 1975, the Khmer Rouge sent between 2 and 3 million people from cities to the countryside.[64] As well as Phnom Penh – the 'great prostitute on the Mekong' – other cities were evacuated.[65] These included the former royal capital of Oudong, where the Khmer Rouge demolished the town and executed schoolteachers and government officials. McCoy describes the remains in Phnom Penh of an assault of 'primal passion': the ruins of the Central Bank leaving an aftermath of strewn paper currency; every light connection torn from the ceiling of a six-storey building at the university; back streets littered with the carcasses of Volkswagens and Toyotas 'shot, burned and beaten'.[66]

Conceivable reasons for the Khmer Rouge to empty urban Cambodia of its population are to ensure food supply, prevent epidemics, protect against possible American bombing and secure the revolution by the dispersal of opponents.[67] Ideology is, however, the most convincing explanation. Soviet Marxism-Leninism, as argued by Marx and followed in Vietnam, regarded cities as necessary: a capitalist, modernizing force which must triumph over a traditional and backward countryside as a prerequisite for socialism. The Khmer Rouge, adopting a Maoist interpretation of Marxism, inverted Marx's city–rural dichotomy: the countryside was the true nation. To realize the nation and achieve socialism necessitated that the countryside overcome the city and eradicate all foreign influence. Because of their integration with the international market as part of globalization, cities were seen as centres of unproductive work as well as alien ideas which had to be eliminated.

Following the end of the Khmer Rouge's regime, people flooded back to Phnom Penh in an uncontrolled way. Some came back to their former dwellings but others squatted where they might, including in churches and a large cinema built during the colonial era. From 1980 to 2018, Phnom Penh grew at 5.7 per cent annually and to about 2 million, dwarfing Cambodia's other larger cities of Siem Reap and Battambang (Table 17.3).

63 Turley, 'Urban transformation', pp. 616–24; Jones, 'Population trends', pp. 798–99.
64 This paragraph is based on McIntyre, 'Geography as destiny', pp. 730–58.
65 Chandler, *Tragedy*, p. 247.
66 McCoy, 'Tale of three cities', p. 28.
67 Chandler, *Tragedy*, p. 247.

Rural–Urban Migration, Urbanization, Squatters and Slums

Inward migration and over-urbanization – an inward flow of migrants beyond the capacity of cities to offer anything other than informal sector work – was the third main explanation for urban growth. As population increased and land became scarcer, migrants were pushed from the countryside. At the same time, and perhaps even more, migrants, both internal and from other Southeast Asian countries, were drawn to cities as places of opportunity created by some combination of the prospect of work and possibly of even a modern sector job in industry or services; large modern sector wage differentials; and an urban bias in the location of infrastructure and amenities.

In the 1950s and 1960s, the age structure of most Southeast Asian cities was relatively young and natural increase a principal factor in population growth. By the 1970s, however, urban birthrates had slowed and cityward migration joined area expansion as the principal features of Southeast Asian urbanization. Between 1970 and 1989, migrants from elsewhere in Thailand accounted for half of Bangkok's growth.[68] Although internal, often circular, migration remained significant, by the later 1980s immigration from poorer Southeast Asian countries became the principal dynamic adding to the population of Bangkok.[69] The same was true of Singapore and Kuala Lumpur as the main cities in Southeast Asia's net immigrant receiving countries.

A large proportion of cityward migration to cities could be termed 'premature': arrivals far exceeded the totality of formal sector work available from industry's both direct and indirect job creation.[70] As Singapore planners were well aware – and as was later formalized in the Harris–Todaro model of migration – industrialization and its high-wage modern sector jobs would attract such a large number of migrants that 'a paradoxical situation would most probably arise. Increasing levels of employment would not decrease unemployment but increase it.'[71] Premature rural–urban migration perpetuated and enhanced a stark pre-World War II urban dualism of the co-existence of large slums and, after the war, squatter communities alongside modern commercial economies. Slum dwellers and squatters exacerbated social problems because they worked in a bloated, low-productivity informal sector of hawkers, petty traders, unskilled labour and pedicab or taxi drivers. Informal sector workers typically suffer from underemployment, low incomes and inadequate recourse to health facilities.

Singapore alone in Southeast Asia had no slums, since it was entirely urban and, after independence, was able to regulate population inflows. However,

[68] Falkus, 'Bangkok', p. 156.

[69] United Nations, *Thailand migration report 2019*, pp. 9–21.

[70] For the concept of premature migration, see International Labour Organization, *Sharing*, pp. 4, 17, 29, 23, 26.

[71] Singapore, *Development plan, 1961–1964*, p. 10. For the model, see Harris and Todaro, 'Migration, unemployment', pp. 126–42.

Table 17.7 *Southeast Asia population living in slums as a percentage of urban population, 2001–22*

	Myanmar	Thailand	Indonesia	Philippines	Vietnam	Cambodia	Laos
2001	29	26	35	50	45	85	54
2010	45	27	27	43	21	57	37
2014	52	25	24	40	11	45	30
2022	58	24	19	36	32	42	55

Notes and Sources: Data for Thailand are for 2005, 2010, 2014 and 2018 and from World Bank, *World development indicators, 2020*. All other data are from World Bank, *World development indicators, 2025*.

the Republic's many construction and factory guest workers were housed on the city's outskirts in dormitories that by historic standards would likely be deemed as constituting overcrowding, and in some respects as replicating the slums of Singapore's 1950s badly overcrowded Chinatowns on either side of the Singapore River. Migrant workers in Singapore frequented their own shopping and hawker areas in central Singapore and congregated in its open spaces such as around St Andrew's Cathedral.

The World Bank did not report statistics for slums in Malaysia, although in the mid-1970s squatters made up between from just under a third to about two-fifths of Kuala Lumpur's population and slum dwellers about a further 10 per cent, some quarter of a million people in all.[72] Data from the United Nations show that in 2000, 37.4 per cent, and in 2022, 21.6 per cent, of Malaysia's urban population lived in slums and informal settlements.[73] In the late 1980s, well over 1 million Bangkok residents were squatters. Additionally, over 1,000 slums housed squatters.[74] In 2001, about half of the urban populations of the Philippines and Vietnam, a third of those in Indonesia and the great majority of city dwellers in Cambodia lived in slums. By 2022, the proportion of slum dwellers in these countries, but not in Thailand, Laos and Myanmar, had fallen considerably (Table 17.7). To some extent, the fall was because industrialization and its associated economic activity helped to soak up labour surpluses.

Nevertheless, slum populations remained considerable in 2022. They ranged from two-fifths of the urban population in Cambodia, to a third in the Philippines and Vietnam, a quarter in Thailand and a fifth in Indonesia. After

[72] Aiken and Leigh, 'Malaysia's emerging conurbation', pp. 559–60.
[73] United Nations, UN-Habitat, *World cities report, 2024*, p. 302.
[74] United Nations, *Population growth: Bangkok*, pp. 1, 27; Krongkaew, 'Changing urban system', p. 311.

2001 in Vietnam and Cambodia, as these Indochinese economies turned outwards to manufacture for export, the incidence of slum populations dropped sharply. An exception to a fall in the share of those living in slums was Myanmar, where the proportion apparently rose from 29 per cent of urban dwellers in 2001 to 58 per cent in 2022 (Table 17.7).

Conclusion

Urban development in Southeast Asia is a story of geography as destiny: first nature locational advantages were strongly and repeatedly reinforced by both government and private investment decisions. Before 1940, government was largely responsible for the siting of ports and other urban infrastructure on optimal or near optimal sites to connect primary producing hinterlands to export markets. The port locations chosen determined the pattern of Southeast Asia's main cities, apart from Kuala Lumpur, for which both colonial politics and Malaysian independence were crucial.

When in the 1950s Southeast Asia began to industrialize, investors favoured locating industry in the region's existing main cities, because population concentrated there and pre-World War II industry centred in them. Main cities offered the benefits of external economies through established industries; infrastructure and services; and afforded the principal internal markets and lowest cost distribution points for manufactures. A centralization of political power further added to urbanization, notably for Kuala Lumpur, Jakarta and Hanoi. In the 1950s, most main cities were already primate, and in 2018 the same group of cities remained so, allowing Southeast Asia to be regarded, as it has long been, as a region of primate cities.

Regional dualism resulting from the emergence of a few economic growing points within countries is a major theme in Southeast Asian economic history and one to which urbanization adds a further dimension. After 1950, urban growth remained highly unbalanced. Populations in areas that comprised the more traditional parts of Southeast Asia's pre-World War II dual economies typically remained too small and too poor to attract much industrialization. New industries very largely clustered in the main cities. Localization gave good access to world markets through existing communications and transport networks and yielded external economies through close spatial proximity to other, similar firms and their existing knowledge, suppliers and labour pools. The concentration of economic activity attracted migrants. Although between the 1950s and the early twenty-first century the urban pattern became more balanced in some countries, polarization effects largely prevailed, especially for manufacturing. Southeast Asia remained, as throughout its pre-World War II development, a region of a few, hugely dominant cities, unbalanced growth and dualistic economies.

18

Development Assessment, Caveats and Conclusion

After World War II, Southeast Asia made remarkable economic progress and greatly raised living standards. In 1991, Malaysia, the most developed of the region's economies outside of Singapore, envisaged being a 'fully developed country' by 2020.[1] Thailand aimed to become a developed economy by 2037 and Indonesia by 2045.[2] Cambodia aspired to be a high-income country in 2050.[3] But in 2025 for the four countries, these remained targets, and it was unclear, even for Malaysia, how, when or if developed status would be achieved.[4]

Much of the post-war progress started in the 1970s, when Southeast Asian trade and growth began to benefit from what Kuznets termed an 'epochal innovation', the electronics revolution, and all the changes in technology, communications and production that came with it.[5] As with the late nineteenth-century epochal transport and communication revolutions, Southeast Asian economies were reactive to the new changes in the global economy. The region was no more than a junior partner in the electronics revolution, a follower rather than being responsible for global innovation. But, as for much of the period between the 1870s and 1939, trade was again a strong Southeast Asian growth engine and through it, the region underwent fundamental economic transformation.

This concluding chapter has two purposes. Both focus principally on post-1970 economic developments, since the effects of World War II and political independence in dividing the region into socialist and capitalist countries were dealt with at length in Parts II, III and IV of the book. One aim of the chapter is to provide some assessment of development policies and how these made possible Southeast Asia's economic transformation through reacting to opportunities created by globalization and world trade expansion. The other

[1] Mahathir Mohamad, *Malaysian: the way forward (vision 2020)*, p. 1.

[2] Thailand, *National strategy*, foreword; Indonesia, Ministry of National Development Planning, 'Indonesia Vision 2045'; World Bank, *Funding Indonesia's vision*, pp. 2, 20.

[3] Menon and Naqvi, 'Structural transformation', p. 81.

[4] Malaysia, National Economic Advisory Council, *New economic model*, pp. iv, 35; Resosudarmo and Abdurohman, 'Is being stuck', pp. 144, 161–62; Negara and Ramayandi, 'Laying the foundations', pp. 9–10.

[5] Kuznets, *Modern economic growth*, pp. 1–16 and 'Modern economic growth', pp. 247–48.

main purpose is to consider how far Southeast Asia's countries traversed a path towards development by achieving modern economic growth. Between the 1870s and the 1930s, Southeast Asian GDP per capita fell further behind the advanced economies. Was the region, or at least some countries in it, after 1970 catching up with the global leaders?

The chapter's initial section looks at the GDP per capita income rankings of countries in the region between 1870 and 2022. This section as well as the second and third sections reflect on the special cases of Singapore and Myanmar, the conditions for growth, the policy choices of countries and why over 150 years country rank order changed so little. The fourth and fifth sections examine the dual economy and plural society respectively, themes highlighted in the Introduction as running throughout the book. How did these two *problematik* of Benda evolve in modern Southeast Asia?[6] In the sixth section, the slowing of growth in some Southeast Asian countries and the region's catch-up in GDP per capita with the world leaders are assessed. The seventh section points to caveats. These suggest that as a path to modern economic growth, the recent Southeast Asian development model is incomplete. The book's conclusion follows.

Growth Rankings

Southeast Asia illustrates Nurkse's 'first law of development': 'To those who have shall be given.'[7] With few exceptions, the rank order of the seven Southeast Asian countries for which statistics are available was the same in 2022 as it had been in 1938 or in 1870. Over a century and a half, Singapore and Malaysia ranked first and second respectively. Burma and Vietnam, in that order, had the lowest per capita incomes in 1870 and still did so in 2022. However, the gap between rich and poor widened sharply. In 1870, Southeast Asian countries were bunched at not too dissimilar per capita incomes: the average of the leading two countries was only about half as much again as the bottom two. By 2022, per capita incomes in Singapore were eight times, and in Malaysia four times, those of the two poorest countries (Table 18.1).

One reason for a relatively unchanging order is that countries stay ahead if they begin with a head start and grow at similar speeds to their poorer counterparts. Second, a land lucky in natural resources and empty at the outset of growth is likely to start ahead. Subsequently, it probably has an edge over

6 Benda, 'Structure', p. 132.

7 Nurkse, *Equilibrium and growth*, p. 288. Nurkse attributes the remark to A. K. Cairncross, who may, however, have been influenced by the Bible, Matthew 12:13: 'For whosoever hath, to him shall be given, and he shall have more abundance: but whosoever hath not, from him shall be taken away even that he hath' (King James Version).

resource-poor, more densely populated areas, because relatively few people share in resource gains and because these can be used to finance development.

Malaysia, mostly jungle in the 1870s, was fortunate both in starting as a lightly populated region and in its rich resource base. Beginning with a low man-to-land ratio in 1870, over the next century and a half the Malay Peninsula offered a succession of resource-intensive staples: first tin, then rubber, the early twentieth-century boom commodity, followed by palm oil and timber and finally the later twentieth-century boom commodities of oil and natural gas. Singapore had in its geographical position an appreciating natural resource. Moreover, since 1819, when Raffles founded modern Singapore, it has consistently made the most of its location, maximizing this 'first nature' natural advantage through 'second nature' advantages of population and built environment and through a policy of free trade.

The countries – Burma, Vietnam and Indonesia until the later 1960s – that began at the bottom remained at or near there. Part of the explanation for why these nations stayed near the bottom lies in their post-World War II attempts to implement some form of socialism. And part of the explanation for a choice of socialist policies may be that starting the post-war period behind other Southeast Asian countries and seeing the example of rapid Soviet Union growth pushed these countries towards some form of socialism. Southeast Asian socialist experiments cost decades of growth. With other policies, growth would almost certainly have been higher. In 1966, when Indonesia abandoned an attempt at building socialism, it grew faster and, between 1938 and 2022, retained its rank order of four above the Philippines, Vietnam and Burma (Myanmar), these last three enmeshed in inward-looking policies for much of the period after 1950. Indonesia had the disadvantage of increasingly overpopulated Java, making it difficult to register per capita income gains despite plentiful Outer Island resources.

Singapore and Myanmar

These countries warrant a section for two reasons. One is their ranking at extreme ends of successful Southeast Asian growth, and why this is so requires a particular attempt at explanation. The other is that, in different ways, the two countries evolved into special cases.

Singapore is a special case partly because it is a city state. That has allowed its development to sidestep the need for an agricultural revolution. As a city on world transport routes, Singapore can draw on an elastic world food supply; and has no need for structural change in agriculture to furnish labour for other sectors of the economy or for higher agricultural earnings to provide a market for local manufactures. In manufacturing for export, Singapore's small size and manufacture for the world market allow the Republic fully to obtain the gains from trade specialization and realize available economies of scale. In the early 1990s, the production in Singapore of half of the world's disk drives is an example of these trade gains which, furthermore, accrued to a population of only a city.

Second, Singapore's geographical location, centred on the most important world sea, air and electronic communication routes and in a time zone linking Asia and Europe, gives it opportunities for the provision of international services unavailable to other main Southeast Asian cities. Even insofar as these cities grow through services provision, the effect on national per capita growth is diluted by large rural sectors. Third, Singapore can regulate labour supply, drawing on migrant labour as needed but terminating work visas in downturns. Migrant inflows, in combination with tight government control over wage increases, allowed Singapore to preserve a relatively low-wage manufacturing economy and to continue to attract foreign investment in search of cheap labour.[8] Singapore shows how governments can further development, but no other Southeast Asian economy fully embraced the Republic's developmental state model in directing the accumulation of physical and human capital.

The Singapore government's single-minded emphasis on growth above, or even to the exclusion of, all else was, however, at the expense of perceived inequality by Singapore citizens. Globalization exacerbated this perception, and in the late 1990s it became a significant problem.[9] In 2018, household members in the top decile had 24 times the income of the bottom decile.[10] More important, however, than the relatively slight changes after 2000 in measures of inequality appears to have been the daily 'felt' or 'lived' inequalities among Singaporeans. In Singapore, 'inequality is palpably experienced at the day-to-day level of the person-in-the-street', an experience partly owing to large influxes of wealthy foreigners and, among the rich, blatant conspicuous consumption such as the purchase of luxury cars.[11] For many Singaporeans, retirement saving came through the Central Provident Fund which was mandatory and fully funded. The scheme's forced saving enabled Singaporeans to own Housing Development Board flats when they were relatively young, but as they aged it left many 'asset rich and cash poor'.[12] A large number of poorer individuals had a house as their main asset and were unable to protect themselves in retirement from poverty and from ill health.

Myanmar is perhaps best described as caught in a politically induced low-level economic equilibrium trap since soon after World War II. In 2011, the government of President Thein Sein replaced rule by the State Peace and

8 Pang and Lim, 'Labour, productivity and Singapore's development', pp. 9–10, 16.
9 Tan, *Singapore*, p. 12.
10 Peng, 'Inequality', p. 359.
11 Tan, *Singapore*, p. 35.
12 McCarthy et al. 'Asset rich and cash poor', pp. 198, 214–15.

Development Council (a renamed and still military-dominated reincarnation of the State Law and Order Restoration Council dating from 1988) and introduced a 20-year National Comprehensive Development Plan. Under the new government, Myanmar's economy was partially liberalized and appeared to have significant potential for economic growth. Elections were held in 2015.

International agencies and a number of knowledgeable observers believed that, after more than 70 years, as the outcome of a 'Burmese spring', Myanmar had relegated its past to history and turned a corner.[13] In 2003, compulsory procurement of rice crops at below market prices and rationing to consumers were abandoned, and the 2011 government completely liberalized the international rice trade. Garment manufacture on the outskirts of Yangon and Mandalay generated exports. Rural–urban migration increased, partly in response to opportunities for manufacturing jobs, and the resulting higher rural wages encouraged agricultural mechanization, all of which suggested rural transformation.[14]

But history and a praetorian state in which the army held all civil as well as military top positions were not so easily overcome.[15] Change was cut short by a military coup in February 2021. Myanmar reverted to a policy of rice self-sufficiency. High inflation was accompanied by currency depreciation. Widespread street protests, strikes, serious civil disobedience and ongoing civil wars, along with Covid, worsened an already dire economy. In 2021, GDP reportedly fell by 18 per cent.[16] The political pre-conditions for Myanmar to escape its low-level equilibrium trap are beyond the scope of this book but imperative for the welfare of the population.

Growth Reflections and Lessons

After World War II, every Southeast Asian leader aspired to growth and industrialization, but the characteristics of economies and politics in the region imposed strict limits on policies to pursue these goals. This section identifies considerations that were important to growth and which help to explain why some countries advanced more rapidly than others. Salient factors, intertwined with one another, were stability, comparative advantage and resources, prices, policy choices, administration and development planning, corruption and war. All these relate to the creation of surpluses and whether they are used to promote growth.

13 Bünte, 'Myanmar's protracted transition', pp. 369–91.
14 Belton and Filipski, 'Rural transformation', pp. 166–67, 170, 173–75.
15 The description praetorian state is used by Callahan, *Making enemies*, p. 18.
16 Boughton et al., 'Agriculture and rural livelihoods', pp. 112, 117–18, 124–26, 131–34; OECD, *Multi-dimensional review of Myanmar*, pp. 59–60.

Political and Economic Stability

Stability – both political and economic – is essential for growth. After the early post-World War II turbulence of revolutions, civil conflict and inter-country wars, by the later 1960s most countries in Southeast Asia were politically and socially stable, although the firm establishment of a region-wide settled political order came later in Indochina and not at all in Myanmar. Agreement between countries within the region was paralleled and reinforced by internal stability within countries.

Three reasons for the region's stability were the steadying influence of the Association of Southeast Asian Nations (ASEAN), described as an 'ecosystem for peace'; the success of most countries in achieving economic growth; and the avoidance of crises as well as, on the whole, sensible and predictable macroeconomic policies.[17] The three reasons worked together, reinforcing one another.

After the formation of ASEAN by the five outward-looking countries in Bangkok in 1967, it seemed a good bet that the Association would have as little influence as most regional organizations or even break apart. ASEAN had as its founding objectives only the somewhat nebulous goals of growth and cultural unity. However, ASEAN became, somewhat against the odds, probably the world's most successful regional organization apart from the European Union.

Several factors explain why ASEAN gained the acceptance of its members and became an important institution promoting regional stability. In the early years, as Mahbubani and Sng argue, two of these were that a fear of communism gave a convincing reason for mutual cooperation and that this could be enforced by a number of strong leaders. Probably, the most important continuing incentive to maintaining peace and stability was that anything else would threaten growth.[18]

By 1999, ASEAN consisted of 10 member states and encompassed all of Southeast Asia. Although maligned for a ponderous, consensus-required, lowest-common-denominator style, ASEAN afforded a forum that institutionalized and promoted regional accord. As such, the Association remained of fundamental importance to supporting a settled Southeast Asia. Members of ASEAN continued broadly to decide to put aside their many historical differences (and grievances) and get along with each other. ASEAN moved progressively to free trade among members with an ASEAN integration scheme in 1992 and the ASEAN Trade in Goods Agreement adopted in Thailand in 2010. Free trade agreements within Asia under the ASEAN+1 scheme – including with China in 2005 as well as with much of the rest of Asia – ensured member states' crucial access to supply chains and export markets.[19]

[17] Mahbubani and Sng, *ASEAN miracle*, p. 12.
[18] Mahbubani and Sng, *ASEAN miracle*, pp. 50–51.
[19] Anas and Narjoko, 'International cooperation', pp. 300–06.

Relative economic stability was as important in accounting for the region's development success as its stable – if authoritarian or semi-authoritarian – politics. Crucially, economic crises were generally averted, if with obvious exceptions like the Philippines in the 1980s and the Asian financial crisis. For most of this period, macroeconomic management was reasonably prudent and safeguarded the international competitiveness essential to countries dependent on their export orientation. Competent central banks, again excepting the Philippines during the 1980s, kept inflation under control, avoided severe exchange rate misalignment and held public debt within acceptable limits, averting the need to finance through wholesale monetary expansion. Macroeconomic orthodoxy conferred a 'regime credibility' which attracted investors. After the fall of Sukarno and with the 'New Order', that credibility extended to Indonesia, and then to Indochina. Myanmar was the regional exception.[20] The post-1966 resurgence of Indonesia could be generalized to elsewhere in Southeast Asia: it was not a miracle but the outcome of an environment in which government 'got its policies "right" more often than it has not'.[21]

Comparative Advantage and Prices

Throughout the period covered in this book, Southeast Asia was a region of small, open economies with limited home markets. International trade was always – and remained – the region's best option as an 'engine of growth'. Southeast Asia's comparative advantage has been, in varying combinations and at different times, the exploitation of land suitable for certain tropical agricultural products, adding value to them through processing prior to export and mobilizing labour surpluses. By the 1970s, comparative advantage lay chiefly in utilizing a factor endowment of abundant labour to produce labour-intensive manufactured goods for export.

Manufactured exports were Southeast Asia's best industrialization and development opportunity. Because of restricted home markets and the scale economies associated with manufactured materials and heavy industry, development based on these manufacturing sectors would be difficult and likely uneconomic. Countries would have to produce at costs competitive on the world market and, until they did, accept that industries would be maintained through subsidies and be confined to import substitution. Such policies risked perpetuating manufacturing through a soft budget constraint and creating a lobby of rent-seeking interests. The socialist countries – Vietnam, Cambodia, Laos, Burma and Indonesia – grew slowly, if at all, partly because they stuck dogmatically to industrialization policies favouring heavy industry and import substitution.

[20] Hill, 'Indonesia's industrial policy', p. 154; see also Yusuf, 'East Asian miracle', pp. 10–15.
[21] Hill, *Indonesian economy*, p. 10.

'Getting the prices right' was basic to Southeast Asian post-1970 growth, because it enabled the region to develop according to its comparative advantage of abundant labour and the export of manufactures.[22] A flexible labour market in which wages were close to the supply price of labour attracted multinationals and foreign investment, a main constituent of the region's development from the 1970s onwards. Countries that grew fastest – Malaysia, Thailand and Singapore – quickly recognized the importance of ensuring competitive pricing for the mobilization of labour. The role in employment creation of attention to the price mechanism and wage levels reflective of comparative advantage were important lessons of Southeast Asian development.[23] The employment that multinationals created, both directly and indirectly, facilitated growth and high domestic saving and so increased capital accumulation.

Market wages did not, however, come about automatically but often were engineered through government intervention. Malaysia and Thailand kept wages low by admitting large numbers of immigrant workers. Thailand offered weak terms of employment, making the dismissal of labour relatively easy.[24] Singapore regulated wage growth through the government taking control of the unions and extensive reliance on foreign, non-resident workers who could be sent home at any time. In 2024, Singapore had some 1.8 million non-residents out of a total population of 6 million. Most non-residents were immigrant workers or domestic servants. Singapore's flexible labour force management was apparent when, during the Covid pandemic, between 2019 and 2021 the number of foreign workers fell by 194,000 but by 2024 had risen by 299,000.[25] For Malaysia, Thailand and Singapore, the lesson is the need, after an exhaustion of labour surplus, to invest in technology, training and education to attract higher value-added and higher-waged employment.

At the same time as exporting manufactures, Thailand and Malaysia continued to exploit a comparative advantage of existing agricultural knowledge and still vacant land to remain as major primary commodity exporters. For both countries, continued large commodity exports and primary export diversification were valuable sources of foreign exchange and buoyed national income. Primary sector exchange earnings helped Malaysia to avoid a balance-of-payments crisis, despite an unsuccessful foray into heavy industry and automobile manufacture initiated under Prime Minister Mahathir Mohamad and his 'Look East' project. Import-substitution phases in Thailand and Malaysia were

[22] The phrase which appears often in the World Bank, *East Asian miracle* is 'getting the fundamentals right', for example, pp. 23, 347. The Bank regards prices as a key ingredient of correct fundamentals and 'market friendly' policies, another commonly used phrase. Dercon makes similar points about stability, credibility and macroeconomic fundamentals. Dercon, *Gambling*, pp. 39–42.

[23] For example, see Little, *Economic development*, pp. 80–85, 358–61.

[24] Hewison and Tularak, 'Thailand and precarious work', pp. 449–55.

[25] Singapore, *Population in brief 2024*, pp. 7–9.

moderate and relatively brief, before both countries, following Singapore's lead, began to grow rapidly through manufacturing for export.

Governments in socialist Southeast Asia largely ignored, both for industry and agriculture, the price system and its allocative and incentive signals. In the socialist countries, declines in agricultural exports to far below pre-World War II levels were the result of low administered prices, which destroyed incentives to production. Indonesia, and even more Burma and Vietnam, became shortage economies. Falls in exports took away a principal source of foreign exchange to finance development and led to repeated balance-of-payments crises. Vietnam and the other Indochinese countries of Cambodia and Laos commenced rapid growth only when governments began to take more account of their citizens and, crucially, after policy reform that abandoned Soviet-style socialism turned the economies towards the world market to export labour-intensive goods. In Vietnam, between 1975 and *doi moi* in the late 1980s, people used the phrase 'Drunk with victory' to explain the mindset of the army and the imposition of 'a time of tyranny and waste, a headless attempt to create a visionary socialist state in defiance of reality'.[26]

Policy Choices

Just as Singapore's development suggests a role for good policies, so does the experience of other countries indicate the problems of poor choices. Southeast Asia lends support to Meier's observation that 'a country is poor because of poor policies'.[27] In the rank ordering of countries, the Philippines, held back by unfortunate post-World War II policies and endemic corruption, fell from third in 1938 to fifth by 2022, while over the same period Thailand, more outward-looking and with more appropriate policies for growth, rose from fifth to third (Table 18.1).

Where post-World War II developmental problems arose, it was often because, as Scalapino observed, leaders were 'skilled primarily in the art of politics. Understandably, economic matters were beyond their competence and, more important, usually outside the mainstream of their interest.'[28] U Nu and Ne Win in Burma as well as Sukarno in Indonesia abundantly demonstrated a lack of economic knowledge and, of greater significance, any concern with economics. Until the late 1980s, Indochina's communist leaders remained convinced that Marxist politics were also the correct economics for their countries.

After World War II, Burma, Indonesia and Vietnam – both as North Vietnam and after re-unification Vietnam – soon encountered severe fiscal difficulties. It was impossible for countries at as early a stage of industrialization as Southeast Asia's after World War II to maintain a plethora of import-substituting,

26 Sheehan, *Two cities*, p. 14.
27 Meier, *Leading issues*, preface to fifth edition.
28 Scalapino, *Politics of development*, p. 45.

Table 18.1 *Southeast Asia GDP per capita and rank ordering, 1870–2022 (2011 US$)*

	1870 GDP per capita	1870 rank	1938 GDP per capita	1938 rank	2022 GDP per capita	2022 rank
Singapore	1,423	1	3,363	1	80,320	1
Malaysia	1,055	2	2,515	2	26,629	2
Philippines	995	3	2,295	3	8,371	5
Thailand	969	4	1,317	5	16,421	3
Indonesia	810	5	1,655	4	12,802	4
Vietnam	805	6	–	–	8,050	6
Burma	803	7	1,180	6 or 7	5,177	7

Source: Maddison Project Database, 2023.

state-sponsored projects without, at the same time, a rapid expansion of exports or taxes to finance the import substitution. Public goods such as education and health, demanded by expectant, post-colonial populations, cannot be successfully increased without finance through taxation. The power to levy taxes effectively requires a government with fiscal or state capacity.[29]

Socialist Southeast Asia neither expanded exports nor taxed effectively, turning to monetary expansion to finance budget deficits. Administered prices and a rejection of incentives for producers undermined exports. Unsurprisingly, these fell. Vietnam failed to mobilize finance through agricultural collectivization and Burma and Indonesia through their tax systems. In Indonesia, declines in tax revenue reflected an inelastic tax system and falls in exports which, through trade taxes, were a major source of revenue. At the same time as budget revenue in Burma and Indonesia came under pressure, strains on government expenditure grew, because rural credit given through cooperatives or other government agencies was inefficiently distributed, because state enterprises were generally poorly managed, and because these ventures, justified partly on grounds of indigenization, were often economically inappropriate to the current stage of economic development.

Development Planning

All Southeast Asian countries, once independent, issued development plans at intervals, usually of five years but in some cases as short as two years and as long as 10. Frequently the plans were blueprints of desirable objectives, and governments, apart from communist Vietnam, lacked adequate means of enforcement. Sometimes the plans, notably in Sukarno's Indonesia, were fantasy or, as in Burma, ill-conceived and over-ambitious.

[29] Besley and Persson, 'Taxation', p. 52.

Southeast Asian planning experience shows, as Lewis reminds us, that: 'The economics of development is not very complicated; the secret of successful planning lies more in sensible politics and good public administration.'[30] Singapore, although with the relatively easy problem of managing a city not a country, provided the one outstanding Southeast Asian example of effective administration. The combination in Vietnam, after the late 1980s, of a communist political system and capitalist mixed private and state economy demonstrated that stable government and rational administration count for more than any particular economic regime.

Corruption and Rent-seeking

Embedded in every Southeast Asian regime, except Singapore's, was historic widespread corruption. Southeast Asia does not accord with the World Bank's 'East Asian miracle' of an unbiased, uninvolved government–business relationship. Neither, excepting Singapore, were Southeast Asian countries developmental states or even strong states as envisaged by the World Bank.[31]

Rapid growth in Southeast Asia and authoritarian or semi-authoritarian regimes provided considerable scope for the accumulation of wealth through rent-seeking. *The Economist* index of crony capitalism divides the source of the wealth of billionaires into rent-seeking and non-rent-seeking sectors and then ranks countries by billionaires' wealth gained in rent-seeking sectors as a percentage of GDP. On that measure, Malaysia ranked third in the world, behind Russia in first place. Singapore came fourth (partly owing to the dominance of government and importance of contacts and with this possibly an easing of vigilance against corruption and acceptance of personal relationships), Thailand ninth and Indonesia fifteenth.[32]

Corruption in Indonesia was firmly institutionalized by the time Sukarno left office in 1966, and flourished on the fertile ground of a labyrinthine regulatory system and large state-owned sector.[33] An estimated 60 per cent of business in Indonesia came under the influence of private lobbying interests.[34] At the least, the conclusion in 2010 of Malaysia's National Economic Advisory Council applied, and continued to apply, throughout Southeast Asia. The Council pointed to a raised cost of doing business 'due to rent-seeking, patronage and opaque government procurement. This has engendered pervasive corruption, which needs to be addressed earnestly.'[35]

30 Lewis, *Development planning*, preface.
31 World Bank, *East Asian miracle*, pp. 7, 11, 26, 86–102; Yusuf, 'East Asian miracle', p. 6.
32 'The 2023 crony-capitalism index', *The Economist*, 2 May 2023.
33 Booth, *Economic change*, pp. 218–23.
34 Verhezen, 'Review of *Ethics, business and capitalism*', p. 161.
35 Malaysia, National Economic Advisory Council, *New economic model*, p. 61, see also pp. 7, 135.

As well as favours to the well-connected, Thai government officials and army officers practised a relatively gentle corruption of bureaucratic capitalism which required cooperation between state power and Chinese business if the latter was to operate at all. Like Thailand, corruption in Malaysia and Indonesia took the form of businessmen needing to enlist the alliance of a patron politician to operate and realize rents. These surpluses could have gone towards development but instead enriched individuals.

Sometimes Malaysian corruption, as with the 1MBD scandal, took the form of the outright theft of state funds by government officials. That episode involved the deposit of approximately US$ 1 billion directly into the bank account of Prime Minister Najib Razak. In Vietnam and Myanmar, socialist Southeast Asia raised corruption to the level of forcing the entire society to trade on the black market and steal from the state merely to survive.

The Marcos regime in the Philippines was a kleptocracy. Yet in this regard it was outdistanced by military governments in Burma after the mid-1960s which made the entire state their personal fiefdom. Malaysia and Indonesia were able to grow and partly compensate for policy mistakes, corruption and extractive regimes through drawing on their rich resource bases. By contrast, Burma's resources were more limited and its policies so extreme and dogmatic that it was not possible to overcome the impediments they imposed.[36]

The Philippines emphasized import substitution far too much and for too long. The creation of a strong lobby of rent-seeking industrialists helped to prolong import substitution and promote an economy of private interests geared towards gaining monopoly profits for themselves, not growth. The 1966 election of Marcos and his 20-year reign elevated already endemic corruption to new heights and led to a sharp reversal in growth. A growth turnaround was not evident until the 1990s, after the implementation of more appropriate policies than had been followed historically. The 2021 coup in Myanmar cut short what might have been an opening towards more outward-oriented policies, and plunged the country into a continuation of widespread civil war.

In Vietnam, corruption and rent-seeking thrived. *Doi moi*, followed by state capitalism and privatization, led to the emergence of 'a political-business complex that commercializes the state's ownership of land, policy, firms and funds for private interests'. In Vietnam, the state owned all the land. Not infrequently, local and central government officials as well as state-owned companies used this state ownership to take land to sell at a profit, often to cronies or family members. Infrastructure development, like that, for example, in Malaysia, was subject to rampant rent-seeking.[37]

[36] Cf. Perkins, *East Asian development*, pp. 55, 108, 120, 152.

[37] Vuving, 'Vietnam in 2018', p. 376 for the quote and see p. 384.

War and Conflict

As well as undermining growth through creating uncertainty and instability, war and civil conflict waste resources. Growth in Indonesia, Myanmar and Vietnam was held back by the predominantly unproductive use of surpluses to channel large funds to the military and the drain of wars. Sukarno in Indonesia appropriated funds that could have gone towards development to support his romantic desire to renew a revolutionary spirit through, first, civil war and then Confrontation with Malaysia. Civil wars have been endemic in Myanmar since it gained independence. One result was to help entrench a military regime serving only its own interests. Almost three decades of two Indochinese wars diverted resources and destroyed physical and human capital.

Dualism

Late nineteenth-century globalization created dual economies and late twentieth-century globalization did not erase these inherited divisions. Rather, post-World War II development concentrated in regions that were already a country's more developed and fastest-growing ones, building on earlier localization and perpetuating dualism. Malaya's pre-war tin and rubber belt centred on the peninsula's west coast and the post-1970 expansion of Metropolitan Kuala Lumpur is an example but not an isolated one. A concentration of economic activity around Bangkok is another instance and the growth of Singapore and Manila are cases in point.

The dominant cities that developed after 1870 retained this same status in the twenty-first century. Post-independence governments invested disproportionately in the region's largest cities. On Malaysia's west coast, government funds were poured into Kuala Lumpur, while the neighbouring state of Perak to the north and its capital of Ipoh looked much the same in 2025 as they had in 1975. The siting of industry in the main cities, together with still large employment in low-productivity agriculture, further sharpened rural–urban dualism.

Dualism and division persisted for three reasons. One was that investors found regions of existing growth the most attractive sites for further investment. They offered already established networks of transport and communications, supplies of power and water, sources of skilled labour, nearness to established enterprises with associated externalities and the largest internal markets. Second, after 1960 in most countries agricultural productivity, measured as value added per worker, remained relatively low. The development of agriculture, despite advances in technology and a green revolution, was insufficient to eliminate the dualism of a low-productivity peasant sector.

Third, historically large cityward migration resulted from a combination of population increase beyond the availability of vacant land, the limited absorptive capacity of agriculture, people's rising expectations and the possibility of urban jobs at wages far above rural earnings. Much of this migration was 'premature': it bore little relation to the availability of jobs created by urban modern sector industrialization and services. Premature migration expanded the urban low-earning, informal component of Southeast Asia's dual economies. The growth of this 'non-modern' sector enhanced an existing urban dualism of formal and informal sectors to stand alongside countryside dualism of a modern and a still only partly modernized agricultural sector, and so a divided rural economy.

Plural Society and Entrepreneurship

Plural Society

After independence, Southeast Asian countries might have moved towards some mutually agreed assimilation that eradicated, if gradually, the plural society's ethnic, religious and regional divisions. That accommodation, or at least some acceptable equilibrium, did not, however, always happen and, where it did, only partially and only in some countries, principally Thailand, the Philippines and Singapore. For much of Southeast Asia, Scalapino's 1989 comment remained broadly true: 'Asian societies have made little if any progress in race relations.'[38]

Perhaps the barriers of past history and ingrained ethnic differences were always too great to overcome. The plural society was, as Furnivall observed, no more than 'a business partnership rather than a family concern, and the social will common to all groups and holding them together is restricted to their common interests'.[39] After independence, historical legacies that discouraged the perception of a common interest included the social divisions inherent in plural societies, their long entrenchment under colonial rule, a lack of majority, indigenous economic participation except mainly as cultivators and early post-World War II oversupplied labour markets allowing choice in hiring. Ethnic conflict during and after World War II, the suddenness of independence and the rise in expectations accompanying it were not conducive to tolerance.

Southeast Asian societies responded to legacies of plural societies in three ways, ranging from the least tolerant to the most. Intolerance was greatest under the socialist regimes of Myanmar (Burma), Indonesia and Vietnam. In all these countries, a principal reaction to the plural society was periodic, or even concerted, attempts to try to eliminate it through the expulsion of minorities.

Efforts aimed at elimination were the most organized in Myanmar and Vietnam, where they had strong government backing. In Myanmar, the government oversaw the purging of an Indian presence, already depleted by World War II. In the 1960s, Indians were forced to leave and stripped of all their

[38] Scalapino, *Politics of development*, p. 122.
[39] Furnivall, 'Political economy of the tropical Far East', p. 204.

possessions. However, the Myanmar government had limited scope to expel the many ethnic minorities who had always lived in the country. Before, during and for decades after World War II, accommodation between the Burman majority and some of the country's many ethnic minorities no more than temporarily occurred. Civil war between the government and at least one, and generally several, of Myanmar's minority groups was almost constant. During the 2020s, there was renewed hostility to the minority Rohingyas and an attempt to drive them out of Myanmar.

After the communist government gained control in North Vietnam, Chinese and Catholic minorities, along with many professionals, perhaps 1 million in all, flooded southwards to the Republic of Vietnam. Following Vietnam's reunification, government reforms in 1978 had the twin objectives of building socialism and, in the south, expropriating ethnic Chinese business which centred in Ho Chi Minh City. Government security officials destroyed Chinese homes, and in 1978–79 alone at least 400,000 people, including large numbers of Chinese, left Vietnam. Mass exodus, most notoriously of the 'boat people', began in 1978 and continued into the 1990s. As departure was sustained, it comprised, as well as ethnic Chinese, an even greater number of other people, mainly those who had opposed the regime.

During the 1950s and 1960s, Indonesian politicians responded to widespread and long-standing popular resentment and envy of Chinese commercial success with highly discriminatory educational and economic policies. Periodic anti-Chinese riots, including the one in 1998, and destruction of Chinese shops, insufficiently policed by the authorities, marked Indonesia's post-World War II history. Although Indonesian Chinese reacted to this violence by leaving the country, they tended to return. A Chinese presence (about 3 per cent to as much as 5 per cent of the population) remained quite firmly in evidence in Indonesia. After overt anti-Chinese discrimination from 1966 to 1996 under the New Order, Indonesian governments became more accepting of ethnic diversity and allowed Chinese participation in the political process.[40]

In 2025, Chinese had full citizenship rights and at the national level official discrimination no longer existed. However, Chinese still faced a 'grassroots racism', often justified on religious grounds, and might be called by the pejorative *aseng* (economic threat, a Trojan horse for China and communism).[41] Assimilated Chinese, often through the marriage of a Chinese businessman to the daughter of a wealthy Indonesian, predominated at the head of Indonesia's large conglomerates. Nevertheless, indigenous Indonesians received preferential treatment: when small business was *pribumi* (indigenous)-owned, that it needed special assistance was an article of faith.[42]

[40] Chin and Tanasaldy, 'Ethnic Chinese', pp. 961–65.
[41] Tanasaldy, 'From official to grassroots racism', pp. 463–64, 467–68.
[42] Hill, 'Myths', p. 265.

Thailand and the Philippines came the closest to an assimilation of their Chinese minorities. Although manifestations of pluralism such as Chinatowns existed in these countries, many leading business figures were Thai-Chinese or Filipino-Chinese. One factor promoting assimilation was probably that ethnic characteristics and religious preferences were not insurmountably different. Perhaps more important, Chinese business ability was useful to the numerically dominant group and could frequently be incorporated through intermarriage. The latter ensured the official acceptability of citizenship. Between the 1980s and 1990s in Thailand, assimilation occurred rapidly enough to eliminate discrimination against wealthy Thai-Chinese. In the Philippines, little ill-feeling existed towards major Chinese businessmen if they were citizens and long-standing residents.[43]

For over a decade following independence, Malaysia maintained a plural society more or less along colonial lines, although with Malay now the national language. Pluralism proved unacceptable, however, to the politically dominant *Bumiputera* (Malays and other indigenous peoples) majority, because business continued to be dominated by foreigners, mainly Europeans, as well as Malaysian Chinese. The New Economic Policy, formulated after the May 1969 riots, aimed to redress economic and social imbalance by giving Malays a greater stake in Malaysian society. An ethnic equalization process ended a plural society accommodation of Malay political power but Chinese business dominance.

Through legislation, Malaysia's Chinese and Indian minorities were relegated to a second-class citizenship, and discriminated against economically, educationally and socially. Malays had preference in university entry, and Chinese, if able to afford the cost, sent their children abroad for tertiary education. Chinese and Indian freedoms were compromised by Malaysia's increasingly Islamic state. By 2019, political Islam was 'now the only game in the Malay polity'.[44] Malaysian Chinese (or Indians) had no hope of equal citizenship rights unless they converted to Islam and adopted Malay culture.[45] Nevertheless, as for the indigenous groups in Thailand and the Philippines, large Malay businesses generally could not do without Chinese business acumen and often incorporated a Chinese partner.

Singapore dealt with the inheritance of a plural society by maintaining a number of its features through a policy of 'multiculturalism' based on the so-called CMIO (Chinese-Malays-Indians-Others) model along with government-enforced social tolerance.[46] One method of forestalling possible conflict was to break up ethnic concentrations through a careful mixing of ethnic groups in

43 Milne, 'Privatization', pp. 11–13, 25.
44 Chin and Tanasaldy, 'Ethnic Chinese', p. 975.
45 Chin, 'Racism', p. 458.
46 Tan, *Singapore: identity*, pp. 20–26.

government-built housing where most Singaporeans lived. However, groups had quite different starting points which prejudiced equality of opportunity.[47] Advancement was judged on the narrowly defined criterion of merit; and Singapore's fierce meritocracy largely ignored historically determined differences in equality and opportunity. Poorer households were at a disadvantage, since they were unable to afford the private tuition which almost three-quarters of Singapore students had. The lagging status of the Malays remained, as it was in 1990, among the most conspicuous failures of the plural society in Singapore. In 2020, Malays were more than three times less likely than Chinese, and four times less likely than Indians, to have a university qualification.[48]

Entrepreneurship, Privatization and Rent-seeking

The mobility of foreign factors – J. S. Mill's 'indirect benefits' of trade – was always fundamental to Southeast Asian development, but beginning in the 1970s assumed a new importance when international capital flowed into the region on an unprecedented scale. Because much of this capital took the form of foreign direct investment, it brought a wave of new entrepreneurship due to a wholesale arrival of multinational corporations. The new skills, technology, management and entrepreneurs that came to Southeast Asia from the 1970s onwards were basic to its development.

The state became a second, new entrepreneurial group. Its role had already started to grow under colonialism, for example in Burma, but expanded much more after independence, for three main reasons. One was that as economies grew, governments generally assumed more responsibilities and their economic presence expanded. Governments were responsible for providing, or at least regulating, services with elements of natural monopoly, like water, gas and electricity, as well as some infrastructure. As the need for these increased so did the role of government. Government also engaged in business as the default option when enterprises would cease to exist in the absence of state ownership. Southeast Asian rail networks established before World War II, and little improved after, were an example. Second, the government owned and operated business for ideological reasons. The communist government in Vietnam and the regime in Myanmar favoured a dominant state-enterprise sector. Indonesia inherited a large state-owned sector from nationalizations during the Sukarno years and built on it.

Third, a number of Southeast Asian governments took enterprises into public ownership to lessen foreign economic influence and after being unable in

[47] See, for example, Teo, *This is what inequality*; Peng, 'Inequality and the social compact', pp. 355–79.

[48] Singapore, *Census 2020*, statistical release 1, p. 19.

the 1950s and 1960s to foster what was seen as an acceptable level of indigenous participation in trade and business. Impatience to achieve this and counter Chinese or Indian commercial dominance left little choice but for the state to become an entrepreneurial substitute, such as in Indonesia with the mass expulsion of the Dutch.

Singapore apart, government enterprise in Southeast Asia tended to be inefficient, lose money and act as a drag on government budgets. Privatization programmes were introduced partly in response to loss-making government enterprise and partly due to pressure from the International Monetary Fund and World Bank for reduced direct government participation in economies. During the 1980s and 1990s, except in the Indochinese economies and Myanmar, an enthusiasm for privatization swept through Southeast Asia.

Privatization had important implications for the evolution of business in Southeast Asia's plural societies, because the transfer of privatized enterprises to individuals or consortiums was not generally competitive but political. While in independent Southeast Asia political power transferred to indigenous groups, business ability did not and largely remained with ethnic Chinese. Because of this post-independence division which separated political influence from entrepreneurship and management experience, in business inter-ethnic cooperation replaced the pre-World War II plural society's separation between ethnic groups. As early as the 1950s, that pattern was already evident in Thailand, and other Southeast Asian countries followed a similar logic of cooperation between ethnic groups, each of which was able to offer something the other group needed (Chapter 13).

Governments can make rents realizable for business in a government–business relationship through discounted privatizations, the sale of assets at artificially low prices or their purchase at unrealistically high prices, the award of franchises and the grant of permits and licences. In all these ways, privatization in Southeast Asia spawned business lobbies of rent-seeking interests; afforded monopoly profits to the politically well-connected; and, in Malaysia, created a new class of wealthy Malays. Southeast Asian Chinese businessmen cultivated and allied with these Malays who, as members of indigenous ethnic groups, could obtain favourable government treatment that created opportunities to obtain rents. In Schumpeter's famous remark that 'the only man [the entrepreneur] has to convince or to impress is the banker who is to finance him', for most of Southeast Asia, indigenous businessmen with good government contacts could be substituted for bankers.[49]

Privatization in the Philippines, as in most other government transfers of the ownership of companies and award of contracts, lacked subtlety.[50] As described in Chapter 14, Marcos shamelessly plundered large parts of the economy and

[49] Schumpeter, *Theory*, p. 89.

[50] This and the next two paragraphs draw on Milne, 'Privatization', pp. 7–29.

handed these to a small group of cronies. Like Marcos, President Aquino had her cronies and, as under Marcos, privatizations generally benefited an existing elite, doing little towards either fostering entrepreneurs or creating a new group of wealthy Filipinos or Filipino-Chinese. Political intrigue, and a degree of nuance, increased when privatizations became bogged down in the bureaucracy of government and the law, but even more in personal conflicts. Delays during the resolution of privatizations enabled civil servants who managed the enterprises awaiting privatization to obtain quite generous salaries.

The inefficiency, lack of accountability and large size of Thailand's public enterprise sector made it an obvious candidate for reform and privatization (Chapter 13). In 2014, the sector consisted of 46 enterprises. Most were the quasi-natural monopolies of transport, energy, water management, communications and power generation. There were also 10 financial entities including state-owned banks. A 2014 military coup led to the establishment of an 'SOE superboard', given sweeping powers to regulate all state-owned enterprises and improve efficiency and performance. The boards of the enterprises had been 'stacked with political appointees and their cronies'. Improved management and efficiency were, however, questionable because the 'SOE superboard' replaced the previous managers and board members with 'junta appointees, mostly in uniform, and their associates'.[51]

In 2025, rather than opting for full privatization, the Thai government preferred, as it had since the 1980s, public–private partnerships and to maintain the control of ownership and supervision of almost all enterprises. The state-enterprise sector still comprised the same range of industries as in 2014, and the government had full or majority ownership of 52 enterprises and stakes of from 10 per cent to 49 per cent in a further six. Although public listings of some companies from the 1980s onwards offered a source of capital and may have improved transparency and governance, the State Enterprise Office, operating under the Ministry of Finance, oversaw and coordinated the management of the 52 state-owned enterprises. The State Enterprise Office collaborated with line ministers in exercising ownership rights and nominating board members. Protectionist, trade union and line ministry lobbies against privatization were strong, and because of this opposition still in 2023 only five state-owned enterprises had been privatized, partially privatized or corporatized.[52]

In Indonesia, many privatizations were only partial, giving equity purchasers a virtual guarantee that enterprises would continue to be supported by the state.[53] Privatizations were in the hands of the political leadership,

[51] Teera Phutrakul, 'Time to rethink our misguided reform policy on state-owned enterprises', *Bangkok Post*, 12 June 2017.

[52] OECD, *OECD review of the corporate governance*, p. 29 and see the report *passim*.

[53] For a list of partial privatizations since 1990, see Asian Development Bank, *Unlocking*, pp. 45–46.

including many of the military, and generally benefited Indonesian conglomerates, which first emerged in the mid-1980s. Ownership of all of the 'top 20' conglomerates concentrated in the hands of either Sino-Indonesian families or groups. The latter consisted of well-connected *pribumi* investors, notably President Suharto's children, or the state.[54]

Politicians extended monopoly privileges to conglomerates whose owners, in exchange for the chance to realize rents, gave payoffs in various forms.[55] Often, the award of economic advantage stayed within the political-business establishment, such as with toll roads. President Suharto's children 'used their connections and other people's capital and expertise … to dominate the toll-road sector. Suharto's eldest daughter, popularly known as Tutut, took control of the lucrative Jakarta Inner Ring Road.' Tariffs on the children's toll roads were higher than on other roads, but high tariffs brought neither efficiency nor innovative gains.[56] Although entrepreneurship among indigenous Indonesians remained weak, and a government aim was to improve it, privatization contributed minimally towards a remedy.

Privatization in Singapore differed from other Southeast Asian countries: the government wanted to demonstrate efficiency and a total absence of corruption. In both regards, the objective was to exhibit a stewardship that confirmed the rightness and popular acceptance of PAP rule. In keeping with Singapore's twin preference for multinationals and tight state social and economic control, foreign firms typically won the bidding for privatized enterprises, but the government retained a controlling stake in them. Singapore was also unlike the rest of Southeast Asia in its lack of interest in privatization as a way to promote local entrepreneurship. If anything, the government seemed to want to discourage Singaporean entrepreneurs, possibly because multinationals were considered more efficient and because local entrepreneurship rested mainly with the China-oriented Chinese. This group had traditionally opposed the English-educated and -speaking Chinese who formed the core of the government.

The Malaysian 'Bargain of 1957' recognized Malay political dominance in exchange for tacit acceptance of the reality of Chinese economic power (Chapter 13). In the 1960s, apart from some small-scale dealings, few *Bumiputera* entrepreneurs existed. There were almost no *Bumiputera* capable of managing larger businesses. Chinese conducted virtually all local retail trade in the towns, and, along with foreigners, mainly Europeans, dominated larger enterprises, including the tin and rubber industries, engineering, manufacturing and banking.

The 1969 New Economic Policy (NEP, renewed as the New Development Policy from 1991 to 2000, and then replaced by the National Vision Policy

54 Hill, 'Myths', p. 260.
55 Mackie, 'Changing patterns', pp. 178–81; Jesudason, 'Chinese business', p. 133.
56 Davidson, *Indonesia's changing political economy*, p. 46.

until 2010 and finally by the National Transformation Programme intended to stretch until 2050) marked the onset of an ongoing departure from Malaysia's early post-independence acceptance of a pre-World War II plural society. Central to this change was much greater Malay participation in business and holding of economic assets. In 1969, *Bumiputera* ownership of Malaysian corporate wealth was just 1.5 per cent of the total. To meet the New Economic Policy's target of 30 per cent wealth ownership by 1990, the government began to acquire corporate equity, and, due to a lack of Malay managers, set up 'trustee institutions' to own and manage it on behalf of the *Bumiputera*. The share of *Bumiputera* corporate equity rose from 12.5 per cent of the total in 1980 to 18.7 per cent three years later and in 1990 reached just over a fifth.[57] Ownership of most of the large British plantation, tin mining and engineering corporations passed to the *Bumiputera* via the government, most famously in its September 1981 'Dawn Raid' in the London stock market to acquire Guthries (a British agency house founded in 1821) in less than four hours.[58] Historically, *Bumiputera* had no bank ownership, but by the late 1980s they held half of the equity of 10 of 22 domestic banks, and the government controlled the two largest banks.[59]

In 1983, the Malaysian government announced privatization, partly in response to an inefficient public sector which had expanded rapidly under the NEP and only a soft budget constraint. Perhaps almost as important, privatization appealed to Prime Minister Mahathir Mohamad, elected in 1981, as a means to realize his vision of a *Bumiputera* commercial participation more genuine than trusteeship and the creation of a *Bumiputera* entrepreneurial class able to practise the 'virtues of accumulation via enterprise'.[60] The outcome of privatization, however, was the emergence of a small number of newly wealthy Malay business interests distinguished not by demonstrated entrepreneurial ability but by a 'subsidy mentality'.[61] Most *Bumiputera* businessmen owed their successful acquisition of privatized assets and various concessions to some degree of state backing; many were able to participate in privatizations because of affiliation with the patronage networks of the political party of United Malays National Organisation (UMNO). The offer price of privatizations depended on political connections. UMNO itself owned privatized corporate equity and the members of the new Malay business elite donated to it.[62]

Chinese business did not disappear, but found itself increasingly squeezed by the increase in multinationals, including those manufacturing for export,

57 Gomez and Jomo, *Malaysia's political economy*, p. 53.
58 Yacob and White, 'Unfinished business'.
59 Gomez, *Chinese business*, p. 185.
60 Gomez and Jomo, *Malaysia's political economy*, pp. 35–36, 75–80, 117–18; Searle, *Riddle*, p. 53.
61 Crouch, *Government*, pp. 196–218.
62 Jesudason, *Ethnicity*, pp. 100–01; Searle, *Riddle*, p. 54.

and by the rise of *Bumiputera* business. While some long-established Chinese entrepreneurs remained independent of involvement with Malay contacts, newer Chinese business sought them for reasons of necessity and advantage. Among these Chinese entrepreneurs, inter-ethnic cooperation was critical and predominated. They affiliated with politically influential Malay businessmen and financially backed Malay politicians and parties.[63]

Most Malays in receipt of privatized assets or government contracts, although maintaining high-profile positions in the business, relied on Chinese to run the enterprise or subcontracted its running to foreign or local firms. Malay businessmen seldom used rents to build other businesses, but Chinese entrepreneurs did, displaying their historic entrepreneurial flair. When *Bumiputera* businesses ran into difficulty, they could usually rely on government help. By the late 1990s, Bank Bumiputera, established for Malays and other local indigenous groups to participate in commerce and industry, had been bailed out three times.

In Vietnam, privatization had similar motivations as elsewhere in Southeast Asia: the inefficiency of state enterprise, its soft budget constraints, subsidization and international government and donor agency pressure. Privatization, or equitization in Vietnamese terminology, also created the same opportunities for rent-seeking in Vietnam as elsewhere in Southeast Asia. Equitization in Vietnam was limited, because state and party leaders were hesitant to surrender any control. The government countered this potential loss of influence in two ways. One, as in Singapore, was to retain a large stake in companies by only partially privatizing them. Second, government authorities kept owners of privatized assets in continuous uncertainty by constantly threatening to exercise political power and regulation, a tactic of creating dependency viewed by Gainsborough as amounting not to a retreat of the state, but a new form of intervention or indeed state advance.[64]

Although in Vietnam state power was even greater than in much of Southeast Asia, government strategies like the Vietnamese one of substituting 'indirect' for 'direct' government and yet retaining a good deal of control operated to some extent throughout the region. Rent-seeking was not absent in Vietnam: its government officials were like those in other Southeast Asian countries in using their power to enrich themselves. Equitization in Vietnam 'has driven the monetization of politics, in which party and government officials trade political influence and positions for cash among themselves and with businesses and individuals in a position to profit from state favours'.[65]

63 Searle, *Riddle*, pp. 220–21; Jesudason, 'Chinese business', pp. 135–36; Gomez and Jomo, *Malaysia's political economy*, pp. 40–48.

64 Gainsborough, 'Privatisation', pp. 257–60, 269–71; Tran, 'Vietnamese economy', p. 130; Chiat, 'Comment', p. 144.

65 Pincus, 'Why doesn't Vietnam', p. 43.

Catch-up and Slowing of Growth

From 1870 to 1929, in catching up with United States income as the world leader, Southeast Asian countries either gained a little ground or at least avoided falling much further behind. However, the 1930s depression and World War II were disastrous for Southeast Asia and catch-up. In 1950 and still in 1970, every country in the region trailed United States per capita income by more, and often much more, than in 1929 (Table 18.2). If between 1929 and 1950 countries in Southeast Asia had grown at the same rate as from 1870 to 1929, the region would have started the 1950s from much higher incomes, and by 1970 have advanced further towards catch-up.

Southeast Asian catch-up only decisively began in the late 1960s, as some countries started growing rapidly. Subsequently, this growth spread to most of the region. But in 2022, the gap remained wide except for Singapore, which had a considerably higher per capita income than the United States (Table 18.2). Even in Singapore, large inflows of high-income expatriates, not least from China, exaggerated per capita income, and high saving, partly government-enforced, limited consumption. Based on 2022 per capita incomes and annual growth rates in Malaysia, Thailand and the United States from 1997 to 2022, Malaysia and Thailand – the countries with the region's second- and third-highest incomes – would match United States per capita income in around 50 and 200 years respectively. Nevertheless, after being far adrift of the United States in 1970, by 2022 all countries in Southeast Asia were catching up with it.

Projected catch-up times depend crucially on current growth rates and also on US dollar conversion rates. Between 1997 and 2022, slower growth in the early industrializers of Malaysia and Thailand, and, in time, a likely replication of the same slowing as in the late industrializers, engenders pessimism about Southeast Asia's chances for catch-up in the near future. So too does the nature of growth achieved as part of the Southeast Asian development model. The slowdown in growth and an assessment of post-1970s development in the region are the subjects of this and the next section.

In the early industrializers of Malaysia, Singapore and Thailand, extremely rapid growth was largely confined to the quarter-century from 1970 to 1997. From 1997 to 2022, GDP per capita in Malaysia grew at 2.8 per cent per annum, in Singapore at 3.4 per cent and in Thailand at 2.0 per cent. These are normal, or even better than, rates of growth for advanced economies, but well short of growth in the early industrializers before the 1997 financial crisis. By contrast, growth between 1997 and 2022 in most other Southeast Asian countries did not experience a similar slowing. Growth in the late industrializing Indochinese economies of Vietnam, Cambodia and Laos was notably rapid. The Philippines, after crises during much of the last half of the twentieth century, grew at a faster pace than it had historically.

Table 18.2 *Southeast Asia and United States GDP per capita and comparative growth, 1870–2022*

(a) Per capita GDP 2011 US$

	1870	1929	1950	1970	1997	2022
Malaysia	1,055	3,220	2,485	3,314	13,345	26,629
Singapore	1,423	3,323	3,572	6,650	34,868	80,320
Thailand	969	1,264	1,302	2,700	9,996	16,421
Philippines	995	2,252	1,706	2,812	3,928	8,371
Indonesia	810	1,702	1,280	1,882	6,056	12,802
Vietnam	805	–	1,049	1,172	2,467	8,050
Cambodia	–	–	768	1,031	1,466	3,944
Laos	–	–	697	850	2,002	7,168
Myanmar (Burma)	803	1,438	631	1,023	1,506	5,177
United States	4,803	10,695	15,240	23,958	41,723	58,487

(b) Annual growth %

	1870–2022	1870–1929	1929–1950	1950–1970	1970–1997	1997–2022
Malaysia	2.1	1.9	−1.2	1.4	5.3	2.8
Singapore	2.7	1.4	0.3	3.2	6.3	3.4
Thailand	1.9	0.5	0.1	3.7	5.0	2.0
Philippines	1.4	1.4	−1.3	2.5	1.2	3.1
Indonesia	1.8	1.3	−1.3	1.9	4.4	3.0
Vietnam	1.5	–	–	0.6	2.8	4.8
Cambodia	–	–	–	1.5	1.3	4.0
Laos	–	–	–	1.0	3.2	5.2
Myanmar (Burma)	1.2	1.0	−4.2	2.4	1.4	5.1
United States	1.7	1.4	1.7	2.3	2.1	1.4

(c) Southeast Asia as % of US

	1870	1929	1950	1970	1997	2022
Malaysia	22.0	30.1	16.3	13.8	32.0	45.5
Singapore	29.6	31.1	23.4	27.8	83.6	137.3
Thailand	20.2	11.8	8.5	11.3	24.0	28.1
Philippines	20.7	21.1	11.2	11.7	9.4	14.3
Indonesia	16.9	15.9	8.4	7.9	14.5	21.9
Vietnam	16.8	–	6.9	4.9	5.9	13.8
Cambodia	–	–	5.0	4.3	3.5	6.7
Laos	–	–	4.6	3.5	4.8	12.3
Myanmar (Burma)	16.7	13.4	4.1	4.3	3.6	8.9

Note: For Myanmar (Burma) for 1929 data are for 1931.
Source: Maddison Project Database, 2023.

Three main considerations account for the growth deceleration in Malaysia, Singapore and Thailand. One is a seeming slowdown beginning in the later 1990s, and particularly after 2006, in the expansion of the value of world electronics and electrical goods exports (Figure 15.9). Exports in the trade grouping SITC 75, 76, 77, 87 and 88 were a principal force in export-led Southeast Asian growth during the last three decades of the twentieth century. The deceleration of these exports cut into Southeast Asian export-led growth, as reflected in falling export–GDP ratios in Malaysia and Thailand after 2008 (Figure 15.8). However, the slower expansion in the nominal value of world SITC 7 and 8 exports was at least partly owing to a decrease in the prices, rather than the volume or the value added, of electronics and electrical goods, and so provides no more than a partial explanation of Southeast Asian growth deceleration.[66]

A second reason for slowing Malaysian, Singaporean and Thai growth was a decrease in their shares of global exports of products in global manufacturing value chains, within which electronics and electrical products were the main constituent. In the late 1990s and early 2000s, the shares in global value chain exports of Malaysia and Singapore peaked at over 2.5 per cent before falling back. Thailand's share grew to nearly 2.0 per cent of world exports in 2011 but then dropped.[67]

Malaysia, Singapore and Thailand lost part of their earlier shares of electronics and electrical products to competition from China and subsequently also from the late industrializers of Vietnam and Cambodia. After China embarked on market-oriented reforms in 1978, there was a significant shift in the final assembly of electronics and electrical goods from Southeast Asia to China. However, during the early stages of China's economic transition, the impact on Southeast Asian exports was more than offset by a surge in parts and component exports to China, a trend that continued until the late 1990s. From then, Chinese competition began to exert a significant contractionary effect on Southeast Asia's exports of both final assembly and parts and components of electronics and electrical goods. This trend intensified following China's accession to the World Trade Organization in 2001: global value chain production bases in China expanded rapidly, with the scope of activities deepening to include parts and component production and assembly, alongside a massive expansion in final assembly operations.[68]

In Vietnam, growth did not slow until the 2019 to 2022 pandemic. Both Vietnam and Cambodia had lower wages than Malaysia and Thailand.

[66] Athukorala, 'Global trade slowdown'; Goldberg and Reed, 'Global economy deglobalizing', pp. 348–50, 353–54, 360–61.

[67] Athukorala, 'Philippines', figure 2, p. 14.

[68] I owe the information in this paragraph to personal correspondence with Prema-chandra Athukorala. See also Athukorala and Kohpaiboon, 'Global production sharing', pp. 151–53.

Furthermore, Vietnam increasingly offered a production base with skilled labour and engineering services. Vietnam started to grow rapidly beginning in the early 1990s and Cambodia from the end of the decade, although much of Cambodian growth depended on garments and footwear. Vietnam's share of world exports of global manufacturing value chain products rose from effectively zero in 1990 to pass 3.0 per cent by 2019.[69] The example of Vietnam emphasizes the importance of low-cost, productive labour and suggests that through being able to offer this Vietnam may have gained export share at the expense of Malaysia and Thailand. The Vietnamese example also underscores the indispensability in Southeast Asian export-led growth of plugging into global value chains.

The third explanation for the divergent growth patterns of the early and late industrializers is to be found in the fundamental nature of growth: the less developed an economy, the greater its potential for rapid growth; and the more successfully an economy achieves catch-up growth, the harder it is to sustain this growth.[70] These considerations imply that the divergent patterns of Southeast Asian slowdown and continued rapid expansion were to be expected, and may well be the principal cause of growth deceleration in the region's highest-income economies.

Development Assessment

This section attempts, from the perspective of the mid-2020s, to analyse Southeast Asian growth and development since 1970 and argues three things. One is that growth, just as before World War II, was largely input-driven. Compared to Southeast Asian economies in the late 1960s, subsequent growth and change in the region seemed a miracle. However, even in Singapore total factor productivity – a residual after 'accounting' for all other contributors to growth and defined as efficiency in the use of all factors of production – remained low. Sustained long-term growth depends on gains in total factor productivity. In achieving these, education, innovation and resource allocation are crucial.

Second, after 1970 globalization was a necessary, though not a sufficient, condition for the accelerated growth that most countries experienced. Swift growth also depended on the response of those in Southeast Asia to new opportunities in the global economy. Even if Southeast Asian countries had not responded so vigorously to the new phase of globalization, they would still have grown, if less rapidly, through exports of primary commodities and the dynamic of their own internal markets.

[69] Athukorala, 'Philippines', figure 2, p. 14.

[70] Summers and Pritchett, *Asiaphoria*, pp. 296–307.

The section's third argument is that the Southeast Asian globalization-dependent model has so far yielded an incomplete development. Successful as the Southeast Asian growth model since the 1970s has been, the special case of Singapore apart, Southeast Asian countries remain, in varying degrees, short of 'fully developed status', defined by Kuznets as the outcome of modern economic growth.[71] Only Myanmar shows no immediate promise of advance towards this goal. Judged by Kuznets' six characteristics of modern economic growth, except in Singapore structural change and urbanization, though accelerated, were only partially accomplished in Southeast Asia. On the criterion set out by Kuznets of reaching out to the world, just some countries arrived at this stage and only as investors. Productivity and so growth were much higher than historically, but, worryingly, this advance stemmed less from an internalization of technology – central to the Kuznets definition – than from labour mobilization and structural change.

Evaluation of Southeast Asian Growth

From the 1970s, exceptionally swift Southeast Asian growth was mostly confined to relatively short bursts of no more than about a decade before falling back. Southeast Asia, Singapore apart, lacked the sustained decades of exceptionally high growth of South Korea and Taiwan. Economic growth depends on labour force expansion, the accumulation of physical capital, the augmentation of human capital through both formal education and on-the-job training, and technical progress.[72]

Estimates for Southeast Asia record low or often negative (a decline in the efficiency of resource use) total factor productivity growth throughout the region. Malaysia alone, and only from 2010 to 2015, showed efficiency or technical progress gains of as much as 2 per cent (Table 18.3). Concerted government attempts in Singapore, Malaysia and Thailand did not succeed in raising total factor productivity above low levels.[73] In these countries, strategies of importing large quantities of cheap migrant labour told against productivity gains.

In the 1960s, Malaysia, Singapore and Thailand had considerable scope for fast growth through extraordinarily high saving and capital accumulation; mobilizing more labour into full-time employment, including previously unemployed workers; continued structural change involving a shift in labour

[71] Kuznets, 'Modern economic growth', pp. 247–51.

[72] See, for example, Yusuf, 'East Asian miracle', pp. 8, 15–17. Stiglitz argues against the finding of numerous studies of low total factor productivity in Southeast Asia. Stiglitz, 'Miracle to crisis', pp. 510–12.

[73] Perkins et al., 'Explaining Malaysia's past growth', p. 19; Tran, 'Vietnamese economy', pp. 129–30; Monetary Authority of Singapore, 'Sources of Singapore's economic growth', pp. 72–73; Lim, 'Singapore's success', pp. 213, 220.

Table 18.3 *Southeast Asia growth in total factor productivity, 1970–2022 (% annual average growth rate)*

	1970–1990	1990–2010	2010–2015	2015–2022
Malaysia	1.0	0.7	2.5	0.8
Singapore	0.7	1.2	0.3	1.1
Thailand	0.4	-0.4	0.6	0.2
Philippines	-0.9	0.7	0.4	-0.2
Indonesia	1.4	-0.9	-0.9	-0.3
Vietnam	-0.9	0.9	0.9	1.8
Cambodia	-2.5	0.9	-1.9	0.3
Laos	0.4	1.3	-1.8	-1.2
Myanmar	-0.9	0.3	-0.8	1.2

Source: Asian Productivity Organization, *APO productivity databook 2024*, p. 16.

from low-productivity agriculture and services to industry; and greater female labour force participation. Industrialization eliminated obvious labour surpluses in Singapore, where between 1966 and 1973 unemployment halved to 4.5 per cent, and in Malaysia, where from 1960 to 1985 widespread underemployment and large unemployment had persisted.[74]

Among the first group of Southeast Asian countries to industrialize, earlier successful catch-up told against continued swift growth because growth relied principally on once-and-for-all changes. Pools of unemployed and underemployed labour were depleted and structural change was irreversible. Saving rates were limited by the need for consumption and at very high levels possibly had a negative effect on growth. With the progression of a demographic transition which accompanies economic growth, the high birth rates of post-World War II Southeast Asia fell. Fewer births, a drop in new entrants to the workforce and an ageing population caused a relative shrinkage in the working-age population, unless augmented by migrant labour. A continuation of the demographic transition and so higher old age dependency ratios cut into saving rates. As these decreased, so did capital accumulation as a source of growth.

Unlike the early industrializers, their later industrializing counterparts still had abundant opportunities for growth through greater inputs of labour and capital. Beginning in the 1990s, the Indochinese economies and the Philippines began to follow the growth path already traversed by Malaysia, Singapore and Thailand. Again, growth was export-led and dependent on the region's new

[74] Bruton, *Sri Lanka and Malaysia*, p. 221.

staples. And once more the late industrializers grew through labour force mobilization, structural change and capital accumulation.

After 1990, the structure of the Indochinese economies moved decisively away from agriculture and towards industry. Saving rates were still no more than 4 per cent in Vietnam at the outset of the 1990s, negative in Cambodia until 1997 and 3 per cent in Laos in 2001, but by the 2010s savings stood at around 20 per cent or more in all three economies. Capital formation in the three economies, which also tapped foreign savings, reached as much as over 30 per cent of GDP in Vietnam and Laos and the mid-20s in Cambodia.

In the 1980s, the Philippines was already a high saver, and before the downturn beginning in 1984 had capital formation of 26 per cent to 28 per cent of GDP. Capital accumulation in the Philippines resembled Southeast Asia's early industrializers (Chapter 15). In contrast to them, however, during the twenty-first century the Philippines still had abundant opportunities for higher growth through labour mobilization. In the 2020s, the Philippines exported large numbers of workers and had comparatively high birth rates and low old age dependency as well as considerable amounts of underemployed and unemployed – surplus – labour. However, the Philippines lacked a booming manufacturing sector to create semi-skilled jobs, so 'the majority of the surplus labor moved out of agriculture to low-end services jobs'.[75]

Trade and Growth

Openness and trade have always been central to Southeast Asian development. Beginning in the 1970s, Southeast Asia swapped its dependence for growth on exports of primary commodities to developed countries for exporting manufactures to them. Both between the 1870s to 1930 and beginning in the 1970s, Southeast Asian growth was at its most rapid when globalization facilitated the free flow of factors and thus the demand for goods in which Southeast Asia had a comparative advantage. Any disruption to the global order and hindrance to the flow of goods impacted Southeast Asia's trade-dependent economies.

When for Southeast Asia globalization stalled or went into reverse, so too did Southeast Asian growth: in the 1930s, during the Asian financial crisis and again between 2019 and 2023 due to the Covid pandemic and accompanying and subsequent interruption to global supply chains (Chapter 15).

After 1970, as during earlier globalization, trade connected Southeast Asia, a collection of economically small countries, to the outside world from which capital, entrepreneurship and ideas came and which afforded markets otherwise unavailable. Trade contributed to moving Southeast Asia away from a reliance on the venting of surpluses, which are merely analogous to the realization

[75] World Bank, *Middle class in the Philippines*, p. xii.

of economic rents or quasi-rents on underutilized natural resources.[76] Without the dynamic of linkages, the gains from exports would soon have been exhausted and trade would have failed to fulfil an engine of growth role.

Trade is not, however, a source of growth but a transmission mechanism – a handmaiden – which induces growth and assists in the acquisition of its fundamental sources: the accumulation of physical and human capital and the promotion of education, learning and technology. Long-term growth depends on technology, of which total factor productivity is a measure. As a handmaiden, trade led to a greater division of labour and had growth-inducing effects in Southeast Asia. Trade served as a leading sector; created production linkages in the services, transport and industrial sectors; encouraged capital accumulation and structural change; introduced new ideas; and supported the emergence of a growing middle class, defined as a household having sufficient economic security to be able credibly to plan for the future and likely having at least one member in a job with a steady pay cheque.[77]

Nurkse distinguished between two types of industrialization: one producing manufactured goods for export to industrial countries, the other catering mainly for domestic markets.[78] Southeast Asian industrialization predominantly focused on export markets and was the easier of the two types, because it did not require a complementary advance in domestic agriculture. While Southeast Asian agricultural diversification and the green revolution in rice production helped to resolve concerns over food supply and were important advances, agriculture did not progress at the same pace as industry. In the mid-2020s, Southeast Asian countries had still to follow the pattern of the advanced countries, where agricultural and industrial revolutions went together to complete an industrial transformation.

Incomplete Development

Southeast Asia, with Singapore the exception, remained partially economically developed. Mega-cities notwithstanding, in 2024 in Southeast Asia except Malaysia and Singapore between about half and three-quarters of populations lived in rural areas. Imported technology and remarkable structural change made industry a greater contributor to GDP than agriculture, but the latter still accounted for a quarter to a third of employment in most countries. In addition to underemployment in large rural populations, many Southeast Asian migrants to cities, hoping for modern sector jobs, joined a bloated informal economy and became slum dwellers. Major cities in almost all Southeast Asian countries had large slum populations, comprising between a quarter and

76 Caves, 'Export-led growth', pp. 408, 435.

77 Birdsall, 'Middle-class heroes', pp. 25–26 and '(Indispensable) middle class', pp. 161–67.

78 Nurkse, *Equilibrium and growth*, pp. 307–22.

around half of urban inhabitants. Dual economies persisted: modern sectors existed alongside low-productivity smallholder agriculture and urban informal sectors in which most slum dwellers found employment (Chapter 17). Even though manufacturing became a Southeast Asian growth engine, export industries could not employ all of the labour available, contributing to the 'lopsided' structure of Southeast Asia's dual economies.

The large amount of labour in low-productivity agriculture and informal urban services revealed the incompleteness of the globalization-dependent Southeast Asian development model. So, too, did an extreme reliance on female labour in Southeast Asian garment factories and substantial migrant outflows from a number of countries. An agricultural revolution is historically a developmental precondition, but in Southeast Asia in the mid-2020s it had yet fully to materialize. Despite advances, notably in the use of fertilizers and high-yielding rice, productivity gains were limited. Except in Malaysia, value added per agricultural worker, although advancing markedly for the decades from the 1990s, remained relatively low (Table 16.3).

In 2010, perhaps a third of the populations of Bangkok, Kuala Lumpur and Jakarta were middle class. However, fundamental as such class formation is in the development process, this urban middle class was a fraction of these countries' populations, and was somewhat divorced from them in being disproportionally ethnic Chinese and rarely venturing into city hinterlands.[79] In the Philippines, the middle class was about 10 per cent of the total population and, as elsewhere in Southeast Asia, largely an urban phenomenon, heavily concentrated in the National Capital Region and Luzon. Although the Philippines middle-class share of the population was low, it probably (even assuming more equal income distributions than in the Philippines) still exceeded Southeast Asian countries with per capita incomes below the Philippines. It would be difficult for these lower-income countries to have a middle class as large as 10 per cent of their populations in light of the World Bank definition of middle class as households with daily per capita incomes of at least 2011 PPP $15.[80]

Growth in Southeast Asia remained dangerously unbalanced due to industrial specialization in a narrow range of the staples of electronics and electrical goods, garments and footwear. More balanced growth would have involved diversification through a widening of industrial development as well as a greater range of primary exports. Relevant models of the latter were Thailand in becoming a world leader in the export of cultivated shrimp, Vietnam as not just a major world exporter of rice but other agricultural products as well, and efforts by the Philippines to promote the export of more resource-intensive manufactured goods.[81]

79 Rimmer and Dick, *City in Southeast Asia*, pp. 15, 36.

80 World Bank, *Middle class in the Philippines*, pp. ix, xi, 5–7, 20–21, 80.

81 Findlay, 'Trade and development', p. 40.

Resource Utilization and Migrant Labour

Southeast Asia, in the half-century after 1970, did not fully utilize the growth sources of labour inputs and structural change, slowing the rate of advance and probably leaving total factor productivity less than it could have been. Labour surpluses persisted in agriculture and the urban informal sector. In Thailand, scope to mobilize this surplus labour remained, even though the mid-1990s have been considered to mark the 'end of the era of cheap labor'.[82] However, in Southeast Asia industrial wages were too near subsistence level and modern sector jobs too few and insecure fully to draw labour from the countryside, as occurs in industrial revolutions.

In Malaysia and Thailand, and also in Singapore, migrant inflows kept factor input-driven growth on track, but were symptomatic of an incomplete model of development. Migration from the poorer Southeast Asian countries helped to supply a large low-wage unskilled industrial workforce but discouraged higher wages. Wage pressure should act as an adjustment mechanism which encourages a transition to a higher-skill, higher-productivity, higher-wage economy, and so the technical change that leads to self-sustaining economic growth.[83] As earlier sources of domestic surplus labour are depleted and labour supply becomes less elastic, a rise in wages should be matched by technical progress to increase labour productivity.[84] To some extent this happened, most apparently in Singapore, where in most years real wages regularly and markedly rose. Even in Singapore, however, and for much of Malaysia's and Thailand's export-oriented industrialization, particularly for electronics and electrical goods production, inflows of low-wage, foreign workers helped to perpetuate cheap-labour, low value-added, often substantially assembly, manufacturing sectors.

Social Capability and Education

Sustained technologically driven growth is difficult to achieve and not automatic. It requires narrowing a technological gap with the leaders through what Abramovitz terms 'social capability'. That demands the ability to assimilate advanced countries' technology. Assimilation requires some mixture of suitable education levels, human capital and appropriate institutions. While education and human capital can, if quite imperfectly, be measured, institutions cannot, and what 'appropriate' means is not clear. Broadly, institutions suited to catch-up growth ensure stability and an openness to ideas, learning

[82] Brimble and Doner, 'University–industry linkages', p. 1022.

[83] Abeysinghe and Choy, *Singapore economy*, p. 85; Choy, 'Singapore's changing economic model', p. 135.

[84] Findlay, 'Trade and development', p. 35.

and innovation. Southeast Asian institutions that favoured particular interest groups and narrowed a society's horizons through cronyism and rent-seeking were not conducive to growth.[85]

Although Southeast Asian economies expanded education so that primary schooling and literacy became near universal, Malaysia and Thailand remained a considerable distance from being able to realize a potential for catch-up through acquiring the technology of the leaders and through possessing sufficient social capability. Barriers to reducing a technological gap with leaders included gaining access to developed country patented technologies, mobilizing them and building international marketing and distribution networks. Beginning to export soon after opening a new, technologically advanced industry was essential for its successful development, since no Southeast Asian country had a large enough internal market to realize available scale economies.

Malaysia and Thailand lacked an educational and institutional framework conducive to social capability. Moving up the technology ladder requires a strong research-oriented university system which complements robust research in corporations or other private institutions.[86] Neither Malaysia nor Thailand, nor any other Southeast Asian country except Singapore, had such a network of universities. Even Singapore lacked a cluster of universities capable of cutting-edge science, although it had a developed country per capita income partly through providing services, establishing itself as a global city and inviting in wealthy foreigners. Malaysian education suppressed a diffusion of global knowledge and ideas through instruction mainly in Malay rather than English, the international language of science and communication. In both Malaysia and Thailand, the availability of rents to businessmen with political connections discouraged entrepreneurship and innovation. Government favouritism inhibited the emergence of new ideas and innovation.

As labour comes under pressure from cheaper cost locations and is expelled from low-wage manufacturing, development requires that workers have the skills to move to higher-tech activities. However, Malaysia and Thailand had shortages of skilled industrial labour. In Thailand, industrialization was long held back by a lack of skilled labour, which university and technical education, despite their expansion, did not remedy. The principal response in Malaysia, as in Thailand, was not to augment the supply of human capital through strengthening education, initiating training programmes and forging close university–industry links to re-adjust a mismatch of skills. Rather, Malaysia welcomed large numbers of low-skill workers to prevent multinationals from moving to lower-wage countries. Beginning in the early 1990s, Malaysia signed

85 Abramovitz, 'Catching up', p. 390; Crafts, 'Historical perspectives', pp. 317–21.
86 Yusuf, 'East Asian miracle', p. 18.

Memorandums of Understanding with at least eight countries to recruit labour for the manufacturing sector.[87]

A move towards a more skill-intensive, technological manufacturing Malaysian export economy through educational upgrading would have promoted economic development. Even in 1986, the Review of the Industrial Master Plan emphasized the shortage of trained manpower: the need to upgrade technology, develop local capabilities and expand R&D 'has reached a critical point'.[88] However, few Malaysian universities concentrated on engineering; and, rather than assuming this role through in-house training, Malaysian firms reverted to 'tried and tested means such as a readily available pool of unskilled foreign workers and underpriced resources to generate profits'.[89] As a result, the Malaysian electronics industry relied heavily on imported foreign workers, many able to do no more than semi-skilled jobs.[90]

In 2024, Malaysia's Cybercity, built near the end of the twentieth century to launch a digital revolution, was still mainly warehouses. Most Cybercity technicians came from India on contracts. As contract manufacturers like Flex, although long established in Malaysia, upgraded, they tended to site this functional upgrading elsewhere than in Malaysia because of its shortages of skills, particularly engineers.[91] When contractors in the electronics industry upgraded to higher value-added activities like design and engineering, they often preferred to locate in China rather than Malaysia because of a lack of skills in the latter.[92] Skill shortages remained chronic. In 2024, Tengku Zafrul Aziz, Minister of Investment, Trade and Industry, declared that Malaysia 'must transition from merely being a production centre to becoming a leader in innovation and technology development … We do not want to be just a country that provides labour.'[93]

Vietnam seemed to have copied the policy of Malaysia and Thailand towards electronics multinationals. Perhaps because of still abundant labour, the Vietnamese government chose to emphasize employment rather than focus on technology and innovation. The thrust of the so-called 'Vietnam's Silicon

[87] World Bank, *Malaysia economic monitor: immigrant labour*, p. 74, 699, 702: Rasiah, 'Industrial policy experience', pp. 136–40; Lee, 'Comment on "Transforming Malaysia's higher education"', p. 26; Raj-Reichert, 'Global value chains', pp. 704–06, 712.

[88] Malaysia, Ministry of International Trade and Industry, *Review of the Industrial Master Plan, 1986–1995*, p. xv and see pp. xvii and 30.

[89] Malaysia, National Economic Advisory Council, *New economic model*, p. 50.

[90] Malaysia, *Eleventh Malaysia plan*, pp. 5.1–5.30 and *Twelfth Malaysia plan*, pp. 10.1–10.27; Edgington and Hayter, 'In situ upgrading', p. 250.

[91] Raj-Reichert, 'Global value chains', pp. 705–10; Selvaratnam, 'Malaysia's higher education', pp. 212–16.

[92] Raj-Reichert, 'Global value chains', p. 710.

[93] 'Malaysia takes Nvidia AI chip smuggling claims to China seriously', *Malay Mail*, 7 February 2024.

Valley' was to attract as many multinational electronics and electrical firms as possible, of whatever kind. That succeeded, but labour-intensive, cheap-labour, low-tech production predominated.[94] The ASEAN integrated free trade area put Malaysian electronics firms under competitive pressure from, as well as China, lower-cost locations like Vietnam.[95]

Singapore had the same barriers to acquiring technology as elsewhere in Southeast Asia but it had many of the ingredients that promoted social capability. Its network of universities was easily the best in Southeast Asia. Close university–industry links turned out the supply of technically trained operatives, supervisors and managers that multinationals required and that enabled Singapore to advance along global value chains. Education also provided the skills needed for an international financial centre. But in manufacturing Singapore was held back by its smallness, weak entrepreneurship and lack of access to the technology and the marketing power of lead firms in electronics production. In this industry, Singapore was a regional centre as a part of global value chains but not a second Silicon Valley. Unlike China and South Korea, Singapore had no lead firms. An overbearing, authoritarian government in Singapore discouraged individual initiative. This seemed to be reinforced by the risk preferences of Singaporeans themselves, especially the English-speaking population. Many of the most able Singaporeans favoured the relative safety of jobs in the civil service and finance or went into politics.

For migrant-sending Southeast Asian countries, the export of cheap labour probably encouraged capital accumulation and certainly contributed to improved living standards for remittance-receiving households. These remittances were, however, the main gain from exporting labour. Its export, as opposed to its use in domestic production of goods for export, worked against both the possibility of creating extensive linkages and the wider gains from trade. Remittances of 10 per cent or more of national income, as in the Philippines, probably negatively impacted development.[96] Like their migrant-importing counterparts, migrant-sending countries needed to implement policies to build social capability and diversify beyond a restricted developmental base.

Conclusion

Initially, Southeast Asia vented both surplus land and surplus labour, but as early as the inter-war years in Myanmar, and by the 1970s in most Southeast Asian countries, land had begun to run short and only labour surpluses existed.

[94] Klingler-Vidra and Wade, 'Science and technology policies', pp. 718, 725; Lim and Nguyen, 'Reinterpreting Vietnamese industrialization', p. 3.

[95] Edgington and Hayter, 'In situ upgrading', pp. 241, 243, 252.

[96] Jongwanich and Kohpaiboon, 'Workers' remittances', pp. 61, 62.

Both between 1870 and the 1930s and beginning in the 1970s, growth in Southeast Asian countries depended heavily on marshalling greater inputs rather than intensive growth achieved through technical progress. In the first, pre-World War II vent-for-surplus expansionary period, resources came chiefly through cultivating more land and mobilizing additional labour to farm it. That mode of growth created overwhelmingly agrarian economies and required relatively little capital.

On the demand side, both late nineteenth-century and post-1970 growth were responses to the needs of developed countries, but on the supply side differed in factor inputs. Growth after 1970 utilized a combination of Southeast Asia's by then abundant, often surplus, labour, the movement of workers out of low-productivity to higher-productivity activities and capital accumulation, the last realized partly through foreign direct investment by multinationals manufacturing for export. Countries that grew most swiftly were those with the greatest success in attracting foreign capital, mobilizing labour and training workers to move into higher value-added occupations. Less successful countries substituted for trade by exporting labour surpluses as migrant workers.

Catch-up with the leading countries – or the goals set by some Southeast Asian leaders of 'fully developed' status by the mid-twenty-first century – were ambitious, and likely unrealistic. Progress was, of course, interrupted between 2019 and 2023 by the Covid pandemic and its aftermath. By 2023, however, almost all countries had regained at least their pre-pandemic GDP per capita levels. Having recovered by the mid-2020s, Southeast Asia will almost certainly continue to grow, albeit more slowly, even if globalization becomes a less important driver of growth because of some rejection of openness in the world economy, such as the 2025 imposition of tariffs. Myanmar alone warrants pessimism. If, in the region's wealthiest countries, growth in GDP per capita settles to the more normal levels of around 2 per cent to 2.5 per cent per annum, national income will double in the next 35 years or less, and these countries will look quite different. In the Indochinese economies, swift growth seems probable for some time so long as more developed countries continue to demand cheap-labour products and trade remains relatively unimpeded. If so, social and economic transformation will follow.

In the mid-2020s, Southeast Asian countries were, however, still searching for the technological acquisition and for the agricultural development that would afford a firm footing for catch-up and becoming fully developed. The implementation of new ideas and technical change are imperative to raising total factor productivity and moving towards self-sustaining economic growth. Policies to build social capability through institutional change, expanding supplies of qualified manpower and learning allow a realization of productivity gains. These enable a country to climb a ladder of dynamic comparative advantage to more skill-intensive, higher-wage occupations, which are an essential component of the realization of total factor productivity growth. Further structural change, the development of the agricultural sector and higher total factor productivity growth are obvious parts of the solution towards reaching a surer footing for continuous growth. But these developments along the lines of the Western model of a genuine industrial revolution are not so easily achieved. Accomplishing this transition will be Southeast Asia's biggest challenge.

REFERENCES

Archives

Burma

National Archives of Myanmar, Yangon (MNA)

France

Centre des Archives d'Outre-Mer, Aix-en-Provence (AOM)
Indochine nouveau fonds (INF)

Japan

National Institute for Defense Studies, Military History Research Centre (NIDS)

Malaysia

Arkib Negara Malaysia (National Archives of Malaysia) (ANM)

The Netherlands

Indische Collectie, Instituut voor Oorlogs-, Holocaust- en Genocidestudies (Collection Netherlands East Indies, Institute for War, Holocaust and Genocide Studies), Amsterdam (IC)
Nederlands Instituut voor Militaire Historie (Netherlands Institute for Military History), The Hague (NIMH)

Philippines

University of the Philippines, Diliman Main Library (UP)
Manuel A. Roxas Papers

Singapore

National Archives of Singapore (NAS)

Thailand

Bank of Thailand Archives (BT)

United Kingdom

Bank of England Records, London (BE)
OV25 (Thailand)
OV65 (Malaya, Singapore and Borneo)
OV79 (Burma)
OV85 (Dutch East Indies/Indonesia)
OV85 (Indochina)
OV98 (South Vietnam 1954–76)
OV149 (Philippines)
Guthrie Corporation Archive, School of Oriental and African Studies (London)
Hongkong and Shanghai Banking Corporation (HSBC) Group Archive (London)
India Office Records, British Library, London (IOR)
Clague Papers Mss Eur E252
National Archives, Kew (NA)
CO273 Straits Settlements original correspondence
WO203 War of 1939–45; military headquarters papers, Far East

United States

National Archives and Records Administration (NARA)
RG59 General records of the Department of State
RG226 Records of the Office of Strategic Services (OSS)
United Press International (UPI) Archives, www.upi.com/Archives/
US Army Center of Military History
Japanese Monographs (JM) (Prepared by the Military History Section of the Headquarters, Army Forces East, distributed by the Office of the Chief of Military History, Department of the Army)
No. 103 *Outline of administration in occupied areas, 1941–1945*

Vietnam

National Archives Center I, Hanoi (VNA)
Fonds de la direction des finances de l'Indochine (FF)

Official Publications

International Organizations

International Bank for Reconstruction, *A public development programme for Thailand* (Baltimore: Johns Hopkins Press, 1959).

International Bank for Reconstruction and Development, *The economic development of Malaya* (Washington, DC, 1955).

International Labour Office, *Report to the government of Singapore on social security measures* (published as Cmd. 56 of 1957, Singapore, 1957).

International Labour Organization, *Sharing in development: a programme of employment, equity and growth for the Philippines* (Geneva: ILO, 1974).

Employment, wages and working conditions in Asia's garment sector: finding new drivers of competitiveness (Bangkok: ILO, 2015).

Regional Office for Asia and the Pacific, Wages, productivity and labour share in China (Bangkok: ILO, 2016).

Wages and productivity in the garment sector in Asia and the Pacific and the Arab states (Bangkok: ILO, *c.*2017).

The footwear sector – new opportunities for Cambodia? (Cambodia Garment and Footwear Sector Bulletin, issue 9) (Bangkok: ILO, 2019).

Opportunities for a just transition to environmental sustainability and Covid-19 recovery in the textile and garment sector in Asia (Geneva: ILO, 2021).

'Empowering women in Viet Nam's textile and garment industry: the importance of training, skills development, and gender equality' (March 2025), www.ilo.org/resource/article/empowering-women-viet-nams-textile-and-garment-industry-importance-training.

International Tin Research and Development Council, *Statistical year book 1938* (The Hague: International Tin Research and Development Council, 1938).

League of Nations, *The network of world trade; a companion volume to 'Europe's trade'* (Geneva: League of Nations, 1942).

OECD (Organisation for Economic Co-operation and Development), *Multi-dimensional review of Myanmar, vol. 1, Initial Assessment* (Paris: OECD, 2013).

OECD review of the corporate governance of state-owned enterprises in Thailand (Paris: OECD Publishing, 2025).

United Nations, *Mobilization of domestic capital in certain countries of Asia and the Far East* (Bangkok: Department of Economic Affairs, Economic Commission for Asia and the Far East, 1951).

A proposed industrialization programme for the State of Singapore (New York: UN Commission for Technical Assistance, 1961).

Population growth and policies in mega-cities: Bangkok (New York: United Nations, 1987).

World urbanization: the 2007 revision (New York: United Nations, 2008).

'Gross domestic product: total and per capita, current and constant (2015) prices, annual', https://unctadstat.unctad.org/datacentre/reportInfo/US.GDPTotal

The world's cities in 2018: data booklet (New York: United Nations, 2018).

The world's cities in 2025: data booklet (New York: United Nations, 2025).

Thailand: migration report, 2019 (New York: United Nations, 2019).

World migration report, 2024 (Geneva: International Organization for Migration, 2024).

United Nations Conference on Trade and Development (UNCTAD), *World investment report*, annual series, 1980–2022 (New York: United Nations).

A case study of the electronics industry in Thailand (New York and Geneva: United Nations, 2005).

United Nations, Department of Economic and Social Affairs, Population Division, *World urbanization prospects: the 2018 revision* (ST/ESA/SER.A/420) (New York: United Nations, 2019).

United Nations Development Programme, *Human development report 1990* (New York: Oxford University Press, 1990).

United Nations, Economic and Social Council, E/CN.1/Sub.1/C.2/W.2. *Economic reconstruction of devastated areas working group for Asia and the Far East, part II country studies. B. Indo-Chinese Federation* (New York: United Nations, January 1947).

United Nations, Economic and Social Council, E/CN.1/Sub.1/C.2/W.5. *Economic reconstruction of devastated areas working group for Asia and the Far East, part II country studies. E. Siam* (New York: United Nations, January 1947).

United Nations, Economic and Social Council, E/CN.1/Sub.1/C.2/W.8. *Economic reconstruction of devastated areas working group for Asia and the Far East, part II country studies. H. Philippine Republic* (New York: United Nations, January 1947).

United Nations, Economic and Social Council, E/CN.1/Sub.1/C.2/W.9. *Economic reconstruction of devastated areas working group for Asia and the Far East, part II country studies. I. British Borneo* (New York: United Nations, January 1947).

United Nations, Economic and Social Council, E/CN.1/Sub.1/C.2/W.10. *Reconstruction of devastated areas working group for Asia and the Far East, part II country studies. J. Burma* (New York: United Nations, January 1947).

United Nations, Economic and Social Council, E/CN.1/Sub.1/C.2/W.11. *Economic reconstruction of devastated areas working group for Asia and the Far East, part II country studies. K. Netherlands Indies* (New York: United Nations, January 1947).

United Nations, Statistics Division, 'Per capita GDP at current prices – US dollars', https://data.un.org/Data.aspx?d=SNAAMA&f=grID%3A101%3BcurrID%3AUSD%3BpcFlag%3A1.

United Nations, UN-Habitat, *World cities report 2024: cities and climate action* (Nairobi: United Nations Human Settlement Programme, 2024).

World Bank, *Proceedings of the World Bank Annual Conference on Development Economics 1990* (Washington, DC: World Bank, 1990).

The East Asian miracle: economic growth and public policy (New York: Oxford University Press, 1993).

World development indicators, annual series (Washington, DC: World Bank, 2010–).

Malaysia Economic Monitor: immigrant labor (Washington, DC: World Bank, 2015).

Philippines urbanization review: fostering competitive, sustainable and inclusive cities (Washington, DC: World Bank, 2017).

Riding the wave: an East Asian miracle for the 21st century (Washington, DC: World Bank, 2018).

PISA 2018: Programme for international student assessment, East Asia and Pacific regional brief (World Bank, 2019).

The middle class in the Philippines: an exploration of the conditions for upward mobility (Washington, DC: World Bank, 2020).

Who is keeping score?: estimating the number of foreign workers in Malaysia (Kuala Lumpur: World Bank Group, 2020).

World Development Report 2022: finance for an equitable recovery (Washington, DC: World Bank, 2022).

Funding Indonesia's vision 2045 (Washington, DC: World Bank, 2024).

World Economic Forum, *The human capital report, 2015* (Geneva: World Economic Forum, 2015).

Brazil

Brazil, *O Brasil em Numeros Apendice do 'Anuario Estatistico do Brasil – 1960* (Rio de Janeiro: IBGE – Conselho Nacional de Estatistica, 1960).

Burma

Baxter, James, *Report on Indian immigration* (Rangoon: Superintendent, Government Printing and Stationery, Burma, 1941).

Bennison, J. J., *Report of an enquiry into the standard and cost of living of the working classes in Rangoon* (Rangoon: Superintendent, Government Printing and Stationery, 1928).

Bingham, R. P., *Report of the Labour Department 1946* (Singapore, 1947).

Burma, *Report on the administration of Burma*, annual series, 1868/69–1935/36 (Rangoon: Office of the Superintendent, Government Printing and Stationery).

Report of the Burma Provincial Banking Enquiry Committee, 1929–30, 3 vols. (Rangoon: Superintendent, Government Printing and Stationery, Burma, 1930).

Interim report of the Committee Appointed to Enquire into the Rice and Paddy Trade (Rangoon: Superintendent, Government Printing and Stationery, 1931).

Burma's new order plan (Rangoon: Bureau of the State Printing Presses, 1944).

Two-year plan of economic development for Burma (Rangoon: Superintendent, Government Printing and Stationery, 1948).

The national income of Burma (Rangoon: Ministry of National Planning, 1951).

Economic survey of the Union of Burma, annual series, 1959–63 (Rangoon: Superintendent, Government Printing and Stationery).

Burma, Census Department, *Towns classified by population with decennial variations from 1881 to 1953* (Rangoon: Superintendent, Government Printing and Stationery, 1954).

Burma Currency Board, *Annual report: Report of the Burma Currency Board for the period 1st April, 1947, to 30th September, 1948 (1947/48); Report of the Burma Currency Board for the year ended 30th September, ... (1948/49–1950/51);*

Report of the Burma Currency Board for the period 1st October, 1951, to 30th June, 1952 (Rangoon: Burma Currency Board, 1947/48–1951/52).
Burma Intelligence Bureau, *Burma during the Japanese occupation*, vol. 2 (Simla: Government of India Press, 1944).
Burma, Office of the Chief Collector of Customs, *Annual statement of the sea-borne trade and navigation of Burma*, annual series, 1912–1913, 1920–1921 (Rangoon: Office of the Superintendent, Government Printing).
Myanmar, Ministry of Labour, Immigration and Population, *2014 Myanmar Population and Housing Census, thematic report on migration and urbanization, census report, volume 4-D* (Nay Pyi Taw: Department of Population, Ministry of Labour, Immigration and Population, 2016).
2014 Myanmar Population and Housing Census, thematic report on population dynamics, census report, volume 4-E (Nay Pyi Taw: Department of Population, Ministry of Labour, Immigration and Population, 2016).
Union of Burma, Ministry of Planning and Finance, *Report to the Pyithu Hluttaw on the financial, economic and social conditions of the Socialist Republic of the Union of Burma*, annual series, 1989/90–1997/98 (Yangon).

India

India, *Census of India, 1901. vol. XV. Madras. Part I. Report* by W. Francis and *Part II* (Madras: Superintendent, Government Press, 1902).
Census of India, 1921. vol. X. Burma. Part I. Report by S. G. Grantham (Rangoon: Superintendent, Government Printing, 1923).
Census of India, 1931. vol. XIII. Madras. Part I. Report by G. T. Boag and *Part II* (Madras: Superintendent, Government Press, 1932).
Census of India, 1931. vol. XI. Burma. Parts I and II. Report by J. J. Bennison (Rangoon: Superintendent, Government Printing and Stationery, 1932).
Madras, *Report of the Census of the Madras Presidency, 1871*, by W. R. Cornish (Madras: Government Gazette Press, 1874).

Indochina and Vietnam

Indochina, *Situation de l'Indochine de 1902 à 1907*, vol. 1 (Saigon, 1908).
Annuaire statistique de l'Indochine, irregular series covering the years 1913–46 and published 1927–48 (Hanoi).
Vietnam, *Annuaire statistique du Viêtnam, 1950–51* (Hanoi: Institut de la Statistique et des Études Économiques du Viêtnam, 1952).

Indonesia

Indonesia, *Koloniaal Verslag 1892* (Batavia: Landsdrukkerij, 1893).
Centraal Kantoor voor de Statistiek, Statistisch Jaaroverzicht van Nederlandsch-Indië, 1925 (Batavia: Departement van Landbouw, 1926).

Volkstelling [Population census] *1930*, 8 vols. (Batavia: Departement van Landbouw, Nijverheid en Handel, 1933–4).

Statistical pocketbook of Indonesia 1941 (Batavia: Central Bureau of Statistics, 1947).

Department of Labour, Report on the labour force sample survey in Java and Madura, 1958 (Djakarta, 1961).

Indonesia, Ministry of National Development Planning, 'Indonesia Vision 2045', https://indonesia2045.go.id/.

Malaya and Malaysia

Federated Malay States, *Census of population, 1901*, by George Thompson Hare (Kuala Lumpur, 1902).

Federated Malay States, review of the census operations and results, 1911, by A. M. Pountney (London: HMSO, 1911).

Table of taxes, duties, fees, etc ... and manual of statistics 1929 (Kuala Lumpur: FMS Government Press, 1929).

Report on the Rice Cultivation Committee, 2 vols. (Kuala Lumpur: Government Printing Office, 1931).

Fifty years of railways in Malaya 1885–1935 (Kuala Lumpur: Federated Malay States Railways, 1935).

Report by the auditor on revenue and expenditure 1939 (Kuala Lumpur: Government Printing Office, 1939).

Federation of Malaya and Singapore, *Report of the war damage commission, Federation of Malaya and Singapore* by Richard Graham (Kuala Lumpur: Government Press, 1953).

Fermor, Lewis Leigh, *Report upon the mining industry of Malaya* (Kuala Lumpur: Government Press, 1939).

Grant, J. W., *The rice crop in Burma*, Agricultural Survey no. 17 of 1932 (Rangoon: Superintendent, Government Printing and Stationery, 1932).

Mackenzie, K. E., *Economic and commercial conditions in the Federation of Malaya and Singapore*, March 1951 (London: HMSO, 1952).

Malaya, *The census of British Malaya, 1921* by J. E. Nathan (London, 1921).

Return of foreign imports and exports, annual series, 1921–28 (Singapore: Government Printing Office).

Foreign imports and exports, annual series, 1930–37 (Singapore: Government Printing Office).

British Malaya, a report on the 1931 census by C. A. Vlieland (London, 1932).

Rubber statistics handbook 1940 (Singapore: Government Printing Office, 1940).

The foreign trade of Malaya 1939 (Singapore: Government Printing Office, 1941).

Malaya, a report on the 1947 census of population by M. V. Del Tufo (London, 1949).

Population census of the Federation of Malaya. Report no. 2, State of Selangor; Report no. 13: Administrative report and Report no. 14: Final report, all by H. Fell (Kuala Lumpur: Department of Statistics, Federation of Malaya, 1957).

Malayan Union, *Report on the British military administration of Malaya* by H. R. Hone (Kuala Lumpur: Malayan Union Government Press, 1946).

Annual report on education in the Malayan Union, 1946 by H. R. Cheeseman (Kuala Lumpur: Malayan Union Government Press, 1947).

Report of the medical department 1946 by R. B. MacGregor (Kuala Lumpur: Malayan Union Government Press, 1947).

Malaysia, *First Malaysia plan 1966–1970* (Kuala Lumpur: Government Press, 1965).

Second Malaysia plan 1971–1975 (Kuala Lumpur: Government Press, 1971).

Mid-term review of the second Malaysia plan, 1971–1975 (Kuala Lumpur: Government Press, 1973).

Third Malaysia plan 1976–1980 (Kuala Lumpur: Government Press, 1976).

Fourth Malaysia plan 1981–1985 (Kuala Lumpur: National Printing Department, 1981).

General report of the population census, 1980: Population and housing census of Malaysia, vol. 2 by T. H. Khoo (Kuala Lumpur: Department of Statistics, 1983).

Population distribution and basic demographic characteristics, 2000 population and housing census of Malaysia by Shaari Abdul Rahman (Putrajaya: Department of Statistics, 2001).

Eleventh Malaysia plan 2016–2020: anchoring growth on people (Kuala Lumpur: Economic Planning Unit, 2015).

Twelfth Malaysia plan 2021–2025: a prosperous, inclusive, sustainable Malaysia (Kuala Lumpur: Economic Planning Unit, 2021).

My Census 2020: Mukim/Town/Pekan by Mohd Uzir Mahidin (Putrajaya: Department of Statistics, Malaysia, 2024).

Malaysia, Department of Statistics, *Current population estimates Malaysia 2023* (Putrajaya: Department of Statistics, 2023).

Malaysia, Ministry of International Trade and Industry, *Review of the industrial master plan 1986–1995* (Kuala Lumpur: Ministry of International Trade and Industry, 1995).

New industrial master plan 2030 (Kuala Lumpur: Ministry of Investment, Trade and Industry, 2023).

Malaysia, National Economic Advisory Council, *New economic model for Malaysia, part 1* (Kuala Lumpur: National Economic Advisory Council, 2010).

Watson, G. M. and Sir Sydney Caine, *Report on the establishment of a central bank in Malaya* (Kuala Lumpur: Government Printer, 1956).

Philippines

Philippines, *Third annual report of the Secretary of Finance and Justice to the Philippine Commission* (Manila, 1904).

Annual report of the Chief of the Division of the Currency, annual series, *1904, 1905* (Manila: Bureau of Public Printing).

Census of the Philippine Islands, 1903, 4 vols. (Washington, DC: United States Bureau of the Census, 1905).

Census of the Philippine Islands, 1918, 4 vols. (Manila: Bureau of Printing, 1921).
Census of the Philippines: 1939 (Manila: Bureau of Printing, 1942).
Handbook of Philippine statistics 1903–1959 (Manila: Bureau of Printing, 1960).
Philippines, Bureau of Commerce, *Statistical bulletin of the Philippine Islands*, annual series, 1918–38 (Manila: Bureau of Printing).
Philippines, Bureau of the Census and Statistics, *Yearbook of Philippine statistics* (irregular series) (Manila: Bureau of Printing, 1940, 1946).
Philippines, Commission of the Census, *Special Bulletin no. 1, Census of the Philippines, 1939* (Manila: Bureau of Printing, 1939).
Philippines, Department of Agriculture and Commerce, *Philippine statistical review, 1937* (quarterly) (Manila: Bureau of Printing, 1937).
Philippines, Division of Statistics, *Bulletin of Philippine statistics 1938* (fourth quarter) (Manila: Bureau of Printing, 1938).
Philippines, National Economic and Development Authority, *NEDA statistical yearbook of the Philippines*, 1970–76 continued as Philippines, National Economic and Development Authority/National Statistical Coordination Board, *Philippine statistical yearbook* (1977–2020).
Port of Manila, Commonwealth of the Philippines, *A year book devoted to foreign commerce and shipping of Manila and the Philippines* (1924–40).

Singapore

Arumainathan, P., *Report on the census of population 1970* (Singapore), 2 vols. (Singapore, 1973).
Hu, Richard Tsu Tau, *Budget statement* (Singapore, 1988).
Khoo Chian Kim, *Census of population 1980 Singapore* (Singapore: Administrative report, 1983; and 9 separate vols., released 1980 and 1981, and 5 census monographs published 1982–85).
Lau Kak En, *Singapore census of population 1990* (Singapore: Advance data release, 1991; Demographic characteristics [statistical release 1], 1992; Households and housing [statistical release 2], 1992; Literacy, languages spoken and education [statistical release 3], 1993; Economic characteristics [statistical release 4], 1993).
Marriott, H., *Census report of the Straits Settlements, 1911* (Singapore, 1911).
Singapore, *Report of the Housing Committee Singapore, 1947* (Singapore: Government Printing Office, 1947).
Annual report on the registration of births and deaths for the years 1940–47 by E. J. Phillips (Singapore: Government Printing Office, 1948).
'An industrial development programme' (Lyle Report), Sessional Paper No. Cmd. 5 of 1959 (Singapore: Legislative Assembly, 15 January 1959).
Development plan 1961–1964 (Singapore, 1961).
Annual report of the Division of Commerce and Industry of the Ministry of Finance Singapore 1960 (Singapore, 1963).
Parliamentary Debates (Singapore), annual series, 1965–.

Report of the public sector divestment committee (Singapore, 1987).

Report of the Economic Strategies Committee: high skilled people, innovative economy, distinctive global city (Singapore: Ministry of Trade and Industry, 2010).

A sustainable population for a dynamic Singapore: population white paper (Singapore: National Population and Talent Division, 2013).

Census of population 2020, statistical release 1: demographic characteristics, education, language and religion (Singapore: Department of Statistics, 2021).

Population in brief 2024 (Singapore: Department of Statistics, 2024).

Singapore, Department of Statistics, *Singapore external trade statistics* (from 1975 *Singapore trade statistics)* (Singapore), annual, quarterly or monthly series, 1956–. From 1989 published by the Trade Development Board.

Singapore, Department of Statistics (or Economic Development Board), *Report on the census of industrial production* (Singapore), annual series, 1959–.

Singapore Economic Development Board, *Annual report* (or *Yearbook*) (Singapore) (1961–1991/92).

Singapore, Economic Planning Committee, *Ministry of Trade and Industry, The strategic economic plan* (Singapore, 1991).

Singapore, Economic Planning Unit, Prime Minister's Office, *First development plan 1961–1964: review of progress for the three years ending 31st December 1963* (Singapore, 1964).

Singapore Legislative Assembly, *Report of the Committee on Minimum Standards of Livelihood* (Singapore, 1957).

Singapore, Ministry of Labour, *Yearbook of labour statistics* (Singapore), annual series, 1976–91.

Report on wages in Singapore (Singapore), annual series, 1986–91.

Singapore, Ministry of Trade and Industry, *Economic survey of Singapore* (Singapore), annual and quarterly series, 1974–.

Highlights of Singapore's economic development plan for the eighties (Singapore, n.d.).

Singapore, Monetary Authority of Singapore, *Annual report* (Singapore), 1971–1991/92.

Singapore, Report of the Economic Committee, *The Singapore economy: new directions* (Singapore, 1986).

Singapore, Statistics Division, Ministry of Labour, 'Wages and earnings in the financial sector, 1979–1982', *Singapore Statistical News*, 6, 2 (1983).

SSLCP (Straits Settlements Legislative Council Proceedings) (Singapore: Government Printing Office, 1923–32).

SSTC: Straits Settlements, *Report of the commission appointed by the Governor of the Straits Settlements to enquire into and report on the trade of the Colony*, 5 vols. (Singapore, 1934).

Straits Settlements, *Blue book* (Singapore), annual series, 1870–1939.

'Protector of Chinese', *Straits Settlements Annual Reports* (Singapore: Government Printing Office, 1881–1911).

Report on the census of the Straits Settlements, 1891 by E. M. Merewether (Singapore: Government Printing Press, 1892).
Return of imports and exports (Singapore), annual series, 1900–27.
Report on the census of the Straits Settlements taken on 1st March 1901 by J. R. Innes (Singapore, 1901).
'Report on the Straits Settlements', *Straits Settlements Annual Reports* (Singapore: Government Printing Office, 1903–38).
Reports of the commissions on the present state of trade depression and the extension of credit facilities (Singapore: Government Printing Office, 1921).
'Chinese affairs', *Straits Settlements Annual Reports* (Singapore: Government Printing Office, 1930–38).
Statistical summary 1934 (Singapore: Government Printing Office, 1934).
'Progress of the Straits Settlements', *Straits Settlements Annual Reports* (Singapore: Government Printing Office, 1934–38).
Wong, Lawrence, *Onward together for a better tomorrow: budget statement 2025* (Singapore: Ministry of Finance, 2025).

Thailand

Kingdom of Siam, *Statistical yearbook of the Kingdom of Siam [or Thailand]*, annual series, 1920–1939/40 (Bangkok).
Kingdom of Thailand, *Annual statements of the foreign trade and navigation of the Kingdom of Thailand 1942–1945* (Bangkok: Department of His Majesty's Customs, *c.*1947).
Report of the financial adviser covering the years 1941 to 1950 (Bangkok, 1951).
Statistics on the import and export trade of Siam, 1901. Port of Bangkok (Bangkok, 1901), continued under various titles and from 1923–24, *The foreign trade and navigation of the Kingdom of Siam* (Bangkok).
Thailand, *National strategy 2018–2037 (summary)* (Bangkok: National Strategy Secretariat Office, Office of the National Economic and Social Development Board, 2018).
Thailand, National Statistical Office, *National income of Thailand, 1951–1996*. www.nesdc.go.th/nesdb_en/ewt_news.php?nid=4289&filename=national_account.

United Kingdom

MacMichael, Sir Harold, *Report on a mission to Malaya (October, 1945–January, 1946)* (London: HMSO, 1946).
Reports on the Federated Malay States for 1901 (P.P. 1902, LXVI).
Reports on the Federated Malay States for 1903 (P.P. 1905, LIV).
United Kingdom, *Commission to Enquire into the Use of Opium in the Straits Settlements and the Federated Malay States*, 3 vols. (P.P. 1909, LXI).
Report of the Committee on the Working of the Monetary System (London: HMSO, 1959).

United States

CIA (Central Intelligence Agency), 'The rice situation in South Vietnam'. www.cia.gov/readingroom/docs/CIA-RDP78T02095R000800020039-7.pdf.

United States Department of Commerce, *Historical statistics of the United States colonial times to 1970, part 1* (Washington, DC: US Government Printing Office, 1970).

United States Department of Labor, *Bureau of Labor Statistics, International comparisons of hourly compensation costs for production workers in manufacturing 1991*, Report 825 (Washington: US Department of Labor, June 1992).

United States Department of State, *Report to the President of the United States by the economic survey mission to the Philippines* (the Bell mission) (Washington, DC: Department of State, 1950).

United States Tariff Commission, *Economic factors affecting the use of items 807.00 and 806.30 of the tariff schedule of the United States* (Washington, DC: US Tariff Commission, 1970).

United States Office of Strategic Services (OSS), Research and Analysis Branch (R&A): Assemblages, Reports and South East Asia Command (SEAC) (published in Washington DC or Honolulu or in NARA)

R&A 1286.1 *An additional strategic objective* (Appendix to selection of *S. O. objectives in the Southeast Asia theatre* R&A 1286), 8 December 1943.

R&A 1713 *The structure of the government of Burma*, 29 September 1944.

R&A 1992 *Burma* (New Delhi area report no. 1), 15 May 1944.

R&A 1992A *Burma (situation report no. 1)*, 25 February 1944.

R&A 2015 *Japanese administration of Burma*, 10 July 1944.

R&A 2137 *Industrial facilities in Malaya*, 15 May 1944.

R&A 2280 *Handbook of Japanese industry in Japan and occupied areas*, 10 June 1944.

R&A 2423 *Singapore under Japanese domination*, 8 September 1944.

R&A 2594 *Selected industrial installations in Indo-China*, 1 January 1945.

R&A 2753, *Japanese use of Burmese industry*, 1 November 1945.

R&A 3186S *The kempei in Japanese-occupied territory*, 15 July 1945.

JISPB (Joint Intelligence Study Publishing Board Studies, University Microfilms, Ann Arbor, MI)

JISPB, *Joint Army-Navy intelligence study of Indochina*, Chapter 7, 'Transportation and communications' (Washington, DC: United States Strategic Bombing Survey, October 1945).

United States Strategic Bombing Surveys and Reports (USSBS)

United States Strategic Bombing Survey, *Summary report (Pacific war)* (Washington, DC: Office of the Chairman, United States Strategic Bombing Survey, 1946).

The effects of strategic bombing on Japan's war economy (Washington, DC: Overall Economic Effects Division, United States Strategic Bombing Survey, 1946).

Oil in Japan's war (Washington, DC: Oil and Chemicals Division, United States Strategic Bombing Survey, 1946).

The war against Japanese transportation 1941–1945 (Washington, DC: Transportation Division, United States Strategic Bombing Survey, 1947).

Newspapers

Business Times (Singapore)
Daily Telegraph
Euromoney
Far Eastern Economic Review
Financial Times
Guardian
Japan Times and Advertiser
Malaya Mail
New York Herald Tribune
New York Times
Singapore Trade and Industry
Straits Times Weekly (Singapore)
The Economist
The Times
Washington Post

Books and Articles

A Correspondent lately in Burma [Reginald Dorman-Smith], 'Burma: the struggle for power', *Round Table*, 37, 146 (1947), pp. 146–52.

Abeysinghe, Tilak and Keen Meng Choy, *The Singapore economy: an econometric perspective* (London: Routledge, 2007).

Abramovitz, Moses, 'Catching up, forging ahead, and falling behind', *Journal of Economic History*, 46, 2 (1986), pp. 385–406.

Abueva, Jose Veloso, 'The Philippines: tradition and change', *Asian Survey*, 10, 1 (1970), pp. 56–64.

Adas, Michael, *The Burma Delta* (Madison, WI: University of Wisconsin Press, 1974).

Ades, Alberto F. and Edward L. Glaeser, 'Trade and circuses: explaining urban giants', *Quarterly Journal of Economics*, 110, 1 (1995), pp. 195–227.

Agoncillo, Teodoro A., *The fateful years: Japan's adventure in the Philippines, 1941–45*, 2 vols. (Quezon City: R. P. Garcia Publishing Company, 1965).

Aiken, Robert S. and Colin H. Leigh, 'Malaysia's emerging conurbation', *Annals of the Association of American Geographers*, 65, 4 (1975), pp. 546–63.

Alburo, F. and G. Shepherd, 'Trade liberalization experience in the Philippines, 1960–84', PIDS working paper, 8601 (Manila: PIDS, 1985).

Aldrich, Richard J., *The key to the south: Britain, the United States and Thailand during the approach of the Pacific War, 1929–1942* (Kuala Lumpur: Oxford University Press, 1993).

Allen, G. C. and Audrey G. Donnithorne, *Western enterprise in Indonesia and Malaya* (London: George Allen & Unwin, 1954).

Allen, Louis, 'Burma: the longest war, 1941–45', in Ian Nish and Mark Allen, eds., *War, conflict and security in Japan and Asia-Pacific, 1941–1952: the writings of Louis Allen* (Folkestone: Global Oriental, 2011), pp. 297–305.

Allen, Robert Loring, 'Burma's clearing account agreements', *Pacific Affairs*, 31, 2 (1958), pp. 147–63.

Anamwathana, Panarat, *Thailand's economy and the Second World War* (Bangkok: Thammasat University, 1994).

Anand, Sudhir, *Inequality and poverty in Malaysia: measurement and decomposition* (New York: Oxford University Press, 1983).

Anas, T. and D. Narjoko, 'International cooperation and the management of globalisation: the Indonesian experience', in A. A. Patunru, M. Pangestu, and M. C. Basri, eds., *Indonesia in the new world: globalisation, nationalism and sovereignty (Books and Monographs.* Singapore: ISEAS–Yusof Ishak Institute, 2018), pp. 294–316.

Anas, Titik and Thaliya Wikapuspita, 'Indonesia's services sector: performance, policies and challenges', in Hal Hill and Siwage Dharma Negara, eds., *The Indonesian economy in transition: policy challenges in the Jokowi era and beyond* (Singapore: Institute of Southeast Asian Studies, 2019), pp. 209–38.

Anas, Titik, Hal Hill, Dionisius Narjoko and Chandra Tri Putra, 'The Indonesian economy in turbulent times', *Bulletin of Indonesian Economic Studies*, 58, 3 (2022), pp. 241–71.

Anderson, Benedict, *Some aspects of Indonesian politics under the Japanese occupation: 1944–1945* (Ithaca, NY: Southeast Asia Program, Department of Far Eastern Studies, Cornell University, 1961).

'Withdrawal symptoms: social and cultural aspects of the October 6 coup', *Bulletin of Concerned Asian Scholars*, 9, 3 (1977), pp. 13–30.

Andrew, E. J. L., *Indian labour in Rangoon* (London: Oxford University Press, 1933).

Andrews, James M., *Siam, 2nd rural economic survey 1934–35* (Bangkok: Bangkok Times Press, 1935).

Andrus, J. Russell, *Burmese economic life* (Stanford, CA: Stanford University Press, 1948).

Apter, David E., 'Ideology and discontent', in David E. Apter, ed., *Ideology and discontent* (Glencoe, IL: The Free Press, 1964).

Arnaud, I., 'Taux moyen de la piastre de 1876 à 1919', *Bulletin économique de l'Indochine* (1920), pp. 267–68.

Arndt, H. W., 'Banking in hyperinflation', *Bulletin of Indonesian Economic Studies*, 2, 5 (1966), pp. 45–70.

Asian Development Bank, *Unlocking the economic and social value of Indonesia's state-owned enterprises* (Manila: Asian Development Bank, 2022).

Key indicators for Asia and the Pacific, 2023 (Manila: Asian Development Bank, 2024).

Asian Productivity Organization, *APO productivity databook 2024* (Tokyo: Asian Productivity Organization, 2024).

Athukorala, Prema-chandra, 'The Philippines in global manufacturing value chains: a tale of arrested growth', ANU working papers in trade and development, no. 2021/22 (2021).

'The global trade slowdown: is it nominal or real?', ANU working papers in trade and development, no. 2024/08 (2024).

Athukorala, Prema-chandra and Hal Hill, *Revisiting globalization: Southeast Asia in the global factory* (Cambridge: Cambridge University Press, 2026).

Athukorala, Prema-chandra and Archanun Kohpaiboon, 'Global production sharing, trade patterns, and industrialization in Southeast Asia', in Ian Coxhead, ed., *Routledge handbook of Southeast Asian economics* (London: Routledge, 2015), pp. 139–61.

Athukorala, Prema-chandra and Wanissa Suanin, 'Saving transition in Asia', *Journal of Development Studies*, 60, 8 (2024), pp. 1211–26.

Atkin, J. M., *British overseas investment 1918–1931* (New York: Arno Press, 1977).

Ayal, Eliezer B., 'Some crucial issues in Thailand's economic development', *Pacific Affairs*, 34, 2 (1961), pp. 157–64.

'Private enterprise and economic progress in Thailand', *Journal of Asian Studies*, 26, 1 (1966), pp. 5–14.

Badgley, John H., 'Burma's zealot wungyis: Maoists or St. Simonists', *Asian Survey*, 5, 1 (1965), pp. 55–62.

'The Union of Burma age twenty-two', *Asian Survey*, 11, 2 (1971), pp. 149–58.

Bailey, Conner, *The sociology of production in rural Malay society* (Kuala Lumpur: Oxford University Press, 1983).

Baker, Chris and Pasuk Phongpaichit, *The history of Thailand* (Cambridge: Cambridge University Press, 2005).

Baldwin, Robert E., 'Patterns of development in newly settled regions', *Manchester School of Economic and Political Studies*, 24 (1956), pp. 161–79.

'Export technology and development from a subsistence level', *Economic Journal*, 73 (1963), pp. 80–92.

Foreign trade regimes and economic development: the Philippines (New York: National Bureau of Economic Research, 1975).

Balisacan, Arsenio M., Hal Hill and Sharon Faye Piza, 'Spatial disparities and development policy in the Philippines', in Yukon Huang and Alessandro Magnoli Bocchi, eds., *Reshaping economic geography in East Asia* (Washington DC: World Bank, 2009), pp. 169–82.

Bankers Almanac, *Bankers almanac and yearbook, 1941–42* (London: Thomas Skinner & Co. and Waterlow & Sons, 1941).

Barker, Randolph, 'Barriers to efficient capital investment in agriculture', in T. W. Schultz, ed., *Distortions in agricultural incentives* (Bloomington, IN: Indiana University Press, 1978), pp. 140–60.

Barker, Randolph, Robert W. Herdt with Beth Rose, *The rice economy of Asia* (Washington, DC: Resources for the Future, 1985).

Barro, Robert J. and José F. Ursúa, 'Macroeconomic crises since 1870', *Brookings Papers on Economic Activity*, 39, 1 (2008), pp. 255–335.

Bassino, Jean-Pascal, 'Public finance in Vietnam under French rule', in J.-P. Bassino, J.-D. Giacometti and K. Odaka, eds., *Quantitative history of Vietnam 1900–1990* (Tokyo: Institute of Economic Research, Hitotsubashi University, 2000).

Bassino, Jean-Pascal and Pierre van der Eng, 'Asia's "little divergence" in the twentieth century: evidence from PPP-based direct estimates of GDP per capita, 1913–69', *Economic History Review*, 73, 1 (2020), pp. 185–208.

Bastin, John and Harry J. Benda, *A history of modern Southeast Asia* (Englewood Cliffs, NJ: Prentice Hall, 1968).

Bauer, P. T., 'Some aspects of the Malayan rubber slump 1929–1933', *Economica*, 11 (1944), pp. 190–98.

The rubber industry (London: Longmans, Green, 1948).

From subsistence to exchange and other essays (Princeton, NJ: Princeton University Press, 2000).

Becker, Abraham S., *National income accounting in the USSR* (Santa Monica, CA: Rand Corp., 1971).

Belton, Ben and Mateusz Filipski, 'Rural transformation in central Myanmar: by how much, and for whom?', *Journal of Rural Studies*, 67 (2019), pp. 166–76.

Benda, Harry J., 'Indonesian Islam under Japanese occupation', *Pacific Affairs*, 28, 4 (1955), pp. 350–62.

The crescent and the rising sun: Indonesian Islam under Japanese occupation 1942–1945 (The Hague: W. van Hoeve, 1958).

'The structure of Southeast Asian history: some preliminary observations', *Journal of Southeast Asian History*, 3, 1 (1962), pp. 106–38.

'Democracy in Indonesia: Herbert Feith, *The decline of constitutional democracy in Indonesia* (book review)', *Journal of Asian Studies*, 23, 3 (1964), p. 449.

'Decolonization in Indonesia: the problem of continuity and change', *American Historical Review*, 70, 4 (1965), pp. 1058–73.

'The Japanese interregnum in Southeast Asia', in Grant K. Goodman, ed., *Imperial Japan: a reassessment* (New York: East Asian Institute, Columbia University, 1967), pp. 65–79.

'The beginnings of the Japanese occupation in Java', in Harry J. Benda, *Continuity and change in Southeast Asia* (New Haven, CT: Yale University Southeast Asian Studies, 1972), pp. 63–82.

'Peasant movements in colonial Southeast Asia', *Asian Studies*, 42 (2006), pp. 31–45.

Bennett, W. J., 'Kuala Lumpur: a town of the equatorial lowlands', *Tijdschrift voor Economische en Sociale Geografie*, 52, 12 (1961), pp. 327–33.

Beresford, Melanie, *Vietnam: politics, economics and society* (London: Pinter Publishers, 1988).

National unification and economic development (New York: St. Martin's Press, 1989).

Bernardelli, H., 'New Zealand and Asiatic migration', *Population Studies*, 6, 1 (1952), pp. 39–54.

Berry, Albert, 'Income and consumption distribution trends in the Philippines, 1950–70', *Review of Income and Wealth*, 24, 3 (1978), pp. 313–31.

Berry, Brian J. and Frank E. Horton, *Geographical perspectives on urban systems* (Englewood Cliffs, NJ: Prentice Hall, 1970).

Bertrand, Trent and Lyn Squire, 'The relevance of the dual economy model: a case study of Thailand', *Oxford Economic Papers*, 32, 3 (1980), pp. 480–511.

Besley, Timothy and Torsten Persson, 'Taxation and development', in A. Auerbach, R. Chetty, M. Feldstein, and E. Saez, eds., *Handbook of public economics* (Amsterdam: Elsevier, 2013), pp. 51–110.

Bevan, David, Paul Collier and Jan Willem Gunning, *The political economy of poverty, equity, and growth: Nigeria and Indonesia* (Washington, DC: World Bank, 1999).

Bird, Kelly and Hal Hill, 'Tiny, poor, land-locked, indebted, but growing: lessons for late reforming transition economies from Laos', *Oxford Development Studies*, 38, 2 (2010), pp. 117–43.

Birdsall, Nancy, 'The (indispensable) middle class in developing countries', in Ravi Kanbur and Michael Spence, eds., *Equity and growth in a globalizing world* (Washington, DC: Commission on Growth and Development, 2010), pp. 157–88.

'Middle-class heroes: the best guarantee of good governance', *Foreign Affairs*, 95, 2 (2016), pp. 25–32.

Birnberg, Thomas B. and Stephen A. Resnick, *Colonial development* (New Haven, CT: Yale University Press, 1975).

Bloomfield, A. I., *Monetary policy under the international gold standard* (New York: Federal Reserve Bank of New York, 1959).

Blythe, W. L., *Methods and conditions of employment of Chinese labour in the Federated Malay States* (Kuala Lumpur: Government Printer, 1938).

Boomgaard, Peter and A. J. Gooszen, *Changing economy of Indonesia*, vol. 11: *Population trends, 1795–1942* (Amsterdam: Royal Tropical Institute, 1991).

Booth, Anne, *Agricultural development in Indonesia* (Sydney: George Allen & Unwin, 1988).

The Indonesian economy in the nineteenth and twentieth centuries: a history of missed opportunities (London: Macmillan, 1998).

Colonial legacies: economic and social development in East and Southeast Asia (Honolulu: University of Hawaii Press, 2007).

Economic change in modern Indonesia: colonial and post-colonial comparisons (Cambridge: Cambridge University Press, 2016).

Borg, Dorothy, 'French considering industrialization of Indo-China', *Far Eastern Survey*, 8 (1939), pp. 44–47.

Boughton, Duncan, et al., 'Agriculture and rural livelihoods: incipient progress aborted', in Adam Simpson and Nicholas Farrelly, eds., *Myanmar: politics, economy and society*, 2nd edn. (Abingdon: Taylor & Francis, 2023), pp. 124–38.

Bown, Chad P. and Dan Wang, 'Semiconductors and modern industrial policy', *Journal of Economic Perspectives*, 38, 4 (2024), pp. 81–110.

Boyce, James K., *The Philippines: the political economy of growth and impoverishment in the Marcos era* (Honolulu: University of Hawaii Press, 1993).

Bredo, William, 'Agrarian reform in Vietnam: Vietcong and government of Vietnam strategies in conflict', *Asian Survey*, 10, 8 (1970), pp. 738–50.

Bredo, William, et al., *Land reform in Vietnam* (Menlo Park, CA: Stanford Research Institute, 1968).

Brimble, Peter and Richard F. Doner, 'University–industry linkages and economic development: the case of Thailand', *World Development*, 35, 6 (2007), pp. 1021–36.

Brocheux, Pierre, *The Mekong Delta: ecology, economy and revolution, 1860–1960* (Madison, WI: Center for Southeast Asian Studies, University of Wisconsin, 1995).

'The economy of war as a prelude to a "socialist economy": the case of Vietnamese resistance against the French', in Pierre Brocheux and Gisele Bousquet, eds., *Viêt Nam exposé: French scholarship on twentieth-century Vietnamese society* (Ann Arbor, MI: University of Michigan Press, 2002), pp. 313–30.

Ho Chi Minh: a biography (Cambridge: Cambridge University Press, 2007).

Brocheux, Pierre and Daniel Hémery, *Indochina: an ambiguous colonization, 1858–1954* (Berkeley, CA: University of California Press, 2009).

Broek, Jan O. M., 'Diversity and unity in Southeast Asia', *Geographical Review*, 34, 2 (1944), pp. 175–95.

Brookfield, Harold, Abdul Samad Hadi and Zaharah Mahmud, *The city in the village: the in-situ urbanization of villages, villagers and their land around Kuala Lumpur, Malaysia* (Singapore: Oxford University Press, 1991).

Brown, McAlister and Joseph J. Zasloff, 'Laos 1976: faltering first steps toward socialism', *Asian Survey*, 17, 2 (1977), pp. 107–15.

'Laos 1977: the realities of independence', *Asian Survey*, 18, 2 (Feb. 1978), pp. 164–74.

'Laos 1979: caught in Vietnam's wake', *Asian Survey*, 20, 2 (1980), pp. 103–11.

Brown, C. P., 'Rice price stabilization and support in Malaysia', *Developing Economies*, 11, 3 (1973), pp. 164–83.

Brown, Ian, 'Some comments on industrialization in the Philippines during the 1930s', in Ian Brown, ed., *The economics of Africa and Asia in the inter-war depression* (London: Routledge, 1989), pp. 203–20.

Economic change in South-East Asia, c.1830–1980 (Kuala Lumpur, Oxford University Press, 1997).

Burma's economy in the twentieth century (New York: Cambridge University Press, 2013).

Bruchey, Stuart, 'Douglas C. North on American economic growth', *Explorations in Entrepreneurial History*, 1, 2 (1964), pp. 145–58.

Brummethuis, Han Ten, *King of waters: Homan van der Heide and the origin of modern irrigation in Siam* (Leiden: KITLV Press, 2005).

Bruton, Henry J., *The political economy of poverty, equity, and growth: Sri Lanka and Malaysia* (New York: Oxford University Press, 1992).

Buck, John L., *Land utilization in China, statistics* (London: Humphrey Milford, 1937).

Buckley, Kenneth, 'The role of staple industries in Canada's economic development', *Journal of Economic History*, 18, 4 (1958), pp. 439–50.

Bünte, Marco, 'Myanmar's protracted transition: arenas, actors, and outcomes', *Asian Survey*, 56, 2 (2016), pp. 369–91.

Burghardt, A. F., 'A hypothesis about gateway cities', *Annals of the Association of American Geographers*, 61, 2 (1971), pp. 269–85.

Buruma, Ian, *God's dust: a modern Asian journey* (London: Jonathan Cape, 1989).

Butlin, N. G., *Australian domestic product, investment and foreign borrowing, 1861–1938/39* (Cambridge: Cambridge University Press, 1962).

Butwell, Richard, 'U Nu's second comeback try', *Asian Survey*, 9, 11 (1969), pp. 868–76.

Butwell, Richard and Fred von der Medhen, 'The 1960 election in Burma', *Pacific Affairs*, 33, 2 (1960), pp. 144–57.

Callahan, Mary P., *Making enemies: war and state building in Burma* (Ithaca, NY: Cornell University Press, 2003).

Callis, Helmut G., *Foreign capital in Southeast Asia* (New York: Institute of Pacific Relations, 1942).

'Capital investment in Southeastern Asia and the Philippines', *Annals of the American Academy of Political and Social Science*, 226, Southeastern Asia and the Philippines (1943), pp. 22–31.

Cameron, Rondo and Larry Neal, *A concise economic history of the world: from Paleolithic times to the present*, 4th edn. (New York: Oxford University Press, 2003).

Carroll, John J., 'Filippino entrepreneurship in manufacturing', *Philippine Studies*, 10, 1 (1962), pp. 100–26.

The Filipino manufacturing entrepreneur: agent and product of change (Ithaca, NY: Cornell University Press, 1965).

Castro, Amado A., 'Philippine-American tariff and trade relations, 1898–1954', *Philippine Economic Journal*, 4, 1 (1965), pp. 29–56.

'Philippine export development, 1950–1965' and 'Comment' by Ken'ichi Odawara in Theodore Morgan and Nyle Spoelstra, eds., *Economic interdependence in Southeast Asia* (Madison, WI: University of Wisconsin Press, 1969), pp. 181–201.

'The central bank of the Philippines: the first twenty years', *Philippine Review of Economics*, 9, 2 (1972), pp. 33–45.

Catton, Philip E., *Diem's final failure: prelude to America's war in Vietnam* (Lawrence, KA: University Press of Kansas, 2002).

Caves, Richard E., '"Vent for surplus" models of trade and growth', in Robert E. Baldwin et al., eds., *Trade, growth and the balance of payments* (Chicago, IL: Rand McNally, 1965), pp. 95–115.

'Export-led growth and the new economic history', in Jagdish N. Bhagwati et al., eds., *Trade, balance of payments and growth* (Amsterdam: North Holland, 1971), pp. 403–42.

Chakravarti, Nalini Ranjan, *The Indian minority in Burma: the rise and fall of an immigrant community* (London: Oxford University Press, 1971).

Chandler, David, *The tragedy of Cambodian history: politics, war, and revolution since 1945* (New Haven, CT: Yale University Press, 1991).

A history of Cambodia, 4th edn. (Boulder, CO: Westview Press, 2008).

Chandler, David P., Joel Steinberg, David K. Wyatt, John R. Smail, Alexander Woodside and William R. Roff, *In search of Southeast Asia: a modern history* (London: Pall Mall Press, 1971).

Cheah Boon Kheng, 'Sino-Malay conflicts in Malaya: communist vendetta and Islamic resistance', *Journal of Southeast Asian Studies*, 12, 1 (1981), pp. 108–17.

Red star over Malaya: resistance and conflict during and after the Japanese occupation, 1941–1946, 3rd edn. (Singapore: Singapore University Press, 2003).

Cheng, Siok-Hwa, *The rice industry of Burma 1852–1940* (Kuala Lumpur: University of Malaya Press, 1968).

Chew Soon Beng, *Small firms in Singapore* (Singapore: Oxford University Press, 1988).

Chiang, Hai Ding, *A history of Straits Settlements foreign trade* (Singapore: National Museum, Singapore, 1978).

Chiat Siow Yue, 'Comment on Tran Van Thot, "Vietnamese economy at the crossroads: new *Doi Moi* for sustained growth"', *Asian Economic Policy Review*, 8 (2013), pp. 144–45.

Chin, James, 'Racism towards the Chinese minority in Malaysia: political Islam and institutional barriers', *Political Quarterly*, 93, 3 (2022), pp. 451–59.

Chin, James and Taufiq Tanasaldy, 'The ethnic Chinese in Indonesia and Malaysia: the challenge of political Islam', *Asian Survey*, 59, 6 (2019), pp. 959–77.

Chin Kee Onn, *Malaya upside down* (Singapore: Jitts & Co., 1946).

Choy Keen Meng, 'Singapore's changing economic model', in Terence Chong, ed., *Management of success* (Singapore: Institute of Southeast Asian Studies, 2010), pp. 123–38.

Christian, John L., *Burma* (London: Collins, 1945).

Burma and the Japanese invader (Bombay: Thacker and Co., 1945).

Clarete, Ramon L., Emmanuel F. Esguerra and Hal Hill, eds., *The Philippine economy* (Singapore: Institute of Southeast Asian Studies, 2018).

Claudio, Lisandro E., *The profligate colonial: how the US exported austerity to the Philippines* (Ithaca, NY: Cornell University Press, 2025).

Clemens, M. A. and J. G. Williamson, 'Wealth bias in the first global capital market boom', *Economic Journal*, 114 (2004), pp. 304–37.

Coclanis, P. A., 'Distant thunder: the creation of a world market in rice and the transformation it wrought', *American Historical Review*, 98 (1993), pp. 1050–78.

Coclanis, P. A. and J. Komlos, 'Time in the paddies: a comparison of rice production in the southeastern United States and Burma in the nineteenth century', *Social Science History*, 11 (1987), pp. 343–54.

Cohen, Jerome B., *Japan's economy in war and reconstruction* (Minneapolis, MI: University of Minnesota Press, 1949).

Cole, A. H., 'The American rice-growing industry: a study in comparative advantage', *Quarterly Journal of Economics*, 41 (1927), pp. 595–643.

Cole, David C. and Betty F. Slade, *Building a modern financial system. The Indonesian experience* (Cambridge: Cambridge University Press, 1996).

Collis, Maurice, *Last and first in Burma (1941–1948)* (London: Faber and Faber, 1956).

Commodity Research Bureau, *Commodity year book 1939* (New York: Commodity Research Bureau, 1939).

Concannon, T. A. L., 'A new town in Malaya: Petaling Jaya, Kuala Lumpur', *Malayan Journal of Tropical Geography*, 5 (1955), pp. 39–43.

Constantino, Renato, *A history of the Philippines: from Spanish colonization to the Second World War* (New York: Monthly Review Press, 1975).

Copeland, Edwin Bingham, *Rice* (London: Macmillan, 1924).

Coppel, Charles A., *Indonesian Chinese in crisis* (Kuala Lumpur: Oxford University Press, 1983).

Coquerel, Albert, *Paddys et riz de Cochinchine* (Lyon: A. Rey, 1911).

Corden, W. M. and J. A. C. Mackie, 'The development of the Indonesian exchange rate system', *Malayan Economic Review*, 7, 1 (1962), pp. 37–60.

Corpuz, O. D., *An economic history of the Philippines* (Quezon City: University of the Philippines Press, 1997).

Crafts, Nicholas, 'Historical perspectives on development', in Gerald M. Meier and Joseph E. Stiglitz, eds., *Frontiers of development economics: the future in perspective* (Washington, DC: World Bank, 2001), pp. 301–34.

Craig, J. Edwin, 'Ceylon', in W. Arthur Lewis, ed., *Tropical development 1880–1913: studies in economic development* (London: George Allen & Unwin, 1970), pp. 221–49.

Cresson, L., *Industrial Singapore: handbook* (Singapore, n.d.).

Creutzberg, P., *Changing economy in Indonesia*, vol. 1: *Indonesia's export crops 1816–1940* (The Hague: Martinus Nijhoff, 1975).

Changing economy in Indonesia, vol. 2: *Public finance 1816–1939* (The Hague: Martinus Nijhoff, 1976).

Cribb, Robert, 'Political dimensions of the currency question 1945–1947', *Indonesia*, 31 (1981), pp. 113–36.

Gangsters and revolutionaries: the Jakarta people's militia and the Indonesian revolution 1945–1949 (Honolulu: University of Hawaii Press, 1991).

Cristina, David C., 'Credit and price policies in Philippine agriculture', in Dale Adams, D. H. Graham and J. D. Von Pischke, eds., *Undermining rural development with cheap credit* (Boulder, CO: Westview Press, 1984), pp. 210–25.

Cronon, William, *Nature's metropolis: Chicago and the Great West* (New York: W. W. Norton, 1991).

Crosby, Josiah, *Siam: the crossroads* (London: Hollis & Carter, 1945).

Crouch, Harold, *The army and politics in Indonesia* (Ithaca, NY: Cornell University Press, 1978).

Government and society in Malaysia (Ithaca, NY: Cornell University Press, 1996).

Cutshall, Aiden, 'Trends of Philippine sugar production', *Economic Geography*, 14, 2 (1938), pp. 154–58.

Dacy, Douglas C., *Foreign aid, war, and economic development: South Vietnam 1955–1975* (London: Cambridge University Press, 1986).

Dales, John H., John C. McManus and Melville H. Watkins, 'Primary products and economic growth: a comment', *Journal of Political Economy*, 75, 6 (1967), pp. 876–80.

Damuri, Jose Rizal and Mari Pangestu, 'Who is afraid of economic openness? People's perceptions of globalisation in Indonesia', in Arianto A. Patunru, Mari Pangestu and M. Chatib Basri, eds., *Indonesia in the new world: globalisation, nationalism and sovereignty* (Singapore: Institute of Southeast Asian Studies, 2018), pp. 109–29.

Dapice, David O., 'An overview of the Indonesian economy', in Gustav F. Papanek, ed., *The Indonesian economy* (New York: Praeger, 1980), pp. 3–55.

Davidson, Jamie S., *Indonesia's changing political economy: governing the roads* (Cambridge: Cambridge University Press, 2015).

Davis, James C. and J. Vernon Henderson, 'Evidence on the political economy of the urbanization process', *Journal of Urban Economics*, 53, 1 (2003), pp. 98–125.

Davis, L. E. and R. E. Gallman, *Evolving financial markets and international capital flows: Britain, the Americas, and Australia, 1865–1914* (Cambridge: Cambridge University Press, 2001).

de Boer, M. G. and J. C. Westerman, *Een halve eeuw paketvaart 1891–1941* [Half a century of package shipping 1891–1941] (Amsterdam, 1941).

de Dios, Emmanuel S., Maria Socorro Gochoco-Bautista and Jan Carlo Punongbayan, 'Martial law and the Philippine economy', UP discussion paper no. 2021-07 (University of the Philippines, 2021).

De Jong, Louis, *The collapse of a colonial society: the Dutch in Indonesia during the Second World War* (Leiden: KITLV Press, 2002).

Dematte, Claudio, 'International financial intermediation: implications for banking and regulators', *Banca Nazionale del Lavoro Quarterly Review*, 136 (1981).

Department of Economic Affairs, Batavia, 'Economic prospects of the Indonesian islands beyond Java and Sumatra', *Economic Review of Indonesia*, 1, 1 (1947), pp. 1–8.

'The industries of the Indies since the Japanese capitulation', *Economic Review of Indonesia*, 1, 2 (1947), pp. 21–24.

'The economic condition of Indonesia in mid-1947', *Economic Review of Indonesia*, 1, 8 (1947), pp. 117–30.

'Economic data on Indonesia to the end of 1948', *Economic Review of Indonesia*, 3, 1 (1949), pp. 5–22.

de Pleijt, Alexandra M. and Ewout Frankema, 'The deeper roots of human capital formation and economic development in Southeast Asia, 1900–2000', *Journal of Development Economics*, 176 (2025), pp. 1–16

Dercon, Stephen, *Gambling on development: why some countries win and others lose* (London: Hurst & Company, 2023).

Dharmapatni, Ida Ayu Indira and Tommy Firman, 'Problems and challenges of mega-urban region in Indonesia: the case of Jabotakek and the Bandung metropolitan area', in T. G. McGee and Ira M. Robinson, eds., *The mega-urban regions of Southeast Asia* (Vancouver: University of British Columbia Press, 1995), pp. 296–314.

Dhiratayakinant, Kraiyudht, 'Public enterprises', in Peter G. Warr, ed., *The Thai economy in transition* (Cambridge: Cambridge University Press, 1993), pp. 265–95.

Díaz-Alejandro, Carlos F., *Essays in the economic history of the Argentine Republic* (New Haven, CT, and London: Yale University Press, 1970).

Dick, Howard W., *Surabaya, city of work: a socioeconomic history, 1900–2000* (Athens, OH: Ohio University Press, 2002).

Dick, Howard W. and Peter J. Rimmer, *Cities, transport and communications: the integration of Southeast Asia since 1850* (Houndmills: Palgrave Macmillan, 2003).

Dick, Howard W., et al., *The emergence of a national economy: an economic history of Indonesia, 1800–2000* (Leiden: KITLV Press, 2002).

Dixon, Chris, 'Development, regional disparity and planning: the experience of northeast Thailand', *Journal of Southeast Asian Studies*, 8, 2 (1977), pp. 210–23.

The Thai economy: uneven development and internationalization (London: Routledge, 1999).

Dobby, E. H. G., *Monsoon Asia* (London: University of London Press, 1961).

Southeast Asia, 9th edn. (London: University of London Press, 1966).

Dodge, Nicholas N., 'Population estimates for the Malay Peninsula in the nineteenth century, with special reference to the east coast states', *Population Studies*, 34, 3 (1980), pp. 437–75.

Doeppers, Daniel F., 'An incident in the PRRI/Permesta rebellion of 1958', *Indonesia*, 14 (October 1972), pp. 182–95.

Manila 1900–1941: social change in a late colonial metropolis (Manila: Manila University Press, 1984).

Dohner, Robert S. and Ponciano Intal, 'The Marcos legacy: economic policy and foreign debt in the Philippines', in Jeffrey D. Sachs and Susan M. Collins, eds., *Developing country debt and economic performance*, vol. 3: *Country studies – Indonesia, Korea, Philippines, Turkey* (Chicago, IL: University of Chicago Press, 1989), pp. 372–614.

Doner, Richard F., *The politics of uneven development: Thailand's economic growth in comparative perspective* (Cambridge: Cambridge University Press, 2009).

Donnell, John C., 'South Vietnam in 1975: the year of the communist victory', *Asian Survey*, 16, 1 (1976), pp. 1–13.

Donner, Wolf, *Five faces of Thailand: an economic geography* (Queensland, Australia: University of Queensland Press, 1982).

Donnison, F. S. V., *British military administration in the Far East 1943–1946* (London: Her Majesty's Stationery Office, 1956).

Dore, Ronald, 'The diploma disease revisited', *IDS Bulletin*, 11, 2 (1980), pp. 55–61.

Dorfman, Joseph, *The economic mind in American civilization*, vol. 3: *1865–1918* (New York: Viking Press, 1959).

Dower, John, *War without mercy: race and power in the Pacific War* (New York: Pantheon Books, 1986).

Drabble, J. H., *Rubber in Malaya, 1876–1922* (Kuala Lumpur: Oxford University Press, 1973).

Malayan rubber: the inter-war years (London: Macmillan, 1991).

Drabble, J. H. and P. J. Drake, 'The British agency houses in Malaysia: survival in a changing world', *Journal of South East Asian Studies*, 12 (1981), pp. 297–328.

Drake, P. J., 'Natural resources versus foreign borrowing in economic development', *Economic Journal*, 82 (1972), pp. 951–62.

'Southeast Asian monies and the problem of a common measure, with particular reference to the nineteenth century', *Australian Economic History Review*, 31 (1991), pp. 90–96.

'Vent for surplus, the subsistence fund, and the evolution of money', in Gerald M. Meier, ed., *From classical economics to development economics* (New York: St. Martin's Press, 1994), pp. 94–103.

Currency, credit and commerce: early growth in Southeast Asia (Aldershot: Ashgate, 2004).

Drea, Edward J., *Japan's imperial army: its rise and fall, 1853–1945* (Lawrence: University Press of Kansas, 2009).

Easterlin, Richard, 'Review of North, *Economic growth of the United States*', *Journal of Economic History*, 22, 1 (1962), pp. 122–26.

'Why isn't the whole world developed?', *Journal of Economic History*, 41 (1981), pp. 1–19.

Eckstein, Otto, 'Capital theory and some theoretical problems in development planning', *American Economic Review*, 51, 2 (1961), pp. 92–101.

Edelstein, Michael, *Overseas investment in the age of high imperialism: the United Kingdom, 1850–1914* (London: Methuen, 1982).

'Foreign investment and accumulation, 1860–1914', in R. Floud and D. McCloskey, eds., *The economic history of Britain since 1700*, 2nd edn. (Cambridge: Cambridge University Press, 1994).

'Imperialism: cost and benefit', in R. Floud and D. McCloskey, eds., *The economic history of Britain since 1700*, 2nd edn. (Cambridge: Cambridge University Press, 1994).

Edgington, David and Roger Hayter, 'The in situ upgrading of Japanese electronics firms in Malaysian industrial clusters', *Economic Geography*, 89, 3 (2013), pp. 227–59.

Ellis, Thomas Flower, 'A brief account of the Malay tin industry', *Proceedings of the Chemical and Metallurgical Society of South Africa*, 2 (1897).

Ellman, Michael, 'Did the agricultural surplus provide the resources for the increase in investment in the USSR during the First Five Year Plan?', *Economic Journal*, 85, 340 (1975), pp. 844–63.

Socialist planning, 3rd edn. (Cambridge: Cambridge University Press, 2014).

Elsbree, Willard H., *Japan's role in Southeast Asian nationalist movements 1940–1945* (New York: Institute of Pacific Relations, 1953).

Elson, R. E., *The end of the peasantry in Southeast Asia: a social and economic history of peasant livelihood, 1800–1990s* (Houndmills: Macmillan Press, 1997).

'International commerce, the state and society: economic and social change', in Nicholas Tarling, ed., *The Cambridge economic history of Southeast Asia*, vol. 3: *1800–1930s* (Cambridge: Cambridge University Press, 1999), pp. 127–92.

Eltis, Walter, *The classical theory of economic growth* (London: Macmillan, 1984).
Emerson, Rupert, *Malaysia* (London: Macmillan, 1937).
Emerson, Rupert, Lennox A. Mills and Virginia Thompson, *Government and nationalism in Southeast Asia* (New York: Institute of Pacific Relations, 1942).
Emery, Robert F., 'The successful Philippine decontrol and devaluation', *Asian Survey*, 3, 6 (1963), pp. 274–84.
The financial institutions of Southeast Asia: a country-by-country study (New York: Praeger, 1970).
Emmerson, Donald K., '"Southeast Asia": what's in a name?', *Journal of Southeast Asian Studies*, 15, 1 (1984), pp. 1–21.
Engerman, Stanley L., 'Review: Douglas C. North's *Economic growth of the United States, 1790–1860* revisited', *Social Science History*, 1, 2 (1977), pp. 248–57.
Erlich, Alexander, 'Development strategy and planning: the Soviet experience' and 'Comment' by Abram Bergson in Max F. Millikan, ed., *National economic planning: a conference of the universities – National Bureau Committee for Economic Research* (New York: National Bureau of Economic Research, 1967), pp. 233–78.
Esguerra, Emmanuel F., 'An assessment of the Masagana 99 credit subsidy as an equity measure', *Philippine Review of Economics and Business*, 18, 3&4 (1981), pp. 168–91.
Esterline, John H., 'Vietnam in 1987: steps toward rejuvenation', *Asian Survey*, 28, 1 (1988), pp. 86–94.
Evans, Grant, '"Rich peasants" and cooperatives in socialist Laos', *Journal of Anthropological Research*, 44, 3 (1988), pp. 229–50.
Lao peasants under socialism (New Haven, CT: Yale University Press, 1990).
Falkus, Malcolm, 'Review of Ian Brown, *The elite and the economy in Siam, c.1890–1920*', *Business History*, 32, 1 (1990), pp. 141–42.
'Bangkok: from primate city to primate megalopolis', in Theo Barker and Anthony Sutcliffe, eds., *Megalopolis: the giant city in history* (Houndmills: Macmillan, 1993), pp. 143–65.
Fall, Bernard B., *The two Vietnams: a political & military analysis* (New York: Praeger, 1963).
Fear, Sean A., 'The ambiguous legacy of Ngô Đình Diệm in South Vietnam's Second Republic (1967–1975)', *Journal of Vietnamese Studies*, 11, 1 (2016), pp. 1–75.
Feenstra, Robert C., 'Integration of trade and disintegration of production in the global economy', *Journal of Economic Perspectives*, 12, 4 (1998), pp. 31–50.
Feeny, David, *The political economy of productivity: Thai agricultural development 1880–1975* (Vancouver: University of British Columbia Press, 1982).
'Extensive versus intensive agricultural development: induced public investment in Southeast Asia, 1900–1940', *Journal of Economic History*, 43, 3 (1983), pp. 687–704.
Feith, Herbert, *The decline of constitutional democracy in Indonesia* (Ithaca, NY: Cornell University Press, 1962).
'President Soekarno, the army and the communists: the triangle changes shape', *Asian Survey*, 4, 8 (1964), pp. 969–80.

Feith, Herbert and Daniel S. Lev, 'The end of the Indonesian rebellion', *Pacific Affairs*, 36, 1 (1963), pp. 32–46.

Fenichel, Allen H. and Gregg Huff, 'Colonialism and the political economy of an independent Burma', *Modern Asian Studies*, 9 (1975), pp. 321–35.

Ferns, H. S., *Britain and Argentina in the nineteenth century* (Oxford: Clarendon Press, 1960).

Ferrara, Federico, *The political development of modern Thailand* (Cambridge: Cambridge University Press, 2017).

Fetter, Frank Whitson, 'Lenin, Keynes and inflation', *Economica*, 44, 173 (1977), pp. 77–80.

Fforde, Adam, 'Economic aspects of Soviet-Vietnamese relations: their role and importance', in Robert Cassen, ed., *Soviet interests in the Third World* (London: Sage, 1985), pp. 192–219.

Figart, D. M., *The plantation rubber industry in the Middle East* (Washington, DC: US Department of Commerce, 1925).

Findlay, Ronald, *Trade and specialization* (Harmondsworth: Penguin, 1970).

'Trade and development: theory and Asian experience', *Asian Development Review*, 2 (1984), pp. 23–42.

Findlay, Ronald and Mats Lundahl, 'Natural resources, "vent-for-surplus", and the staples theory', in Gerald M. Meier, ed., *From classical economics to development economics* (New York: St. Martin's Press, 1994), pp. 68–93.

'Natural resources and economic development: the 1870–1914 experience', in R. M. Auty, ed., *Resource abundance and economic development* (Oxford: Oxford University Press, 2001).

Fisher, Charles A., 'The Thailand–Burma railway', *Economic Geography*, 23, 2 (1947), pp. 85–97.

'The railway geography of British Malaya', *Scottish Geographical Magazine*, 64, 3 (1948), pp. 123–36.

South-East Asia: a social, political and economic geography (London: Methuen, 1964).

'Economic myth and geographical reality in Indonesia', *Modern Asian Studies*, 1 (1967), pp. 155–89.

'Review: Willmott, Chinese in Cambodia', *Modern Asian Studies*, 4, 4 (1970), pp. 368–71.

Fisk, E. K., 'Productivity and income from rubber in an established Malay Reservation', *Malayan Economic Review*, 6, 1 (1961), pp. 13–22.

Fletcher, Max E., 'The Suez Canal and world shipping, 1869–1914', *Journal of Economic History*, 18, 4 (1958), pp. 556–73.

Floro, Sagrario L. and Pan A. Yotopoulos, *Informal credit markets and the new institutional economics: the case of Philippine agriculture* (Boulder, CO: Westview Press, 1991).

Forbes, Dean K., *Asian metropolis: urbanisation and the Southeast Asian city* (Melbourne: Oxford University Press, 1996).

Frederick, Katharine and Elise van Nederveen Meerkerk, 'Local advantage in a global context: competition, adaptation and resilience in textile manufacturing in the "periphery", 1860–1960', *Journal of Global History*, 18, 1 (2023), pp. 1–24.

Frederick, Stacey and Gary Gereffi, *The Philippines in the electronics & electrical global value chain* (Durham, NC: Center on Globalization, Governance & Competitiveness, Duke University, 2016), https://dukespace.lib.duke.edu/items/88a06165-8a8e-462b-a2c1-1a3d29f7fb49.

Freedman, Maurice, *Chinese family and marriage in Singapore* (London: HMSO, 1957).

Frézouls, A., 'Tableau du movement commercial de l'Indo-Chine de 1890 à 1900 inclusivement', *Bulletin économique de l'Indochine* (1901), p. 274.

Friedman, Milton, 'A welfare state syllogism', speech to the Commonwealth Club, San Francisco, 1 June 1991.

Friedman, Milton and Anna Jacobson Schwartz, *A monetary history of the United States, 1867–1960* (Princeton, NJ: Princeton University Press, 1971).

Friend, Theodore, 'The Philippine sugar industry and the politics of independence, 1929–1935', *Journal of Asian Studies*, 22, 2 (1963), pp. 179–92.

Between two empires: the ordeal of the Philippines 1929–1946 (New Haven, CT: Yale University Press, 1965).

The blue-eyed enemy: Japan against the West in Java and Luzon, 1942–1945 (Princeton, NJ: Princeton University Press, 1988).

Fruin, T. H. A., 'Popular and rural credit in the Netherlands Indies', *Bulletin of the Colonial Institute of Amsterdam*, 1 (1938), pp. 106–15, 161–75.

Het economisch aspect van het Indonesisch vraagstuk [The economic aspect of the Indonesian issue] (Amsterdam: Vrij Nederland, 1947).

Fujita, Masahisa and Tomoya Mori, 'The role of ports in the making of major cities: self-agglomeration and the hub-effect', *Journal of Development Economics*, 49 (1996), pp. 93–120.

Furnivall, J. S., 'Land as a free gift of nature', *Economic Journal*, 19, 76 (1909), pp. 552–62.

'The political economy of the tropical Far East', *Journal of the Royal Asiatic Society*, 29, 3 (1942), pp. 195–210.

Educational progress in Southeast Asia (New York: Institute of Pacific Relations, 1943).

Colonial policy and practice: a comparative study of Burma and Netherlands India (Cambridge: Cambridge University Press, 1948).

'Twilight in Burma: independence and after', *Pacific Affairs*, 22, 2 (1949), pp. 155–72.

An introduction to the political economy of Burma (Rangoon: People's Literature Committee and House, 1957).

'Safety first: a study in the economic history of Burma', *Journal of the Burma Research Society*, 40, 1 (1957), pp. 24–38.

A study of the social and economic history of Burma (British Burma), 8 parts (Rangoon: Ministry of National Planning, 1960).

'Industrial agriculture', *Journal of the Burma Research Society*, 48, 1 (1965), pp. 89–97.

Gainsborough, Martin. 'Privatisation as state advance: private indirect government in Vietnam', *New Political Economy*, 14, 2 (2009), pp. 257–74.

Gamba, Charles, 'Poverty and some socio-economic aspects of hoarding, saving and borrowing in Malaya', *Malayan Economic Review*, 3 (1958), pp. 33–66.

Geertz, Clifford, 'The integrative revolution: primordial sentiments and civil politics in new states', in Clifford Geertz, ed., *New states: the quest for modernity in Asia and Africa* (Glencoe, IL: Free Press, 1963), pp. 105–57.

Gelb, Alan and Associates, *Oil windfalls: blessing or curse?* (New York: Oxford University Press for the World Bank, 1988).

Gittinger, J. Price, 'Communist land policy in North Vietnam', *Far Eastern Survey*, 28, 8 (1959), pp. 113–26.

Glassburner, Bruce, 'Economic policy-making in Indonesia, 1950–1957', *Economic Development and Cultural Change*, 10, 2 (1962), pp. 113–33.

'The role of economic interest in the Indonesian politics of the 1950's: a rejoinder', *Economic Development and Cultural Change*, 11, 2, part 1 (1963), pp. 177–80.

ed., *The economy of Indonesia: selected readings* (Ithaca, NY: Cornell University Press, 1971).

'Indonesia: windfalls in a poor rural economy', in *Alan Gelb and Associates, Oil windfalls: blessing or curse?* (New York: Oxford University Press, 1988), pp. 197–226.

Goh Keng Swee, *Urban incomes and housing: a report on the social survey of Singapore, 1953–54* (Singapore, 1956).

Decade of achievement (budget speech, 1970) (Singapore: Minister for Finance, 1970).

The Asian, 20 August 1972.

Golay, Frank H., 'Economic consequences of the Philippine Trade Act', *Pacific Affairs*, 28, 1 (1955), pp. 53–70.

'Commercial policy and economic nationalism', *Quarterly Journal of Economics*, 72, 4 (1958), pp. 574–87.

The Philippines: public policy and economic development (Ithaca, NY: Cornell University Press, 1961).

'Malaya', in Frank H. Golay et al., *Underdevelopment and economic nationalism in Southeast Asia* (Ithaca, NY: Cornell University Press, 1969), pp. 341–89.

'Southeast Asia: the "colonial drain" revisited', in C. D. Cowan and O. W. Wolters, eds., *Southeast Asian history and historiography* (Ithaca, NY: Cornell University Press, 1976), pp. 368–87.

Goldberg, Pinelopi and Tristan Reed, 'Is the global economy deglobalizing? if so, why? and what is next?' with comments and discussion, *Brookings Papers on Economic Activity* (Spring, 2023), pp. 347–423.

Goldsmith, Raymond W., 'The power of victory: munitions output in World War II', *Military Affairs*, 10, 1 (1946), pp. 69–80.

The financial development of India, 1860–1977 (New Haven, CT: Yale University Press, 1983).

The financial development of India, Japan, and the United States (New Haven, CT: Yale University Press, 1983).

The financial development of Japan, 1868–1977 (New Haven, CT: Yale University Press, 1983).

Gollin, Douglas, David Lagakos and Michael E. Waugh, 'The agricultural productivity gap', *Quarterly Journal of Economics*, 129, 2 (2014), pp. 939–94.

Gomez, Edmund Terrance, *Chinese business in Malaysia: accumulation, accommodation and ascendance* (Richmond: Curzon Press, 1999).

Gomez, Edmund Terrance and K. S. Jomo, *Malaysia's political economy: politics, patronage and profits*, 2nd edn. (Cambridge: Cambridge University Press, 1999).

Gooszen, Hans, *A demographic history of the Indonesian archipelago, 1880–1942* (Singapore: Institute of Southeast Asian Studies, 1999).

Goscha, Christopher E., *The Penguin history of modern Vietnam* (London: Allen Lane, 2016).

Gough, Kathleen, 'The Vietnamese economy: interview with Nguyen Kach Vien', *Journal of Contemporary Asia*, 12, 3 (1982), pp. 376–81.

Grant, Bruce, *Indonesia* (Harmondsworth: Penguin, 1967).

Grenville, Stephen, 'Monetary policy and the formal financial sector', in Anne Booth and Peter McCawley, eds., *The Indonesian economy during the Soeharto era* (Kuala Lumpur: Oxford University Press, 1981), pp. 102–25.

Grove, D. L. and J. Exter, 'The Philippine Central Bank Act', *Federal Reserve Bulletin*, 34 (1948), pp. 938–49.

Gullick, J. M., 'The entrepreneur in late 19th century Malay peasant society', *Journal of the Malaysian Branch of the Royal Asiatic Society*, 58 (1985), pp. 59–70.

Gurley, John G. and E. S. Shaw, 'Financial structure and economic development', *Economic Development and Cultural Change*, 15, 3 (1967), pp. 257–68.

Guyot, Dorothy, 'The Burma Independence Army: a political movement in military garb', in Josef Silverstein, ed., *Southeast Asia in World War II: four essays* (New Haven, CT: Yale University Southeast Asia Studies, 1966), pp. 51–65.

Haberler, Gottfried, *International trade and economic development* (Cairo: National Bank of Egypt, 1959).

Hainsworth, Geoffrey B., 'Economic growth and poverty in Southeast Asia: Malaysia, Indonesia and the Philippines', *Pacific Affairs*, 52, 1 (1979), pp. 5–41.

Hainsworth, Reginald G. and Raymond T. Moyer, *Agricultural geography of the Philippine Islands* (Washington, DC: United States Department of Agriculture, Office of Foreign Agriculture Relations, 1945).

Hammer, Ellen J., 'Progress report on Southern Vietnam', *Pacific Affairs*, 30, 3 (1957), pp. 221–35.

Hanke, Steve H. and Kurt Schuler, *Currency boards for developing countries* (San Francisco, CA: ICS Press, 1994).

Harper, T. N., *The end of empire and the making of Malaya* (Cambridge: Cambridge University Press, 1999).

Harris, John R. and Michael P. Todaro, 'Migration, unemployment and development: a two-sector analysis', *American Economic Review*, 60, 1 (1970), pp. 126–42.

Harrison, Mark, 'The Soviet Union: the defeated victor', in Mark Harrison, ed., *The economics of World War II* (Cambridge: Cambridge University Press, 1998), pp. 268–301.

Hart, G. H. C., 'Recent development in the Netherlands-Indies', *Geographical Journal*, 99, 2 (1942), pp. 81–102.

Hartendorp, A. V. H., *History of industry and trade of the Philippines* (Manila: American Chamber of Commerce of the Philippines, 1958).

The Japanese occupation of the Philippines, 2 vols. (Manila: Bookmark, 1967).

Hawati Abdul Hamid, 'Malaysian higher education and economic growth: a causality analysis', Khazanah Research Institute, working paper 3/22 (October 2022).

Hawkins, Everett D., 'Job inflation in Indonesia', *Asian Survey*, 6, 5 (1966), pp. 264–75.

Hayami, Yujiro, 'Conditions for the diffusion of agricultural technology: an Asian perspective', *Journal of Economic History*, 34 (1974), pp. 131–48.

'Ecology, history and development: a perspective from rural Southeast Asia', *World Bank Research Observer*, 16, 2 (2001), pp. 169–98.

Hazelwood, Arthur, 'The economics of colonial monetary arrangements', *Social and Economic Studies*, 3 (1954), pp. 291–315.

He Wen-Lit, *Syonan interlude* (Singapore: Mandarin Paperbacks, 1991).

Helleiner, G. K., *Peasant agriculture, government, and economic growth in Nigeria* (Homewood, IL: Richard D. Irwin, 1966).

'Manufactured exports from less-developed countries and multinational firms', *Economic Journal*, 83, 329 (1973), pp. 21–47.

Hendry, James B., 'Economic development under conditions of guerrilla warfare: the case of Viet Nam', *Asian Survey*, 2, 4 (1962), pp. 1–12.

Hensley, Roy J., 'Development banks and economic development in Indonesia', *Economic Development and Cultural Change*, 12, 4 (1964).

Hewison, Kevin and Woradul Tularak, 'Thailand and precarious work: an assessment', *American Behavioural Scientist*, 57, 4 (2013), pp. 444–67.

Higgins, Benjamin, *Indonesia's economic stabilization and development* (New York: Institute of Pacific Relations, 1957).

Indonesia: the crisis of the millstones (New York: Van Nostrand Co., 1963).

Economic development: problems, principles and policies, revised edn. (New York: W. W. Norton & Co., 1968).

Higgins, Benjamin H. and William C. Hollinger, 'Central banking in Indonesia', in S. Gethyn Davies, ed., *Central banking in South and East Asia* (Hong Kong: Hong Kong University Press, 1960).

Hill, David T., *Journalism and politics in Indonesia: a critical biography of journalist Mochtar Lubis (1922–2004) as editor and author* (London: Routledge, 2010).

Hill, Hal, 'Indonesia's industrial transformation, part I', *Bulletin of Indonesian Economic Studies*, 26, 2 (1990), pp. 79–120.

'Indonesia's industrial policy and performance: "orthodoxy" vindicated', *Economic Development and Cultural Change*, 45 (1996), pp. 147–74.

'Myths about tigers: Indonesian development policy debates', *Pacific Review*, 10, 2 (1997), pp. 256–73.

The Indonesian economy, 2nd edn. (Cambridge: Cambridge University Press, 2000).

'Industry', in Arsenio M. Balisacan and Hal Hill, eds., *The Philippine economy: development, policies, and challenges* (Oxford: Oxford University Press, 2003), pp. 219–53.

'Asia's third giant: a survey of the Indonesian economy', *Economic Record*, 94, 307 (2018), pp. 469–99.

'The challenge for Jokowi 2.0': how to revitalise the economy', *East Asia Forum* (2020), https://eastasiaforum.org/2020/01/12/the-challenge-for-jokowi-2-0-how-to-revitalise-the-economy/.

Hill, Hal and Siwage Dharma Negara, eds., *The Indonesian economy in transition: policy challenges in the Jokowi era and beyond* (Singapore: Institute of Southeast Asian Studies, 2019).

'Setting the scene – the Jokowi era and beyond', in Hal Hill and Siwage Dharma Negara, eds., *The Indonesian economy in transition: policy challenges in the Jokowi era and beyond* (Singapore: Institute of Southeast Asian Studies, 2019), pp. 1–33.

Hill, Hal and Deasy Pane, 'Indonesia and the global economy: missed opportunities', in Arianto A. Patunru, Mari Pangestu and M. Chatib Basri, eds., *Indonesia in the new world: globalisation, nationalism and sovereignty* (Singapore: Institute of Southeast Asian Studies, 2018), pp. 267–93.

Hill, Hal, Budy P. Resosudarmo and Yogi Vidyattama, 'Economic geography of Indonesia: location, connectivity, and resources', in *World Bank, World Development Report: reshaping economic geography* (Washington, DC: World Bank, 2009), pp. 116–34.

Hiratsuka, Daisuke, '*Production networks in Asia: a case study from the hard disk drive industry*', ADBI working paper 301 (Tokyo: Asian Development Bank Institute, 2011).

Hirschman, Albert O., *The strategy of economic development* (New Haven, CT: Yale University Press, 1958).

'A generalized linkage approach to development, with special reference to staples', in Manning Nash, ed., *Essays on economic development and cultural change in honor of Bert F. Hoselitz* (Chicago, IL: University of Chicago Press, 1972), pp. 67–98.

'Linkages', in John Eatwell, Murray Milgate and Peter Newman, eds., *The new Palgrave: economic development* (London: Macmillan, 1989), pp. 210–21.

Hiscock, Mary E. and David E. Allan. 'Law modernization in South-East Asia: colonial and post-colonial land tenures in Indonesia and Malaysia', *Rabels Zeitschrift für Ausländisches und Internationales Privatrecht/Rabel Journal of Comparative and International Private Law*, 46, 3 (1982), pp. 509–29.

Hlaing, U Aye, *A study of the economic development of Burma, 1870–1940* (Rangoon: Department of Economics, University of Rangoon, 1964).

'Trends of economic growth and income distribution in Burma, 1870–1940', *Journal of the Burma Research Society*, 47 (1964), pp. 89–148.

'Public finance and public policy in Burma, 1870–1940', *Journal of the Burma Research Society*, 56 (1973), pp. 1–29.

Ho, Robert, 'Land settlement projects in Malaya: an assessment of the role of the Federal Land Development Authority', *Journal of Tropical Geography*, 20 (June 1965), pp. 1–15.

Ho, Samuel Pao-Sen, 'Agricultural transformation under colonialism: the case of Taiwan', *Journal of Economic History*, 28 (1968), pp. 313–40.

Hobday, Michael and Howard Rush, 'Upgrading the technological capabilities of foreign transnational subsidiaries in developing countries: the case of Thailand', *Research Policy*, 36 (2007), pp. 1335–56.

Hodder, B. W., 'Racial groupings in Singapore', *Malayan Journal of Tropical Geography*, 1 (1953).

Hodjera, Zoran, 'The Asian currency market: Singapore as a regional financial centre', *IMF Staff Papers*, 25, 2 (1978), pp. 221–53.

Holcombe, Alec, *Mass mobilization in the Democratic Republic of Vietnam, 1945–1960* (Honolulu: University of Hawaii Press, 2020).

Holmes, Robert A., 'Burmese domestic policy: the politics of Burmanization', *Asian Survey*, 7, 3 (1967), pp. 188–97.

Hon Sui Sen, *Economic pattern in the 1970s* (budget speech) (Singapore, 1972).

Hooley, Richard, 'A century of Philippine foreign trade: a quantitative analysis', in E. de Dios and R. Fabella, eds., *Choice, growth and development* (Manila: University of the Philippines Press, 1996), pp. 255–303.

'American economic policy in the Philippines, 1902–1940: exploring a dark age in colonial statistics', *Journal of Asian Economics*, 16 (2005), pp. 464–88.

Hooley, Richard and Vernon W. Ruttan, 'The Philippines', in R. T. Shand, ed., *Agricultural development in Asia* (Canberra: Australian National University Press, 1969), pp. 215–50.

Horvat, Branko, 'The optimum rate of investment reconsidered', *Economic Journal*, 75, 299 (1965), pp. 572–76.

Huff, Gregg, 'Barter, money, credit and Singapore's international rice trade, 1870–1939', *Explorations in Economic History*, 26, 2 (1989), pp. 161–89.

'Sharecroppers, risk, management and Chinese rubber estate development in inter-war British Malaya', *Economic Development and Cultural Change*, 40 (1992), pp. 743–73.

'The development of the rubber market in pre-World War II Singapore', *Journal of Southeast Asian Studies*, 24, 2 (1993), pp. 285–306.

The economic growth of Singapore: trade and development in the twentieth century (Cambridge: Cambridge University Press, 1994).

'Singapore's economic development: four lessons and some doubts', *Oxford Development Studies*, 27, 1 (1999), pp. 33–55.

'Entitlements, destitution and emigration in the 1930s Singapore Great Depression', *Economic History Review*, 54, 2 (2001), pp. 290–323.

'Boom-or-bust commodities and industrialization in pre-World War II Malaya', *Journal of Economic History*, 62, 4 (2002), pp. 1074–115.

'Currency boards and Chinese banks in Malaya and the Philippines before World War II', *Asia-Pacific Economic History Review*, 43, 2 (2003), pp. 125–39.

'Monetization and financial development in Southeast Asia before the Second World War', *Economic History Review*, 56, 2 (2003), pp. 300–45.

'Globalization, natural resources and foreign investment: a view from the resource rich tropics', *Oxford Economic Papers*, 59, 5 (2007), pp. 127–55.

'Finance and long-term development issues in Southeast Asia', *Asian-Pacific Economic Literature*, 25, 1 (2011), pp. 56–78.

'Export-led growth, gateway cities and urban systems development in pre-World War II Southeast Asia', *Journal of Development Studies*, 48, 10 (2012), pp. 1431–52.

'Causes and consequences of the Great Vietnam Famine, 1944–1945', *Economic History Review*, 72, 1 (2019), pp. 286–316.

'The great World War II Vietnam and Java Famines', *Modern Asian Studies*, 54, 2 (2020), pp. 618–53.

World War II and Southeast Asia: economy and society under Japanese occupation (Cambridge: Cambridge University Press, 2020).

'Vent-for-surplus in Southeast Asian development since 1870', *World Development*, 181 (2024), pp. 1–20.

Huff, Gregg and Luis Angeles, 'Globalization, industrialization and urbanization in pre-World War II Southeast Asia', *Explorations in Economic History*, 48, 1 (2011), pp. 20–36.

Huff, G. and G. Caggiano, 'Globalization, immigration and Lewisian elastic labor in pre-World War II Southeast Asia', *Journal of Economic History*, 67 (2007), pp. 33–68.

Huff, Gregg and Gillian Huff, 'Urban growth and change in 1940s Southeast Asia', *Economic History Review*, 68, 2 (2015), pp. 522–47.

Hummels, David, 'Transportation costs and international trade in the second era of globalization', *Journal of Economic Perspectives*, 21, 3 (2007), pp. 131–54.

Humphrey, Don D., 'Indonesia's national plan for economic development', *Asian Survey*, 2, 10 (1962), pp. 12–21.

Hutchinson, Francis Edward, '"Developmental" states and economic growth at the sub-national level: the case of Penang', *Southeast Asian Affairs* (2008), pp. 223–44.

'I. G. M. I.', 'L'effort d'industrialisation de l'Indochine', *Bulletin Économique de l'Indochine*, part 1 (February 1943), pp. 161–93.

Imperial Shipping Committee, *British shipping in the Orient* (London: HMSO, 1939).

Ingram, James C., 'Thailand's rice trade and the allocation of resources', in C. D. Cowan, ed., *The economic development of South-East Asia* (London: George Allen & Unwin, 1964), pp. 102–26.

Economic change in Thailand 1850–1970 (Stanford, CA: Stanford University Press, 1971).

Intarakumnerd, P. and A. Jutarosaga, 'The evolution of university–industry linkages in Thailand', *Asian Economic Policy Review*, 18, 2 (2023), pp. 262–82.

Intarakumnerd, Patarapong, Pun-Arj Chairatana and Preeda Chaiyanajit, 'Global production networks and host-site industrial upgrading: the case of the semiconductor industry in Thailand', *Asia Pacific Business Review*, 22, 2 (2016), pp. 289–306.

Iriye, Akira, 'Japan's drive to great-power status', in Marius B. Jansen, ed., *The Cambridge history of Japan*, vol. 5 (Cambridge: Cambridge University Press, 1989), pp. 721–82.

Jackson, Karl D., ed., *Cambodia, 1975–1978: rendezvous with death* (Princeton, NJ: Princeton University Press, 1989).

'Intellectual origins of the Khmer Rouge', in Karl D. Jackson, ed., *Cambodia, 1975–1978* (Princeton, NJ: Princeton University Press, 1989), pp. 241–50.

Jao, Y. C., 'The rise of Hong Kong as a financial center', *Asian Survey*, 19, 7 (1979), pp. 674–94.

'Hong Kong's future as a financial centre', *Three Banks Review*, 145 (1985).

Jesudason, James V., *Ethnicity and the economy: the state, Chinese business and multinationals in Malaysia* (Singapore: Oxford University Press, 1989).

'Chinese business and ethnic equilibrium in Malaysia', *Development and Change*, 28, 1 (1997), pp. 119–41.

Joel, Clark, 'The foreign exchange operations fund for Laos: an interesting experiment in monetary stabilization', *Asian Survey*, 6, 3 (1966), pp. 134–49.

Johnson, Harry G., *Economic policies towards less developed countries* (Washington, DC: Brookings Institution, 1967).

Johnston, Bruce F. and John W. Mellor, 'The role of agriculture in economic development', *American Economic Review*, 51, 4 (1961), pp. 566–93.

Johnston, David B., 'Rice cultivation in Thailand: the development of an export economy by indigenous capital and labor', *Modern Asian Studies*, 15, 1 (1981), pp. 107–26.

Jomo, K. S., *Growth and structural change in the Malaysian economy* (Houndmills: Macmillan, 1990).

'Whither Malaysia's new economic policy', *Pacific Affairs*, 64, 4 (1990–91), pp. 469–99.

Jones, F. C., *Japan's new order in East Asia: its rise and fall 1937–45* (London: Oxford University Press, 1954).

Jones, Gavin W., 'Population trends and policies in Vietnam', *Population and Development Review*, 8, 4 (1982), pp. 783–810.

Jones, Ronald W., 'Production fragmentation and outsourcing: general concerns', *Singapore Economic Review*, 53, 3 (2008), pp. 347–56.

Jongwanich, Juthathip and Archanun Kohpaiboon, 'Workers' remittances, capital inflows, and economic growth in developing Asia and the Pacific', *Asian Economic Journal*, 33, 1 (2019), pp. 39–65.

Kahin, George McTurnan, *Nationalism and revolution in Indonesia* (Ithaca, NY: Cornell University Press, 1952).

'In memoriam: Sjafruddin Prawiranegara (1911–1989)', *Indonesia*, 48 (October 1989), pp. 101–5.

Kalecki, Michal, 'An outline of a method of constructing a perspective plan', in *Essays on planning and economic development: teaching materials*, vol. 8 (Warsaw: Szkola Glówna Planowania Statystyky, 1963).

Kakizaki, Ichiro, *Laying the tracks: the Thai economy and its railways 1885–1935* (Kyoto: Kyoto University Press, 2005).

Kaothien, Utis, 'Regional and urbanization policy in Thailand: the tertiary sector as a leading sector in regional development', *Urban Studies*, 28, 6 (1991), pp. 1027–43.

'The Bangkok metropolitan region: politics and issues in the seventh plan', in T. G. McGee and Ira M. Robinson, eds., *The mega-urban regions of Southeast Asia* (Vancouver: University of British Columbia Press, 1995), pp. 328–40.

Katzen, Leo, *Gold and the South African economy* (Cape Town and Amsterdam: A. A. Balkema, 1964).

Keesing, Felix M., *The Philippines: a nation in the making* (Shanghai: Kelly and Walsh, 1937).

Kemmerer, E. W., 'Agricultural bank for the Philippines', *Yale Review*, 16 (1908), pp. 262–79.

Kerkvliet, Benedict, 'Land reform in the Philippines since the Marcos coup', *Pacific Affairs*, 47, 3 (1974), pp. 286–304.

'Village-state relations in Vietnam: the effect of everyday politics on decollectivization', *Journal of Asian Studies*, 54, 2 (1995), pp. 396–418.

The power of everyday politics: how Vietnamese peasants transformed national policy (Ithaca, NY: Cornell University Press, 2005).

Kesner, Richard M., *Economic control and colonial development* (London: Bloomsbury, 1981).

Keynes, John Maynard, *Collected writings*, vol. 1: *Indian currency and finance* (London: Macmillan, 1971).

Khin Maung Kyi, et al., *Economic development in Burma: a vision and a strategy* (Stockholm: Olaf Palme International Centre, 2000).

Khin Myo Chit, Daw, *Three years under the Japs* (Sanchaung: Khin Myo Chit, 1945).

Khin Win, *A century of rice improvement in Burma* (Manila: International Rice Research Institute, 1991).

Khoman, Sirilaksana, 'Education policy', in Peter G. Warr, ed., *The Thai economy in transition* (Cambridge: Cambridge University Press, 1993), pp. 325–54.

Kimura, Fukunari and Lurong Chen, 'Value chain connectivity in Indonesia: the evolution of unbundlings', *Bulletin of Indonesian Economic Studies*, 54, 2 (2018), pp. 165–92.

Kimura, Tetsusaburo, 'Vietnam – ten years of economic struggle', *Asian Survey*, 26, 10 (1986), pp. 1039–55.

King, Frank H. H., *Money in British East Asia* (London: HMSO, 1957).

Klingler-Vidra, Robyn and Robert Wade, 'Science and technology policies and the middle-income trap: lessons from Vietnam', *Journal of Development Studies*, 56, 4 (2020), pp. 717–31.

Klump, Rainer and Klaus Gottwald, 'Financial sector reform in Vietnam', in Maximilian J. B. Hall, ed., *The international handbook on financial reform* (Cheltenham: Edward Elgar, 2003), Chapter 12.

Knorr, K. E., *World rubber and its regulation* (Stanford, CA: Stanford University Press, 1945).

Knowles, L. C. A., *The economic development of the British overseas empire* (London: George Routledge & Sons, 1928).

Koh Ai Tee, 'Saving, investment and entrepreneurship', in Lawrence B. Krause, Ai Tee Koh and Yuan Lee Tsao, *The Singapore economy reconsidered* (Singapore: Institute of Southeast Asian Studies, 1987), pp. 78–106.

Kornai, János, *The socialist system: the political economy of communism* (Oxford: Clarendon Press, 1992).

Korthals Altes, W. L., *General trade statistics 1822–1940*, published as vol. 12a, *Changing economy in Indonesia* (The Hague: Royal Tropical Institute, 1991).

Kousted, Jens, John Rand and Finn Tarp, *From monobank to commercial banking: financial sector reforms in Vietnam* (Singapore: Institute of Southeast Asian Studies, 2005).

Kratoska, Paul H., *The Japanese occupation of Malaya and Singapore: a social and economic history* (Singapore: NUS Press, 2018).

Krause, Lawrence B., 'Hong Kong and Singapore: twins or kissing cousins?', *Economic Development and Cultural Change*, 36, 3 (1988), pp. 45–66.

Krause, Lawrence B., Ai Tee Koh, and Yuan Lee Tsao, *The Singapore economy reconsidered* (Singapore: Institute of Southeast Asian Studies, 1987).

Krongkaew, Medhi, 'The changing urban system in a fast-growing city and economy: the case of Bangkok and Thailand', in Fu-chen Lo and Yue-man Yeung, eds., *Emerging world cities in Pacific Asia* (Tokyo: United Nations University Press, 1996), pp. 286–334.

Krugman, Paul, 'History and industry location: the case of the manufacturing belt', *American Economic Review*, 81, 2 (1991), pp. 80–83.

'Increasing returns and economic geography', *Journal of Political Economy*, 98, 3 (1991), pp. 483–99.

'First nature, second nature and metropolitan location', *Journal of Regional Science*, 33, 2 (1993), pp. 129–44.

'Urban concentration: the role of increasing returns and transport costs', *International Regional Science Review*, 19, 1&2 (1996), pp. 5–30.

Krugman, Paul and Raul Livas Elizondo, 'Trade policy and the Third World metropolis', *Journal of Development Economics*, 49 (1996), pp. 137–50.

Kubo, Ryō, 'Higashi Ajia no sō-dōin tōsei' [Total war system in East Asia], in Wada Haruki et al., eds., *Higashi Ajia kingendaishi* [East Asian modern history] (Tokyo: Iwanami Shoten, 2011), vol. 6, pp. 48–72.

Kumar, Dharma, *Land and caste in South India: agricultural labour in the Madras Presidency during the nineteenth century* (Cambridge: Cambridge University Press, 1965).

Kuncoro, Ari, 'Trends in the manufacturing sector under the Jokowi presidency: legacies of past administrations', in Hal Hill and Siwage Dharma Negara, eds., *The Indonesian economy in transition: policy challenges in the Jokowi era and beyond* (Singapore: Institute of Southeast Asian Studies, 2019), pp. 180–208.

Kurasawa, Aiko Iromata, 'Mobilization and control: a study of social change in rural Java, 1942–1945', Ph.D. diss., Cornell University, 1988.

Kurihara, Kenneth K., *Labor in the Philippine economy* (Stanford, CA: Stanford University Press, 1945).

Kuroiwa, Ikuo, '"Thailand-plus-one": a GVC-led development strategy for Cambodia', *Asian-Pacific Economic Literature*, 30 (2016), pp. 30–41.

Kuznets, Simon, *Modern economic growth: rate, structure and spread* (New Haven, CT: Yale University Press, 1966).

'Modern economic growth: findings and reflections', *American Economic Review*, 63, 3 (1973), pp. 247–58.

Kuznets, Simon and Ernest Rubin, *Immigration and the foreign born* (New York: National Bureau of Economic Research, 1954).

Kyaw Ying Hlaing, 'Reconsidering the failure of the Burma Socialist Programme Party government to eradicate internal economic impediments', *South East Asia Research*, 11, 1 (2003), pp. 5–58.

'L. A.', 'L'Indochine depuis la guerre', *Bulletin Économique de l'Indochine*, part 1 (February 1942), pp. 1–27.

Landon, Kenneth Perry, *Siam in transition* (London: Oxford University Press, 1939).

'The problem of the Chinese in Thailand', *Pacific Affairs*, 13, 2 (1940), pp. 149–61.

The Chinese in Thailand (New York, 1941).

Larkin, John A., *Sugar and the origins of modern Philippine society* (Berkeley, CA: University of California Press, 1993).

Latham, A. J. H. and Neal, Larry, 'The international market in rice and wheat, 1868–1914', *Economic History Review*, 36, 2 (1983), pp. 260–80.

LeBar, Frank M. and Adrinne Suddard, eds., *Laos: its people, its society, its culture* (New Haven, CT: Human Relations Area Files, 1964).

Lebra, Joyce C., *Japanese-trained armies in Southeast Asia* (Singapore: Institute of Southeast Asian Studies, 2010).

Lee Boon Thong, 'Challenges of superinduced development: the mega-urban region of Kuala Lumpur-Klang Valley', in T. G. McGee and Ira M. Robinson, eds., *The mega-urban regions of Southeast Asia* (Vancouver: University of British Columbia Press, 1995), pp. 315–27.

'Emerging urban trends and the globalizing economy in Malaysia', in Fu-chen Lo and Yue-man Yeung, eds., *Emerging world cities in Pacific Asia* (Tokyo: United Nations University Press, 1996), pp. 335–76.

Lee, Cassey, 'Comment on "Transforming Malaysia's higher education: policies and progress"', *Asian Economic Policy Review*, 18 (2023), pp. 261–62.

Lee Kuan Yew, *Social revolution in Singapore* (speech to the British Labour Party Conference) (Singapore, 1967).

The Singapore story (Singapore: Times Editions, 1998).

Lee Poh Ping, *Chinese society in nineteenth century Singapore* (Kuala Lumpur: Oxford University Press, 1978).

Lee Sheng-Yi, 'Business elites in Singapore', in Peter S. J. Chen and Hans-Dieter Evers, eds., *Studies in ASEAN sociology: urban society and social change* (Singapore: Chopmen Enterprises, 1978).

'Income distribution, taxation, and social benefits of Singapore', *Journal of Developing Areas*, 14 (1979), pp. 71–98.

'Developing Asian financial centres', in Augustine H. H. Tan and Basant Kapur, eds., *Pacific growth and financial interdependence* (Sydney, Allen & Unwin, 1986).

Legarda, B., 'Foreign exchange decontrol and the redirection of income flows', *Philippine Economic Journal*, 1, 1 (1962), pp. 18–27.

Legge, J. D., *Sukarno: political biography* (Harmondsworth: Penguin, 1972).

Le Manh Hung, *The impact of World War II on the economy of Vietnam 1939–45* (Singapore: Eastern Universities Press, 2004).

Lenin, Vladimir Ilyich, 'On cooperation', in *Collected works*, 2nd edn., vol. 33 (Moscow: Progress Publishers, 1965), pp. 467–75.

Leong Mun Keong, *Wage levels of selected countries* (Singapore: Ministry of Finance, 1971).

Leurence, F., 'Étude statistique sur le développement economique de l'Indochine de 1899 à 1923', *Bulletin économique de l'Indochine*, 28 (1925), pp. 127–61.

Lewis, John P. and Devesh Kapur, 'An updating country study: Thailand's needs and prospects in the 1990s', *World Development*, 18, 10 (1990), pp. 1363–78.

Lewis, W. Arthur, *Economic survey 1919–1939* (London: George Allen & Unwin, 1949).

'Economic development with unlimited supplies of labour', *Manchester School of Social and Economic Studies*, 22, 2 (1954), pp. 139–91.

Development planning: the essentials of economic policy (London: George Allen & Unwin, 1966).

Aspects of tropical trade, 1883–1965 (Stockholm: Almqvist and Wicksell, 1969).

'The export stimulus', in W. Arthur Lewis, ed., *Tropical development 1880–1913* (London: Allen & Unwin, 1970), pp. 13–45.

Evolution of the international economic order (Princeton, NJ: Princeton University Press, 1978).

Growth and fluctuations 1870–1913 (London: Allen & Unwin, 1978).

'Development economics in the 1950s', in Gerald M. Meier and Dudley Seers, eds., *Pioneers in development* (New York: Oxford University Press, 1984), pp. 119–37.

Racial conflict and economic development (Cambridge, MA: Harvard University Press, 1985).

Lim Chong Yah, *Economic development of modern Malaya* (Kuala Lumpur: Oxford University Press, 1967).

'The NWC as I see it', in S. Jayakumar, ed. *Our heritage and beyond: a collection of essays on Singapore, its past, present and future* (Singapore, 1982).

Lim Chong Yah and Associates, *Policy options for the Singapore economy* (Singapore: McGraw-Hill Book Co., 1988).

Lim, Guanie and Nhat Anh Nguyen, 'Reinterpreting Vietnamese industrialization: another Southeast Asian (paper) tiger?', *GRIPS discussion paper* 24 (2024).

Lim, Linda Y. C., 'Singapore's success: after the miracle', in Robert E. Looney, *Handbook of emerging economies* (London: Routledge, 2014), pp. 203–26.

'Fifty years of development in the Singapore economy: an introductory review', *Singapore Economic Review*, 60, 3 (2015), pp. 1–13.

Lim, Linda and Pang Eng Fong, 'Rethinking Singapore's economic model' (2024). www.academia.sg/academic-views/rethinking-singapores-economic-model/#:~:text=LINDA%20LIM%20(University%20of%20Michigan,is%20inefficient%2C%20inequitable%20and%20unsustainable.

Trade, employment and industrialisation in Singapore (Geneva: ILO, 1986).

Lindblad, J. Thomas, 'Foreign investment in late-colonial and post-colonial Indonesia', *Economic and Social History of the Netherlands*, 3 (1991), pp. 183–208.

Foreign investment in Southeast Asia in the twentieth century (London: Macmillan, 1998).

'The late colonial state and economic expansion, 1900–1930s', in Howard Dick et al., eds., *The emergence of a national economy: an economic history of Indonesia, 1800–2000* (Leiden: KITV Press for Asian Studies Association of Australia, 2002), pp. 111–52.

Bridges to new business: the economic decolonization of Indonesia (Leiden: KITLV Press, 2008).

Lindsey, Charles W., 'Economic crisis in the Philippines', *Asian Survey*, 24, 12 (1984), pp. 1185–208.

Lindsey, Charles and Gustav Ranis, *Evidence to the Subcommittee on Asian and International Affairs, US House of Representatives* (1984).

Lintner, Bertil, 'Drugs and economic growth in Burma today', in Morten B. Pedersen, Emily Rudland and Ronald J. May, eds., *Burma-Myanmar: strong regime, weak state?* (Adelaide: Crawford House Publishing, 2000), pp. 164–94.

Little, Ian M. D., *Economic development; theory, policy and international relations* (New York: Basic Books, 1982).

Look Lai, Walton, 'Asian contract and free migrations to the Americas', in David Eltis, ed., *Coerced and free migrations: global perspectives* (Stanford, CA: Stanford University Press, 2002), pp. 229–58.

López Jerez, Montserrat, 'Factor endowments, vent-for-surplus and involutionary process in rural developing economies', *Economic History of Developing Regions*, 37, 1 (2022), pp. 50–74.

Low, Linda, 'Public enterprises in Singapore', in You Poh Seng and Lim Chong Yah, eds., *Singapore: twenty-five years of development* (Singapore: Nan Yang Xing Zhou Lianhe Zaobao, 1984), pp. 253–87.

'The Singapore economy in 1987', *Southeast Asian Affairs*, 15 (1988), pp. 253–65.

Low, N. I., *When Singapore was Syonan-to* (Singapore: Eastern Universities Press, 1973).

Low, N. I. and H. M. Cheng, *This Singapore (our city of dreadful night)* (Singapore: Ngai Seong Press, 1946).

Lowy, Stephen, *Century of growth: the first 100 years of Siam Commercial Bank* (Singapore: Editions Didier Millet, 2007).

Lucas, Anton, *One soul, one struggle: region and revolution in Indonesia* (Sydney: Asian Studies Association of Australia in association with Allen & Unwin, 1991).

Luthringer, George Francis, *The gold-exchange standard in the Philippines* (Princeton, NJ: Princeton University Press, 1934).
McArthur, J. W. and Sachs, J. D., 'Institutions and geography', National Bureau of Economic Research working paper 8114 (2001).
McCarthy, David, Olivia S. Mitchell and John Piggott, 'Asset rich and cash poor: retirement provision and housing policy in Singapore', *Journal of Pension Economics*, 1, 3 (2003), pp. 197–222.
McCoy, Alfred, 'A tale of three cities: Hanoi, Saigon, Phnom Penh', *Geo: Australasia Geographical Magazine* (July–August 1983), pp. 18–39.
McFadyean, Sir Andrew, ed., *The history of rubber regulation, 1934–1943* (London: George Allen & Unwin, 1944).
McGee, T. G., *The Southeast Asian city* (London: G. Bell and Sons, 1967).
McIntyre, Kevin, 'Geography as destiny: cities, villages and Khmer Rouge orientation', *Comparative Studies in Society and History*, 38, 4 (1996), pp. 730–58.
McKendrick, David G., Richard F. Doner and Stephan Haggard, *From Silicon Valley to Singapore: location and competitive advantage in the hard disk drive industry* (Stanford, CA: Stanford University Press, 2000).
McVey, Ruth, ed., *Indonesia* (New Haven, CT: Southeast Asian Studies, Yale University, 1963).
'The post-revolutionary transformation of the Indonesian army, part I', *Indonesia*, 11 (1971), pp. 131–76.
'The post-revolutionary transformation of the Indonesian army, part II', *Indonesia*, 13 (1972), pp. 147–81.
ed., *Southeast Asia capitalists* (Ithaca, NY: Cornell University Southeast Asia Program, 1992).
Mackie, Jamie (J. A. C), *Problems of the Indonesian inflation* (Ithaca, NY: Cornell University Southeast Asia Program, 1967).
'The Indonesian economy, 1950–1963', in Bruce Glassburner, ed., *The economy of Indonesia: selected readings* (Ithaca, NY: Cornell University Press, 1971), pp. 16–69.
'A preliminary survey', in *The Chinese in Indonesia: five essays* (Melbourne: Nelson, 1976), pp. 1–9.
'Changing patterns of Chinese big business in Southeast Asia', in Ruth McVey, ed., *Southeast Asia capitalists* (Ithaca, NY: Cornell University Southeast Asia Program, 1992), pp. 161–90.
Maddison, Angus, 'The historical origins of Indian poverty', *Banca Nazionale del Lavoro Quarterly Review*, 23 (1970), pp. 31–81.
'The colonial burden: a comparative perspective', in Maurice F. G. Scott and Deepak Lal, eds., *Public policy and economic development* (Oxford: Oxford University Press, 1990), pp. 361–75.
The world economy: historical statistics (Paris: OECD, 2003).
Maddison Project Database, version 2020. www.rug.nl/ggdc/historicaldevelopment/maddison/releases/maddison-project-database-2020?lang=en.
Maddison Project Database, version 2023: Bolt, Jutta and Jan Luiten van Zanden, 'Maddison style estimates of the evolution of the world economy: a new 2023 update', *Journal of Economic Surveys* (2024), 1–41.

Mahbubani, Kishore and Jeffrey Sng, *The ASEAN miracle: a catalyst for peace* (Singapore: Ridge Books, 2017).

Main, Par M. F., 'La culture du riz en Indochine', *Journal d'Agriculture Tropicale*, 137 (30 November 1912), pp. 321–25.

Manarungsan, Sompop, *Economic development of Thailand, 1850–1950: response to the challenge of the world economy* (Groningen: University of Groningen, 1989).

Mangahas, Mahar, 'What happened to the poor on the way to the next Philippine development plan?', *Philippine Economic Journal*, 21, 3–4 (1982), pp. 126–46.

Mao Tse-tung, *The writings of Mao Tse-tung, 1949–1976*, vol. 1: *September 1949–December 1955* (New York: Routledge, 1987).

Marr, David G., *Vietnamese tradition on trial 1920–1945* (Berkeley, CA: University of California Press, 1981).

Vietnam 1945: the quest for power (Berkeley, CA: University of California Press, 1995).

Vietnam: state, war and revolution (1945–1946) (Berkeley, CA: University of California Press, 2013).

Marr, David G. and Christine P. White, eds., *Postwar Vietnam: dilemmas in socialist development* (Ithaca, NY: Cornell University Southeast Asia Program, 1988).

Marriott, H., 'Population of the Straits Settlements and Malay Peninsula during the last century', *Journal of the Straits Branch of the Royal Asiatic Society*, 62 (1912), pp. 31–42.

Marshall, Alfred, *Principles of economics*, 8th edn. (London: Macmillan, 1920).

Marx, Karl, *Capital: a critique of political economy*, vol. 2: *The process of circulation of capital* (London: Lawrence & Wishart, 1974).

Mason, E. S., et al., *The economic and social modernization of the Republic of Korea* (Cambridge, MA: Council on East Asian Studies, Harvard University, 1980).

Maung Maung, 'Central banking in Burma', in S. Gethyn Davies, ed., *Central banking in South and East Asia* (Hong Kong: Hong Kong University Press, 1960), pp. 1–8.

Mears, Leon, 'Indonesia', in Adamantios Pepelasis, Leon Mears and Irma Adelman, eds., *Economic development: analysis and case studies* (New York: Harper & Row, 1961), pp. 418–67.

Meehan, Patrick, 'Drugs, insurgency and state-building in Burma: why the drugs trade is central to Burma's changing political order', *Journal of Southeast Asian Studies*, 42, 3 (2011), pp. 376–404.

Meier, Gerald M., *Leading issues in economic development: studies in international poverty*, 5th edn. (New York: Oxford University Press, 1989).

Menon, Jayant and Kaukab Naqvi, 'Structural transformation and inclusive growth in Cambodia: country diagnostic and product space analyses', ISEAS–Yusof Ishak Institute economics working paper (2024).

Menon, Jayant and Peter Warr, 'The Lao economy: capitalizing on natural resource exports', *Asian Economic Policy Review*, 8, 1 (2013), pp. 70–89.

Mieno, Fumiharu, 'The eastern seaboard development plan and industrial cluster in Thailand: a quantitative overview', in Machiko Nissanke and Yasutami

Shimomura, eds., *Aid as a handmaiden for the development of institutions* (Houndmills: Palgrave Macmillan, 2013), pp. 81–105.

Miller, Marcus and Pongsak Luangaram, 'Financial crisis in East Asia: bank runs, asset bubbles and antidotes', *National Institute Economic Review*, 165 (1998), pp. 66–82.

Milne, R. S., '"National ideology" and nation-building in Malaysia', *Asian Survey*, 10, 7 (1970), pp. 563–73.

'The politics of Malaysia's new economic policy', *Pacific Affairs*, 49, 2 (1976), pp. 235–62.

'Privatization in ASEAN states: who gets what, why, and with what effect', *Pacific Affairs*, 65, 1 (1992), pp. 7–29.

Milward, Alan S., *War, economy and society, 1939–1945* (London: Allen Lane, 1977).

Mitchell, B. R., *International historical statistics: Africa, Asia and Oceania 1750–2000* (London: Palgrave Macmillan, 2003).

Mitchell, Kate L., *Industrialization of the western Pacific* (New York: Institute of Pacific Relations, 1942).

Moerman, Michael, *Agricultural change and peasant choice in a Thai village* (Berkeley, CA: University of California Press, 1968).

Mohamad, Mahathir bin, *Malaysian: the way forward (vision 2020)* (Kuala Lumpur: Malaysian Business Council, 1991).

Mohammed, S. I. S. and J. G. Williamson, 'Freight rates and productivity gains in British tramp shipping 1969–1950', National Bureau of Economic Research working paper 9531 (2003).

Monetary Authority of Singapore, 'Sources of Singapore's economic growth, 1990–2009', *Macroeconomic Review*, 9, 1 (2010), pp. 66–81.

Montesano, Michael J., 'Revisiting the rice deltas and reconsidering modern Southeast Asia's economic history', *Journal of Southeast Asian Studies*, 40, 2 (2009), pp. 417–29.

Motooka, Takeshi, 'The conditions governing agricultural development in Southeast Asia', *Developing Economies*, 5, 3 (1967), pp. 425–45.

Mukherjee, Hena and Poh Kam Wong, 'The National University of Singapore and the University of Malaya: common roots and different paths', in Philip G. Altbach and Jamil Salmi, eds., *The road to academic excellence: the making of world-class research universities* (Washington, DC: World Bank, 2011), pp. 129–66.

Murphey, Rhoads, 'New capitals of Asia', *Economic Development and Cultural Change*, 5 (1957), pp. 216–43.

Murray, Martin J., *The development of capitalism in colonial Indochina (1870–1940)* (Berkeley, CA: University of California Press, 1980).

Muscat, Robert J., *Development strategy in Thailand: a study of economic growth* (New York: Praeger, 1966).

The fifth tiger: a study of Thai development policy (Armonk, NY: M. E. Sharpe, 1994).

Mya Maung, 'The Burmese Way to Socialism beyond the welfare state', *Asian Survey*, 10 (1970), pp. 535–51.

'Burma's economic performance under military rule: an assessment', *Asian Survey*, 37, 6 (1997), pp. 503–24.

Mya Than and Joseph L. H. Tan, eds., *Myanmar's dilemmas and options: the challenge of economic transition in the 1990s* (Singapore: Institute of Southeast Asian Studies, 1990).

Myat Thein, *Economic development of Myanmar* (Singapore: Institute of Southeast Asian Studies, 2004).

Myint, Hla, 'An interpretation of economic backwardness', *Oxford Economic Papers*, 6, 2 (1954), pp. 132–63.

'The gains from international trade and the backward countries', *Review of Economic Studies*, 22 (1954–55), pp. 129–42.

'The "classical" theory of international trade and the underdeveloped countries', *Economic Journal*, 68 (1958), pp. 317–37.

'The universities of Southeast Asia', *Pacific Affairs*, 35, 2 (1962), pp. 116–27.

'The inward and outward looking countries of Southeast Asia', *Malayan Economic Review*, 12, 1 (1965), pp. 1–13 and reprinted in Hla Myint, *Economic theory and the underdeveloped countries* (New York: Oxford University Press, 1971), pp. 271–90.

'Economic theory and the underdeveloped regions', *Journal of Political Economy*, 73, 5 (1965), pp. 477–91.

The economics of the developing countries, 5th edn. (London: Hutchinson, 1980).

'Inward and outward-looking countries revisited: the case of Indonesia', *Bulletin of Indonesian Economic Studies*, 20 (1984), pp. 39–52.

'The neoclassical resurgence in development economics: its strengths and limitations', in G. M. Meier, ed., *Pioneers in development economics, second series* (New York: Oxford University Press, 1987), pp. 107–36.

Naing Oo, 'Urbanization and economic development in Burma', *Sojourn*, 4, 2 (1989), pp. 233–60.

Nakahara Michiko, '"Comfort women" in Malaysia', *Critical Asian Studies*, 33, 4 (2001), pp. 581–89.

National Archives of Singapore, *Reflections and memories of war*, vol. 2: *Syonan years 1942–1945: living beneath the rising sun* (Singapore: National Archives of Singapore, 2009).

Naval Intelligence Division, *Indo-China* (London: Naval Intelligence Division of the Admiralty, 1943).

Netherlands East Indies, vol. 2 (London: Naval Intelligence Division of the Admiralty, 1944).

Naya, S., 'Natural resources, factor mix, and factor reversals in international trade', *American Economic Review*, 57 (1967), pp. 561–70.

Nazrin, R., 'Historical statistics of Malaya, 1900–1939: progress and perspectives', paper presented at the XIII International Economic History Congress, Buenos Aires (2002).

Negara, Siwage Dharma and Arief Ramayandi, 'Laying the foundations for future growth acceleration?', *Bulletin of Indonesian Economic Studies*, 56, 1 (2020), pp. 1–21.

Nenryō Konwa Kai [Fuel Study Group], ed., *Nihon kaigun nenryō shi* [History of Japanese naval fuels], 2 vols. (Tokyo: Hara Shobō, 1972).

Nevin, Edward, *Capital funds in underdeveloped countries* (London: Macmillan, 1961).

Ngo Vinh Long, 'Some aspects of cooperativization in the Mekong Delta', in David G. Marr and Christine P. White, eds., *Postwar Vietnam: dilemmas in socialist development* (Ithaca, NY: Cornell University Southeast Asia Program, 1988), pp. 163–73.

Nguyen Thy, 'Urbanization processes in North Vietnam', *Soviet Geography*, 15, 6 (1974), pp. 352–57.

Nguyen Tien Hung, *Economic development in socialist Vietnam, 1955–80* (New York: Praeger, 1977).

North, Douglass C., *The economic growth of the United States, 1790–1860* (New York: W. W. Norton, 1966).

Nu, U, *Saturday's son* (New Haven, CT: Yale University Press, 1975).

Nuechterlein, Donald E., 'Thailand after Sarit', *Asian Survey*, 4, 5 (1964), pp. 842–50.

Nurkse, Ragnar, 'International investment to-day in the light of nineteenth-century experience', *Economic Journal*, 64, 256 (1954), pp. 744–58.

Patterns of trade and development (Stockholm: Almqvist and Wicksell, 1959).

Equilibrium and growth in the world economy (Cambridge, MA: Harvard University Press, 1961).

Nwe, Than Than, 'Yangon: the emergence of a new spatial order in Myanmar's capital city', *Sojourn*, 13, 1 (1998), pp. 86–113.

Nyberg, A. J., 'Growth in the Philippine coconut industry, 1901–1966', *Philippine Economic Journal*, 7, 1 (1968), pp. 42–52.

Oanh, Pham Thi, Luc Thi Thu Huong and The Tuan Tran, 'Participation of Vietnamese enterprise in the global footwear supply chain', *International Journal of Advanced and Applied Sciences*, 11, 8 (2024), pp. 80–88.

Ocampo, Romeo B., 'The Metro Manila mega-region', in T. G. McGee and I. M. Robinson, eds., *The mega-urban regions of Southeast Asia* (Vancouver: University of British Columbia Press, 1995), pp. 282–95.

Ooi Keat Gin, *The Japanese occupation of Borneo, 1941–1945* (London: Routledge, 2011).

Osborne, Milton, *Region of revolt: focus on Southeast Asia* (Harmondsworth: Penguin Books, 1971).

Oshima, Harry T., 'Growth and unemployment in Singapore', *Malayan Economic Review*, 12 (1967), pp. 32–58.

Ouyyanont, Porphant, 'Bangkok as a magnet for rural labour: changing conditions, 1900–1970', *Southeast Asian Studies*, 36, 1 (1998), pp. 78–108.

Owen, Norman G., 'The rice industry of mainland Southeast Asia 1850–1914', *Journal of the Siam Society* (July 1971), pp. 75–141.

Prosperity without progress: Manila hemp and material life in the colonial Philippines (Manila: Ateneo de Manila, 1984).

'Economic and social change', in Nicholas Tarling, ed., *The Cambridge history of Southeast Asia*, vol. 2, part 2: *From World War II to the present* (Cambridge: Cambridge University Press, 1999), pp. 139–99.

ed., *The emergence of modern Southeast Asia* (Honolulu: University of Hawaii Press, 2005).

Paauw, Douglas S., *Financing economic development: the Indonesian case* (Glencoe, IL: Free Press, 1960).

'From colonial to guided economy', in Ruth McVey, ed., *Indonesia* (New Haven, CT: Southeast Asian Studies, Yale University, 1963), pp. 135–247.

Pang Eng Fong and Linda Y. C. Lim, 'Labor, productivity and Singapore's development model', *Singapore Economic Review*, 60, 3 (2015), pp. 1–30.

Pante, Michael D., *A capital city at the margins: Quezon City and urbanization in the twentieth-century Philippines* (Manila: Ateneo de Manila University Press, 2019).

Parmer, J. Norman, *Colonial labor policy and administration* (Locust Valley, NY: J. J. Augustin, 1960).

Parr, J. B., 'A class of deviations from rank-size regularity: three interpretations', *Regional Studies*, 10 (1976), pp. 285–92.

'A note on the size distribution of cities over time', *Journal of Urban Economics*, 18 (1985), pp. 199–212.

Patterson, Neil K., Marie Montanjees, Colleen Cardillo and John Motala, 'Key concepts in the measurement of FDI', in *Foreign direct investment: trends, data availability, concepts, and recording practices* (Washington DC: International Monetary Fund, 2004), Chapter 5. www.elibrary.imf.org/display/book/9781589063471/ch05.xml.

Pauker, Guy J., 'Indonesia's eight-year development plan', *Pacific Affairs*, 34, 2 (1961), pp. 115–30.

Pe, U Hla, *Narrative of the Japanese occupation of Burma* (Ithaca, NY: Southeast Asia Program, Cornell University, 1961).

Pelzer, Karl J., *Pioneer settlement in the Asiatic tropics: studies in land utilization and agricultural colonization in Southeastern Asia* (New York: Institute of Pacific Relations, 1945).

'Physical and human resource patterns', in Ruth McVey, ed., *Indonesia* (New Haven, CT: Southeast Asian Studies, Yale University, 1963), pp. 1–23.

Peng, Nathan, 'Inequality and the social compact in Singapore: macro trends versus lived realities', *Journal of Southeast Asian Economics*, 36, 3 (2019), pp. 355–79.

Penn World Table, version 10.0. www.rug.nl/ggdc/productivity/pwt/?lang=en.

Perkins, Dwight H., *East Asian development: foundations and strategies* (Cambridge, MA: Harvard University Press, 2013).

Perkins, Dwight, Rajah Rasiah and Wing Thye Woo, 'Explaining Malaysia's past growth and future prospects', unpublished ms (2017).

Phongpaichit, Pasuk and Chris Baker, *Thailand: economy and politics* (New York: Oxford University Press, 1995).

Thailand's boom and bust (Chaing Mai: Silkworm Books, 1998).

Pincus, Jonathan, 'Why doesn't Vietnam grow faster?: fragmentation and the limits of vent for surplus growth', *Journal of Southeast Asian Economics*, 32, 1 (2015), pp. 26–51.

Pluvier, Jan M., *Confrontations: a study of Indonesian politics* (Kuala Lumpur: Oxford University Press, 1965).

South-East Asia from colonialism to independence (Kuala Lumpur: Oxford University Press, 1974).

Power, John H., 'Import substitution as an industrialization strategy', *Philippine Economic Journal*, 5, 2 (1966), pp. 167–204.

'The structure of protection in West Malaysia', in Bela Balassa and Associates, eds., *The structure of protection in developing countries* (Baltimore, MD: Johns Hopkins Press, 1971), pp. 203–22.

'The structure of protection in the Philippines', in Bela Balassa and Associates, eds., *The structure of protection in developing countries* (Baltimore, MD: Johns Hopkins Press, 1971), pp. 261–87.

Power, John H. and Gerardo P. Sicat, *The Philippines industrialization and trade policies* (London: Oxford University Press, 1971).

Prince, G. H. A., 'Monetary policy in colonial Indonesia and the position of the Java Bank', in J. Thomas Lindblad, ed., *Historical foundations of a national economy in Indonesia, 1890s–1990s* (Amsterdam: North Holland, 1996), pp. 55–70.

Pryor, Frederic L., *The red and the green: the rise and fall of collectivized agriculture in Marxist regimes* (Princeton, NJ: Princeton University Press, 1992).

Purcell, Victor, *The Chinese in Malaya* (Kuala Lumpur: Oxford University Press, 1967).

Raben, Remco, 'The Indonesian *rōmusha* and coolies under naval administration: the eastern archipelago, 1942–45', in Paul H. Kratoska, ed., *Asian labor in the wartime Japanese empire* (Armonk, NY: M. E. Sharpe, 2005), pp. 197–212.

Rabenau, K. V., 'Trade policies and industrialization in a developing country: the case of West Malaysia', *Malayan Economic Review*, 21, 1 (1976), pp. 23–46.

Rabino, Joseph, 'The statistical story of the Suez Canal', *Journal of the Royal Statistical Society*, 50, 3 (1887), pp. 495–546.

Rafael, Vincent L., 'The war of translation: colonial education, American English, and Tagalog slang in the Philippines', *Journal of Asian Studies*, 74, 2 (2015), pp. 283–302.

Raffles, Lady, *Memoir of the life and public services of Sir Thomas Stamford Raffles* (London: John Murray, 1830).

Raffles, Sir T. S., 'The founding of Singapore', *Journal of the Malaysian Branch of the Royal Asiatic Society*, 42, 1 (1969).

Raj-Reichert, Gale, 'Global value chains, contract manufacturers, and the middle-income trap: the electronics industry in Malaysia', *Journal of Development Studies*, 56, 4 (2020), pp. 698–716.

Ranis, Gustav, 'Brief reflections on the Philippine economy, summer 1984', prepared statement before the subcommittee on Asian and International Affairs, US House of Representatives, 20 September 1984.

'Comment' on article by Myint, in Gerald M. Meier, ed., *Pioneers in development, second series* (New York: Oxford University Press, 1987), pp. 144–50.

'Marcos's economic legacy: problems, policies and prospects for President Aquino and how the United States can help', in Carl H. Landé, ed., *Rebuilding a nation: Philippine challenges and American policy* (Washington, DC: Washington Institute Press, 1987), pp. 111–21.

'Two memoranda from G. Ranis', *Philippine Review of Economics*, 55, 2 (2018), pp. 198–217.

Rao, V. V. Bhanoji and M. K. Ramakrishnan, 'Economic growth, structural change and income inequality, Singapore, 1966–1975', *Malayan Economic Review*, 21, 2 (1976), pp. 92–122.

Rasiah, Rajah, 'Expansion and slowdown in Southeast Asia electronics manufacturing', *Journal of the Asia Pacific Economy*, 14, 2 (2009), pp. 123–37.

'Garment manufacturing in Cambodia and Laos', *Journal of the Asia Pacific Economy*, 14, 2 (2009), pp. 150–61.

'The industrial policy experience of the electronics industry in Malaysia', in John Page and Finn Tarp, eds., *The practice of industrial policy: government–business coordination in Africa and East Asia* (Oxford: Oxford University Press, 2017), pp. 123–44.

Rasiah, Rajah and Hing Ai Yun, 'Industrializing Southeast Asia', *Journal of the Asia Pacific Economy*, 14, 2 (2009), pp. 107–15.

Rattanakhamfu, Saowaruj, 'Comment on "The evolution of university–industry linkages in Thailand"', *Asian Economic Policy Review*, 18 (2023), pp. 283–84.

Rawson, Rees, 'Two new railways in South-East Asia', *Geographical Journal*, 103, 13 (1946), pp. 85–88.

Raymond, Chad, '"No responsibility and no rice": the rise and fall of agricultural collectivization in Vietnam', *Agricultural History*, 82, 1 (2008), pp. 43–61.

Reid, Anthony, *Southeast Asia in the age of commerce*, vol. 2: *Expansion and crisis* (New Haven, CT: Yale University Press, 1993).

Reitsma, S. A., *Gedenkboek der Staatsspoor- en Tramwegen in Nederlandsch-Indië 1875–1925* (Weltevreden: Topografischie Inrichting, 1925).

Remolona, Eli M. and Mario B. Lamberte, 'Financial reforms and the balance of payments crisis: the case of the Philippines, 1980–83', *Philippine Review of Economics and Business*, 23, 1–2 (1986), pp. 101–41.

Resosudarmo, Budy P. and Abdurohman, 'Is being stuck with a five percent growth rate a new normal for Indonesia?', *Bulletin of Indonesian Economic Studies*, 54, 2 (2018), pp. 141–64.

Reynolds, E. Bruce, 'Anomaly or model? Independent Thailand's role in Japan's Asian strategy, 1941–1943', in Peter Duus, Ramon H. Myers and Mark R. Peattie, eds., *The Japanese wartime empire, 1931–1945* (Princeton, NJ: Princeton University Press, 1996), pp. 243–73.

'History, memory, compensation and reconciliation: the abuse of labor along the Thai–Burma railway', in Paul H. Kratoska, ed., *Asian labor in the wartime Japanese empire* (Armonk, NY: M. E. Sharpe, 2005), pp. 326–47.

Reynolds, Lloyd G., 'The spread of economic growth to the Third World', *Journal of Economic Literature*, 21, 3 (1983), pp. 941–80.

Economic growth in the Third World, 1850–1980 (New Haven, CT: Yale University Economic Growth Center, 1985).

Richardson, Harry W., 'Theory of the distribution of city sizes: review and prospects', *Regional Studies*, 7 (1973), pp. 239–51.

Riggs, Fred W., *Thailand: the modernization of a bureaucratic polity* (Honolulu: East-West Center Press, 1966).

Rimmer, Peter J. and Howard W. Dick, *The city in Southeast Asia: patterns, processes and policy* (Honolulu: University of Hawaii Press, 2009).

Robequain, Charles, *The economic development of French Indo-China* (London: Oxford University Press, 1944).

Malaya, Indonesia, Borneo and the Philippines (London: Longmans, 1958).

Robertson, C. J., 'The rice export trade from Burma, Siam and French Indo-China', *Pacific Affairs*, 9, 2 (1936), pp. 243–53.

Rocamora, Joel, 'From regime crisis to system change', in Rodolfo C. Severino and Lorraine Carlos Salazar, eds., *Whither the Philippines in the 21st century* (Singapore: Institute of Southeast Asian Studies, 2007), pp. 18–42.

Rosenstein-Rodan, P. N., 'Some problems of industrialization in eastern and south-eastern Europe', *Economic Journal*, 53 (1943), pp. 202–11.

Rosenthal, Stuart S. and William C. Strange, 'How close is close?: the spatial reach of agglomeration economies', *Journal of Economic Literature*, 34, 3 (2020), pp. 27–49.

Rotary Club of Singapore, *Singapore as an industrial centre* (Singapore: Rotary Club of Singapore, 1931).

Rothe, Cecile, 'Industrial development and home consumption in the Netherlands Indies', *Bulletin of the Colonial Institute of Amsterdam*, 1 (1938), pp. 1–13.

Rowe, J. W. F., *Studies in the artificial control of raw material supplies, no. 2 rubber* (London: London & Cambridge Economic Service, 1931).

Rōyama, Masamichi and Tatsuji Takéuchi, *The Philippine polity: a Japanese view*, ed. Theodore Friend (New Haven, CT: Southeast Asian Studies, Yale University, 1967).

Rudner, M., 'The Malaysian general election of 1969: a political analysis', *Modern Asian Studies*, 4, 1 (1970), pp. 1–21.

Runes, I. T., *General standards of living and wages of workers in the Philippine sugar industry* (Manila: Philippine Council Institute of Pacific Relations, 1939).

Saito, T. and K. K. Lee, *Statistics on the Burmese economy* (Singapore: Institute of Southeast Asian Studies, 1999).

Sallaz, Jeffrey J., *Lives on the line: how the Philippines became the world's call centre capital* (New York: Oxford University Press, 2019).

Samuelson, Paul A. and William D. Nordhaus, *Economics*, 14th edn. (New York: McGraw-Hill, 1992).

Sanders, J. O., 'The Malayan railway', *Malaya* (Sept. 1952),

Sandhu, Kernial Singh, *Indians in Malaya: some aspects of their immigration and settlement (1786–1957)* (Cambridge: Cambridge University Press, 2010).

Sandilands, R. J. and Tan Ling Hui, 'Comparative advantage in a re-export economy: the case of Singapore', *Singapore Economic Review*, 31, 2 (1986).

Sansom, R. L., *The economics of insurgency in the Mekong Delta of Vietnam* (Cambridge, MA: MIT, 1970).

Sato, Shigeru, *War, nationalism and peasants: Java under the Japanese occupation 1942–1945* (Armonk, NY: M. E. Sharpe, 1994).

'Relocation of labor and the rōmusha issue', in Peter Post et al., eds., *The encyclopedia of Indonesia in the Pacific War* (Leiden: Brill, 2009), pp. 245–61.

Saw Swee-Hock, *Singapore population in transition* (Philadelphia: University of Pennsylvania Press, 1970).

Scalapino, Robert A., *The politics of development: perspectives on twentieth-century Asia* (Cambridge, MA: Harvard University Press, 1989).

Schumpeter, Joseph, *The theory of economic development: an inquiry into profits, capital, credit, interest and the business cycle* (Cambridge, MA: Harvard University Press, 1934).

Schwartz, Anna J., 'Currency boards: their past, present, and possible future role', *Carnegie-Rochester Conference Series on Public Policy*, 39 (1993), pp. 147–87.

Schwulst, E. B., 'Report on the budget and financial policies of French Indo-China, Siam, Federated Malay States and the Netherlands East Indies', in *Report of the Governor General of the Philippine Islands* (Washington, DC: US Government Printing Office, 1931).

Searle, Peter, *The riddle of Malaysian capitalism: rent-seekers or real capitalists* (St Leonards, NSW: Allen & Unwin, 1999).

Selth, Andrew, 'Race and resistance in Burma, 1942–1945', *Modern Asian Studies*, 20, 3 (1986), pp. 483–507.

Burma's armed forces: power without glory (Norwalk, CT: EastBridge, 2002).

Selvaratnam, V., 'Malaysia's higher education and quest for developed nation status by 2020', in D. Singh and M. Cook, eds., *Southeast Asian affairs 2016* (Singapore: ISEAS, 2016).

Sen, Amartya Kumar, 'On optimising the rate of saving', *Economic Journal*, 71, 283 (1961), pp. 479–96.

'Development: which way now?', *Economic Journal*, 93, 372 (1983), pp. 745–62.

Development as freedom (New York: Alfred A. Knopf, 1999).

Sendut, Hamzah, 'The structure of Kuala Lumpur: Malaysia's capital city', *Town Planning Review*, 36, 2 (1965), pp. 125–38.

Severino, Rodolfo C. and Lorraine Carlos Salazar, eds., *Whither the Philippines in the 21st century* (Singapore: Institute of Southeast Asian Studies, 2007).

Shabad, Theodore, 'Economic developments in North Vietnam', *Pacific Affairs*, 31, 1 (1958), pp. 36–53.

Shah, Sultan Nazrin, *Charting the economy: early 20th century Malaya and contemporary Malaysian contrasts* (Kuala Lumpur: Oxford University Press, 2017).

Striving for inclusive development: from Pangkor to a modern Malaysian state (Kuala Lumpur: Oxford University Press, 2019).

Shand, R.T., ed., *Agricultural development in Asia* (Canberra: Australian National University Press, 1969).

Shaplen, Robert, 'Letter from Malaysia', *New Yorker*, 18 April 1977.

'The Philippines: from Marcos to Aquino – I', *New Yorker*, 25 August 1986.

'The Philippines: from Marcos to Aquino – II', *New Yorker*, 1 September 1986.

Sharpston, Michael, *International sub-contracting* (Washington, DC: World Bank, 1975).

Shaw, William, *Tun Razak: his life and times* (London: Longman, 1976).

Shee Poon Kim, 'Singapore in 1991', *Asian Survey*, 32, 2 (1992), pp. 119–25.

Sheehan, Neil, *Two cities: Hanoi and Saigon* (London: Jonathan Cape, 1992).

Shein, Maung, *Burma's transport and foreign trade (1885–1914)* (Rangoon: Department of Economics, University of Rangoon, 1964).

Shein, Maung, Daw Myint Myint Thant and Daw Tin Tin Sein, '"Provincial contract system" of British Indian Empire, in relation to Burma – a case of fiscal exploitation', *Journal of the Burma Research Society*, 52 (1969), pp. 1–26.

Shepherd, Jack, *Industry in Southeast Asia* (New York: Institute of Pacific Relations, 1941).

Short, Brock K., 'Indigenous banking in an early period of development: the Straits Settlements, 1914–1940', *Malayan Economic Review*, 16 (1971), pp. 57–75.

Shrestha, Rashesh and Ian Coxhead, 'Can Indonesia secure a development dividend from its resource export boom?', *Bulletin of Indonesian Economic Studies* 54, 1 (2018), pp. 1–24.

Siam Commercial Bank, *1904–1932 laying the foundations of Thai banking* (Bangkok: Siam Commercial Bank, 2010).

Siamwalla, Ammar, 'A history of rice policies in Thailand', *Food Research Institute Studies*, 14, 3 (1975), pp. 233–49.

Siamwalla, Ammar, Suthad Setboonsarng and Direk Patamasiriwat, 'Agriculture', in Peter G. Warr, ed., *The Thai economy in transition* (Cambridge: Cambridge University Press, 1993), pp. 81–117.

Sicat, Gerardo P., 'The Philippine economy', in Gerardo P. Sicat, ed., *The Philippine economy in the 1960s* (Quezon City: Institute of Economic Development and Research, University of the Philippines, 1964).

A historical and current perspective of Philippine economic problems, Monograph series no. 11 (Manila: Philippine Institute for Development Studies, 1986).

'The Philippine economy during the Japanese occupation, 1941–1945', in Marcel Boldorf and Tetsuji Okazaki, eds., *Economies under occupation: the hegemony of Nazi Germany and Imperial Japan in World War II* (London: Routledge, 2015), pp. 191–204.

Silcock, T. H., 'Promotion of industry and the planning process', in T. H. Silcock, ed., *Thailand: social and economic studies of development* (Canberra: Australian National University Press, 1967), pp. 258–88.

ed., *Thailand: social and economic studies of development* (Canberra: Australian National University Press, 1967).

The economic development of Thai agriculture (Canberra: Australian National University Press, 1970).

Silcock, T. H. and E. K. Fisk, eds., *The political economy of independent Malaya; a case-study in development* (Canberra: Australian National University, 1963).

Silverstein, Josef, 'Politics and railroads in Burma and India', *Journal of Southeast Asian History*, 5, 1 (1964), pp. 17–28.

'The importance of the Japanese occupation of Southeast Asia to the political scientist', in Josef Silverstein, ed., *Southeast Asia in World War II: four essays* (New Haven, CT: Yale University Southeast Asia Studies, 1966), pp. 1–11.
Burma: military rule and the politics of stagnation (Ithaca, NY: Cornell University Press, 1977).
Simpson, Adam and Nicholas Farrelly, eds., *Myanmar: politics, economy and society*, 2nd edn. (Abingdon: Taylor & Francis, 2023).
Singapore manufacturers' exhibition: a light on local industries, 2–9 January 1932 (Singapore, 1932).
Sitsen, Peter H. W., *Industrial development of the Netherlands Indies* (New York: Netherlands Indies Council of the Institute of Pacific Relations, 1943).
Sivaram, M., *The road to Delhi* (Rutland and Tokyo: Charles E. Tuttle, 1967).
Skinner, G. William, *Chinese society in Thailand* (Ithaca, NY: Cornell University Press, 1957).
Leadership and power in the Chinese community of Thailand (Ithaca, NY: Cornell University Press, 1958).
'The Chinese minority', in Ruth McVey, ed., *Indonesia* (New Haven, CT: Southeast Asian Studies, Yale University, 1963), pp. 97–117.
Smith, C. A., 'Modern and premodern urban primacy', *Comparative Urban Research*, 11 (1982), pp. 79–96.
'Types of city-size distribution: a comparative analysis', in Ad van de Woude, Akira Hayami and Jan de Vries, eds., *Urbanization in history* (Oxford: Clarendon Press, 1990), pp. 43–46.
Smith, Martin, 'Burma and World War II', *Cultural Survival Quarterly*, 13, 4 (1989), pp. 1–4.
Smolski, T., 'Les statistiques de la population indochinoise', *Actes du Congrès International de la Population*, 6 (1937), pp. 56–67.
Snider, Nancy L., 'Race, leitmotiv of the Malayan election drama', *Asian Survey*, 10, 12 (1970), pp. 1070–80.
Snodgrass, Donald R., *Inequality and economic development in Malaysia* (New York: Oxford University Press, 1980).
Sokoloff, K. L. and S. L. Engerman, 'Institutions, factor endowments, and paths of development in the New World', *Journal of Economic Perspectives*, 14 (2000), pp. 217–32.
Solow, Robert M., 'A contribution to the theory of economic growth', *Quarterly Journal of Economics*, 70, 1 (1956), pp. 65–94.
Somers, Mary F., *The Peranakan Chinese politics in Indonesia* (Ithaca, NY: Southeast Asia Program, Cornell University, 1964).
Spate, O. H. K., 'Beginnings of industrialization in Burma', *Economic Geography*, 17, 1 (1941), pp. 75–92.
Burma setting (London: Longmans, Green & Co., 1943).
'The Burmese village', *Geographical Review*, 35, 4 (1945), pp. 523–43.
Spencer, J. E., *Land and people in the Philippines* (Berkeley, CA: University of California Press, 1954).

'The cities of the Philippines', *Journal of Geography*, 57 (1958), pp. 288–94.

Spoor, Max, 'Finance in a socialist transition: the case of the Democratic Republic of Vietnam (1955–1964)', *Journal of Contemporary Asia*, 17, 3 (1987), pp. 339–65.

Stamp, L. Dudley, 'Siam before the war', *Geographical Journal*, 99 (1942), pp. 209–24.

Asia: a regional and economic geography, 9th edn. (London: Methuen, 1957).

Steinberg, David, I., *Burma: the state of Myanmar* (Washington, DC: Georgetown University Press, 2001).

'An ambiguous legacy: years at war in the Philippines', *Pacific Affairs*, 45, 2 (1972), pp. 165–90.

Stern, Lewis M., 'The overseas Chinese in the Socialist Republic of Vietnam, 1979–82', *Asian Survey*, 25, 5 (1985), pp. 521–36.

Sternstein, Larry, 'A critique of Thai population data', *Pacific Viewpoint*, 6, 1 (1965), pp. 15–35.

'The growth of the population of the world's pre-eminent "primate city": Bangkok at its bicentenary', *Journal of Southeast Asian Studies*, 15, 1 (1984), pp. 43–68.

Stifel, Lawrence D., 'Economics of the Burmese Way to Socialism', *Asian Survey*, 11, 8 (1971), pp. 803–17.

'Technocrats and modernization in Thailand', *Asian Survey*, 16, 12 (1976), pp. 1184–96.

Stiglitz, Joseph E., 'From miracle to crisis to recovery: lessons from four decades of East Asian experience', in Joseph E. Stiglitz and Shahid Yusuf, eds., *Rethinking the East Asian miracle* (New York: Oxford University Press, 2001), pp. 509–26.

Stoler, Ann Laura, *Capitalism and confrontation in Sumatra's plantation belt, 1870–1979*, 2nd edn. (Ann Arbor, MI: University of Michigan Press, 1995).

Stone, I., *The global export of capital from Great Britain, 1865–1914: a statistical survey* (London: Macmillan, 1999).

Storer, Thomas Perry, 'The Philippines', in W. Arthur Lewis, ed., *Tropical development 1880–1913* (London: George Allen & Unwin, 1970), pp. 283–308.

Stover, Charles C., 'Tropical exports', in W. Arthur Lewis, ed., *Tropical development 1880–1913* (London: George Allen & Unwin, 1970), pp. 64–99.

Straits Chinese British Association, *Golden jubilee souvenir* (Singapore, 1950).

Stuart-Fox, Martin, 'The French in Laos, 1887–1945', *Modern Asian Studies*, 29, 1 (1995), pp. 111–39.

A history of Laos (Cambridge: Cambridge University Press, 1997).

Sturgeon, T. and M. Kawakami, 'Global value chains in the electronics industry', Policy Research working paper 5417 (Washington DC: World Bank, 2010).

'Global value chains in the electronics industry: characteristics, crisis, and upgrading opportunities for firms from developing countries', *International Journal of Technological Learning Innovation and Development*, 4, 1 (2011), pp. 120–47.

Suehiro, Akira, *Capital accumulation in Thailand, 1855–1985* (Tokyo: Centre for East Asian Cultural Studies, 1989).

Sukarno, *Sukarno: an autobiography as told to Cindy Adams* (Indianapolis: Bobbs-Merrill, 1966).

Summers, Lawrence H. and Lant Pritchett, 'Asiaphoria meets regression to the mean', National Bureau of Economic Research working paper 20573 (2014).

Sundrum, R. M., 'Urbanisation: the Burmese experience', *Journal of the Burma Research Society*, 40, 1 (1957), pp. 105–27.

Surianta, Andree and Arianto A. Patunru, 'Repositioning Indonesia in the post-COVID-19 global value chains', *Southeast Asian Affairs* (2021), pp. 122–38.

Suryadinata, Leo, 'Indonesian Chinese education: past and present', *Indonesia*, 14 (October 1972), pp. 49–71.

Sutter, John O., *Indonesianisasi: politics in a changing economy, 1940–1955*, vol. 1: *The Indonesian economy at the close of the Dutch period and under the Japanese* (Ithaca, NY: Southeast Asia Program Cornell University data paper 36-I, 1959).

Swift, M. G., 'The accumulation of capital in a peasant economy', *Economic Development and Cultural Change*, 5, 4 (1957), pp. 325–37.

Tai, Hue-Tam Ho, *Millenarianism and peasant politics in Vietnam* (Cambridge, MA: Harvard University Press, 1983).

Tambunlertchai, Somsak, 'Manufacturing', in Peter G. Warr, ed., *The Thai economy in transition* (Cambridge: Cambridge University Press, 1993), pp. 118–50.

Tan, Kenneth Paul, *Singapore: identity, brand, power* (Cambridge: Cambridge University Press, 2018).

Tan Tek Soon, 'Chinese emigration', *Straits Chinese Magazine*, 6 (1903), pp. 44–45.

Tanaka, Yuki, *Japan's comfort women: sexual slavery and prostitution during World War II and the US occupation* (London: Routledge, 2002).

Tanasaldy, Taufiq, 'From official to grassroots racism: transformation of anti-Chinese sentiment in Indonesia', *Political Quarterly*, 93, 3 (2022), pp. 460–68.

Tarling, Nicholas, *Nations and states in Southeast Asia* (Cambridge: Cambridge University Press, 1999).

Taylor, Milton C., 'South Vietnam: lavish aid, limited progress', *Pacific Affairs*, 34, 3 (1961), pp. 242–56.

Taylor, Robert H., 'Perceptions of ethnicity in the politics of Burma', *Southeast Asian Journal of Social Science*, 10, 1 (1982), pp. 7–22.

Marxism and resistance in Burma, 1942–1945: Thein Pe Myint's 'Wartime traveler' (Athens, OH: Ohio University Press, 1984).

'Disaster or release: J. S. Furnivall and the bankruptcy of Burma', *Modern Asian Studies*, 29, 1 (1995), pp. 45–63.

The state in Myanmar (Honolulu: University of Hawaii Press, 2009).

Teo You Yenn, *This is what inequality looks like* (Singapore: Ethos Books, 2018)

Tham, Siew-Yean and Pui-Yee Chong, 'Transforming Malaysia's higher education: policies and progress', *Asian Economic Policy Review*, 18 (2023), pp. 243–60.

Thant Myint-U, 'What to do about Burma', *London Review of Books*, 29, 3 (February 2007), pp. 31–33.

Thien Ton That, 'Economic development in South Vietnam 1954–60', *Malayan Economic Review*, 6, 1 (1961), pp. 55–80.

Thomas, Terry, *My story: justice in the wilderness* (Petaling Jaya, Malaysia: Strategic Info Research Development, 2021).

Thomas, W. A., 'An intra-empire capital transfer: the Shanghai Rubber Company boom 1909–1912', *Modern Asian Studies*, 32, 3 (1998), pp. 739–60.

Thomas, K. D. and B. Glassburner, 'Abrogation, take-over and nationalization: the elimination of Dutch economic dominance from the republic of Indonesia', *Australian Outlook*, 19, 2 (1965), pp. 158–79.

Thompson, Virginia, *Thailand: the new Siam* (New York: Macmillan, 1941).

Thrift, Nigel J. and Dean K. Forbes, *The price of war: urbanization in Vietnam, 1954–1985* (London: Allen & Unwin, 1986).

Tilman, Robert O., 'Malaysia: the problems of federation', *Western Political Quarterly*, 16, 4 (1963), pp. 897–911.

Times Higher Education, 'Asia university rankings 2024'. www.timeshighereducation.com/world-university-rankings/2024/regional-ranking#!/length/100/sort_by/rank/sort_order/asc/cols/stats.

Timmer, C. Peter, 'The agricultural transformation', in Hollis Chenery and T. N. Srinivasan, eds., *The handbook of development economics* (Amsterdam: Elsevier, 1988), pp. 275–331.

Tin Maung Maung Than, *State dominance in Burma: the political economy of industrialization* (Singapore: Institute of Southeast Asian Studies, 2007).

Tinker, Hugh, *The Union of Burma*, 4th edn. (London: Oxford University Press, 1967).

Totani, Yuma, *The Tokyo War Crimes Trial; the pursuit of justice in the wake of World War II* (Cambridge, MA: Harvard University Asia Center, 2008).

Touwen, Jeoren, *Extremes in the archipelago: trade and economic development in the Outer Islands of Indonesia* (Leiden: KITLV Press, 2001).

Trager, Frank N., *Building a welfare state in Burma, 1948–1956* (New York: Institute of Pacific Relations, 1958).

'The failure of U Nu and the return of the armed forces in Burma', *Review of Politics*, 25, 3 (1963), pp. 309–28.

Tran Van Thot, 'Vietnamese economy at the crossroads: new *Doi Moi* for sustained growth', *Asian Economic Policy Review*, 8 (2013), pp. 122–43.

Treadgold, Malcolm and Richard Hooley, 'Decontrol and redirection of income flows: a second look', *Philippine Economic Journal*, 6, 2 (1967), pp. 109–28.

Tregonning, K. G., *Home port Singapore: a history of the Straits Steamship Company Limited, 1890–1965* (Singapore: Oxford University Press, 1967).

Trocki, Carl A., 'Political structures in the nineteenth and early twentieth centuries', in Nicholas Tarling, ed., *The Cambridge economic history of Southeast Asia, vol. 3: 1800–1930s* (Cambridge: Cambridge University Press, 1999), pp. 75–126.

Trued, M. N., 'South Viet-Nam's industrial development center', *Pacific Affairs*, 33, 3 (1960), pp. 250–67.

Tsao, Yuan, 'Growth without productivity: Singapore manufacturing in the 1970s', *Journal of Development Economics*, 18, 1/2 (1985), pp. 25–38.

Tun Thet, U, 'Outline of a socialist economy for Burma', *Journal of the Burma Research Society*, 38 (1954), pp. 59–76.

Tun Wai, U, *Burma's currency and credit* (Bombay: Orient Longmans, 1962).

'Myanmar', in Pradumna B. Rana and Naved Hamid, eds., *From centrally planned to market economies: the Asian approach, vol. 3: Lao PDR, Myanmar and Vietnam* (Hong Kong: Oxford University Press, 1996), pp. 149–331.

Turley, William S., 'Urbanization in war: Hanoi, 1946–1973', *Pacific Affairs*, 48, 3 (1975), pp. 370–97.

'Urban transformation in South Vietnam', *Pacific Affairs*, 49, 4 (1976–77), pp. 607–24.

Turnbull, C. M., *A history of Singapore, 1819–1975* (Kuala Lumpur, Oxford University Press, 1977), and 2nd edn. *A history of Singapore, 1819–1988* (Singapore, Oxford University Press, 1989).

Turnell, Sean, *Fiery dragons: banks, moneylenders and microfinance in Burma* (Copenhagen: NIAS Press, 2009).

'Fundamentals of Myanmar's macroeconomy: a political economy perspective', *Asian Economic Policy Review*, 6 (2011), pp. 136–53.

Twang Peck Yang, *The Chinese business élite in Indonesia and the transition to independence* (Kuala Lumpur: Oxford University Press, 1998).

Twining, Charles H., 'The economy', in Karl D. Jackson, ed., *Cambodia, 1975–1978: rendezvous with death* (Princeton, NJ: Princeton University Press, 1989), pp. 109–50.

Twomey, Michael J., *A century of foreign investment in the Third World* (London: Routledge, 2000).

Ulep, Valerie Gilbert, 'The future of children in the Philippines', in Valerie Gilbert Ulep, ed., *Raising the bar: understanding and solving chronic malnutrition in the Philippines* (Quezon City: Philippine Institute for Development Studies and United Nations Children's Fund, 2025), pp. 1–22.

Ullman, E. L., 'Trade centers and tributary areas of the Philippines', *Geographical Review*, 50, 2 (1960), pp. 203–18.

Ungphakorn, Puey, 'Thailand', in Cranley Onslow, ed., *Asian economic development* (London: Weidenfeld and Nicolson, c.1965).

Urquhart, M.C. and K. A. H. Buckley, eds., *Historical statistics of Canada* (Cambridge: Cambridge University Press, 1965).

Usher, Dan, 'Income as a measure of productivity: alternative comparisons of agricultural and non-agricultural productivity in Thailand', *Economica*, 33, 132 (1966), pp. 430–41.

Van Can, Luc and Tu Ngoc Dang, 'Challenges in searching for Vietnam's growth drivers through 2030', *Asian Economic Policy Review*, 19 (2024), pp. 252–67.

van der Eng, Pierre, 'Marshall aid as a catalyst in the decolonization of Indonesia, 1947–1949', *Journal of Southeast Asian Studies*, 19, 2 (1988), pp. 335–52.

'Growth and productivity change in Indonesian agriculture, 1880–1985', Institute of Economic Research, Faculty of Economics, University of Groningen, Research Memorandum no. 348 (1990).

'The real domestic product of Indonesia, 1880–1989', *Explorations in Economic History*, 29, 3 (1992), pp. 343–73.

'The silver standard and Asia's integration into the world economy', Australian National University, Department of Economic History, working paper no. 175 (1993).

Agricultural growth in Indonesia: productivity change and policy impact since 1800 (Houndmills: Macmillan, 1996).

'Indonesia's growth performance in the twentieth century', in A. Maddison, D. S. P. Rao and W. F. Shepherd, eds., *The Asian economies in the twentieth century* (Cheltenham: Edward Elgar, 2002).

'Productivity and comparative advantage in rice agriculture in South-East Asia since 1870', *Asian Economic Journal*, 18, 4 (2004), pp. 345–70.

'Capital formation and capital stock in Indonesia, 1950–2007', Australian National University, Arndt-Corden Department of Economics, working paper 2008–24 (2008).

'Government promotion of labour-intensive industrialization in Indonesia, 1930–1975', in Gareth Austin and Kaoru Sugihara, eds., *Labour-intensive industrialization in global history* (London: Routledge, 2013), pp. 176–200.

'Why didn't colonial Indonesia have a competitive cotton textile industry?', *Modern Asian Studies*, 47, 3 (2013), pp. 1019–54.

van Eeghen, Geertrui M., 'The beginnings of industrialization in Netherlands India', *Far Eastern Survey*, 6, 12 (1937), pp. 129–33.

van Laanen, J. T. M., 'Between the Java Bank and the Chinese moneylender: banking and credit in colonial Indonesia', in Anne Booth, W. J. O'Malley and Anna Weidemann, eds., *Indonesian economic history in the Dutch colonial era* (New Haven, CT: Yale University Southeast Asian Studies, 1990), pp. 245–66.

van Leeuwen, Robert J., 'Indonesia', in W. Arthur Lewis, ed., *Tropical development 1880–1913* (London: George Allen & Unwin, 1970), pp. 256–82.

Vaughan, J. D., *The manners and customs, of the Chinese of the Straits Settlements* (Singapore: Mission Press, 1879).

Verhezen, Peter, 'Review of *Ethics, business and capitalism: Thailand and Indonesia in an Asian perspective*', *Bulletin of Indonesian Economic Studies*, 61, 1 (2025), pp. 159–62.

Vickerman, Andrew, 'A note on the role of industry in Vietnam's development strategy', *Journal of Contemporary Asia*, 15, 2 (1985), pp. 224–34.

The fate of the peasantry: premature transition to socialism in the D.R.V. (New Haven, CT: Yale University Southeast Asian Studies, 1986).

Villamil, Winfred, 'Education and training', in Ramon L. Clarete, Emmanuel F. Esguerra and Hal Hill, eds., *The Philippine economy* (Singapore: Institute of Southeast Asian Studies, 2018), pp. 151–89.

Vlieland, C. A., 'The population of the Malay Peninsula: a study in human migration', *Geographical Review*, 24, 1 (1934), pp. 61–78.

Vo Nhan Tri, *Vietnam's economic policy since 1975* (Singapore: Institute of Southeast Asian Studies, 1990).

Vos, R. and J. T. Yap, *The Philippine economy: East Asia's stray cat? Structure, finance and adjustment* (London: Macmillan, 1996).

Vries, Jan de, *European urbanization 1500–1800* (Cambridge, MA: Harvard University Press, 1984).

Vuving, Alexander L., 'Vietnam in 2018: A Rent-Seeking State on Correction Course', in Daljit Singh and Malcolm Cook, eds., *Southeast Asian affairs 2019* (Singapore: ISEAS–Yusof Ishak Institute, 2019).

Wade, Robert, *Governing the market* (Princeton, NJ: Princeton University Press, 1990).

Walinsky, Louis J., *Economic development in Burma, 1951–1960* (New York: Twentieth Century Fund, 1962).

'The role of the military in development planning', *Philippine Economic Journal*, 4, 2 (1965), pp. 310–26.

'The rise and fall of U Nu', *Pacific Affairs*, 38, 3/4 (1965/66), pp. 269–81.

Walker, Andrew, *Thailand's political peasants: power in the modern rural economy* (Madison, WI: University of Wisconsin Press, 2012).

Wallace, Peter, 'Investment climate and business opportunities', in Rodolfo C. Severino and Lorraine Carlos Salazar, eds., *Whither the Philippines in the 21st century* (Singapore: Institute of Southeast Asian Studies, 2007), pp. 180–201.

Walters, Alan, 'Currency boards', in John Eatwell, Murray Milgate and Peter Newman, eds., *The new Palgrave: money* (London: Macmillan, 1989), pp. 109–14.

Warr, Peter G., 'The Thai economy', in Peter G. Warr, ed., *The Thai economy in transition* (Cambridge: Cambridge University Press, 1993), pp. 1–80.

ed., *The Thai economy in transition* (Cambridge: Cambridge University Press, 1993).

Warr, Peter G. and Archanun Kohpaiboon, 'Thailand's automotive manufacturing corridor', Asian Development Bank working paper no. 519 (Manila: ADB, 2017).

Warr, Peter G. and Bandid Nijathaworn, 'Thai economic performance: some Thai perspectives', *Asia-Pacific Economic Literature*, 1, 1 (1987), pp. 60–74.

Watkins, Melville H., 'A staple theory of economic growth', *Canadian Journal of Economics and Political Science*, 29 (1963), pp. 141–58.

Weiman, David F., 'From Old South to New: metropolitan and regional development in the Lower South, 1860–1920', in Emery Castle and Barbara Baldwin, eds., *The changing American countryside: past, present, and future* (Corvallis, OR: National Rural Studies Committee Conference. Western Rural Development Center, 1995), pp. 37–51.

Werner, Jayne, 'Socialist development: the political economy of agrarian reform in Vietnam', *Bulletin of Concerned Asian Scholars*, 16, 2 (1984), pp. 48–55.

Wernstedt, Frederick L., 'Cebu: focus of Philippine interisland trade', *Economic Geography*, 32, 4 (1956), pp. 336–46.

Wernstedt, Frederick L. and Joseph E. Spencer, *The Philippine island world* (Berkeley, CA: University of California Press, 1967).

Wheelwright, E. L., 'Reflections on some problems of industrial development in Malaya', *Malayan Economic Review*, 8, 1 (1963), pp. 66–80.

Industrialization in Malaysia (Parkville, Australia: Melbourne University Press, 1965).

White, Christine Pelzer, 'Alternative approaches to the socialist transformation of agriculture in postwar Vietnam', in David G. Marr and Christine P. White, eds., *Postwar Vietnam: dilemmas in socialist development* (Ithaca, NY: Cornell Southeast Asia Program, 1988), pp. 133–46.

Wikkramatileke, L., 'State aided rural land colonization in Malaya: an appraisal of the FLDA program', *Annals of the Association of American Geographers*, 55, 3 (1965), pp. 377–403.

'Federal land development in West Malaysia 1957–1971', *Pacific Viewpoint*, 16, 1 (1972), pp. 62–86.

Williamson, Jeffrey G., *Globalization and the poor periphery before 1950* (Cambridge, MA: MIT Press, 2006).

Trade and poverty: when the Third World fell behind (Cambridge, MA: MIT Press, 2011).

Willis, H. P., 'The Philippine National Bank', *Journal of Political Economy*, 25 (1917), pp. 409–41.

Willmott, William E., *The Chinese in Cambodia* (Vancouver: University of British Columbia, 1967).

Wilson, Constance M., *Thailand: a handbook of historical statistics* (Boston, MA: G. K. Hall, 1983).

Wilson, David A., *Politics in Thailand* (Ithaca, NY: Cornell University Press, 1962).

Wilson, Peter, 'Monetary policy and financial sector development', *Singapore Economic Review*, 60, 3 (2015), pp. 1–25.

Wisaweisuan, Nitinant, 'Spatial disparities in Thailand: does government policy aggravate or alleviate the problem?', in *World Bank, World Development Report: reshaping economic geography* (Washington, DC: World Bank, 2009), pp. 184–95.

Wong, Kwok-Chu, *The Chinese in the Philippine economy 1898–1941* (Manila: Ateneo de Manila, 1999).

Wong, Lin Ken, *The Malayan tin industry to 1914* (Tucson, AZ: University of Arizona Press, 1965).

Woo, Wing Thye and Anwar Nasution, 'Indonesian economic policies and their relation to external debt management', in Jeffrey D. Sachs and Susan M. Collins, eds., *Developing country debt and economic performance*, vol. 3: *Country studies – Indonesia, Korea, Philippines, Turkey* (Chicago, IL: University of Chicago Press, 1989), pp. 18–149.

Woo, Wing Thye, Bruce Glassburner and Anwar Nasution, *Macroeconomic policies, crises, and long-term growth in Indonesia, 1965–90* (Washington, DC: World Bank, 1994).

Woodside, Alexander B., *Community and revolution in modern Vietnam* (Boston, MA: Houghton Mifflin, 1976).

Worcester, Dean C., *The Philippines and past and present* (New York: Macmillan, 1930).

World Population Review (n.d.) https://worldpopulationreview.com/world-cities.

Yacob, Shakila and Nicholas J. White, 'The "unfinished business" of Malaysia's decolonisation: the origins of the Guthrie "dawn raid"', *Modern Asian Studies*, 44, 5 (2010), pp. 919–60.

Yang, Shu-Chin, *A multiple exchange rate system: an appraisal of Thailand's experience, 1946–1955* (Madison: University of Wisconsin Press, 1957).

Yap Pheng Geck, *Scholar, banker, gentleman soldier: the reminiscences of Dr. Yap Pheng Geck* (Singapore: Times Books International, 1982).

Yasin, Muhammad Yazrin, Muhammad Azmi bin Mohd Zain and Muhammad Haniff bin Hassan, 'Urbanization and growth of Greater Kuala Lumpur: issues and recommendations for urban growth management', *Southeast Asia: A Multidisciplinary Journal*, 22, 2 (2022), pp. 4–19.

Yip Yat Hoong, *The development of the tin mining industry of Malaya* (Kuala Lumpur: University of Malaya Press, 1969).

Yoichi, Itagaki, 'Some aspects of the Japanese policy for Malaya under the occupation, with special reference to nationalism', in K. G. Tregonning, ed., *Papers on Malayan history* (Singapore: Journal of South-East Asian History, 1962), pp. 256–67.

Yong, C. F., 'A preliminary study of Chinese leadership in Singapore, 1900–1941', *Journal of Southeast Asian History*, 9, 2 (1968), pp. 258–85.

Yoon, Won Z., 'Military expediency: a determining factor in the Japanese policy regarding Burmese independence', *Journal of Southeast Asian Studies*, 9, 2 (1978), pp. 248–67.

Young, Alwyn, 'A tale of two cities: factor accumulation and technical change in Hong Kong and Singapore', *NBER Macroeconomics Annual*, 7 (1992), pp. 13–64.

Yusuf, Shahid, 'The East Asian miracle at the millennium', in Joseph E. Stiglitz and Shahid Yusuf, eds., *Rethinking the East Asian miracle* (New York: Oxford University Press, 2001), pp. 1–53.

Zasloff, Joseph, 'Rural resettlement in South Viet Nam: the agroville program', *Pacific Affairs*, 35, 4 (1962/63), pp. 327–40.

Zimmerman, Carle C., *Siam rural economic survey* (Bangkok: Bangkok Times Press, 1931).

Zipf, George Kingsley, *Human behavior and the principle of least effort: an introduction to human ecology* (Cambridge: Addison-Wesley Press, 1949).

INDEX

Page numbers in **bold** indicate a Table, and in *italics* a Figure.

Printed in the United Kingdom by TJ Clays Ltd.